P9-BIV-729

Newfoundland in the North Atlantic World, 1929-1949

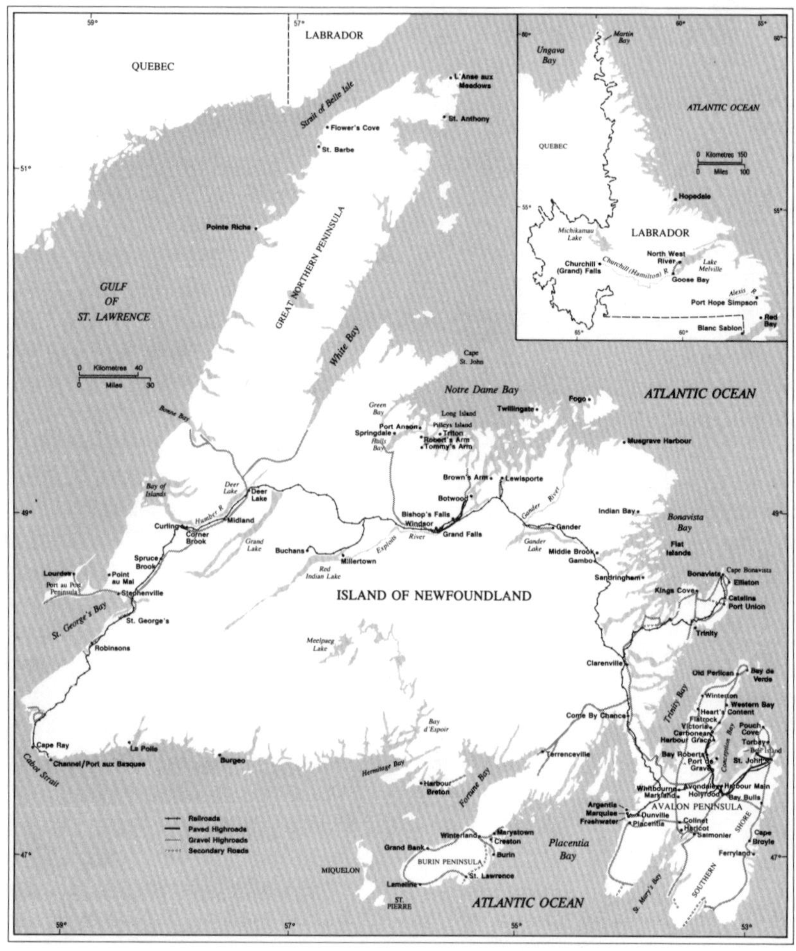

Newfoundland and Labrador in the Era of the Commission of Government (including 1949 Road and Rail Networks). *Credit*: Patricia Chalk, Cartographic Section, Department of Geography, University of Western Ontario

Newfoundland in the North Atlantic World, 1929-1949

PETER NEARY

McGill-Queen's University Press
Kingston and Montreal

ISBN 0-7735-0668-3

Legal deposit fourth quarter 1988
Bibliothèque nationale du Québec

Printed in Canada on acid-free paper

This book has been published with the help of a grant from the Social Science Federation of Canada, using funds provided by the Social Sciences and Humanities Research Council of Canada.

Canadian Cataloguing in Publication Data

Neary, Peter, 1938–
Newfoundland in the North Atlantic world, 1929–1949

Includes index.
Bibliography: p. 427
ISBN 0-7735-0668-3

1. Newfoundland – History – 1934–1949.
2. Newfoundland – Politics and government – 1934–1949.
I. Title.
FC2174.2.N43 1988 971.8'03 C88-090304-X
F1123.N43 1988

For Hilary
Nicholas
John

Contents

Preface

In recent years a great deal has been written about Newfoundland's entry into the Canadian Confederation. However, the history of the British-appointed Commission of Government which governed Newfoundland from 1934 to 1949 has not been the subject of much detailed investigation. What I attempt to do in this book, therefore, is to survey the history of the Commission and to weigh the constitutional outcome of 1949 against developments in Newfoundland itself during the preceding twenty years. In sum, I seek to broaden the debate about a critical but somewhat neglected period in Newfoundland's modern history. To this end, I have attempted to describe the general thinking of the Commission and the way in which events in Newfoundland and events in the North Atlantic world generally were interconnected. My work, I believe, reveals many subjects in the history of Newfoundland worthy of detailed study in themselves, and I hope that these will eventually be taken up by other scholars. Above all, perhaps, my work is a reminder that Newfoundland was a country before it became a province and that therefore its history is more than a mere record of those events, important as they were, which led to Confederation. The Commission era, like pre-1949 Newfoundland history generally, deserves study for itself and not merely as a prelude to what followed. Part of my purpose, then, has been to bring to light again an important time in the Newfoundland past and to counteract any Whiggish tendency that would reduce the history of the Commission period and much else to one theme with its inevitable outcome.

In arranging my material, I have followed what seem to be the obvious divisions in the chronology of events. I have therefore written my narrative with five distinct periods in view, namely, 1929–34, 1934–39, 1939–42, 1942–45 and 1945–59. At the end of my discussion of each of these, I provide an interpretive synopsis. For the years 1945 to 1949 this is in two parts. The first deals with the administrative and diplomatic history of the period and the second with political and constitutional history. My final chapter attempts to develop themes suggested by the work as a whole. With few exceptions, my use of place names follows the listings in the *Gazetteer of Canada: Newfoundland Terre-Neuve,* 2d ed. (Ottawa 1983). Italicized lines in the table of contents are quoted in context at the beginning of chapters 2 to 11. In both places, italics have been added. I have made every effort to identify, credit appropriately, and obtain publication rights from copyright holders of illustrations in this book. Notice of any errors or omissions in this regard will be gratefully received, and correction made in any subsequent editions.

Like all researchers who seek to understand the workings of modern governments, I have needed a great deal of help along the way. My debts to archivists and librarians in Canada, the United States, and the United Kingdom are many, and I am grateful to all those who have helped me. In the United Kingdom, I extend special thanks to Rear Admiral James H. Walwyn, J.B. Hope Simpson, and the second Baron Amulree. Transcripts of Crown-copyright records in the Public Record Office appear by permission of the Controller of H.M. Stationery Office. I acknowledge special help on this project from F.H. Armstrong, D.H. Avery, Erich Hahn, A.M.J. Hyatt and Hector Mackenzie of the Department of History at the University of Western Ontario. At the same university, for their generosity in discussing my research with me at every stage in my progress, I especially thank Robert A. Young of the Department of Political Science and Sam Clark of the Department of Sociology from whom I always learn. In like manner, I thank J.L. Granatstein of York University, James Struthers of the Canadian Studies Programme at Trent University, and W.A.B. Douglas and Carl Christie of the Directorate of History, Department of National Defence.

In Newfoundland, I have always found a warm welcome and astute advice in the Department of English Language and Literature at Memorial University, and I thank Patrick O'Flaherty and George Story for that. Other present and former residents of Newfoundland to whom I am indebted include Melvin Baker, Ed Chafe, Mona Cramm, Campbell Eaton, Brother E.B. Foran, Nancy Grenville, Michael Harrington, Anne Hart, Harold Horwood, Phillip McCann, Tony Murphy, James Overton, Gregory Power, Shannon Ryan, Shelley Smith and G. Bernard Summers.

At McGill-Queen's I received invaluable assistance, which I gratefully acknowledge, from Philip Cercone, Joan McGilvray, and Mary Norton. For the typing of a difficult manuscript, I thank Lori Morris, Joanne Burns, and Linda Tupholme. I thank the Social Sciences and Humanities Research Council for supporting my work financially, the University of Western Ontario for research funds, and the J.B. Smallman and Spencer Memorial Fund, University of Western Ontario, for a grant-in-aid of publication.

My thanks finally go to my immediate and extended families in London, St. John's, and Gander. Margaret and Mary Neary made my way easy in Newfoundland, as, editorially, did A.P. Bates in London. I salute in particular his command of the Queen's English and his expert knowledge of World War II, in which he so gallantly served. Hilary, Nicholas, and John, always considerate and involved, have made my every step worthwhile. Having thanked so many, far and near, I hasten to add that I alone am responsible for any errors or misjudgements the book may contain.

A long time ago I saw warships in Conception Bay, was awakened by an enemy submarine raid, and watched planes climb away from the new Canadian air base at Torbay, heading north to Gander. After the United States dropped anchor at Argentia, one of my brothers went to work there, a big family event. On VE day my father, an air raid warden, took me by the hand to the celebration in St. John's where, off in the distance, I do believe I saw Governor Sir Humphrey Walwyn. In small ways, then, I glimpsed something of Newfoundland's emergence from the Great Depression and the drama of the political round that followed World War II. My intention in writing this book has been to call back times when a little people, inured to toil and well acquainted with adversity, joined in memorable transatlantic undertakings and took some big steps forward.

Newfoundland in the North Atlantic World, 1929-1949

CHAPTER ONE

Introduction

Newfoundlanders often refer to their island home as "the rock," and this description, at once defiant and wary, is hardly misplaced. In area, 43,359 square miles, Newfoundland has a long and ragged coastline, eaten into, especially on its eastern and southern aspects, by several large bays which historically have separated the population and produced highly self-conscious local communities.[1] The capital city, St. John's, is located on the Avalon Peninsula, a rough appendage joined to the main part of the island by an isthmus so slender that on a fine day, from the height of land, one can see across it. In latitude St. John's is south of Paris, and except for its northernmost reaches Newfoundland lies south of Ireland. But in this case latitude belies geographical reality, for Newfoundland's climate, though full of surprises, is definitely northern.

Proximity to the sea moderates the coastal climate, especially in the southeast, but everywhere the weather is unsettled. Winter can begin early and, while usually punctuated by mild spells, drags on for many months. Spring is damp and cold, held back by the annual arrival of arctic drift ice which on the east coast can and often does fill the bays to the shoreline for many weeks at a time. Summer arrives late, is almost invariably brief, and in some years limited amounts of sunshine and warmth are a great disappointment. Autumn is decidedly cooler but hardly less variable. Wind, sometimes fierce, is an almost constant companion. Residents are inured also to rain, sleet, snow and, last but not least, fog, for which the island is justifiably famous. Truly, as the novelist and critic Paul West has written, life in Newfoundland pits "hope against the foretaste."[2]

Yet, for all the trials of its climate, the island has considerable natural resources. Though trees tend to be small, large parts of the island are forested, and there are areas where limited agriculture is possible. In addition there are sizeable mineral deposits. The most famous resource, abundant and diverse fish stocks, lies offshore, especially on the Grand Banks. Not surprisingly, therefore, Newfoundland is best known as a fishing country, and it was the pursuit of maritime enterprise that first attracted Europeans to the island after its rediscovery by them – there had been Viking visitors centuries before – around the turn of the sixteenth century. Initially, the fishing at Newfoundland was transatlantic and multinational in character, but by the Treaty of Utrecht in 1713 Great Britain obtained sovereignty over the island and thereafter dominated the region. Nonetheless, France retained important fishing and landing rights for her subjects on a part of the Newfoundland coast that became known as the French Shore. By the same token, citizens of the newly formed United States were granted their own special status on parts of the Newfoundland and Labrador coasts in 1783.[3] These complex international arrangements indicated that Newfoundland was located at the conjunction of various national interests, a consideration that would take on an entirely new dimension in the twentieth century.

Within the British Isles, it was the West Country, the counties of Devon, Dorset, Cornwall, and Somerset, that dominated the lucrative Newfoundland fish trade. It was also mainly from this region and from the southeast counties of Ireland, whose port of Waterford enjoyed a close economic connection with the West Country, that Newfoundland gradually acquired a resident population of European descent. In the era of the American Revolution, as the end of the third century of continuous European exploitation of the offshore resource approached, this group probably numbered only around 10,000 to 12,000.[4] By 1857, however, the population of the island stood at 122,638,[5] and St. John's had long since replaced the West Country ports as the commercial centre for the fishing industry. With the latter change had come also administration, modelled on the practices of English local government, the emergence of a small but ethnically mixed and religiously divided business and professional elite, a modicum of gentility and intellectual life, newspapers and, inevitably, advocacy of reform. In short, Newfoundland entered the colonial mainstream after 1815, a change acknowledged by the calling of a bicameral legislature in 1832. At the head of Newfoundland's typically British colonial system of government stood a British governor, appointed by London.

In 1842, after a decade of fractious politics which variously pitted St. John's against the scattered rural coastal communities or outports, merchant against producer, and Protestant against Roman Catholic, the constitution was changed and a unicameral or "Amalgamated Legislature," with appointed and elected members, was introduced. This variation on normal procedure showed the difficulty of applying British parliamentary practice in the Newfoundland setting, something that would become a recurrent theme of local history. Nonetheless, in 1847, the bicameral legislative system was restored. Responsible Government followed in 1855 with Roman Catholic liberal reformers, both Irish-born and of Irish descent, leading the way and the largely Protestant merchant and office-holding community of St. John's opposing them. The first years of Responsible Government were relatively calm, but there was a big sectarian blow-up in 1861 when the premier of the day was dismissed from office. Thereafter, politics in Newfoundland, while never wholly without incendiary potential, settled into a pattern of elite accommodation which mixed class and denominational elements. Roman Catholics, concentrated on the Avalon Peninsula and forming a majority in St. John's, were the largest single religious group, a distinction they have retained to this day, but their leadership potential visibly declined with their numbers – from 46.4 per cent in 1847 to 39.9 per cent (including Labrador) in 1874.[6] The Roman Catholic elite, aided and abetted by the Church, had fought in the 1850s for a fair share of patronage, and once this was obtained it became a staunch defender of the new status quo and a decidedly conservative force in local society.

Another factor favouring accommodation at the top across an otherwise fractured Newfoundland society after 1855 was the general belief that the colony was both threatened and constrained by the existence of French rights on the island and by France's possession since 1763 of the islands of St. Pierre and Miquelon. In the second half of the nineteenth century, St. John's produced its own variety of economic nationalism which featured a series of disputes with the imperial government over the extent and meaning of the extraterritorial rights granted on the French Shore and about the jurisdictional rights of the Newfoundland government in the area. Thereafter the French Shore question became a staple of Newfoundland politics; the sense it produced that the country was labouring under disadvantages which were the product of agreements made against its interest and without its full consent cast a long shadow over the later history of the island. Rhetorically at least, there has usually been good mileage to be made in Newfoundland politics by charging governments past and present with having sold the country down the river and by challenging the legitimacy of allegedly perfidious agreements. At one level, indeed, Newfoundland history is a record of attempts to undo the past. If a foreign bogeyman can be made part of the story all the better, although the greatest loathing in this particular tradition is perhaps reserved for local politicians who are believed to have aided or engineered the betrayal of their own people. In St. John's especially, a paranoid outlook in such matters has, going back to the nineteenth century, never been very far below the surface. In sum, the scapegoat, either at home or from abroad, has figured prominently in Newfoundland's political history.

Newfoundland rejected Confederation in the 1860s, and indeed there was no economic basis at the time for her union with the other British North American colonies. Having done so, she set off on a course of economic development the purpose of which was to escape over-dependence on the export-oriented and therefore highly vulnerable fishing industry, whose principal product was dried salt cod. The centrepiece of the colony's program was the building of a trans-island railway, which was completed in 1897 after many political and financial upheavals. As a result of this venture, the Reid Newfoundland Company, formed in 1901 to operate the line, became a major landowner and an influential voice in future plans for developing resources.[7] Newfoundland also tried to better her economic position by seeking closer ties with the United States. A reciprocity agreement between the two countries, actually negotiated in 1890, was overruled by the imperial government at Canada's request.[8] This might have created testy relations between Newfoundland and Canada; instead, following the 1894 failure of Newfoundland's two main financial institutions, the Union and Commercial banks, talks on Confederation were opened. When Newfoundland could not get satisfactory terms, this second attempt at union failed. Nonetheless, the events of 1894–95 had important long-term consequences for relations between the two countries, the chief of which were financial.[9] In the wake of the bank crash in St. John's, the Bank of Nova Scotia quickly established itself in the country. It was followed soon after by the Bank of Montreal and eventually by the Canadian Bank of Commerce and the Merchants' Bank of Halifax (later the Royal Bank of Canada). These Canadian banks took over Newfoundland's banking business, leaving only a government-owned savings bank under local control. Furthermore, the Bank of Montreal became the government's financial agent, and the local currency was made interchangeable with Canada's. These developments paralleled the closing of many small banks in the Maritime Provinces of Canada in the same period. Thus, while Newfoundland had stayed outside Confederation in 1867, in banking and monetary terms she now went the way of the Maritimes within Canada: internal control gave way to outside domination, mainly from Montreal.

In 1902, Newfoundland negotiated another reciprocity agreement with the United States, but because of opposition to it in New England, this deal also eventually fell through. The whole episode showed again nevertheless how an independently minded Newfoundland had the potential to complicate Anglo-American-Canadian relations. Moreover, despite her failure to achieve a reciprocity agreement with the United States, Newfoundland scored some notable economic successes around the turn of the century, though not necessarily because of her railway investment. In 1895 large scale mining of iron ore was started at Bell Island in Conception Bay, and in 1905 the Anglo-Newfoundland Development

Company, a creation of the British newspaper magnates, Alfred and Harold Harmsworth (Viscounts Northcliffe and Rothermere), completed arrangements leading to the opening of a paper mill at Grand Falls. Newfoundland also benefited from the Anglo-French *entente cordiale* of 1904, which included an agreement whereby Paris exchanged rights in Newfoundland for financial compensation and territorial concessions in West Africa, while retaining St. Pierre and Miquelon.[10]

The first decade of the twentieth century was notable in Newfoundland for the formation in 1908 of the Fishermen's Protective Union. Founded and led by William F. Coaker, an able speaker and journalist who appealed to the independent fisherman-producer, the union made great headway in the mainly Protestant northern bays of the east coast. Then through the Union Party, it made a spectacular entry into politics in the general election of 1913 when it won eight of the thirty-six seats in the House of Assembly. Like contemporary agrarian movements elsewhere in North America, the Fishermen's Protective Union called for an order of things in which the small producer would get fair value for his work and product and in which the middlemen and other exploiters would be eliminated. This would be achieved through co-operative buying and selling and by the construction of a new and truly democratic political order based on co-operative rather than competitive principles. To show what could be achieved in outport Newfoundland, Coaker promoted with considerable success a model community at Port Union, Trinity Bay.[11]

Coaker's movement ran into strong opposition from the political and economic elite of the country and from the Roman Catholic Church. It was then deflected from its original goals by the Great War in which Newfoundland, like Canada and all the countries of the British Empire, was automatically involved. Many Newfoundlanders served overseas in the Royal Navy during the war, and the country raised an infantry regiment of its own which suffered devastating losses at Beaumont Hamel on the opening day of the Battle of the Somme, 1 July 1916. At home the war effort, which proved expensive,[12] was managed by a Newfoundland Patriotic Committee, to which the government of the day deferred in a striking break from normal constitutional practice. Eventually, the war produced both an all-party national government and conscription for overseas service, with highly divisive results. Coaker entered the national government and supported conscription, which many outport residents resisted.[13]

The union movement did not regain its momentum after 1918, even though the 1920s turned out to be a rough decade for the country both economically and politically. As minister of marine and fisheries in a Liberal Reform government formed in 1919, Coaker introduced regulations to co-ordinate the activities of Newfoundland's highly individualistic fish exporters. However, this attempt to regulate co-ordination into existence failed, a failure with profound long-term consequences for Newfoundland. As the economic historian David Alexander has written, "the failure to expand the [fishing] industry and, more importantly, to transform it in terms of the diversity of output and the technologies of catching, processing, packaging and organized marketing, simply left Newfoundland fishermen less competitive than their rivals.[14] Evidence of this would now be seen in the invasion of Newfoundland's own fishing grounds by the fleets of a number of European countries, by a high level of emigration, and by economic and social stagnation. In 1911 Newfoundland's approximately 43,800 fishermen had accounted for about 53 per cent of her labour force; by 1935 these figures were down to 35,000 and 40 per cent.[15]

On the bright side, in the 1920s the country got another pulp and paper mill – and another company town – when the Newfoundland Power and Paper Company, which was controlled by Armstrong Whitworth and Company of the United Kingdom, began operations at Corner Brook.[16] In 1927 the Corner Brook operation was taken over by the International Paper Company of New York, whereupon it became the International Power and Paper Company of Newfoundland. There was good news for Newfoundland also, if no immediate jobs, in a 1927 ruling of the Judicial Committee of the Privy Council on the location of her boundary with Canada in Labrador. This decision awarded Newfoundland an area of 112,826 square miles, an outcome that was later described by one resident of Quebec as "equivalent to a terrible defeat on a battleground."[17]

Newfoundland also achieved an enhanced constitutional position within the British empire in the 1920s thanks to the definition of dominion status formulated by the imperial conference of 1926. The country was covered by the Statute of Westminister (1931), which subsequently codified the new relationship between the Dominions and the United Kingdom. She did not, however, assume the operative powers consequent on dominion status, provided for in sections 2-6 of that statute.[18] Nor did she become a member of the League of Nations.[19] Nevertheless, she was clearly on the same constitutional track in the post World War I period as Canada and the other self-governing dominions. Like Canada, although as a much smaller country, she had emerged as a "Dominion of the North," becoming a recognized, albeit not very active, presence both in imperial affairs and on the world stage.

Thus as the 1930s approached, Newfoundland was decidedly in transition, socially, economically, and constitutionally. By 1921, the population of the country (including Labrador) had grown to 263,000; by 1935, to 289,588. Trans-national business enterprise had helped create significant mining and forestry sectors in the local economy, but because the country remained highly dependent on exports, it was very sensitive to changes in world market conditions. Furthermore, although the division of labour was more pronounced in the 1920s than ever before, there was still a striking dependence on the fishing economy which had led to settlement by Europeans in the first place. Moreover, within that economy, despite the growth of secondary enterprises, especially the annual spring seal hunt, financial success or failure for a sizeable segment of the population and much of the traditional commercial establishment depended on the export trade in salt cod. Trade also determined the financial position of the Newfoundland government for about three-quarters of its revenue still came from customs. Income tax, introduced as a wartime measure in 1918 and the subject of further legislation in 1922, was abolished in 1925 by a merchant-led government.[20] Reintroduced in 1929, it was thereafter kept within strict and narrow limits by the small but politically well-placed, monied class that could be expected to pay it.[21]

At the apex of the country's traditional fishing economy stood a merchant elite that was largely located on Water Street in St. John's, just as it had been for generations. In 1931, fifty-one traders qualified for membership in "the Salt Codfish Exporters' Association of Newfoundland,"which was to oversee a new system for licencing exporters in a further attempt to achieve orderly marketing.[22] Those exporters from St. John's who were members of the Association wielded great influence in the country collectively and in many cases individually. Water Street, largely Protestant, had been for a long time suspicious of democracy; before 1914 it had been given a bad scare by Coaker. It played the game of electoral politics but had an important second line of defence in the appointed Legislative Council. It also promoted its interests through the Newfoundland Board of Trade, which had been formed in 1909.[23] In practice the Board "consisted of two or three dozen of the prominent merchants and importers of St. John's and was divided into four or five family groups who shared the honors of holding the offices of the Board from year to year."[24]

Water Street was connected to the outports in several ways but largely through small merchant intermediaries, who in turn provided credit to individual fishermen proprietors. Those at the bottom of the hierarchy operated in a truck or barter system which, although varying somewhat in different localities and regions, was one in which fish were traded for supplies with little or no money changing hands. The outport ideal was the self-sustaining, independent (though in reality, highly dependent) commodity producer. Rural Newfoundlanders were indeed as a group remarkably versatile; work was seasonal and there were many fishermen-farmers, fishermen-miners, fishermen-loggers,[25] and various combinations thereof. The frequently itinerant Jack of all trades flourished in outport Newfoundland, where a tradition of self-help was deeply ingrained. But the country also had a long history of rural poverty and dependence on the state. Further, the line between self-sufficiency and need was a fine one for many families. After a poor catch or when the price for saltfish fell or overseas sales lagged, the relief rolls of the government grew quickly. For those at the bottom rungs of society, life in Newfoundland was dominated by what one British historian has aptly termed mankind's "perennial problem of keeping body and soul together."[26] Seasonally, the greatest demand on the government by the able-bodied poor came in the spring when supplies in the country generally began to run low.

Administratively, Newfoundland was highly centralized in the 1920s with denominational considerations still very much to the fore. Government did not reach very far into the lives of rural dwellers, whose social leaders tended to be merchants, clergymen, and, when present, magistrates, doctors and teachers. An outport member of the House of Assembly was expected to give priority to the interests of his locality and fight for its share of whatever funds were available for local road and other public works. Relief programs were administered by local relieving officers appointed from St. John's. For the able-bodied destitute, relief was always paid in kind with food rations consisting chiefly of tea, flour, pork, and molasses. A higher scale of relief was applied in the capital than in the outports on the assumption that outport residents, however poor, could always provide at least some of the necessities of life because of their traditional skills and proximity to resources.

Education had made considerable headway in Newfoundland by the post World War I period, but the school system was the jealously guarded preserve of the churches. In 1927 a new Education Act, said to have been a denominational "Magna Carta," created a bureau of education to run the school system.[27] The membership of this body consisted of the prime minister; three already functioning denominational superintendents, one each for Roman Catholic, Church of England, and Nonconformist (United Church of Canada) schools; the educational secretary of the Salvation Army; "six other persons proportionally representative of the several religious denominations to be appointed from time to time by the Governor-in-Council and to serve on the Bureau for three years at a time"; and a secretary for education, a permanent official who acted as the bureau's executive officer. By contrast, higher education, attracting only a few students, was the responsibility of the Memorial University College and Normal School, which had opened its doors in September 1925 and was at least nominally undenominational.[28]

Viewed from outside, such arrangements could make Newfoundland seem unique, but in reality the country had much in common with the staple-producing and export-oriented regions of Canada. Her economy depended on the export of the products of three basic industries: fishing, forestry (principally pulp and paper manufacturing), and mining. Newfoundland resembled some of the Canadian provinces, too, in that, while depending on primary production and international markets, she carried a substantial debt load. In 1920–21 this amounted to $43,032,285 with railway and war expenditures the leading items; but by 1929 it had risen to $79,477,478. In the meantime the country had gone to the money markets every year. Under the terms of arrangements with its bondholders, the government had to make interest payments semi-annually. Clearly, if Newfoundland's trade should decline, so too would her ability to meet this obligation; like many other traders, she operated in the 1920s on a narrow margin. With large fixed costs arising from her debt, there was little room for manœuvre in the face of a sudden loss of revenue. Her most obvious choices were retrenchment, more borrowing abroad or, as was more likely, both. It was not her dependence on exports or the growth of her indebtedness that made Newfoundland distinctive, as much as an extreme vulnerability to shifts in demand. In a crisis the neighbouring Maritime Provinces of Canada could look for assistance to a national government, which, however begrudging it might be and often was, could hardly disown them. At worst, Confederation permitted the Maritimes a "shabby dignity,"[29] while Newfoundland, like many small countries, lived dangerously and alone. Constitutionally, Newfoundland's progress had paralleled Canada's, but in effect the status she had achieved within the British empire had given her attributes of sovereignty without great substance, and responsibility without many compensating advantages. Individually, many Newfoundlanders could absorb a sudden loss of income by falling back on a household economy that was still remarkably versatile and comprehensive, but collectively they had no such solution. If Newfoundland were ever to approach the end of her own limited financial resources, she could, barring default, rely for help only on her membership in the British family of nations.

In February, 1927, at a tense political moment, one of many in the troubled decade of the 1920s, Governor Sir William Allardyce wrote from St. John's: "the political atmosphere is heavily charged, the glass is low and falling, and it looks as if there might be a hurricane."[30] This forecast was not immediately borne out by events; but, after 29 October 1929, the chill wind of the Great Depression began blowing around the world, and it soon struck Newfoundland with devastating force.

CHAPTER TWO

Crisis and Change, 1929-34

I am looking forward to the economic conference at Ottawa which I trust will be under your chairmanship for the development of a practical policy of inter dominion trade relations and cooperation which like the gutta percha and steel of the trans oceanic cables will form the material protection of *that thin red cord of sentiment and of blood* which if unprotected may fail efficiently to function or be utterly destroyed under pressure of new world conditions economic scientific and racial.

Prime Minister Richard Squires to
Prime Minister R.B. Bennett,
January 1932

In the realm of public finance the story of what the Great Depression did to Newfoundland is, at one level, disarmingly simple. By 1 July 1933, the country's debt had grown from the $79,477,478 of 1928-29 to $98,453,865, an increase of 23.9 per cent. Of this sum, the net funded total was $87,776,198.78. The holders of Newfoundland paper for this amount were principally in the United Kingdom and the United States. A portion of the funded debt – sterling loans to the value of £2,014,000 – was in "Trustee Stocks" issued under the provisions of the United Kingdom's Colonial Stock Act of 1900. The interest rates applicable to Newfoundland's funded debt varied from a low of 3 per cent to a high of 6 1/2 per cent, and the average rate of interest on the whole debt, funded and floating, was "just under 5 per cent."[1] Everything considered, the 1933 figures and what lay behind them were nothing short of disastrous.

Sir Richard A. Squires, who was in power in St. John's when the Depression struck and whose name came to be closely associated with the alarming increase in the public debt that followed, had played to mixed reviews in his political career.[2] Born at Harbour Grace in 1880 and a lawyer by profession, he was first elected to the House of Assembly in

1909. In 1919, with William Coaker's help he became premier and subsequently scored a big success in the development of Corner Brook. Reelected in May 1923, he was soon caught up in a complex scandal which forced him from office two months later. He was charged with theft and, although acquitted by a grand jury, his name became a byword in London for sharp practice. When an election was held in Newfoundland the next June, the hastily formed Liberal-Conservative Party of Walter S. Monroe, a St. John's businessman, obtained a majority. Monroe governed until August 1928, when he made way for his cousin and business colleague, Frederick C. Alderdice. Alderdice was the managing director of the Colonial Cordage Company in St. John's and a director of several other companies in spite of being seriously disabled as the result of a rugger accident. He, like Monroe, had been born in Ireland of Protestant stock. Both were notable for a conservatism which stood out even in mercantile St. John's. They were true believers in the British Empire, an unfettered financial system, minimal government, and the right of business to a free hand. It was the Monroe government that abolished the modest income tax introduced in 1918. In time this and other conciliatory gestures to privilege cleared the way for the return of a clever populist: when Alderdice went to the polls on 29 October 1928, it was Squires redux.

Squires came back on a rising economic tide, as Newfoundland benefitted from the investment boom and the general good times of the late 1920s. Exports, especially in the forest and mining sectors, were rising in value; a promising new market for fish had been found in Brazil; and there was a sizeable American investment being made at Buchans, where lead and zinc had been discovered. In 1928-29, excluding its railway loss, the government recorded a deficit on current account of $1,107,173, but in 1929-30, by the same accounting, it was able to realize a surplus of $144,902, the first such surplus since 1924-25. During the next year, however, the bubble burst as markets for Newfoundland products turned soft, revenue fell precipitously, and expenditure soared. In 1929-30 interest on the public debt amounted to a stiff 35.9 per cent of current revenue, but worse followed. In 1930-31 this figure rose to 44.8 per cent, in 1931-32 to 59.7 per cent, and in 1932-33 to a breathtaking 63.2 per cent.[3] In September 1931, the United Kingdom's departure from the gold standard struck an especially hard blow at the local economy as the Canadian dollar rose sharply in value against sterling. Since most of Newfoundland's fish trade was in sterling, this change favoured her competitors in what was already a crowded and difficult market.[4]

Squires attempted to deal with the sudden crisis by borrowing more money. In 1930, with the assistance of the Bank of Montreal, the government was able to float a loan of $5,000,000; in 1931, an $8,000,000 loan was authorized by the Legislature, but this time there were no takers. In early summer, a syndicate of the four Canadian banks operating in the country loaned the government $2,000,000, on condition that it ask the British Treasury to appoint an official to investigate its whole financial situation, a task to which Sir Percy Thompson, deputy chairman of the Board of Inland Revenue, was assigned.[5] During the autumn of 1931, Newfoundland tried bargaining with Canada for the sale of Labrador at an asking price of $110,000,000; the idea remained alive in some circles, but nothing came of it.[6] To cover its year-end interest payments, a now desperate Squires government obtained another loan, which the Canadian government backed, from the Syndicate Banks. The condition imposed on Newfoundland on this occasion put the country on the brink of receivership.[7]

On 1 February 1932, Squires's fiery minister of finance, Major Peter J. Cashin, a prominent war veteran and the son of a former premier, broke with him, subsequently charging misappropriation of funds.[8] In April, a riot, from which Squires was lucky to escape, forced the temporary closing of the House of Assembly.[9] Subsequently, legislative authority was obtained for the raising of a "Prosperity Loan" of $2.5 million. Of this amount, Imperial Oil took $1.75 million in return for a monopoly on the sale of certain oil products in the country.[10] Dissolution soon followed and an election was scheduled for 11 June. In the campaign leading up to this, Alderdice led a reorganized opposition which now called itself the United Newfoundland Party. If elected, this party promised to appoint an unpaid committee "to enquire into the desirability and feasibility of placing the country under a form of Commission Government for a period of years." If the committee recommended this course of action, Alderdice promised to submit the proposition "to the electorate for their approval." Nothing would happen that did "not first have the consent of the people."[11] Thus committed, Alderdice won a big victory; only two Liberals, F. Gordon Bradley (Humber) and Roland G. Starkes (Green Bay) were returned.[12]

In office, Alderdice contemplated a unilateral rescheduling of Newfoundland's debt but was talked out of this by J.H. Thomas, the Secretary of State for Dominion Affairs, who predicted that such drastic action would bring financial crisis to Newfoundland and blacken the name of the Commonwealth generally.[13] In the event Newfoundland was able to meet its 1932 year-end payments thanks to an Anglo-Canadian loan of $1,250,000 (half supplied, with Ottawa's backing, by the Canadian banks). This was offered on condition that the country accept "a mixed Commission composed of United Kingdom, Canadian and Newfoundland personnel to examine into the Dominion's future, with a view to reaching decisions and making appropriate arrangements before the debt interest due on the 1st July, 1933, matures."[14] Pending the report of this commission of enquiry, Newfoundland would be required to consult the United Kingdom before alienating any substantial asset by sale or lease. The commission itself would have three members. St. John's could choose whether the United Kingdom would name two members and Newfoundland one, or whether the United Kingdom would select all three. Whichever formula was adopted (Newfoundland opted for the first), London would reserve the right, in consultation with Ottawa, to name a Canadian to the enquiry. To set events in motion, the British insisted on a two-part assurance from St. John's, which could be given to Parliament. The Newfoundland government had to promise to recommend at once to the legislature the measures put forward from London and to seek from that body the authority needed to carry them out. Beyond this, the government had to agree to appeal at once to the electorate should the powers asked for not be immediately obtainable from the legislature. If these commitments were not given and default ensued, the United Kingdom would have no choice but to make public the offer to Newfoundland and the fact of her refusal of it.[15] The political scientist S.J.R. Noel, author of the finest work on twentieth century Newfoundland history, has described this particular juxtaposition of alternatives as "a classic combination of diplomatic pressures in the form of a small but adequate 'carrot' and an implied 'stick,'" and so it was.[16] Not that Alderdice and his colleagues had difficulty in making up their minds: they quickly and gratefully agreed to everything asked of them.[17] Preparing for default had been out of character for Newfoundland's conformist leader, who welcomed enthusiastically a solution that put him back in the imperial mainstream, if only in tow.

To chair the commission of enquiry thus agreed upon, the United Kingdom chose William Warrender Mackenzie, first Baron Amulree, a Scottish Labour peer. Called to the bar in 1886, Amulree was a veteran investigator and conciliator who had served as Secretary of State for Air and President of the Air Council in 1930–31.[18] Remarkably, no Newfoundland public figure was asked to serve on the commission: instead, the Alderdice government rather naively nominated Sir William Stavert. Born at Summerside, Prince Edward Island, in 1861, Stavert had served as a trustee and liquidator, and as an intermediary in the merger with the Bank of Montreal of several small banks in the Maritimes and elsewhere.[19] In the autumn of 1932, he had become financial advisor to the Newfoundland government in succession to Thompson, whom Alderdice suspected became of his previous association with Squires. Whatever

Stavert's appointments, first as financial advisor and then as commissioner may have done for Newfoundland, they gave the Canadian banks a known and reliable presence at the highest level of her government.

From Ottawa, Prime Minister R.B. Bennett nominated as commissioner, Charles A. Magrath, the chairman since 1914 of the Canadian section of the International Joint Commission. A native of North Augusta in Ontario, Magrath had worked early in his career in western Canada as an irrigation engineer and land surveyor. He had been a member of the legislature of the North West Territories, had represented Medicine Hat in the Canadian House of Commons, and most recently had been chairman of the Ontario Hydro-Electric Power Commission.[20] If Stavert's career had emphasized consolidation, Magrath's had favoured expansion. Both were businessmen but of very different types. All three nominees to the commission, however, were septuagenarians.

On 17 February 1933, the commission was appointed by royal warrant issued on the advice of the King's ministers in the United Kingdom, Canada, and Newfoundland.[21] According to this document, whose provenance was said to be unique in the history of the British empire,[22] the task of the Royal Commission was "to examine into the future of Newfoundland and in particular to report on the financial situation and prospects therein."[23] Peter Alexander Clutterbuck of the Dominions Office was named secretary to the commission. Thirty-five years old at the time of his appointment, Clutterbuck was a product of Malvern College and Pembroke College, Cambridge, and had won the military cross in the Great War while serving with the Coldstream Guards.[24] Industrious, informed, discreet, and highly literate, he exemplified the ideals of the British civil service and in time would rise to the top administrative position in his department. Beginning with his work for the Amulree commission, he would have an influential say over British policy towards Newfoundland for many years to come.

Amulree set to work in London immediately, chairing meetings at the Treasury on 18 February and at the Dominions Office six days later.[25] On these occasions, which brought together officials of the two offices, the Newfoundland question was canvassed in all its aspects and important understandings were reached about the future of the Royal Commission. In the course of the discussions, it was pointed out that because of Newfoundland's dominion status, her constitution could not be suspended by order-in-council. While it was true that Newfoundland had not taken up the powers under the Statute of Westminster to which she was entitled, the United Kingdom's relationship with her was governed by section 1 of this statute and by its preamble which made this provision: "It is in accord with the established constitutional position that no law hereafter made by the Parliament of the United Kingdom shall extend to any of the said Dominions as part of the law of that Dominion otherwise than at the request and with the consent of that Dominion."[26] Amulree and his associates would have to bear this in mind in their deliberations. Amulree was also given a pointed message from Thomas, communicated by Sir Edward Harding, Permanent Under-Secretary of State in the Dominions Office. It was essential, Harding said, that any solution the commission might recommend be acceptable not only to Newfoundland but to the United Kingdom and Canada. When the commission reached the stage of formulating recommendations, therefore, Amulree would be expected to seek by private telegram Thomas's view of what was afoot. The Canadian and Newfoundland governments would have to be similarly approached either by Amulree himself or by their respective nominees on the commission.[27] Amulree in other words would not only have to investigate and recommend but strike a bargain. His solution in short would have to be the occasion not of further debate but of speedy action. With Newfoundland reeling from payment to payment, time was clearly of the essence.

Having been thus briefed in London, Amulree and Clutterbuck sailed for Halifax, where they met Stavert and Magrath.[28] The whole party then arrived in St. John's on 13 March and established itself in the government-owned and deficit-ridden Newfoundland Hotel, which Amulree pronounced as "very comfortable."[29] On 16 March the Royal Commission held a formal opening sitting in public, and four days later hearings were started in the capital with witnesses appearing in private. The approach of the commission to its work was judicial: they would hear all the evidence before attempting to draw conclusions from it.[30] Amulree soon had reason to write to Harding that "the stories of corruption, incompetence and nepotism" heard by the commissioners were "continuous." Alderdice was "all right," but it was said that some other members of the government were not much of an improvement on their notorious predecessors. Amulree was clearly shocked by the poverty of the island and by the unequal truck system which operated between merchants and fishermen and which, through price manipulation, made many of the latter permanent debtors. Looking ahead, Amulree reported that Alderdice and apparently his whole cabinet were "against Confederation, Crown Colony, Government by Commissioner, sale of Labrador (unless on advantageous terms), or any further borrowing."[31] The prime minister still favoured some scheme of partial default. Given this reality, Amulree recommended to Thomas, as "the only course now open," that Newfoundland be incorporated directly into the United Kingdom.[32]

While this fanciful scheme was being considered in London, the commission completed its business for the moment in St. John's, and on 17 April (without Magrath, who had returned to Canada) it left the capital to hold hearings in other parts of the island.[33] At the end of the month the commissioners went to Ottawa. There Amulree received a message from Thomas which peremptorily dismissed the idea of a parliamentary union between the United Kingdom and Newfoundland. Noting that Newfoundland was not alone in having trouble balancing her books, Thomas now argued that the prevailing pessimism in St. John's did not take sufficient account of the changed financial position that would come about, in Newfoundland as elsewhere, with a revival in trade. Accordingly, it might be desirable for the Royal Commission to differentiate in its report between short-term and long-term solutions to Newfoundland's problems. If Alderdice clung to the "shameful" idea of default, then either the whole commission or, barring general agreement, Amulree himself, should put forward "whatever temporary solution" seemed appropriate. If this were accepted by Canada and the United Kingdom but refused by Newfoundland, the world at large would know that the blame for default rested with Newfoundland rather than the empire. Any proposition put forward by the commission, however, would have to take account of the fact that nothing in the nature of a "mere dole" for Newfoundland could be carried through Parliament. If the United Kingdom were to render assistance, she must have effective control of "financial policy and financial administration" in Newfoundland while the Dominion was her dependent. If the commission were able to devise a plan for Newfoundland acceptable to the British government, it would be important for Amulree to state plainly that Newfoundland should accept it rather than default. It was assumed also in London that the chairman would do "everything possible" to ensure that any further assistance to Newfoundland would be contributed to equally by the United Kingdom and Canada. Assuming equality of financial sacrifice, the United Kingdom would not object in principle to joint control with Canada of Newfoundland's finances, but practically it might make sense to centralize direction in London.[34]

The Dominions Office followed up Thomas's telegram with the details of a "measure of temporary control" over Newfoundland which might meet the Treasury's requirements. This was sent over the signature of Sir Edward Harding to Clutterbuck, who was instructed to show it to Amulree at his discretion. If Amulree liked the proposals, he could then put them forward as his own, it being desirable that the other commissioners not know of London's involvement. The underlying purpose of the scheme advanced was to secure "effective control in practice ... with the minimum of constitutional alteration." To this end Newfoundland's revenue would be paid into an account operated by a controller of finance, who, "appointed and paid" by London, would be "solely responsible for the due payment of the debt service." The amount of assistance Newfoundland needed would be decided annually and approved by the controller of finance in consultation with London before the estimates were submitted to the legislature. Newfoundland would have to maintain existing taxes unless the United Kingdom permitted change. If the legislature balked at any action needed to keep up the tax level, the measure in dispute could simply be authorized by the governor. The government of Newfoundland would also have to agree not to exceed the approved annual level of expenditure; supplementary spending would require the prior consent of the controller, who would have to consult London. To keep expenditure within approved bounds, key departments of the Newfoundland government might be supervised, under normal ministerial control, by officials on loan from the United Kingdom. This whole scheme would be formally agreed to by the two governments and then ratified by their respective legislatures. The duration of the agreement might be three years, with termination possible beforehand should Newfoundland be able to meet her "contractual obligations" in full.[35]

In contrast to these well-laid British plans, Canadian thinking about the future of Newfoundland remained amorphous. Based on his preliminary observations, Magrath argued for a policy of "generosity." Though Confederation was not yet practical, it was, he thought, Newfoundland's ultimate destiny and Canada's policy towards her neighbour should therefore be co-operative and helpful. Like other debtors, Magrath believed, Newfoundland was being required to pay interest rates that were "excessive under present conditions."[36] Accordingly, he wrote favourably of the plan Newfoundland had devised the previous year for scaling down payments, placing this solution in the context of a general international repayments problem.[37]

If Newfoundlanders received fair export prices and had a lighter financial load, they would "get along nicely."[38] Even with a reduced debt load, however, they would need outside help pending the revival of world trade. Practically speaking, there were only two ways this could be obtained. One, often alluded to in St. John's, was for the United Kingdom to assist Newfoundland in recognition of the country's war debt, just as she had cancelled sums owed her by various European nations as a result of the 1914–18 conflict. The other was by the sale of Labrador to Canada. Magrath did not attempt to name a price that Canada should pay and suggested that Newfoundland be given the option of repurchasing the territory within a specified period. This latter provision would both allow Newfoundland to accept "a reasonable figure and refute the criticism that Canada took advantage of its neighbour in distress."[39] Instead, Newfoundland might be given a share of the net revenue from Labrador for a fixed period.[40] In Magrath's scheme of things, a Labrador deal would involve providing Newfoundland with some of the services of the Geological Survey of Canada, the Department of Fisheries, and the Dominion Bureau of Statistics. Canada would also assist in the development of local air service, the improvement of St. John's, and the movement of people, so as to reduce, in the interest of more efficient public administration, the number of outports. This help would be given without any change in Newfoundland's existing system of government. Its effect would be to steer Newfoundland towards Confederation while forestalling "anything that might be unsound in connection with any portion of its territory."[41]

This was constructive analysis. After an initial meeting with Bennett on 4 May, Magrath and Stavert were optimistic that a settlement involving Canada could be reached, but Amulree was less sanguine.[42] Nevertheless, he reported to London the following day that the prime minister "seemed anxious to help," was "genuinely sympathetic," and had intimated that he wanted the commission to meet with the whole cabinet.[43] On the evening of the sixth, however, Amulree had a stiff encounter with the Minister of Finance, Edgar N. Rhodes, a Nova Scotian who "was against Confederation as the Newfrs would really in effect become another Ireland – not in the racial sense, but a nuisance and always grumbling and wanting something. Labrador was not worth possessing [and] default would not make the slightest difference."[44] Following the dropping of this bombshell, negotiations stalled for a week as the commissioners endured one postponement after another in their attempts to meet again with Bennett, who was immersed at the time in trade negotiations with France. While they cooled their heels, the commissioners grappled with the very real possibility that Canada would reject what had become their preferred solution to the Newfoundland problem – the acquisition of Labrador by the Dominion "at such a figure as would enable Newfoundland to carry on with a balanced budget."[45]

On 11 May Amulree sounded London about a scheme, pushed by Stavert, whereby Newfoundland, having made "full explanation" to her bondholders, would offer to exchange her existing bonds for a new series. The new bonds would mature in thirty to forty years, bear interest of 2 per cent, and be backed by Canada in return for the transfer to her of Labrador. Should Canada balk at this scheme, there were two positions to fall back on: the United Kingdom could join Canada in guaranteeing the new bond issue, or she could assume full liability and take Labrador herself. In any event, since it would take time to put the whole plan into effect, Newfoundland would have to be provided with $2,000,000 in order to meet her mid-1933 interest payment.[46]

In effect this scheme, which would have strengthened the position of the banks vis-à-vis the bondholders by freeing money for their needs, was a variation on the plan of default advanced by Alderdice in the autumn of 1932. As such, it was promptly rejected by the United Kingdom, although not before it had been discussed in Ottawa when Bennett and his cabinet finally received the Amulree commission. [47] At this meeting, which a frustrated Amulree had been led to believe would be with a cabinet committee, Bennett picked up on the conversion idea and promised to discuss it further with his colleagues. Subsequently, while awaiting further word from Bennett, Amulree heard from Thomas that "any form of conversion which could be described as default" was anathema to London. No part of the British Empire had ever defaulted and for this to happen now "would be disastrous," the more so since prices seemed to be rising again and the forthcoming World Economic Conference offered further hope. At the end of the day, if no other way out could be found for Newfoundland, the United Kingdom would, for about three years at least, contribute what was needed to avoid default. But she would never join "in a guarantee in respect of a balance payable upon a deliberately defaulted Bond."

Canada, however, posed no problem in this regard, for on the nineteenth Amulree heard from Bennett that the Dominion government would suggest nothing for the moment but would "give immediate and sympathetic consideration" to any proposal coming from Newfoundland. Amulree subsequently heard from O.D. Skelton, the Canadian Under-Secretary of State for External Affairs, that Bennett had cooled to the guarantee idea on the grounds that "it would ... likely ... cause much heart-burning both in Newfoundland and among bondholders and would thus land Canada in difficulties." Skelton's own view, Amulree reported, had been that Confederation was the solution which would command the greatest support in Canada but Newfoundland would have to take the first step, "and no modified form of political union would be acceptable unless it provided for full Confederation after [a] short interval." On a more pressing matter, Skelton had said that Bennett wanted to discuss the question of Newfoundland's July interest payment in England, whither he would depart at the end of the parliamentary session. To facilitate this discussion, Skelton advised that the commission prepare a memorandum for the two governments stating the facts of the case. He had also told Amulree that he anticipated another fifty-fifty split between the United Kingdom and Canada on the money Newfoundland would need in July. Later, however, he had telephoned Amulree to say that the cabinet opposed any further Canadian advance to Newfoundland and that Bennett would act accordingly. Amulree discounted this pessimistic second report on the grounds that Bennett was protecting himself against "premature disclosure" and would hardly have sought to discuss the 1 July payment in London if his country did not intend to contribute to it.[48] In fact this was wishful thinking, but on the strength of it Amulree decided to pack his bags and return to St. John's. In truth the Royal Commission's visit to Ottawa had been a fiasco.

As its final act in the Canadian capital, the commission completed the memorandum Skelton had solicited. A copy of this document, which was classified as secret, was mailed to London by Amulree, while Stavert and Magrath undertook to give copies to Alderdice and Bennett respectively.[49] The British hoped that the memorandum would "make it difficult for Canada to decline participation" in helping Newfoundland with her next scheduled payment.[50] But though their purpose was "to pave the way for a further joint advance," the commission did not actually make a specific recommendation about the July payment because of Alderdice's vocal opposition to any further enlargement of Newfoundland's debt.[51] On the other hand, Amulree did not see any "serious difficulty" in dealing with the Newfoundland leader provided a further advance could be presented to him as the "necessary preliminary to [the] working out of [a] constructive solution in [the] best interest not only of Newfoundland itself but of the Empire as a whole."[52]

From St. John's, where the commission resumed hearings on 30 May, Amulree gave the Dominions Office seven arguments above and beyond those "based on Imperial considerations" to employ in dealing with Bennett when he came to London. The appeal of these was to Canada's self-interest since the collapse of Newfoundland would have "serious consequences" for Canada's own credit. This collapse could only be avoided by devising a long-term solution, and it would be "unthinkable" for Canada to "stand aside" while the commission was attempting to achieve this. By backing out now, Canada would herself appear financially strapped and the loss of face involved might cost her as much on the New York money market as if Newfoundland defaulted. While Canada claimed to be indifferent about Labrador, she might be compromised later on if, as seemed likely, the territory came to be regarded more favourably but had in the meantime come under the sway of American speculators. Equally, as some of her own officials understood, Canada might, through inaction, lose out in the coming international air age to "United States interests" in the competition to take advantage of Newfoundland's prime location. Lastly, since Canada placed such importance on the outcome of the World Economic Conference, it only made sense for her to pay the small amount needed to carry Newfoundland until that conference met.[53]

In a supplementary message, intended primarily for information rather than as ammunition for use against Bennett, Amulree set these arguments in the larger historical contest of Canada-Newfoundland relations. There were, he wrote, many institutional and economic links drawing the two countries closer together all the time. The "inevitable conclusion" of this was that the "destiny of Newfoundland" lay with Canada. Accordingly, whether she liked it or not, Canada could not "avoid special responsibility" for events in Newfoundland. Her present attitude, therefore, was myopic. By thinking they could stand back until Newfoundland came "crawling to them on her hands and knees," Canadians invited a situation in which Newfoundland would never be a "contented partner" in Confederation. It would be equally futile for Canadians to say "they would not mind taking over Newfoundland" provided she did not bring her debt with her. This approach would make Confederation seem less advantageous to Newfoundlanders, breed bitterness among them, and postpone a decision indefinitely. The two countries would never unite "so long as one is afraid of humiliation and the other insists on standing aloof until appealed to as by a supplicant." The commission's opportunity, Amulree mused, ignoring the hard knocks received in Ottawa, was to bring the parties together and so eliminate what might become a "source of perpetual trouble."[54]

Magrath's thinking at this stage continued to be directed towards the eventual achievement of Confederation. In forwarding the commission's memorandum of 20 May to Bennett, he told the prime minister that the welfare of Newfoundland's people should take precedence over the claims of her bondholders.[55] Magrath favoured the adoption of a three year plan. At the start of this Newfoundland would make a "frank statement" to her bondholders, promising to issue a revised payment schedule in three months. During this time a team of experts drawn from the Newfoundland and Canadian civil services would determine the capital expenditure needed to revive the country's economy. Assuming a satisfactory outcome to this, for a trial period, perhaps three years, the United Kingdom and Canada would assist Newfoundland to maintain interest payments on her debt at a reduced rate, say 2 1/2 per cent. Under the authority of the Newfoundland legislature, an Anglo-Canadian advisory board would also be created. The Newfoundland government would have to approve appointments to this board, which would be empowered to pass judgment on all legislation relating to the raising or spending of money. Confederation, Magrath believed, though desirable, "should not be forced ... Let the Island," he wrote, "collect its own revenue and pay for its own services. It would not be very long until the people themselves would seek entry into our Canadian family, thereby avoiding the question becoming a political issue in Newfoundland, which might happen if pressed upon the people."[56]

Magrath's plea for magnanimity was lost on Ottawa. There, in the grim summer of 1933, a fearful government, numbed by adversity, sought not fresh commitment in relation to Newfoundland but escape from her troubles. At the close of 1932 the British had their way once they had been able to work on Bennett alone in England, but this time the prime minister, even in person, was unyielding. True, he agreed to consult his colleagues once again, by telegraph, about joining in the further advance Newfoundland would soon need; but their reply that the "continuous and heavy demands" of the western provinces and the Dominion's "own necessities" made this impossible, ended the matter.[57] Canada had cut loose from a badly listing Newfoundland; if she was to be salvaged, the United Kingdom would have to do the job alone. Reluctantly the British accepted the full burden,offering to loan Newfoundland the extra amount needed to avoid a July default.[58] This loan, approved in a supplementary vote, and eventually fixed at $1,850,000, would be subject to the same terms and conditions as its December 1932 predecessor. When these arrangements were promptly and gratefully accepted by Newfoundland, the immediate difficulty passed.

In the weeks following, the full implications of Canada's withdrawal from the scene and of the United Kingdom's enhanced responsibility for Newfoundland were explored in London and a scheme devised for the future of Newfoundland which was later embodied in the report of the Amulree commission. Amulree participated in these discussions but his colleagues, who went back to Canada after the commission completed the second phase of its Newfoundland work at the beginning of July, did not.[59] Amulree was also apparently active during the summer in further behind the scenes negotiations to secure a Labrador "windfall" for Newfoundland from private capital, but nothing came of this either.[60] In a memorandum dated 17 July the commission concluded that the business before it had boiled down to one item: did the United Kingdom consider a default by Newfoundland important enough to continue assisting the country to meet its financial obligations? If the answer was yes, consideration would have to be given to the constitutional changes which would have to be made in Newfoundland to justify the financial help to be proffered. If the answer was no, attention would have to be focused henceforth on various schemes of default. Nine possible plans of action were briefly sketched by the commission: the first three for consideration if it were decided to avoid default, and the remaining six if default was to be tolerated.[61]

On 18 July the commission's memorandum was discussed at the Treasury. Present were two officials each from that department and the Dominions Office along with Clutterbuck, who had returned from Newfoundland with Amulree. The conclusion of this working group was that "the best course would be that the United Kingdom should take over the responsibility for the administration of Newfoundland until such time as the country could pay its way." Financial assistance in other words would have to be linked to "a strict form of control," which could be justified by reference to Newfoundland's prodigal past. Although Newfoundland had suffered greatly from the effects of the world depression, there was no doubt that her difficulties were largely the result of her own reckless extravagance in more prosperous times. If, therefore, assistance was to be given her now, "it was only right that it should be accompanied by conditions which would bring home the lesson that misgovernment on such a scale could not be tolerated with impunity. To give assistance, on terms which would provide for firm control for some time to come, would be more likely to bring home the lesson than the adoption of any other course."[62]

Provided Thomas and Chancellor of the Exchequer Neville Chamberlain accepted this advice, the recommendation was that they should next see Bennett and explain to him what the United Kingdom intended unless Canada had a change of heart about sharing responsibility. If Bennett was not forthcoming, Amulree should then be approached by the ministers to determine whether he would be willing to recommend what was suggested. Assuming he was, the details would be worked out among him, the Treasury, and the Dominions Office, so that the report of the commission would "contain a complete scheme for immediate adoption."[63]

On two grounds Thomas was "not very happy" with the proposals thus placed before him: an outcry could be expected in Parliament if it was proposed to help Newfoundland "indefinitely"; and there was reason to worry about establishing a precedent in Newfoundland that could be cited should another Dominion, or even an Australian state, find its debt overwhelming. Complicating this latter point was the fact that the "drastic nature of the changes in the form of Government" contemplated for Newfoundland "could not be suggested to any other Dominion or State," because such changes "would have no chance of acceptance." In the last analysis, however, Thomas deferred to the Treasury's insistence that default had to be avoided to maintain "the general credit of the Empire," and preparations for an intervention in Newfoundland proceeded apace.[64] By early August opinion had crystallized as to the form this should take both constitutionally and financially.

Constitutionally, the proposal was that Newfoundland would be administered by a governor and an executive council, ultimately the Commission of Government, which would have Newfoundland as well as British members. This administration would be responsible not to the legislature, which would be suspended, but to the secretary of state for dominion affairs. The financial package was more complex and represented, in response to lobbying from the Dominions Office, a considerable shift in Treasury thinking. What it proposed in effect was "a disguised default" that would simultaneously save the United Kingdom money by reducing

Newfoundland's interest payments, make the drastic political changes envisaged more acceptable to Newfoundlanders, and, above all, forestall criticism that "the United Kingdom taxpayer was being bled to enable the bondholders to receive their pound of flesh."[65] The United Kingdom must be seen as a trustee rather than as a bailiff. As eventually explained by Neville Chamberlain to Amulree, the settlement proposed for Newfoundland was one in which the country would "declare itself unable to carry on upon the present basis" and "address to the King a petition in two parts." The first part would ask the United Kingdom to assume temporary responsibility "for the internal administration of Newfoundland." The second part would ask the United Kingdom to make whatever arrangements were "just and practicable in the circumstances in relation to the island's debt." Provided all this was done, Newfoundland's bonds could then be rolled over to produce a lower annual interest payment. Bondholders who did not convert to the new series to be issued "would have to wait for any interest or repayment of capital on their old bonds until such time, if ever" as Newfoundland could make the payments. Chamberlain justified the proposed financial measure as follows: "In considering what we could do with the debt if the responsibility for it is thus passed to us, I adopt the standpoint that a bankrupt who goes out of business is not disgraced if with the aid of his friends he pays 20s in the £ and that the bondholder of a bankrupt debtor has not much reason to grumble if he gets his money back, although he may be deprived of benefits which would accrue from the continued fulfilment of his bond."[66] In short, a rescheduling of debt that would have been anathema while Newfoundland was a self-governing dominion would be perfectly acceptable should she forego that constitutional status.

Tactically, Chamberlain had two suggestions. The first was that if Amulree and his colleagues agreed with this plan, they should attempt to obtain the Newfoundland government's acceptance of it in advance of their report. This would enable the United Kingdom to act quickly and so avoid awkward speculation in Newfoundland bonds. Logically, therefore, the commission would have to lobby Alderdice to act on the report without calling an election. To go to the people would be to invite an "unfortunate period of suspense and speculation" and force another supplementary estimate on the British government to enable Newfoundland to meet her end-of-the-year payments. Chamberlain's other suggestion concerned the content of the report itself. While this document should spell out the constitutional changes, it should "allude to the debt arrangement only in general phrases."[67] This latter vagueness would permit the United Kingdom to tailor the financial proposal to the market circumstances at the time of its announcement.

During the first week of September, with his departure for Newfoundland scheduled for the eighth, Amulree worked over Chamberlain's scheme in London and attempted to sweeten it. Two issues dominated discussion: the specifics of the constitutional proposal to be put forward, and the rate of interest to be attached to the new bonds. On the first Amulree took the position that Alderdice's hand would be strengthened when it came to suspending the legislature "if he could say that under the scheme contemplated, Newfoundland would be given a constitution which would place her far above an ordinary Colony, something quite new which had been specially worked out to suit both her special needs and her position as 'Britain's oldest colony.'"[68] This requirement, it was agreed, could be met by providing in the new system that the governor could act only "by and with the advice of the new Commission." Authority would not devolve on him personally and he would not be given any general enabling or specific right to override his advisers. In these respects, Newfoundland's constitution would be unlike that of any colony. At the same time the United Kingdom's interest would be protected by the appointment of equal numbers, three being the suggested figure, of British and Newfoundland commissioners. In a crunch the British commissioners and the governor could defeat the Newfoundlanders four to three.[69]

Various means for providing a "safety valve" for Newfoundland public opinion were also considered. One possibility was the creation of an "Advisory Council of Newfoundlanders," but this was dismissed on several grounds: good members would be hard to find, the council might perpetuate the existing "political and denominational jealousy and intrigue," and, moreover, it might be tempted to play to the gallery and thereby compete with the Commission itself. Allowing the Newfoundland members of the Commission to be elected would also be dangerous. The case the Amulree commission would make for constitutional change was "that the difficulties of Newfoundland were due not so much to the depression as to a generation of mismanagement; that the political life of the Island was corrupt from top to bottom, as the main object both of the individual politician and the individual elector was to get what each could out of the public till; and that the process of demoralisation had, after 25 years, reached such extremes that only by a rest from politics could the people be trained anew to independence and self-reliance." Having said this, to allow the election of Newfoundland commissioners and the "acute party struggle it would entail," would be a blatant contradiction. Giving the Newfoundland members of the Commission renewable yearly appointments was equally questionable. This would be seen "as a means of getting rid of any Newfoundland Commissioner who was not readily amenable to the views of the United Kingdom members." It would be anomalous to have different terms for the British and Newfoundland members, and a rapid turnover of commissioners would work against long-term planning and sound departmental administration. Nonetheless, Amulree might broach this procedure in his negotiations in St. John's. Yet another way of gauging public opinion, emergency situations aside, might be to require the publication of proposed legislation "at least one month prior to enactment." This might slow the Commission down but again Amulree was given the green light to use it as a bargaining point. Not so the proposition that to become law any measure would require majority support among the commissioners exclusive of the governor. The effect of this would be to give the Newfoundland commissioners collectively a veto and tempt them to court public favour. Equally repugnant was the notion that the right be given to any three commissioners who found themselves in a minority "to submit their views in writing to the Secretary of State." This might encourage dissidence among the Newfoundland members in order to save their local reputations. The best "safety valve," it was agreed, was that a dissatisfied Newfoundland commissioner could resign.[70]

On the financial side Amulree accepted in principle Chamberlain's scheme but wanted a lower rate of interest on the new bonds than the 3 1/4 per cent Chamberlain proposed. The rationale for this rate had been that it would allow investors to redeem the new bonds in present market conditions at face value, thereby upholding the principle that they were recovering the whole of their capital. But Amulree argued that a lower interest rate was needed to prevent the idea from catching hold in St. John's that the conversion scheme involved replacing one impossible debt load with another and therefore "perpetual subservience" to the United Kingdom. Faced with this prospect, the Newfoundland government might choose to default.[71]

Amulree agreed with Chamberlain, however, that trustee securities should not be subject to conversion, but he forecast trouble on this issue with his colleagues on the commission, especially Stavert, who believed that no such distinction should be made. On the other hand, Amulree himself questioned the assumption that the banks were "specially secured" and should therefore forthwith be paid in full. In his estimation if "the contract with the Bondholders was to be broken that with the Banks might be broken also." They were "highly unpopular" in Newfoundland and "were to some extent the villains of the piece." Accordingly, "any discrimination in their favour would ... be strongly resented." Paying off the "Prosperity Loan" as planned would be different: this was in order because it would be to Newfoundland's advantage to be clear of Imperial Oil's monopoly. Looking to his forthcoming negotiations in St. John's, Amulree also sought assurance that the United Kingdom's grants-in-aid to Newfoundland once the Commission of Government was established would be gifts rather than loans. Otherwise, the country could never hope to escape its burden of debt. By the same token, Amulree sought authority to say in St. John's that the United Kingdom would not demand repayment of her recent loans to Newfoundland.[72]

On the eve of their departure for Newfoundland, Amulree and Clutterbuck, together with two Treasury officials, attended a final meeting at the Dominions Office during which the interest rate question was considered once more. This gathering heard that Chamberlain, having considered Amulree's position, remained convinced that a 3 1/4 per cent rate would be required to carry the conversion scheme: "the reduction of interest was ... a strong measure, but under the present plan the Chancellor would at least be able to say that he was offering the bondholders their nominal capital ... If the rate was to be reduced from 3 1/4 per cent. to 3 per cent. he would not be able to say this and the scheme would be liable to severe criticism." Amulree's request that Newfoundland might tax bond payments at source was also rejected. Nor would the Treasury budge on the necessity of creating before very long a sinking fund for the new bonds. This would eliminate the possibility of any future surplus in Newfoundland against which bondholders who had refused to convert might make claims. The importance of this precaution was indicated by the 30 per cent depreciation which had occurred in the value of the Canadian dollar during 1933, a change that could be expected to increase Newfoundland's revenues. Although deferring to these views, Amulree remained critical of a plan which Newfoundlanders on first hearing might well regard as "unpalatable." He feared that if his commission reported the proposals of the British government as they now stood, it might well be accused of having produced "a bondholders' report" leading to a "bondholders' régime": "Newfoundland would sacrifice her independence temporarily and the United Kingdom taxpayer would be called upon to stand behind the country; but the third party, the bondholder, would sacrifice nothing at all, since he would get his full pound of flesh, *i.e.*, 20s in the pound." However only in relation to the proposed grants-in-aid was there any give in the Treasury's position. Though the intention was that these should be regarded as "advances-in-aid" and therefore repayable, a "reassuring formula" could be drafted for Newfoundland's benefit if they became a stumbling block in negotiations. The United Kingdom could go no further. Yet if the door was closed, it was not locked: unwelcome as failure in Newfoundland would be, Amulree was instructed to telegraph a report to London for cabinet consideration should he not succeed with his colleagues on the Royal Commission or with Alderdice.[73]

On 15 September 1933, the Newfoundland Royal Commission reassembled in St. John's, and two days later Amulree sent Alderdice, to whom he had already given a verbal summary, a memorandum detailing the United Kingdom's offer.[74] By the twenty-first he was able to report to London that Magrath and Stavert had fallen into line, subject to Alderdice's acquiescence.[75] At the best of times Newfoundland's capital was a centre of gossip and intrigue, but in the autumn of 1933 it was alive with rumour. Alderdice, Amulree told Prime Minister Ramsay MacDonald, could not even discuss matters with his colleagues; and his own meetings with the Newfoundland leader had to be held after dark at the latter's residence.[76] At these sessions Amulree pitched his appeal to Alderdice's deeply felt sense of imperial solidarity; the United Kingdom was not moved by any desire to interfere in Newfoundland's internal affairs but "by a feeling of special responsibility towards the Island as the Oldest British Colony." What she offered was "co-operation in a joint plan of reconstruction," which could only be carried out "on the willing initiative of the Newfoundland Government and Legislature."[77] Alderdice responded favourably to this, only hesitating over three points. Not surprisingly, the first was the interest rate to be paid on the conversion bonds. A 3 per cent maximum, he told Amulree, would strengthen his hand politically, though even this figure would provoke opposition. Alderdice also wanted to know whether the United Kingdom would back Newfoundland in redeeming the new bonds if the country had not become self-supporting when that necessity arose. Lastly, he sought assurance that the grants-in-aid under commission of government would be gifts rather than loans. His concerns, of course, included the items on which Amulree himself wished to be conciliatory and the chairman now pressed his case for amendment afresh. If 3 per cent was impossible, could the United Kingdom not herself pay the difference between that and a higher figure?[78]

Alderdice was a "lonely" figure, Amulree cautioned MacDonald, and faced a terrible decision. He was "not a politician but a businessman who [had] entered the House a few years ago to do his best to save his country from the 'politicians.'" His circumstances were "almost pathetic" and invited "a few lines of encouragement" from the prime minister.[79] MacDonald dutifully complied with this request, and the exchange of letters with Alderdice that followed typified the overly sentimental, even lachrymose tone that by 1933 was a general feature of the correspondence of both men.[80] The real decision makers in London were less accommodating: nothing less than 3 1/4 per cent could be promised, and the United Kingdom could not make up the difference between 3 per cent and a higher interest figure. Better terms, it was reiterated, could only be secured if the market for Newfoundland bonds improved, and Alderdice would have to live with this uncertainty. On the other hand, Amulree was authorized to say that the United Kingdom would, if necessary, stand behind the redemption of the new bond issue. The question of grants-in-aid was trickier, but here too there was a concession. The United Kingdom had a "special reason" for reserving the right to treat the sums to be paid over to Newfoundland as loans rather than gifts. Loans would have second claim on Newfoundland's revenues, after the payments on the new bonds but before any payments on previous bond issues. This would add to the pressure on bondholders to convert. Although the situation facing the government in Parliament dictated caution on this issue, Amulree was authorized to tell Alderdice that the advances already made to Newfoundland together with any others that might be made over the next three years would be "treated as free gifts." Thereafter the conditions attached to the United Kingdom's financial aid would be subject to Treasury review as conditions required, but this did not necessarily mean the repayment of either capital or interest. Amulree was given leeway, too, on Stavert's suggestion that the offer to the bondholders be conditional on acceptance by 85 per cent of their number. The United Kingdom could not accept this figure, which was too high, but would willingly tie her offer to acceptance "by a sufficient number" of Newfoundland's creditors.[81]

With these instructions in hand, Amulree was quickly able to bring matters to a conclusion in St. John's. By 13 October the Royal Commission had "arrived at [a] unanimous report," and Amulree had in hand a letter in which Alderdice accepted the British plan "unreservedly in principle" and pledged "his utmost endeavour to carry it through [the] Executive Council and Legislature." The understanding thus reached with Alderdice was, in Amulree's opinion, "highly satisfactory." The Newfoundland leader's cabinet colleagues would be "left in the dark until the last moment."[82] Before leaving St. John's for Liverpool on 17 October, Amulree handed over copies of the draft report of the commission confidentially to both Alderdice and Governor D. Murray Anderson, who had taken up duty in January.

Interestingly, though he had not pressed his point, Magrath had been critical of the explanation offered in this document for the crisis that had engulfed Newfoundland. Magrath agreed that Newfoundland should have commission of government, a change which had been advocated by nearly all the witnesses who had appeared before the Royal Commission. He believed, however, that Newfoundland's new administration should be given the best possible start. To denounce those who had previously governed Newfoundland would not serve this purpose; rather it would breed resentment among the accused and possibly opposition to the new system. Nor did Magrath believe that Newfoundland's politicians were as culpable as it was proposed to say they were. The big expenditures of the past in Newfoundland had no doubt been "made for developing the resources of the Island and thereby expanding the opportunities of the people." Newfoundlanders were North Americans, a fact not always appreciated even in St. John's, and like Canadians they had been influenced by the "tremendous prosperity" and "vast public expenditure" of the United States. "Loose spending" had indeed been common "in all countries in recent years." If a group had to be singled out for criticism, he wrote, it was not perhaps the politician patrons or their fishermen clients but "that section of the people who had the greatest opportunities" – Newfoundland's commercial elite, who now led the assault on the party men. With their considerable influence, they should have been able to restrain the politicians they now denounced. But looking ahead it would be unwise to fix blame: nothing would be gained by "more or less degrading a people whom we wish to get moving along sound lines, by exposing to the outside world their stupidity resulting in graft and other weaknesses, and which has been told with considerable force on past occasions." The Royal Commission was "not giving sufficient weight to world factors" which had "brought about business depression and governmental difficulties in Newfoundland as in all other countries." These were telling points. Why then did Magrath knuckle under to London's wishes? The answer is that he believed the Newfoundland problem rested "entirely between the United Kingdom and the Island." If the United Kingdom was to pay the piper, she must also be allowed to call the tune. The Canadian government's decision in the summer of 1933 not to lend any further assistance to Newfoundland had rendered ineffective the one dissident voice on the Royal Commission.[83]

Back in London Amulree sent Harding a memorandum detailing various points Alderdice had raised about the workings of commission of government.[84] In his reply Harding promised sympathetic consideration to all these except one, namely, Alderdice's request that four of his ministers be retained under the Commission "in an advisory capacity." The ministers in question were John G. Stone (Marine and Fisheries), William J. Walsh (Agriculture and Mines), Kenneth M. Brown (Labour), and Capt. William C. Winsor (Posts and Telegraphs). His reason for intervening on their behalf was that he "could not be certain of putting through the requisite legislation" if he were not "in a position to assure my Ministers that their support of Government by Commission would not involve their being cast adrift.[85] But as events unfolded, Alderdice was put in the position of promising what he could not deliver. Harding told Amulree "that the objections, political, administrative and financial" to what Alderdice proposed were "so strong that his suggestion is not one which could be accepted by the government here." He did, however, venture that "some alternative method of meeting the situation" might be possible.[86] This, Governor Anderson was subsequently told in a private letter, perhaps lay in appointing the future ex-ministers to the magistracy.[87] If Alderdice were to raise the troublesome issue again, the governor should "bear this in mind." Amulree, while in St. John's, had already discussed the possibility of magisterial appointments with Alderdice; but the prime minister had apparently resisted this particular solution because the salary of a magistrate was only about half that of a cabinet minister and therefore "insufficient."[88] Alderdice, Anderson wrote from St. John's on 17 November, was "quite firm that the 'adviser' solution had been agreed to by Lord Amulree." The governor himself favoured a compromise whereby the ex-ministers would serve temporarily as advisers and then go to the magistracy.[89] This roughly accorded with Alderdice's subsequent version of what had been agreed upon but in truth a crucial matter had been left hanging.[90] At a decisive moment in Newfoundland's history Alderdice acted on a false assumption, but whether the fault lay with him or his British opposites is debatable.

In any event, on 10 November Amulree informed Thomas that the report of the Royal Commission, which he would sign in his own right and also on behalf of Stavert and Magrath, was ready for submission to the King.[91] Proceeding from the analysis of Newfoundland's failings that Magrath had questioned, the report prescribed thus:

> We therefore recommend that the Newfoundland Government, recognising that it is impossible for the Island to surmount unaided the unprecedented difficulties that now confront it, should make an immediate appeal for the sympathetic co-operation of Your Majesty's Government in the United Kingdom in the adoption and execution of a joint plan of reconstruction, of which the following would be the main features:
>
> (a) The existing form of government would be suspended until such time as the Island may become self-supporting again.
>
> (b) A special Commission of Government would be created which would be presided over by His Excellency the Governor, would be vested with full legislative and executive authority, and would take the place of the existing Legislature and Executive Council.
>
> (c) The Commission of Government would be composed of six members, exclusive of the Governor, three of whom would be drawn from Newfoundland and three from the United Kingdom.
>
> (d) The Government Departments in the Island would be divided into six groups. Each group would be placed in the charge of a Member of the Commission of Government, who would be responsible for the efficient working of the Departments in the group, and the Commission would be collectively responsible for the several Departments.
>
> (e) The proceedings of the Commission of Government would be subject to supervisory control by Your Majesty's Government in the United Kingdom, and the Governor-in-Commission would be responsible to the Secretary of State for Dominion Affairs in the United Kingdom for the good government of the Island.

> (f) Your Majesty's Government in the United Kingdom would, for their part, assume general responsibility for the finances of the Island until such time as it may become self-supporting again, and would, in particular, make such arrangements as may be deemed just and practicable with a view to securing to Newfoundland a reduction in the present burden of the public debt.
> (g) It would be understood that, as soon as the Island's difficulties are overcome and the country is again self-supporting, responsible government, on request from the people of Newfoundland, would be restored.
> (h) The appropriate procedure for bringing a joint plan of this character into operation would, we suggest, be the submission of an Address to Your Majesty by both Houses of the Newfoundland Parliament, followed by legislation in the United Kingdom.[92]

In consideration of the working hours of the bond markets, the plan of the British government was to present the report to Parliament at 2:30 PM on 21 November, and to have it released at the corresponding local times in Ottawa and St. John's.[93] Simultaneously, a parliamentary paper would be published in London incorporating, after a brief introduction, an exchange of telegrams between Alderdice and Thomas dealing with the action the British government would, assuming Parliament was agreeable, be willing to take on the recommendations of the report.[94] The message from Thomas to Alderdice, dated 19 November, marked a further and final refinement of the plans, both constitutional and financial, which had been in the making since the summer. The three United Kingdom commissioners, it was now announced, would be paid from British funds and their three Newfoundland colleagues from local funds. Public service appointments could be made by the governor-in-commission, but when a proposed salary "exceeded a specified figure," London would have to agree first. The business of the commission "would be decided, by unanimity or, if on any matter there should not be unanimity, by a majority of the votes given." In the governor's absence meetings would be presided over by a vice-chairman elected by the commission as a whole from the Newfoundland members. The governor would "be given powers in executive matters to act in [an] emergency on his own initiative." While the office of governor was vacant or an incumbent was absent from the colony, the chief justice would assume the governor's powers.[95]

On the financial side, the interest rate announced for the new Newfoundland bonds was the much debated 3 per cent, a reduction made possible in the end by an improvement in the United Kingdom's own credit position. Another change altered the arrangement originally proposed for holders of trustee securities. These bonds were now also to be convertible, but holders who decided against this option were to be given additional protection: by act of the local legislature they were to become

Newfoundland's preferred creditors. The purpose here was to protect the holders of trustee stock in the event that their paper had not matured when the United Kingdom gave up her financial control over Newfoundland. Without the additional legislative guarantee, the holders of trustee securities would not be as well placed as holders of ordinary Newfoundland bonds who had converted and would therefore still enjoy the benefit of the United Kingdom's guarantee, an unacceptable situation. At the British end, the financial plan called for an estimate to be submitted to Parliament in order to provide Newfoundland with the advance she would need to meet in full the interest due on 1 January 1934 to two classes of creditors: the holders of trustee securities, who would be paid on schedule, and holders of other Newfoundland bonds who decided to convert. The latter group would be paid retroactively at the 3 per cent conversion rate and as soon as possible after they had exchanged their old paper. By this arrangement, holders of Newfoundland paper, other than trustee securities, who did not convert would go to the back of the queue with very little prospect of ever being paid. Under the enabling legislation to be passed in Newfoundland to allow the financial plan to be carried out, "recalcitrants" would "be deprived by law of any right to further payments of interest or any payment of principal for a period which though indefinite would certainly be a good many years."[96]

When it was released on 21 November, the report of the Royal Commission was widely praised in the press on both sides of the Atlantic, some of the most flattering comments appearing in the two principal St. John's papers, the *Daily News* and the *Evening Telegram*.[97] Magrath may have raised a few official eyebrows by saying publicly that the plan promulgated for Newfoundland had been hatched entirely in London but Stavert believed that this indiscretion could be safely ignored.[98]

For Alderdice, of course, the publication of the report was a signal for urgent action in desperate circumstances. On the morning of the twenty-third, with a government caucus scheduled for that evening, Alderdice invoked the understanding he believed he had with London about future employment for selected colleagues.[99] He did so apparently to forestall an attempt to enlist support among ministers in favour of a referendum. His ministers of posts and telegraphs, Capt. William C. Winsor, and of agriculture and mines, William J. Walsh, are specifically mentioned in his correspondence, but others seem also to have been involved. "I do not know," he later told Amulree, "what would have been the result of these overtures had not these department heads had the assurance of consideration after the Commission Government begins to function." To Alderdice's great dismay, E.N.R. Trentham, the Treasury official superintending Newfoundland's finances, had let it be known that such promises were out of order "as the English Commissioners must take their positions without trammels of any sort." Alderdice's difficult position was compounded when Trentham persuaded the governor to write him what was presumably a cautionary letter. "This," Alderdice mused, "in spite of the fact that when the acceptance or otherwise of the plan was in doubt His Excellency stated to me the few thousand dollars annually to be spent to ensure acceptance would be well invested."[100] Yet if these exchanges behind the scenes disrupted the previously very cordial relations between Alderdice and Trentham and eventually created difficulties, they did not interrupt the timetable of events being pressed by London.

On 27 November, the Newfoundland legislature was called into session, and the following day resolutions introduced by Alderdice and incorporating an Address to the King were debated and carried by the House of Asembly.[101] These asked in effect that the recommendations of the Royal Commission and the detailed proposals of the British Government as described in the parliamentary paper be carried out. Two days later they were carried unanimously in the Legislative Council.[102] That same day Gordon Bradley, the leader of the opposition in the House of Assembly, and Roland G. Starkes, his lone colleague, moved a complex amendment to the customary motion thanking the governor for the address with which he had opened the session. Their amendment called for either an immediate general election or a referendum on what the government proposed. In addition, the governor would be required to appoint a delegation consisting of the speaker of the House of Assembly, the president of the Legislative Council and the prime minister to go to London to negotiate "terms that will not involve loss by Newfoundland of representative Government."[103]

Alternatively, the opposition amendment proposed either that the Newfoundland members of the Commission of Government be elected; or, in view of the full legislative power to be granted the Commission, including the right to tax, that Newfoundland be given representation in the British House of Commons. Barring this, citing the Royal Commission's attribution of Newfoundland's problems to previous maladministration, the opposition proposed that anyone who had sat in the House of Assembly during the previous twenty-five years be ineligible for service on the proposed Commission and that anyone sitting in the existing house be excluded from holding or being appointed to a civil service position during the first three years of the new regime. In defence of his motion, Bradley claimed that there were "blacks and untouchables" in the British Empire who had "more rights to a voice in their own Governments" than Newfoundlanders would have in theirs, if Alderdice succeeded. Newfoundland would not be self-supporting for "many many years," and it was only "reasonable" that the people should retain some voice in their own affairs. But the opposition leader was not a root and branch dissenter. If the new system came in as the government intended, he said, the Liberal Party, not being out "to make trouble" in the country, would co-operate with it. Nor would the opposition campaign in an election for the "total rejection of the British Government's offer." What was needed was time to consider and sober second thought: Alderdice must keep the bargain he had made with the electors in 1932 to consult them before giving way to Commission of Government.[104] On division the opposition amendment was defeated 20 to 2, whereupon the government motion carried by a like majority. The other item dealt with in this brief session was the bill enabling the financial arrangements to be put into effect.[105] To avoid the technical problems that might arise from independent legislative action on both sides of the Atlantic on so tangled a topic, the finance bill was sent over word for word from London and passed precisely as it was sent. The term of the new 3 per cent bonds would be to 1 July 1963, but they would be redeemable at par from 1 July 1943 onwards. A 1 per cent sinking fund was required within five years of issue.[106]

Two Newfoundland critics outside the legislature heard from in London in the dramatic days after the release of the Amulree report were Coaker and Squires. The career of the latter embodied in the minds of the architects of the report everything that had gone wrong in Newfoundland. Like Bradley, Coaker was not against Commission of Government as such; though not a candidate in the general election of 1932, he had written in favour of the commission idea during the campaign and believed the people would endorse it now if given a chance. The sticky point for him was Alderdice's electoral pledge to go to the people before acting. If the changes contemplated were pushed through without a vote, he warned, there would be an "immediate agitation for repeal" which would be justified "on ground of treachery and surrender [of the] country's rights without [the] people being given [the] time properly [to] study the question."[107] For his part, Squires predicted that when Newfoundlanders realized what had been done to them in such a rush, they would "feel and express resentment as loyal and devoted subjects of the King should do when fundamental principles of British rule have been violated."[108] Weighing against such individual protests, however, were the collective expressions of support for the British plan sent across the Atlantic from the Newfoundland Board of Trade (St. John's), the Bay of Islands Board of Trade (Curling), the Newfoundland Co-operative Self-Help Association (Harbour Grace), the Great War Veterans' Association of Newfoundland, and the Army and Navy League (St. John's).[109]

Once the Newfoundland hurdle was passed, matters were brought to a swift conclusion in London. On 7 December a resolution was considered by the House of Commons in committee to empower the government to make the constitutional changes desired by Newfoundland and to authorize the financial arrangements contigent thereon.[110] Since money was involved, this was introduced by Chamberlain. It succeeded 227 to 38 and was reported to the House the next day without a division, whereupon the bill so anticipated was introduced.[111] The debate on second reading of this bill was held on 12 December, with Thomas leading off for the government in a well-rehearsed performance.[112] He was answered by a variety of opposition spokesmen, chief among them the deputy leader of the Labour Party in the House of Commons, Clement Attlee, who was destined to play an important role in relation to Newfoundland in the 1940s.[113] The government's purpose, he claimed, was not "to tide Newfoundland over" but to save the bondholders, for fear of opening the floodgates of default. This was a "nineteenth century attitude," since "all the best countries," including the United Kingdom itself (in relation to the United States), now defaulted. The real sin in the Government's eyes, apparently, was not for one country to default to another, a common occurrence, but to "make a default to a private individual." In Newfoundland's case investors had had ample warning and should have read the danger signs; they had gone in "with their eyes open," and there was consequently no reason "to meet their losses." The Newfoundland situation typified the larger economic crisis: "It is about time that the Government faced the fact that the world cannot stand the interest demanded by the money lenders. Because of the mass of indebtedness piled up and the fall in prices, the burden is too great, and if you say that it has to be put on the back of the working man, you will have severe trouble." The report of the Royal Commission showed "the utter failure of competitive capitalism" in Newfoundland, and to "put the bailiffs in" only to perpetuate an economic order of "fundamental viciousness" would be "cruel." What was needed instead was a plan that would end the iniquitous merchant-fisherman relationship and make "Newfoundland for the Newfoundlanders." These were inflamatory remarks but the amendment they were employed to defend was lost 250 to 42.[114]

On 14 December the bill was considered in committee and reported without amendment.[115] Four days later it was given third reading but not before the House had heard the Labourite Aneurin Bevan, in full oratorical flight, deliver a savage indictment of what the government was about. A democratic constitution, he said, was being set aside "not for the benefit of the people but against their interests" in order that "a certain class of property holder" might "have his securities retained unimpaired."[116] Inexorably, however, the bill was moved forward to the Lords for first reading the same day.[117] During its passage through the upper chamber, which was completed on the twentieth, amendments were made in keeping with an understanding the government had given in the Commons.[118] These involved changes in the references made in the bill to Newfoundland's letters patent, which were to be suspended rather than revoked as originally indicated. After the amendments made in the Lords had been accepted by the Commons on 20 December, the bill, henceforth styled "the Newfoundland Act, 1933," was given royal assent on 21 December, less than a fortnight before the next interest payments were due from St. John's.[119] Clause 5 of the act further sweetened the financial package by making Newfoundland eligible for loans from the Colonial Development Fund established under the Colonial Development Act of 1929. But it was on the first schedule of the legislation that Newfoundland's future would ultimately hinge. This incorporated the address to the King which had come from the House of Assembly and Legislative Council in St. John's. Annexed to this address, were the principal recommendations of the Royal Commission's report including the understanding that when Newfoundland was "self-supporting" again Responsible Government would be restored "on request" from her people.[120] But no definition was given to "self-supporting," and no procedure was spelled out whereby an appropriate request could be made. In later years these omissions would be of critical importance, but for now attention focused on the inauguration of the Commission of Government. This, it was decided from London, would take place in St. John's on 16 February 1934.[121]

SYNOPSIS: 1929-34

Given a downturn in her export trade of the magnitude that occurred after 1929, Newfoundland could scarcely have avoided a sudden payments crisis. There was nothing inevitable, however, about the resolution through Commission of Government of the particular crisis that arose in the 1930s. This outcome resulted from the interplay of many factors. Well into 1933 the United Kingdom was anxious to limit her involvement in Newfoundland's internal affairs, if only to save herself the spending on local services, by now pared to the bone, that direct responsibility would bring. On the other hand, because of their fear of the consequences of a national default, the British had insisted that Newfoundland meet her debt payments in full. The key to achieving this latter objective and of forestalling the plan of default Alderdice was promoting, without paying too high a price for intervention, lay in Ottawa. Ideally, the United Kingdom wanted Newfoundland to become part of Canada. This was a longstanding wish and would have removed the burden from her entirely. Barring this, she wanted Canada to share with her the cost of carrying the bankrupt. For Newfoundland, already on a short leash held by the bankers, this could have meant additional stern financial controls from outside but not necessarily the loss of parliamentary institutions. The maintenance of a facade of self-government might even have been to the convenience of her backers. In December 1932, the British were able to get what they wanted from Canada, that is to say money to assist Newfoundland with her next interest payment and participation in a Royal Commission that would look into the country's future. But in the summer of 1933, after the commission's fruitless sojourn in Ottawa and Bennett's continuing intransigence in London, the British were forced to turn to a less desirable policy. Canada's decision to turn her back on Newfoundland was, therefore, crucial to the coming of commission of government.

What explains Ottawa's attitude? J.L. Granatstein has noted the disarray and amateurism in this period across many fields of Canadian policy making.[122] Certainly an ad hoc approach was well evident in relations with Newfoundland. Whereas the British proceeded by carefully laid plan, expressed in taut Oxbridge English and flowing from one well-crafted position paper to another, Prime Minister Bennett was moved, seemingly, by instinct. As a corporation lawyer and businessman, his fear of financial collapse became the well-spring of his government's whole attitude towards the depression which by the summer of 1933 was at its lowest depth, an attitude which favoured the British plan. But working against the British point of view in this instance was Bennett's growing belief, fed by cabinet ministers more atavistic than himself, that the mounting debt problems of Canada's own provinces precluded any more help for Newfoundland, let alone taking her into Confederation. In the end it was this beggar-thy-neighbour view, increasingly evident as well in inter-regional relationships within Canada, that prevailed. Bennett could abandon Newfoundland, of course, knowing full well that if the British really meant what they said about the effect of default, they would have to act. This attitude was eased by the conviction in Ottawa that history had made the United Kingdom rather than Canada responsible for the rescue of Newfoundland. The wild card in all this was Labrador and it was never played. Bennett toyed with a Labrador deal, which might have brought him advantage in Quebec, but the asking price was daunting, especially for a region of unproven worth, which it was possible, perhaps reasonable, to believe would in the long run be incorporated, along with the island, into Confederation anyway.

Left to carry Newfoundland on their own, the British understandably decided they would need greater political control than previously contemplated in order to safeguard their investment. Alongside their plans for this, they devised a scheme for pressuring most of Newfoundland's bondholders into converting their paper to a new issue at a lower interest rate. This, as was understood in Whitehall, was default by another name.

The effect of the conversion would be to lower the cost of carrying Newfoundland's debt, which is what Alderdice had wanted, but by acceptable means. A unilateral reduction of interest payments would not be justified while Newfoundland was still in business, but a conversion would be legitimate were she, in effect, to go out of business. This was a neat distinction but its origin lay as much in British self-interest as in high financial principle. For his part, the individual bondholder would be denied the interest rate he had contracted for, though he would now have the British government's guarantee of both interest and principal.

The public argument made for intervening in Newfoundland picked up a characteristic idea of the 1930s, a thought encouraged perhaps by hard times generally. This was that democracy and economic efficiency could sometimes conflict, that left to his own devices the party man would often seek to bribe the electorate and so invite economic disaster through overspending. What was needed to restore economic health was an end to partisanship and the introduction of impartial administration according to business precepts. Echoes of this were heard in Canada in the attempt Mackenzie King made after he returned to power in 1935 to police the spending of the provinces in return for helping them with their debt problems, and in the remarkable but unsuccessful proposal that Mitch Hepburn, the Liberal premier of Ontario, made to his Conservative opposition in 1937 for a union government dedicated to saving the province from "the CIO's Communist threat" and to greater administrative efficiency.[123] But only in Newfoundland was the idea of "a rest from politics" embodied in a whole scheme of government.[124]

In the carrying out of the British plan for Newfoundland, the Royal Commission acted virtually as an extension of the normal Whitehall government machinery. Magrath's presence on the commission might have posed a problem, but Canada's abdication silenced him. Stavert could be counted on for full support because the British plan was very satisfactory to the Canadian banks; they would recover forthwith the sizeable loans they had made to Newfoundland in the initial phase of the crisis while continuing to do business there. Nor was there any great obstacle to overcome in Newfoundland herself. Fear, a lopsided House of Assembly, and widespread support for the notion that the country had the trappings of an elephant on the back of a mouse, all helped to smooth the progress of the British plan. Newfoundland's largely Protestant mercantile elite had fought the introduction of Responsible Government in the 1850s and had ever since looked to the appointed Legislative Council to protect its interest. For the business community the 1933 Royal Commission Report simply articulated in mandarin English what had always been instinctively believed about the evils of popular rule. When the American-born but British and Canadian-educated Leonard C. Outerbridge, one of the leading businessmen and officer veterans in St. John's and a notable philanthropist, gave evidence before the Royal Commission as part of a Merchants' Committee, he advocated the publication of pauper lists in post offices throughout the country and the disenfranchisement at the next general election of the persons named on them.[125] From the point of view of the leaders of the Roman Catholic community, what was important was not the form of government but the maintenance of their denomination's limited but secure share of public largesse. In April 1934, when Archbishop E.P. Roche of St. John's visited the Dominions Office on his way back to Newfoundland from Rome, he gave Harding the impression that he was "glad to see the change in the form of Government" and felt "that self-government had gone for good."[126] Such was the metamorphosis of a once incendiary element on the local political scene. Moreover, the Fishermen's Protective Union, the other menace to established authority the country had produced, had also lost its sting by the 1930s. Coaker's name had formerly been feared in monied and office-holding St. John's, but his 1933 protest, which was in any case muted, could be safely ignored. He was an old man, and his movement had grown old with him. If the Irish had been tamed, senescence had overtaken the Fishermen's Protection Union.

As for Alderdice, he swallowed the bitter medicine served up by the Amulree commission manfully. "Your report," he told Amulree in December 1933, "has made a very striking impression upon all who have read it. Your strictures on our political life are strong but unfortunately only too true."[127] More to the point, after getting his fingers burnt over his plan for default, the prime minister almost stopped bargaining. Newfoundland might not have been able to get many more changes in the British scheme than Alderdice was able to obtain in his talks with Amulree in September 1933, but bankrupts are not without influence and even marginal changes in the circumstances of their demise may have important future consequences. In Newfoundland's case the retention of even a vestige of local self-government, the provision for a later review of the commission system, or the definition of a precise scheme whereby full parliamentary self-government might have been recovered, could have been very important. But such claims were not pressed by Alderdice and, to be fair to him, might well have been impossible to achieve. Intriguing as they are, these possibilities belong not to the facts but to the might-have-beens of history. And in Alderdice's defence it must also be remembered that though Squires may have been a bolder negotiator, at the end of 1931 he too had knuckled under. Alderdice was a gentleman in a world of British and Canadian players. At root, he believed that the honour of the British Empire would see Newfoundland through, and though this faith was never shaken, he did write these bitter words to Lord Amulree in 1935:

"To you alone I would say, if I had had any idea the present plan of Government was to turn out as it has I am afraid I would not have been so ready to accept it. And in justice to you, I feel you, yourself, would have hesitated before suggesting it. 'A word to the wise is sufficient.'"[128] Typically, having rejected the message, Alderdice still believed in the messenger. Regrets notwithstanding, "that thin red cord of sentiment and of blood," as Richard Squires had once described the imperial connection, had held.[129] Newfoundland's ship of state was salvaged, but where her crew would be landed was left an open question.

CHAPTER THREE

The Commission Begins, 1934-36

The administration of this country has been the cause of *ceaseless anxiety* to us. A great deal has been done here in an endeavour to rehabilitate and build up the morale of the people.
Some of the measures such as road building, land settlement, lumber and mineral development, having a long range view, should lead to better conditions, much however remains to be done.

Governor Sir Humphrey Walwyn to
Sir Edward Harding, September 1936

The original British members of the Commission of Government, chosen by the Dominions Office, were Thomas Lodge, Sir John Hope Simpson, and E.N.R. Trentham, the last of whom was already in St. John's.[1] The first chairman was Governor Sir David Murray Anderson. According to Prime Minister Ramsay MacDonald, who visited Newfoundland on holiday in the autumn of 1934, the selection of the first United Kingdom commissioners emphasized "industrial and economic experience."[2] Lodge, a "strong personality,"[3] whose Newfoundland career would be flamboyant, was an experienced civil servant who also had a background in private business. At the time of his appointment to the Commission he was representative of the United Kingdom on the Anglo-Australian-New Zealand Phosphate Commission which operated mines at Nauru and Ocean Island in the Pacific. In a private capacity he was chairman of the Danube Oil Company.[4] Sir John Hope Simpson had served in the Indian Civil Service and as a Liberal member of parliament. Most recently he had been special British envoy to Palestine and Director-General of the National Flood Relief Commission in China.[5] Sixty-five years old at the time of his Newfoundland appointment, he was clearly going to St. John's to round off his career. By contrast, Trentham, a career civil servant, and Lodge, respectively forty-five and fifty, were men whose future prospects depended on their performance as members of the Commission of Government.

The choice of the British commissioners promised change in Newfoundland; the selection of their local colleagues suggested continuity. At the invitation of the Dominions Office, Governor Anderson forwarded a list of possible members and in a private letter came out in favour of the three men eventually chosen. They were Alderdice, John C. Puddester, secretary of state in the outgoing Newfoundland government, and William R. Howley, a lawyer and former member of the House of Assembly. According to Anderson, the range of people to choose from was small: Newfoundland had "no leisured class" whose members could be counted on to serve for patriotic reasons and no public servants equal to the work at hand. Alderdice and Puddester bore the stigma of coming straight from the world of politics, but they were better than anyone else available. Alderdice had "the confidence of the people" and was financially honest. Puddester, who would serve on the Commission until his death in 1947, was formerly business manager of the St. John's *Daily News*, in which he still held shares. His knowledge of the country's social services would serve the Commission well, and though probably only "75 % honest" he could, believed Anderson, "be kept in check." Since Alderdice was Anglican and Puddester a member of the United Church of Canada, the third Newfoundland commissioner, because of the support Archbishop Roche had given to the idea of Commission of Government, had to be a Roman Catholic. One possibility was Lewis Edward Emerson, the Minister of Justice, later to become a key figure on the Commission, but passed over now by Anderson with this comment: "He is not popular, is very inclined to split hairs and I am told is very bumptious and self-opinionated at Meetings of the Committee of the Executive Council, and there are also certain doubts about his strict honesty." William R. Howley, who was eventually chosen, had served briefly as attorney general under Alderdice in 1928. He was "a quiet reserved man" and therefore a good candidate to preside again over the administration of justice.[6]

While the appointments to the Commission were being considered, Alderdice left for England to discuss matters arising out of the impending transfer of power. Anderson told Harding in advance of this visit that Alderdice was "very tired mentally" from the events of the last hectic and crisis-ridden months. The prime minister was also exhibiting an "inferiority complex" and feared that the United Kingdom commissioners might "adopt a superior and perhaps domineering attitude." What must be avoided, Alderdice believed, was the appointment of a "staff of Englishmen," who, coming to St. John's with the British commissioners, "might form an English 'Colony,'" and then "look down on the Newfoundland people generally and be unpopular." "You know far better than I can tell you how to deal with 'Colonial Premiers,'" Anderson wryly observed, "but I thought an indication of Mr. Alderdice's attitude may be useful."[7]

In fact the prime minister's visit to London went smoothly, although the delicate matter of the employment of ex-ministers was left hanging. On 9 January, Harding introduced Lodge, Hope Simpson, and Alderdice to one another over lunch.[8] The Newfoundlander approved of his future colleagues and soon after he and his family sailed with them and their wives for Halifax on board the SS *Montclare*, arriving in St. John's on 15 February. The next day Anderson presided over the inauguration of the Commission of Government at a public ceremony held in the ballroom of the Newfoundland Hotel. Instructions for this event were sent in such detail from London that even the seating arrangements on the platform were laid down.[9] At the start of the proceedings, which were broadcast, Anderson called on the Deputy Secretary of State, Arthur Mews, to read out the new Letters Patent, dated 30 January 1934. The governor declared the Letters in effect and signed a proclamation which was published the same day in the *Newfoundland Gazette*. After this Anderson made a speech, in the course of which he read an inspirational message from Thomas. Then, following a short speech by Alderdice, the ceremony ended, whereupon Anderson privately administered the oath of allegiance to the commissioners.

The preamble of the Letters Patent together with clauses I and II (there were twenty-three clauses altogether) suspended earlier Letters of 28 March 1876, and 17 July 1905; defined the boundaries of Newfoundland; signified the governor's power and authority; and constituted the Commission of Government, the members of which were to hold office at the pleasure of the Crown, though in practice they were given three-year renewable terms. The Commission was to conduct business only at the call of the governor and a quorum was to be three members, not counting the governor or other presiding member. The governor was directed to chair the meetings of the Commission "unless ... prevented by some necessary or reasonable cause." The style of enacting laws was to be "The Governor, by and with the advice of the Commission of Government." No law was to take effect until signed by the governor, and any law could be disallowed from London within one year of such consent being given. By clause XXII the Crown reserved the "full power and authority ... to revoke, alter, or amend" the Letters Patent as it deemed fit.[10]

In a separate document, the governor was given his "Royal Instructions." Embodied in ten clauses, these were also dated 30 January 1934. Among other things, they defined the governor's emergency powers, spelled out the terms of his power of pardon, and specified eight classes of bills to which, generally speaking, he was to refuse assent. Clause VIII specified that any appointment made by the governor which carried an annual emolument exceeding $1200 was to be regarded as "temporary and provisional" until decided upon by royal authority.[11] Superficially, the Letters Patent and the Royal Instructions, framed in high officialese, seemed to cover all contingencies; but in fact constitutional difficulties, especially involving the relationship between the governor and his colleagues on the one hand, and between the Commission of Government and the Dominions Office on the other, would bedevil the new administration in its early years.

At 10:15 AM on 17 February 1934, the first meeting of the Commission of Government, which along with its individual members was styled "the Honourable," was held at Government House with Anderson in the chair.[12] Alderdice was elected vice-chairman of the Commission and departmental responsibilities were distributed as follows: Trentham, "Commissioner for Finance, including Customs, Income Tax, and Post Office"; Hope Simpson, "Commissioner for Natural Resources, comprising Marine and Fisheries, Forests, and Agriculture and Mines"; Lodge, "Commissioner for Public Utilities, comprising Public Works, Railway, Steamship Services and other communications and the Newfoundland Hotel"; Alderdice, "Commissioner for Home Affairs and Education"; Howley, "Commissioner for Justice, Police, Liquor Control, and Attorney General"; and Puddester, "Commissioner for Public Health and Welfare, Labour and Pensions." With adjustments to take account of changed circumstances, this division between the British and Newfoundland commissioners, which in effect put control of finance and the economy in the hands of the former, was maintained throughout the life of the Commission. It was also decided that the senior civil servant in each branch of government would henceforth be known as "Secretary" rather than "Deputy Minister." The secretary appointed to the Commission itself was William J. Carew, a Roman Catholic. In a country famous for its fondness of gossip, he personified discretion; his distinction was recognized in the CBE awarded to him in 1947. One duty assigned him now was the preparation after each meeting of a press communiqué. This was to cover "such matters as it should be deemed desirable to make public." The secretary was also made the "sole channel" of communication for the bringing of business before the Commission.[13] Any matter proposed for discussion at Commission meetings was to focus on policy rather than administrative detail which, according to Hope Simpson, had wasted a great deal of the time of the now defunct Executive Council.[14] To streamline procedures, the minutes would record only the Commission's decisions, though the secretary was enjoined to "keep a record of deliberations for purposes of reference."[15] Procedurally at least, the Commission made a strong start.

What international status had Newfoundland now assumed? While her self-government was suspended, she was juridically still a Dominion, however hollow the distinction. The Commission of Government would perforce at times enjoy great latitude in bargaining internationally on Newfoundland's behalf, but it always acted on sufferance for in practice as well as in theory sovereignty over Newfoundland belonged to the United Kingdom during the Commission era. This was demonstrated in March 1934, when British representatives abroad were given instructions on "Phraseology and Procedure in Correspondence relating to Newfoundland Affairs." The phrase "His Majesty's Government in Newfoundland" was to be dropped and replaced with the less exalted "The Government of Newfoundland." Equally, the United Kingdom was "once more the sole channel of communication" between the governments to which officials were accredited and Newfoundland.[16] Further proof of the country's diminished status was given in May 1934, when the Commission decided to abolish the office, in existence since 1921, of High Commissioner for Newfoundland in London.[17] In international as much as in domestic affairs, Newfoundland had become the United Kingdom's ward.

Hope Simpson and Lodge, the two commissioners who were new to Newfoundland, were appalled by the condition of the country. With so many living on a miserably inadequate dole, Hope Simpson reported in a family letter, the morale of the people was "dreadful." Dependence on government was endemic and the Commission's most pressing and demanding task was to cultivate "a sense of honesty" in relations between government and the governed.[18] Lady Hope Simpson was equally blunt. Potentially a beauty spot, St. John's was "just a dirty foul-smelling slum." Had the British commissioners known what awaited them (Trentham presumably excepted), she doubted whether they would have agreed to serve. Newfoundland lacked "the simplest amenities" and the poor of the country had "nothing but their sects and the gambling game of the fishery." "Every day," she commented shortly after arriving, "seems to unfold new revelations of wickedness in the past, and maladministration in the present as a result. It is all very startling." On the bright side, Lady Hope Simpson quickly developed a friendship with Thomas Lodge's wife, Isobel. This, she observed, would temper the social isolation in which they would now both have to live: "We shall not be able to be very friendly with anyone else so it is lucky that we like each other."[19] Carew thought the British commissioners were left-leaning and would favour "the under-dogs."[20] Though an exaggeration, this remark was discerning. Certainly, Lodge and Hope Simpson would be no strangers to controversy in Newfoundland.

One of the first issues to test the mettle of the new government arose when Alderdice attempted to make good on the promises of employment he had made to former ministerial colleagues. While Alderdice had been in London at the beginning of 1934, the former minister of marine and fisheries, John G. Stone, had died. Walsh had resigned from the agricultural and mines ministry after being arrested and charged with the theft of stamps from the Newfoundland Museum, but his subsequent acquittal re-opened his claim to a job.[21] Alderdice also took up the cause of Herman W. Quinton, his former minister of public works, who had been sent what appeared to be his last salary cheque on the day after the Commission's inauguration. Alderdice challenged Trentham about this but Quinton was nonetheless "relegated to a room on the top floor of the Public Works Building" where he was "completely ignored by all and sundry." Reporting this affront, Alderdice asked Amulree to confirm in writing that there was indeed an agreement between them whereby four ex-ministers would be employed.[22] Clutterbuck attributed this demand to Alderdice's general fatigue and thought that his letter need not be taken "too literally."[23] For his part, Amulree confirmed to Clutterbuck that he had not given the assurances Alderdice claimed to have received. At the same time, however, Amulree sympathized with Alderdice's "political difficulties" and did not want "to make matters worse for him by 'giving him the lie direct.'"[24]

This conciliatory approach was endorsed at the Dominions Office. As a first step towards devising some face-saving settlement, the governor was asked whether the Commission had actually discussed the situation of the stranded ex-ministers and to what effect.[25] This telegam crossed one from Anderson advising that public opinion in Newfoundland was "very strongly opposed" to the employment of such individuals, whose services were in any case not wanted by the United Kingdom commissioners.[26] In short, Alderdice must desist. The next day Anderson telegraphed that what Alderdice wanted would "be prejudicial to the new form of Government ... and would be contrary to the recommendations in the Royal Commission's report."[27] If a commitment had been made that had to be honoured, the "only satisfactory solution" was to compensate the individuals involved financially. In another message Anderson reported that Winsor, who had been kept on as Secretary for the Post Office, would not be retained in that position.[28] Further, no magistracies were vacant and no other openings for which the ex-ministers might qualify were soon anticipated. In view of all this, the next telegram from London agreed that ex-ministers could not be kept on as "advisers" but argued the case for magnanimity being pressed by Amulree. Alderdice had no doubt acted on his own in making the promises but it would be useful to "stretch a point" in his favour in order to avoid "an element of friction in the

Commission." Seemingly, the way to do this was by making the requisite appointments outside St. John's, perhaps in the magistracy or in fishery or relief work.[29] But this proposal drew another unyielding reply from Anderson, who told London that such appointments would be disastrous "to [the] prestige of [the] Commission." "I did not realize," he cautioned, "how unanimous and strong is public opinion in all classes against all politicians until [the] Commission started work. I am most unwilling to cause Alderdice any difficulty. I am however concerned that the Commission's work will be devoid of result and they will not keep the goodwill of the people unless they can establish themselves as being firmly opposed to politics and wire pulling."[30]

In lieu of jobs, Anderson again urged a cash settlement, this time specifying a figure of $2,000 for each man. But the notion of additional spending to save Alderdice embarrassment had already encountered a Treasury roadblock.[31] Moreover, from the point of view of the Dominions Office, the payments envisaged by the governor would create an "impossible situation" in Parliament for the secretary of state, who would in effect have to defend blackmail. An impasse had been reached, and to overcome it London had decided to come down hard on Alderdice. Anderson was to tell the former prime minister that while Thomas appreciated and was willing to relieve "his difficulties," having been urged to do so by Amulree, there was no practical means of doing this.[32] Alderdice should therefore drop the issue. Anderson was asked to confirm his own support for this position and to say that by persisting Alderdice would leave open only one course of action. This was to bring the matter formally to the attention of the Commission, which could be expected to receive Alderdice's case unfavourably. As had happened so often before, Alderdice swallowed his pride and accepted the British lead, but this episode, echoes of which were heard for the remainder of the year, left him thoroughly disillusioned. On the other side of things, Hope Simpson, a good phrasemaker, once told Amulree that though Alderdice was "a very courageous man, with a fine memory and a highly developed sense of humour – an attractive person," he had "an outlook restricted to the coasts of N.F.L."[33] For Alderdice, to serve was now to be patronized. But at least he escaped the indignity of his old colleague William Walsh who, in a pathetic appeal for help, told Amulree in September 1934, that he had been "seven months idle."[34]

While this sorry sub-plot was being played out in the background, a more constructive side of the Commission was also in evidence. One manifestation of this was a push for greater administative efficiency. This involved many procedural and personnel changes, the effect of which was to give the government the appearance of initial dynamism. Early on, the

Commission invited visiting experts (often from the United Kingdom) to report on a particular policy area as a prelude to action. A number of officials were also seconded from the British civil service to occupy key positions in selected branches of the Newfoundland government. In contrast, by 1936 the Commission was planning to send Newfoundland civil servants to London for short courses.[35] Between 1935 and 1939 the Commission reported on its plans and activities in six parliamentary papers published in the United Kingdom.[36]

In one of its most important administrative initiatives, the Commission sought to improve communications between the central government and the rural population. The only elected local government in Newfoundland was the Municipal Council in St. John's, which the British commissioners believed to be as badly run as the Newfoundland government itself had been.[37] Part of the Commission's answer to the problem it perceived in local administration outside the capital was the creation in 1935 of a Newfoundland Ranger Force, which operated under its direct control.[38] This step had been recommended by the Royal Commission, and the new organization was modelled on the familiar colonial "district commissioner" concept. Captain Leonard T. Stick, who had the distinction of having been the first enlistee in the Newfoundland Regiment during the Great War, was made chief ranger, but much of the actual training of the force was left to Sergeant-Major Fred Anderton, a Royal Canadian Mounted Police drill sergeant who was loaned to Newfoundland for this purpose.[39] By the end of 1936 there were thirty-eight ranger detachments across Newfoundland and Labrador; and the total personnel of the force, which established its headquarters at Whitbourne, was fifty-two. The work of a ranger in the field was diverse: he might simultaneously be police officer, customs collector, inspector of weights and measures, game warden, sawmill inspector, and salvage commissioner – in brief, a general factotum for whatever the government wanted done in his neighbourhood. By mid-1936 the rangers had completed 150 patrols, covering some 42,104 miles. The work done on these patrols was sub-divided as follows: 48 per cent for the Department of Natural Resources, 35 per cent for the Department of Public Health and Welfare, and 17 per cent for the Department of Justice.[40]

In 1935 the Commission also reorganized the country's stipendiary magistracy. St. John's and vicinity had a central district judge who was ex-officio stipendiary magistrate for the area. The rest of the island was divided into seven magisterial districts. The result was a system wherein, according to the Commission's 1936 annual report, seven district magistrates enjoyed the help of fourteen assistant magistrates. Eight of these officials had been recruited in 1935 to replace retirees; most members of this new group were under thirty and all were well educated. The intention of the 1935 judicial reform was that the magistrates, in addition to dispensing justice, should undertake some of the work previously done by members of the House of Assembly: they were to be the government's "principal agents" in local social and economic affairs, initiators of ideas as well as supervisors of approved schemes. As their first task in this role, the magistrates worked on a settlement by settlement survey, the results of which were intended to give the various departments of government a body of factual information on which to base future policy. In keeping with their changed status, the magistrates also began gathering in annual convention under the sponsorship of the Department of Justice.[41]

The original commissioners attempted also to recast the health and welfare services. Hospitals in St. John's were given increased facilities and staff, and a public health clinic was provided there for the "Sick Poor." In addition it was decided to close the city's Home for the Aged and Infirm, which had housed a poor infirmary, and to board out the destitute old in approved accommodation. A clinic for the treatment of venereal disease was also opened in the capital. Outside St. John's a cottage hospital scheme, which would be a great boon to the rural population, was launched. The first such institution was opened at Markland, a new community that, as will be seen, was itself a notable Commission experiment. By the end of 1936, cottage hospitals were also in operation at Old Perlican, Argentia, Come-by-Chance, Grand Bank, Harbour Breton, and Burgeo. Another building had been completed and was ready for occupation at Stephenville. The need for this additional hospital space was pressing. In its 1935 annual report, the Commission noted that whereas Newfoundland required at least one thousand hospital beds, it had only five hundred available. Moreover, a health survey undertaken by the Rotary Club of St.John's in the previous year had found that there were about four hundred crippled children in the country whose special needs were ignored altogether in the existing public health arrangements.[42]

Given the difficulty of attracting doctors to the Newfoundland outports, the Commission's plans for improving rural health care stressed the role of nurses and midwives. A district nursing service was organized to take over the functions of the voluntary Newfoundland Outport Nursing and Industrial Association (NONIA), and to train nurses for public health work in challenging circumstances. Whereas only eight nurses were available for such service in 1934, fifty-four were on assignment at the close of 1936. In the latter year the Midwives Act was also amended to provide for a system of licensing and registration; thirty women were trained in St. John's for this work. On the south-west coast of the island, from the summer of 1934 onwards, the M/V *Lady Anderson*, which would become a Newfoundland icon, provided a travelling clinic for one of the country's most hard pressed regions. In 1935 the Commission also reported that a sick bay was being provided at public expense on the steamer that annually transported large numbers of island fishermen to and from the rich fishing grounds off Labrador. Generally, however, the Commission relied for medical service in northern Newfoundland and Labrador on the famous medical mission which Sir Wilfred Grenfell had established there in 1895, even though it was in many respects fiercely independent with its own international network of fund raisers.

Special attention was given in the Commission's health care plans to the control of communicable diseases, especially tuberculosis which was rife in Newfoundland. Indicative of this was the fact that when the male patients at the Mental Hospital in St. John's were surveyed in 1936, it was found that in addition to their psychiatric problems, 15 per cent of them were suffering from tuberculosis. This dread disease would cast a long shadow over Newfoundland for years to come, but the Commission intensified the fight against it just as it did against diptheria, typhoid fever, and smallpox, all of which had often spread terror in the population. Immunization became more readily available in Newfoundland after 1934, and the methods of modern child health care became better known. Sensibly, the Commission linked health care and education, as is shown by this observation in its 1936 annual report: "In a country where somewhat extreme conservatism characterizes the adult population, it is obvious that satisfactory progress with health education can be made only if those in the formative period of life, pre-school and school children, are properly and generally trained."[43] During 1936 the government distributed free milk in the schools of St. John's to about a quarter of the children in attendance in order to combat undernourishment. In schools located in outport nursing districts, cocoa was distributed instead, as milk was not available for general distribution. In this period also, the government promoted the organization in the schools of branches of the Junior Red Cross; at the end of 1936 these numbered some 350 and involved about 20 per cent of all school children. In the same spirit, the Commission sponsored health broadcasts over VONF, St. John's. Attention was also given to improving the water supply; existing food and drug laws were revised with better provision being made for their enforcement. In 1935 the Department of Health and Welfare hired two officials, de facto social workers, who began a program of home visits, concerning themselves with the welfare of rejected and illegitimate children, the problems of abandoned wives, and family difficulties generally. In August of the same year, the department mobilized 270 workers for a country-wide census, the first since 1921.

Important changes were likewise made in the country's public relief system; but while the Commission may have been bureaucratically more efficient in this area than previous governments, at root it was moved by time-worn precept. Virtue lay in paring costs and keeping the able-bodied on relief below the standard of living that work could provide. Implicitly, this meant adherence to the same principle of "less eligibility" that dominated Canadian thinking about relief in this period.[44] According to this doctrine, those who did not work had always to be less eligible for society's benefits than those who did. Otherwise the will to work would generally be eroded. In its annual report for 1936, the Commission noted that 2,998 needy individuals had qualified during the year for payments, at the annual rate of $150, from the $150,000 it had available for old age pensions. At the same time, there were 4,300 individuals on the "permanent poor lists," a group consisting of "widows, orphans and the infirm," to whom $115,000 had been paid during the year. This represented a decrease in payment of $18,000 from the previous year, a reduction that had been "largely secured by stricter supervision." The beneficiaries of this allowance were now being paid directly by cheque; but the mass of the government's dependents, the recipients of able-bodied relief, were still given assistance in kind.[45]

During 1934 the Commission began purchasing relief commodities in bulk and with the savings thus realized increased the value of relief orders to a general average of $1.85 per person per month from the existing $1.57.[46] Even so the government was able to save $181,445.51 during the months March to September 1934 as compared to the same months in 1933 because of a drop in the number of people on the dole.[47] The list of products made available to relief recipients was also improved in 1934; more foods were provided as well as soap and kerosene oil. The effect of this change, however, should not be exaggerated considering the fact that the lean food list the Commission set out to improve had featured only seven items, "flour, tea, molasses, pork and beef, salt and yeast."[48]

Mercifully, one of the government's bulk purchases was of vitamin B enriched flour, which it began importing from England to counteract beriberi. In its 1935 report on unemployment the Commission observed that in St. John's, where there was still a separate relief administration, the value of public assistance to the individual was now 25 per cent greater than ever before.[49] A larger ration was being given in the capital than in the outports because city residents could not grow food for themselves. Additionally, in St. John's the "sick poor" were being given "special food orders," and elementary school children were receiving free milk and buns daily. On weekdays two kitchens in the capital made deliveries of soup to indigents, amounting to 1,500–2,000 gallons per week. During the winter of 1934–35 also, clothing valued at about $10,000 had been distributed to more than 6,000 St. John's residents by the Service League of Newfoundland, a voluntary organization supported by the government. In Placentia Bay and on the southwest coast the Commission reported that it had distributed 2,000 barrels of Newfoundland-grown potatoes to residents unable to provide this staple for themselves.[50]

What was the effect of these changes? Publicly the Commission wondered in its May 1935 report whether it was going too far in its reform of public assistance: "So far from the relief of the outports being insufficient, apprehension is felt and has already been voiced by independent observers lest the liberality in this connection should result in permanent pauperization of a considerable part of the population."[51] Such sanctimony notwithstanding, the outlook for Newfoundland's poor remained bleak. In 1936 the Dominions Office was told from Government House in St. John's that the dole was "not of itself a living ration and could not possibly be reduced." It should, but could not be, increased, because "however low the scale may appear in English eyes, it is too near the average standard of existence in Newfoundland, for the Government to make idleness more attractive than work."[52]

The same grim logic also inspired remarks made from the Newfoundland side at a meeting held in the Dominions Office in April 1939. The record made of this gathering described the views of the representatives of the Commission of Government present as follows:

> The dole rations, though admittedly meagre, were yet sufficient to provide a bare subsistence for those concerned. Account had also to be taken of the natural resources available to the people in most parts of the Island. The standard of dietary would better be described as rough rather than low, and people on the dole, even if having no other resources, could manage to keep going without impairment to their health, provided they did not undertake any hard work or expose themselves to severe winter conditions. The margin between the value of the dole rations received by the average family on relief and the value of the earnings of the average fisherman not on relief was, in fact, very small; and if in present circumstances the dole rations were to be increased, this ... would inevitably mean that many thousands of fishermen who were courageously struggling to maintain themselves without recourse to public relief would give up the struggle and flock on to the dole.[53]

Reduced to its essence, this was the relief policy of Newfoundland's new administration in the 1930s.

In educational matters the Commission was otherwise constrained. Hope Simpson was appalled by an educational system that divided funds denominationally. In one small community, he wrote home, there were, incredibly, separate Roman Catholic, Anglican, United Church, and Salvation Army schools serving only 120 families. His example was extreme, but it was powerful ammunition nonetheless. "The next generation," he believed, "is the hope, but will be no better than the present one unless we can get a better system of education."[54] Lodge agreed, writing that education was "the most important question of all." "I doubt," he ventured, "whether there is a purely white community in the world on such a low cultural level or where complete ignorance of anything outside the daily toil is so widespread." The barrier to education posed by a scattered population had been overcome in Norway, and, in Lodge's view, a better school system had to be the Commission's first priority for Newfoundland. This meant both compulsory attendance and "some departure from the present ultra denominational system." Lodge acknowledged the "special position" of the Roman Catholic Church locally and declared that he would not press for anything the church had not accepted elsewhere. But he insisted that the moment was ripe for fundamental change and must not be lost.[55]

Given that Lodge thought the Protestant Newfoundlanders were indifferent to the religious backgrounds of their children's teachers, he defined the job of the Commission as providing "efficient schools managed by efficient teachers." This meant "a state school system and a body of teachers appointed by the State and looking to the State for advancement in their careers." If the Roman Catholic Church wanted to maintain "a parallel system," it could do so on its own; but the religious authorities would have to assume full responsibility for the quality of the education given under their auspices and accept state supervision to ensure compliance with established requirements. When the Commission grasped the educational nettle, it would start Newfoundland on the road to permanent prosperity.[56]

By contrast, Alderdice, who had departmental responsibility for education, favoured a policy of gradual change in the school system. With an eye to local political and religious realities, he told Amulree in September 1934, that "for some time ... it would be inadvisable to upset the present system of denominational education."[57] Equally, curriculum reform and compulsory school attendance would have to be achieved over time, tactfully and patiently. His point was well taken, for when early in 1935 the government addressed itself to the overhaul of the administration of education, it soon clashed with Archbishop Roche and Bishop William C. White, his Church of England counterpart.[58]

According to Hope Simpson, the more formidable opponent was Archbishop Roche. He apparently threatened to require Howley's resignation from the Commission should it go through with its plans, to have the legislation under consideration denounced from the pulpit, and to forbid Newfoundland Roman Catholics from participating in the King's Silver Jubilee Celebrations of 1935 or accepting the Jubilee medal.[59] Eventually, a compromise was arrived at between church and state and embodied in an act given assent on 6 April 1935.[60] This acknowledged the denominational principle while permitting greater administrative efficiency and more government control. Specifically, the act abolished the existing board of education which functioned through the three denominational superintendents. In future the link between the churches and the government would be a committee appointed by the governor in Commission. This would have a chairman and six members, two each from the Roman Catholic, Church of England, and United Churches, nominated by the heads of these denominations. Appointments to local school boards, which were to remain denominational in character, would be on the recommendation of the religious sub-groups of this committee as circumstance required. The government, however, would now be free to appoint as it saw fit a secretary of education and whatever other officials the Department of Education might need to carry out its work including superintending inspectors, one-third of whom would have to be drawn from each of the major denominations. Moreover, "as far as possible" each of these inspectors was to be assigned duties relating to his own denomination. With these changes Newfoundland had a "secularised" department of education "administering a denominational school system."[61] At the department level the key official was now Lloyd Shaw, a Prince Edward Island native and graduate of Columbia University, who had been appointed secretary of education when the Commission set off on the high road of reform.

Hope Simpson considered this legislation a major achievement,[62] but in fact the denominational system outlived the Commission, which never again challenged the basic educational interests of the churches. This retreat was signalled after the 1935 deal had been made when the Commission committed itself in writing to the heads of the denominations not to alter the educational status quo in its essentials without giving them "opportunity for consideration and representation."[63] In May 1935, during a visit to London, Howley had opportunity to pursue still further the Roman Catholic case against unilateral government action in the field of education. While overseas Howley had received a troubled letter from Roche which he circulated in the Dominions Office on the understanding that it would not be shown to Lodge, who was also in England.[64] In his letter Roche described an interview he had had with Alderdice during which two issues of vital importance to the church had been discussed but left unsettled. The first was the question of Roman Catholic representation in the new administrative structure at the Department of Education. Without naming a specific post, Roche's expectation in this regard was that there should be "a Catholic official with statutory powers ... at the head and centre of educational administration." His second concern was the method of appointing teachers. Having inferred from Alderdice's remarks that the Commission was considering taking this out of the hands of the school boards and making it the responsibility of the department, Roche told Howley that this change "would mean a definite break with the Catholic body throughout the country." "Our principle," he wrote, "of Catholic teachers in Catholic schools necessarily implies the appointment of teachers by Catholic authorities." Presumably, he continued, the Commission would refrain from making any more changes in education while its one Roman Catholic member was out of the country. What was needed now was for the Commission "to make known clearly and in detail their educational policy as a whole, and thus afford an opportunity for frank and intelligent discussion."[65]

In passing this letter to Clutterbuck, Howley repeated a rumour from Newfoundland that the Commission proposed spending $40,000 during 1935-36 on state schools for St. John's. This project, he said, had been considered earlier, but he had reserved judgment on it then and had subsequently assumed that it had been abandoned with the passing of the new education act. He understood that this legislation had disposed of "educational questions for the time being." The present difficulty with the archbishop, Howley maintained, resulted from the Commission's failure to take the churches into its confidence. This was a defect traceable to a habit of the United Kingdom commissioners of first framing legislation and then springing it on their Newfoundland colleagues.[66]

For his part Harding heard from Howley that "Sir J. Hope Simpson's experience with native races was not exactly what was required for the administration of a country of European inhabitants like Newfoundland." Harding's own response to the points of educational policy raised by the Newfoundlander was on the surface unyielding: qualifications had to take precedence over denominational considerations in making administrative appointments; the question of how schools should be run and teachers chosen devolved initially on the Commission and had to be settled "in the light of local considerations." As such, it was not something on which the under-secretary could properly comment.[67] Clearly, however, the Dominions Office, which liked to keep Newfoundland out of the news, was anxious for a cooling-off period on the whole educational issue. For his part Governor Anderson welcomed this policy of "sympathy and conciliation to the Churches."[68] In early September 1935, Alderdice told Amulree that the new organization of his department was working well and that a revised curriculum was about to be tested in the schools. If educational reform was to proceed, he observed, "one must be sure of one's ground in every step taken."[69] After their initial flare up, the government and the churches learned to live with one another, for in truth each had too much at stake to risk a pitched battle. This was a reality the

Commission also faced in its dealings with other well-entrenched local interests.

Economically, the newly appointed Commission faced the harsh reality of the continuing world depression. Nonetheless, from a budgetary standpoint the case could be made in the first years of its existence that things were getting better. With the bond conversion the government's interest burden from 1933–34 onwards was lightened by over $2,000,000 annually.[70] On the revenue side, the 1934–35 and 1935–36 figures were affected by a reduction in the customs duties on certain essential consumer items. This took effect in two stages, on 1 January and 1 July 1935, and followed a study of the Newfoundland tariff undertaken by officials seconded from the United Kingdom Board of Customs and Excise.[71] The result was to make flour duty-free and to reduce customs charges on some other foodstuffs as well as on boots, shoes, clothing, and piece goods. For 1935–36 the revenue lost by these changes was estimated at $1,000,000, but in actual fact the total customs revenue was only $258,000 less than had been collected the previous year.

Although the economic facts were construed optimistically in the Commission's public pronouncements, industrially the country remained stagnant. By the spring of 1934 conditions in the fishing industry had deteriorated to such an extent that the government itself had to outfit some men, using relief funds for this purpose.[72] Its investment proved worthwhile as a better season followed than that in 1933. But in 1935, when the government assisted fishermen on a hire-purchase basis, the industry suffered another reverse. This was partly due to weather conditions but the main problem lay in the markets overseas. Italy, which came under League of Nations sanctions in October 1935 because of her invasion of Abyssinia, virtually stopped taking Newfoundland fish. Moreover, prices obtained in Portugal fell off drastically, partly because of the activities of the government-backed importing agency there and partly because Newfoundland exporters undermined one another. At the same time, exchange difficulties handicapped the Newfoundland industry in Brazil and Spain.[73] In 1936, when the Civil War began in Spain, market conditions were marginally better, but the catch declined, producing still more hardship.[74]

Initially, with assistance from the Colonial Development Fund (Hope Simpson wrote privately that he and Lodge would resign if it was not forthcoming),[75] the government concentrated on improving the productive capacity of the fishing industry, drawing on the recommendations of the 1933 Royal Commission in this regard. Among other things, a shipbuilding program was started, bait depots were built, research was stimulated at the government fishery research laboratory, and an educational campaign was begun among saltfish producers to raise the quality of the Newfoundland product. Attention was also given to improving cod liver oil production and to building up the "subsidiary fisheries" in which whales, lobster, herring, and salmon were taken.[76] In all this the government had looked towards incremental, long-term gain but the disastrous events of the 1935 fishing season brought about a crisis requiring immediate attention. In November of that year Hope Simpson, whose department was responsible for fishery matters, told Harding that the Commission was "having an anxious time" and that there were signs of a "breakdown in the economic structure as affecting the fishery." On the South Coast in particular conditions were "desperately bad," and many local merchants had become insolvent. In this area indeed there was reason to fear that the whole of the population would need dole during the winter and would need it permanently unless new supply arrangements could be made for them.[77]

In June the Commission had strengthened the powers of a board the legislature had established in 1933 to regulate the export of saltfish.[78] What it offered as a solution to the gloomy situation at season's end was a commission of enquiry, appointed "in response to a general desire, and in the hope both of maintaining morale and of receiving support for a policy of reform.[79] Justice James M. Kent of the Newfoundland Supreme Court was appointed to chair the commission; other members were Herbert R. Brookes of Harvey and Company and Ernest Watson, a chartered accountant.

Privately, Hope Simpson believed that the commercial elite of the country which ran the fishing industry from its Water Street base constituted the main obstacle to progress. "The St. John's merchants," he once wrote, "are a reactionary crowd. They see no further than the end of their noses and have no interest outside their own profit. They dislike me and they dislike the Commission Government, because our main interest is prosperity for the common folk."[80] Elsewhere, he noted that the "woodsmen and the fishermen ... are in fact serfs. For 300 years ... the major part of their earnings has gone to create about 300 wealthy families. And that system of sweating still exists. It is a dreadful problem."[81] After hearing an economist speaking to the St. John's Rotary Club condemn "a state of society in which the great mass of the people have no say whatever in fixation of the price of what they buy, and equally no say whatever in the price of what they sell," Hope Simpson observed: "That is the case in N.F.L. and ... [the speaker] might have pointed his finger at any individual in the audience (except myself) and have truly said 'thou art the man': that is the most important and radical problem for the government, and we have not yet tackled it."[82] Lady Hope Simpson was just as scathing: "I have never been in a position before," she wrote, "to see what selfishness and greed in commerce mean to the people. Here the merchants have exploited the fishermen ... grown richer and richer and then gone away to enjoy their wealth in England and America. The money made here is not, as a rule, spent here ... The morale of the people has been undermined by all the conditions of their lives.[83]

These were strong sentiments; but just as denominational education survived the Commission's tendency to reform, so too did the fundamental relationship between capital and labour in the fishing industry. Regulation and innovation might be forced on Water Street, but the right of business to own, buy, sell, and profit would remain intact. As with education indeed, the effects of the Commission's efforts in relation to the fishing industry may in the long run have been to stabilize rather than undermine the old order – the opposite of what Hope Simpson and Lodge intended. Certainly this could be argued with respect to the government's main legislative initiative of the 1930s in the fisheries area, the creation in 1936 of the Newfoundland Fisheries Board.[84] In effect the board, which was Hope Simpson's finest legacy to the country, operated as a department of fisheries within the Department of Natural Resources, through which it reported. Consisting of three members, including a chairman, all government appointees, it was given sweeping powers to regulate production and export.[85] Its establishment was intended to calm an increasingly restless and worried business community; under the lawyer Raymond Gushue, its first and only chairman, the new organization sought not to compete with established enterprises but to co-operate with them to mutual advantage; that is, its approach was gradualist and conciliatory.[86]

In its initial dealings with the paper companies, the Commission also set about reform cautiously. When it took office, the immediate problem in the forest sector was a rising tide of complaint about both conditions in the country's logging camps and the wages being paid to loggers, especially those employed by contractors and sub-contractors supplying wood to the paper mills. It was represented to St. John's that in some areas, loggers were not making enough to maintain themselves on the job, let alone contribute to the welfare of their families.[87] In April 1934, using a Public Enquiries Act it had just passed, the Commission responded to this agitation by appointing Gordon Bradley, the former leader of the opposition, to enquire into and report on conditions in the woods.[88] "It is the Congo over again," Hope Simpson indignantly wrote, "so we are putting on a Commission of Enquiry into the labour situation in the forests. Lord Rothermere and the *Daily Mail* are likely to have something to howl about, and we are going to be most unpopular in high quarters ... These two Companies [Rothermere's Anglo-Newfoundland Development Company and the International Power and Paper Company of Newfoundland] have hitherto been all-powerful. And they have lived on sweated labour." This outburst accorded with Hope Simpson's general belief that Newfoundland's forest, water-power, and mineral resources had been "given away with both hands."[89] Yet when Bradley produced his own indictment of the paper companies and their contractors, perhaps the best contemporary account of what life was really like at the bottom in Newfoundland in the 1930s, the commissioner and the government as a whole backed away from it. What Bradley found was that cutters were "grossly underpaid" and fell short by $33.10 the $50.00 per month he estimated the average outport family workman needed to maintain "a reasonable standard of living." In sum the logger had been "reduced to a standard below even tolerable existence."[90] To remedy a desperate situation, he recommended a minimum wage of $2.00 per cord (the International Power and Paper Company paid its loggers $1.40 to $1.80 per cord in 1934).[91] Hope Simpson rejected Bradley's $50.00 per month figure on two grounds: it postulated a living standard way beyond the normal outport standard, and it failed to take account of what the industry could afford.[92]

The report, Hope Simpson told Harding, was a disappointment because Bradley had forgotten about the particular matter he had been assigned to investigate in favour of "a political attack on the foreign companies." His report was "particularly vicious" in its condemnation of the treatment by the paper companies of the loggers they employed directly, a group from whom no complaint had been heard. Publication of the report would put Bradley "in the position of champion of the workers, as against a reactionary Government, whose interest was in favour of foreign capital."[93] It might also, the Commission feared, touch off a strike in the woods.[94] Faced with this danger on one side and an outraged response from the companies on the other, the Commission retreated. The result was a negotiated rather than a legislated settlement, whereby the paper companies agreed to guarantee all loggers employed directly by them minimum net earnings of twenty-five dollars per month.[95] This arrangement, taking effect on 1 January 1935, certainly made things better for the loggers, but it also showed the power of the companies. In another test of strength, more limits had been set on the new government.

Less dramatically, but with modest success, the Commission attempted in its first phase to stimulate the export of pulpwood and pitprops. To this end, a substantial loan was made in 1935 to the Labrador Development Company. This enabled the company to expand the operations which, despite initial labour difficulty, it had begun the previous year at Alexis River.[96] In the interest both of conversation and development, the government sought to regulate better the harvesting of trees and to encourage development of the usable forest resources of the country.[97] In the same spirit it gave a fresh start to geological surveying, although the mining industry itself continued to languish. Thanks principally to improved sales of Bell Island iron ore and higher prices for lead and zinc, the value of mineral exports rose significantly during 1935, but only a small increase was realized the next year as German customers were in financial difficulty.[98] The substantial turnaround for Bell Island came as Germany rearmed in the late 1930s. The Commission had simply waited for the problems of the mining industry to right themselves; in truth, they could not have done much else.

Yet another item on the Commission's agenda for development in the formative 1934–36 period was assistance to agriculture. It was common practice in Newfoundland to supplement work at sea and in the woods with subsistence farming. To increase the return from this, the government proposed improved methods and offered production incentives. The country's few full-time farmers were likewise encouraged, and a program of placing agricultural representatives in the most promising farming areas according to the generally poor Newfoundland standard was started. By January 1936, three of these officials were in the field and six more were being trained in Canada. In addition, "a model and experimental farm" was opened and steps taken to encourage livestock production.[99] In October 1935, a vegetable grading act was passed.[100]

To facilitate commerce generally and to provide employment in construction, the Commission launched an ambitious road program in 1934. Financed by a loan of $500,000 from the Colonial Development Fund, this was designed to upgrade the few existing roads, mainly on the Avalon Peninsula, and to connect isolated centres to the railway.[101] In October 1935, another loan was secured from the Colonial Development Fund towards the cost of a highway linking Port aux Basques and Botwood. Survey work and bush clearing for this formidable undertaking went on the same year. When the building of a bridge was undertaken at Robinsons, each local man employed on the project gave six days of free labour. This example of local co-operation was trumpeted by the government in its 1935 annual report.[102] To increase the operating revenue of the railway, again using funds borrowed from the Colonial Development Fund, the government extended the docks at Port aux Basques. Now paper produced by the International Power and Paper Company of Newfoundland could be shipped through that port when Corner Brook was ice-bound.[103] Steady, progress was made also on reducing the railway's operating deficit, another accomplishment for which the Commission duly took credit.[104]

While considering measures to sustain and revitalize established industry to be most urgent, the Commission soon became convinced that Newfoundland's economic future could be assured only by looking beyond existing enterprises. The case for this was forcefully put by Lodge in a memorandum on general policy completed in January 1935. The country was undoubtedly better off than it had been a year before, he wrote, and if the Commission's "sole objective" – Lodge raised it only as a theoretical point – was a balanced budget, this might be achieved "within a comparatively short time." But to act thus would mean economizing on social expenditure and avoiding the issue of unemployment – a "short sighted policy" that would soon lead to another collapse. "I should not myself," Lodge wrote, "be content with such a policy because to me it involves acquiescence in the existence of an appallingly low standard of life both materially and morally. It would mean a people living just at, or just above, the bare minimum, with no reserve resources and therefore at the mercy of uncontrollable seasonal fluctuations." Lodge's alternative strategy flowed from a belief that Newfoundland's adversity arose from the dominance of fishing – "from the dependence of a population of nearly 300,000 on one calling and that calling one which is prosecuted in a highly individualistic way." In an argument greatly at variance with the analysis of the Amulree Royal Commission, he concluded that it was "easy to exaggerate the effect in the life of Newfoundland of the mistakes in policy of its Governments. The roots of the trouble ... [were] to be found," he argued, "not in the shortcomings of Government, but in the inability of the main industry to adjust itself to modern methods and modern circumstances." Yet the modernization of the fishing industry would lead to fewer people being employed in it. At the same time, the most that could be expected from the forest and mining sectors was that they would "absorb the natural increase of their own populations." How then was full employment to be achieved? Lodge's answer, accepted by his fellow commissioners, was "to put our surplus population on the land." This was, of course, an economic panacea widely favoured in the 1930s in Canada and elsewhere as an alternative to industrialization and urbanization which appeared to have failed. Newfoundland was not "an ideal country for agriculture," but if the right means were employed, the country could produce enough "food, clothing and shelter to satisfy nearly all the ordinary needs of human beings."[105]

A successful example, Lodge believed, of what could be achieved along these lines was to be found at Markland on the Avalon Peninsula between Whitbourne and Colinet. This land settlement, named in recognition of the Viking connection with Newfoundland, was founded in May 1934. Markland was administered by a private trust but backed financially by the government. Its original settlers were ten ex-servicemen and their families, all from St. John's and all on relief. The success of this first group led to the addition of more families in September 1934 and to the appointment of a full-time manager for the project.[106] During the winter of 1934–35, the men of the community harvested 250,000 board feet of wood.[107] In another experiment in the autumn of 1934, ten fishermen from the south coast were resettled at Lourdes on the Port au Port Peninsula, where it was hoped they could combine fishing, farming, and logging to provide a decent living.

Heartened by these developments, the Commission pressed ahead with a larger program, telling Parliament in its May 1935 report on unemployment that the launching of four or five more land settlements was anticipated during the year. In this document the case for resettlement was tied directly to the relief situation in the capital. During and after the war and in better times, it was argued, many outport families had moved to St. John's. Now, without prospect of further employment there, they no longer had houses to which they could return. The land settlement scheme answered their particular needs, helping to put those thus stranded in the capital back to work.[108]

During the summer of 1935 Markland was visited by two experts on the reclamation of bog land, this a prominent feature of the Avalon Peninsula, for agricultural use. Subsequently a drainage experiment was started in the area, and another settlement was launched at nearby Haricot. By the end of that year Markland itself consisted of "120 homes ... two saw mills, a store, two folk schools and 17 community buildings." The folk school idea was borrowed from Scandinavia and featured a curriculum which combined academic and vocational subjects.[109] Children prepared their own meals at school and were well-nourished members of a community which enjoyed "exceedingly good" health. Markland was the Commission of Government's beacon of hope – what New Lanark had been to the followers of Robert Owen and what, earlier in Newfoundland's own history, Port Union, another model community, had been to William Coaker and the Fishermen's Protective Union. The trouble was that the Commission's beacon did not cast much light. Two more new communities – Brown's Arm (near Lewisporte) and Midland (near Deer Lake) were founded after Haricot, but at the end of 1938 there were altogether only 171 families in all the land settlements and the number at Markland had actually declined.[110] Set beside the number of the Government's dependents, this figure was pitifully small. In May 1933, counting the sick, aged, and infirm as well as the able-bodied, Newfoundland's relief population was 87,412. During the same month in 1934 and 1935 the equivalent figures were respectively 72,691 and 66,900; but in 1936, in the aftermath of a disastrous fishing season, this downward trend reversed itself and a May total of 68,690 was recorded.[111]

More than the comforting annual reports of the Commission of Government, these statistics told the real story of Newfoundland in the mid 1930s. Incredibly, in August, 1936, as the crisis in the fishery intensified, there were 7,012 more people on relief than there had been three years earlier when the depression generally was at its worst. After an initial upswing under its new administration, Newfoundland was running hard to stand still, and, not surprisingly, the strain showed both within the Commission and without.

The episode that revealed most about the restless state of public opinion in Newfoundland during the first years of the Commission and about the outlook of the government itself began in November 1934. In that month the Customs Department was tipped off that Captain Westbury Kean of the government-owned steamer *Portia*, which plied between St. John's and Halifax, was about to smuggle beaver skins out of the country.[112] It was revealed to customs officials that the skins could be found in his cabin at a given hour before the ship was scheduled to depart St. John's on one of its regular runs. When this lead was followed up, customs officials found a parcel containing three skins where they had been encouraged to look. Kean denied all knowledge of the contraband but was nonetheless charged with a customs offence and relieved of his command. The trial that followed in December produced an acquittal.[113] Yet early in the new year, acting on the recommendation of Lodge, who was administratively responsible for the steamer service, the Commission of Government voted unanimously to dismiss Kean from his job. When Kean immediately appealed his dismissal, Lodge, Howley, and Puddester were named by the Commission as a whole to hear his case. Kean appeared before them, accompanied by his lawyer, L.E. Emerson, the Minister of Justice before Commission of Government, but to no avail; on 18 January, by another unanimous vote, the Commission affirmed its original decision. Still the matter refused to die.

In Emerson, Kean had found a formidable advocate and a man whose political career had been thwarted by the initial Newfoundland appointments to the Commission. Born in 1890, Emerson had first attended St. Patrick's Hall School and St. Bonaventure's College in his native St. John's. He continued his education at Ampleforth College (Yorkshire), one of England's foremost Roman Catholic schools. This period in England was an important factor when it came to his understanding of the British mores of the Commission of Government. Both through his marriage to Ruby Edith Ayre, daughter of a prominent business family, and in his own right, he was well connected in the small, tightly knit elite that dominated local society. He was a Roman Catholic with a Protestant name (these were important distinctions in Newfoundland), a colonial with metropolitan airs (he was known in London as a hard drinker), an intimate of Archbishop Roche, and a highly talented and ambitious public figure.[114] To add to the government's troubles, moreover, Kean's father,

Abram, was Newfoundland's most famous sealing captain. The family had close ties both to Water Street and to their home region of Bonavista Bay as they had been a long time supplier of common labour to the one and of employment to the other. The Commission in other words had engaged in combat a totemic figure whose abrupt dismissal reverberated through local society. In July Kean obtained another unsuccessful review of his case; another unanimous vote was recorded against him in the Commission's minutes. That same month, the government turned down the request of a public petition that the case be reopened, while former prime minister Walter Monroe appealed to Harding to investigate the Captain's grievance. Monroe contended that Kean had been charged on the word of "an informer who expected to be paid" and that the attitude of the authorities in St. John's towards the matter raised "the question ... whether British justice can be obtained in this country under our present Commission Government."[115]

In response, Harding asked the governor for an account of the case. Monroe, he wrote, had acted out of turn by appealing directly to London, but when his former political standing was considered his letter merited "a considered reply." The startling answer that came from St. John's to this request triggered a constitutional crisis, for in effect the Commission of Government told the Dominions Office to mind its own business. The issue was "a question of local administration." The Commission had unanimously reached a decision. This decision had then been reviewed twice and confirmed with a majority of Newfoundland commissioners present. Intervention by London in this matter would not only compromise but even undermine established authority in the country.[116] In short, Monroe should be informed from London that the Commission's word on the matter he had raised was final.

This bold advice was promptly rejected in London, and in early October Harding again asked Governor Anderson for a statement of the facts of the case. Monroe, he now revealed, had also written William Lunn, the Labour member of Parliament for Rothwell, who in turn had followed the matter up with the secretary of state. Questions could be expected in Parliament and the secretary of state had to be ready for them, since he was responsible for "all the activities of the Commission of Government," matters of personnel included. Furthermore, the secretary of state needed the information requested because Kean undoubtedly had the right to petition him through the governor. In particular, Anderson was asked to address in his report Monroe's specific claim "that Captain Kean had been dismissed by administrative action on grounds akin to the charge on which he had just been acquitted by the courts." For his part, Anderson now took the position that information to be given Parliament should rest not on his authority but that of the Commission, which had made the decision in the Kean case. Accordingly, on 28 October, he requested permission, which was granted, to pass Harding's latest request for information on to the commissioners for reply. While this answer was being prepared, the Dominions Office heard directly from Kean's lawyers, who forwarded copies of both the July petition to the governor and another, also denied, which had been submitted to him in October.[117] The latter document bore the signatures of many prominent citizens of St. John's. It called on Anderson to refer all documents relating to the Kean affair to the secretary of state and to ask him to act on them as justice demanded. These would have included still another petition addressed to the governor by the residents of Flat Islands, Bonavista Bay.[118]

The developing crisis over Captain Kean's dismissal brought all the latent antagonisms within the Commission of Government to the surface. In June, Anderson had told Harding in a secret and personal letter that Lodge had "strong and ... impracticable views on how the Commission should be run and the number of Commissioners." What he seemed to favour was "the U.K. Commissioners acting as 'Mussolinis' and the Governor acting the part of the King of Italy." It was "essential," Anderson cautioned, that the governor continue to chair the Commission to prevent the United Kingdom commissioners from racing ahead without bringing their Newfoundland colleagues with them. Of the United Kingdom commissioners, Anderson considered Trentham the most reliable, though he led a lonely bachelor life in St. John's and had recently been "under the weather and rather seedy." Hope Simpson was "too impulsive" and inclined to get "carried away by people who are not too reliable," while Lodge lacked "consideration of the human element and the 'custom of the country.'" He wanted "to work out everything as a mathematical calculation" and was "very self opinionated, not to say pig headed." Of the Newfoundland commissioners, Anderson considered Puddester the "most useful," but he was unpopular with his local colleagues because he tended to side with the British members.[119]

In October, as the Kean affair was coming to a head, but before the Commission had heard through Anderson of London's insistence on having the full facts of the case, Lodge offered his own savage commentary on selected local figures to Eric Machtig, an assistant secretary at the Dominions Office and another key official in Newfoundland matters.[120] His outburst was triggered by a letter he apparently had received from the St. John's-born but British-resident Sir Edgar Bowring, who had been Newfoundland's high commissioner in the United Kingdom and who helped direct from overseas the operations of one of Water Street's leading merchant houses. The letter in question was written the day before Bowring, whom Lodge called on "old devil," was to complete a visit to St. John's.[121] In it Bowring came out in support of Kean and apparently raised doubts about the loyalty of Puddester and Alderdice to the position the Commission had taken. Lodge attributed Alderdice's alleged equivocation to personal weakness: "I expect that when he said it he was at his fifth whisky – semi-truculent and semi-maudlin. The Commission meets in the morning and 10 a.m. is the hour when few alcoholics have got any moral courage left. Certainly Alderdice hasn't got enough then to argue with Hope Simpson, Trentham or myself. So all we get is a sentimental assurance that he is going to the stake with his colleagues." Puddester was a stronger personality and Lodge did not believe that he was backsliding on the Kean issue: "It is quite obvious that Alderdice feels that Puddester has deserted his old pal and gone over to the English, and that Puddester knows that Alderdice feels this. Consequently his interests are completely bound up with the English Commissioners who do treat him as a human being. Moreover, whether under our influence or not Puddester (when his wife isn't looking) now drinks an occasional glass of sherry, even smokes one cigarette a month and has left the strait and narrow path of United Church-ism. He hasn't yet been ex-communicated but he certainly does not live in the odour of sanctity. On the whole I acquit him." Howley's behaviour in relation to the Kean affair had been "extremely correct" but he too had to be watched closely: "If he weren't a Catholic I should certainly acquit him – as it is I give him the benefit of the doubt. But you can never be quite certain as to what he would say after the fifth whiskey."[122]

Looking beyond the Commission, Lodge found two other weak links in the government's defences in the Kean affair. One was the chief of police, Patrick J. O'Neill, "a suave Catholic"; he would not dare give away any damaging information directly but "might not be sorry if his hearer drew wrong deductions from what he said." The other was Brian E.S. Dunfield, the secretary in the Department of Justice, "an odd bird, an ex-associate of Squires, intelligent, very hard working but with a kink in his brain somewhere." Dunfield, Lodge believed, had poked into the Kean case while Howley had been in England earlier in the year and had then fed information to Emerson. In addition to serving his client, Emerson was "very probably" out to embarrass the Commission and would almost certainly welcome the opportunity "to dish Alderdice" for passing him over when the government's Catholic member was being chosen." Lodge's conclusion about how the parliamentary situation should be handled was categorical:

So there you are! If the Secretary of State repeats monotonously that it is a matter of local administration which must be left to the Commission on which Newfoundland has three members, emphasising in answer to any annoying supplementary [question] what you can deduce from the minutes that the decision was taken at a meeting when the Newfoundlanders were in a majority, it will die a natural death. In the limit I don't think that either [Sir Edgar] Bowring or [Walter S.] Monroe (stupid as the latter is) will put Alderdice into an impossible situation.

But what you are going to do when you have to find another Newfoundlander beats me completely. I do not believe that there is a single man in this island who would take the job who would be acceptable to us. And this would apply to Protestants, Catholics or Pagans.[123]

Despite London's repudiation of this tactic, which it soon heard about through the governor, the Commission persisted in the claim that the secretary of state had no right to call it to account and that a fundamental constitutional principle was at stake. The Newfoundland government's case was put in a despatch from Anderson dated 14 November. While the government of the United Kingdom undoubtedly had "a general power of control" over the Newfoundland government's financial affairs because of the latter's dependent status, it did not under the Letters Patent and Royal Instructions have "general supervisory control" over the administration in St. John's. Nor could these documents be amended to provide it with such authority since it was constrained by the terms of the offer it had made to Newfoundland on 19 November 1933, which could not be altered unilaterally.[124] This was a flimsy argument, easily and quickly demolished in London: the Letters Patent and Royal Instructions had to be read in the context not only of that November offer, but also the report of the Royal Commission, the Address to the Crown of the Newfoundland Legislature, and the Newfoundland Act. Taken together, these provided clear proof that the United Kingdom government's supervisory control over the government of Newfoundland was unqualified.[125]

In December 1935, the Commission was convinced of the reality of this when Malcolm MacDonald, who had succeeded Thomas as secretary of state, met with Lodge, Hope Simpson, and Howley in London. Brought face to face with the minister, the three commissioners had to acknowledge his overriding authority across the board, although they were allowed to record "their considered opinion that any general exercise by the Secretary of State of a right to review the decisions of the Commission on matters of purely local administration would make government by Commission very difficult if not impossible in practice."[126] This was a harmless sop; concomitantly the commissioners promised to co-operate in providing the full information required in London about the Kean case.[127]

What happened over the next year on the issue was revealing. Formally, the Dominions Office backed up the action of the Commission of Government in dismissing Kean, but informally it sought a solution which would conciliate local opinion and lower the political temperature in St. John's. Kean's lawyers and Monroe were told through the governor that the secretary of state saw no reason to interfere in the matter they had raised. Privately, however, Whitehall pressed for Kean's re-instatement, a possibility the three British commissioners flatly rejected.[128] More complications followed when charges were brought against Ernest W. Gaze of St. John's, whom Kean accused of having framed him in the first place.[129] While this litigation was in progress, the Commission decided "as an act of grace" that Kean should be taken back into the Newfoundland railway service as of 1 January 1937 if a suitable position could be found for him.[130] As events unfolded, action on this decision was delayed pending the conclusion of Gaze's trial.[131] After Gaze was acquited, Kean was rehired. If the Newfoundland skipper had been unable to score a knockout in his long bout with the Commission, he had certainly won on points. He had also enjoyed the support of a large and influential cheering section whose political importance was not lost on London.

Kean's rehabilitation was eased by a change during 1936-37 in the Commission's dramatis personae. In February 1936, Sir Humphrey T. Walwyn arrived in St. John's as Anderson's replacement. During the same month, Alderdice died suddenly, and, in April, James A. Winter was appointed to fill the Newfoundland vacancy thus created. Then, in July, Robert B. Ewbank was appointed to succeed Sir John Hope Simpson. In January 1937, Sir Wilfrid Woods succeeded the combative and vitriolic Thomas Lodge, who had returned to England the previous November.[132] Walwyn was a product of Dartmouth and had spent his whole career in the Royal Navy, from which he had retired in 1934 with the rank of vice admiral.[133] His attitudes were those of an old fashioned English squire: he was a grace and favour, pomp and circumstance tory. He strode about Government House as if on a quarter deck while Lady Walwyn carried out with aplomb the social and charitable duties attendant upon being a governor's wife. Some of his private letters read like the pages of a ship's log. Newfoundlanders, he wrote shortly after arriving at Government House, "have rather an inferiority complex but welcome being dealt with in a friendly way and respond accordingly." By the same token, he reported that the Humber Snipe automobile he had brought with him from England was "much admired," people being "pleased to see such a car in use out here."[134] Sir John Hope Simpson, who made his own public farewell to Newfoundlanders on 27 August 1936, once described Walwyn during their brief tenure together as "an Admiral with a fine quarter-deck manner and an astonishingly free use of the broadside." The new governor was "irrepressible" but his brain was "very much a second-rate article."[135] An Anglican, Winter was the son of former prime minister Sir James Spearman Winter. He was a lawyer by profession and had been speaker of the House of Assembly, 1933-34.[136] Ewbank, a clergyman's son, was a graduate of Queen's College, Oxford, and, like Hope Simpson, a veteran of the Indian Civil Service.[137] Sir Wilfrid Woods, also an Oxford graduate, had behind him a long and diverse career as a colonial administrator in Africa and Asia.[138]

Walwyn went to St. John's determined to be the Commission's leader in fact as well as in name. In short order he wanted to reassert the governor's power and become "a strong presiding authority" who would give the struggling administration both energy and direction. The main obstacle in the way of achieving this, he believed, was Lodge, who had "practically run the Commission." Accordingly, when Lodge arrived back from England having heard Secretary of State MacDonald's verdict on the constitutional point raised by the Kean affair, Walwyn confronted him directly. He gave Harding this account of what had passed between them:

> Lodge returned Wednesday night and I had a long talk to him on Thursday. We are perfectly friendly and I appreciate his brain.
>
> He rather surprised me by taking the line that I am not a Governor in an administrative position ...
>
> He expected me to be a passive sort of puppet who would take no part in debates nor express any opinion at the Commission Meetings ...
>
> I very soon explained to him who was Captain of the Ship out here.
>
> I talked over this very point with you at Home and expressed myself very clearly that I did not anticipate being a puppet to open Maternity Homes only. I like dealing with questions of importance and flatter myself I can, and *do* have a lot of influence with the Commission.[139]

With this exchange Walwyn thought he had put Lodge firmly in his place, but in fact he had fired only the first shot in a battle that would convulse the government intermittently until the pugnacious British commissioner was removed from the Newfoundland scene nearly a year later.

In attempting to foster a fresh start economically, Walwyn soon came up against other harsh realities – the complexity and intractability of Newfoundland's problems for one, and the thorny issue of just how much the United Kingdom was willing to spend towards solving them for another. In March 1936, the governor sent London a forecast of the financial aid the Commission believed it would need "over the next few years," above and beyond what would be required to meet normal budget deficits, if it was to make "any real and lasting improvement" in the Newfoundland economy. The information provided was based on a memorandum prepared by Lodge which repeated the arguments in favour of giving priority to land settlement. The 1935 census, it was pointed out, had shown that 34,000 men were employed in fishing, a total that included 21,000 family heads. This was quite simply too many people for the industry to support as presently organized. Logically, therefore, to pick up the slack, new jobs would have to be created. Of the 70,000 current relief recipients, 20,000 were "probably beyond recovery" and would have to be provided for permanently by the government, but the remaining 50,000 – 8,000 to 10,000 families – might be restored to economic health. Where could work be found for them? The forest sector was the most obvious source, as timber was the "one known raw material susceptible of immediate increased exploitation." If the whole of the island's timber resources were used, existing production could be increased by 150,000 cords annually, enough to provide "a tolerable living for say 1,500 workers and their families." In time, the Commission believed, this was an attainable objective, but its realization would be expensive and involve co-operation with the Reid Newfoundland company. This company, in receivership since 1931, still controlled most of the country's surplus timber. Mining was much less promising as a source of new jobs. There was no great mineral discovery awaiting development, and in any case mining ventures tended to grow slowly and were capital intensive. This left only land settlement as an outlet for the country's surplus labour. "If Newfoundlanders want to live in Newfoundland they must in the long run get their living out of the resources of the country. It may not be a luxurious living, but it will be at any rate better than that of the majority of those who are to-day attempting to live by catching and drying codfish." Assuming that 6,000 families would have to be resettled on five-cleared acres each at a cost of $150 per acre, the Commission estimated a total bill for the land development scheme, including provision for housing, of $6,000,000. On an annual basis the appropriate level of expenditure on land settlement would likely work out at "some figure between $1,000,000 and $1,500,000." In addition to the $6,000,000 needed for resettlement, the Commission estimated that it would require "$1,000,000 for Miscellaneous Development" and another "$1,000,000 for capital expenditure on Railway and Boats."[140]

Far from hearing that these amounts would be forthcoming, Walwyn was led to wonder during the summer of 1936 whether the United Kingdom would keep up even her present level of aid to Newfoundland. Prompting his doubt was a Treasury comment on Newfoundland's accounts which came to him through the Dominions Office. The substance of this was that, unforeseen circumstances and unavoidable difficulties notwithstanding, Newfoundland's huge 1935–36 deficit, calculated finally at more than $2,000,000, was "a matter for grave concern." Walwyn's reading of this was that the Treasury might be about "to force an early return to budgetary equilibrium regardless of other considerations."[141] This alarming possibility was immediately denied by Edward Hale, one of the main Treasury officials connected with Newfoundland affairs, who was visiting St. John's.[142] Nonetheless, Walwyn unburdened himself on the subject to Harding.[143]

At its inception, Walwyn wrote, the Commission had a choice of two policies. These were "to give the Island the best possible administration whilst studiously watching every detail, and avoiding undue demands being made on the British Treasury," or to "enforce a steady reduction of the Grant-in-Aid by keeping expenditure down to its most economical limits short of creating severe local protests." Sensibly, it had opted for the former and this policy had been supported in practice by the Treasury ever since. To change course now would be catastrophic. Governing Newfoundland was a "ceaseless anxiety," and while much had been accomplished since 1934 further measures of rehabilitation were urgently needed. No doubt money could be saved by cutting back on social services, but the human cost of this would be unacceptable: "Unemployment with its heavy demands for relief, including fuel and clothing, is more critical to-day than it has ever been in the history of the Island. There is an ever increasing population with little or no opening for the rising generation and practically no opportunities for emigration." The government needed to spend more instead of less; no significant improvement in its budgetary situation could be anticipated without a revival in the country's trade. In the case of the recent downturn in the vital fishing industry, the Commission was up against "factors ... beyond the control of any government." The generation of Newfoundland politicians condemned by the Amulree commission would have appreciated this remark. To add to its woes, the Commission, beginning in 1938, would have to start paying into the sinking fund provided for in the 1933 finance act. Walwyn wondered where this money - approximately $1 million a year - could be found. Newfoundland had fallen on hard times over "a number of years"; economic recovery was a slower process than economic decay. It would, therefore, take "a considerable time" for "a really substantial improvement" to occur. Meanwhile, the Commission was preoccupied with "the struggle for existence," although it "would like nothing better than to be able to turn ... to an ordered programme for the promotion of better social conditions, education, housing and public welfare."[144]

This then was the bleak reality in Newfoundland more than two years after the noble experiment of 1934 had been launched. The Commission of Government was adrift, responding to events rather than shaping them, and the Dominions Office knew it.

CHAPTER FOUR

Renewed Economic Crisis, 1936-39

During the present decade it has been a hard struggle for the people even to maintain the too frail structure of the country's export industries by which this formidable weight of imported necessities is supported. *Every part of the structure is exposed to economic tempests* and nothing but the broadening of its base will made it safe.

Governor Sir Humphrey Walwyn to
Secretary of State for Dominion Affairs,
February 1939

From the British perspective, to prevent a bad situation from becoming worse, a change in direction for Newfoundland was urgently required, and in October 1936 this was forthcoming. It took the form of a request from Malcolm MacDonald to the Commission to submit "something in the nature of a general long-term programme calculated ultimately to make the Island self-supporting again, and to train and equip the people of Newfoundland so that they are then in a position to administer their own affairs unaided once again." Hitherto the Commission had perforce dedicated itself "to adjustment and experiment designed to relieve the immediate necessities of the situation"; but the moment had now arrived "to take stock of the position." Under the general heading of "economic reconstruction," the Commission was asked to weigh in its submission the relative importance in the future of fishing, forestry, mining, and agriculture to the local economy and to prescribe means for eliminating the credit system in favour of cash transactions for all Newfoundlanders. To prepare the people to resume self-government, the Commission was to spell out its future educational policy and to specify additional measures for reform of the civil service. Assuming that the execution of a lengthy reconstruction program of the type contemplated would require "a long period of political peace," the Commission was asked to consider whether an "Advisory Council ... of prominent Newfoundlanders" should be appointed. This group would then be available for the Commission to consult "as occasion required and especially in matters of important legislation." If the Commission were to oppose the creation of such a consultative body, it was asked to suggest other means for informing itself about public opinion and for giving that opinion a safe outlet.[1] This whole proposal reflected MacDonald's belief that the "chief danger" in Newfoundland under Commission of Government was "an irresistible outbreak of hostility to the constitution by a people accustomed to democratic government who have now no representatives in the Govt. except the appointed Newfoundlanders." It was crucial to "devise a means of anticipating this." Lastly, the Commission was invited to comment on anything else it believed needed to be taken into account in connection with the major shift in policy now proposed.[2]

The Commission's reply to MacDonald's request was painstakingly prepared over many weeks. The result was a ninety-seven paragraph despatch which Walwyn forwarded to London the day before Christmas 1936. A separate document, sent later, dealt with – and flatly rejected – the proposal for an advisory council. Lodge, who saw his term out in England after his return there in November, did not participate in the preparation of this document, which was highly critical of his administration and of the whole approach to Newfoundland's difficulties that he had espoused.[3] Underlying the Commission's latest analysis of the situation before it was the assumption that "substantial recovery" for Newfoundland was "a long way off." This was most of all evident in the fishing industry. While this industry, taken as a whole, offered "only a wretched livelihood" to those involved in it, the possibility of transferring fishermen to different and more lucrative employment – the objective of the land settlement policy previously advocated – was unrealistic. Helping fishermen, therefore, meant fostering better methods of production and marketing in their industry and encouraging them to supplement their income from fishing by undertaking other forms of work. The framing of a detailed program of fishery improvement would have to await the recommendations of the Kent Commission, but otherwise what the situation called for was "an active policy of agricultural and general rural improvement." The purpose of this "reasoned programme of rural improvement" would be to bring hope to the outport population and to enlarge its economic opportunities.[4]

Behind this strategy lay a belief in the essential maritime outlook of the country: "The average Newfoundlander is a seaman by birth and choice, and will not willingly leave the sea for another occupation, so long as he can earn a fair living from it." Consequently, it made more sense to augment economic opportunities in the existing outports than to move large numbers of people away from them. The Commission in other words would build from existing strength; fishermen must become fishermen-farmers. In the process, the Commission hoped that the principles of co-operation and local self-government would take hold in rural society. If the government's plan succeeded, "the great majority of the fisher population" would be able to stay put. Only those without access to a sufficient resource base where they now resided would have to be moved "to more promising sites." No attempt, however, would be made to resettle those who had become "so slack and demoralized" that spending to give them another chance would be wasted. Such persons would simply be carried along on relief but made to work for their keep. Their children, however, might possibly be redeemed through the establishment "of industrial boarding schools of a cottage type in outport areas."[5]

In resettling those who could profitably be moved, the Commission intended to avoid past mistakes. At Markland the government had invested heavily, but financial independence for the community was not yet in sight. One source of Markland's difficulty had been the "joint possession and working of communal land." This defied the "highly individualistic" outlook of the inhabitants and tested their "idealism ... too highly." If, at an early date, land had been handed over to individuals, perhaps on a rental or mortgage basis, the experiment would be farther along the road to success. Another problem at Markland had been a top heavy, salaried bureaucracy with "too much power." This had stifled "the spirit of self-help and initiative in the individual," the very qualities that were vital to success. Future land settlement, the Commission hypothesized, might proceed in two stages. Initially, men would go to a site, clear land, and build houses. Only when this work was done, would they be joined by their families. Furthermore, each man would be given to understand from the start what he might come to own by dint of hard work and at what cost. Henceforth, individual initiative would bring tangible reward.[6]

If the Commission could still see attractive, albeit reduced, possibilities in land settlement, it was much less sanguine about moving the country very quickly towards a full cash economy. In the logging industry, the government had been able to make headway in this regard by requiring cash payments to workers as a condition of export licences, but the credit system operating in the fishing industry was much more intractable. It was doubtful whether fishermen, if paid in cash, could be relied upon to save enough to outfit themselves for the next season, so ingrained was their dependence. They had "very little knowledge of the value of money" and were, moreover, "inclined to resent any radical interference with existing habits." Their conservatism, combined with merchant self-interest, posed a formidable obstacle to change. As with so much else in Newfoundland, the way forward lay in the introduction of producer and consumer co-operation, but this was a delicate plant, slow to grow. "Even if it were administratively possible, and it is not, the Commission of Government could hardly face the opposition involved in the immediate adoption of a 100 per cent co-operative policy throughout the Island, with the fishermen uneducated and bewildered and the merchants in full opposition. A number of more or less co-operative undertakings are now being fostered, and they are being extended as opportunity allows. But if they are extended prematurely and with insufficient education in the communities concerned, the money spent will be wasted and the undertaking will disintegrate."[7]

In continuation of what it had previously reported, the Commission also forecast limited opportunities in forestry and mining. Overall, its sense of what could be expected from forestry-related industry was as follows: "We see no prospect of developing our forest resources in such a way as greatly to increase their economic importance in the near future." Qualifying this was the possibility, already mooted, of getting a pulp mill started on the Gander River, using the timber resources of the Reid lands. This development promised a substantial return and would be pursued vigorously. Otherwise, the government believed, the main requirements of this area of policy were "a better knowledge of ... resources" and "closer administration and fuller utilization of the forest generally." The Commission saw a similar role for itself in relation to mining: "We are of opinion that at present our chief object should be to obtain and disseminate accurate information regarding mineral resources, and to establish confidence in our general policy and administration."[8]

Elsewhere in its 1936 reconstruction plan, the Commission detailed its intentions in relation to education, public health and welfare, the civil service, transportation, the improvement of living conditions in St. John's, local government, broadcasting, and the establishment in Newfoundland of units of the Royal Naval Reserve and Royal Naval Volunteer Reserve. The sections on education and public health laid out a truly formidable agenda. As evidence of where matters stood educationally, the Commission cited a report by the country's new corps of school inspectors, based on a survey carried out in the autumn of 1935. This showed an appalling lack of facilities and a "peak age of school attendance" of "nine plus." While annual expenditure on education in Newfoundland was in the order of $3.60 per head of population and $17.40 per pupil, the equivalent figures for Canada were $11.00 and $53.00 respectively. Moreover, the 1935 census had revealed that in the 6 to 14 year old age group there were 14,000 children who were not attending school at all. To overcome these problems, the Commission proposed additional measures of reform in curriculum and examinations, better salaries and improved training for teachers, a higher standard of school inspection, an enlarged program of adult education, and, ultimately, the introduction of compulsory school attendance.[9]

The public health and welfare needs of the country were also seen as requiring concerted action on a broad front. Statistically, the case for this was manifest: infant mortality in Newfoundland was at the rate of 102.8 per 1000 live births compared to rates of 73.1 in Canada and 64.0 in England and Wales; the death rate from tuberculosis per ten thousand population was 18.0 compared to 8.2 in England and Wales; and fully 60 per cent of Newfoundlanders were "unable to secure medical or nursing attention when ill." To change all this the government would, among other things, step up its program for training midwives; introduce a universal child welfare service (an existing voluntary service, which operated with government help, was confined to St. John's); enlarge hospital facilities and provide many additional sanitorium beds for tuberculosis patients; and send out into the field many more district nurses who could "by example, by effort and by precept ... contribute more than almost any factor to the rehabilitation of the people and especially to the raising of the standard of home life and conduct."[10]

Carrying out the entire reconstruction program put forward, the Commission ventured, would take "something between seven and ten years at least." The total cost of the whole program over this period would be in the neighbourhood of $7,000,000 - $8,000,000, but might be higher. Peak annual expenditure would be about $800,000. The whole of the cost involved would have to be borne by the United Kingdom, because the Commission had reached the limit of its own financial capacity. Newfoundland had already borrowed or arranged to borrow $4,000,000 from the Colonial Development Fund, and it would be folly to pile up any more debt with that agency. Indeed the government was undecided whether it should draw the $1,000,000 still in account with the fund for its roads program, about which it was having sober second thoughts. The truth was that without aid Newfoundland would be unable either to live up to its repayment schedule to the Colonial Development Fund or to meet its pending sinking fund payments under the 1933 Finance Act. If the country was to progress in the direction favoured, the United Kingdom would obviously have to pay the bills. Nor was it reasonable to expect that the size of the relief budget could be reduced during the phasing-in period of the reconstruction program. In the short run at least, relief and reconstruction would necessitate a "double expenditure." In addition, to keep the peace, money would have to be spent on public works projects to employ people until the better day that reconstruction would bring. Newfoundlanders had "expected miracles" from the constitutional change of 1934; now "political agitators" could be expected to exploit the continuing hardship. To counter this the Government would have to spend money on "semi-productive employment," though as far as possible this would be co-ordinated with the goals of reconstruction.[11] In connection with its new direction in policy, the Commission had decided on 11 December 1936, to divide the Department of Natural Resources into two sections – one to deal with "Fisheries, Forests, Rangers, Surveys, and minor subjects connected with these major heads," while retaining the old departmental name; and the other to deal with "Agriculture, Co-operation, Land Settlement and kindred subjects," and to be known as the Department of Rural Reconstruction. To serve as the latter department's first secretary, Brian Dunfield was seconded from the Department of Justice.[12] Claude A. Fraser would continue as secretary of the Department of Natural Resources itself.

Walwyn's private assessment of the reconstruction plan was that it marked "a turning point on which we shall pin our faith and reputation." Its adoption would have "a beneficial moral effect out here, and lead to a renewal of confidence in the Commission of Government, which is so desirable."[13] If there was a note of alarm in this, nobody in London should really have been surprised, for if the Commission's hold on the country had never been seriously challenged, there had been a persistent threat of public disorder, especially among the unemployed and those on relief, in Newfoundland since 1934. One prominent critic of the government considered dangerous in official circles was J.T. Meaney, an experienced political operative, a local correspondent of the British press, and an associate of former prime minister Richard Squires, whose name now always spelled trouble for the authorities.[14] In the autumn of 1934 Meaney founded a newspaper, *The Newfoundlander,* and attempted to further his cause through the formation of "The League of Newfoundland," an effort which proved abortive. Another newspaper, the *Fishermen's Advocate* of Port Union, the voice of the Fishermen's Protective Union, was a continuous source of criticism of the government. A more ominous development from the government's perspective, however, was a riot among the unemployed of St. John's on 10 May 1935. This followed a series of demonstrations during the preceding months and a decision of the government that it would give no ground to the demand that the leaders of the unemployed themselves be responsible for the distribution of road work. During the riot, windows were smashed, stores were looted, and the red flag was flown. In the wake of this disturbance, four of the leaders of the unemployed were tried, convicted, and sentenced to short terms in the penitentiary.[15] Two other opposition groups active in 1935 were the "Crusaders" and the "Young Newfoundlanders." In their statement of purpose the Crusaders, having declared their loyalty to the Crown, condemned the Commission as follows: "During their tenure of office, they have shown themselves to be utterly incapable of constructive administration, and have demonstrated an unbearable attitude towards the citizens of this country, bordering on despotism." Accordingly, the Crusaders promised "to work assiduously for the return of Representative and Responsible Government, and the administration of our own affairs."[16] Publicly, the Commission conceded nothing to its mixed bag of critics but behind the scenes it maintained undercover police surveillance of anybody whose activities it feared might lead to a disturbance of the peace.[17]

Walwyn wrote to MacDonald on 15 March 1937 about the existing political situation in the country. Included with his letter was a petition he had received in favour of the restoration of self-government. This had been endorsed at a public meeting in St. John's and presented to him by a five-man delegation. The members of this delegation were not prominent citizens but, Walwyn explained, the background to the petition they had presented was a period of "six months or more" during which there had been "a gradually increasing movement of public opinion against the Commission of Government." This trend had not yet led "men of standing" to advocate the restoration of Responsible Government, but should it do so, "a difficult situation might arise." In sum, Newfoundland was a political tinder-box.[18]

To his great relief, the governor soon heard that, generally speaking, Whitehall accepted the Commission's reconstruction ideas. Although MacDonald's despatch, dated 31 March 1937, did not commit the United Kingdom to a fixed schedule of payments, the Commission was authorized to begin submitting detailed schemes of reconstruction to London for approval on the assumption that, following initial outlays of $100,000 in 1936–37 and $550,000 in 1937–38, $800,000 would be available for them annually through the life of the program. According to MacDonald, three considerations dictated the flexible budgetary stance which had been decided upon: growing defence spending at home might in the future limit the United Kingdom's ability to assist Newfoundland; the Commission's own revenues might yet be greater than forecast; and spending on reconstruction, as the Commission had itself observed, must not be allowed to "outrun organization." Finance aside, MacDonald supported the basic strategy of economic development now proposed for Newfoundland, which he summarized as encouraging the people "to support themselves by following a combination of occupations instead of relying on any one occupation alone."[19]

The Commission's agenda for social services was likewise well received, though MacDonald reserved comment on the "denominational difficulty" in the Newfoundland school system for a "secret and personal" letter which he addressed to Walwyn on the same day. This issue, he noted, had been avoided "for obvious reasons" both in Walwyn's despatch on reconstruction and in his own official reply thereto now forthcoming. Yet progress educationally in Newfoundland would ultimately hinge on the elimination of the denominational system in favour of state schools, what MacDonald understood Walwyn himself to mean by "a free and compulsory system." The case for this reform was undeniable because the denominational system was "unsound in principle" and had "most unfortunate results in practice." Education in Newfoundland could "never be put on a wholly satisfactory footing" while it remained. But given how entrenched the denominational system was, MacDonald accepted that "any sudden change" to a "secular State system" would not be possible. Still he wanted the removal of "the denominational barrier" to be the long-range objective of the Commission's educational policy, towards which public opinion could be gradually moulded.[20] In a spring of wishful thinking, this was an especially hopeful thought.

No sooner had the reconstruction plan been agreed upon between London and St. John's, at least in skeleton form, than it was challenged by John H.Penson who had been Sir Percy Thompson's successor in Newfoundland and who in April was chosen to go back there to succeed Trentham as commissioner for finance.[21] In a letter to Eric Machtig in the Dominions Office on 14 April, he questioned the likely effect both of the economic diversification planned for the outports and the modified scheme of land settlement proposed for those who would have to be uprooted. The first would no doubt be beneficial, but it would not deliver Newfoundland from "the devastating fluctuations characteristic of the fisheries." Equally, land settlement would encounter the same difficulties as in the past: a small local market, transportation obstacles, and the problem of recruiting settlers who could make a go of it without great cost to the government. Agriculture should certainly be expanded in Newfoundland, but this could best be done by encouraging established farmers to increase production.[22]

Another failing Penson detected in the reconstruction plan was that it did not take sufficient account "of local views," ignoring in particular the fact "that the general opinion of serious people in Newfoundland has all along been opposed to extensive schemes of land settlement." Had the Commission paid more attention to this sentiment, it would not have gone so far into debt. By the same token, it missed the mark with its reconstruction proposals, which were animated by a "bureaucratic and ultra-paternal spirit." The Commission was "foredoomed to failure" unless it led the populace "to look away from the Government [and] to themselves and to their own people." Newfoundlanders were "by nature individualistic and self-reliant," and it was to these traits, which previous "political corruption" had unfortunately eroded, that a policy of reconstruction should be directed. The pending scheme of rehabilitation manifestly did not do this, and to proceed with it would be dangerous. In the name of reconstruction, it would be folly to set loose "an army of officials" whose expense the country could never bear on its own. Penson's own prescription for Newfoundland was a policy of limiting imports by means of tariffs in order to stimulate domestic industry. Newfoundland could and should make for herself many things she now bought abroad at great expense; in some cases she even imported raw materials that should have been obtainable locally.

Penson's analysis forecast stormy days ahead within the Commission but was poorly received both in the Dominions Office and the Treasury. Protectionism, Whitehall maintained, posed many difficulties for a small export-oriented country like Newfoundland.[23] In any case, an arrangement had been made with the Commission which could not be altered because of an objection heard in London from somebody who was preparing to assume duties in St. John's. The "correct procedure" (Clutterbuck's phrase) for Penson was to go to Newfoundland, survey the scene and then, if he was still so inclined, attempt to advance his views with his new colleagues.[24] Ironically, the first installment of the Commission's reconstruction program was duly announced to the public by Penson himself in the 1937–38 budget speech, which he delivered, as was now customary under the Commission, before the Newfoundland Board of Trade in July, shortly after he arrived back in St. John's.[25]

A critic of the course now being charted in Newfoundland who could not be deflected by Whitehall was Thomas Lodge. In September 1937, almost a year after his resignation, the disgruntled former commissioner sent MacDonald a highly flavoured memorandum putting on public record his own version of events since 1934. Lodge defended the Markland experiment and expressed regret at having acquiesced in the ruling MacDonald had made on the constitutional point raised by the Kean affair. That pronouncement had "made it impossible for the Commission to function satisfactorily." The minister had declared that "his responsibility was unlimited" in relation to Newfoundland, but the performance of the Dominions Office completely contradicted this. "All my efforts," Lodge complained, "to force a discussion of fundamentals with a view to arriving at a wholehearted agreement between the Dominions Office and the Commission failed." At bottom, what the Dominions Office had sought in Newfoundland was nothing more than "that the machine turn over gently without causing unnecessary trouble at home." This ambition typified officialdom but the consequences of it were grave: "A good third of the population of Newfoundland is living in conditions of poverty and squalor which would shock the conscience of England, were they known here. The responsibility of the Secretary of State is no light one."[26] With this screed

Lodge was launched into a crusade which led eventually to the publication of his *Dictatorship in Newfoundland* after he had revisited and lectured in St. John's in July 1938.[27] Lodge's highly unorthodox behaviour out of office horrified his former superiors in the Dominions Office, but in reality he was an isolated, powerless figure whose efforts they were easily able to contain.[28] In any event, the Commission of Government had made a fresh start - or so it was thought.

Much was expected from the 1936 reconstruction plan, but Newfoundland was headed into another slump, the result of the downturn - the so-called Roosevelt Recession - that affected the North American economy generally in 1937-38. The effect of this reversal on Newfoundland's budgetary position was dramatic. In 1937-38 the country had a revenue of $12,275,000, the largest in its history and considerably more than had been anticipated.[29] But this figure masked an erosion that was already well underway, and the 1938-39 budget forecast a very different outcome; revenue of only $11,403,000, expenditure of $15,352,000 and a deficit of $3,949,000, the largest in the Commission's history to date.[30]

The improved 1937-38 record had been achieved despite another disastrous year for the fishing industry. The 1937 catch in the codfishery was about 20 per cent below normal. As this drop occurred mainly in the inshore fishery where labour was concentrated, its injurious effect was widely felt in the population. There were also adverse developments during 1937 on the market side, most notably the closing of Spain to Newfoundland traders because of the outbreak of civil war in that country. Early in 1938 local exporters were dealt yet another blow when Brazil, which took more Newfoundland fish than any other country, imposed stiff duties on fish imports.[31]

The Commission responded to this new round of difficulties with a variety of measures. In the autumn of 1937 it introduced an insurance scheme to cover risks which could not be insured privately in connection with the export of fish to Italy. This, together with benefits Newfoundland obtained through Anglo-Italian trade negotiations, permitted local exporters to make new headway in a traditional market. Additionally, during the summer of 1938 the Commission, working through the Newfoundland Fisheries Board, introduced a scheme whereby exporters organized themselves into marketing groups for sales to Brazil, Italy, Greece, and Puerto Rico (a like arrangement was already in effect for Portugal). Government assistance to the new export arrangement amounted to $300,000, in return for which exporters guaranteed the prices producers would be paid. The latter group was further assisted by an increase in the salt subsidy the Commission had introduced earlier.[32] Paradoxically, as the economy generally went down, the output of the cod fishery rose. In February 1939, the Commission reported that its general policy towards the fishing industry aimed "to improve marketing methods and results, and to cheapen the cost of production."[33]

The industry that bore the brunt of the recession in Newfoundland was pulp and paper manufacturing, which, relatively, had fared reasonably well earlier on.[34] In 1937, approximately 500,000 cords of wood were cut to supply the pulp and paper industry; a year later only about 200,000 cords were taken, mainly because of the greatly reduced demand for Newfoundland newsprint in the United States. In 1937–38, Newfoundland's newsprint production was 324,000 tons with a value of $13,874,000. Of this output, 215,000 tons went to the United Kingdom and 108,000 tons to the United States. In 1938–39, production fell back to 288,000 tons with a value of $12,664,000. While the British market remained reasonably firm, taking 202,000 tons, only 79,000 tons were shipped to the United States, the principal market of the International Power and Paper Company's mill at Corner Brook.

The social cost of this economic reversal in the forestry sector and of the continuing difficulties of the fishing industry quickly showed up in the country's relief statistics. During the autumn of 1937 and the winter following fewer people were on relief than usual, but as the recession caught hold this trend reversed itself; by April 1939 the government had 84,659 able-bodied dependents, more than in any month since March 1934.[35] Thus to the Commission's great dismay, what followed the acceptance in London of its reconstruction plan was not the period of ordered progress it had anticipated but another full-scale social and economic crisis. In its own defence, the Commission noted in its 1938 annual report that "the dominating factor in Newfoundland economic life" remained "the dependence of the country upon external trade and the conditions existing in international markets."[36] But such reasoning was cold comfort to a public which had been led to believe in 1934 that a new economic day had dawned. Not surprisingly, as hard times got worse, the Commission's political troubles mounted, not least with the local St. John's business community which had so staunchly supported the ending of self-government.

The episode in the late 1930s that caused the greatest political uproar concerned the Commission's attempt to get a third pulp mill started in the country. This was a longstanding dream of Newfoundland governments, and, following the completion of its reconstruction plan, the Commission pursued it with fresh determination. Most of Newfoundland's timber lands were committed to the Anglo-Newfoundland Development Company and the International Power and Paper Company, but there was one block of land, some 4,500 square miles in area, which lay undeveloped. This was owned by the Reid Newfoundland Company and, roughly speaking, constituted the watershed of the Gander River. It was in this area, known as the Gander properties, that successive Newfoundland governments had sought to promote a new mill. In Clutterbuck's words, the Gander properties had "long been regarded by Newfoundland public opinion not only as the most important undeveloped asset in the country, but as the one visible remaining asset capable of transforming the economic life of the Island through the attraction of large-scale manufacturing enterprise." This outlook had bred "the most exaggerated hopes" and made "a mill on the Gander" the "slogan for a new Utopia in which Newfoundland's economic troubles would vanish in a healing wave of industrial activity."[37] In practical terms, the construction of a mill in the area depended on two separate but interconnected agreements being made: a potential developer would have to purchase the properties from the Reid Newfoundland Company, and the developer and the government would have to come to an agreement on mutual responsibilities and benefits in connection with the new enterprise. Despite numerous attempts, Reid Newfoundland had never been able to find a purchaser for its lands. However in the spring of 1937 the company's receiver, the St. John's businessman, V.S. Bennett, was able to negotiate an option to purchase with the Bowater-Lloyd Group of the United Kingdom. Since Bowater-Lloyd was Europe's largest newsprint manufacturer, its expression of interest in the Gander properties was "warmly welcomed" in St. John's.[38] Providentially, the Commission seemed poised for the developmental breakthrough which had tantalized the country for many years; a successful outcome with Bowaters would clearly bring it great political as well as great financial reward.

In June 1937, A.G. Allen, one of the company's solicitors, and Arthur Baker, its managing director, opened talks in St. John's with representatives of the Commission of Government. These led to the initialling in September of a provisional draft agreement, which was then referred for final approval on one side to the head office of the company and on the other to the full Commission of Government and the secreatry of state. The Bowaters negotiators had ruled out from the start the construction of another paper mill and had offered instead to erect a pulp sulphite mill which would essentially export its product to the company's mills in England. It was this arrangement that was provided for in the provisional draft agreement, the terms of which were explained to the Newfoundland public by Commissionner Ewbank on 4 November in an enthusiastic radio address. The proposed mill was to have a productive capacity of 70,000 short tons of sulphite pulp per annum, consume 154,000 cords of wood yearly, and be operational by the end of 1940. In return for this boon, the government was to build and operate a railway to connect the mill site with the main line of the Newfoundland railway. This branch line was not to exceed twenty miles in length and its maximum cost was estimated to be in the order of $1,500,000. The company was to have the right to export 115,000 cords of rough wood annually, but this total was to be reduced if production at the mill fell to less than three-quarters of capacity. The company's timber rights in relation to the Gander properties were to be for ninety-nine years and renewable. In addition, the company was to have a timber licence for ninety-nine years over 3,000 square miles of Labrador in return for certain promises to work the property. Wood cut by the company on the Gander properties was to be exempt from royalty, as was wood cut by it until 1945 in Labrador. As well, the company was to be free of municipal taxation on all property connected with its operations at or within twenty miles of the mill site. Customs exemptions included the right to import, duty-free, the coal it would need to run its mill. By the same token, the company was to be given the water-power rights on the Gander River as well as on all streams emptying into Bonavista Bay from Middle Brook to Indian Bay Brook.[39]

Just prior to Ewbank's speech, Bowaters had been involved locally in a nasty strike in the area of Roberts Arm, Notre Dame Bay, the site of a pulpwood export operation the Commission had authorized in July.[40] The main issue was the workers' demand that the payment for the coming winter season be "$2.50 to $2.75 per cord at the stump." On the workers' side the principals in this strike, in which Sergeant-Major Fred Anderton of the Newfoundland Rangers played a key role, were Joseph J. Thompson of the recently formed Newfoundland Lumbermen's Association and the former prime minister Sir Richard Squires, the union's lawyer, who, to the dismay of the authorities, had actually appeared at the scene of the trouble. On the employer's side the key players were H.M. Spencer Lewin of Bowater-Lloyd, a buccaneering businessman who ultimately came to personify his company in the country, and A.J. Hewlett, the local contractor through whom Bowaters was working in the area. On 27 October negotiations began offshore aboard the anchored SS *Argyle,* but when Lewin was heard to be unyielding the ship was boarded by about 500 men. Shouting for the Bowaters official, they made it known "that if he did not make a settlement they would have his hearts blood over the stern of the ship." A tense standoff lasting three-quarters of an hour ensued during which Lewin was holed up in the saloon. Anderton and another Ranger separated him from the angry invaders by blocking the companion-way doors so that only crew members and union delegates were allowed through. A memorable chapter in Newfoundland labour relations ended when Squires emerged from the negotiations to announce that a contract had been signed specifying a rate of $2.50 per cord. The crowd then abandoned the ship and paraded in triumph on shore. Next Bowaters decided to close its operations at Roberts Arm and appealed to the government for police protection to get out their stores and equipment. In response, the government chartered the *Argyle* and sent fifty policemen to the area. On its arrival on 1 November the vessel was met by Anderton, who by this time detected "a very quiet and different attitude ... amongst the men." In these circumstances he advised St. John's that the *Argyle* should go to Lewisporte for supplies and drop off all but ten of the policemen on board. When Anderton next heard from Hewlett that Bowaters might reconsider their decision to pull out, he called a meeting of union men to explain the situation to them. They now agreed, Anderton reported, that "they had made a sad mistake and wished to call a meeting of council men of the Union from nearby settlements." In the course of this meeting, delegate Sidney Rice of Pilley's Island apologized to Bowaters and to Hewlett, thanked them for giving the men "another chance to go back to work and earn their living" and promised loyal service in future. The men, he said, "realized they had been wrongly advised and that a strike should not have been called." Henceforth they "would compel their Union Representative to properly discuss" with them, any difficulty that arose.[41] At the end of the day, Anderton, who, by his own account, left to the sound of cheers for the rangers and the government, believed that if Thompson ventured into the area he would "suffer bodily injury."[42] After all that had happened this was an astonishing reversal, but it showed just how precious a commodity work was in Newfoundland during the Depression. Thompson's union lived on but in the hard equation of work and wages, work perforce came first. This lesson was not lost on the Commission and was indeed employed to great advantage in the final stage of the larger negotiations now in progress with Bowaters.

As matters developed, changes in the draft agreement worked out between the government and the company in September were required on all sides, and to facilitate these, negotiations were resumed in London in December 1937. Newfoundland was represented at these talks by Woods, Penson, and L.E. Emerson, who, in a move that showed the willingness of the Dominions Office to co-opt important local critics of the Commission, had succeeded Howley in October as commissioner for justice and the government's Roman Catholic member. Woods and Emerson were called to London specifically for this round of negotiations; Penson was already there on other business. To the chagrin of the Newfoundland party and the Dominions Office, just as agreement seemed in sight, Bowaters drew back when a more promising prospect elsewhere in Newfoundland presented itself. This reversal, MacDonald wrote Sir Eric Bowater on 13 January 1938, had came as a "bombshell to all of us concerned with the matter on our side." Bowater sought to assure MacDonald that the new scheme the company was considering would please him. The only potential difficulty it posed – events proved Bowater to be greatly understating the case – "was the removal of the mill from the Gander area elsewhere." But this would save Newfoundland the expense of a branch railway and lead to lower operating costs for the company, a matter of "vital importance." When MacDonald enquired further whether the new scheme might "involve some political difficulty which did not attach to the old," Bowater replied "that he thought not." "What he had meant," MacDonald noted in his record of the conversation, "was that the word 'Gander' had been used in Newfoundland in such a way that the Gander project was regarded as an Eldorado. The people seemed to have become convinced that all sorts of things were possible in the Gander project which, in fact, would never have been possible. The idea of changing the site of the project might therefore cause a difficulty. But he was convinced, that properly handled, it could be shown that the Gander project would not have achieved anything which the new project was not also going to achieve."[43]

Subsequently, MacDonald was told that the alternative possibility Bowaters had in view was the purchase of the International Power and Paper Company's mill at Corner Brook. When Woods and Emerson were also informed of this possibility (Penson had already left for Newfoundland), they accepted "that there was no practicable alternative but to acquiesce in a reasonable period of delay to enable the Company to carry their investigations further." To expedite matters, however, should the company's latest quest prove fruitless, the revised draft of the original Gander agreement was initialled on 26 January, with the two commissioners acting for Newfoundland.[44] This was done on the understanding, embodied in a covering minute, that the agreement could only be made formal and binding if each party notified the other by 31 May that it wished to proceed. It was now also agreed that the Commission of Government could publish the revised draft agreement with an explanatory memorandum once its negotiators arrived home. This action was taken on February 17th.[45]

Here matters rested as far as Newfoundland was concerned until Sir Eric Bowater informed the Secretary of State in May that his company had reached agreement with the International Power and Paper Company and would shortly become the owner of the properties of that organization in Newfoundland. Given this outcome, he explained, Bowaters would not proceed with the agreement initialled in January. On the other hand, the company was anxious to resume negotiations with Newfoundland, looking towards a different agreement. Briefly, what Bowaters now proposed was a deal whereby, in return for the relevant concessions Newfoundland had previously offered, it would still acquire the Gander properties but build new facilities for the manufacture of sulphite pulp at Corner Brook.

This addition would have the same productive capacity as that of the mill originally proposed for the north-east coast. Although admittedly less ambitious than its predecessor, this scheme would provide considerable employment, while relieving the Newfoundland government of the cost of building a branch railway line. Adding to the existing operation at Corner Brook would also lead to lower production costs and therefore a more secure future for the operation.[46]

From the Newfoundland point of view, of course, things looked very different. What Bowaters now wanted represented a conderable retreat from the heady prospect of an entirely new manufacturing centre with its promise of many jobs. In short, the government had suffered a serious setback. Nonetheless, faced with a rapidly deteriorating general economic situation, it decided to pursue the company's latest offer, however disappointing. To this end, negotiations were resumed in St. John's, and an agreement was eventually reached. This was executed on 29 November 1938, and published the following day, together with the text of a bill the government proposed to pass confirming it.[47]

The new agreement, which was to run for ninety-nine years and was conditional on Bowaters acquiring the Gander properties, committed the company to add to its manufacturing capacity at Corner Brook by 31 December 1941, so as to produce 30,000 additional tons of sulphite pulp annually. This increment was less than half the production which had been planned for the proposed east coast mill, but the company also agreed to increase the paper-making capacity of the Corner Brook operation by 30,000 tons annually as soon after 31 December 1940 as it and the government agreed economic conditions warranted. During the first two years of operation of its new pulp sulphite facility, the company committed itself to manufacture for export not less than 15,000 short tons of pulp, a figure that was to rise to 22,500 tons the following year. In addition, beginning with the 1938–39 cutting season, the company agreed, as a condition of holding its timber licences, to export not less than 50,000 cords of raw wood annually. If it failed to reach this quota, it was to pay the government twenty-five cents for every cord by which it fell short. On the other hand, the company could export more than 50,000 cords annually provided it met certain specified conditions. Until its new pulp sulphite operation had been in production for four years, additional exports of wood were limited to 70,000 cords annually. Thereafter, the export of additional quantities of wood would be tied to additional production of pulp sulphite and paper. On all timber exports the company was to pay a royalty of thirty cents per cord. There was no reference to Labrador in the new agreement, but the water power rights, customs and other concessions the company received were in line with those specified in the agreement initialled in January.[48]

The second Bowaters agreement was explained and defended to the Newfoundland people in a radio address which Ewbank gave from the Newfoundland Hotel on the evening of 29 November. In his opening remarks the commissioner for natural resources sought "to make one point perfectly clear." The St. John's rumour mill to the contrary, there was no other developer available to purchase and work the Gander properties, should the government break off its negotiations with Bowaters. The choice before the Commission and the country was therefore plain: either to accept a deal worked out in hard bargaining over many months, or to allow the "opportunity to slip" and ask "the people ... to tighten their belts and wait until some other opportunity should offer itself." In uncertain economic times the second alternative manifestly carried too high a price, and for this reason, and because it believed a fair bargain had been arrived at, the government had decided to press forward:

> To talk of tightening belts and waiting for better days sounds well enough, and in present conditions many of our people have, alas, no choice but to do it. Times have indeed often been worse in the past, but that is not much consolation to the man who sees a chance of earning a living for himself and his family being denied to him. Every member of the Commission of Government hears daily by post or by talks tales of distress which move them deeply. Men who have never been on the dole are today desperately fighting to keep off it. Men who have long been on the dole are beginning to despair of ever finding any way of getting back to independence. Young men just coming to full manhood find themselves denied an outlet. One cannot but be struck with the fortitude with which these hard conditions are being faced, but it is inevitable that in time they will sap the fine spirit on which this country has been built up. We are bound to ask ourselves what is to happen to the people to whom these operations would afford employment if we reject this chance which is going to mean work and cash wages to so many of them. It is easy to say that conditions are bound soon to improve, and that things will soon right themselves. It may be so, but then again it may not. Even so, had the Commission believed that this Agreement was not, on the whole, in the interests of the country, they would have rejected it. But that is not their view, and therefore the needs of the people in the North East of the Island are one of the facts that have weighed very heavily in the scales.

The government was placing "the resources of the Gander ... in strong hands" and had faith that the agreement with Bowaters would "pave the way to other developments and add to the economic strength of the country." "We believe," Ewbank concluded, "that time will justify the step we have taken, and we believe that the great majority of the people of this country will, in their hearts, be glad that the greatest natural resource still remaining in this country is at last to be developed and to play its part in bringing us back the prosperity for which we are all working."[49]

One Newfoundlander not of this view was Emerson, who had played a prominent role in the negotiations. The day after Ewbank's radio address, in a minute of dissent which he circulated to his Commission colleagues, Emerson came out against the agreement on the grounds that it was weighted too heavily in favour of the company. He argued that if the government waited until market conditions improved, it could strike a better bargain either with Bowaters or some other potential developer.[50] Emerson was close to the St. John's business community, and the view he expressed within the government, though confidential, quickly manifested itself in the capital after the agreement and the bill to give it force were published. Another of the government's critics was J.P. Powell, formerly of the engineering department of the Reid Newfoundland Company, who had been the "chief exponent" for many years of a mill on the Gander.[51] Having heard from Powell, the Newfoundland Board of Trade, on the evening of 6 December, passed resolutions which were forwarded to the governor, the Commission, and the secretary of state, condemning the government's action. The Bowaters agreement, the board argued, would permit "the export of unmanufactured wood from the Gander areas for an unreasonably long period" and did not require the company "to undertake that large scale industrial development of the Gander areas warranted by the timber resources and water power of the territory." Instead of ratifying the agreement, the government should "adopt such policy only as will assure the development of the Gander areas as an industrial entity," pending which "the export of unmanufactured wood" should be permitted from the region "up to a maximum quantity of 100,000 cords per annum upon short-term licenses subject to such conditions as may be considered proper in the interests of the Country."[52]

The next day the St. John's Municipal Council also came out against the agreement, which was further attacked in petitions submitted to the authorities from a number of outports along the east coast.[53] A plea to the *Daily Express* for its help in stopping the government was signed by the mayor of St. John's and a number of figures who would be important in post-1945 Newfoundland politics. These included John B. McEvoy, Harry G.R. Mews, Eric Cook, Philip J. Lewis, James D. Higgins, and Chesley A. Crosbie, a talented young entrepreneur and the son of Sir John Crosbie, one of the country's earlier political heavy-weights. The claim of their submission, which had wide support in the business community, was that the Newfoundland public was "deeply incensed at the arbitrary method adopted by the Government in consummating this Agreement." In calling on the secretary of state to use his "powerful influence to prevent ... a grave injustice," the petition predicted that if the government proceeded with the bill it had in hand "a grave constitutional crisis" would arise and the Newfoundland people would "appeal direct to the British Parliament for redress."[54] Yet another critic of the government's action, especially noteworthy in retrospect but socially far removed from the local establishment, was Joseph Roberts (known variously as J.R., Joey and Joe) Smallwood, an author, organizer, and publicist who after dabbling in many occupations, would in time become Newfoundland's most successful twentieth-century politician. In a letter to the St. John's *Daily News*, he described the Bowaters deal as "suidical" and predicted that it would "drive another nail in the national coffin that will doom us to the status of southeastern European peasants." "It is our country," he boldly proclaimed, "and Mr. Ewbank and his colleagues are only temporarily in charge of it."[55]

In a telegram to the secretary of state on 9 December, the Commission assessed the rising tide of complaint against it. Opposition to the Bowaters agreement, it noted, had so far been confined mainly to the St. John's area (the outport petitions came in later). Moreover, given the high hopes that had existed in Newfoundland for so long about a Gander mill, "natural and widespread" disappointment was to be expected in the face of an agreement that did not deliver one, even though this possibility had been ruled out since May. Significantly, it was not the detail of the agreement which was drawing the fire of the critics but the fact that a Gander mill would not be built "within any period that can reasonably be foreseen." Furthermore, the controversy had to be understood in the larger context of Newfoundland history. Thus, there was a "rooted tendency" in the country to "regard with suspicion any scheme which brings in outside companies to develop local resources."[56] This had manifested itself at the time of the building of the Grand Falls mill during the first decade of the century and had inspired an agitation the previous year against a proposal by General Seafoods, an American company, to establish a cold storage plant on the south coast, an initiative the government had welcomed and about which negotiations were still in progress.[57] The Commission understood and appreciated the sentiment it had encountered but believed also that "substantial progress towards rehabilitation" in Newfoundland required the "assistance in many directions of powerful outside interests." Undoubtedly, too, there was a "political element" in the campaign against the Bowaters deal. The fact that the public did not have a direct say in government in itself bred a critical attitude towards the Commission's actions. Looked at from this point of view, what the Bowaters issue offered was "a convenient peg for attacking the Government at ... [a] time when the outlook for the coming winter [is] gloomy." Given this background, the Commission believed that the agitation against it would be short-lived. On the other hand, it was convinced that it would have faced an "equally vigorous agitation" if it had not gone through with the deal. Three commissioners, it was reported, had just visited Grand Falls and two of them had also been in Corner Brook. They had found public opinion in both places indifferent to the controversy which was stirring the capital. At the same time, the former labour minister, Kenneth M. Brown, who had been elected President of the Fishermen's Protective Union, had spoken out in favour of the agreement, claiming that he was "supported by the whole of the north-east coast."[58] These were hopeful signs and, having taken stock of the full position, the Commission proposed to pass the bill ratifying the agreement "towards the end of the month."[59]

This was in fact done on 31 December after the government's case had been defended in another radio address. This time the speaker was Puddester (soon to be Sir John), a counterweight on the administration's Newfoundland side to the dissenting Emerson.[60] The bill as passed contained only one really substantial amendment. This increased to $2.00 the amount Bowaters would have to pay the government per cord on the difference between its actual export of raw wood in a given year and the 50,000 cord annual export target specified in the agreement.[61] Interestingly, this change was made to assuage the one fear the Fishermen's Protective Union had about the agreement, namely, that Bowaters was not firmly enough committed to the export total.[62] Whereas important elements in the St. John's business community looked to the eventual scaling down of such exports in favour of domestic industry, the Fishermen's Protective Union wanted a long-term guarantee of jobs for its fisherman-logger members through the direct sale abroad of the resource on which new manufacturing capacity might be built. This difference in view point permitted the Commission to present itself as the champion of the working man and to appeal to the masses over the heads of the local business elite, a familiar populist alignment of forces that had a considerable future in Newfoundland politics.

Early in January, Walwyn reported to London that Powell had answered Puddester in a radio address of his own on 30 December and that a special meeting of the Newfoundland Board of Trade had been held on 4 January to protest the enactment of the Bowaters legislation and "to consider further steps." This meeting, however, had been attended by only about half the number present at the previous meeting, and there had been "a considerable division of opinion" among the participants.[63] When the meeting had voted on a resolution condemning the Government's action and calling for the formation of a committee to carry the fight to London, thirty-seven members had voted in favour, thirteen against. The mover and seconder of the resolution had been respectively Leslie R. Curtis, a lawyer and future attorney general of Newfoundland, and Ches Crosbie. But Leonard Outerbridge of Harvey and Company, a doyen of the local establishment, had declined nomination to the committee thus launched, an outcome decidedly to the government's advantage.[64] "We are satisfied," Walwyn concluded in his despatch of 6 January, "that the bulk of sound public opinion is coming round to our view that the Agreement will prove to be in the interest of the country."[65] In this tense episode the Commission had prevailed, but the glad confident morning of 1934 was now far behind it.

The other preoccupation of the Commission during the troubled year of 1938 was the future of its reconstruction plan, the critical rural side of which in particular was off to a shaky start. Dunfield had proved a disappointment in his new role as head of the Department of Rural Reconstruction, had clashed with Ewbank, and had returned after a few months to the Department of Justice.[66] In December 1937, Puddester told Machtig and Clutterbuck in London that the Newfoundland government had "little to show for the long-term policy" and that public opinion in the country was "showing signs of impatience."[67] The occasion for this observation was a discussion of a corrective measure under consideration for some time and soon afterwards taken. This was the secondment of John H. Gorvin, a principal in the British Ministry of Agriculture and Fisheries, to advise the Commission of Government in the difficult policy area of rural development.[68] Gorvin, fifty-two years old at the time of his Newfoundland appointment, had uncommon credentials for the work he was now to undertake. He had joined the Ministry of Agriculture and Fisheries in 1906. During the Great War he had served as Director of Requirements to the Allied Food Council and after the war had been involved in refugee and relief work, mainly in Russia. This postwar experience was said to have given him "a valuable insight into rehabilitation problems among rural communities."[69] Returning to the Ministry of Agriculture and Fisheries in 1926, Gorvin had subsequently served on the Jamaica Banana Commission in 1935-36, and as special commissioner in 1936 to the Turks and Caicos Islands. A friend of Lodge, he was known in Whitehall not only for his energy and originality but also for a prickly temperament and singleness of purpose which could land him in difficulty with colleagues. These last-mentioned attributes almost cost him the Newfoundland job, but working in his favour was the argument, put succinctly by Puddester, that the need in St. John's for an advisor of his calibre was "a matter of urgent importance."[70]

During the spring and summer of 1938 Gorvin travelled extensively in Newfoundland, visiting the agricultural areas of the west coast in April, the land settlements in May and June, and then the entire coast of the island between June and September.[71] While he was thus engaged, the rapidly deteriorating economic condition of the country heightened the significance of his already important mission; if the Commission's need for fresh plans and ideas had been urgent before, it was now becoming desperate.

Just how tricky matters actually were for the government was shown in June, when there was an outbreak of lawlessness, involving interference with road workers, at Bonavista. To head off further trouble there, the Commission made an emergency appropriation of $400,000 to provide additional work in the area - on the construction of a breakwater at Bonavista itself and on the ballasting of the branch line connecting the hard-pressed town with the main line of the Newfoundland Railway.[72] It was hoped that these projects, along with the reconstruction of the highway linking Bonavista and King's Cove, would provide "work for practically all who are in need of assistance." Time had literally been bought by the government; but the Commission was forced to receive a delegation representing the protesters, and the whole episode clearly rattled Governor Walwyn. In a gloomy letter to Harding, he described a rising tide of resentment in the country which had the potential for "demonstrations, marches and mass petitions." Should a big movement for change get underway, Walwyn feared the resignation "of one or more of the Newfoundland Commissioners" who naturally could be expected to look to their own local futures. Such a development would be "a serious blow" to the existing system of government. The Commission was doing its utmost to handle a difficult situation with "good judgment and equanimity"; but having "little or no control" over the forces causing unemployment, operating within a "limited financial margin," and lacking a police force able "to ensure firm handling of any violation of law and order," the task before it was "not an easy one."[73]

It was with this foreboding commentary from Government House in the background that Gorvin submitted a four-part preliminary report to the Commission on 29 September 1938.[74] In the first part Gorvin described the situation as he had found it. He then in turn analyzed the major problems of rural Newfoundland, suggested solutions to them, and described the administrative changes that would be needed to carry out his recommendations. Though he had discovered that there were families in Newfoundland "living for periods of the year below minimum physiological requirements and having insufficient clothing," they did "not present a problem of great dimensions" and were "confined to a few areas." Even so, this situation was one which "in a British community ... should not be allowed to continue." The problem facing Newfoundland was "to place men in work and improve the standard of living in the settlements." There was "no single cure" for this problem but Gorvin had many suggestions for tackling it, chief among them, a scheme for the rehabilitation of unemployed fishermen.[75] In the words of a concise and penetrating Dominions Office summary of his findings, this would "involve revolutionary changes both in fishery organization and also in the administration of the dole."[76] Gorvin arrived at this scheme through an analysis which held that the morale of the Newfoundland people had been so eroded by the long years of depression that the government had to abandon its "present negative policy of merely keeping those in distress alive on public relief pending the return of better times" in favour of "a positive policy of finding work for them," despite the fact that this could not be done "as a strictly commercial proposition." Logically, "the best and quickest results" in this regard could be obtained not by directing the people to unfamiliar work but "by assisting them to re-establish themselves in the calling which by tradition and environment comes most naturally to them, i.e. in the main fishing."[77]

The main objective of the plan Gorvin proposed in relation to unemployed fishermen was "to link the distribution of relief with work of a constructive and reproductive character." Hitherto assistance had been given to the able-bodied unemployed either gratis or by requiring work on local road projects at the nominal rate of twenty-five cents per hour. This practice encouraged "idleness" and must be stopped. What was required instead was a fresh approach that would provide work for men trapped in the relief system without undermining existing arrangements whereby "the merchant equips the more efficient and trustworthy fishermen." Since the "individual credit supply system" offered no hope to the unemployed and was obviously breaking down in many parts of the country, the government had no choice but to modify it. If the "interests concerned" would not co-operate in this, the government must have ready "a scheme whereby the individual merchant credit system could be replaced by a regional supplying and marketing scheme." Specifically, Gorvin proposed that the assistance recommended take the form of "grants from relief funds" made "to a non- or limited-profit making, or public utility type of organisation." This approach would overcome the lack of financial acumen among Newfoundland fishermen, which made it difficult to go straight into a co-operative system. "The fishermen's sense of responsibility in financial matters," Gorvin wrote, "is undeveloped, and it will take at least five years to educate him sufficiently in co-operative principles to enable him to derive benefit from the system."[78] Hence, the recommended scheme: it had the potential to develop into a full co-operative system and in effect envisaged the eventual withering away of the merchant class.

Under Gorvin's proposal, a regional development corporation, which would involve local merchants and work side by side with established supply arrangements, would be formed in a given area. If the activities of the corporation worked against a fisherman in receipt of credit from an individual merchant, he could seek redress through a claims committee. The corporation would advance cash through "merchants or organised trading societies" and hold signed certificates of issue in return. Repayment of its loans would be "a first charge" on the assets of a fisherman thus helped. Unemployed fishermen thus assisted would, however, have the benefit of a ten year moratorium on past debts. The marketing of the catch of fishermen participating in the scheme would be "through merchants or organised trading societies as in the ordinary course of business." But the corporation would reserve the right to act against "lack of co-operation or profiteering or ... failure to provide proper facilities for processing fish." In these circumstances, the corporation could, without compensation, move an assisted individual's business to the "more progressive" of its members.[79]

The capital for the corporation would be "subscribed by merchants or organised trading societies in nominal shares, limited as to dividend." Funds available to the corporation to loan to fishermen would come "in the first instance out of grants from Government relief or from special Government funds and be made against nominal share capital." The corporation would be administered by a regional board consisting of a "manager-secretary" and "a chairman and five representatives of merchants or trading organisations of whom at least one ... [would] be a representative of organised trading societies." Working alongside the corporation would be a regional development council. When the whole system was operating countrywide there would be twenty of these, corresponding roughly to the former electoral divisions. Each council would be chaired by a magistrate and would have the following other members: three representatives each from the churches and the fishermen, at least one of the latter from an organized group; a representative from each of the logging, mining, and agricultural industries; one merchant; one schoolmaster; and either a lawyer, bank manager, or other prominent person in the region. The council would have a paid secretary who would also manage a labour bureau. Meetings of council would be attended by "the Head Ranger and Police Officer for the Region." The council would take over the administration of relief within its jurisdiction, act as an employment agency, and in effect provide a form of local government. It would also collaborate with the regional development corporation in determining which unemployed fishermen that body would assist. If an unemployed fisherman were refused assistance by the corporation, his claim would "be examined impartially" by the council. To begin, Gorvin proposed that his whole scheme for the rehabilitation of unemployed fishermen should be tested in one region, Placentia Bay, where in his view the problem to be addressed was most severe.[80]

Coincident with this experiment, Gorvin proposed significant changes in the organization of the central government. At the top, a co-ordinating committee would constitute "the Reconstruction Authority." This authority, acting primarily through a reorganized and greatly expanded Department of Rural Reconstruction, would "ensure a common drive towards rehabilitation." The restructured department would have "three main divisions – Relief and Reconstruction; Agriculture; and General." The general division of the department would be given the task of promoting co-operative practice in the country, but within this unit there would also be branches devoted to organized marketing, technical and vocational education, rural industries, and road development in relation to agricultural extension. Gorvin's immediate agenda in the latter regard included the provision of five-acre lots for fishermen and loggers (his report contained a list of possible sites) and the reorganization of existing land settlements to provide bigger (25 to 50 acre) individual holdings.[81]

In November 1938 Gorvin's report was published in St. John's, together with (1) a December 1937 report by Professor J.A. Hanley of King's College, Newcastle-upon-Tyne, on the development of agriculture in Newfoundland; (2) edited versions of Walwyn's crucial despatch of 24 December 1936 on reconstruction and Malcolm MacDonald's reply thereto of April 1937; and (3) extracts dealing with the Commission's reconstruction policy from Penson's budget speeches of 1937 and 1938.[82] The Dominions Office had previously refused the Commission's request to allow publication of this seminal correspondence on reconstruction, but it relented now lest the Newfoundland government be accused of having had no ideas of its own before Gorvin came along.[83] In the Commission's view, the simultaneous publication of the documents in question and the Gorvin report was a "matter of paramount importance" to its prestige.[84]

Beginning on 13 December 1938, in the midst of the flare-up over the Bowaters agreement, the Commission gave long and hard consideration to Gorvin's proposals in a series of meetings that ran until early February. In January when the Commission voted on whether his fishery scheme should be adopted, the vote was three to three.[85] The governor put off breaking this deadlock, and eventually the impasse was overcome. Thus in a despatch Walwyn sent to London on 13 February the Commission declared itself ready to launch a modified version of the Placentia Bay experiment once the "general reconstruction machinery" was functioning and provided that "good technical management" was available for the project.[86]

Gorvin was correct, the Commission asserted, in concluding that an alternative method of financing the fishing industry in general had to be found. The merchant-lender who had previously met this need was "progressively curtailing his operations" and might "in the not distant future ... disappear altogether." Gorvin was right too in his assessment that an "intervening period" was needed to set the stage for "a co-operative system," and that the first step forward should be "an experiment in a limited scale." On the other hand, his plan for unemployed fishermen, as originally submitted, had presented difficulties.[87]

The first of these arose from the fact that there were some areas of Newfoundland where conditions were such that even "in normal years" inshore fishermen could not operate profitably; in these places, it was now clear, "it would naturally be no part of Mr. Gorvin's scheme to base reconstruction ... on a fishery which, on the basis of average marketing values, would not contribute to the support of the family." Another matter that had "weighed heavily" with the Commission was the effect on working fishermen of the special assistance to be given the unemployed. This was an especially serious consideration in Newfoundland because, as things stood, throughout "the greater part of the Island ... the independent fisherman" fared "very little better than the fisherman on the dole." If those who had "given up the struggle" were assisted by the government while those just above the dole line were not, the latter might "throw in their hand" to get their share of the development corporation's largesse. Equally, merchants might be tempted to push the whole task of outfitting fishermen, their own employees excepted, onto the development corporation, confining themselves "to retail trade on a cash basis." Either of these developments would, of course, greatly increase the cost to the government of the experiment to be undertaken. Gorvin had answered this problem with an ingenious modification of his original plan. This involved the creation in Placentia Bay under one regional corporation of three "special trading areas each covering about thirty miles of coast." Within these, provided public opinion was favourable, all fishermen, except for those excluded by the regional council as "hopelessly incompetent or otherwise ineligible" would form a supply and marketing co-operative. All members of the co-operative would then receive assistance from the regional corporation. Local supply merchants would not be "authorized bodies" under these arrangements, but there were few of them left in business anyway. Vessel building as well as fishing would be supported by the corporation. An added advantage of the revised plan was that geographically small operational units would facilitate the centralization of bait supply and curing functions. Within the "special trading areas" it would also be possible "to keep a check on disloyalty to the outfitting organization." It was on this basis, the Commission explained, that it was willing to proceed with the Placentia Bay experiment while maintaining, albeit perhaps in modified form, its other "special forms of assistance" to the fishing industry.[88]

The cost of carrying out Gorvin's amended plan was estimated by the Commission at roughly $2,000,000 in 1939–40, $2,800,000 in 1940–41 and

$3,000,000 in 1941–42. When already planned expenditure was deducted from these totals, the net addition to the government's requirements over the three years would be $1 million, $2 million and $2.5 million respectively. Admittedly, these were much larger amounts than the Commission's original reconstruction program had called for, but the need for "a plan ... of wider scope" which could be pressed forward with "greater rapidity" than "previously considered advisable" was urgent. No doubt Gorvin's proposals "increased demands on the already over-burdened Treasury of the United Kingdom," and "their adoption might have the appearance of pushing further into the future the financial independence and political autonomy of Newfoundland," which were the Commission's "ultimate objectives." But economic conditions were such that financial independence for Newfoundland was "impossible except at a price payable in human misery." "It is true," the Commission concluded, "that Newfoundland's history is largely a story of the ebb and flow of national income, the flow succeeding the ebb independently of attempts at contrivance on the part of the people and their governments. History may yet repeat itself, but all the signals we can read give warning of the danger of relying on time alone to reverse the tide ... Every part of the structure is exposed to economic tempests and nothing but the broadening of its base will make it safe." When it had put forward its own long-range reconstruction plan in 1936, the Commission had believed that the "resiliency of the country's economic fabric" was such that it "would respond with reasonable rapidity ... to indirect ameliorative action." Alas, this faith was now shaken and the time had come for "a direct attack upon poverty."[89] Interestingly, Emerson, who had dissented from the decision to go forward with the Bowaters agreement, also qualified in writing his support for the policy on which the Commission was now embarked. His point was that, considering the gravity of the unemployment problem in the country, the Commission could not just wait to see how the Placentia Bay experiment worked out. While this experiment was in progress special, though lesser assistance, should be given to two or three other areas. His tentative suggestions for these were Bonavista and Harbour Breton, "the sorest spots on the face of Newfoundland."[90]

In a telegram dated 20 March 1939, the Dominions Office accepted in principle the plans outlined in Walwyn's despatch. In doing so, however, it sounded a note of caution: the fisheries rehabilitation scheme called for "very close examination" as it involved "the reversal of traditional methods and the establishment of a new and complicated co-operative system" in a population which was "for the most part unversed in business and strongly individualist." By definition, the scheme proposed would tempt people to take advantage of public funds and "continuous skilled supervision would be essential to success." Nonetheless London accepted "that the declining merchant-lender system should be gradually replaced by organizations of producers" and declared itself "impressed by [the] arguments in favour of [a] new and radical method of approach to [the] fishery problem in the outports." Accordingly, the Commission was authorized to frame its 1930–40 estimates on the assumption that the plans it had worked out with Gorvin would take effect. The only constraint in this regard was that the grant-in-aid to be sought from Parliament to carry Newfoundland to 31 March 1940 (the end of the United Kingdom's financial year), could not now be increased.[91] In order to settle various administrative and financial questions resulting from all this, the British asked that one of the United Kingdom commissioners come over to London to join Walwyn and Emerson who were already there.[92] Subsequently, Woods was chosen for this mission.

On 4 April 1939, at a meeting held in the Dominions Office, the Newfoundland party discussed the state of affairs facing the Commission with Sir Thomas Inskip, who had become secretary of state in January, and his parliamentary under-secretary, the Duke of Devonshire. Also present on this occasion were Harding, Machtig, and Clutterbuck. Emerson now said that while he agreed that the Placentia Bay experiment should go forward, he doubted whether the problem of unemployment in the Newfoundland fishery "could be solved by the development of cooperative institutions among the fishermen." The industry was by nature "highly speculative," and "though in good times the merchants had made handsome profits (and though their charges for outfitting allowed a margin not merely for profit but also for bad debts) it was very difficult to say that, taking the bad times with the good, the merchants had in fact done well out of the fisheries; indeed, the small merchant almost invariably came to grief sooner or later, and it was the common experience that the names of the small merchant firms in the outports changed every two generations." Co-operatives would face the same risks, and the effect of inevitable periodic losses might be "too great a strain on them." Moreover, "the average Newfoundlander was highly individualistic," and "it would take a great deal of education and propaganda to get the fishermen to work smoothly together in a cooperative organisation." Still a "trial and error" approach was necessary, and now that Gorvin's plan had been "published and favourably received ... it would ... be a great political mistake not to proceed with it." For his part, Walwyn maintained that Gorvin "had caught the popular imagination" and that the announcement of a decision to go forward with his plans would be "warmly welcomed" in Newfoundland. According to Woods, while the ultimate effect of Gorvin's strategy for the fishery would be to displace merchants from "active business" in the industry, they would still be able to function "as storekeepers, freed from the risks which direct investment in the fisheries involved." This was circumspect.[93]

When discussion turned to how the Commission might bring itself into "closer contact with public opinion," a perennial Dominions Office concern, Walwyn argued in favour of maintaining the existing lines of authority. Matters would be helped by the introduction of the consultative process Gorvin proposed and perhaps also by the appointment of a government public relations officer, but the creation of an advisory council, as previously suggested from London, would be going too far. Without "direct responsibility," such a body "would be bound to make all kinds of recommendations which could not be accepted by the Government, and constant clashes, which would seriously embarass the Commission, would have to be expected." Emerson agreed, noting that while "the average Newfoundlander, accustomed as he was to self-government, naturally did not like the present form of Government," the existing system could not at present be changed "without great danger to the true interests of the country." Woods concurred, observing that "there was no real demand for any change" locally "except in so far as such change might assist Newfoundland to screw a larger amount of financial assistance out of the United Kingdom." This was not said disparagingly but in recognition of the fact that, given world conditions, the British government was the only possible source of funds to make the country self-supporting again. Picking up on this, Emerson commented that "if the United Kingdom could spare £4,000,000 as a gift, and many more millions as a loan, to Czechoslovakia, apart altogether from the millions spent in assisting parts of the Empire where the population was not of British stock, surely the amount needed to develop Newfoundland should not be grudged." In reply, Inskip said that money in itself posed "no difficulty," and that a larger grant-in-aid from the United Kingdom could be expected in 1940-41. The real challenge was to apply financial aid to "genuinely productive purposes," as would now be done.[94]

Following this round of talks, consideration was given in London to Gorvin's appointment as a member of the Commission of Government. As a first step in this direction, Harding and Machtig arranged for Gorvin's release for duty in Newfoundland. At the same time, Gorvin's home ministry agreed to co-operate in "producing a reason" should the Dominions Office ever want him removed from his new posting. This unusual precaution was taken because of lingering doubts at the Dominions Office about Gorvin's ability to "'get on' with his fellow Commissioners." Next Gorvin himself was approached and told, among other things, that his proposed appointment "would be somewhat experimental"; "though ordinarily for three years," his would be "terminable, after three months' notice, at the end of the first and second years, at the instance either of the holder or of the Government."[95] When Gorvin agreed to what he had heard, a formal offer was made to him, whereupon he was appointed. In the course of a conversation with Inskip on 2 May, Gorvin admitted that he could be "mulish" but promised "to do his best to work in well" in St. John's.[96] Finally, on 5 July he was sworn in as a member of the Newfoundland government and made commissioner for natural resources, a portfolio which, of course, included the existing Department of Rural Reconstruction.[97]

As part of its original assessment of Gorvin's proposals, the government had commissioned and received a report itemizing the vessels and gear that would be needed to get unemployed fishermen back to work in Placentia Bay.[98] Moreover, on 20 February, pending word of London's attitude towards the recent turn of events in the field of reconstruction, Magistrate Quinton had been put to work completing tasks necessary for carrying out the whole regional development proposal.[99] From this planning base, Gorvin plunged into his new job with characteristic energy and determination, gradually building up the expert team he needed, a group that eventually included C.A.L. Irving, who also came from the Ministry of Agriculture and Fisheries, and the American, Mary Arnold, who had previously been involved in labour, co-operative, and rural development work in the United States and Nova Scotia.[100] In July 1939 ad hoc regional development councils were approved for east and west Placentia Bay, and the groundwork was laid for a Special Areas Development Act.[101] The Commission had turned another corner, but it had now to cross a veritable minefield of vested interests, great and small. In short, it had embarked on a reform which, with the possible exception of the attack it had contemplated in 1935 on the denominational system of education, was at once the most fundamental and politically the most dangerous it had yet attempted.

SYNOPSIS: 1934–39

Between 1934 and 1939 the Commission of Government passed through several phases. During the years 1934–36 the government was dominated by two of its United Kingdom members, Thomas Lodge and John Hope Simpson. They were both highly independent men who took a broad and ultimately foolhardy view of the mandate the government had been given. Appalled by the physical conditions and the social structure they found in Newfoundland, they set off on the high road of reform. In the course of this journey, as they were not directly accountable to any local constituency, they occasionally rode roughshod over groups and organizations, in particular, the businessmen and the churches, which had strongly supported the introduction of the Commission system in the first place. Newfoundland's conservative economic and social elites had looked forward to Commission of Government as an administration that would be peculiarly their own. Not surprisingly, they were sorely disappointed by the performances of Lodge and Hope Simpson, whose contempt for the local squirarchy was deeply felt.

Generally speaking, Lodge and Hope Simpson prevailed over their Newfoundland colleagues who were men of lesser ability, grateful for their positions, appointed on a denominational basis and in the expectation that they would never break ranks. But when the British commissioners stepped onto the sacred ground of local interest groups who were able to defend themselves, for example, the churches and the pulp and paper companies, they were forced to retreat. Their downfall was the Kean affair which, in the absence of normal political opposition, gave a reading of the extent to which disaffection with Commission policy had spread in the upper ranks of Newfoundland society. In truth, root and branch reform in Newfoundland after 1934 would have required either a strong body of local public opinion behind it, a willingness in London to fight economic and political battles in the country to final victory, or, preferably, both. The fact was the neither of these conditions existed. Lodge and Hope Simpson were transients in Newfoundland, their political standing a function of appointment alone. Moreover, when they became embroiled in controversy, Whitehall demonstrated its willingness to act over their heads to lower the political temperature. What the Dominions Office really wanted in Newfoundland was progress with economy and without adverse publicity. This was a typically bureaucratic goal and showed just how much the Commission of Government was at heart an administration of civil servants. Having been burned by Lodge and to a lesser extent by Hope Simpson, who tested the limits of the new system, the permanent officials in London - Harding, Machtig and Clutterbuck - who devised policy towards Newfoundland were afterwards more careful in recommending appointments to St. John's from the United Kingdom. The result was that, with the exception of Gorvin, Newfoundland never again saw spirits as free as Lodge and Hope Simpson. Commissioners came and departed but their civil service chiefs in Whitehall remained the same, a factor which in itself weighted authority under the Commission system towards London.

Yet for all the bad feeling that gradually enveloped it, the Commission had some solid accomplishments in the first years of its rule. The administrative machine was overhauled and, within a small range, significant improvements were made in health, welfare, and education, though in the latter area the denominational principle survived attack. In addition, to better communication with the outport population, the Commission established the Newfoundland Ranger Force and reformed the magistracy. With the help of sizeable loans from the Colonial Development Fund, it launched an ambitious road building program and improved various other transportation facilities. Economically, the government attempted to revive, and where possible extend, established enterprise. In the case of the hard-hit fishery, still the country's basic industry, its most important achievement was the creation in 1936 of the Newfoundland Fisheries Board. This was a characteristic Commission innovation: it did not threaten established patterns of ownership or control but sought to co-ordinate efforts to achieve better results. In particular, the Commission tried to save Newfoundland saltfish exporters from one of their worst vices – unbridled competition among themselves in overseas markets. In this instance as in many others, the reforms brought in by the Commission, whatever their provenance and no matter how much they were resented by their ultimate beneficiaries, amounted to state intervention to prop up the old order. This was an essentially conservative outcome. At the close of the Commission era, Newfoundland would have a much more modern and efficient educational system, but it would still be organized denominationally. Though refurbished and changed remarkably in outward appearance, many other local institutions and structures would be similarly recognizable.

A fundamental conviction of the first body of commissioners was that Newfoundland's traditional resource industries could not support the population dependent on them. To solve this problem of surplus labour, new means of employment had to be found since for practical purposes emigration had ceased to be a viable option. The Commission's answer to this need was the land settlement program: beginning with the Markland experiment, the expectation was that thousands of outporters would be resettled. Land settlement, however, encountered many obstacles, and in the meantime, though the government's budgetary situation improved somewhat after 1934, Newfoundland remained in the grip of depression. The result was that in 1936, after Governor Walwyn had established himself in St. John's and Hope Simpson had departed with Lodge soon to follow, the Dominions Office requested the Commission to prepare a long-range reconstruction plan. In effect, having been given new blood, the government was invited to regard the first unhappy years of its rule as experimental and, with the benefit of hindsight, to chart a course that would finally revive the Newfoundland economy.

Its response was embodied in Walwyn's key despatch of 24 December 1936 to Malcolm MacDonald. This criticized current road policy (and by implication Lodge), called for a revised and greatly reduced land settlement program (another black mark against Lodge), and advocated placing the main emphasis in economic development on enlarging the scope of the outport economy. In short, it was agreed that the future of Newfoundland lay in occupational pluralism as another generation of planners would call it. Fishing would remain the basis of the rural economy, but it would be supplemented by a variety of other forms of productive activity. In this way most Newfoundlanders would be able to go on living where they were. The cost of the 1936 reconstruction plan, which was to run for about ten years, was estimated at approximately $8,000,000. In practice, though accepted by London, the Commission's long-range reconstruction program got off to a slow and shaky start. It then came up against the grim general recession of 1937–38 in the North American economy. This devastated in particular the forestry sector of the local economy which, as far as the mill towns were concerned, had been a reasonably bright spot and put the government on the defensive. Faced with falling revenues and a rapidly rising relief population, the Commission proceeded to make a deal with the Bowater-Lloyd company involving the Gander properties of the Reid Newfoundland Company. This in turn brought important elements of the St. John's business community into open and organized opposition against it. Within the government the Bowaters agreement was opposed by Emerson, one of the Commission's main critics during the Kean affair, who now emerged as the leading figure on its Newfoundland side. Emerson's presence on the Commission was in itself evidence of just how delicate a political game Whitehall was playing in Newfoundland.[102] Still, in the case of the Bowaters controversy, an instructive episode that revealed much about underlying political realities in Newfoundland, the Commission was able to fight off its opponents. It did so using the argument that its policy favoured the common man, not the narrow selfish interests of those who could afford to wait for better times in the false hope of achieving a mill on the Gander.

In a further attempt to revive its sagging fortunes, the Commission accepted, with some qualifications, the drastic alteration recommended by Gorwin to its original reconstruction plan. His scheme for getting unemployed fishermen back to work was ingenious in that it sought to conciliate local merchants and credit-worthy fishermen. Nonetheless, its ultimate object was the restructuring of the fishing industry on a co-operative basis, an undertaking that called for government intervention on a scale never before imagined. The economic benefits to be derived from this change were thought to be substantial, but considering the number of interests that would be disturbed in pushing the reform through, the political risks were correspondingly great, a point recognized in the position taken by Emerson. In any event, with the assignment of the portfolio of natural resources to Gorvin in July 1939, the Commission began moving full steam ahead in the new direction, hazardous and unknown as the waters before it were.

In January, 1939, the London *Daily Express* sent its own "Commissioner," the reporter Morley Richards, to investigate conditions in Newfoundland. As was usual in such cases, the Dominions Office and its agents in St. John's did their best (short of outright interference) to steer him away from controversy,[103] but in fact his five inflammatory articles about Newfoundland, published between 27 March and 1 April 1939, added up to a blanket condemnation of the British record in the country since 1934.[104] Within the Dominions Office the task of preparing an answer to Richards's arguments, in case the secretary of state should needs it, fell to the prolific Clutterbuck. In a superbly written memorandum, he ranged over the whole history of the Commission experiment, arguing that the real measure of success or failure was not so much what had been achieved in Newfoundland since 1934, which was considerable, but what would have happened to the country had not its present administration "been there to stand between it and disaster."[105] This was persuasive, for there can be no doubt about the Commission's ameliorative work or that Newfoundland's continuing economic difficulties after 1934 were at root a function of unfavourable external market conditions which no government in the country could have controlled. Without outside assistance to cope with the adverse effect of those conditions, Newfoundland's situation would have been very dismal indeed. At the same time it could hardly be expected that Newfoundlanders would measure events by the same yardstick as that of Clutterbuck and his superiors. Newfoundlanders had taken a big step in 1934 and, rightly or wrongly, they had been led to expect big results. When these were not forthcoming, disillusionment naturally followed. By 1939 this was bordering on disaffection, and the real question facing the United Kingdom in Newfoundland, Clutterbuck's detached logic notwithstanding, was whether or not the situation there could be contained.

CHAPTER FIVE

The Onset of World War II, 1939-41

She also became *one of the sally-ports of freedom*, for many of the bombers which dominated the skies over Germany like an avenging host from out of the West were ferried across the broad Atlantic to the United Kingdom either direct from Gander or by way of Greenland and Iceland from Goose Bay.

A.M. Fraser, "History of the Participation by Newfoundland in World War II"

The United Kingdom's declaration of war on Germany on 3 September 1939 changed the course of the Commission and made the defence of Newfoundland its first priority. Unlike Canada, Newfoundland was automatically a participant when the United Kingdom went to war.[1] This was no doubt a mark of her dependent status but it is doubtful whether a self-governing Newfoundland would have chosen differently. Despite their many criticisms of the British record in their country since 1934, Newfoundlanders, especially the largely Protestant elite, were intensely loyal. This was demonstrated anew in June 1939 when the King and Queen visited the country at the end of their Canadian tour. Before this event the police warned the Commission that agitators might take advantage of the occasion to provoke demonstrations by the unemployed, a frightening prospect.[2] Moreover, in deference to the wish of their Majesties, the government rushed through legislation to prevent "the indiscriminate firing of guns and fireworks" - traditional forms of greeting in Newfoundland - in the royal presence.[3] In fact nothing untoward occurred. As happened everywhere they went, the visit of George VI and his gracious wife Elizabeth was a great success and a drawing together of kinsmen before the hour of battle. In 1938, after visiting Newfoundland at the time of the Munich agreement, Clutterbuck had noted that the "general assumption" locally was that "if the United Kingdom was forced to war, Newfoundland 'would be there.'" "Generally," he wrote, "the fact that Newfoundland would be automatically included in any war was taken for granted, and to have suggested that there was any possibility of the people wishing otherwise would have been regarded as an insult."[4] And so it was.

There was much to defend in Newfoundland. In March 1939 the Commission listed the most likely targets of enemy attack as: "(a) The Newfoundland Airport (b) The Bell Island Iron Mine (c) The cable terminals at Bay Roberts and other places [and] (d) The City of St. John's."[5] The airport, which had only recently been completed, had a complex history. Under an agreement made at Ottawa in 1935, the United Kingdom, Canada, the Irish Free State, and Newfoundland had set out to develop, in two stages, a transatlantic air service. The first exploratory stage would involve "survey and experimental flights ... and other investigations," and would be carried out by Imperial Airways. Thereafter, a regular service would be started, to be run by a joint operating company, which the United Kingdom, Canada, and the Irish Free State would form. Each of the countries represented at Ottawa also agreed to "arrange for the provision, within its own territory, of the airports, and the radio and meteorological services and other aids to air navigation" which would be necessary for the scheme to go forward.[6] In Newfoundland's case, the United Kingdom was made responsible for the provision of radio facilities during the experimental stage. Subsequently, radio and meteorological services were to be provided in Newfoundland by the government of Canada, under an agreement to be negotiated between the two parties. Nominally, however, the Newfoundland government stood committed to providing the airport facilities needed on the island, through it was understood that the lead in this regard would be taken from London.[7]

Two British officials, Ivor McClure, operations adviser in the Department of Civil Aviation, and Maurice Banks, a technical assistant in the same department, had visited Newfoundland in August and prepared a report on where the required facilities would best be located. The primary need was for a seaplane base, since for the moment flying boats offered the only practical means of introducing a scheduled transatlantic service. Looking to the future, however, it was proposed to experiment with land-based planes, and for this an airfield would also have to be built. The site recommended by McClure and Banks for the seaplane base was Botwood, as it was considered to be relatively fog free. Another advantage of this location was a large harbour, which was not affected by swell and which for its size had the most favourable ice conditions on the east coast; it was usually completely open from June to November. Botwood, which is 1,987 statute miles by the great circle route from Galway, Ireland, was also linked to the mainline of the Newfoundland railway by a branch line owned by the Anglo-Newfoundland Development Company. The most promising site found for the proposed airfield was on the north shore of Gander Lake; McClure and Banks were flown over the area by the pioneer Newfoundland aviator, Douglas Fraser. Here, at 400 feet above sea level there was a large plateau believed to have enough firm ground for a landing field. Confirmation of the suitability of this location would, of course, have to await surveyor's reports, but superficially its advantages were manifest. It was on the Newfoundland railway, and the weather was thought to be the best to be found anywhere on the eastern side of the island served by that line. By the great circle route the Gander site was 1,950 miles from Galway. Another advantage of the location was that Gander Lake, though not as well situated as Botwood, afforded an acceptable alternative landing place for flying boats.[8]

The task of completing the assessment of the Gander Lake area was entrusted by the British mission to T.A. Hall, the engineer assigned by the Commission to the airport job. Working under him was Allen Vatcher, said to be "the most experienced bushman surveyor in the island".[9] Their further investigations confirmed the initial promise of the Gander location. In the last analysis the British decided on the building of a seaplane base at Botwood, the development of an auxiliary water landing facility at Gander Lake, the construction of an airfield at nearby Hattie's Camp and the building of a main meteorological facility at Botwood, with back-up radio services at Gander Lake and Hattie's Camp.[10] In the summer of 1936, while work proceeded on the clearing of the Hattie's Camp area, mauarauding bears notwithstanding, Squadron Leader Harold A.L. Pattison, a Royal Air Force Signals Officer, was sent to Newfoundland to oversee the installation by the Marconi Company of the wireless station at Botwood and to act for the time being as civil aviation liaison officer.[11] He was soon followed by Lewis Dale, the deputy director of Works and Buildings in the Air Ministry, who came out to advise on construction at Botwood.[12]

The commissioner responsible for airport matters was Lodge, who had represented Newfoundland at the 1935 Ottawa conference. In what followed that event, he showed his usual opinionated, prickly self. In July 1936, he asked Sir Harry Batterbee of the Dominions Office "whether any of you have any conception of what living in Botwood will really mean." Apart from fishing, which he described as "a device for suffering excruciating agony from mosquitos and flies," there was nothing to do there but drive to Bishop's Falls, which was itself "little better" than Botwood. The nearest "civilised community" was Grand Falls. Hattie's Camp was even more daunting:

There you will have a square mile of cleared land in the middle of a wilderness. A man can walk along the railway track for miles and miles in either direction

> before coming to any kind of habitation. Some sort of a track will have to be made to the lake but otherwise the Airport will be completely surrounded by forest through which a man could only progress by hacking his way with an axe, and one has to have a very peculiar temperament to enjoy much of that! The only event will be the passing of a passenger train three times a week in each direction in Summer, and twice a week in Winter, and most of these will be in the middle of the night ... I can only imagine one thing more deadly than living there in Summer and that is living there in Winter![13]

The immediate problem, however, was money. Lodge's view was that Newfoundland should not have to pay anything towards the cost of building and maintaining the air facilities now required. Planes, he argued, would land in Newfoundland only because the state of aircraft design made it necessary for them to do so, and it was the beneficiaries of the service to be provided who should bear the expense. Newfoundland had "something to give, not something it ought to be expected to pay for." In any case, given the other urgent needs of the country, it would be impossible for the government to justify expenditure simply to facilitate transatlantic air travel.[14] These were telling points, but Lodge's influence was on the decline when he made them; the eventual financial arrangement for all airport construction in Newfoundland was one that he had rejected. By it the ownership of the airports was vested in Newfoundland in return for a contribution of one-sixth of their capital cost and the payment of one-half of the cost of operating them. The difference in both cases was to be made up by the Air Ministry of the United Kingdom. Newfoundland was also made responsible for the running of the airports.[15]

Following the Ottawa talks in 1935, representatives of the United Kingdom, Canada, and the Irish Free State went to Washington, where an understanding was reached regarding reciprocal landing rights with the United States in future transatlantic air service. In keeping with this, the United Kingdom, in February 1937 issued a permit to Pan-American Airways which, inter alia, gave that carrier landing rights in Newfoundland for fifteen years from 1 June 1936. The permit authorized the "carriage of passengers, goods and mail" between the United States and the United Kingdom and allowed the carrier, unless otherwise permitted, two round trips per week via Canada, Newfoundland, and the Irish Free State or via "Bermuda and other countries."[16] The next spring the United States, issued a permit giving Imperial Airways operating rights there on equivalent terms.[17]

The diplomatic way was now clear for the pilots to take off in order to determine whether the service envisaged was indeed possible. Accordingly, on 5 July 1937, with Governor Walwyn present to bid farewell, Pan

American Airway's *Clipper III* departed Botwood for Foynes, Ireland, and Southampton.[18] The next day the Imperial Flying Boat *Caledonia* of Imperial Airways landed at Botwood en route to Montreal and New York. In May 1939 by which time the flying boat service was well established, the first plane landed at the Hattie's Camp aerodrome. It had been named the Newfoundland Airport and was the administrative headquarters for the local transatlantic air operation.[19] Thus thanks to her geography and the air travel aspirations of other countries, Newfoundland had acquired some first class air facilities by 1939.

Defending and, more especially, running these facilities in wartime was another matter. In defence terms, the threat to the Newfoundland Airport, the Commission believed, would come from "a small raiding party from a lone cruiser or submarine, or an aircraft flown from a vessel." The other major targets on the island, Bell Island, St. John's, and the cable terminals, were thought to be "very well vulnerable to attack from the sea in the form of bombardment or landing parties."[20] To counter these threats, the Commission had the benefit of a plan for the defence of Newfoundland drawn up in 1936 in St. John's by a committee chaired by Trentham.[21] When this scheme was reviewed at the request of the Dominions Office by the Committee of Imperial Defence, particular note was made of the fact that there was "no plan of any sort ... for the active defence of Newfoundland" and that the only forces available on the island consisted of "255 Constabulary and 50 Rangers armed with obsolete and inefficient weapons." Agreeing that these "must be 'regarded as practically unarmed for purposes of modern warfare,'" the British Committee called for the creation of a local defence force as a matter of priority. Trentham's committee, it was noted, had found that men were readily available to form such a unit to a strength of 1,000 to 2,500.[22]

In January 1938 the Commission decided that responsibility for defence would lie with the commissioner for home affairs and education, and a council was appointed to advise him. This consisted of Captain C.M.R. Schwerdt, Walwyn's private secretary, who had served on Trentham's committee, and eight departmental secretaries, including the secretary for justice, who was to act as secretary to the advisory council unless his departmental duties prevented his undertaking this responsibility.[23] In March of the next year the government decided to act on the recommendation that a defence force be formed, and a proposal in this regard was put to London.[24] What the Government initially suggested was the enlistment of twenty-five men per month to a total over a year of 250 to 300. The recruits would be given one month of intensive training during which they would be housed in a fire hall in St. John's. Thereafter they would have to report once a month for drill and rifle practice. Once formed, the defence force might be assembled each year for a week or two of "training under canvas." The Commission anticipated "a good response" to its initiative from the unemployed of St. John's, but it also wanted recruiting done on Bell Island and at Bay Roberts, so that members of the force would be readily available at these places "in case of need." The members of the force would be put in uniform and paid at the same rate as members of the Newfoundland constabulary. The total expenditure forecast for the defence force during 1939–40 was $60,000. If the formation of the unit was approved in London, the Commission asked that a warrant officer be found in the United Kingdom to instruct the Newfoundland recruits. While admitting that the scheme proposed was neither "elaborate" nor "exhaustive," the Commission submitted that it represented what the government could afford. If it was thought necessary to base aircraft or anti-aircraft guns in Newfoundland in order to defend the country, these would have to be provided by others.[25] During the spring of 1939 informal negotiations for carrying out the Commission's plan for a defence force, which was accepted by the Dominions Office, were conducted in London by Captain Schwerdt. Captain Claude Fanning-Evans of the Durham Light Infantry was chosen to go out to St. John's to train the new unit, but when war broke out in September he had not yet arrived and preparations for the defence of Newfoundland were still largely confined to paper.[26]

The Commission responded to the outbreak of war in Europe with a variety of legislative measures. On 1 September 1939, an Act for the Defence of Newfoundland became law.[27] This provided the Governor in Commission with sweeping powers to regulate social and economic life and to appropriate whatever was needed to defend the country. Using its new authority, the government issued the Newfoundland Defence Regulations the same day.[28] These contained seventy-seven sections dealing with a wide range of defence and economic matters. On 3 September laws took effect to prevent trading with the enemy and "to confer certain emergency powers on the customs."[29] On the twelfth the *Newfoundland Gazette* announced the creation of the position of food controller, to which Pudester was named. To advise him a board of businessmen and officials was appointed. On the same day the governor issued a proclamation authorizing the Supreme Court of Newfoundland "to take cognizance of any judicial procedure in matters of Prize."[30] Emerson was named King's Proctor for prize cases, one of which, involving a German registered ship, the *Christopher V. Doornum*, was pending.[31] Yet another important public action taken by the government in the opening days of the conflict was the publication, on 16 September in an extraordinary issue of the *Newfoundland Gazette*, of foreign exchange control regulations.[32] Under the authority of the Defence Act, these created a Foreign Exchange Control Board consisting of the commissioner for finance as the chairman, the commissioner for natural resources, and the secretary for customs.[33]

Behind the scenes, meanwhile, the government was scrambling to provide a modicum of protection for the country's vital installations. Since the home defence force was still in the planning stage when the war began, the government decided to send fifty policemen to Bell Island to guard the mine heads and landing piers. To relieve them and to serve until longer term arrangements could be effected, Emerson, whose department was responsible for getting the defence force started, asked the Great War Veterans' Association to recruit a group of thirty veterans, with preference being given to "the youngest available unemployed and unmarried."[34] On 3 October, after Fanning-Evans had arrived in St. John's and Brian Dunfield had visited Ottawa in search of equipment and supplies for the new unit, Emerson put before the Commission a draft act authorizing its establishment.[35] This legislation, modelled on the 1914 act creating the regiment that had gone overseas in the Great War, came into effect on 31 October for one year.[36] The home defence service was to be a volunteer force known as the Newfoundland Militia. Its members were to be subject "to the Army Act of the Imperial Parliament and the King's Regulations and Orders for the Army" to the extent that these could be applied locally. The force was to be under the command of a "Lieutenant-Colonel of Militia," who would be responsible for appointing all non-commissioned officers. On the day the act became law, W.F. Rendell CBE, who had served his country with distinction at Gallipoli and in France in the Great War, was named to this particular post.[37] Other appointments followed on 21 November when Fanning-Evans was made staff captain.[38]

Four days before this, responsibility for recruiting and defence matters generally had been transferred from the Department of Home Affairs and Education to the Department of Justice.[39] With this change Emerson had moved from being one of the Commission's most dangerous critics in the mid-1930s, to being one of its most independent members after 1938, and then in 1939 to occupying its most important position in wartime. On 23 November Emerson gave his colleagues a memorandum concerning the accommodation of members of the Newfoundland Militia while they were being trained in St. John's. This called for the construction of barracks near Fort Townshend, and noted that the YMCA building, now being used by the unit along with the accommodation available in the two city fire halls, was needed as a community centre so as to ensure "the peace and good order of St. John's during the winter months."[40] War or no war, some things remained the same in the capital, where for many the misery of the 1930s lived on into the next decade.

The defence of St. John's and of the airports in the northeast of the island, of course, posed problems for the government which went far beyond the creation of the militia. In the case of the former, it was decided, on the advice of the Commander-in-Chief of the North America and West Indies Naval Squadron, to place a net, which could be raised and lowered, across the narrow entrance to the harbour.[41] The Commission's answer to the defence problem it faced at the Botwood seaplane base and the Newfoundland Airport was to suggest to London on 15 September that these facilities be turned over to the Royal Canadian Air Force for the duration of the war. The suggestion was consonant with the commitment Prime Minister Mackenzie King had made in the Canadian House of Commons on 8 September to contribute "as far as we are able to the defence of Newfoundland and the other British and French territories in this hemisphere." Behind this commitment lay the belief that "the integrity of Newfoundland and Labrador" was "essential to the security of Canada." The terms on which Newfoundland proposed that the airports be transferred were simple: Canada would "assume entire responsibility for maintenance and operation of the Bases and for all expenditure attributable to meteorological and wireless services and for other expenditure insofar as it is attributable to military as distinct from civil requirements."[42] This plan was, however, rejected out of hand by the Air Ministry. According to J.W. Herbertson of the Air Civil Administration, War Group, his department had always understood the United Kingdom's policy to be "that Newfoundland, the oldest British Colony, should remain a separate entity and that anything tending to increase Canadian domination should be avoided as far as possible." It was this policy which had led to the building of the bases in the first place and it would be "a great mistake" to hand them over to the Royal Canadian Air Force now. "It is one thing," Herbertson bluntly wrote, "to let them in, but it would be another thing to get them out." Newfoundland was destined to play a big role in future transatlantic air service and afforded "an important bargaining counter" which it would be "folly" to give away. The Royal Canadian Air Force might be permitted full use of the Newfoundland bases, but allowing the Canadians to run them was a different matter altogether.[43] It was this view that for the moment prevailed in London, and Newfoundland was told that this suggestion regarding the air bases could not be entertained.[44]

The Commission had much better luck at home with its recruitment efforts for overseas service. On 14 September the Admiralty authorized the calling up of 625 local men the first 198 of whom sailed out the Narrows on 27 November; as in the Great War of 1914–18, it was seafaring men who first left the shores of Newfoundland to fight for King and Country.[45] In the meantime, a director of recruiting had been appointed and a recruiting committe formed under his leadership.[46] Recruiting meetings soon followed at Pouch Cove, Bay Bulls, Western Bay, and Winterton, and a weekly recruiting program was started on radio station VONG of the Broadcasting Corporation of Newfoundland. This corporation, established by the Commission in January 1939, thereafter formed a vital link between it and the people.[47] By January of the next year, the 625 men originally sought by the Admiralty had been found, and the governor asked for the enlistment of 1,000 more volunteers, this time for general naval service.[48] Other such requests soon followed with the result that by the end of 1942 about 5,000 Newfoundlanders had offered themselves for service under the white ensign. Of this total, approximately 2,000 were medically unfit while 2,889 had actually been taken into the service.[49]

On the army side, a start on recruiting was also made in the autumn of 1939. When Clutterbuck was in St. John's in 1938 he heard over and over "that Newfoundland would not in any future war repeat the experiment of raising a Newfoundland regiment." The expense involved would be too great and in any case it would be a "mistaken policy for a small country to raise a regiment of its own and to run the risk of all its best men becoming casualties together in one action". A better course, it was generally agreed, would be for Newfoundlanders to enlist in the British forces "so that casualties might be more evenly distributed."[50] Roughly speaking, this was in fact what happened. The first step was taken when it was decided through negotiations with the War Office in November and December that 1,375 men should be recruited for two heavy regiments in the Royal Artillery.[51] Walwyn's proclamation calling for volunteers explained that the Newfoundlanders who joined up would "form one complete Heavy Royal Artillery Regiment, and as far as possible, other complete Heavy Royal Artillery Regiments."[52] Late in March a recruiting team arrived in St. John's from the United Kingdom. On 14 April 1940, 404 volunteers, drawn from the St. John's area, Carbonear, Holyrood, and Bell Island, embarked for Canada en route to the United Kingdom, where they were welcomed by Anthony Eden, who had become Secretary of State for Dominion Affairs the previous autumn. A second draft, 212 men from the Grand Falls and Corner Brook areas, followed them on 12 May. By the close of 1942 more than 3,000 Newfoundlanders had offered themselves for service with the Royal Artillery. About 1,500 of these failed to meet the physical or educational requirements of enlistment, but 1,608 were accepted and left the country. In December 1940, the government began distributing rejection badges to those Newfoundlanders who had volunteered for active service and had not been accepted for one reason or another.[53]

Two other British services, the Merchant Navy and the Royal Air Force, also began recruiting in Newfoundland in 1940. For the former the call for volunteers was issued by the commissioner for public utilities in a public notice dated 13 March.[54] Recruiting for the Royal Air Force began when Walwyn issued a proclamation in May, asking skilled tradesmen to volunteer for ground staff.[55] The men accepted in St. John's for this duty were also enlisted in the Royal Artillery, to which they would revert if, on arrival in England, their qualifications did not meet the needs of the Royal Air Force.[56] A June 1940 proclamation by the governor invited volunteers to come forward to be trained as Royal Air Force air crew under the British Commonwealth Air Training Plan which a number of Commonwealth countries had started in Canada shortly before.[57] Selection of candidates by a mixed Royal Canadian Air Force/Royal Air Force recruiting team commenced in St. John's in August, and fifty-two recruits were soon on their way to Canada to become airmen.[58] By the close of 1942, 276 Newfoundlanders had enlisted in this highly dangerous branch of His Majesty's forces.

One of the biggest recruiting drives in Newfoundland in the opening phase of the war had nothing to do with the military at all. During the Great War, Newfoundland had sent a forestry corps to work in the United Kingdom, and in the autumn of 1939 it was agreed that this should be done again. Provision was made for this in an Act which, when it became law on 18 November 1939, created the "Newfoundland Forestry Unit." The purpose of this unit was the cutting of "pitprops or timber" in the United Kingdom, mainly in Scotland. The unit, whose expense would be borne by the United Kingdom, was to be under the "control and management" of the commissioner for natural resources and was to be commanded by a "Chief Overseas Forestry Officer" and such other officers as he might name. The pay and allowances of members of the unit were to be determined by the Governor in Commission. Each member of the Unit would have to sign "Articles of Engagement for a definite term of service," subject to discharge or dismissal.[59] In practice, command was given to Captain Jack Turner, Chief Forestry Officer in the Department of Natural Resources and a prominent veteran of the Great War.[60] On 11 December 1939 he sailed from St. John's aboard the SS *Antonia* with a party of 300 men, arriving in England a week later. To the end of 1942, 3,597 Newfoundland loggers had joined the forestry unit, thirty-three of them in the United Kingdom. Of this total, twenty-one died overseas, thirty had been discharged there, and 1,495 had returned to and been discharged in Newfoundland. Of the remainder, 554 had entered the armed forces in the United Kingdom and 1,497 were still with the unit, which had its operational headquarters at Carr Bridge and divisional centres at Beauly, Ballater, and Newtonmore.[61] Thanks to war-induced demand, things had started looking up for the Newfoundland woodsman in 1939, if only in the Highlands of Scotland.

While the Commission was busy with recruiting, it also repulsed a couple of attempts to question its authority. On the outbreak of the war, the

Great War Veterans' Association had offered its services to the Government "in any capacity in which they could be utilized." Disappointed with the response their offer received, the Dominion Executive of the Association proceeded to pass a resolution criticizing the government for its "studied indifference" to the veterans' organization.[62] To rectify the situation, the Executive represented to the Commission that it should be "constituted an Advisory Council to assist and co-operate with the Government in the carrying out of the war policy of Newfoundland." This drew a polite but firm rejection. In a letter from the commissioner for home affairs and education, the Great War Veterans' Association was thanked for the contribution it had made to date, including the raising of men to guard the Bell Island mines; encouraged to co-operate with the Director of Recruiting; and assured that its offer of help, together with the offers of "various other organizations" would be taken up as necessity arose.[63]

This response provoked a sharp reply from the executive of the veterans' body. It deplored the fact that organized ex-servicemen had been relegated by the government to "the same category as 'various other organizations' who had offered help."[64] More complications followed when the Great War Veterans' Association accepted an invitation from the Newfoundland Board of Trade to join forces to revive the Newfoundland Patriotic Association, the men's organization which had managed the country's military effort in the Great War.[65] An organizing committee was promptly formed and a statement detailing the purposes of the revived organization (a Women's Patriotic Association was already functioning) agreed upon. The Patriotic Association, according to this document, should be representative of "all sections of the people and country," and should assume an important role in running Newfoundland's war effort, while not interfering "with the executive functions of the Government."[66] In January 1940, Cyril J. Fox, a prominent St. John's lawyer and president of the Newfoundland Board of Trade, Leonard Outerbridge, who had served with the Canadian forces in the Great War, and Major F.W. Marshall, the president of the Great War Veterans' Association, called on Walwyn on behalf of the organizing committee of the Patriotic Association to ask him to become the nascent organization's patron. He immediately agreed, whereupon arrangements proceeded for the holding of an inaugural meeting at the Pitts Memorial Hall. Former prime minister Walter S. Monroe undertook to serve as chairman elect of the association, and several important officials were invited personally to attend. All went smoothly until Emerson and Puddester met with Walwyn and questioned the wisdom of what was now afoot.

Emerson told the governor that while the memorandum which had been drafted by the organizing committee "was in itself quite harmless," it would take on quite a different meaning if adopted at a public meeting held under official auspices. In these circumstances it would in fact "create something in the nature of a binding undertaking between the Government and the Association to consult on Government matters connected with the War." This was unacceptable.[67] When Walwyn showed the two commissioners the agenda he had been given for the meeting, they found further evidence of the difficulty they had perceived in the statement. The next day Walwyn sent for Outerbridge, told him that questions had arisen over the plans he and his colleagues had made, and referred him to Emerson for details. The meeting that followed between Emerson and Outerbridge on the morning of 1 February proved a stiff encounter indeed. The government, the commissioner said, welcomed the proposal to revive the Patriotic Association but could not be party to a proceeding whereby "it was in honour bound to consult a committee or committees of the Association before taking executive action in connection with Newfoundland's War Effort." When Outerbridge countered that consultation might be limited to military matters, this too was turned down by the commissioner: "The Government's responsibility for the conduct of Newfoundland's War Effort," Emerson asserted, "and its constitutional position in general, were such that it would be impossible for my colleagues or myself to bind ourselves even in most general terms as to matters upon which we would be debarred from acting without prior consultation." This, of course, did not rule out consultation as such with the Patriotic Association, but this would have to be at the sole discretion of the administration. In other words, the Commission's mandate was to govern, and govern it would.[68]

Following this rebuff, Outerbridge reported the same day to a joint meeting of the organizing committee of the Patriotic Association and the Council of the Newfoundland Board of Trade.[69] The result was a decision to cancel the public meeting and to notify individually the dignitaries to whom personal invitations had been issued of this change. One of the recipients of this notification was Brian Dunfield, who had been named a judge of the Supreme Court in November 1939.[70] The letter he received from Harry Renouf, the acting secretary of the organizing committee, explained that the meeting had been cancelled because "official approval" had been withdrawn from the Patriotic Association proposal.[71] When Dunfield showed this letter to Emerson, the latter immediately disputed its contents in a sharp letter to Outerbridge. This ranged over the interview the two men had had and pointed out that the government welcomed the formation of a Patriotic Association as such, and objected only to the constitutionally impossible role proposed for it.[72] After further negotiations behind the scenes, the government's point of view was accepted all round. The Men's Patriotic Association (or the

Newfoundland Patriotic Association as it was commonly known) was launched finally at a meeting held on 26 February, but its relationship to the government was not at all what its organizers had originally anticipated.[73] Led by the diminutive Emerson – his nickname was 'Cocky' – the Commission had won an important political skirmish; constitutionally, the war notwithstanding, it would be business as usual. Thereafter, the Patriotic Association performed many useful functions, including presenting to the government in August 1940 the complaints of some of the Newfoundlanders enrolled in the Royal Artillery about the treatment they were receiving in England.[74] The Patriotic Association also joined with other organizations, including the Women's Patriotic Association, which had opened a clubroom for recruits, in supporting the work of the St. John's War Services Committee.[75] In early January 1940 the committee was incorporated as the St. John's War Services Association and opened "The Caribou Hut" later the same month. Located on Water Street, this establishment was run with great élan and provided until June 1945 warm hearted hospitality to thousands of men of the armed services and merchant navy.[76] It exemplified the gallant spirit of wartime St. John's.

Understandably, the financial implications of the changes brought on by the war were also high on the Commission's agenda. Penson announced new economic measures on 20 November 1939. His speech, entitled "Newfoundland Finance in Time of War," was given at a meeting of the Board of Trade and was also broadcast. In his budget for 1939–40 the Commissioner for Finance had forecast that the country would need a grant-in-aid of $5,735,208 on an expenditure of $17,116,908 and a revenue of $11,381,700. What he now revealed was that, as a patriotic gesture, Newfoundland would immediately reduce its grant-in-aid request for the duration of the war to the amount it spent in the United Kingdom itself on debt service and other charges. This would relieve London of the need to expend on Newfoundland's behalf, money that the mother country badly needed herself for the purchase of essential war equipment and supplies. During the financial year in progress the change meant that the Government would have to find elsewhere $1,500,000 which it had counted on as part of the grant-in-aid. Of this amount, the customs revenue, which was running ahead of what had been forecast, would yield $250,000. The remainder would be made up by reductions in expenditure of $750,000 and a tax increase of $500,000. The tax changes introduced placed surtaxes on the existing income tax and estate duties, increased the import duty on gasoline by three cents per gallon, and raised the same imposition on matches from fifty cents to one dollar per gross. Penson's estimate of the cost of war services for 1939–40 was $250,000 and was taken into account in his revised budget. Despite this unforeseen expenditure and the retrenchment the war now required of the country, the government recognized, Penson assured his listeners, "that the Reconstruction Programme should be maintained."[77]

In the case, however, of that program's most vital component – Gorvin's plan for reorganizing the fishing industry – Penson's statement was belied by later events. In March 1940 while work was proceeding on the Placentia Bay experiment, Gorvin brought his regional development plans a stage further when he submitted to the Commission a bill entitled "An Act to Facilitate the Economic Development of Special Areas of Newfoundland."[78] This was given detailed consideration by the government and various amendments were made, but on 24 March the amended bill was passed by only four votes to three.[79] Gorvin, Emerson, Woods, and Winter voted for the bill, and a formidable opposition of Penson, Puddester, and Walwyn voted against it. Walwyn also asked that his vote be recorded. So divided was the government at this stage that the Dominions Office contemplated replacing Penson who, along with the ailing Winter, was nearing the end of his initial three-year term. This, however, was opposed by Walwyn who although he gave Machtig a vivid account of the battles in progress within the government between Gorvin and Penson, succeeded in keeping his unruly crew intact.[80] On 29 April the highly complex Special Areas Bill was published in a fifteen-page extraordinary issue of the *Newfoundland Gazette*, together with an introductory statement of "objects and reasons."[81] This was now a frequent Commission legislative practice between the introduction of a bill and the final decision on it. A leaflet explaining the bill clause by clause was published separately. The public was informed that the bill had been read a first time by the Commission and was invited to comment on it. Comments were to be addressed to the secretary of the Department of Agriculture and Rural Reconstruction, and to reach him no later than 1 June.

The proposed legislation met fierce opposition in newspapers attuned to Water Street, which were in any case clamouring for constitutional change on the grounds that the Commission had failed and that the war demanded a government of national unity. Some of the harshest criticism came from the *Daily News* and the *Observer's Weekly*, the latter paper edited by Albert B. Perlin, a prominent local writer and man of affairs who had been all for Commission of Government in 1934. The Special Areas Bill, Perlin's paper trumpeted on 7 May, contained "the legislative authority for the establishment of a ferocious dictatorship" and should be withdrawn immediately. Otherwise the fishing business would be brought to a halt, for no supplier would "invest his capital in circumstances which may make him the victim of a despotic Special Areas Board." If the government so desired, the bill could be brought forward again in the autumn, when the fishing season was over and there would be "plenty of time for dispassionate discussion."[82] Not that there could be any doubt about what the outcome of that discussion would be. Whenever the bill came forward, the *Observer's Weekly* was convinced, "it must prove utterly unpalatable to Newfoundlanders who value their liberty and do not wish to see themselves or their fellow men delivered into bondage." In its 21 May issue the paper attacked the bill from another angle in an article entitled "Lets get on with the war." As long as Gorvin persisted, this piece claimed, he must "accept the grave responsibility of maintaining bitter controversy at a time when all should be working in the utmost harmony." His bill was "highly contentious" and did "violence to every sane concept of democracy." Accordingly, it must be "either withdrawn or postponed."[83]

Faced with such acerbic criticism and the determined lobbying of the Newfoundland Board of Trade, which once described the Special Areas Bill as the "most radical and revolutionary piece of Legislation ever introduced into Newfoundland,"[84] the Commission decided to extend the deadline for the submission of public comment first to 1 July and then to 31 December.[85] In early July in the meantime, Penson's 1940–41 budget scuttled the whole enterprise. The central feature of this document was the decision of the government to run the country forthwith without any grant-in-aid whatever; "if at all possible," Newfoundland would not ask the United Kingdom for any further financial assistance while the war was in progress. In practical terms this meant more retrenchment and more taxes. Estimated expenditure was reduced to $15,449,965 which included $730,771 for war services. This was a sum approximately $1,500,000 less than the equivalent figure in the original 1939–40 budget and nearly $1,000,000 less than had been provided for in the revised budget of November 1939. By contrast, the revenue estimate of $13,525,116 was roughly $2,000,000 more than in the original 1939–40 budget and approximately $1,000,000 more than the revised estimate for that year. This increase was to be realized through a further rise in the income tax rates and in certain customs and excise duties, higher licence fees, a special war tax on alcoholic liquors, and higher postal and telegraph rates. Yet for all these new impositions the government would still be short $2,000,000.[86]

Where would this be found? On 17 June an act had become law which authorized the government to raise an internal loan of $1,500,000 by the sale of bonds at 3 3/4 per cent interest. The purpose of this issue, which had a twenty-five year term, was to cover the cost of the interest and sinking fund payments due in London at the end of June. The loan took only five and a half working days to raise, a decided contrast to the last time a Newfoundland government had tried to borrow money at home, and was in fact oversubscribed by $131,600.[87] Following this success and with an eye to drawing in the small investor, the government passed a War Savings Certificate Act, which became law on 29 June. This provided for the sale of certificates with $3.00 face value, which were to be marketed at $2.50, have a six-year term and earn income tax exempt compound interest of 3 per cent. An upper limit of $500 per annum, based on market price, was placed on individual purchases of the new certificates.[88] To cover its anticipated 1940–41 deficit, the government looked to sales of these savings certificates and further expenditure cuts, which it hoped to make as the year progressed. Beyond that it would have to improvise. In keeping with this whole strategy, a further act authorized the sale of savings stamps. These were to be affixed to savings certificate cards, which could in turn, when the value of the stamps on them reached $2.50, be exchanged for war savings certificates.[89]

Following these developments, Gorvin told his colleagues, on 4 September in a lengthy and reflective memorandum, that "the policy of retrenchment necessitated by the war, and implemented in the Budget" had made "impracticable, for the present, Government-assisted measures for economic development on any important scale in the more depressed regions of the country along the lines contemplated in the Special Areas Bill." While standing by the principles of the bill, Gorvin declared himself willing to recommend now that it be "indefinitely postponed" and that the public be informed of this change.[90] His recommendation was accepted by the Commission, and a press communiqué to this effect was issued.[91] In announcing its change of course, the Commission emphasized the financial difficulty which had arisen but assured the public that it shared the anxieties felt by many about what might happen economically after the war and stood ready "to take any measures within its powers and resources ... likely to lead to the development of the resources of the country and the augmentation of the national revenue."[92]

Once the Special Areas Bill was put in limbo, Gorvin's own days in Newfoundland were numbered. Walwyn immediately began pressing London to have the commissioner for natural resources recalled, and in April 1941 he got his wish.[93] Gorvin himself was given the word in a letter from the governor. This explained the action being taken as "owing largely to the position brought about by the war and the impossibility in present circumstances of proceeding with your reconstruction programme on any effective scale." His transfer, Gorvin was told, was back to the Ministry of Agriculture. After taking leave there, he would be sent to the Ministry of Food, where his services were required as an Assistant Secretary. To this end his Newfoundland appointment would be terminated on 4 July. Manfully, Walwyn personally handed his letter to Gorvin, telling the commissioner at the same time "that during the period of his tenure of office his attitude towards his colleagues had shown him to be unsuited to a position which called for responsibility and unity of purpose."[94]

If Gorvin's removal was calculated to please the business community, to which he had become a bogeyman, it touched off sizeable complaints elsewhere. In time, letters were received in London in favour of keeping Gorvin in Newfoundland from the West Coast Cooperative Council, the Avalon Cooperative Council, three co-operative and credit societies, the heads of the four Corner Brook mill unions, the superintendent of the International Grenfell Association in Newfoundland, and the Newfoundland Federation of Labour (formed in 1937 as the Newfoundland Trades and Labour Council and renamed in 1939).[95] Walwyn's opinion of these missives was that "while some might be spontaneous, others were directly or indirectly prompted by Mr. Gorvin." Observing that the Newfoundland Federation of Labour did "not by any means speak for Unionism in Newfoundland" and that Gorvin's recall had been "accorded scant notice by the Newfoundland press," Walwyn's advice to London was to hold steady and to send the complainants routine, calming replies.[96] Gorvin himself commented on his impending removal in a letter to H.N. Tait, an assistant secretary in the Dominions Office. He disputed the claim that "effective action" on the reconstruction program was now impossible. This was not only possible, he wrote, but essential, albeit on a limited scale and as long as spending was "restricted to developments likely to assist directly in the war effort". Keeping the planned reconstruction going would not only bring "definite economic results" (they were shown in what had been accomplished already) but set "a precedent for future action on sound and approved lines." In view of all that was at stake, Gorvin suggested that an enquiry might be in order into the circumstances surrounding his recall. At the very least, he told Tait, he was owed "an opportunity to express my views on the advice which has been given to the Dominions Office, advice which may be inspired by considerations that might call for some investigation."[97]

Not surprisingly, this plea also fell on deaf ears, and Gorvin left St. John's on schedule, after having reported on his Newfoundland work in an address to the St. John's Rotary Club on 3 July.[98] His replacement in September was P.D.H. Dunn, another civil servant who had served earlier in Newfoundland, first as customs advisor to the government and then as chairman of the Board of Customs from 1935 to 1937. In July, Ira Wild, another Treasury man, succeeded Penson, who went to the British Purchasing Commission in Washington, and it was announced that Walwyn's term, originally for three years, had been extended for a second time by an additional year; he remained in Newfoundland until 1946.[99] In September, the St. John's lawyer Harry A. Winter, replaced J.A. Winter as commissioner. The latter had become chief clerk and registrar of the Supreme Court and official receiver under the Companies Act.[100]

With both Penson and Gorvin gone, Walwyn told Machtig the government would "have more peaceful meetings."[101] No doubt this was true, but much had been lost as well. Despite the rough handling he received from the St. John's business establishment, Gorvin was perhaps the most genuinely popular British commissioner ever to come to Newfoundland, and his ideas for the regeneration of the country's rural society were truly visionary. It can be argued that, on the home front in Newfoundland, these ideas were among the biggest casualties of the war. Instead of setting out to refashion Newfoundland from the ground up as Gorvin intended, the Commission would stay on the age-old path of paternalism towards the outports. In matters of policy as in so many other ways, the 1930s would fade fast in the memory of Newfoundlanders after Gorvin's abrupt exit.

In Newfoundland, as elsewhere in the North Atlantic, the pace of wartime events quickened in the spring of 1940. Much had happened in the country during the period of the "phoney war," but the unleashing of the full force of the Nazi war machine against western Europe heralded a period of truly astonishing change for Newfoundlanders. The Commission reacted to the harsh new realities of the conflict with further and more far reaching defence measures. In April, Charles H. Hutchings, the former inspector general of police, was appointed air raid precautions director, acting under the authority of the commissioner for justice.[102] He was ultimately director of civil defence. Then on 25 May as the struggle for France approached its devastating finalé, a partial blackout was instituted in St. John's.[103] On 31 May Emerson reported to his colleagues that he had received a delegation from Corner Brook proposing the creation there of a volunteer force, the members of which, though unpaid, would supply their own uniforms.[104] In response to this initiative, the Commission decided to introduce legislation to facilitate the formation of the proposed force and, in addition, to provide the Corner Brook volunteers with arms and ammunition if these could be found. This legislation, becoming law in June, created the "Newfoundland Auxiliary Militia," which the Governor in Commission was empowered to raise "by voluntary enlistment … for home defence service." The Auxiliary Militia was to consist "of men armed and equipped in accordance with regulations to be made by the Governor in Commission," the first of which were in fact issued on 5 November.[105] Except for permanent staff, the members of the Auxiliary Militia (or Home Guard as it was also called) were to be "employed about their ordinary avocations and called together only for such training as may be deemed appropriate to the force, or for service against the

King's enemies." The legislation further authorized the division of the island into military districts and the appointment of officers commanding them. Overall command of the Auxiliary Militia was to rest with the commanding officer of the Newfoundland Militia, of which the new organization was "deemed to form part". The provisions of the Militia Act of 1939 were also made applicable to the auxiliary body.[106]

On the same day that this legislation took effect, another act created a department of defence. This was given responsibility "for the administration of military affairs including home defence, the fortifications, ordnance, ammunition, arms, armouries, stores, amunitions and habiliments of war, and the control, regulation, management and supervision of the Newfoundland Militia and recruiting for service at home and abroad."[107] To run the new department, Emerson was appointed "Commissioner for Defence," and his full title now became "Commissioner for Justice and Defence."[108] At first the functions of justice and defence were carried out by the same personnel, but eventually a separation was effected between them.[109] By yet another enactment on 22 June, the government extended the operation of daylight saving time so as to allow essential war work to be carried on with maximum efficiency and to promote public safety.[110]

Meanwhile, Emerson, Penson, and Woods were working as a committee of the Commission on plans "to meet any emergency that might arise in connection with public administration in the event of an enemy raid on St. John's."[111] The seriousness of the situation was underlined when the government amended the blackout regulations and issued further regulations which restricted the use of lights, defined "prohibited places," and severely limited the private possession of firearms, ammunition and explosives.[112] Regulations provided for the establishment of defence alarm areas, and the St. John's area was so designated on 1 August.[113] Otherwise during the fearful summer of 1940, the Commission sought to determine whether it was feasible to ship scrap metal to the United Kingdom, issued new regulations for the control of shipping, in coordination with Canada brought into operation a wartime system for the display of navigational lights, and, in response to a request from the Royal Canadian Air Force, set out to establish an Air Raid Detection Corps in Newfoundland.[114] In addition, this time at the request and expense of the United Kingdom, the Commission began work on a camp, at Victoria, near Carbonear, for the reception of one thousand civilian internees from the United Kingdom.[115] A sign of the times was the decision to cancel the St. John's regatta, an annual event dating from the early nineteenth century.[116] Another was the Emergency Powers (Defence) Act, which became law on 20 September.[117]

This act was needed, Emerson told the Commission, because the 1939

Defence Act was "very narrow so far as the powers of the Governor in Commission are concerned." It would be possible to amend the 1939 act to meet contingencies as they arose, but this might be politically awkward. If the government, for example, had to legislate in order to deal with labour troubles, it stood to be accused on one side or the other of bias. In any case, it would be "awkward and cumbersome" to be constantly amending legislation as important as the Defence Act.[118] The Emergency Powers (Defence) Act itself was based on legislation of the same name which Parliament had passed in 1939 and had since twice amended. It authorized the Governor in Commission to make "by Order in Commission ... such regulations (... referred to as "Defence Regulations") as appear to him to be necessary or expedient for securing the public safety, the defence of the realm, the maintenance of public order and the efficient prosecution of any war in which His Majesty may be engaged, and for maintaining supplies and services essential to the life of the community."[119] In short, it provided for governmnt by fiat. The term of the act was two years from the date it was passed, but this could be extended during the life of the legislation for another year by the simple expedient of an Order in Commission. In fact the legislation would not finally expire until 1949.[120] As with other governments, once the Commission tasted the heady elixir of wartime power, it did not readily revert to previous practice.

Important as these changes were, it was what happened after Dunkirk at Gander, as the settlement, post office and railway station adjoining the Newfoundland Airport were officially known from 22 August 1940,[121] and at Botwood, that best indicated where Newfoundland was heading. Earlier that year Emerson had visited Ottawa and Halifax, in part to discover the extent to which Canada's war plans "envisaged the defence of Newfoundland." What he found was unsettling. Canada had agreed to provide two guns and two searchlights for the defence of Bell Island and to lend the personnel needed to show the Newfoundland Militia how to use these. But beyond that, except for those parts of the Newfoundland coast which could not be ignored in the defence of Canada itself, the Dominion government had no plans for the protection of her neighbour. Nor was Emerson able to get any idea in Ottawa of the risk the two countries now ran of enemy attack. Guesswork, it seemed, was the order of the day in the Canadian capital as much as it was in St. John's. This was decidedly unsatisfactory, and in Emerson's view the time had come to determine once and for all what the United Kingdom and Canada each intended in relation to the defence of Newfoundland. In sum, the country's "present state of uncertainty and unpreparedness" must be changed forthwith.[122]

To this end a telegram was sent to London on 8 April, seeking clarification of the whole defence position. This stated what Emerson had concluded from his visit to Ottawa, namely, that Canada was only considering the defence of Newfoundland to the extent that her own defence was involved. Confirmation of this, it was noted, was to be found in various requests Ottawa had made of St. John's, all of which had been met. Thus Canada had been promised land at Red Bay on the Labrador coast for a seaplane base and granted the use of the Newfoundland Airport and Botwood. In addition, Newfoundland had installed radio equipment on the navigational aids along her south and west coasts so that these could be switched off at Canada's request. Emerson had also learned from the chiefs of Canada's navy and air force that neither patrol vessels nor reconnaissance aircraft could be provided at present for Newfoundland's defence. While it was true that Canadian air and sea defence measures to safeguard Halifax and Sydney would of necessity provide some protection to the south and west coasts of Newfoundland, the vital east coast of the island would remain exposed - hence Newfoundland's desire to have the existing uncertainty about her defence resolved.[123]

At the end of April, the Commission reported to London that the Canadian minister of transport had told Penson privately during a visit the commissioner for finance had recently made to Ottawa that "he wished Canada could take over the use and responsibility of the Newfoundland Airports for the period of the war." Penson had replied only that he would let his colleagues know this, but with a party of Canadian officers due in St. John's shortly to discuss the future operation of the Royal Canadian Air Force in the country, the Commission urged London to reconsider the position it had taken on the transfer of the local air bases. Such a transfer, it was argued, would have great benefit. If Canada had the "full use of and responsibility for" Newfoundland's airports, she would perforce have to interest herself in the aerial reconnaissance of the country's whole coastline. Furthermore, this would lessen Newfoundland's dollar requirements and thereby assist the United Kingdom financially.[124]

To begin with the Commission did not get its way. In fact London's response to the Newfoundland government's telegram seeking clarification of the whole defence situation was couched in generalities. To the extent that Newfoundland could not defend herself, the Commission was told, the responsibility lay with the United Kingdom. Assistance from Canada in this regard "would on general grounds be welcome" but "specific proposals" relating thereto, whether emanating from Ottawa or St. John's, would have to be approved in London before being accepted. In any event, the defence of Newfoundland rested "primarily upon [the] protection afforded by [the] Royal Navy rather than upon local defence measures," and for the moment that service considered the likelihood of an attack on the island, either by submarine or surface vessel, a "remote" possibility. Because of more urgent demands elsewhere, no "special Naval or Air Forces" could be assigned to patrol duty in Newfoundland as the Commission had requested. Nor, by the same logic, would it be possible to provide the guns and mines for the defence of St. John's which had also been sought.[125]

Undeterred, the Commission responded on 14 May that the planned discussions with the Canadians would be postponed until an answer was received from London to the specific proposal it had made in April regarding the transfer of the air bases. On 25 May, in order to give St. John's some protection, Newfoundland asked to be allowed to take possession of a gun and ammunition from the SS *King Edward*, which had been damaged in convoy and was now in port in St. John's. This request was refused but in the meantime the Commission had issued an urgent appeal to London to accede to its request about the airports. In view of the most recent developments in the war, the British were told as they were making their last stand in France, the "defenceless condition" of Newfoundland was causing "public alarm." Prime Minister King was reported to have assured the Canadian Parliament that Canadian troops were "assisting in [the] guardianship of Newfoundland," but the Newfoundland Government itself had heard nothing of this. Nonetheless, assuming Canada was ready to act, a decision about the airports was imperative, and, the Commission ventured, "at this stage post war problems should not be a decisive factor." The logic of Newfoundland's position was now inescapable and, with their own backs to the wall, the British agreed on 5 June to the transfer of the bases. The next day discussions were held in St. John's with Air-Vice Marshal George M. Croil and Air Commodore N.R. Anderson of the Royal Canadian Air Force, who had just visited the Newfoundland Airport. At these talks Croil took the view that the airport might become "a positive menace" in that its capture "by a landing party and planes operating from a raider" was not impossible. Equally, he held, the base could only be used by aircraft if its local defences were secured. After this message was carried back to Ottawa, Canada requested permission from Newfoundland to move both air and ground forces to the island. These would consist of one flight each of reconnaissance and fighter aircraft (the latter when available) and an infantry battalion "with personnel of other arms attached as required." Pending the despatch of these, Canada asked for permission to send a reconnaissance party to the island, and asked for the Commission's attention to the matter of sharing the cost of the measures now contemplated.[126]

Newfoundland immediately agreed to the Canadian defence plan, gave permission for the visit of the reconnaissance party, and accepted in principle that she should carry part of the financial burden. Canada was told, however, that Newfoundland's share of the cost would of necessity be "small" and that London would have to be consulted before any amount could be agreed upon.[127] As a result, at 10:50 AM, on 17 June, five Digby aircraft of the Royal Canadian Air Force's No. 10 (Bomber Reconnaissance) Squadron arrived at the Newfoundland Airport from Dartmouth, Nova Scotia, and in so doing forged a link that would endure. They were followed on 22 June by 900 men of the first battalion of the Black Watch (RHR) of Canada, commanded by Lt. Col. Kenneth G. Blackader, who landed at Botwood from the SS *Antonia*.[128] Canadian military intervention in Newfoundland had great strategic and ultimately political importance. Historically, the United Kingdom's control of Newfoundland had rested on seapower, but she had now admitted that the island could not be defended by this or any other means at her disposal. In the northwest Atlantic, as in so many other parts of the world, her retreat from empire was thus signalled by the wartime situation.

The emergency arrangements made by Newfoundland and Canada in June 1940 left in abeyance for the moment the question of control of the airports, but this issue soon arose again. In August, Canada asked Newfoundland for permission to put up new buildings and install additional service facilities at the Newfoundland Airport to the value of $1,370,000.[129] These, it was explained, were needed as part of a planned expansion of local air defence forces, and Newfoundland was asked to provide the required "land, and right of way, etc." free of charge. By return telegram the Commission granted what was asked for,[130] whereupon a meeting on "Bilateral Defence Questions" was held between representatives of the two countries at St. John's on 20 August. The Canadian party was led by Charles G. Power, minister of national defence for air, who stated that "what was required was for Newfoundland to help Canada and Canada to help Newfoundland" without the latter's "autonomous rights" being encroached upon. Next he asked "if the principle could be admitted that Canada should be in charge of Newfoundland's defences without any modification." To this Emerson replied that the question was too broad to answer by a simple yes or no; "modifications" might have to be made and the Commission would have "to consider just what these might be." Principle aside, progress was made on a number of important matters in Canada's proposed plans for the defence of the region. These included the establishment of Canadian army and navy headquarters at St. John's and a build up of Canadian forces in the country. Newfoundland offered to pay "a fixed sum which would not be inconsiderable" within her means towards the defence effort Canada was now undertaking. This could not, however, be "commensurate with the expense involved." Speaking personally, Power said that while he "appreciated the desire of Newfoundland to do its share ... he thought it would be repugnant to the ideas of both countries that Newfoundland should, as it were, pay tribute to Canada and thus appear in a somewhat subservient role." A better course, he suggested, would be for Newfoundland to provide "certain services and concessions." On the latter point, Newfoundland agreed, "subject to certain safeguards" to "absorb the cost of transport of fighting forces while travelling on duty or being moved from point to point." Equally, a member of the armed forces travelling privately would be given a return ticket for the price of a single one, in keeping with existing Canadian practice. Newfoundland further agreed that her soldiers could be recruited into the Canadian forces. More importantly, she agreed to a unified command for her forces and those of Canada stationed in the country. This would operate according to Canadian practice in "civil and military affairs."[131] In order to give effect to this agreement and to accommodate the Canadian forces more generally, the Commission passed the Visiting Forces (British Commonwealth) Act, which became law on 15 October.[132] This followed the lines of legislation already passed in the United Kingdom, Canada, and other Dominions, and dealt in part with the operation in the country of the military courts of visiting forces.[133] Section 5 of the act defined the terms on which Newfoundland forces could be combined with visiting forces from Canada, Australia, New Zealand, South Africa, and Eire. In accordance with this, on 22 November the military forces of Canada in the country were deemed to be acting in combination with the Newfoundland Militia, and Brigadier Philip Earnshaw, the local Canadian commander, was appointed commander of the combined force.[134] Meanwhile, on 13 September Canada had asked Newfoundland to give her control of the Newfoundland Airport for the duration of the war. Newfoundland responded favourably to this initiative, but the issues involved were complex and as matters developed negotiations about them dragged on into 1941.[135]

Operationally, however, by the late summer of 1940 Gander was starting to hum. During the winter of 1939-40 experiments had been undertaken there by the Air Ministry to see whether the runways, of which there were three, could be used in snowy conditions.[136] The results were encouraging and thereafter Gander figured prominently in plans for the highly dangerous work of ferrying military aircraft from North American production centres to the United Kingdom. This vital service was initially organized by the Canadian Pacific Railway Company of Montreal with the assistance of personnel sent to Canada by British Overseas Airways and Lord Beaverbrook's Ministry of Aircraft Production.[137] At the British end, the required wireless organization, needed because the existing radio service for transatlantic flight was located at Foynes in neutral Ireland, was established during the summer of 1940 by the Royal Air Force.[138] To facilitate matters in Newfoundland, Squadron Leader Griffith Powell of the Royal Canadian Air Force, a former transatlantic pilot with Imperial Airways, was sent to Gander.[139] There, the biggest problem was accommodation. It was at first proposed to solve this difficulty by erecting tents, but eventually the Newfoundland Railway came to the rescue with three sleeping coaches and a dining car which it continued to service. On 29 October the first plane scheduled to be flown overseas under the new system (a PBY flying boat had been ferried via Botwood in 1939), arrived at the Newfoundland Airport. A Hudson bomber, manufactured by the Lockheed Company of Burbank, California, it was one of an initial shipment of fifty planes.[140] By 10 November six other Hudsons had arrived safely. Then, on the evening of the tenth, under the command of Captain D.C.T. Bennett, who had brought the last of the planes in, all seven Hudsons lifted off from Gander and headed out over the Atlantic on what would become one of the war's most celebrated runs.[141] The crews of the first planes to go departed to the strain of bagpipes laid on by Colonel Blackader and on arrival at Aldergrove, Northern Ireland, they disembarked wearing poppies. At a single stroke Newfoundland had become "one of the sally-ports of freedom."[142]

The men who flew the early ferry missions were a motley company, with their nucleus "roughly half a dozen British Overseas Airways Captains." To these were added pilots loaned by the United Kingdom's Air Transport Auxiliary, numerous American volunteers, bush pilots from Canada, and Free French, Dutch, Egyptian, Australian, and South African aviators.[143] The group that flew out of Gander on 10 November consisted of nine Americans, six British, six Canadians, and one Australian.[144] In March 1941 the ferry operation passed under the direct control of the Atlantic Ferry Organization ("Atfero") of the Ministry of Aircraft Production. The flying boat base which had been planned before the war was then built at Gleneagles on Gander Lake,[145] in order to centralize both land and water operations in one general area. From 1 August 1941 the ferry service was run by the Royal Air Force Ferry Command with Air Vice Marshal Sir Frederick Bowhill, who was based at the newly completed aerodrome at Dorval, Quebec, in charge.[146] In 1943 Ferry Command was itself absorbed into the Royal Air Force Transport Command as No. 45 (Atlantic Transport) Group and from 20 July 1944 Transport Command's Gander unit was known as "Staging Post 83."[147] Meanwhile, many other types of aircraft had passed through the Newfoundland base.[148] On 17 December 1940, Francis W. Coughlan of St. John's, a radio officer, became the first Newfoundlander to serve on a ferry mission, when he crossed the Atlantic on a Hudson bomber.[149]

Another pressing concern of the Commission during the summer of 1940 was the situation created on the islands of St. Pierre and Miquelon by the fall of France. There, Gilbert de Bournat, a Vichy sympathizer, held sway as governor. On 19 June 1940 after Petain had assumed office in France, Newfoundland asked London for permission to take over these islands "at the appropriate moment," and suggested that Canada should be approached to help in this enterprise. The thinking behind this bold proposal was eminently straightforward. Because of what had happened in France, the prospect had now arisen of a "virtually independent" St. Pierre and Miquelon. Should this come about, a "serious gap" would be opened up in Newfoundland's wartime "administrative control" which in turn would tempt others to take the French islands over for the duration of the war. To head off this possibility Newfoundland must act first. A rival fishing industry, it was pointed out, was carried on from the islands, which also drained revenue from Newfoundland through smuggling. If another country, even Canada, were to intervene in St. Pierre the effect would be to transfer to itself "the cause of constant irritation" Newfoundland had historically endured because of their possession by France. Hence the need for prompt and decisive action.[150]

The British declined this proposal, and pointed out that the integrity of France's North American possessions was assured by the Monroe Doctrine.[151] Instead, Newfoundland was asked to work out with Canada what forces would be needed to occupy the islands should this need ever arise. In addition, London requested urgent consideration between St. John's and Ottawa as to the despatch of a prominent official to St. Pierre who would "encourage [the] local authorities there to maintain an independent attitude." On receipt of these instructions, the Commission sent Emerson to Ottawa for discussions and, on his return from a visit to the United States and Canada, Raymond Gushue of the Newfoundland Fisheries Board was sent to St. Pierre to size up the situation there.[152] Gushue found the islanders despondent over the stunning defeat of France and expecting a takeover by some neighbouring government. Their preference in this regard was to "become part of the United States," an outcome which, it was believed, would benefit the islands "more than association with Canada or Newfoundland." The islanders knew Newfoundland mainly through nearby settlements like Lamaline on the poverty stricken south coast and wanted to avoid for themselves what they saw there. "Some say," Gushue memorably reported, "they would rather fight than be associated with Newfoundland."[153]

For the next year a vigilant Commission kept close watch on developments on the islands from where a dozen trawlers staged a getaway for France in the autumn of 1940.[154] In Canada, Mackenzie King's attitude towards the islands was governed by the belief that "a resort to force would place a severe strain" on his country's national unity (Petain was popular in Quebec), especially if there was "an open break with Vichy."[155] The

Newfoundland government, of course, was under no such constraint, nor were the British. In the long run their policy hardened as part of a general shift in London in favour of the takeover of France's overseas territories by the forces of General Charles de Gaulle. And, indeed, the islands were taken on 24 December 1941 by a Free French force under the command of Vice-Admiral Emile Henri Muselier. They had sailed from Halifax two days before on the pretext of conducting exercises at sea.[156] Canada denied any connection with Mustelier's action, which the United States condemned, but the deed had been done and was soon endorsed in a plebiscite held on the islands themselves.[157] The United Kingdom's policy had been vindicated, and if Newfoundland did not get the direct control of the islands which she originally wanted, she had at least avoided the two developments she most feared: domination of the French territories by an openly hostile regime, or their occupation, to her lasting political and economic disadvantage, either by Canada or, worse still, by the United States. On the whole, both the Commission and Newfoundlanders generally could be pleased with this outcome.

By now Newfoundland was internationally more prominent also by virtue of one of the most celebrated achievements of Anglo-American wartime diplomacy. This was the famous agreement of 2 September 1940, completed by an exchange of notes between the Marquess of Lothian, the United Kingdom's ambassador in Washington, and Cordell Hull, the United States Secretary of State. By this agreement the United Kingdom obtained fifty American destroyers in return for making available to the United States base sites and related facilities on a number of West Indian Islands and in British Guiana and for promising to secure the lease to the United States, "freely and without consideration," of base sites in Newfoundland and Bermuda. Like their counterparts in the Caribbean and South America, the bases in Newfoundland and Bermuda would be leased to the United States for a period of ninety-nine years, "free from all rent and charges other than such compensation to be mutually agreed on to be paid by the United States in order to compensate the owners of private property for loss by expropriation or damage arising out of the establishment of the bases and facilities in question." In the leases to be negotiated the United Kingdom was to grant to the United States "all the rights, power and authority within the bases leased, and within the limits of territorial waters and airspace adjacent or in the vicinity of such bases, necessary to provide access to and defence of such bases and appropriate provisions for their control." The "exact location and bounds" of the bases, together with related defence matters, were likewise to be determined between the United Kingdon and the United States, for which purpose Lothian proposed that "experts" from the two countries should begin meeting.[158]

For its part the Commission of Government was drawn into the diplomacy leading to the bases agreement, which was a milestone in the advance of the United States from neutrality to belligerency, on 15 August. Three days later, in a related development aimed at hemispheric defence, President Roosevelt and Prime Minister Mackenzie King, meeting at Ogdensburg, New York, agreed to establish a Permanent Joint Board on Defence.[159] Initially, the Newfoundland government was told that the United Kingdom's greatest weakness was the shortage of destroyers. Congress could only be persuaded to transfer ships if Roosevelt could show that the security of the United States would be enhanced.[160] This was the reason for the scheme to establish bases on Newfoundland. The stakes were high, but the United Kingdom would "naturally wish to carry Newfoundland public opinion with it." As the need for secrecy was paramount, the Commission was asked whether it would be able to handle public opinion and ensure that no difficulty would arise when the announcement of the agreement was made. If the Commission was sure of its ground, the United Kingdom would proceed. The Newfoundland government's answer, given the following day, was unqualified: there would be "no difficulty with public opinion" either to the lease or the sale of the areas the United States needed.[161]

Over the course of the next few days, the Commission was kept abreast by London of developments as they occurred. Following C.G. Power's visit to St. John's (he had been kept in the dark about the big news Newfoundland was now hearing from London), the Commission told the Dominions Office that it had stressed to the Canadian minister of national defence for air the need for open diplomacy: Newfoundland had to be kept fully informed of any discussions between Canada and the United States involving her interests. Equally, while disavowing any attempt to delay the agreement the United Kingdom was so anxiously seeking with the United States, the Commission now pointed out something else which had to be emphasized to the Americans: that in Newfoundland's case the base proposal would involve "a Government of a temporary nature and of unrepresentative character" in "serious steps vitally affecting the future of a country used to representative Government which must be restored." It was, therefore, "vitally necessary" in the interest of the United States itself that the agreement to be negotiated "should bear the hallmarks of being reasonable and fair so as to ensure its meeting with the wholehearted approval of future Governments and not of the appearance of being forced upon a small country by powerful nations." Since the bases proposed must inevitably require Newfoundland to make special customs and immigration arrangements for the United States, the Americans might be approached to signify their willingness to give "favourable and sympathetic consideration to certain compensating advantages" to

Newfoundland in tariff and immigration matters once the existing emergency had passed. Nothing more than "a record in general terms" was suggested for the moment, but a commitment by the United States along the lines indicated would create a "most favourable impression" in Newfoundland and put "beyond doubt any question of opposition."[162]

Nothing was heard in St. John's in reply to this before the agreement was actually made, but on 4 September Newfoundland was told how the United Kingdom intended to proceed. London would first consider the "maximum concessions" which could be given the Americans in each of the jurisdictions where property was to be leased. The "provisional conclusions" reached about Newfoundland would be communicated to St. John's and Ottawa for comment before any proposals were actually made to the United States. Then, the discussions between British and American "experts" envisaged in the exchange of letters between Lothian and Hull would be held. Since in the present circumstances it would be difficult for the United Kingdom to spare the personnel needed for these discussions, it would be suggested to the United States that the talks should be held in London. The British plan was that both Newfoundland and Canada should be represented at these talks, and the Commission was asked to decide who would be sent when the appropriate moment came. Canada was being included because it was "essential" to co-ordinate Canadian-American and Anglo-American plans for the defence of Newfoundland.[163] Subsequently, Newfoundland was told that it could expect an American mission headed by Rear Admiral J.W. Greenslade and Brigadier General J.L. Devers to visit the country.[164]

The reaction of the Commission of Government to these opening moves set the tone for much that followed in a long, complex, and, at times, highly charged round of bargaining. The negotiators chosen in St. John's to represent Newfoundland at the forthcoming London talks were Emerson and Penson, the former because he was already experienced in defence negotiations and was a Newfoundland member of the Commission and the latter because of the financial and customs issues the talks would inevitably involve.[165] On 12 September, the Commission spelled out for London what its approach would be in future dealings with the Americans. On the specific question of base location, the Commission agreed with the British that the Conception Bay area presented difficulties because of Bell Island, but pointed out that public opinion on the east coast might still favour an American presence there because of the economic advantage this would bring to one of the most heavily populated parts of the country. Generally speaking, however, the Commission's expectation was that public opinion "would wish broad imperial considerations to be given [the] fullest weight." At the same time, the Commission itself questioned "the apparent assumption" that Canada and Newfoundland had "equal interests" in relation to the establishment of American bases locally. "Our view," London was told from St. John's, "is that this is a matter which primarily concerns Newfoundland and we hope you will do everything possible to disabuse the Canadians of any idea that they are in a position to settle the destinies of Newfoundland in negotiations with the United States." The Commission also urged the United Kingdom not to countenance any proposal about Newfoundland to the United States that had not first been passed to St. John's for comment. Since "sovereign rights" were not at issue in the negotiations now to be undertaken, the Commission's view was that an appropriate bargaining stance would be to regard the Americans, whether telling them so or not, as "private applicants seeking rights in an undeveloped country."[166] This, it turned out, was very wishful thinking.

Against this background of understanding on Newfoundland's side, the eight-member board of experts under the chairmanship of Admiral Greenslade that had been appointed by President Roosevelt to investigate possible base sites arrived aboard the warship *St. Louis* in St. John's at 6:50 AM on 16 September. Captain Schwerdt was on hand to greet Greenslade, who then went directly to Government House to meet Walwyn himself. The governor at once granted the Americans permission to begin their planned survey of the country, and a full-scale meeting of officials of both sides followed. This brought together men of remarkably different backgrounds, careers, and expectations: on one side sat Walwyn, Schwerdt, the six commissioners, and Carew – depression survivors to a man; opposite them were Greenslade, Devers, and three other members of their party – all braid and big Yankee ideas.[167] The Americans quickly busied themselves with their investigations in several parts of the country, and two days later the *St. Louis* sailed for Placentia Bay. On the same day, the Commission reported to London on events so far. It complained that the Permanent Joint Board on Defence had apparently been making plans for the defence of Newfoundland without any reference to it. While the Newfoundland people, the Commission cautioned, had welcomed the visit of the American mission, their attitude would change if decisions were taken over the head of their government. If this should happen, the reaction in Newfoundland would, in the Commission's view, be "extremely adverse."[168] Newfoundland followed up this warning with a stiff telegram to Ottawa telling the Canadian authorities that she was not committed to the defence plan which had been worked out by the Permanent Joint Board on Defence and which she was now hearing about indirectly from the Greenslade mission because she was not party to it.[169]

The next messages received in St. John's were reassuring. The Commission was told from London that Lothian had mentioned to Secretary of State Cordell Hull Newfoundland's request for "compensating advantages." The idea had been well received; Hull in fact had thought it "quite reasonable that Newfoundland should ask for sympathetic consideration of its desire when [a] suitable time came."[170] The following day the Newfoundland government was told that the United Kingdom would not put forward proposals to the United States with regard either to base sites, or the jurisdictional and many other administrative problems which the establishment of bases would present. Rather, she would wait for proposals to come from the United States. These would form the agenda of the forthcoming conference of experts in London, where of course Newfoundland (along with all the other host jurisdictions and Canada) would be represented. In the meantime, the issues likely to be raised by the American proposals were being examined in London in order to work out a satisfactory negotiating position, and Newfoundland could expect to be fully consulted. As for the Commission's worry that Canada might be dealing with the United States behind its back, London countered that it had no reason to believe that anything untoward was happening along these lines.[171]

Meanwhile, the Greenslade mission had completed its Newfoundland work, and the *St. Louis* left Argentia on Placentia Bay for Boston on 22 September. At a final session with Newfoundland officials held at Government House on the morning of the twenty-first, the Americans submitted a memorandum outlining the recommendations they would be making to their government.[172] As things now stood, the Commission afterwards reported to London, the United States would need land at Argentia and St. John's. Two sites were needed at each place including a harbour front property in the capital. In addition, the Americans had requested the right to build an air field near St. John's if Canada did not. Canada was in fact considering building such a facility - the future Torbay air base - as part of the developing plans of the Permanent Joint Board on Defence. If Canada did act, the Commission reported, the United States would also want to use the new base.[173]

On the same day as the Americans announced their requests, Newfoundland agreed to them in principle, and this decision was communicated by Walwyn to Greenslade in a brief letter.[174] In November, after they had undertaken further investigations in Newfoundland, the Americans were granted permission to build an additional facility which had been talked about only during Greenslade's visit.[175] This was a landing field to be located near St. George's on the western side of the island; a site at Stephenville was finally chosen.

In the wake of the Greenslade mission, Newfoundland was given a direct assurance by Canada about the work of the Permanent Joint Board on Defence. The organization was described in a telegram from the Department of External Affairs as "purely an advisory body" to the

United States and Canadian governments. While it was true that the board was at work on a defence plan for the eastern seaboard of the continent, this was still in the draft stage. The decisions the board had actually made in relation to Newfoundland were routine, including only "prospective action" about which Newfoundland would naturally be consulted by Canada and the United States as required. To expedite the defence plan being prepared, Canada would, the Commission was told, recommend to the board that it invite Newfoundland to send representatives to a meeting it had arranged in Halifax for early October.[176] The board accepted this advice with the result that Emerson and Penson were present when it discussed Newfoundland business on 4 October.[177]

The Newfoundland representatives went along with all the defence plans explained to them on this occasion, but one problem remained: by law the United States could not begin construction work abroad until it had clear title to a particular property on which money was to be spent. Emerson and Penson told the board that if the law meant that every issue connected with the establishment of bases had to be dealt with before leases could be executed, a lengthy delay would ensue. To avoid a serious setback, the board suggested that once the boundaries of the properties in question were agreed upon, Newfoundland "should grant leases for ninety-nine years at once and leave to the future negotiating of terms, solving immediate problems as they arise." Not surprisingly, this vague and simple-minded approach was immediately contested by Emerson and Penson, who reported back to their colleagues that, until they had raised the subject, the board had not even been aware of the pending negotiations to be held in London. Agreeing nonetheless that speed was of the essence, Newfoundland put forward its own solution to the dilemma which had been debated in Halifax, and asked London to approach the Americans with the suggestion to accept "a simple lease" in the first instance. The simple lease would be preliminary to the general leased bases agreement about which each party would rely on "the good faith of the other" while work processed.[178]

In fact, the Americans were already working on a draft lease of their own, which Colonel Frank Knox, the secretary of the navy, showed to Lothian on 9 October.[179] But this document – here was a clear sign of things to come – was rejected out of hand by the British Ambassador: it attempted, he told London in a message repeated to St. John's, "to provide legally for every conceivable contigency from [the] American point of view" and, if adopted, "would lead to every kind of legalistic dispute." This view was heartily endorsed in St. John's when a copy of the draft lease finally reached there, after the Commission had to ask for it twice and long after the offending document had been withdrawn at Lothian's request from consideration.[180] In its place, having negotiated further with the Americans and exchanged telegrams on the subject with both London and St. John's, the embassy wrote a letter to resolve the problem. It authorized the United States, "pending the settlement of the terms of a formal lease," to begin work in the three areas in Newfoundland it had chosen to date. The exact boundaries of these areas (once more described in general terms only) would be given in the formal lease which, in keeping with the original understanding about the bases, would have a ninety-nine year term. This was all simple and straightforward, but the letter also required the United States "forthwith" to work out an agreement with Newfoundland concerning the procedure to be followed for compensating property owners "for loss or damage ... caused by expropriation."[181] Such an agreement, it soon became clear, would not be easy to reach.

The approach favoured by the Commission of Government was to appoint an arbitration board to adjudicate claims. The board would be headed by a judge of the Newfoundland Supreme Court and would have two other members, one a businessman and the other someone experienced in land evaluation. Its job would be to recommend settlements to the government which, if satisfied with their amount, would refer them to the United States for payment.[182] From the Newfoundland point of view the advantages of this procedure were twofold: it would circumvent an existing cumbersome expropriation law, and would be more acceptable to public opinion than direct government action to determine payments.[183] In sum, a board, operating at arm's length from the government, would be perceived in the country as eminently fair. The Americans were willing to go along with this procedure, but only on two conditions: awards recommended by the board had to be subject to their agreement, and they had to be allowed to investigate matters for themselves in Newfoundland in the case of awards they deemed excessive.[184] In other words, they had to have the final say on all payments. Newfoundland resisted these conditions for properties which would have to be turned over before the amount of compensation was fixed. But with United States contractors arriving in the country, the Commission had to allow American personnel to begin work on private holdings at Argentia. In fact, an order for this purpose was issued under the Defence (Requisition of Land) Regulations without a formula having been agreed on for compensation.[185] To ease matters, however, the Americans transferred to Newfoundland a lump sum out of which interim payments could be made to the first Newfoundland property owners to be affected by base construction.[186] Moreover, even though the future status of its decisions was in doubt, Newfoundland proceeded to establish the Board of Arbitration it had proposed, appointing Judge William J. Higgins of the Newfoundland Supreme Court as chairman.[187] Its services were urgently needed as people were already being moved in the Argentia area – a tough operation at the best of times but far worse in the middle of a Newfoundland winter.

Prior to the appointment of the Board of Arbitration, the Commission wrote to the British Embassy in Washington explaining the factors which in its opinion had to be considered in determining compensation in rural areas and asked that the substance of the letter be passed to the Americans. In a key passage, the Newfoundland government argued: "Many of these people by the exercise of inherited aptitudes have wrested a living out of extremely unpromising physical conditions but they cannot be expected to re-establish themselves in a short time in a new undeveloped area at approximately the same economic level as that on which they are now living without financial assistance in excess of a normal appraisement of their existing lands and buildings, and we ask your assistance in bringing this home to the United States Government."[188] In other words, in giving up a house, many Newfoundlanders would also be giving up a means of livelihood. This claim made sense, but selling it in Washington would be another matter.

As the Americans began their construction drive in Newfoundland, there was also uncertainty in the Commission about many other complex administrative questions the September bases agreement posed. These included tax, customs, postal, port, and immigration issues, as well as the delicate question of the legal position of Newfoundlanders inside the leased bases. To expedite the start of work, Newfoundland made interim arrangements with the Americans as required on these matters, which indeed had been discussed back and forth with the British authorities through the autumn and early winter as a prelude to the London talks where, it was anticipated, they would be disposed of once and for all. Newfoundland's quest for "compensating advantages" was also deferred as Americans began pouring into the country, but the Commission, in consultation with various influential St. John's businessmen and the Newfoundland Board of Trade, had worked out what in general it wanted: mainly freer access to the American market for Newfoundland fresh and frozen fish and immigration arrangements which would make it easier for Newfoundlanders to go to the United States.[189]

Emerson's sense of how Newfoundland should go about bargaining with the Americans was characteristically bold. In a memorandum he submitted to his colleagues in November, he challenged the assumption being made both in St. John's and Washington that the Americans were entitled under the exchange of notes of 2 September to concessions above and beyond the simple lease of property. Hitherto, he wrote, the Commission had concerned itself with the extent of these concessions, but it was questionable whether there should be any concessions at all:

> There appears to be no reason, based either upon the logical results that follow from the Agreement, nor upon the principles of equity, why, merely because we have freely and generously acceded to the desire of the United States Government to erect in Newfoundland a first line of defence for the United States, we should add a further gift in the nature of monetary contributions. The logical result of the Americans coming here to defend their own land should be that they will obey the laws of this country in all respects, and will pay all the taxes and duties which fall to be paid by any other residents of this country. From the equitable point of view it seems to me that not only should we not make monetary sacrifices, but we should be receiving monetary considerations. It is true that we have waived these, we are not charging rent, but it would be both illogical and inequitable if, having waived the payment of rental we also give to the United States the equivalent of actual cash contribution ...
>
> When the whole story is told the intelligent public will readily grasp the point that the Agreement does not go further than I have previously stated and if we grant one iota to the United States more than we are bound to grant within the text of the letters of September 2nd. we will be censured and very properly censured, unless of course we have obtained a quid pro quo for such grants.[190]

As might be expected, the Newfoundland Board of Trade was thinking along the same lines. Arguing that the negotiations underway with the United States presented Newfoundland with an "unequalled opportunity" to make economic gains, the Board maintained that the government must not act "without first informing itself fully of the local viewpoint through the establishment of a consultative commmittee which shall be fully representative of all sections of the population."[191] Earlier, the Dominions Office had itself broached the possibility that a prominent Newfoundlander outside the government might accompany Emerson and Penson to London, but in the end nothing came of this idea.[192] Another critical juncture had been reached, but the Commission would continue to go it alone.

CHAPTER SIX

The Base Building Boom, 1941-42

I would only ask the people of Newfoundland, of whose loyalty we have, in this testing time as throughout her long and eventful history, had ample proof, to bear in mind the wide issues which hang upon this Agreement ... It is with these considerations in our minds that, recognizing to the full the considerable sacrifices made by Newfoundland to the cause which we all have at heart and her splendid contribution to the war effort, we ask her to accept the Agreement. It will be yet one more example of what she is ready to do for *the sake of the Empire, of liberty and of the welfare of all mankind.*"

Prime Minister Winston S. Churchill to
Commissioner for Justice and Defence L.E. Emerson,
22 March 1941

On 17 January 1941, the two Newfoundland representatives to the London conference on leased bases, Commissioners Emerson and Penson, flew to England from New York on the same clipper that carried the American delegates across.[1] The tenacious Emerson, had come a long way from the days when his main claim to fame was his defence of Wes Kean, but he and Penson were to leave the British capital fearful and bitterly disappointed men. What happened in the negotiations, which began on 28 January at the Colonial Office, was that the United States brought forward again the draft lease that Lothian had rejected and Knox had withdrawn in November. Faced with this intransigence, and with the celebrated lend-lease bill - pointedly numbered 1776 and crucial to the United Kingdom's whole war effort - now hanging in the balance in Washington, the British accepted the American document as the basis for discussion. They attempted to modify it only where the "vital interests" of Newfoundland and the various colonies involved were concerned. But even this conciliatory approach failed to satisfy the Americans and led to a further British retreat. The result was that by 8 February the subcommittee of the British cabinet dealing with the bases question had accepted the American point of view on most of the issues dealt with so far, even though it "recognised that very real hardship to the inhabitants of the territories and Newfoundlanders might well be involved.[2]

Even so the Americans wanted more; they not only disputed the British position on the remaining points to be settled but sought to reopen issues on which, apparently, agreement had already been reached. This development led Lord Cranborne, the chairman of the conference, to tell his government colleagues that the negotiations were unlikely to come "to a rapid or successful conclusion." Rather there was a "real danger" that the conference would "merely drag on, with increasing irritation on all sides." According to Cranborne there were two reasons for this difficulty. In the first place the Americans regarded "their own interest in the bases and in adjacent territory as paramount and all local and other considerations ... quite subordinate."[3] Secondly, the American representatives in London were relatively junior officials who could not act independently but had to seek authority from Washington for even the slightest change, a requirement that seriously undermined progress in the talks. After the Bermuda delegates had threatened to walk out of the conference (over the question of American land requirements in the islands), Cranborne advocated a change of direction: either the Americans must send "a more substantial representative" to London or else the talks must be continued in Washington. If the talks were moved to the American capital, "great care," Cranborne admitted, would have to be taken to reassure public opinion in Newfoundland and the colonies affected that a deal was not being made behind the backs of their representatives. Otherwise the United Kingdom would find herself in the embarrassing position of having to overrule colonial legislatures to which the agreement with the Americans would have to be submitted. But it was better to run this risk, he believed, than to allow the present stalemate in the talks to continue.[4]

His advice was not heeded. Instead, after further haggling had taken place across the bargaining table in London, the issues still in dispute were taken up, exceptionally, by Prime Minister Churchill and President Roosevelt themselves. On 3 March Cranborne and Lord Moyne, the latter of whom with Churchill eventually signed the agreement on the United Kingdom's behalf, summarized for the prime minister the six matters about which agreement could not be reached. The peacetime "general powers" being sought by the United States outside the leased bases were "excessive." Nor did the Americans want any reference in the agreement to the United Kingdom's "mutual interest in the defence of the Territories and the Leased Areas." Furthermore, beyond what the British negotiators were willing to concede in relation to the respective legal rights of American personnel and local inhabitants, the United States wanted "jurisdiction (i) over British subjects for any offences committed in a Leased Area if they are arrested in the area and (ii) over aliens for any offence committed in the area and not merely against the security of the United States." Equally, the Americans wanted to import duty free all goods for the use of their military personnel and families. The objections to this, Cranborne and Moyne explained, were threefold: the Americans would become a "privileged class" in the several jurisdictions where the bases were being established; their status would create a smuggling problem for their host governments; and in any case the concession being sought was irrelevant from the defence point of view. The other matters remaining in contention, Churchill was told, were the location of the land to be leased in Bermuda and the refusal of the United States to allow the United Kingdom the same right to use the leased bases she had already offered to her sister American republics.[5]

The day after this submission was made in London, President Roosevelt went over some of the same ground with Viscount Halifax, the deceased Lothian's successor as British ambassador to the United States. Roosevelt pronounced himself in favour of a division of authority within the leased areas for British subjects; offences which involved American "security" would be tried by United States courts, while all other offences would be tried by British courts. As for customs, Roosevelt essentially spoke out in favour of duty-free importing, as was being urged by his country's negotiators in London.[6]

At the end of the day, these and other American views prevailed. On 18 March Churchill personally saw Emerson and Penson to appeal for their forbearance in the face of an agreement that went against much the Newfoundland government held dear. What was at stake, he said, was the "whole of the United States co-operation in the ... war" without which success in the conflict would be "gravely jeopardized.[7] The Newfoundland representatives readily deferred to Churchill's opinions, and, to cushion the blow, the prime minister afterwards addressed a letter to Emerson. This was drafted by Charles W. Dixon, an Assistant Secretary in the Dominions Office, and was intended for publication in St. John's.[8] It praised Newfoundlanders for their self-sacrifice and contribution to the war effort, and asked them generously to accept the agreement to be made with the United States "for the sake of the Empire, of liberty and of the welfare of all mankind." In the name of duty, Newfoundland would have to rely on the administration of the agreement with the Americans being not so much according to the compromising letter of the document as to the "spirit" which now animated Anglo-American relations.[9] Emerson loyally replied that Churchill's recommendation of the agreement would "not fail to impress" Newfoundlanders with the importance of their role "in strengthening the co-operation between the two great democracies in the struggle for the freedom of mankind."[10] To their colleagues in St. John's, however, he and Penson described the terms negotiated with the Americans as "one-sided throughout and often extremely harsh."[11]

The leased bases agreement, signed on 27 March 1941, contained thirty-one articles and had annexed to it the forms of the leases that were to be executed in respect of all the base sites.[12] Article I gave a "general description" of the American position. By this the United States was granted "all the rights, power and authority within the Leased Areas ... necessary for the establishment use, operation and defence thereof, or appropriate for their control, and all the rights, power and authority within the limits of territorial waters and air spaces adjacent to, or in the vicinity of, the Leased Areas ... necessary to provide access to and defence of the Leased Areas, or appropriate for control thereof." Article IV of the agreement dealt with the controversial subject of jurisdiction. In sum, the Americans obtained "the right to try, if they so desired" the following classes of persons:

(i) a member of the United States forces or any other foreigner who has committed an offence of a military nature (including sabotage and espionage) either within or without a leased area;
(ii) a British subject who committed any such offence within a leased area and was arrested there;
(iii) a foreigner who committed any other offence in a leased area.[13]

The United States had insisted on the jurisdiction it was given over British subjects – here surely was something quintessentially American – "partly owing to reluctance to see offences against the security of the United States tried by a local Court which in the case of the Colonies might include black judges or juries." By the terms of the article dealing with customs and duties (no. XIV), the United States secured exemptions which effectively made the bases extensions of the American homeland itself, a like regime being applied by Article XVII in the case of taxation. The host countries were even forbidden by Article XII to charge taxes or fees for licensing United States government motor vehicles to operate within their borders outside the base boundaries.[14] In short, with the United Kingdom reeling from the body blows of war, the United States pressed its bargaining advantage to a practical limit in the London agreement, something well understood at the time on the British side. As a subsequent Colonial Office memorandum on leased bases explained, the Americans had exploited an advantageous situation "to the full."[15] If the United States had not been granted sovereignty over the bases, she had obtained many of its attributes.

Emerson and Penson were so worried about the effect this outcome might have in Newfoundland that they advised their colleagues from London on 24 March to begin lining up newspaper and other support for the agreement before it was published. One suggestion made to St.John's was that consideration be given to making "frank confidential disclosures" to a number of prominent members of the business and professional communities. What should be impressed on the members of this group was "the necessity for creating [a] proper atmosphere." Three urgent considerations prompted the effort to influence public opinion: Churchill's personal appeal to Newfoundland; the "prime importance" of not criticizing the United States while Newfoundland's representatives at London were on their way home via Washington, where they hoped "to clear up certain points" and secure economic aid; and the fact that the future of Anglo-American relations generally hinged on a good beginning being made with the bases. If, it was argued, the country's newspapers "could be induced to be editorially broadly patriotic," and if at an early moment Charles E. Hunt, a prominent lawyer, would defend the agreement before the prestigious St. John's Rotary Club and other speakers do the same elsewhere, the battle for public opinion might be won before the critics got going.[16]

To assist their colleagues in what would admittedly be an "exceedingly difficult task," Emerson and Penson suggested several points that might be made.[17] The first involved an Anglo-American-Canadian protocol which would be issued with the Leased Bases Agreement (Emerson, Penson, and the Canadian negotiators in London had pushed for a separate agreement covering Newfoundland but had to settle for this protocol when the Americans refused to make the exception they wanted).[18] The protocol recognized "that the defence of Newfoundland was an integral feature of the Canadian scheme of defence" and therefore a matter "of special concern to the Canadian Government." Accordingly, it was agreed that in whatever was done under the bases pact in relation to Newfoundland, Canada's defence interests would "be fully respected." The protocol further guaranteed the inviolability of defence arrangements affecting Newfoundland already made by Canada and the United States on the recommendation of the Permanent Joint Board on Defence. The document further accorded Ottawa and St. John's the right to participate in all Anglo-American consultations arising out of the bases agreement which touched "considerations of defence."[19] Emerson and Penson maintained that together the protocol, the exchange of letters with Churchill, and various references in the bases agreement itself proved that Newfoundland's "separate position" was recognized. The case could also be made that the jurisdiction given the United States over British subjects was confined to one class of offence and in the view of Newfoundland's negotiators would probably not be applied locally. Similarly, in defence of the customs and taxation provisions of the agreement, it could be pointed out that they were "limited broadly to leased areas." "We believe," Emerson and Penson optimistically concluded in a message that did credit to their inventiveness and adaptability, "the United States has no intention of exercising its rights to the detriment of Newfoundland Revenue Administration or to impose financial or administrative burdens upon the country."[20]

For all the misgivings felt about it within the Commission of Government, the bases accord was accepted in Newfoundland without serious incident after it was made public. Following the advice of Emerson and Penson, a subcommittee of the Commission consisting of Puddester and Woods held two meetings, one with the editors of the *Evening Telegran* and *Daily News* and the other with a group of about ten citizens. The result was "surprisingly good"; there was only one dissenter (unnamed in the documents), and general agreement was reached that the government was acting in the only way it could.[21] Leonard Outerbridge and Charles Hunt spoke on the radio in support of the bases deal, and it was also defended in this same critical period in the *Evening Telegram* and *Daily News*. The chiefs of both papers were later thanked in writing by the government for their patriotism.[22] Puddester told Emerson, in a telegram sent to Washington, that the effect was also to bring into line the two weekly papers which might have been expected to make trouble.[23] These were the *Fishermen-Workers Tribune*, since 1938 a publication of the Fishermen's Protective Union and a perennial source of criticism of the Commission; and *The Express*, edited by Smallwood, which had first appeared on 15 February 1941. Another source of concern to the authorities was the Newfoundland National Association. This short-lived organization, which had been formed in July 1940 to lay the groundwork for the return of self-government to the country, drew its membership mainly from the disaffected commercial and professional elite of St. John's that had risen in protest against the 1938 Bowaters deal.[24] All in all, Puddester reported, the government was "highly pleased" with what had happened: the agreement had been given a "unanimously favourable reception," and the opposition anticipated had undergone a "sudden collapse." At the same time, Churchill's letter had had a "magnificent appeal." Indeed, according to the commissioner for public health and welfare, the question of the hour in St. John's about United States bases was something much more mundane: whether something could be done about the city's streets and feeder roads which had been reduced to "deplorable condition" by heavy truck traffic as a result of the work the Americans had in progress at the base site they had chosen on the north side of Quidi Vidi Lake.[25]

The news coming from St. John's was good, and what Emerson and Penson heard in Washington was also generally reassuring, though it left some important matters still unresolved. While in the United States capital, the Newfoundland representatives met briefly with Hull, Knox, and Colonel Henry L. Stimson, the secretary of war, but the main spokesman on the American side was John D. Hickerson, assistant chief of the State Department's Division of European Affairs, the secretary of the American section of the Permanent Joint Board on Defence and the resident expert on Newfoundland. Hickerson assured his visitors that his country did not claim sovereignty within the leased areas and that "it was the hope and expectation of the United States Government that it would not have to exercise jurisdiction over Newfoundlanders even for security offences." In Newfoundland's case the jurisdiction the United States had obtained would be treated as a "reserve" power, and Emerson and Penson were authorized to say this when they returned home. At the same time, Hickerson rejected the idea advanced by the commissioners that the United States should send to Newfoundland a "Political Officer" versed in the problems of resettlement. Such an appointment, he said, might justifiably be regarded by the officers of the war and navy departments already in the country as interfering with their work, and, moreover, "might involve both the United States and Newfoundland in considerable expense in the not unlikely event of his ideas on resettlement proving somewhat lavish." In the end the best that Emerson and Penson were able to do with respect to resettlement was to obtain a commitment that the war and navy departments would instruct their representatives in Newfoundland "to give every possible assistance" in carrying out whatever plans the Commission decided upon.[26]

The Newfoundland negotiators also did not get very far with the representations they made on economic questions and immigration. Nevertheless, Hickerson reiterated that "the Bases Agreement did constitute a ground for expecting closer economic relations between the two countries" and authorized a statement in Newfoundland along the lines Hull had earlier specified: once the "present emergency" ended, the United States would "be prepared to consider sympathetically the commercial relations between the two countries with a view to the development of mutual trade." Other matters discussed during this round of talks were the future channel of communication between Washington and St. John's (the Americans wanted business routed through their consulate general in the Newfoundland capital); the compensation formula (adjustments were agreed upon to be incorporated in a final document); roads expenditure (this was left to be worked out locally between United States and Newfoundland officials); the removal of the Argentia hospital (the Americans agreed to pay for this); the resolution of postal and customs questions (these also were left to be dealt with on the spot); the use of local labour and materials (written assurances, copies of which Emerson and Penson brought back to St. John's, had already been given the British

Embassy in relation to each of these); Newfoundland's participation in the deliberations of the Permanent Joint Board on Defence (at Hickerson's suggestion Emerson and Penson discussed this matter in Ottawa on their way home, whereupon it was announced that the board expected to confer periodically with representatives of the Newfoundland government); the defence of St. John's (two eight-inch guns would be installed there and more planes would be sent to the Newfoundland Airport); and the coverage Newfoundland was receiving in the United States press (the commissioners complained about damaging magazine articles that had appeared in *Harper's* and *Collier's*, were told that the United States government did not control the country's press, and then took up the suggestion that they hold a press conference, an event that occurred on 11 April with representatives of the Associated Press, United Press, International News, and two Washington newspapers in attendance).[27]

On their return to St. John's, Emerson and Penson reported to the Newfoundland people on the bases agreement in radio speeches. In his speech on 25 April Emerson concentrated on sovereignty, jurisdiction, and defence. The United States, he told his listeners, had neither sought nor been granted sovereignty. While it was certainly true that the "powers and authorities" granted the Americans were "quite extensive," it would be "a grave error to overestimate them." The truth was that exceptional circumstances had dictated the grant of exceptional authority. Turning to the issue of jurisdiction, Emerson told his audience that it was the provision of the agreement relating thereto - the cession to the United States of "a certain limited right to try British subjects for offences commited against American property or security" - that had given him and Penson the "gravest anxiety." The establishment of foreign courts on Newfoundland soil was "repugnant" to them both, but here again Newfoundlanders had to be "reasonable" and remember how things looked from the American perspective. In any event, Emerson continued, playing his trump card, the jurisdiction the Americans had obtained was "optional" and Newfoundland had now been assured that it would not be exercised locally "except under exceptional circumstances." Hence "there need be no fear of any person being tried by any court other than a Newfoundland Court." Following a brief explanation of the meaning and significance of the protocol and an acknowledgement of the help he and Penson had received in London from the Dominions Office, Emerson concluded his speech on a high note: Newfoundlanders could "face the future" fully confident that they were playing their part "in uniting the two great English speaking democracies."[28]

In the address he gave the following evening, Penson dealt mainly with economic issues, revealing to his audience the promise, however nebulous, made by Washington about future trade relations between the two countries.[29] As usual, the Commission of Government had made its public case cogently and comprehensively – if nothing else, this was an administration of strong rhetoric and good grammar – but for all its claims Newfoundland had undeniably taken some hard diplomatic knocks.

In June 1941, the arrangement for compensating private property owners in Newfoundland was finally completed.[30] Under this the Newfoundland Government would first attempt to reach agreement with an individual owner. If this effort succeeded, "an authorized representative of the United States" would be notified of the result. If he concurred in the amount decided upon, the owner would be paid, whereupon the United States would reimburse "His Majesty's Government" for the amount involved. If the Newfoundland government could not reach agreement with a particular owner, or if the United States disputed the amount agreed upon, the case would be referred to the Board of Arbitration Newfoundland had established. The owner in question would then be paid whatever the board decided upon. Payment from the United States would then follow as previously noted. If, however, the United States disputed the findings of the board in a particular case, the matter would "be settled under arrangements to be determined and agreed by the United States Government and His Majesty's Government." In carrying out this whole procedure Newfoundland was "invited" to consult with the appropriate American officials in the country before making any compensation offer and, to the extent possible, provide the United States representative responsible for compensation matters with information, under seven headings, about the history, assessment, tax status, and comparative worth of the properties affected.[31] For their part the Americans agreed that when Newfoundland resumed its pre-1934 constitutional status, the words "His Majesty's Government" in the compensation formula would be "taken to mean the Government of Newfoundland."[32] This arrangement flowed logically from an existing understanding about the Leased Bases Agreement itself, something that was embodied in notes which Churchill and John G. Winant, the American ambassador in London, had exchanged on 27 March in connection with the signing of the agreement.[33] Not surprisingly, Emerson had made much of this understanding in his public defence of what had been done in the British capital.

Following these developments, on 11 June 1941, The American Bases Act became law in Newfoundland.[34] This incorporated, in Annex I and Schedule A respectively, both the exchange of letters of 2 September 1940 between Lothian and Hull and the Leased Bases Agreement. The act set Newfoundland's seal of approval on that agreement, made "lawful," American actions under its terms since 27 March 1941, and authorized the Governor in Commission to execute a lease with the United States in a form specified in its Schedule B. This document which laid down "the exact metes and bounds" of the American bases was signed by Walwyn on 14 June and executed the same day by J.A. Winter acting on behalf of Newfoundland, and by Harold B. Quarton, the United States Consul General in St. John's since 1934, acting on behalf of his country.[35] Upon the completion of the lease, all the properties assigned by it "became the absolute property of the Crown in right of the Government of Newfoundland." These were described in the lease under six headings: Argentia; Quidi Vidi (St. John's), 2 parcels of land; Quidi Vidi Lakeside; White Hills (near St. John's), 4 parcels of land; Stephenville, 3 parcels of land and Signal Hill Battery (the St. John's harbour front property).[36]

By the time this formality was disposed of, work was humming at the base sites themselves. Some of the most dramatic changes were seen in the Argentia area where two facilities, a large naval base and a much smaller army base, were being constructed on adjacent properties. A crew of American construction workers arrived in the area in early January aboard the SS *Richard Peck*, which was subsequently used as a floating camp for American personnel. On the twenty-fifth a detachment of marines arrived on the SS *Niblack* and shortly afterwards erected a monument to commemorate their flag raising.[37] Two Newfoundland communities stood in the way of American plans for this area: Argentia itself and Marquise which, according to the 1935 census, had populations of 477 and 283 respectively, almost all of whom were Roman Catholics.[38] On 1 January 1941 at a public meeting, the residents of Argentia had formed a committee to defend their interests. At the same time they pronounced themselves in favour of resettlement on a site where they could "live together in one town, with their own Parish Church and schools, as at present constituted."[39]

In pursuit of this goal, the Argentia committee subsequently engaged the service of Philip J. Lewis, a well known St. John's Roman Catholic lawyer and one of the Commission of Government's prominent critics at the time of the Bowaters deal. Lewis was quoted in the *Evening Telegram* to the effect that the base development had descended on Argentia "like an avalanche" and that the people there were bewildered."[40] The Commission's own plans for the local population were spelled out in a statement published on 21 February. This announced the forthcoming establishment of the Board of Arbitration, guaranteed payment (on the authority of the United Kingdom Government) of its awards, and promised to "meet the wishes" of those residents who wanted to be "settled as a community." But there were two conditions. The first was that a site would have to be "agreed upon between the Government and a clear majority of the total number of all property owners in the two areas (Naval base and Army base)." The second was that "each and every one of those forming such majority" would have to undertake in writing to move to the site chosen and to have "his claim to compensation ... dealt with on this basis."[41] Lewis described the government's whole position as "evasive,"[42] but given the unsettled diplomatic background it could hardly have been otherwise. Still, his statement was a warning of many skirmishes to come on both the resettlement and compensation fronts.

In mid-March 1941, Lt. J.W. Silliman, the American naval officer in charge at Argentia, asked that the whole local base area be cleared of residents by 11 April.[43] This was a tall order to say the least. Faced with a severe problem of temporary accommodation, and with the residents "apparently averse from going any distance afield, even temporarily" and "likely to take advantage of every circumstance in order to postpone the evil day," the deadline proposed put the government on the spot.[44] The only way out, the Commission decided, was to get the American contractors to put up temporary accommodation for fifty-three families. The question of payment for this would be left to be settled later, though as an opening gambit, the ever cautious Newfoundland government put on record its view that the expenditure proposed should be borne by the United States.[45] More complications followed as Silliman's deadline passed without the desired result. On its side the Board of Arbitration found during its initial foray into the area that the general desire with regard to resettlement of those appearing before it was still "to go with a crowd." Woods, the commissioner responsible for administering government policy on the issue, interpreted this "as a general desire to be re-settled quite near Argentia and probably at Herring Bay."[46] Acting on this assumption, he asked the Argentia committee to tell the government where the people wanted to go and what "communal facilities" they would need there, offering at the same time the Commission's services in advising on the engineering and agricultural problems the move would entail.[47] Eventually, a survey of the Herring Bay (Dunville) site was undertaken by the government, but this location was later deemed unsuitable after a review in which Father Adrian Dee, the parish priest of Argentia (but not of Herring Bay), had most to say on behalf of its prospective residents.[48] On 17 July the people of Argentia and Marquise directed a telegram of protest to the governor. This condemned the government for its apparent procrastination and announced that the residents still in their homes intended to stay until the administration produced a plan that was satisfactory to them. "Flesh and blood," Walwyn was told, were "equally important as war emergency."[49] In time the Commission was able to piece together a solution whereby most of the residents, heeding the call of Father Dee and anxious to take advantage of the employment opportunities offered by the base, moved to the nearby hamlet of Freshwater. In July 1942, in what must surely be counted the ultimate act of resettlement in Newfoundland's long twentieth-century experience of this process, the remains of six hundred and twenty-five individuals were exhumed from the old graveyard at Argentia and reinterred in the new cemetery at Freshwater.[50] Circumstances were indeed changing for Newfoundlanders – even for some long deceased.

Things went more smoothly in St. John's. There were only a few private owners at Quidi Vidi and White Hills, and the fishermen who worked out of the Battery property decided early on that "it was in their interest to move quickly," even though those who chose to remain in fishing would not be able to find as convenient a location around the harbour.[51] The biggest problem in the capital was not resettlement, but the adjustment of the local population to the influx of so many newcomers, both Canadian and American. The first contingent of American troops sent to St. John's arrived in January 1941 on board the *Edmund B. Alexander* which, like the *Richard Peck* at Argentia, was then used as a floating camp and headquarters.[52] Later on, pending the completion of permanent quarters at the Quidi Vidi base, the troops moved into tents at "Camp Alexander" on the "Carpasian Estates" to the north of the city.[53] Ultimately, the base built at Quidi Vidi, St. John's, was named Fort Pepperrell after Sir William Pepperrell, the New England commander who in 1745 had captured the French fortress at Louisbourg. By contrast, the naval base built at Argentia continued to be known by its local name, but bases built at Marquise and Stephenville were designated Fort McAndrew and Ernest Harmon Airbase.

Not surprisingly, rents began a sharp climb in St. John's in 1941. The dawn of a new era was visible also in a memorandum issued by the Headquarters of the United States Army's Newfoundland Base Command to all its personnel. This put "*off limits*," because of unsanitary conditions, sixteen St. John's cafes and thirteen beer shops; the liquors served in the latter were declared so bad as to "frequently" produce "temporary insanity." In the same document thirteen St. John's restaurants which met "the minimum requirements of U.S. Public Health" were graded on a scale in which class four meant excellent, class three, very good, and class two, good; the restaurant in the government-owned Newfoundland Hotel was placed in class two.[54] At Stephenville the experience with the Americans was more like that at Argentia than at St. John's in that the main issue was resettlement. The Commission cautioned the Americans, for what it was worth, that the reestablishment of the population to be moved from the west coast base site would of necessity have to be on underdeveloped land.[55] The cost of this would obviously not be covered by the market value alone of what was to be expropriated.

A problem the Commission had to face on all the base sites, American and Canadian, was what should be paid to the Newfoundlanders employed on them. Here the Government's policy, as developed in a memorandum submitted by Woods on 17 January, was to arrange informally for foreign defence contractors in the country to stay within established local wage rates. In the case of common labour this meant a rate of thirty cents per hour in St. John's and the government's own rate of twenty-five cents per hour elsewhere. The higher wage in the capital arose from a decision of the city council. According to Woods, adherence to these rates was justified on several grounds. The basic need of the country was for more employment rather than employment at higher rates. Moreover, the effect of higher wage rates brought on by "transient conditions" would be to reduce government employment, threaten established enterprise (the fluorspar mine at St. Lawrence was cited as an example), to "accentuate the tendency for the fishing industry to be manned by those too unenterprising to escape from it altogether or to react to modern requirements," and to make Newfoundland less attractive for investment in new industries. Nor, Woods maintained, did the argument that the payment of higher wages on defence jobs could be localized (as was the case in Corner Brook and Grand Falls where the paper companies went beyond common local practice), apply. In these centres, he claimed, the higher wages paid went to permanent residents, whereas on the bases workers from many parts of the country would be affected. The "psychological effect" of paying such a diverse group on a higher scale would be to set "a new standard" for everybody: "the argument will be irresistible that anything less than the Canadians and Americans are willing to pay must be too low; that this Government should treat its own labour at least as well as the Canadians and Americans treat their labour in this country." Hence the need for Newfoundland employers, including the government itself, to set the rates for the foreign employers rather than the reverse. Underlining all this was something else: "one of the difficulties and dangers" of the situation that had suddenly been created in the country was that it provided "a golden opportunity for the growth of mushroom Trade Unions." This development could not be headed off simply by raising wages, because unions could "always ask for more." On balance, therefore, the "wisest course" for the government would be "to refuse point blank" to reveal, on the grounds of confidentiality, anything about its discussions with the visiting employers on the subject of wage rates, and to leave its own rates where they were unless it had to do otherwise. If the government later contemplated an increase in its own basic labour rate, then Woods recommended that it consult the country's "private employers" before acting.[56]

As might be expected, some of the Newfoundlanders who went to work on the American bases saw things in a different light, though there was not much they could do about the informal understanding that existed between their employers and the Newfoundland government. A meeting in February 1941 at the Victoria Hall in St. John's, attended by the executives of the city's fourteen unions, appointed a committee to protest working conditions at Quidi Vidi. In resolutions subsequently drafted, this committee denounced the Commission for "laxity" in its attitude to the "welfare of the working people." Specifically, the committee made three complaints: the absence of proper facilities for the men to eat and take shelter in when the weather was bad; the American practice of making deductions from pay for time legitimately taken off when on the job; and the fact that the thirty cents per hour being paid unskilled workers was below the true going rate in the city. Accordingly, the committee passed resolutions in favour of better accommodation for the workers, a forty cents per hour wage for unskilled workers, an eight hour day ("9 a.m. to 5 p.m. with one hour for lunch"), and an overtime rate of one and a half times the normal hourly wage.[57] Similar signs of labour dissatisfaction were also evident at Argentia where in early March of the same year an "Argentia Labour Union" was formed at a general meeting. Among the speakers were Father Dee and William J. Frampton of the carpenter's union in St. John's, the latter speaking on behalf of the Newfoundland Federation of Labour.[58] What the organized Argentia workers or any other Newfoundland union could expect from the Americans in bargaining tactics had been made plain shortly before by Lt. Col. Philip G. Bruton, the district engineer in charge of army construction in Newfoundland. After he had announced a new wage scale to take effect from 1 March on all army projects in the country, he explained to the press that the governing principle behind the American policy on wages was to match local rates; the same policy, effective March 1, was introduced at Argentia by the United States navy over Silliman's signature. The Americans considered all Newfoundland as one wage area. Any trade union which sought a wage increase for local base employees would have to produce a signed contract with a Newfoundland employer showing that a higher rate was being paid elsewhere in the country than that offered by the United States for the work in question. The matter would be then taken up with Washington. Within the existing framework, however, local base workers could increase their wages by showing adaptability and thereby improving their job classification.[59]

In April 1941, a group of labour leaders pressed the government to increase the wages paid common labourers in the Newfoundland construction industry generally to forty cents an hour from 1 June, an appeal poorly received by Woods. The Americans and Canadians, he noted, might well match this rate if it were adopted by the Commission for its own employees, but the effect of this development on the

Newfoundland economy as a whole would be harmful. The government should stick to its "rate of 25¢ an hour for common labour on road work and similar jobs" and adjust this rate upward only if it encountered difficulty finding takers. If labour resorted to strike action to push up construction wages, the government should respond with a twofold policy. In the case of its own jobs, it should simply wait the strikers out; where the bases were concerned it would have to be ready to protect men willing to work at going rates from union intimidation.[60] While the septuagenarian Woods advocated these heroics, the Newfoundland workers on the leased bases who might be affected by them were having to make other kinds of adjustments. For example, they had to work alongside Americans who could buy duty free cigarettes at seven cents a pack, and to learn to live with a right hand rule of the road on the bases. This was the opposite of the system in force elsewhere in Newfoundland, which kept with British practice. At the base gate, entering Newfoundland drivers switched from left to right, a circumstance that made plain just how much parts of their country had been taken over by others.[61]

If the United States set the pace in defence spending and construction on the island of Newfoundland during 1941, Canada ran hard to stay in the race. Following on what had been accomplished as a result of Power's visit to St. John's in August 1940, a further discussion on Canada-Newfoundland bilateral defence issues was held there from 28 November to 1 December.[62] Canada was represented at these talks by a group led by Colin Gibson, her minister of national revenue. The Commission of Government's team on this occasion consisted of Puddester, Penson, Woods, Emerson, and two public servants. During that winter the matters left over from this meeting were pursued by correspondence, usually telegraphic. This led finally to direct negotiations on the question of the transfer of Newfoundland's air bases to Canada for the duration of the war. Talks were held at the Newfoundland Airport in April 1941 with Woods as chief negotiator for Newfoundland and Gibson for Canada.[63] The outcome of their talks was a nineteen-term memorandum of agreement which they signed in St. John's on 17 April.[64] To take effect, the agreement needed the concurrence of the United Kingdom, and this was later received.

This document, which helped to shape the future relations of Canada and Newfoundland, was negotiated in accordance with a detailed understanding between London and St. John's. If it gave the Canadians many advantages, it also saddled them with numerous responsibilities, while simultaneously ensuring the restoration for all practical purposes of the status quo ante once the need for their assistance had passed. Subject to a long list of conditions and understandings the bases were to be transferred to Canadian administration for "the duration of the war." Thereafter, they would be transferred to Newfoundland control. Except in one area, however, Newfoundland would be obligated after the war to lease to Canada for fifty years any land at the Newfoundland Airport on which, at her own expense, Canada had constructed, or might construct during the period of her control of the base, "hangars, works and buildings" needed by the Royal Canadian Air Force. In the penultimate term of the memorandum, Newfoundland's "intention" with regard to the bases once she had resumed control of them was specified: this was that they had to revert to being civil airports devoted to the promotion of transatlantic flight. The "extent" of Canada's "continued use" of the bases for military purposes once the changeover occurred was thus made subject to future consultation between the two signatories. Unquestioningly, Canada could look forward to having some long-term standing at the Newfoundland bases, but what she would be left with paled beside what the Americans had obtained on the island under the Leased Bases Agreement of the month before. The Americans were established in some of the most densely populated parts of Newfoundland with extensive rights that would last long into the future. By contrast, Canada had come to the island to do war service, and her exact role in the country after that remained to be worked out.[65]

This fact was not lost on Ottawa, where a defence was quickly worked out to be employed in case of adverse domestic comment on what had been arranged with Newfoundland. If invidious comparison were made between the ninety-nine year span of the Leased Bases Agreement and the control and lease provisions of the Newfoundland bases deal, the reply would be made that the two arrangements were "designed for different purposes." The Anglo-American agreement spelled out "in exact detail the precise rights and obligations of the United States Government over certain minutely specified areas." On the other hand, the Canada-Newfoundland agreement had "to do only with arrangements for control and operation of certain air defence facilities" and did not deal with Canada's "larger commitments ... for the defence of Newfoundland as a whole." "In other words," so this argument ran, "it is a specification of certain arrangements for the effective accomplishment of a common service operation to which Newfoundland and the United Kingdom will contribute, although Canada will have control. It does not attempt to spell out a solution for all the problems involved in Canadian-Newfoundland relations." Furthermore the agreement left Canada completely free "in regard to political or other relationships with Newfoundland in the post-war period."[66]

This reasoning was plausible, if somewhat strained, but there can be no doubt that worry about the growing role of the United States in Newfoundland was mounting in Ottawa at this stage of the war. When Woods reported back to his colleagues about the negotiations at the Newfoundland Airport, he noted that the discussions with the Canadians had been dominated "by what became a veritable 'King Charles' head', the possibility that the United States would try to obtain a dominating position (more especially in regard to problems involved in the use of land and air forces) in Newfoundland."[67] Woods's analysis was discerning, for in reporting to his colleagues about events in Newfoundland, Colin Gibson spoke in a similar vein. Canada, he said, was spending "large sums" in Newfoundland, but the United States was spending "much larger" sums there. That the "eventual investment" of the United States would be "many times that of Canada ... could not fail to have an important practical effect upon our position on the island."[68]

After the air bases question was disposed of, there was a quick succession of other important developments in relations between Canada and Newfoundland. On the same day the bases transfer deal was signed, Newfoundland also formally agreed, in a letter from Woods to Gibson, to the establishment of the projected aerodrome in the Torbay area near St. John's. Consent for this was given on the understanding that Canada would bear the whole cost of the project and that the use of the facility for civil aviation would require Newfoundland's permission. Subject to satisfactory administrative arrangements being made with the departments of the Newfoundland government concerned, Canada was authorized to begin acquiring land needed for the aerodrome. Any Crown land needed for the base, Gibson was told, would be provided by Newfoundland "free of charge either as an outright grant or on a lease commensurate with the capital investment of the Canadian Government, as may be agreed in due course."[69] During the summer of 1941, work on the Torbay Base was pushed forward with great speed, and the first aircraft landed there in October. Militarily, the purpose of the field, which was built in accordance with the evolving general defence plans of the Permanent Joint Board on Defence, was to provide cover for St. John's and extend the zone through which protection could be given the convoys, which were now a common sight in Newfoundland waters.

While work was progressing at the Torbay site, Newfoundland also agreed to allow Canada, again acting at the behest of the Permanent Joint Board on Defence, to build another air base.[70] The site for this was to be in the North West River area of Labrador. As Canada would once more bear the whole cost of this ambitious enterprise, Newfoundland, having consulted the United Kingdom, agreed informally to lease to her for ninety-nine years the Crown land to be occupied by the base.[71] This was done on the understanding that the lease "was to be for military purposes only," that "no transfer of Newfoundland's sovereignty was to be involved," and that the question of the use after the war of the proposed airport for civil aviation purposes would be decided between Newfoundland and Canada in talks to be held within twelve months of the end of the conflict.[72] Negotiations over the conditions of the lease in question would drag on, amidst increasing rancour, until 1944. But thanks to one of Canada's remarkable wartime engineering feats, the base itself was operational by December 1941, even though runways had yet to be paved.[73] The role of the new base, built at Goose Bay and so named, was to serve as an alternate to Gander, to enhance air defence generally, and to provide another resource in the Battle of the Atlantic.[74] A northern ferry route via Greenland and Iceland was later established. Among other things the Goose and Torbay projects brought into the country the McNamara Construction Company, which continues to this day to do business locally.[75]

To clear the way through a diplomatic maze and so proceed on the work she had undertaken at Goose Bay and elsewhere, Canada now had the benefit of a High Commission in St. John's, as arranged in July 1941.[76] Her first high commissioner was Charles J. Burchell, a Nova Scotian who could claim local connections.[77] The rationale for his appointment was given in a memorandum which the Canadian under-secretary of state for external affairs addressed to Mackenzie King on 15 July. During the previous six months, this document noted, Canada had had in total "more varied, more important and more urgent business with Newfoundland than with all the self-governing Dominions" to which she sent representatives. Newfoundland was now indeed "economically, socially and strategically closer to Canada than to any other part of the British Empire," although her "international position" was determined by a "three-way pull - to the United Kingdom, to the United States and to Canada." Present circumstances placed Newfoundland in a "precariously balanced position," any change in which was "of direct interest" to Canada. Hence the need for Ottawa to be "adequately and directly" represented there.[78] In effect this analysis dropped the curtain on the bad old days when Richard Squires, whose death in 1940 had elicited only the usual empty official regrets, had met on the run, cap in hand, with Canadian officials.

In May 1942 yet another link was forged between the two countries, though its far-reaching effect on popular taste and behaviour in Newfoundland was perhaps not fully anticipated. An agreement was made between Canada and Newfoundland to establish an air service which would use the new Torbay airport.[79] The first flight of the new service, which was operated by Trans-Canada Air Lines, reached Torbay on 1 May. The publicly owned Canadian carrier quickly established itself as an indispensable link between Newfoundland and the outside world.

Through 1941 and 1942, therefore, Canada undoubtedly improved her standing in Newfoundland but what the future would hold for her there was problematic. The circumstances surrounding the building of an advance naval base at St. John's for convoy protection typified the situation she faced. The decision to build this important base was made by the Admiralty in 1941, but even though it would be manned and mainly used by the Royal Canadian Navy, Newfoundland resisted the idea that the property on which it stood should be transferred to Canada. The Commission was apprehensive "as to the political consequences if the Canadian Government obtained a foothold in the Island through actual ownership of a considerable area in St. John's."[80] The result was that, even though taking on a burdensome and demanding duty, Ottawa had to accept Admiralty ownership. The British, however, did agree to consult the Royal Canadian Navy before abandoning the base once the war was over.

Generally, of course, the public was not aware of such dealings. What the Commission naturally emphasized to the people it governed was the partnership of the various parties now represented in the country and the strategic importance of Newfoundland to the Allied war effort. There was much to indicate that Newfoundland was indeed the "Gibraltar of the West."[81] In August 1941 the emergence of the country from the grim obscurity into which it had sunk during the 1930s was underscored by the famous meeting between Churchill and Roosevelt in Placentia Bay, where Walwyn and Outerbridge had lunch with the prime minister aboard HMS *Prince of Wales*.[82] Churchill also privately ventured ashore in Newfoundland, and amused himself by "rolling boulders down a cliff."[83] The Atlantic Charter, proclaiming a message of freedom and democracy for all mankind, resulted from this meeting of the British and American leaders. Subsequently the occasion inspired an enduring and defiant image of Newfoundland at war in the poet E.J. Pratt's graphic phrase "Argentia's Smoking Funnels,"[84] a reference to the smoke stacks of the Anglo-American fleets which brought the president and prime minister to their conference. But if Newfoundlanders glimpsed glory through this event and the arrival of a steady stream of other distinguished wartime visitors (among them the Duke of Kent and Mayor Fiorello La Guardia of New York and his fellow members of the Permanent Joint Board on Defence, including John Hickerson), they also saw and tasted some of the bitter fruit of armed conflict. When ninety-two merchant marine survivors of the famous action in which HMS *Jervis Bay* under Captain E.F.S. Fegen was lost arrived in port at St. John's on 12 November 1940, a wave of shock and revulsion at a formidable enemy swept the country.[85] When two of three Newfoundland survivors of the *Jervis Bay* sinking, George Squires and Louis Tilley, arrived back in St. John's by train on the twenty-first, they were welcomed with an enthusiastic public reception.

They greeted their countrymen with the words "There'll Always be an England."[86] Suddenly the war was real.

Newfoundlanders were also hit by a stream of casualty reports from overseas and by a series of grim events closer to home. In February 1941 a plane carrying Sir Frederick Banting crashed near Musgrave Harbour. His would-be rescuers found only "the torn tissues of his healing hands."[87] A year later the destroyer USS *Truxton* and the supply ship USS *Pollox* were lost near St. Lawrence in a disaster that evoked once more in Newfoundlanders "their master passion of giving shelter and of sharing bread."[88] In gratitude the Americans later erected a hospital in the community. Submarines made two raids at Bell Island. The first, on 5 September 1942, was by day. A night raid followed on 9 November 1942, one of the author's earliest memories. Four ships were sunk in these raids with a considerable loss of life.[89] In the early hours of 14 October 1942, the ferry steamer *Caribou*, which sailed between Port aux Basques, Newfoundland and North Sydney, Nova Scotia, was torpedoed and sunk in the Cabot Strait.[90] A popular poster afterwards celebrated "the *Caribou* and her gallant crew." To this list in any chronology of wartime tragedy in Newfoundland must be added the devastating fire that destroyed the St. John's Knights of Columbus hostel, a servicemen's haunt, in early December of the same year.[91] The popular "Uncle Tim's Barn Dance" was being performed before a Saturday night audience of about 350 people when the fire started just after 11 PM. Ninety-nine lives were lost. Though not related to enemy action, the blaze evoked widespread rumours of sabotage and was the subject of investigation by Justice Dunfield.[92] Many years later it became known that German forces had landed at Martin Bay on the coast of Labrador in October 1943 and established an automatic weather station.[93] Still, for all the terrible occurrences of the times, Newfoundland was materially better off. Thanks largely to American and Canadian investment to provide forward defences for themselves, Newfoundland after 1939 was undoubtedly a case in point that, though rightly identified with death and destruction, war can sometimes incidentally and unexpectedly improve the social order. If "the Cinderella of the Empire," as Newfoundland has sometimes been called, had been fitted with a boot rather than a slipper, she had reason to be grateful all the same.

The economic consequences of recruitment and of the defence construction boom that followed were truly impressive. In its annual report for 1941 the Commission noted that the demand for labour during the year had been "unprecedented" and that a market existed in the country "wherein any man, and a large number of women, capable of working could secure employment at attractive rates of remuneration."[94] This was a startling turnaround indeed, but 1942 brought even better results; the Commission described the economic improvement that occurred during that year as "phenomenal."[95] At the height of the base building boom about 20,000 Newfoundlanders were employed in military construction, which in effect had suddenly, some would say providentially, given the country a major new industry. Amazingly, in 1942 the government did not have to pay out any able-bodied relief, and was able to confine itself to the support of the sick, aged, and infirm.[96] From a figure of $1,382,000 in 1939–40, relief expenditure fell away by 1942–43 to a wartime low of $280,000.[97] In short order, Newfoundland's most corrosive social and economic problem had been almost magically solved.

Better times also came to the country's primary industries. In 1939, to keep the dilapidated fishing industry going, the Commission introduced legislation guaranteeing fishermen a minimum price for salt codfish exports.[98] This scheme had much to recommend it but cannot be given credit for the recovery that followed, which was a result of world market forces. Exports of salt codfish dropped from 1938–39 through 1941–42 but thanks to price increases the value of production was greater in 1940–41 than in the preceding two years, and this upward trend continued through the war.[99] Moreover, as salt codfish shipments fell, export of fresh and frozen cod grew by leaps and bounds, an increase encouraged by a Newfoundland Cold Storage Development Committee on which government and business were represented.[100] The number of men engaged in codfishing declined from 25,220 in 1939 to 18,643 in 1941, but rose to 20,019 in 1943 as the boom in defence construction passed.[101] Anticipating this development, the Commission decided in February 1942 to issue a notice about employment prospects on the bases. The purpose of this would be to caution fishermen about the need to keep in good repair the equipment they used in their primary occupation.[102] Altogether, the early war years marked a period of profound change for Newfoundland's oldest industry, not only from bad times to relatively good ones, but from one large scale mode of production to two, salting and refrigeration. Of these, the future belonged to the second.

The mining industry, which had picked up considerably of its own accord in the late 1930s, also continued to do well after the war started though its market situation changed considerably. In 1939 and again in 1940, employment fell back slightly, but in 1941 the 1938 figure was equalled, and in 1942 a wartime high of 3,040 employees was reached. Thanks to German rearmament, much of the renewed activity in the immediate pre-war period had been at Bell Island, where the number of employees rose from 1,295 in 1935 to 1,781 in 1938 and to 1,894 in 1942.[103] Ironically, an ore carrier sailed from Bell Island for Germany as late as 26 August 1939. The effect of the loss of the German market thereafter was eased by exporting to the United Kingdom and, after this became too hazardous, by sales to Canada.[104] At St. Lawrence, where fluorspar had been mined by the St. Lawrence Corporation of Newfoundland since 1933, a second operation, run by Newfoundland Fluorspar, a subsidiary of the Aluminum Company of Canada, was started up in 1942.[105]

The turnaround in the forest sector of Newfoundland's economy was nothing short of spectacular. In 1938–39 newsprint exports fell to 288,000 tons, but in 1939–40 they surged ahead to 346,000 tons and the next year rose to a wartime peak of 352,000 tons.[106] In 1942 the new sulphite mill built by Bowaters at Corner Brook under the terms of its controversial 1938 agreement with the Newfoundland government produced at greater than intended capacity.[107] In that year too, labour was in such demand in Newfoundland that the supply of wood in the country fell short of the needs of the pulp and paper industry going flat out. The result was that the Commission actually agreed to allow the duty free import of pulpwood by Bowaters, a step that would have been inconceivable a few years before.[108] The war also brought with it the possibility of increased pitprop sales to the United Kingdom, for which purpose Newfoundland producers formed themselves in 1940 into a Roundwood Exporters' Association.[109]

From the standpoint of public finance the effect of the economic revival was not so much restorative as redemptive. When the books were closed for 1940–41, the year in which Penson had cut back, the Commission had an unexpected surplus of $696,531, on slightly higher than forecast expenditure. This did not include a return of $534,000 from the sale of war savings certificates. The windfall thus realized was put to four uses: $100,000 went into a reserve fund for redeeming war savings certificates; $250,000 was paid against the $625,000 loan the syndicate banks, on the guarantee of the Canadian government, had given Newfoundland in 1933; $300,000 was issued to the United Kingdom as an interest free loan to be paid back after the war; and the remainder was kept on hand. Out of its war savings certificate returns, the Commission made a gift of $500,000 to the United Kingdom towards the cost of a unit of the Royal Air Force, designated in time the 125th Newfoundland Squadron. As its name implied, this was to be manned by local servicemen. In short order a government that had never been able to support itself had become a lender – and a lender to its former benefactor. Yet despite this surprising change of fortune, Penson produced a budget for 1941–42 that again reduced expenditure to $14,865,475 against estimated revenue of $17,463,295. This left a surplus of $2,597,820, the "greater part" of which, Penson said, would be treated by the government as a "general reserve" for future use. The "paramount objective" of the new budget was "giving the maximum help possible towards winning the war." To this end, at least $2,000,000 of the surplus anticipated would also be lent to the United Kingdom interest free for the duration of the war. Newfoundland would have a nest egg when she needed it, but in the meantime her savings would be put to good use to defeat Hitler.[110]

In practice, the budgetary outcome for 1941–42 repeated the experience of 1940–41 but on a grander scale; this time the projected surplus was $7,211,182 or 57.5 per cent of the country's total revenue in 1939–40.[111] Up to 14 July 1942 when Penson's successor, Ira Wild, read his first budget speech, Newfoundland had lent $4,100,000 interest free to the United Kingdom.[112] In addition the government had paid out $1,977,000, which it also stood to recover, on the United Kingdom's behalf. Included in this amount, which covered various war expenses, was the sum of $1,460,000 issued to date to property owners for land expropriated for the leased bases. Though the United Kingdom was ultimately responsible for this expenditure, Newfoundland expected, of course, to be reimbursed by the United States for the full amount issued. Proceeds from war savings certificates sold during 1941–42 came to $809,900, which in time was also lent to the United Kingdom interest free. For 1942–43 the Commission at last set its expenditures higher, and Wild forecast an outlay of $17,722,300 on revenue of $18,744,100. These were numbers that would warm the heart of any finance minister, let alone a member of a government that had known the travail of the Commission. Yet another notable wartime financial development was an agreement in 1941 whereby the Newfoundland Railway obtained a loan of $2,100,000 on the credit of the country from the United States Defence Supplies Corporation for improving its facilities.[113] This loan was prompted by the transportation requirements of the American bases.

As prosperity spread and its revenues soared, the Commission was, despite its cautious approach to spending, at last able to carry out some of the social reforms it had envisaged in the 1930s. One of the most important of these was in the field of education. In late August 1942, school attendance was made free and compulsory for children "over seven and under fourteen years of age."[114] In deciding on this change, the Commission also proposed a major reorganization of the Department of Education.[115] In 1939, under pressure from the churches, the department had again been reorganized, this time in a denominational direction.[116] In April 1942, the Commission decided to place the office of secretary of education, held by the secularist Lloyd Shaw, in abeyance. Instead, the duties of the Secretary would be performed jointly by the four denominational representatives (one each from the Roman Catholic, Church of England, United Church, and Salvation Army populations) who served on the

"Council of Education" which under the 1939 act had responsibility "for all educational policy."[117]

The Commission's plans received a mixed reception in London. The changeover to free and compulsory education was heartily endorsed, but the reorganization proposed for the Department of Education was perceived as "a retrograde step" because, as Woods argued, the change in the secretaryship would remove "the one influence ... free of official loyalty to any particular denomination." To act as the Commission wanted would bring Newfoundland to a "parting of the ways" educationally and "end ... any hope of progress towards a state system of education in any foreseeable future." Still, if the plans which had been worked out in St. John's went "strongly against the grain," it was acknowledged in London that it would be difficult for the Dominions Office to press its views against what seemed like "an almost unanimous public opinion in Newfoundland."[118] The outcome was, in keeping with what had happened in 1935, a compromise that really favoured denominationalism. Lloyd Shaw was made director of vocational education, a new position, but the post of secretary was retained and filled by I.J. Sampson, the Church of England representative on the Council of Education.[119] That his denominational colleagues on the council should have consented to his elevation was no surprise, for, as Shaw had explained to the Commission in April, they all had "direct access to the commissioner."[120]

An area of policy in which the Commission renewed its effort to make a definite break with the past was local government. A local administration act had been passed in 1937 under which local government areas could be established and councils appointed to administer them.[121] Four years later, the government approved a system for financing the local councils whereby it would match the revenue raised by them to a maximum of $3,000.[122] However, by virtue of the Local Administration (Military Areas) Act which became law in June 1941, the commissioner for public health and welfare, or any other commissioner appointed by the Governor in Commission, was empowered to act in lieu of a local council within a fifteen mile radius of any military or naval base.[123] The government's purpose in passing this law, as Emerson explained to the public, was to prevent the creation of "shack towns." The Commission, he continued, would keep its newly acquired powers only while "absolutely necessary" and would welcome the formation of local councils willing to exercise authority under the 1937 act in the areas in question.[124] On 14 June, in accordance with this shift in policy, a local government area was created encompassing "all the area within a circle extending five miles in all directions from the Court House in the town of Placentia, excluding therefrom all land leased to the United States of America."[125] Exactly one week later Puddester was appointed "to act in place of a local

Council" in this area. The same authority was given him in September over a local government area created adjacent to the American base at Stephenville.[126] By an Act dated 5 November 1942, the town of Windsor, which had had an appointed Board of Management since 1938, became the first Newfoundland community outside St. John's to be incorporated and given elective local government.[127] Three days later another act accorded the same status to the town of Corner Brook West.[128] Needless to say, these positive developments were employed by the Commission to considerable public relations advantage.

As the war progressed, the government made further changes in economic policy. Following a suggestion in Gorvin's report, a New Industries Committee had been formed in 1939. This was typical of Gorvin's co-operative and corporatist approach and brought together representatives of government, business, and labour.[129] In September 1940 at the invitation of this committee, three economic experts from the United States visited the country to advise on industrial development policy.[130] The consultants, G.H. and J.V.N. Dorr, and W.O. Faxon, endorsed the basic fishery policy of the Commission; suggested that overall more could be gained by sending Newfoundlanders abroad to take advantage of fishery research being done elsewhere than by bringing experts into the country; suggested "as a tempting field for investigation" the possibility of getting chemical or other industry going which would use Bay d'Espoir and east coast water power; recommended that water power development in Labrador should "be regarded as a task for future generations"; and praised the tripartite approach of the New Industries Committee. In general the American experts advised that "efforts should be made to create industries along diversified lines rather than to expect some spectacular development in any one particular direction."[131] Following the demise of Gorvin's special areas scheme, the government emphasized this approach, and in January 1942 a Newfoundland Industrial Development Board was created. This board was not itself to "engage in trade or carry on any enterprise or project" or to "devote any part of its funds to making a grant, advance or loan to any trade or industry." Rather it was to encourage development by gathering and disseminating information, bringing interested parties together, and generally promoting expansion and innovation. By the terms of the legislation that created the board, the government's grant to it was not to exceed $12,500 per annum.[132] In 1942 also the Commission went into shipbuilding at Clarenville.[133] Here, by 1946, at a cost of $2,750,000, it would build ten 350-ton wooden coastal freighters equipped with diesel engines as well as two vessels designed for specialized fishery use.

If wartime conditions greatly altered the framework of government-business relations, they also sped the development of a new and more modern system of labour relations. In 1938 T.K. Liddell, the chief conciliation officer in Manchester for the Department of Labour, had undertaken for the Commission a study of labour conditions in Newfoundland. His report, which was published in 1940 under the title *Industrial Survey of Newfoundland*, recommended new labour relations procedures based on contemporary British practice.[134] While the Commission was still considering what he had to say, it was overtaken by events. In January of 1940 the Longshoremen's Protective Union, a perennial thorn in the side of the Government, threatened a strike in St. John's over wage rates.[135] The immediate issue was the loading on board the SS *Newfoundland* of a shipment of fish for the United Kingdom. The government decided that if the union tried to stop this work from being done, it would call for volunteers to load the cargo, assuming the local manager of Furness Withy & Company, the owners of the vessel, was agreeable. At the same time, however, it was agreed by the commissioners that the time was ripe for an "impartial economic investigation" into the conditions of work on the St. John's waterfront, provided the union would go along with this.[136] In fact a decision to go ahead with such an enquiry was made on 17 January and a four-member investigative committee chosen.

While this committee was going about its work, the government considered passing legislation modelled on the Canadian Industrial Disputes Investigation Act, but nothing came of this.[137] For the moment the government could still manage to operate on an ad hoc basis in the labour field although the days of this approach were numbered. Already a change had been made in the handling of labour relations for the logging industry. In April 1940 the government approved the formation of a Woods Labour Board which was to solve problems as they arose in order to prevent wartime strikes.[138] The brainchild of Gorvin, this board, which from the beginning worked well, brought together representatives of the two pulp and paper companies and the four unions active among loggers: the Fishermen's Protective Union (1908), the Newfoundland Lumbermen's Association (1936), the Newfoundland Labourers' Union (1937), and the Workers' Central Protective Union (1938).[139] The board's first chairman was Albert Walsh, the assistant secretary for justice and an official destined soon to become an important figure in Newfoundland public life. Born at Holyrood, Conception Bay, Walsh was a Roman Catholic lawyer who had been educated at St. Bonaventure's College, St. John's and Dalhousie University, Halifax. After being speaker of the House of Assembly from 1928 to 1932, he had served from 1935 to 1940 as magistrate at Grand Falls and Corner Brook.[140]

With the demand for labour growing apace, the government issued, on 27 June 1941, under the authority of the Emergency Powers (Defence) Act, the Defence (Avoidance of Strikes and Lockouts) Regulations. These empowered the commissioner for public utilities to intervene in the event of "an actual or apprehended lockout or stike" which threatened "the efficient prosecution of the war or the maintaining of supplies and services essential to the life of the community." Several forms of intervention were provided for: the Commission could, by order, establish "a tribunal or tribunals for the settlement of any trade dispute or trade disputes"; prohibit any strike or lockout; impose "terms and conditions" of work on employers; vary "any rule, practice or custom in respect of the employment, non-employment, conditions of employment, hours of work or working conditions, of any persons"; and deal with any related "incidental and supplementary matters" as circumstances required. Contravention of an order issued under the regulations could lead to a variety of fines or imprisonment. If a convicted person was "a body corporate," each of its directors or officers at the time the offence was committed would ipso facto also stand convicted unless he could prove "that the offence was committed without his knowledge or that he exercised all due duty to prevent the commission of the offence."[141]

These regulations were put to the first and a severe test in August 1941, when the Buchans' Workers Protective Union went on strike. A tribunal was promptly appointed and the strike outlawed. The confrontation that followed between strikers and government was limited, and the report of the tribunal formed the basis of an eventual satisfactory settlement reached a month later.[142] In October the Commission faced another emergency on the St. John's docks when a dispute arose between the Employers' Association and the Longshoremen's Protective Union whose working agreement had lapsed. This concerned the unloading of three ships carrying cargo destined for the United States bases. Having already suggested to the two parties who had been negotiating for many months that their differences be referred to a board of arbitration to be set up by the government, the Commission decided to give police protection to men who wanted to work during a union slowdown. A military guard was proposed but did not have to be used as the union went along with the prompt unloading of the three ships whose arrival had brought matters to a crisis.[143] Nonetheless, the government decided it could no longer delay settling the dock situation in St. John's once and for all, and, accordingly, informed the two parties that it would forthwith establish a tribunal to investigate the differences between them.[144]

That same month, the Commission issued new regulations to strengthen even more its hand in labour matters. The Defence (Control and conditions of employment and disputes settlement) Regulations authorized the commissioner for public utilities to direct "any person in Newfoundland" to perform service which in his view that individual was capable of doing. In addition, the commissioner could, subject to certain provisos, determine the "remuneration and conditions of service" of those ordered by him to work. He could also "make provision for regulating the engagement of workers by employers and the duration of their employment." Any trade dispute reported to the commissioner could be referred by him to a specially constituted trade dispute board for binding arbitration. At the same time no employer could "declare or take part in a lockout" and no worker take part in a strike without giving the commissioner twenty-one days notice of his intention to do so. During that time the commissioner could, if he deemed fit, act within the framework of the regulations to head off the threatened work stoppage, and if necessary appoint a trade dispute board to impose a settlement on the disputing parties.[145] While this arrangement did not ban strikes and lockouts as such, it ensured that they would only occur when and where the government was willing to tolerate them. The first trade dispute board under the new regulations was appointed on 6 December to settle a long festering dispute between the St. Lawrence Workers' Protective Union and the St. Lawrence Corporation of Newfoundland. Its membership included William J. Walsh, the former minister of agriculture and mines.[146] The second board was appointed on 27 December to enquire into the St. John's dock situation. Sir Lionel Warner, the General Manager of the Mersey Docks and Harbour Board, of Liverpool, England, agreed to chair this board. Judge J.L. Ryan of Bathurst, New Brunswick, and the increasingly useful Albert Walsh were the other members named.[147] As the months passed, the extensive use of this new machinery proved that the Commission had created it in the nick of time.

In his 1940 report T.K. Liddell had recommended the establishment of a section of a government department to deal "exclusively with labour matters."[148] Warner's enquiry gave similar advice, calling on the government to appoint "one or more officers whose duty shall include rendering assistance in the settlement of disputes arising between employers and workmen."[149] In April 1942 after having been urged on by London as well, the Commission answered these calls and decided to create the post of labour relations officer.[150] Albert Walsh was appointed to this position, and the new office, which administratively came under the commissioner for public utilities, was opened in June. For the moment, however, the Commission resisted pressure from London to go beyond the wartime regulations it had introduced in labour relations and to effect permanent reform by bringing in legislation based on the British Conciliation Act. What lay behind this response, it was explained in one Dominions Office memorandum, was a situation in Newfoundland whereby employers regarded "any industrial legislation with the suspicion of an industrialist of the Victorian era," while employees saw "the strike weapon" as "the simplest of short cuts to the settlement of all disputes imaginary or real."

In reacting as it had, according to this same source, the Commission had revealed its "profound distrust of any advancement in the field of industrial conciliation." Formally, it was explained, the Newfoundland government's case was as follows: "that, whilst employers would be able to refuse to arbitrate, Government as an employer would be unable to exercise this option; that to legislate would imperil the financial stability of the country and would be an unfair legacy to hand down to any successive independent Government; that there were not sufficient competent people on the Island to form arbitration boards; and that the legislation proposed was too complicated." But these arguments were all swept aside in London; the secretary of state told the Commission that in his view "no time should be lost in bringing Newfoundland conditions into line with modern ideas" on labour relations.[151] Nothing happened immediately in response to this July 1942 directive, but in 1944 a Trade Disputes (Arbitration and Inquiry) Act became law.[152] This did not entirely satisfy all the requirements of the Dominions Office and did not cover Crown employees (London had specifically conceded this point);[153] but it ensured that the regulatory approach adopted during the war would carry over into the post-war period. One matter left hanging through the war and after, to the consternation of the Newfoundland Federation of Labour, was that procedure whereby a union could be certified by the government as an exclusive bargaining agent. This change was not made until 1950, when a new labour relations act was passed in radically different constitutional circumstances.[154]

By the time the 1944 act was passed, the Labour Relations Office had established itself as an indispensable arm of government. In August 1942 in order to be able to allocate labour as the war situation required, the Commission decided on a national registration. This was "for the purpose of ascertaining and recording the extent of the manpower employed or employable in the country, its distribution throughout the various industries or avenues of employment and the amount available for any industry considered essential to the efficient prosecution of the war and the general welfare of the country."[155] The registration was carried out under Walsh's direction and employed the services of, among others, teachers and rangers.[156] From 31 December 1942 nobody could obtain employment in Newfoundland or leave the country by ship or aeroplane without producing a certificate of registration.[157] The age of the identity card had come to a society that prided itself on its informality.

Other far-reaching government controls were also an accepted part of everyday life in Newfoundland by this time. Following the outbreak of war, the cost of living in the country rose steadily. Assuming a base figure of 100 on 1 October 1938, the cost of living index, as worked out by the government, stood a year later at 104.4. By December 1941, however, it had jumped to 131.6 and twelve months later it reached 150.2.[158] These substantial increases were attributed by the Commission largely to higher prices for imported goods, inflated transportation and insurance costs, and enhanced consumer purchasing power. To prevent a bad situation from becoming worse, the government in late 1941 brought in a series of new control measures. In November the advisory committee appointed in 1939 to assist the food controller was dissolved and replaced by a committee of the Commission itself.[159] Next, two sets of regulations were issued under the versatile and serviceable Emergency Powers (Defence) Act, one, the Defence (Price of Goods) Regulations, dealing with prices and the other, the Defence (Rent Restrictions) Regulations, with rents. Under the provisions of the first of these, Puddester issued what was known as the Food (Current Prices) Order. This exemplified the approach of the Commission, which was to control the prices of individual products rather than impose a general regime of restriction, a course which would have been administratively very complex in a country as dependent on imports as Newfoundland. Thus by the food prices order a "specified good" could not be sold above its "current price." For the moment the only product singled out in this way was liquid cow's milk, the price of which was set from the first of the new year at its 15 December 1941 level.[160] But in May 1942, many other dietary items, most of them Newfoundland staples, were also brought within the price control framework. According to one estimate, by the end of 1942, "60 % of all foodstuffs had been brought under some form of price control." Other products whose price at one time or another during the war came under government regulation included coal, tires and tubes, motor fuel used by fishermen, gasoline, axes, and various agricultural implements.[161]

As far as rent was concerned – and this was an especially important factor in St. John's where there was much rental property and a growing demand for more – the Commission's 1941 regulations fixed rents on houses let on 30 June 1941 at what was being charged on that date.[162] In the case of houses let thereafter, the commissioner for public utilities was authorized to set maximum rates. He was also empowered at his discretion, to appoint, in an advisory capacity, a rent control board to advise him on landlord and tenant grievances. What the government intended in all this, Puddester explained in a radio address at the end of the year, was to prevent "the man of moderate or poor means being penalized unduly by having his rent increased to such an extent that it would be impossible for him to pay it without his family suffering undue hardship."[163] This was a familiar refrain in Newfoundland politics; it allowed the Commission to claim it was a champion of fair play in the market place for the little man working to get by on his own.

Yet another feature of the government's wartime regulatory machinery involved the working out of supply arrangements with Canada and the United States. The nerve centre of this operation was the Supplies Division of the Department of Public Works, headed by W.E. Curtis, who reported to the commissioner for public utilities. In October 1941 the government sent an official to Washington to work with the British Purchasing Commission there on its Newfoundland supply business. Subsequently, Newfoundland opened its own Supply Liaison Office, headed by Frank Hue, in the American capital. At home after October 1941, applications from importers seeking preference in supply were assessed by a government-appointed priorities committee, which included two representatives of the Newfoundland Board of Trade.[164]

In May 1942 the Kentucky native George D. Hopper, who had been transferred a year earlier from Winnipeg to succeed Harold B. Quarton as United States Consul General at St. John's, reported to Washington that he detected a "state of mind" among many Newfoundlanders which indicated "complacency and indifference as to the war effort."[165] In support of this contention he sent the State Department a copy of an editorial from the 4 April 1942 issue of the *Trade Review*, which was published by the Newfoundland Board of Trade.[166] This asked the startling question "Is there a war on," a query justified as follows: "Business is not 'as usual' but very much better than usual. Shopping crowds positively throng the streets in fine weather. Covetous renters are charging abnormal rentals to families of servicemen of one or other of the United Nations. There appears to be no diminution of social life or amusement." Hopper was surprised and evidently dismayed by what he perceived to be the "tendency of many Newfoundlanders to lag behind" his own countrymen "in willingness to undergo personal sacrifice of long enjoyed privileges," but then he had not been in Newfoundland during the 1930s.[167] If he had been, the indulgence he claimed to see about him would have been more understandable. Collectively, Newfoundlanders had been let out of the poor house, and if they paused to enjoy the view, this was understandable. Perhaps Governor Walwyn came closer to the mark when he told Eric Machtig in August 1943, that Newfoundlanders were "dazzled by American dollars, hygiene and efficiency."[168]

Politically, the consequences of the economic revival were fundamental. Having emerged unscathed from what it perceived as a period of grave political danger following the announcement of the terms of the Leased Bases Agreement, the Commission handily repulsed all later challenges to its authority. Several factors aided the government's position in this regard. The great distraction of prosperity was obviously one. Then again the Commission system could be defended while the war was in progress on the grounds that constitutional change would disrupt the military effort and be unfair to those serving and working overseas who would be denied a say in what was being done. To engage in political agitation in wartime, moreover, carried the clear risk of appearing disloyal. Advocacy of a change in the system of government was possible but had to be dressed up as somehow helping the war effort, not an easy case to make. Furthermore, Newfoundlanders lacked political parties to mobilize their discontents. Working to the government's advantage also was the fact that the people, when they thought about it at all, were divided as to what the next constitutional step should be. This made it easy to play one group off against another. The noisiest criticism of the Commission system continued to come from the St. John's business community, but its opposition could always be portrayed as self-serving, as indeed it was. By contrast, important elements of the labour movement, which grew in strength during the war from approximately 35,000 unionists in 1939 to about 42,000 in 1945 accepted the continuation for the time being of the constitutional status quo.[169] Their basic position was expressed in a letter which F.A.F. Lush, the secretary of the Newfoundland Federation of Labour, addressed to the secretary of state in May 1941, appealing for Gorvin to be kept in the country to continue his good work: "It is probably regarded as essential that for the duration of the war, Newfoundland will be ruled by the present form of government. It is natural that a British people should regard some of its immediate implications with disfavour. But it is true that the vast majority of Newfoundlanders are reasonable and knowledgeable enough to take advantage of the opportunities which it presents as a period of transition."[170] With labour thus pulling one way and business another, the Commission had a clear field to go on presenting itself as the disinterested advocate of the common good, an administration above politics and grubby self-seeking.

Still for all the tactical advantage the war gave the Commission, there was good reason to believe that strategically another constitutional turning point had been reached. The post-war political situation would clearly be very volatile, and in the age of the Atlantic Charter the country's constitution was an anomaly that would become harder and harder to defend. As one British document would put it in 1944, "the objections to the present form of Government on grounds of constitutional theory are greatly reinforced to-day. It is constantly stated both here and in the United States that the war is being fought 'for democracy' and 'the democratic way of life'. The more this note is struck, the more glaring becomes the exceptional form of Government in Newfoundland - a white community, on the very doorstep of the American continent, self-governing for the best part of a century, enjoying Dominion status at the time of the Statute of Westminster, yet to-day with no representative institutions and with its constitution in suspense."[171] In 1943 Governor Walwyn wrote that what Newfoundlanders "universally" wanted was "to be on their own with a comfortable grant-in-aid, and little responsability,"[172] but his salty views were out of date, and the belief in London was, as one official wrote in June 1942, that "a new and vigorous policy with regard to Newfoundland" had become imperative.[173] In the making of this policy it was assumed that the existing good times in Newfoundland were accidental and that the island faced a difficult post-war adjustment, a view that persisted even though the base building boom was followed by a period of continuing high demand for Newfoundland's export staples and still further improvement in her public accounts.

The issues at stake for the United Kingdom were brought sharply into focus after Clement Attlee, now leader of the Labour Party, became deputy prime minister and secretary of state for dominion affairs in February 1942. Several months later, having received a scathing indictment of the Commission experiment from Grant McKenzie, his personal assistant, Attlee went to Newfoundland to size up the situation there at first hand.[174] The purpose of his visit, Walwyn was told, "would be to inform himself of conditions in the Island" and to discuss with the governor and the commissioners "the large questions of policy which are likely to arise in relation to the Island as soon as the war is over."[175] No announcement was to be made of Attlee's plan until he arrived in Newfoundland, when the object of his visit was to be "related to the present rather than to the future in order to avoid embarrassing speculation in the Island." Clutterbuck preceded Attlee to St. John's; Attlee himself arrived on 14 September.[176] The following day the readers of the city's *Evening Telegram* were told that he had come "to discuss current matters relating to Newfoundland with the Commission of Government."[177] On the evening of the seventeenth in an address broadcast from Government House over radio station VOCM, a private outlet, and VONF and VONG, the stations of the Broadcasting Corporation of Newfoundland, Attlee praised Newfoundlanders for "maintaining the age long tradition of loyalty and courage which is their heritage from their forefathers." When victory was won, "a new chapter" would open in their country's history.[178]

Attlee recorded his impressions of Newfoundland in a witty and trenchant note. Politics, he wrote, was regarded locally as something of a "national sport," and the Commission system had not only ended self-government but "a form of amusement." Newfoundlanders believed that government was something from which one took rather than to which one gave and, alas, the absence of democratic practice since 1934 had not been offset by any attempt to teach them democratic theory. The Commission had been remiss most of all in its failure to prepare Newfoundlanders to resume self-government. Emerson thought that the Commission should rule for twenty years but had no suggestions about how his countrymen could be made fit to govern themselves again. "He would," Attlee observed, "keep his football team all the season in the dressing room without even a punt about and expect them to be fit to win a match at the end." On the other hand, it was doubtful if the pre-1934 Newfoundland politicians who had been so totally discredited had been any worse than their Canadian and Australian counterparts. What had really distinguished them was their "narrower margin." The Commission of Government had been ill-conceived and was the creation of the administrative mind. It was aloof, and its members tended to work in "watertight compartments" without general purpose: "the machine was running but it was not progressing to any clear goal and there was no one at the steering wheel. All were busy keeping the engine running." Newfoundlanders were disappointed that the Commission had not attracted more British capital, but "hardly anyone" thought Responsible Government could be restored during the war. There was, however, a widespread desire to find some constitutional "half way house," though the schemes Attlee had heard about "would clearly breed irresponsibility." The United Kingdom, he concluded, had these choices:

> We can with general assent continue the Commission till the end of the war. There will then be an irresistible demand supported by all the weight of democratic sentiment for a return to self government. If we accede to this we shall probably have a Government which will spend the available balances in an effort to cope with depression with a consequent return to bankruptcy.
>
> We can refuse self government with the result that we shall have to meet all the odium of the post-war slump which will be laid to our charge because we refused to let the people run their own affairs.
>
> We can try to formulate some system less than full self government keeping the brake in our own hands. We shall then promote irresponsibility and probably get the blame for everything that goes wrong.
>
> We can concede self government now while the going is good and while war conditions impose a certain restraint on the Government.
>
> We can try to devise some different form of Government which, while democratic, does not conform to the Westminster model. We can put off the evil day by appointing a commission of inquiry.[179]

Characteristically, Attlee did not procrastinate and a new policy on Newfoundland was soon forthcoming from London, where contingency planning was second nature. At a decisive moment, British rather than Newfoundland spokesmen once again had seized the initiative.

SYNOPSIS: 1939–42

In 1939, as in 1914, Newfoundland, unlike Canada, went to war automatically when the United Kingdom did. This showed her dependent status. Militarily, however, the country was largely unprepared for conflict. Although a defence plan for Newfoundland had been drawn up in 1936, when the fighting started in Europe, the Commission had to scramble to provide even a modicum of protection for the country's vital installations. Sensibly, however, in laying its plans for the war, the government benefited from past experience. Early on, the notion of sending a Newfoundland regiment overseas, something that had cost the country dearly in 1914-18, was ruled out. Instead Newfoundlanders were encouraged, as needed, to join the British forces in which a few distinctive Newfoundland army and air force units were ultimately formed. In time Canada was also allowed to recruit both men and women in Newfoundland for certain branches of her armed forces.[180] Conscription, which badly divided Canadians in both world wars and which had met stiff resistance in Newfoundland when it had been introduced in 1917, was avoided by the Commission. Given what Newfoundland set out to do in the war, voluntary enlistment satisfied the need for recruits and also favoured social peace. Typical of the Commission's pragmatic approach to the conflict was the recruiting of a Forestry Unit which was to do for the Allied war effort what its members were best equipped to do, cut trees.

From the early days of the war, the Commission insisted that in an age of submarine and air warfare Newfoundland could not defend herself. Its answer to one of the most urgent defence problems in the country, the safeguarding of the Newfoundland Airport and the seaplane base at Botwood, was to turn the job over to Canada. This expedient was at first resisted in London, but, after the disastrous turn the war took in the spring of 1940, the British gave way on the issue with the result that Canadian forces began pouring into Newfoundland. In 1933, Canada had been able to walk away from Newfoundland's troubles; in the military crisis of 1940 she had to admit that her destiny and Newfoundland's were inextricably linked. During the war Newfoundland badly needed Canada, but, unquestionably, Canada also badly needed Newfoundland. Diplomatically, the expression of this interdependence was a complex set of undertakings and agreements which, on balance, proved highly favourable to the Newfoundland and, by extension, to the British position. The essence of this position was to meet the wartime need while keeping as free a hand as possible for the post-war period.

Acting in accordance with the plans of the Permanent Joint Board on Defence, before which the Commission asserted its right to be heard but on which it was not given separate representation, Canada undertook diverse and expensive defence responsibilities in Newfoundland although she could look forward to only limited compensating advantages in the country once the victory was won; after the war, Gander, Botwood, and

Gleneagles were scheduled to be returned to Newfoundland control. Moreover, at Newfoundland's insistence, the United Kingdom had retained the ownership of the naval base in St. John's even though it was being run by the Royal Canadian Navy. Again while it was true that Canada owned Torbay Airport, her position there left much to be desired. An October 1943 Department of External Affairs memorandum pointed out that "at any time, at the sole discretion of the Newfoundland Government, Canada might find herself unable to use the Torbay Airport for either civil or military purposes."[181] At Goose Bay Canada had the promise of a ninety-nine year lease, but a final agreement would have to be negotiated with a newly enhanced Commission of Government, which after the Anglo-American Leased Bases Agreement was more sensitive than ever to being accused of giving away the country's assets. Without doubt, Canadian influence grew dramatically in Newfoundland after 1939,[182] yet it was far from being predominant, considering that the Newfoundland Government was accountable to the United Kingdom, and that once the United States burst on to the scene, it set the pace in defence spending. According to a 1946 Canadian estimate, United States military investment in Newfoundland was over $300,000,000, roughly more than three times Ottawa's defence spending there.[183]

The contrast between what the United States had secured in Newfoundland and what Canada had obtained there was striking. In the Leased Bases Agreement, to the dismay of the Newfoundland government, the United States had carved out extensive extra-territorial rights on the island for ninety-nine years, rights far beyond anything conceded to Canada. Why this disparity? On the surface, the fact that the United Kingdom and Newfoundland had actually built the bases at Gander and Botwood justified the arrangements made for them. But beyond this was a larger reality: Canada was in the war and could be counted on for support, while the United States had to be won over. In other words, in the complex process of give and take which went on behind the scenes in relation to Newfoundland, the United States and Canada were in fundamentally different positions vis-à-vis the United Kingdom, the final arbiter of what would obtain there because she controlled the Commission of Government. What happened diplomatically in Newfoundland after 1939, therefore, did not illustrate "the North Atlantic triangle" in action. J.B. Brebner's clever 1945 title would comfort a generation of Canadians about the nature of their role in the war and in international affairs generally, but it is doubtful whether the metaphor of a triangle can be sustained.[184] Certainly, events in Newfoundland do not lend it credence. There Canada was very much the junior partner of both the United States and the United Kingdom and reacted to rather than shaped events. When all was said and done, the United States had come into Newfoundland with a first class ticket, while Canada came with a second class ticket which only the British could upgrade. In a diplomatic round for sizeable stakes, the United States played a strong hand boldly; the United Kingdom, because she could no longer defend Newfoundland and desperately needed American support in the war, had a difficult hand but played it cleverly; Canada had a modest hand, and, as so often in her history, played it modestly.

When the United Kingdom had created the Commission of Government in 1934 as an answer to Newfoundland's economic and political troubles, she did not appear to have had strategic advantage in mind. Nevertheless, a co-operative administration in St. John's had a big pay-off for her in the Anglo-American diplomacy in the summer of 1940. Whether an elected Newfoundland government would have responded to her needs differently can only be a matter of speculation. No dollar figure can be put on the worth to the United Kingdom of being able to offer the United States bases in Newfoundland "freely and without consideration." However unexpected, this was a kind of return on the investment she had made since 1934. Certainly, the Commission of Government placed a high value on what the Americans were being given, even though it completely misread its own ability to bargain with them. Newfoundland's administration expected to obtain revenue and trade advantages from the United States, but the truth was that once the Americans, amidst great international fanfare, were promised the bases, they were pretty well able to write their own agenda about how they would be established and operated, especially since Lend-Lease was being negotiated in the background.

Not surprisingly, the Americans proceeded to take full advantage of the situation. The best the Commission could do was seek exemptions from the worst features of what the United States was about overall – a foreign policy expedient that Canada would soon raise to the level of an art form.[185] Newfoundland had hoped for a separate deal with the Americans; when this project failed, she sought and obtained relief from what was regarded in St. John's as a harsh arrangement. Luckily for the Commission, the agreement devised in London brought its critics up against the problem of loyalty, which had always limited political activity among the conservative St. John's elite and was especially potent in wartime. Moreover, shaken as the Newfoundland government was by what happened at the London talks, the establishment of the American bases proved immensely popular in the country at large, notwithstanding what became a legal uproar over compensation for those who had to be moved to make way for them. In the spring of 1941, the Commission was judging the Leased Bases Agreement by what might have been, but even at this early stage in the proceedings public attention was focused on the many employment opportunities the Americans were opening up. In this way, a deal whose political consequences the Commission of Government at first feared, ultimately became synonymous in Newfoundland with high times, quick development, and an end to the misery of the 1930s. It can be argued indeed that one of the most lasting effects of the whole bases boom was to add a new dimension to that strain in the Newfoundland political culture which identifies prosperity with the application of foreign capital to untapped local resources. After the economic miracle of 1941-42, Newfoundland's politicians would long scan the horizon for another ninth wave.

Ironically, even in the boom times that the war brought, the Commission's initial financial response was to cut planned spending. This was done in order to meet defence expenditure and to limit the country's demand on the British Treasury to what it actually spent in the United Kingdom. As part of this general policy of retrenchment, and because of rising opposition to it both within the administration and without, Gorvin's reconstruction scheme, as embodied in the Special Areas Bill, was discarded and the commissioner for natural resources himself recalled. His visionary program was the major policy casualty of the war. More to the point, it had projected a line of development for Newfoundland greatly at variance with that brought on by base construction and the resultant massive influx of foreign capital. Once dropped, Gorvin's plan was never revived. Yet in the year of his departure, after having decided against grants-in-aid for the duration of the war, the Commission began accumulating the surpluses which might one day have made possible the reconstruction of rural Newfoundland he had wanted. But by stimulating employment through recruitment and defence construction, the war obviated the need for the fundamental economic and social shakeup Gorvin had advocated and allowed the Commission to drop with impunity the most controversial item in its 1930s agenda. With prosperity, however, and the great reduction in relief expenditure, the government was able to carry out many other parts of that agenda, refurbishing and modernizing without antagonizing vested interests as Gorvin had. Sticking to his thorny ideas simply did not make political sense when the problem he was addressing had for the moment at least solved itself. Instead the government began setting aside money for the rainy day it, in company with many other depression survivors, believed must surely come again. In this instance, at least, its governing financial principle was once bitten twice shy.

If there was a time in this period of upheaval when Newfoundland might have regained some measure of self-government, it was probably after the Leased Bases Agreement. "For the sake of the Empire, of liberty and of the welfare of all mankind," the country had made a big sacrifice which was publicly acknowledged by Churchill. Furthermore, as Penson explained in his 1941–42 budget speech, the Newfoundland government was not only paying its own way but was actually embarked on a policy of giving and loaning money to the United Kingdom. In the midst of a war being fought for democracy, a situation ripe for constitutional change was created. This was understood by Attlee, who told the Commission in November 1942, that "if Newfoundland could be regarded as self-supporting and there were a general demand in Newfoundland for the restoration of self-government, it would not be practical to refuse it."[186] But in fact no such "general demand" was ever forthcoming. For various reasons public opinion in Newfoundland was split several ways on the constitutional issue, and in any case the 1933 Act establishing the Commission of Government had not spelled out any procedure for the re-introduction of self-government. Nor did the Newfoundland commissioners, all loyal men and true, and busy administering expanding portfolios, express any sentiment in favour of constitutional change.[187] With great authority and no electorate to satisfy, what they seemed to want was more of the same. In these circumstances, the moment in which Newfoundland might conceivably have struck out on her own passed by. The war was transforming an old land and people, and the Dominions Office, which agreed with the Commission's view that the prosperity was fleeting, moved adroitly to cover the contingency created. If the war made criticism difficult in Newfoundland, it did not inhibit planning in London. Needless to say, the British began laying their plans for constitutional change in Newfoundland far away from public view at home or abroad.

P.A. Clutterbuck personified this British adaptability. While he had been to the fore in devising and defending the Commission experiment, he was also quick to move with the times. The very model of the model Whitehall mandarin, he was able to reverse himself and bring the same energy and skill to one minister or policy as to another. In the event, he proved as clever in negotiating the United Kingdom's exit from the administration of Newfoundland as in 1933 and 1934 he had been in negotiating her entry. Revealingly, when he was in St. John's prior to Attlee's visit there, Charles Burchell consulted Ottawa as to whether Clutterbuck was important enough to be invited to a lunch he was organizing for the Governor General of Canada, who was himself about to arrive in the Newfoundland capital.[188] This was a small incident, no doubt, but it is indicative of just how far removed, at a critical juncture, one important Canadian official was from understanding who governed Newfoundland. Skillfully, what the British eventually did was not to propose a particular constitutional solution for Newfoundland – this would be decided by the people themselves – but to establish a timetable and a procedure for political change there. To outward appearance this put them above the fray; but in truth, by asserting their right to establish how political change would occur in Newfoundland, they positioned themselves brilliantly to influence strongly what that change would be.

CHAPTER SEVEN

Continuing Prosperity, 1942-45

The problem of venereal disease prevalence is one which has caused and is still causing the Medical Officers of my Department much concern ... As a direct result of the advent here of so many thousands of members of the Armed Forces, this public health problem and several others of major importance has been greatly accentuated. Our existing facilities were relatively inadequate to the pre-war situation. Later developments have hopelessly swamped them altogether.

There are other public and general health results of the transformation of Newfoundland into *a garrison country* that I think I should point out.

Commissioner for Public Health and Welfare Sir John Puddester to Major General J.B. Brooks, Newfoundland Base Command, Fort Pepperrell, July 1943

Happily, Newfoundland's sudden prosperity outlived the defence-construction boom of 1941-42. Contrary to the government's own expectations, employment on the bases and at military construction fell off only slightly in 1943, but by the close of 1944 the work force in this sector of the economy was down to about 5,000.[1] This was a big drop from the peak year of 1942 when approximately 20,000 were employed, but even so the bases remained some of the country's major employers and provided jobs on a scale the Commission could only have dreamt of matching a few years before. Moreover, as workers moved out of defence construction, they were readily absorbed into other forms of employment, both at home and abroad. The transformation of the fishing industry in those years was especially notable. Though the production of salt cod was down in 1943 because nature was somewhat unco-operative, both producers and exporters of this product got the best prices they had obtained since 1919.[2] Their good fortune was a result of Newfoundland's participation in a scheme for the production and sale of salt cod and related species worked out by the Combined Food Board, which the United States and the United Kingdom had formed in June 1942, "to co-ordinate and obtain a planned and expeditious utilisation of the food resources of the United Nations."[3] Under this arrangement, which would remain in effect until 1946,[4] Newfoundland, Canada, Iceland, Greenland, and St. Pierre and Miquelon were allotted market quotas, in order to ensure that supplies went where they were most needed and to prevent "the effects of an unbridled play of competition and speculation." Greater co-operation than ever before was also the order of the day domestically, as the prices to be paid fishermen in consequence of what was decided internationally were worked out at a series of meetings of the Newfoundland Fisheries Board, which were attended by the commissioner for natural resources and representatives from the producers and merchants. Having recorded this "distinct accomplishment," the board looked forward to "an era in which a full exchange of information, engendering mutual confidence, understanding and respect," would "become the keynote of relationships between producer and merchant."[5] Another development that also pointed in this direction was the extension in 1943 of the policy of group marketing to Newfoundland's entire saltfish production. Under the aegis of war, predictability, profitability, and planning had come to an industry long used to living on an economic roller coaster. The crowning touch was the 1943 appointment of Raymond Gushue (who had to be talked out of resigning as chairman of the Newfoundland Fisheries Board at the time of the uproar over the Special Areas Bill) as chairman of the fisheries branch of the International Combined Food Board.[6] Newfoundland's foremost fisheries administrator had become an important figure in world fishing affairs as well.

Paper manufacturing continued to be adversely affected during 1943 and 1944 by a shortage of labour. Because of this and persistent difficulties with shipping, the two mills worked below capacity in 1943, when the sulphite mill at Corner Brook was actually shut down so that newsprint production could be increased.[7] In 1944 the Anglo-Newfoundland Development Company operated at full capacity for three months, but was limited to 80 per cent capacity during the rest of the year. In 1944 also, Bowaters could have employed an average of 2,000 more loggers than were available.[8] Conversely, while the mining industry in general continued to prosper, there was a major lay-off at Bell Island in 1943, and employment remained a problem there through 1944.[9]

Abroad, there was a sizeable demand for Newfoundland labour from 1943 onwards in both Canada and the United States.[10] In the spring of 1943, the United States made an informal agreement with Canada not to recruit Newfoundlanders for its domestic labour market.[11] This gave Canada a free hand in Newfoundland and was in return for a continued supply of Quebec lumbermen for work in the Maine woods. The following November, however, the War Manpower Commission in Washington let the Canadian Department of Labour know that it would now begin seeking Newfoundland workmen for American industry.[12] This step was taken against the advice of Hopper who in April 1943 reported to Washington that Newfoundland workers were "not suited for agriculture or mining due to poor physical condition, inexperience and climatic conditions in the United States plus desire to make frequent visits to homes." Expert labour opinion on the local American bases was against the recruitment of Newfoundland labourers "for any purpose" in the United States because of their "slow methods of work and habits of quitting on numerous holidays and other trivial excuses."[13] Whatever the worth of this advice, it was ignored and the United States soon surpassed Canada in the number of local workers recruited.[14]

In dealing with the various requests that came from Canada and the United States about the hiring of Newfoundland workers, the Commission was able to put newly acquired labour market skills to good use.[15] Its purpose was twofold: to ensure that no workers went out of the country who were needed at home and to protect the interests of those who were actually recruited for work elsewhere. By July, 1946, as result of wartime developments, companies hoping to hire in Newfoundland for work abroad had to submit information under sixteen headings to the Labour Relations Office.[16] This office was thus not only protecting the interests of the Newfoundland labour market but, in effect, performing some of the functions of a trade union for Newfoundlanders going abroad to work. This was commendable and showed that if the Commission's approach to labour matters was paternalistic, it was also protective, a combination that went to the heart of the government's whole philosophy of public administration.

On the domestic labour scene, there was a major change in July 1945 when the national employment registration system ended, although this did not mean the end of state involvement in labour market planning. Selby Parsons, who had become acting labour relations officer in July 1944 after Walsh's appointment to the Commission of Government, had visited Canada and observed the Dominion's employment administration.[17] On his recommendation, a labour exchange was opened in August 1945 in St. John's on an experimental basis for one year. The service of the new exchange was "limited to male workers in St. John's," but in practice requests from outside the capital were also handled.[18] The purpose of the exchange, which was supervised by the Labour Relations Office, was to bring together persons looking for work and employers seeking to hire.

By the end of November 1945, 2,142 workers had registered with the exchange, 1,016 referrals had been made to employers, and 679 men placed in jobs. The work of the exchange may have seemed routine beside some of the dramatic wartime developments, but it showed just how much government had now assumed a permanent responsibility as an intermediary between workers and employers.

The buoyancy of the job market after 1942 sustained the upward trend in public revenue. Beginning in 1942-43, the end of the budget year was changed from 30 June to 31 March, so that the out-turn for that year was for nine months only. Even so, the government had a higher return than in any previous twelve month period except for 1941-42.[19] By the close of the 1945-46 financial year, after record expenditures in the meantime, the surplus the country had realized since June 1940 added up to $28,669,000.[20] At the same time public borrowing since the start of the war amounted to $6,500,000 while $12,300,000 was now on loan to the United Kingdom.[21]

Impressive as this record was, the government's handling of the country's financial affairs did not go unchallenged. The noisiest protest occurred in the spring of 1943 when the Newfoundland Board of Trade came out swinging against the tax increases announced by Wild prior to his 1943-44 budget speech.[22] The increases in question affected both the income tax and an excess profits tax, which had been first applied in the 1942-43 budget. In both cases the increases, approved in advance by the Dominions Office and designed to raise an additional $740,000, were to apply to taxes payable for the year ending on 31 December 1942. On 8 March, the Newfoundland Board of Trade held what was said to have been probably their "largest and most widely represented" meeting ever. One wit dubbed it "a Boston Tea Party without the tea." The Board's resolution, condemning the government's action and calling for the withdrawl of the tax increases, was sent to the governor, the Commission, and the secretary of state. Arguing against the increased taxes on the grounds that the additional money to be raised was not needed to fight the war, the Board claimed that the retroactive character of the imposition went against "the most elementary idea of what is right and just" and was "repugnant to the long established customs and conventions of the British constitution, strictly honoured and observed everywhere else in and throughout the British Empire."[23] By a separate resolution the Board set in motion the establishment of a committee to consider how a "satisfactory form" of representative government might be instituted in the country "as a first step towards the ultimate [restoration] of complete self-government."[24] The result of the deliberations of this committee was the adoption of a resolution by the Board of Trade on 29 March petitioning the King to appoint a royal commission to "determine the popular will with respect to the form that self-government should take."[25] The Commission vacillated at first on the tax issue but ultimately, at London's insistence, dealt with the Board of Trade's tax revolt as it had handled that organization's previous uprisings – by staring the opposition down.[26] The government's position was made plain in a statement Wild broadcast on 27 March. He argued that there was nothing unconstitutional about the tax increase, that only a small number of well-to-do taxpayers would be affected by it, that the money was needed to ensure a smooth post-war transition, and that there was widespread public support for what the government was doing.[27] The Commission would not, therefore, alter its plan one jot or tittle. The board's constitutional resolution similarly failed, and in the process revealed once more just how uncertain and divided Newfoundlanders really were about their constitutional future.[28] The idea of a royal commission was supported by the West Newfoundland Association but vigorously opposed within the labour movement. In April six labour leaders, who were attending a conference in St. John's and whose unions were said to represent about 15,000 workers, adopted a resolution, to be forwarded to the secretary of state, denouncing the Board of Trade's resolution.[29] While declaring themselves in favour of the restoration of responsible government, these labour leaders argued that "if and when" this change was desirable, it should be effected in accordance with promised procedure, that is to say "upon a petition to His Majesty" in favour of the restoration of the previous constitution "signed by the electors of Newfoundland."[30] Until such a petition was forthcoming, the existing system of government should be retained. The labour leaders who advanced this position also "drafted and approved" the requisite petition with the intention of circulating it throughout the country.[31]

On 24 April, acting on the labour leaders' instructions, Richard Cramm, a St. John's lawyer, forwarded copies of this and seven other relevant documents to the British parliamentarians James Maxton and Earl Winterton, the first a left-wing Labourite and the second a right-wing Conservative. These two members, one in the Commons and the other in the Lords, were thus singled out because they had both participated in the 1933 debate on the Newfoundland bill. "You will appreciate, I am sure," Cramm wrote to Maxton, "the feelings of the people of Newfoundland generally, because of the fact that they have no voice whatever in the conduct of the government of their country. This is particularly important at the present time when we have become the Gibraltar of the North Atlantic, and decisions which are bound to affect the future of our country are being made without our consent and very often without our knowledge." Looking back over Newfoundland's recent history, Cramm claimed that it had "long ago been recognized" that the country's difficulties in the early 1930 had been "brought on by the collapse of world trade." Thus "the slanderous and vilifying statements appearing in the Amulree Report," especially those about Newfoundland public men, were "without the slightest foundation." The truth was that the "public mind in Newfoundland" had been so panicked by the financial crisis that it had been "willing to accept its own public men as a scape goat."[32] Clearly, in Cramm's view, the moment had come to right an historic wrong. Yet in practice, the initiative of the six labour leaders and their lawyer spokesman got no further than that of the Board of Trade. They too could be accused of speaking for only one segment of the population, granted a numerically larger one. More to the point, the British, having prepared the ground well, were now almost ready to spring into action with a plan of their own.

For his part, Clutterbuck noted that the labour initiative did not have the support of Kenneth M. Brown, the president of the Fishermen's Protective Union, and "the most prominent Labour spokesman" in the country. Indeed, Brown's publicly voiced opinion that the time was "not yet ripe" for the restoration of self-government was a perceptive assessment.[33] More evidence of labour's divided outlook was forthcoming later on in 1943 when a resolution favouring immediate constitutional change was submitted to the annual convention of the Newfoundland Federation of Labour by the Newfoundland Protective Association of Shop and Office Employees.[34] This called for "responsible government based on representation in the ratio of one member per 20,000 population," with the proviso that "the Auditor General be appointed by the British Government for a period of three years, renewable if they so desire." After discussion, however, the association's resolution was referred back for further study, a move that was in keeping with the cautious approach of the executive of the federation to the constitutional question.[35] Following the convention Walwyn reported on a conversation he had had with Harry Oxford of the International Brotherhood of Paper Makers and the president of the federation. "He is a most able man," the governor wrote of Oxford, "with very sensible views on the whole Newfoundland problem, and a far better type of labour leader than Mr. Ken Brown, who is more brawn than brain. He considers that the Commission of Government have done and are doing a very good job and although he wants representation he does not advocate any change in the present form of constitution for some time to come."[36] Clearly Newfoundlanders did not speak with one voice and in any case had lost the opportunity, if indeed there had been one, to catch London on the defensive.

Having repulsed these further challenges to its authority, and with its nest egg growing, the Commission continued along the path of cautious, measured reform. In April 1944 a Workmen's Wages Act became law. This prohibited "the payment of the wages of workmen in goods or otherwise than in money" and marked a major advance towards the creation of the full cash economy the Commission had aimed for in the 1930s.[37] Another major reform initiative of the late war years would in due course change the face of St. John's. In 1942, under pressure from municipal politicians in the capital, the government had appointed a Commission of Enquiry on Housing and Town Planning in St. John's with Justice Brian Dunfield as chairman.[38] After this commission, which drew many of its ideas from contemporary British thought about cities, had produced six reports, the government in April 1944 passed the Act to Incorporate the St. John's Housing Corporation and the Act for the Acquisition of Lands for Housing Purposes.[39] Other notable departures in the Commission's post-1942 legislative record included, in 1943, the Food and Drugs Act, and in 1944, the Education (Teacher Training) Act, the Venereal Disease Prevention Act, and the Welfare of Children Act.[40] The timing of the last two statutes was indicative of the extent to which Newfoundland had truly become, in Puddester's words, "a garrison country."[41]

The Commission's conduct of Newfoundland's own war effort after 1941 was built on the achievements of the formative 1939–41 period and took advantage of the country's new-found wealth. Overseas the experience of Newfoundland's fighting men was varied both operationally and geographically.[42] The first three drafts of army recruits to arrive in England from Newfoundland were assigned to the 57th Heavy Regiment, Royal Artillery, which came into existence on 4 April 1940, and soon afterwards had the word "Newfoundland" added to its name. In late 1941 after the threat of a German invasion of the United Kingdom had passed, this regiment was reorganized into the 166th (Newfoundland) Field Regiment, which then served in North Africa and Italy. The sister regiment of the 166th was the 59th (Newfoundland) Heavy Regiment, Royal Artillery. Formed on 15 June 1940, this unit absorbed the 191-man fourth draft of army recruits despatched to the United Kingdom from St. John's. The 59th did coastal defence duty in the United Kingdom and on 5 July 1944, one month less a day after D Day, landed at "Juno" beach, Normandy, in the vicinity of Courseulles-sur-Mer. The Newfoundlanders crossed the Rhine on 27 March 1945 and at war's end in Europe occupied Bergedorf in suburban Hamburg. The other unit of the United Kingdom forces to be specifically identified with Newfoundland, the 125th (Newfoundland) Squadron of the Royal Air Force, dated from 16 June 1941. It was kept flying by No. 6125 Servicing Echelon, of which Newfoundland ground personnel formed a substantial part, and acted mainly in defence of the British homeland. The record of service of the thousands of Newfoundland men and women who were scattered world-wide through many other units of the Allied fighting forces forms part of the larger military history of the war. When an atomic bomb was exploded over Nagasaki on 9 August 1945, a Newfoundland member of the RAF, John Ford of Port aux Basques, was a prisoner-of-war there working at the Mitsubishi naval dockyard.[43] Fortunately, he survived to impress on others the living hell of that apocalyptic day. Such was the measure of just how much the war had drawn a largely forgotten land and people into the mainstream of international events.

In keeping with the country's seafaring traditions, the single largest group of Newfoundland enlistees volunteered for sea duty, principally with the Royal Navy. Like their counterparts in World War I, they were known for their versatility, endurance, and singular skill as handlers of small boats. In a much quoted line Winston Churchill once called Newfoundlanders "the most skilful seamen in small boats in rough water who exist."[44] The compliment was well deserved.

Though its activities were not primarily military in nature, the Forestry Unit won its share of credit for Newfoundland as a gallant little ally, a reputation that government spokesmen on both sides of the Atlantic played for all it was worth as the war progressed. Individual Newfoundland foresters were quick to join local units of the United Kingdom Home Guard.[45] In September 1942 this participation was taken a step further when a battalion of the guard, under the command of Colonel Jack Turner, was formed entirely of Forestry Unit personnel. At the end of their service with the unit, many Newfoundland woodsmen in the United Kingdom also found their way into the ranks of the Royal Navy, Royal Artillery, and the Royal Air Force.

In the autumn of 1942, following Attlee's visit to Newfoundland, Emerson went to the United Kingdom to see at first hand how Newfoundland servicemen and foresters were faring here. He broadcast to the Newfoundland people from London during the course of his tour and on his return gave a full account of his visit in a radio address delivered on the evening of 8 December 1942. He asked his audience to increase the supply of cigarettes and sweets going overseas, items which were "far more important to the boys in the forces than socks, or gloves, or mufflers."[46] (To raise money to send more cigarettes overseas, the St. John's Kinsmen sold nuts using the slogan "Nuts to you, smokes to them."[47]) Emerson was ably assisted in his efforts overseas – as indeed was the Commission of Government generally – by D.J. Davies, Newfoundland's trade commissioner in the United Kingdom, whose busy office at 58 Victoria Street, London, had, by force of circumstance, quickly become a social centre for Newfoundland forces once they began arriving in the country.[48] Davies and his daughter Margot also made separate fifteen-minute broadcasts to Newfoundland on the BBC each week.[49] The trade commissioner's contribution took the form of a newsletter, while Margot Davies hosted a program in which servicemen chatted and sent messages to their families and friends. She became the wartime sweetheart of Newfoundlanders serving and working in the United Kingdom and her broadcasts to their homeland made her a household name there as well. A Newfoundland Committee functioned in London early in the conflict to assist the Commission of Government in its war effort, and a Newfoundland War Contingent Association was established there later on.[50] From July 1943 onwards Newfoundland service men and women with time to spare in London could find a warm welcome at the "Newfoundland Caribou Club" in Trafalgar Square. The club, opened by the Duchess of Kent, had been launched by funds raised in a public appeal by the St. John's Rotary Club. It was run by the War Contingent Association.[51]

The contribution of the Commission of Government to the defence of Newfoundland itself remained limited in scope throughout the war but was significant nonetheless. One of the most important duties of the Newfoundland Militia was the defence of Bell Island, an undertaking which led in time to the formation, within the larger organization, of a coastal defence battery.[52] In March 1943 the Newfoundland Militia was renamed the Newfoundland Regiment, and its former name given to what had hitherto been the Auxiliary Militia.[53] With headquarters at Shamrock Field, St. John's, the Newfoundland Regiment at the close of 1943 was 569 members strong, including 26 officers. By this time also there were well established units of what was now the Newfoundland Militia operating at Grand Falls, Corner Brook, and Deer Lake. As the war progressed, many of the volunteers who went overseas to reinforce the two regiments of Royal Artillery the country had undertaken to man, did so after a period of service in the Newfoundland Militia/Regiment. Thus it served the double purpose of home defence and of recruitment and training for overseas duty. Though they had volunteered rather than been conscripted, the position of men in the Newfoundland Regiment was somewhat analagous to that of members of the Canadian armed forces who had been brought into service under the terms of the National Resources Mobilization Act of 1940. They were not required to go overseas (though this changed in Canada in 1944) but were encouraged to volunteer for such service.

After the initial rush to defend the country, the Commission also built effectively on the preliminary measures it had taken in the name of civil defence. In November 1941 new blackout orders were made. The following month the Commission set up a committee to discuss with the commanding officers of the Canadian and United States forces in Newfoundland the emergency measures that might be required should St. John's be attacked.[54] Thereafter, on 5 January 1942, Leonard Outerbridge was named director of civil defence.[55] Later the same month the Commission authorized the formation of a Joint Local Defence Committee which would be chaired by Emerson and would have members from the United States and Canadian forces in the country.[56] Outerbridge had his headquarters at Bishop Feild College in St. John's, and by the end of 1942 the capital was divided for civil defence purposes into four divisions, twelve zones, and thirty-six sections.[57] Bell Island constituted a separate division with a chief civil defence officer who was responsible to Outerbridge. Under the government's plan of civil defence, the rest of the Avalon Peninsula was divided into sections managed by volunteer wardens. The civil defence scheme as finally worked out made provisions for the enforcement of blackouts, the installation of an alarm system to warn of possible enemy attack, the provision of extra fire fighting equipment and firemen, the development of an auxiliary water supply, and the setting up of an emergency communication network for use should the telephone system fail. Plans were made for extra medical facilities to deal with casualties and even for the evacuation of whole segments of the population. For preventing food shortages, emergency food depots were established. As part of its campaign to educate the public, Outerbridge's organization began publishing in January 1942 a series of information bulletins.[58] "Don't say later you never knew," the sixth and later issues of these bulletins admonished the citizenry in a manner that typified the atmosphere of suspicion of the times.[59]

The censorship operation of the Commission was run out of the Department of Posts and Telegraphs, presided over by Major James Haig-Smith, a Scottish born British career civil servant, who had been appointed secretary of the department and Chief Censor in 1939.[60] On 27 July 1942 another restriction was placed on the free flow of information when the government published defence photography regulations, which were invoked for the first time the following day.[61] In May 1942 Newfoundland had been visited by two British security officials, and thereafter the government received a series of reports from a defence security officer. In November 1942 a Commission-sponsored committee was formed, under the chairmanship of Emerson, which brought together the intelligence officers of the Canadian and American forces in the country with various Newfoundland officials. A year prior to these particular security developments, the Commission had issued draconian regulations, arguably understandable in wartime, known as the Defence (Prohibited Organizations) Regulations, to deal with any association, society, group, or organization it considered subversive. Under these regulations all the government had to do to declare an organization illegal was to publish an order to that effect in the *Newfoundland Gazette*. Moreover, in any prosecution under the regulations, an individual who had attended meetings of an illegal organization or spoken publicly in its favour would be deemed, unless there was good evidence to the contrary, to be a member of such organization.[62] To require the accused to prove his innocence went totally against the British common law tradition which assumes a person to be innocent until proven guilty, but such was the perceived exigency of the war situation. Surprisingly, the first groups to be investigated with a view to determining whether they should be declared illegal were not political but religious in nature: these were the Jehovah's Witnesses and the International Bible Association (a separate assessment had been made earlier of the attitude of the German-speaking Moravian missionaries in Labrador).[63] From 1941 onwards the publications of the Jehovah's Witnesses coming into Newfoundland were either held or destroyed, an embargo that was not lifted until 1945.[64] In acting against the Jehovah's Witnesses in this fashion Newfoundland was following the lead of the Canadian and British governments. Rightly or wrongly the government believed that certain of the publications in question contained language likely "to cause disaffection among the population" or to affect recruiting adversely.[65]

On the economic side of the war effort, there was a significant change in December 1942, when to the satisfaction of George Hopper who continued to be scandalized by what he perceived as the laissez faire and opportunistic attitudes of Newfoundlanders and their government in the war situation, rationing was finally introduced.[66] At first just tea was rationed, and only on a voluntary basis, but by the end of 1944 the list of products rationed included sugar, coffee, preserved meat, various categories of footwear (but not including hip and thigh rubbers), and fishermen's motor fuel.[67] Rationing books were distributed under the terms of regulations published in the *Newfoundland Gazette* in May and June 1943.[68] In the case of sugar, special rations were authorized for the months of July, August, and September 1943 to permit housewives to preserve the annual berry harvest.[69] The rationing operation was under the jurisdiction of Puddester in his capacity of food controller, but administratively, the system was run by a group of civil servants working out of a wing of the Newfoundland Hotel. In January 1944, a new public building was opened on Harvey Road which put under one roof the Supplies Division of the Department of Public Works, the Department of Defence, the various officials who dealt with food and price controls and labour relations, a variety of other government offices, and the YWCA.[70] In 1944 the government's supply setup was reformed by the creation of a separate Department of Supply, of which W.E. Curtis became secretary.[71] The new department amalgamated the Supplies Division of the Department of Public Works and the Food and Price Control Division of the Department of Public Health and Welfare.[72] Woods became commissioner for public utilities and supply. The foreign exchange and other economic controls set up by the Commission seem to have worked out reasonably well, perhaps because of the general prosperity of the country. The restrictions brought by the war provided a good talking point for government and people alike but did not in fact demand any great mortification. J.K. Galbraith has written that "never in the long history of human combat have so many talked so much about sacrifice with so little deprivation as in the United States in World War II."[73] This could also be said about Canada and Newfoundland. In truth the de jure rationing of war was but a shadow of what the de facto rationing of the great depression had been in the 1930s.

In Newfoundland some of the biggest complainers, as always, were businessmen, simply because they were unable to stock their shelves with enough goods to take advantage of the cash circulating in the country. In November 1943 Gerald S. Doyle, an important local manufacturers' agent, complained to Hopper about the export restrictions in the United States. Doyle had the exclusive right to distribute Camay soap, and because of these restrictions he could not meet local demand.[74] He had, he wrote, invested "a considerable sum ... in advertising and building goodwill for Camay Soap," and an insufficient supply would mean "great hardship" and "a considerable business loss" for himself and "serious inconvenience to many users" of the toiletry. The existing unsatisfactory supply situation also posed the danger after the war "of the entire loss" of the Newfoundland market for this product. In a scathing reply, which apparently did not fully register with its recipient, Hopper told Doyle that he could do nothing much to help him for the simple reason that oils for the manufacture of soap were in short supply in the United States and that exports of the latter item had accordingly been "drastically reduced." "As you are aware," Hopper acidly wrote, "it has been necessary to set up quotas for about forty different countries that are more or less dependent upon the United States and Canada for supplies of all kinds. The population of these countries having the same standard of living as Newfoundland amounts to three hundred million, while the population of the same group with lower standards of living runs to slightly over one billion." Hopper recommended that Doyle take his grievance up with the Proctor and Gamble Company, makers of the soap, but he noted in conclusion that, to the best of his knowledge, "the allotments of toilet soap made to Newfoundland by the United States and Canada" appeared "ample for normal requirements." If this was not the case, the issue was one that should be taken up with the supply branch of the Newfoundland government.[75]

A striking feature of Newfoundland's import trade during the war was a major change of direction away from the United Kingdom and towards Canada. This was a trend helped along, no doubt, by the fact that the country operated on the Canadian dollar, a vital consideration in a period of exchange control. In 1938-39 the United Kingdom, Canada, and the United States accounted respectively for 24, 37, and 32 per cent of Newfoundland's import trade, but for 1942-43 the equivalent figures were 4, 57, and 36 per cent and for 1944-45, 4, 61, and 33 per cent.[76] In addition to finding a forward line of defence in Newfoundland during the war, Canada also found there a growing market for her export products.

In April 1942 faced with intense competition for shipping space among traders and between traders and the military, the Commission decided to establish a Transportation Control Board under the chairmanship of the general manager of the Newfoundland Railway.[77] Later a representative of the United Kingdom Ministry of War Transport joined this board.[78] The Commission also issued regulations governing the discharge and storage of cargo along the busy St. John's waterfront.[79]

Even in the early stages of war, governments are inevitably called on to deal with returned servicemen whose claims on the resources of the state are hard to deny. In this the Commission was not exempt. As early as 30 August 1940, the Commission had to set out policy regarding men of the Forestry Unit who for one reason or another had not stayed the course in the United Kingdom; in their unwelcome case the government was severe, and the commissioner for public health and welfare undertook "to exercise the strictest possible supervision in connection with any applications for relief."[80]

Returned members of the fighting forces were, of course, altogether different, and with them in mind the government decided in December 1940 that the commissioners for home affairs and education and for natural resources should meet with a committee of the Newfoundland Patriotic Association to discuss the question of their civil re-establishment, a phrase that would henceforth appear often in the Commission's minutes.[81] It has been suggested that technical training for returnees should be provided, and the two commissioners were instructed to enquire if those who had been thus trained would be able to find employment. Having taken this modest first step, the Commission decided, after correspondence with the ever vigilant Great War Veterans' Association, that the committee it had launched the previous year to consider civil re-establishment should become "a permanent body" and have added to its membership the commissioners for public health and welfare and for finance, the first of whom would act as convenor of the group.[82] By November 1941, the Commission agreed that "a compassionate allowance, issued in cash and exceeding, where necessary, the limit of the relief scale," should be paid to discharged members of the fighting forces or merchant navy suffering from handicaps which, while not pensionable, placed them at a disadvantage on the labour market. The amount of this allowance was to be decided in each case at the discretion of the commissioner for public health and welfare. He was now also detailed with the commissioner for finance to "work out the financial arrangements for dealing with the medical examinations, necessary treatment, and return to their homes of repatriated members of the Fighting Forces after their arrival in Newfoundland."[83] These arrangements would be separate from existing pension procedures, but information gathered under them would be available to the veterans for future pension claims. Following these developments, the Commission decided that the committee it had earlier established, now referred to as dealing with "demobilization, civil re-establishment and post-war planning," should have attached to it an advisory committee.[84] As eventually constituted, this advisory body, though dominated by St. John's businessmen, included labour spokesmen and two representatives each from Corner Brook and Grand Falls.[85] Subsequently, subcommittees of the demobilization, civil re-establishment, and post-war planning committee, to which Carew was appointed secretary,[86] undertook with the help of its influential citizen advisory panel detailed studies in the following areas: the rehabilitation of the fishery, forestry and forest products, industrial development, agriculture and land settlement, vocational and technical education, and the provision of education for those whose schooling had been interrupted.[87]

Eventually the planning effort thus undertaken in St. John's, and the very different one launched at the Dominions Office after Attlee's Newfoundland visit, would mesh, – only to be supplanted by still larger policy considerations. Meanwhile, in April 1942, as a further interim measure to assist men returning from overseas service with the imperial forces, the Commission had agreed that, at his discretion, the commissioner for public health and welfare could supply anyone arriving back so in need with a suit of clothes, underclothing, an overcoat, and boots.[88] By this and other carefully calculated gestures, none of them very expensive, a cautious government sought to show its solicitude for a new generation of veterans, pending full demobilization and the maturation of its larger plans for their future welfare and, by extension, that of the society they would be rejoining. As in many other allied countries, winning the war and the promise of a better tomorrow were in Newfoundland two sides of the same coin. "The war and the revolution are inseparable," George Orwell wrote in 1941 in his celebrated essay "The Lion and the Unicorn." "We cannot," he continued, "establish anything that a western nation would regard as Socialism without defeating Hitler; on the other hand we cannot defeat Hitler while we remain economically and socially in the nineteenth century. The past is fighting the future and we have two years, a year, possibly only a few months, to see to it that the future wins."[89] With the possible exception of J.H. Gorvin, heretical views of this sort would probably not have got very far with Newfoundland's remote and highly orthodox wartime leaders. Still, as the conflict advanced, they acknowledged the compelling necessity to be seen as fighting *for* something as well as *against* someone.

On the diplomatic front the government was kept busy after 1941 settling the many matters left over from the big burst of activity that had accompanied the arrival of American and Canadian forces in the country. Simultaneously, the Commission sought to defend Newfoundland's interests under the agreements already negotiated, while dealing with the numerous supplementary requests from the Canadian and United States authorities to be allowed to establish other defence installations and ancillary facilities on the island and in Labrador.

In relation to Canada the biggest item by far was the determination of the Goose Bay lease. A first step in this direction was taken on 28 September 1942 when the High Commission in St. John's submitted a draft lease to the Commission of Government for its consideration.[90] This incorporated a preamble and six articles, and was referred by the Commission to a committee of four of its members for consideration and negotiation.[91] Early the next year, this committee met in St. John's with a Canadian negotiating team. Much was altered in the Canadian draft at this session, which left undecided the important matter of the size of the area to be leased. The Canadian submission called for an area of 160 square miles, a property of such magnitude that Emerson asked whether "the Canadian Government had an aerodrome of this size" anywhere in the world. One of the Canadian negotiators replied that he "thought they had," but later in the meeting Emerson noted that the areas Newfoundland had leased to the United States under the Anglo-American Leased Bases Agreement of 1941 did not "equal one quarter" of what Canada wanted at Goose Bay.[92] Finally, he and his colleagues, with an eye to public opinion in Newfoundland, recommended to the Commission that the area to be leased be 120 square miles, a recommendation that was accepted on the Canadian side.[93]

On 6 February 1943, Walwyn forwarded the revised draft lease to London for approval.[94] This document incorporated the original Canadian preamble but substituted eleven articles for the original six. The term of the lease was for ninety-nine years. During that period Canada was to have on the leased property (called the Air Base in the document) "the right to construct, maintain, operate, manage and control an air base." Incidental to this right she was to be entitled both on and off the property to take various specified actions to make the Air Base functional. While the war was in progress and thereafter as agreed for mutual defence purposes, the Air Base was to be managed and controlled by the Royal Canadian Air Force. But during this whole time the facility was "to be made available to the Royal Air Force and the United States Navy and Army Air Forces."[95]

Civil aircraft would be permitted to use the Air Base "insofar as such use" was "a necessary part of the war effort;" otherwise the base would be "available for ... civilian use" only by mutual agreement. By the same token, and in keeping with what had previously passed between the two parties, the draft agreement provided that the "development of the Air Base" was "primarily for defence" and that the matter of its post-war "use for civil or for commercial operations," would be taken up by the two governments within a year after the war ended. By article 5, disagreement over which would block the completion of the deal for many months, "Civil and military aircraft owned by the Newfoundland Government" would "have the right to use the Air Base on terms not less favourable than those of the government of Canada." Newfoundland labour would have to be used on the base "as far as practicable," and the government of Canada would have to transfer without charge land on the Air Base needed by the government of Newfoundland for official business. The laws of Newfoundland would apply "throughout the Base, and to all persons therein or thereon," and "duly authorised officials" of the Newfoundland government would "have access at all reasonable times to the Air Base in the course of the carrying out of their duties." Lastly, the Canadian government would undertake not to "transfer to any third part[y] in whole or in part the rights, powers and authority" to be granted it by the agreement without Newfoundland's consent.[96]

In a covering letter requesting permission to make a "definite offer" of these terms to Canada, Walwyn explained that Newfoundland had accepted "the view of the Canadian Government that the Goose Bay base must be regarded as a factor in a permanent plan for the strategic defence of Newfoundland, Canada, and the United States." Since Newfoundlanders themselves would not be able to defend Labrador in the foreseeable future, it was necessary to give Canada the means to do so. Hence the ninety-nine year term. Nevertheless, the Newfoundland draft made it plain, in the preamble and in article ten, that the primary purpose of the base was "for defence." The question of the commercial and civil aviation use of the airport had been "definitely relegated to post-war settlement." Moreover, not only had the Canadian negotiators ágreed to a reduction in the size of the property to be leased from 160 to 120 square miles, but they had agreed to drop altogether a provision that would have given them wide latitude to use various resources within a thirty-mile radius of the centre of the base. Newfoundland had no economic reason, so this explanation continued, for refusing to lease the 120 square miles in question because mineral rights in the area were "reserved," and the govcernment had no reason to suppose that there was anything else of particular value in the area. The only foreseeable difficulty, therefore, arose from the fact, based on the evidence of the Canadian side, that the property, with its "fairly extensive plateau," might turn out to be not only the best but perhaps the only good site in Labrador for building an airport. Theoretically, therefore, Newfoundland might find hereself after the war unable to agree with Canada about "civil or commercial operations" at Goose Bay and unable also to build another airport elsewhere. Nonetheless the Commission was willing to proceed because it was "satisfied" that Canada had "sound military reasons for asking for an extensive area."[97]

In fact, negotiations over the draft lease dragged on for many more months, as London raised one objection after another to its terms. To lease the Canadians 120 square miles for ninety-nine years under the pressure of "war conditions," the Commission was told, would be "unwise and inappropriate." Woods, who was directly responsible within the Newfoundland government for the negotiations, strongly disagreed. He denounced the view that there was anything to be gained in post-war terms by holding "back from Canada a few square miles of Labrador wilderness." Indeed, the course of action advocated by London was "well calculated to drive Canada into the arms of the United States so far as post-war trans-Atlantic civil aviation ... [was] concerned."[98] Walwyn also favoured a conciliatory approach on the issue. After visiting Goose Bay in September 1943, he told Lord Cranborne, who succeeded Attlee at the Dominions Office the same month, that if Canada "had not 'jumped the claim' America would have done so." The airport aside, the land in question was valueless and no "water powers, mineral rights or timber rights" had been conceded. The "right thing" had been done and it was "no good Newfoundland being like a dog in a manger." She had "got the use and privilege of a first rate airfield without spending a cent" and a great deal of employment to boot.[99]

Eventually, the British climbed down on the size of the area to be leased, but the negotiations then stalled over their insistence that United Kingdom as well as Newfoundland civil and military aircraft must have access to the base "on terms not less favourable than those of the Government of Canada."[100] The justification for this was that Newfoundland was "under United Kingdom control."[101] Canada rejected this claim on several grounds. It conflicted, High Commissioner to the United

Kingdom Vincent Massey told Attlee, with the provision of the draft whereby the use of the airport after the war for civil or commercial operations would be decided in post-war discussions between Canada and Newfoundland. Canada, moreover, had deliberately avoided making any commitments about the post-war civil use of air bases in her own territory, preferring to leave this matter to be settled either after the war or when "suitable arrangements" could be made through "general international discussions." What the British now wanted at Goose Bay would undermine this policy, for if the United Kingdom obtained the rights proposed, "very great pressure" could be expected from the United States for "similar or equivalent rights" both at Goose Bay and at other bases. Furthermore, by making "special arrangements" among themselves, the Commonwealth countries might compromise wider discussion of post-war civil aviation now pending.[102] The Canadian case was categorically rejected in London, but various modifications of their original demand put forward by the British were likewise spurned in Ottawa.[103] While in London in October 1943 for general civil aviation talks, C.D. Howe, one of the most powerful ministers in the government of Canada, "half seriously" told a group of British officials that they had "no greater rights in relation to ... [Newfoundland] than say Australia." What they were "really out to do," he said, "was to get an air-base for nothing ... [Newfoundland] contributing the territory and Canada the cost."[104] On 30 December negotiations entered a new phase when High Commissioner Burchell wrote to Woods urging that the version of the draft agreement Canada had been ready to sign for many months should now be quickly acted upon. Having explained afresh his government's position in the negotiations, Burchell told Woods that "it would come as a great shock to the Canadian public if they were informed that the only reason for the agreement not having been signed" was the "demand of the United Kingdom for the use of the airport for the full term of the lease." Canadians knew that their country had spent large sums at Goose Bay ($20,500,000 so far with additional spending of $2,000,000 planned) but had been offered no explanation why the arrangement covering the base had not been completed. This situation threatened good relations between Canada and the United Kingdom.[105] The British response to this particular initiative was to propose the postponement of further discussion of the draft agreement among the three governments involved until the war was over.[106] In June 1944 Ottawa flatly rejected this course, but in doing so put forward two conciliatory amendments to the draft agreement. The first of these called for a new clause which would state that "the right of the United Kingdom to use the base for military aircraft" would "be the subject of consultation and agreement between the Governments of Canada, the United Kingdom and Newfoundland after the war." Pending this the United Kingdom's existing right to use the base would "continue unimpaired." The second Canadian amendment would change the format of the discussions to be held after the war concerning the subsequent use of Goose Bay "for civil and commercial operations." Instead of these being discussions between the "Governments of Canada and Newfoundland," they would become discussions between "the Governments of Canada, the United Kingdom and Newfoundland."[107]

While these changes were still being considered in London, the Canadians served notice about what was now at stake in the negotiations. The occasion for this was the visit to Ottawa of a financial mission headed by Lord Keynes, the purpose of which was to settle mutual aid problems between the two countries. On the morning of 15 August, Under-Secretary of State for External Affairs Norman Robertson told the deputy British high commissioner that Canada's financial offer to Keynes would be contingent on the United Kingdom coming to an agreement about Goose Bay.[108]The difficulty which had arisen in relation to that matter, Robertson explained, had become a source of "growing resentment among Ministers" and was now linked by them "with Mutual Aid problems." If the Goose Bay item were left on the agenda of the war committee of the Cabinet, where it had been for months, it was likely "to be [a] constant source of prejudice to all negotiations" between the two countries. In the end, a formal condition about Goose Bay was not actually applied to the Canadian financial assistance under negotiation, but the British had been put on notice nonetheless. Finally, on 23 August the Commission of Government was told that the United Kingdom was ready to accept the Goose Bay draft with the amendments put forward by Canada in June.[109] The agreement was then signed at St. John's on 10 October by Woods and J.S. Macdonald, Burchell's successor as Canadian high commissioner in Newfoundland.[110]

A bitter debate followed in Newfoundland after the Commission published the bill by which it proposed to give effect to the agreement.[111] In answer to the government's call for comment on the proposed legislation, the Newfoundland Board of Trade, the most vocal and well organized lobby in the country, submitted a lengthy memorandum. Macdonald claimed this had been drafted by a committee of legal experts headed by Eric Cook, the Deputy Mayor of St. John's. In effect, it accused the Commission of yet another giveaway to an outside party of an asset that was vital to the country's whole future. Even from a military point of view, the board argued, the agreement presented was for too long a time. Nor was the ninety-nine year term that applied to American base sites in Newfoundland relevant in the present case. That arrangement, made "in special circumstances" and "without consultation with or objection from Newfoundland," was the product of "a critical period of the war" when the United States was "a neutral state with which the British Commonwealth was bargaining for essential assistance." It was not to be expected that the attitude of one British Dominion towards another now, Newfoundland's temporary constitutional inequality notwithstanding, would be "that of a foreign power." Yet this was the apparent reality of the situation. In seeking an agreement of the character now proposed, the Canadian government showed "an attitude of unfriendliness towards Newfoundland, a lack of respect for her national sensitivity and a disregard for ... her reasonable ambition for material advantage." This being so, for an "unrepresentative Newfoundland Government" to have entered into the negotiations now revealed was both "unstatesmanlike and unpatriotic." What Canada was really after in wanting a ninety-nine year lease was "to exercise a prior authority over civil operations for the period of the Agreement." "To expect that she would not do so," the board's spokesmen continued, "is to ask Newfoundland for a measure of confidence in Canada's goodwill towards this country which her attitude in this matter impairs, if not altogether destroys." If the agreement were ratified, Newfoundland would have to negotiate with Canada in order to use a "site on her own territory for military or civil aviation." This would constitute a "national humiliation." It would also involve the imposition of a double standard - one rule for Goose Bay and another for United States bases in Canada, in relation to which Ottawa was following a protective policy. An unprecedented claim was being made against Newfoundland which must not be countenanced: "Financial expenditure by an ally for strictly military purposes has never previously been put forward as a criteria for long term concessions, even in a military sense, much less when they may have such important practical bearing on questions of sovereignty, and commercial activities in time of peace." Either no agreement should be made, the board submitted, or else the document in hand should be amended in three respects: to provide for the expiry of the lease no later than six months after the war, to give Newfoundland the option of acquiring under an arbitration procedure "all fixtures of permanent value" at Goose Bay, and to delay negotiations concerning "long-term rights for civil operations" until the Commission of Government gave way to "a form of Government fully representative of the people of Newfoundland."[112]

On 15 November Harry Winter answered the board on the government's behalf in a letter that was made public. He itemized fifteen criticisms in the board's submission, offered an answer in turn to each, and concluded with a general defence of the agreement.[113] The board countered with a supplementary brief which called for amendment of the agreement so as to provide that there would be no negotiation on "the use of Goose Bay for civil purposes" before the end of the war; that

Newfoundland's freedom "to operate, control, dispose of or grant rights ... for civil purposes" at Goose Bay would not "be prejudiced or affected by its lease to Canada for military purposes"; and that, as previously urged, Newfoundland should be entitled to acquire "all fixtures of permanent value" at the base under an arbitration procedure.[114] These changes, however, were also rejected by the Newfoundland government which, consistent with its behaviour in earlier confrontations with the board, stood firm throughout, with the result that the act covering the Goose Bay Agreement became law on 12 January 1945.[115] After so much hard bargaining, Canada had reason to be pleased with this outcome, but R.A. MacKay, special assistant to the under-secretary of state for external affairs and one of Canada's leading experts on Newfoundland, had some important reservations. He believed that the Newfoundland Board of Trade had won its argument with the Commission of Government and had thereby made the Goose Bay Agreement "indefensible from the Newfoundland point of view." He asserted that to this and other festering defence problems involving Newfoundland there was only one "practical solution."[116] This was to bring that country into Confederation, a cause that the Department of External Affairs soon made its own.

Reinforcing Ottawa's growing uneasiness about having an independently minded Newfoundland off her east coast was the continuing uncertainty about the future both of Torbay Airport and the Admiralty owned, but Canadian run, naval base at St. John's. In the case of the former the Commission broached with the Dominions Office in February 1944, the passing of an act confirming Canadian ownership of land purchased for the airport, an action deemed necessary because of various difficulties which had arisen over title in relation to some of the private properties acquired.[117] Ottawa naturally welcomed this initiative but ultimately, influenced by the uproar over the Goose Bay Agreeement, the Commission backed off, leaving the Torbay land question, together with the issue of the long-term civil and military uses of the airfield, to be settled after the war.[118] Exactly the same approach was adopted by the Newfoundland government in relation to various properties Canada had acquired at Gander and Botwood with the expectation of continuing ownership and use.[119]

More problematic still from the Canadian point of view was the post-war disposition of the St. John's naval base, over which Ottawa made no formal claim during the war.[120] Such a development was anticipated in the Dominions Office when, in 1943, Canada undertook to carry out a needed expansion of the busy and vital facility. But the arrangement actually made required the United Kingdom to pay for the work out of its dollar earnings and did not involve post-war rights, an outcome that was noted with satisfaction in London.[121] Quite clearly, despite the concession eventually wrung out of them in relation to Goose Bay, which in fact was but one move in a larger game, the British, thanks to skillful contingency planning, remained well placed to bargain with Canada after the war concerning her long-term interests in Newfoundland. Conversely, the events of the war demonstrated to Canadian officialdom that there were assets in Newfoundland well worth acquiring.

The Commission of Government's dealings with American officials after the signing of the Leased Bases Agreement and the passing of the 1941 Bases Act were, however extensive, mainly housekeeping in nature. Not surprisingly, an aspect of the presence of American bases in the country on which the Newfoundland government kept an especially close watch was the administration of justice. When the *Edmund B. Alexander* arrived in St. John's an ad hoc agreement on jurisdiction was worked out between the commander of the troops on board, Colonel Maurice D. Welty, and Emerson.[122] This established rules which came to apply generally in judicial matters between the Newfoundland and United States base authorities, though in the early days of their operations in the country the Americans were later said by the Commission to have shown a tendency, the Leased Bases Agreement notwithstanding, "to seek to exercise exclusive jurisdiction over their own personnel in all circumstances."[123] The division of authority worked out, beginning with the Welty-Emerson agreement, left offences committed by American service personnel within the leased areas to the United States military authorities. Conversely, an offence committed on a base by a British subject was prosecuted by the Newfoundland authorities. In the case of offences committed by members of the United States forces outside the base areas, there was initially "a sort of contest for jurisdiction between the civil and military powers," but here too a modus vivendi was arrived at. The workings of this were described by the Commission in a 1945 report as follows:

> Where no civilian or civilian property was affected, such as when a service man was arrested for drunkenness or a minor breach of the Highway Traffic Act, the police would turn the offender over to his military command for treatment. In other matters, not being offences of a military nature and involving civil rights, the offender appeared in the first instance before a local Court, the appropriate military authority being advised of the charge and given the right to attend the hearing. As a rule, in such cases, a remand was granted, during the course of which it often happened that the Base commander would request the Commissioner for Justice to waive jurisdiction and permit trial by court martial. Unless the case were essentially a breach of military discipline, such request was invariably refused and the case went to trial before the civil court. In the rare instances in which a court

martial was substituted, the Department of Justice was always permitted attendance at the proceedings. Conversely, where a service man is the aggrieved party, the civil courts have always been open to him as plaintiff.[124]

This arrangement, the Commission observed, had worked out well but had "not been reached without occasional differences of opinion expressed politely but firmly on both sides."[125] Not mentioned in this summation but important at the time was the difficult personal relationship between Emerson and Major-General G.C. Brant, the American army commander in Newfoundland, 1941-43, once described by Walwyn as an "impossible character ... a better sportsman than soldier."[126] Perhaps the trickiest moment of the whole war period came in 1942 after a Newfoundlander was arrested at Fort Pepperrell in connection with the cutting of a telephone cable in a building under construction there. No formal charge was laid against him by the American authorities, but he was nonetheless held in detention on the base, despite his poor health. When the Newfoundland Department of Justice was handed the American dossier on the case with a request that he be taken into custody and prosecuted, it concluded that there was no evidence against him on which to proceed. Accordingly, the Americans were informed that they should either release the man or launch an action of their own against him in the Newfoundland courts. Instead, they began talking about a court martial, whereupon Newfoundland appealed to the British government for help. Finally, after holding the employee for three weeks, the base authorities obtained a warrant for his arrest from a Newfoundland magistrate. He was then turned over to the local police at the base boundary, but at the hearing that followed the charge against him was dismissed.[127]

In March 1943 the United States proposed that the United Kingdom take action under its United States of America (Visiting Forces) Act so as to give American officials exclusive jurisdiction over criminal offences in British territories where American leased bases were located.[128] The Commission got wind of this sweeping proposal when the United States naval authorities, in anticipation of the proposed change, suddenly became more assertive.[129] Having requested and received information from London about what was now afoot, the Commission told the Dominions Office that the new arrangement sought by the Americans was unnecessary so far as local circumstances were concerned and would cause "real resentment" among the Newfoundland people.[130] Prior to the sending of this message, Emerson told his colleagues that if the government gave "away the right to protect our own people with our own police in our own Courts, the claim for return to Responsible Government would be justified."[131] Subsequently, the United Kingdom agreed to separate the position of Newfoundland if the general arrangement called for by the

United States were actually made.[132] But in fact this step did not have to be taken; the Americans withdrew their proposal, which had been made irrelevant by the passage of time and the progress made in the war.[133]

From the Commission's point of view a successful conclusion was also reached over the payment of compensation to the Newfoundland owners of property expropriated to make way for the bases. Diplomatically, however, this matter was fraught with difficulty well into 1943. In August 1942 under a procedure worked out with the United States Consul General in St. John's, the Commission submitted an accounting to the appropriate officers of the United States' army and navy in Newfoundland with supporting evidence of the claims it had paid to date. In the Army's case these amounted to $1,201,537 and in the Navy's to $362,254. Noting that it had so far been reimbursed only $180,000 by the United States – the sum advanced by the American contractors at Argentia – the Commission requested the British Embassy in Washington to press on its behalf for early payment. The embassy was also asked to take up with the State Department the matter of the payment of the expenses of the Board of Arbitration Newfoundland had established. The Commission explained that because of a telegram sent by the embassy to the Foreign Office in January 1941, the Newfoundland government had assumed that these expenses would be met by the United States. However, the State Department through the consul general in St. John's had recently denied that any such commitment had been given. Since the Board of Arbitration was still hearing cases, a final total of its expenses could not yet be provided but these were estimated by the Commission to be $43,500. Of this amount $40,000 would be charged to cases arising out of the establishment of the American bases and the rest to cases referred to the board in connection with the acquisition of land required either by the Admiralty or the Canadian authorities.[134]

In November, while it awaited Washington's response to this approach, the Commission telegraphed the Dominions Office that it intended to proceed to lease additional areas to the United States. This action, London was told, had been requested by Washington in an application submitted by Hopper on 29 July. The Americans proposed the following changes: the enlargement of Harmon Field at Stephenville from 1,742 to 5,938 acres; the enlargement of Fort McAndrew at Marquise to 4,538 from the existing 3,398 acres for the Argentia and Marquise properties combined; and the enlargement of the whole property on which Fort Pepperrell was situated from 549 to 1,086 acres. According to the application, the additional land sought was needed for both defence and operational purposes. The Commission reported that it had requested "a full statement of the strategic and military reasons" justifying the American application but had received in reply United States military reports that did not add much to what it had already been told. Thereafter it had sought the advice of Major-General L.F. Page, the current commander of the combined Canadian and Newfoundland military forces in the country, but he had declined comment. The government had decided to act now, London was told, "on [the] grounds of general policy and the necessity of cordial co-operation with the United States Government in the administration of their leased areas in Newfoundland." But the American request would not be met in full, as one area they had asked for could not be turned over to them. This incorporated the public road that marked the southern boundary of Fort Pepperrell and the land between there and Quidi Vidi Lake. The lease of this property, the Commission believed, would meet with strong resistance from the people of St. John's. Even without this controversial item the announcement of the supplementary leases could be expected to produce a "loud outcry" in Newfoundland. Since the properties in question were not worth much in themselves, the basis of this agitation would likely be the claim that concessions should have been obtained from the Americans in return for accommodating their latest property requirement.[135]

With the prospect of an unpleasant quarrel on the horizon, the Commission heard from Hopper that the United States Army authorities were not satisfied with all the recommendations of the Board of Arbitration affecting them. The Army wished to reduce to approximately $900,000 the claim, amounting to roughly $1,300,000, which Newfoundland had submitted for those property owners who had been required to make way for its bases. The Commission told London after hearing this news that in determining its awards the board had taken "disturbance" into account. This consideration did not apply in similar circumstances in the United States. Hence the United States Army's objection to what had been claimed, an objection the American naval authorities could be expected to emulate. The Commission's own assessment of the awards was that some of them "might reasonably be held by the Americans to be excessive," but that this case, which lent itself to honest differences of opinion, could not be proven one way or the other. As for what should happen next, the Commission maintained that it would be neither "expedient" nor "altogether reasonable" to take the position with the Americans that the findings of the board were beyond discussion.[136]

Newfoundland sought and obtained authority from London to begin direct talks with the United States about the payments it was presently seeking. On the understanding that no reduction would be made in the amount submitted without prior agreement from London, Woods went to Washington and in early January 1943 met with Hickerson. Woods defended the award of compensation for "disturbance" by pointing out that in Newfoundland productive land had been made fertile "only by dint of the hard labour of many generations." Hickerson said that it was not the size of Newfoundland's bill that concerned him so much as what might happen when Congress was asked to meet charges that did not accord with United States practice in similar claims. Woods stated that he personally would be willing to drop from Newfoundland's claim three items objected to by the United States: the amounts submitted for lawyers' fees (calculated according to Newfoundland custom as part of each award), the expenses of the Board of Arbitration, and "disturbance."[137] Substantial as the concession contemplated by Woods unquestionably was, it had no practical effect. But thanks to a timely British suggestion, a way out was soon found.

In February the Newfoundland government sent the Dominions Office a further statement of its relevant expenses for compensation. In accordance with a procedure now being followed by colonies with leased bases, it was to be submitted to the government of the United States by the British Embassy in Washington. The statement showed that under the heading of compensation over leased bases the amount spent by the Commission had risen to $1,757,751.22.[138] Subsequently, London delayed action on the Newfoundland brief pending the working out of policy on various claims issues affecting it that had arisen elsewhere. Meanwhile, however, the embassy continued to press the State Department for a payment on account to Newfoundland, but without success. The State Department contended that since Newfoundland was in a healthy financial state, any payment to her was best deferred until the whole amount due could be agreed upon.[139] What finally broke this impasse was a British offer to the United States to assume responsibility for compensation for all payments under the whole leased bases arrangement. This offer was readily accepted by the United States, whereupon the understanding arrived at between the two countries was made public on 9 August 1943.[140] The advantages of this outcome were various. From the Newfoundland point of view, the settlement ensured payment in full. At the same time the arrangement relieved the United States administration of the task of seeking an appropriation from Congress that might have proved embarrassing. Lastly, for the United Kingdom, the cost involved could be seen as a charge against good public relations in the United States and in simplified dealings on a complex and touchy subject with a variety of junior governments. By a single act, a variety of conflicting interests had been reconciled.

The attitude of United States officials towards Newfoundlanders as a people was both critical and complimentary, with the balance tipping decidedly towards the latter view as the construction of the bases ended and military-civilian relations generally in Newfoundland became routine. The Americans believed that Newfoundlanders were conservative and backward but on the whole trainable and deserving. In a revealing 1941 letter, Pierrepont Moffat, the discerning United States ambassador to Canada, inquired of Hopper about the impact of the base building drive on "the shell-backed old Tories of the Island."[141] A major irritant to the Americans while they were getting themselves established - and this echoed Canadian views - was an apparent lack of application on the part of Newfoundland workers. In December 1941 after hearing complaints through Emerson about living conditions for local men employed at Argentia, Hopper sent the commissioner a cross rejoinder. The commander at Argentia, he told Emerson, had reported "a steady turn over in Newfoundland personnel caused by dissatisfied workmen ... not accustomed to working through out the day at the speed set by their foremen. The natural habits" of these employees, the consul general continued, "accumulated through years of slow motion at their usual jobs at their outports and other places," made it difficult for them to meet the precise production requirements of their American foremen. Complaints about the quality of the meals being served at Argentia were attributed by Hopper to the fact that many Newfoundlanders working there were "not accustomed to the variety of the food served as directed by the management in accordance with well-known principles of providing a properly balanced diet for men engaged in that kind of work." This inexperience led "quite a few" of the workmen in question to want a daily diet of "fish and potatoes" instead of the variety normally served. Nevertheless, most local employees at the base "seemed to enjoy the food and often returned for a third helping."[142] A month later Hopper reported to the State Department that Newfoundlanders who had earlier been inclined to ask why Americans were in such a hurry when they had "99 years to finish the job" were beginning to wake up to the realities of the war. In the labouring population, however, the tradition of "hibernating during the long winter months" lived on. Thus, despite appeals to their patriotism, many local employees at the bases had quit work before Christmas and gone home on "extended holidays." In one two-week period at Argentia only ten per cent of 3,800 Newfoundland labourers employed had continued to work. Moreover, many of the absentees had departed with the intention of not returning before spring, their purpose, according to Hopper, being to "loaf at home" until they ran out of money.[143]

Carping as this was, the public reputation the United States forces were acquiring and would henceforth assiduously cultivate in Newfoundland was one that emphasized generosity and good works. Having made a clean sweep at the diplomatic bargaining table, the Americans then wanted to be appreciated. When the St. John's arena caught fire in December 1941, fire-fighters from Fort Pepperrell helped to put out the blaze and prevent its spread to other buildings. At Christmas 1941, a $4,000 fund raised at this same base brought cheer to many poor children in the Newfoundland capital, as did a quarter ton of coal to each of three hundred local families.[144] Such humanitarian gestures, multiplied many times over as the war progressed, and invariably well publicized, won the Americans great goodwill. So impressed were some Newfoundlanders with a new road the Americans built to connect Argentia with the Salmonier Line – which was also improved – and thus St. John's, that they petitioned in 1942 to have the Salmonier Line renamed the Bruton Highway, in honour of the United States Army engineer under whose direction the work was done.[145]According to Hopper, Bruton declined the honour; whether or not this was the case the Newfoundland Nomencalture Board declined to accede to the request, and the road in question went on being called by its old name.[146] The Americans also won plaudits for themselves by giving medical assistance, by sponsoring apprenticeship programs for Newfoundland workers, and by supporting the work of the Caribou Hut.[147] On 7 February 1942 the United States Organization opened a recreational centre in St. John's, which raised an already heady local wartime entertainment scene to even dizzier heights.[148] A second Newfoundland branch of the USO was opened in Corner Brook in February 1944.[149] Newfoundland opinion and popular taste were also moulded in a direction favourable to American interests by the introduction of armed forces radio into the country, when VOUS (Voice of United States), Fort Pepperrell, went on the air in the autumn of 1943.[150] With its chatty style, which was a decided contrast to the BBC-like stuffiness of the Broadcasting Corporation of Newfoundland, this station pointed the way to the future pattern of Newfoundland broadcasting.

Inevitably, American men became involved romantically with Newfoundland women. In St. John's, marriages between American servicemen and Newfoundland women took place while the Americans were still under canvas at Camp Alexander.[151] Such unions were, however, frowned on by the American authorities, both civil and military. Hopper told the State Department that "at least ninety per cent" of the marriages in question were being "contracted by enlisted men or noncommissioned officers, or defence base workers below the position of foremen, with waitresses, housemaids, clerks and unemployed Newfoundland girls." The consul general's explanation for the intermarriages taking place was decidedly unsentimental: "The American men," he wrote, "are rendered more susceptible by changed surroundings and absence from home ties, also by the feeling of prosperity resulting from regular pay checks, regardless of their previous financial situation. On the other hand the Newfoundland girls are influenced, in some instances at least, merely by a desire to immigrate to the United States to enjoy the better living conditions they believe to exist there."[152] In fact, a Newfoundland woman who married an American man had to go through normal immigration procedures to enter the United States and, having married an alien, lost her right to a Newfoundland passport, in effect becoming stateless.[153]

In October 1943 another complicating factor was an order issued by Major General J.B. Brooks, G.C. Brant's successor as Army commander in Newfoundland.[154] Citing military necessity as the reason for his action, he decreed that, under pain of punishment, no member of the United States Army's Newfoundland Base Command could marry without the approval of the unit's commanding general. This was harsh in itself, but the order also stated that permission would not be given for marriages between base personnel and aliens. It further required that before the commanding general could given permission for the marriage of two Americans in Newfoundland each had to assure him in writing that one or other would leave the country immediately after the wedding. After the entry of the United States into the war, Washington had ordered the dependents of American servicemen out of Newfoundland and since then had been restricting travel by American civilians to and from there.[155]Hence Brooks's requirement, made presumably in the interest of consistency, that newly wed American couples live apart.

Not surprisingly, Hopper welcomed these changes, telling the State Department in April 1944, that an earlier increase in the allowances paid to the dependents of American servicemen had led to an upswing in the number of marriages in Newfoundland between base personnel and local women. Under existing arrangements, he noted, the wife of a serviceman with one child was entitled to payments from the United States government of $924 Canadian per year. With this income a Newfoundland spouse could live with her parents and support the entire extended family. In fact, some local wives of American enlisted men had already returned home from the United States because their husbands had been posted elsewhere, or because they disliked the climate, were homesick, or could not get along with their in-laws. Expanding upon the views he had earlier expressed, Hopper now wrote as follows:

It is my candid opinion that the types of girls who marry enlisted personnel in Newfoundland is far from desirable. The great majority of them are waitresses, domestics, and shop girls who have endured years of poverty in Newfoundland and who desire to better their situation in life by acquiring an American husband (an ambition for which no one will blame the girl). Many of these domestics had secured employment at the Bases where they formed acquaintances with the soldiers and thus concluded the alliances. It might also be said that a majority of the marriages are between privates, corporals and the waitress-type of girl, and that

> frequently the soldier himself comes from the same stratum of society in the United States. One might therefore claim that it is an "even match" and that it should result in happiness for both parties. Unfortunately the records show that almost two thirds of these marriages are marriages of necessity, caused by misconduct of the parties before the marriage, and which is a severe reflection upon the morals of the soldiers as well as the girls. This condition naturally leads one to conclude that many of these young girls are determined to win their soldier-husband by foul means if not by fair means, and that their consent to misconduct is often a means to force the careless soldier into a position where he cannot refuse marriage.[156]

Elsewhere in his letter Hopper estimated that from January 1942 to 1 April 1944, there had been 350 to 400 marriages between American enlistees and Newfoundland women. During this period also the consultate general had issued visas to 216 alien wives and passports to 135 children of American service fathers and Newfoundland mothers. His own research, Hopper wrote, had revealed that two-thirds of these children had been born within seven and one-half months of their parents being married, but an American clerk in his visa section believed that fully 85 per cent of the unions between forces' personnel and Newfoundland women were "marriages of necessity." Nor were the observations of the consulate in this regard likely to be modified substantially by subsequent applications for visas and passports. Newfoundland Base Command records showed that as of 1 February 1944, there were 130 mixed couples still living in the country, but it was expected that when these came forward for visas the "bad cases" among them would be proportionate to what they had been in the group the consulate already knew about.[157]

Newfoundland seems not to have protested the restrictions on marriage imposed by Brooks, but Canada did, though without effect, when a Canadian servicewoman at Gander ran afoul of the United States regulations after becoming pregnant by an American serviceman.[158] He, in short, could not do the honourable thing, as he wished, and marry her. Overall, Hopper reported in the spring of 1944, the marriage ban was working out well. A few marriages had taken place in secret, but the offenders had been court martialled. If there was a problem, it was that the military courts were being too lenient: "A sentence of not more than four months, with forfeiture of two-thirds pay, but permitting re-instatement in the army does not seem to be a strong deterrent to violation of regulations. In the meantime the wife is on the government pay-roll, and receives her allowance in spite of her husband's court-martial. When the soldier is reinstated his full pay is again in effect, and, if he is transferred from Newfoundland, the wife may be able to qualify for an immigration visa. (It should be stated here that these applicants are required to present evidence of assured means of support other than the husband's pay and allowances, unless it be a case of a high ranking officer who has been in the military service for several years)."[159]

Harsh as such private sentiments undoubtedly were, they apparently did not endanger the good working relationship which had developed between the United States and the local authorities in Newfoundland. In comparison with their Canadian counterparts in the country, the American forces were given high marks by Newfoundland officialdom, a view which might have been encouraged by lavish American entertainment of local higher ups.[160] As Walwyn told Machtig in 1944, "The behaviour of the Americans, except in isolated incidents in the early days, has been infinitely better than that of the Canadians, and is so to-day."[161] In a similar vein the governor reported in October 1945, that "the conduct of the United States forces outside the bases and in relation to Newfoundland citizens" had, generally speaking, "been exceedingly good." They had been "distinctly better behaved in the mass than their Canadian friends and than the gangs of civilian toughs who were often at the bottom of international street fights for which the visitors were too readily blamed." Moreover, the Americans had done and would continue to do "much towards the modernization of Newfoundland building, architecture, communication systems and the art of better and more comfortable living generally."[162]

This latter point was not lost on London, where it had long since been recognized that the existence of the leased bases had aroused in those Newfoundlanders who had mixed with the Americans "a demand for a better standard of living in almost every direction."[163] As they contemplated Newfoundland's constitutional future after the war, the United Kingdom's policy makers recognized that this was a new political reality their plans would have to take into account.

CHAPTER EIGHT

Planning for War and Peace, 1942-45

The Governor, Sir Humphrey Walwyn, left St. John's about the middle of March for one of his periodic trips to the northern and western sections of the Island ... It is interesting to note that the Governor, who is not particularly eager to appear on the public platform, delivered a short address on March 25 at Grand Falls. He discussed the labor situation in Newfoundland and urged workmen not to be tempted by high wages for temporary work (meaning work on the Bases). He urged workmen to return to the woods and to the fisheries. His appeal for more wood cutters was naturally well received at Grand Falls as the paper mills are suffering from a serious shortage of wood cutters. The Governor also referred to the present controversy over increased taxes and stated that representative government is desirable and that Newfoundland should have it, but after the war. He added "*Let us win the war first*, the lads over seas do not want representation handed down to them on a platter while they are away."

George Hopper to Secretary of State, Washington, D.C., 2 April 1943

Shortly after his return to London from Newfoundland, Attlee took the first step in drawing up the United Kingdom's plans for Newfoundland which the events of the war had made necessary. This resulted in a lengthy telegram to the Commission dated 25 November 1942. So as not to be caught unprepared, it was important, he wrote, to devise plans for constitutional change in Newfoundland for when the war was over. For the time being Confederation had to be ruled out as it was unacceptable to public opinion in both Canada and Newfoundland. This left three possibilities: continuing the existing system, self-government, or a constitutional "half-way house." Of these only the second and third were realistic since the existing form of government would not be appropriate after the war. What Newfoundlanders seemed to favour, to the extent that they had considered the matter, was not "self-government at a single plunge" but a two-stage process whereby Whitehall would at first retain some financial control. The United Kingdom was not, of course, an entirely free agent in the matter because a "contract" had been made with the people of Newfoundland in 1933. In a different vein, noting how "undesirable" it was to have "all political activity ... focussed on St. John's," Attlee advocated the creation of regional citizens' committees along the lines of the West Newfoundland Association already functioning in Corner Brook. These would not merely provide an outlet for expressing grievances, but would animate the political life of the country through general discussion of both local and island-wide problems. Lastly, Attlee asked the Commission's opinion of the worth of a special enquiry into Newfoundland's post-war economic prospects.[1]

In its reply the Commission agreed that there were economic difficulties ahead for Newfoundland; the prevailing prosperity was "accidental" and was already being eroded. With public expectations rising, Newfoundland would need assistance "for a number of years" to meet her obligations. This being so, the Commission contended, a wider range of possible forms of government than that proposed by London should be examined. In particular, the continuation of the existing system and Confederation should be considered. While there undoubtedly were some Newfoundlanders who desired to return to Responsible Government after the war, there were others, perhaps a larger group, who feared that such a change, without proof that the country could support itself, would be economically unfortunate. A majority would probably support change, but many believed that Newfoundland could have Responsible Government *and* grants-in-aid. If the latter were deemed impossible, incorporation into a larger state would look more attractive and a constitutional vote might produce a different result. Here two possibilities suggested themselves: association with the United Kingdom on the model of Northern Ireland or Confederation. There was, of course, reason to believe that Canada might be more receptive to union than ever before. Her interest in Newfoundland was growing, she feared United States influence there, and she wanted Labrador. Newfoundland's bargaining position vis-à-vis Canada had never been so favourable. Accordingly, Confederation might "be explored in secret between persons in the highest quarters."[2]

Procedurally, the Commission argued, one of two conditions would have to be met before any change other than the restoration of Responsible Government could be effected: either the people would have to be consulted and approve, or a royal commission would have to make such a recommendation. The Commission balked at Attlee's idea of regional councils. Local self-government was readily available for those who wanted it; all that was required was willingness to pay taxes. This was the sticky point, for there was "a profound conviction everywhere, except perhaps St. John's, that the taxation which a man pays to the Central Government is all the taxation he ought to be asked to pay and there is no hope of breaking down this conviction by argument." Regional associations might well encourage political debate but it would be a mistake for the government to sponsor them. It would be better to "stimulate" their formation informally and encourage them once established. The Commission was also critical of Attlee's suggestion of a further economic enquiry. Newfoundland had been the subject of many such investigations, and another would be useful only if it brought together "men of high standing with national reputations" who would be willing to devote a year or two to this work so as to appreciate fully local circumstances.[3]

Next Attlee decided to send three members of Parliament to Newfoundland. This typified an approach which also led him to promote a series of lectures on local and parliamentary government for Newfoundland soldiers and forestry personnel serving in the United Kingdom: the members would educate and animate Newfoundland public opinion and inform their colleagues at home.[4] "Nothing could be more dangerous," the Commission of Government was told in the 17 March 1943 telegram inviting its acceptance of the proposed mission, "than that the Newfoundland people, now for some nine years without representative institutions, and without even any system of local or district government to give them training and experience in the management of public affairs, should suddenly be called upon, as it were overnight, to resume a form of self-government. In other words, there should be some preparation without delay for possible developments." The proposed mission would not have a formal structure but would be "goodwill" in nature. Its members would survey the local scene "and form some idea both of the potentialities of the country and of the capacity of Newfoundlanders to take charge of their own affairs." This approach would have the advantage of showing Newfoundlanders that their "special problems" were being considered by the United Kingdom, without distracting attention from the war effort. It would encourage constitutional debate while "helping the Commission guide it in a useful direction."[5]

When the Commission was consulted about his proposal, it argued for the appointment instead of a royal commission to examine the whole constitutional position.[6] Affecting its response was the business tax revolt touched off by the budget plans for 1943–44. The Dominions Office, however, was not swayed. Thus on 5 May 1943, Attlee announced to the Commons the despatch of the parliamentary mission, pointing out in subsequent debate that Newfoundlanders were "kinsmen" and that by emphasizing "personal contacts" the government was acknowledging this fact. Charles G. Ammon, the Labour member for Camberwell, would lead the mission and would have as colleagues Sir Derek Gunston, the Conservative member for Thornbury, and A.P. Herbert, the senior member for Oxford University and an Independent.[7] After arriving in St. John's, the three men, with G.W. St. John Chadwick of the Dominions Office as secretary, travelled extensively about the island and as far north on the Labrador coast as Hopedale.[8] They were conducted on their tour by W.J. Carew, and by the time they returned to England in September they had canvassed the views of a wide range of people and developed clear and strong opinions of their own. The one bad moment for the mission came towards the end of its stay when Ammon presented Gunston and Herbert with a report he proposed to make on behalf of the whole group.[9] His proposal was rejected by his colleagues and separate reports were eventually given to the secretary of state.[10] These were circulated to St. John's for the private information of the Commission, but the Dominions Office rejected the latter's suggestion that they be published.[11] In 1944, however, to the shock of Whitehall, Ammon published a revised version of his report as a Fabian booklet entitled *Newfoundland: The Forgotten Island.*[12]

Ammon, Herbert, and Gunston agreed that a vote should be held in Newfoundland after the war, though they differed on its timing and substance.[13] Ammon and Herbert also favoured a ten-year development plan, to be carried out with British support. There was altruism in their advocacy of this, a desire to see the United Kingdom live up to her overseas responsibilities, do well by a plucky ally, and ensure Newfoundland a place in the better tomorrow for which the war was being fought; but the development proposed also recognized that political and economic change in Newfoundland were inseparable and that "there must be no Imperial slum on the back doorstep of the United States."[14] In Ammon's scheme the development plan would be the subject of the election. If approved at the polls, it would be carried out by a Commission of Government, modified to include elected Newfoundland members. A second vote would then be held in ten years. If the development plan and the constitutional changes it involved were rejected by the electorate, self-government would immediately be restored. Herbert favoured the early announcement that a vote on the constitution would be held two years after the war, together with a commitment by the United Kingdom to help Newfoundland regain Responsible Government within the next year unless her people chose otherwise. One year after the announcement of the vote to be taken on the constitution, an election would be held for the three Newfoundland seats on the Commission of Government. Before the constitutional vote a "Citizen's Council," soon universally referred to as a national convention, would be appointed to consider possibilities for future government. With the recommendations of this body before them, the people would then decide on the form of government they wanted and the date of its inauguration. For his part, Gunston wanted a vote five years after the war to decide whether Responsible Government should be reintroduced or not. In the meantime the Newfoundland seats on the Commission would be filled by election and the governor return to being the King's representative alone. This latter change was also favoured by Ammon and Herbert. While differing on timing and method of selection, the members of the mission agreed that the governor's place at the head of the Commission table should be taken by a chairman.[15] Walwyn, however, now advanced the view that the election of the Newfoundland commissioners would be a "fiasco." "The elected three or four would probably be Mr. [Gordon] Bradley, Ken Brown, Al Vardy [Editor, *Fishermen-Workers Tribune,* 1937-43] and [Albert B.] Perlin. They would be perfectly useless, and I doubt if British Commissioners could work with them."[16]

On 8 November 1943 with these recommendations in hand, Lord Cranborne submitted a lengthy memorandum on Newfoundland to the War Cabinet. The parliamentary mission, he told his colleagues, had found local opinion on the constitutional question "very fluid and divided." Still, there was general agreement in the country on three principal matters: that the Commission system should not be altered during the war; that when a change was made, it should not be to "full responsible government" on the pre-1934 model; and that Confederation was "wholly out of the question." Union with Canada might well be the best solution, Cranborne asserted, but it was "a matter in which His Majesty's Government in the United Kingdom could not directly intervene." Opposition to it in Newfoundland had several sources: the fear of direct taxation was one, the belief that small regional business would be "swamped" by large Canadian enterprise another, and the worry that "Newfoundland's interests would be sacrificed to those of Toronto and Montreal" a third. Confederation was thought of as a "drastic" step and would not be possible while there was "money in the till." On the other hand, union with the United Kingdom along the lines of Northern Ireland flew in the face of geography, advances in air travel notwithstanding. "What most Newfoundlanders would like to look forward to after the war," Cranborne submitted, "would be some form of self-government which, while leaving the Island free to manage its own affairs, would provide for the retention by the United Kingdom of a general supervision over its finances and would thus enable it to turn for assistance to the United Kingdom Exchequer in case of need. In other words, they would like both to eat their cake and have it." While a "clear-cut solution" would be preferable, the United Kingdom had to be prepared to accommodate Newfoundlanders if they wanted to return to full self-government in stages. What the United Kingdom must avoid at all costs, however, was backing any future Newfoundland government free to borrow and spend as it saw fit.[17]

From this analysis Cranborne recommended that a public announcement of British intentions be made immediately to satisfy the expectations the parliamentary mission had aroused. Such a statement, he argued, would have a "steadying effect" on Newfoundland and should reflect a five-point policy: no constitutional change during the war; the promise that "as soon as practicable" after the war in Europe, Newfoundlanders would be provided with "machinery" by which to consider their constitutional future in the light of prevailing circumstances; a commitment to restore full self-goverment if that was what Newfoundlanders then wanted and if they were self-supporting; a commitment "to examine ... sympathetically" proposals representative of the "general wish" of Newfoundlanders, for either the continuation of the Commission or the introduction of a system that was less than "full responsible government"; and the promise that, pending the post-war review, local government would be advanced and general reconstruction plans devised. At the same time Cranborne rejected the view that the Commission at once be made more representative through the election of its Newfoundland members. There were objections to this both in theory and practice. Such a change would not only confuse the existing chain of command, but by producing "unsuitable men," might breed "disharmony" and, possibly, the "premature break-up" of the established order.[18]

While Cranborne was consulting the Commission about his wording of the proposed statement to Parliament, an alternative plan for Newfoundland was put to the cabinet by Lord Beaverbrook. His position was that the Commission had lost its legal foundation, now that Newfoundland had become self-supporting. Moreover, it was now believed in Newfoundland that corruption had not caused the breakdown of the 1930s, and that Responsible Government had been given up in the interest of the country's bondholders and the Canadian banks. With Newfoundlanders pushing for the restoration of self-government (seven local newspapers were said to be supporting the cause), the United Kingdom should respond generously, thereby strengthening her hand in relation both to Canada's unjust claim over Goose Bay (the lease to this site was still being negotiated) and to the demand that could be expected from the Americans over the use of their bases in Newfoundland for civil aviation purposes. A self-governing Newfoundland would defend the imperial position in the western Atlantic against any "ganging up" by Canada and the United States.[19] Not surprinsingly, this highly combative view did not prevail, and the policy advocated by Cranborne was adopted by the War Cabinet on 19 November with only minor amendments. There was to be a preamble in the statement indicating that the United Kingdom's "whole policy" was governed by the commitment she had made in 1933 concerning the restoration of Responsible Government, and "soundings" were to be taken immediately to determine what particular constitution-making machinery would be acceptable to Newfoundland opinion.[20]

On 2 December 1943, the announcement presaged in these discussions was made in the House of Commons by P.V. Emrys-Evans, parliamentary under-secretary at the Dominions Office. Constitutional means had now been spelled out for Newfoundland, however vaguely, but the British remained open-minded about constitutional ends and still saw themselves economically assisting a new administration in St. John's if they could retain a political control commensurate with their financial involvement. "I would like to add," Emrys-Evans told the House after outlining the main policy points, "that there is no desire on the part of the Government to impose any particular solution. The Government will be guided by the freely expressed views of the people. It is for Newfoundland to make the choice, and the Government, with the assent of Parliament, will be very ready to give effect to their wishes."[21]

In mid-December all three members of the parliamentary mission were heard in a full scale debate on Newfoundland affairs in the House of Commons. Then, on 6 January 1944, in a lengthy telegram to St. John's, Cranborne addressed the definition of the procedure to be followed after the war.[22] He had earlier informed the Commission that he was attracted by Herbert's suggestion of a national convention.[23] He now dealt with the problem of selecting its members and listed three possibilities: nomination by the governor; election by popular vote on a district by district basis, perhaps using the pre-1934 constituencies; appointment by the governor of representatives of selected organizations together with nominees of his own, the whole to form a "complete cross-section" of local society. Of these Cranborne preferred the third, but he invited the Commission's views, while suggesting further that a British constitutional lawyer be attached to the convention to advise and perhaps chair it. On the crucial question of what would happen after the convention had completed its business, Cranborne insisted that the United Kingdom must keep a free hand. The recommendations of the convention would have to be considered in London. How the Newfoundland people would then be called upon to decide would depend on the nature of the proposals put forward and the extent of the support for them in the convention.[24]

Cranborne also asked the Commission to submit a comprehensive program for long-term reconstruction to be considered jointly by the Dominions Office and the Treasury. Assuming negotiations between London and St. John's went well, this program would be approved in principle and published in Newfoundland with a statement indicating the United Kingdom's willingness to assist financially in carrying it out. Because of Newfoundland's present prosperity, such assistance, it was assumed, would not be needed at first. The help to be given later on would be decided in accordance with the decisions Newfoundlanders made about their constitutional future. The plan would be adopted on the understanding that it could be reviewed by any Newfoundland government that took office before its completion. From London's perspective this approach had two advantages: it would forestall criticism that the economic development of Newfoundland was being held back by the procedure that had been adopted on the constitutional issue and it would get reconstruction going while leaving the United Kingdom free to determine its contribution as the constitutional situation changed. In the case of projects which would not detract from the war effort, the carrying out of the plan was to proceed at once. The request for a master economic plan was favourably received in St. John's, where a great deal of work had, of course, already been done along the lines suggested. As a result of the Commission's own planning, the Dominions Office had in principle already approved projects for fisheries, land settlement, and agricultural development.[25] In effect, therefore, Cranborne's new economic proposal was the logical extension of what had already been achieved.

Though it would fuss as always, the Commission was clearly ready to march forward with the planning; but it bristled over what London was now proposing constitutionally, fearing it would be tried or supplanted by a national convention. In keeping with such worries, the Commission argued, in its reply of 12 February 1944 to Cranborne's proposals, that though public opinion in Newfoundland had been relatively quiet since the December statement in Parliament, opposition might yet well up against what was intended. The groundwork for such a protest had been laid in various letters to the editor that had appeared after Emerson had chided Newfoundlanders for their seeming indifference to the big decisions presently being made about their future. The commissioners foresaw two possible lines of attack. Opponents of the national convention could argue that a pact had been made in 1933 between the United Kingdom and Newfoundland which allowed only two constitutional choices: Commission of Government or the status quo ante. This pact could not be changed unilaterally and on the Newfoundland side could only be altered by "the same kind of body" which had originally accepted it, a Responsible Government. Much might also be made of the argument, already being advanced, that the United Kingdom would be guilty of "a breach of faith" if she did not offer Newfoundlanders their old constitution back once they had shown definitively that they could support themselves. If there had to be a convention, however, it would have to be territorially based. A body formed in this way would at least have the strength of democratic theory behind it and could be deemed the legitimate heir of the elected assembly which had made the 1933 arrangements. Members might be returned to the convention in a two-stage procedure. As suggested by Puddester, delegates from towns and settlements would be elected in primary elections. They in turn would meet to decide the representation for the whole region. In this reply Newfoundland's government also returned to its earlier advocacy of a commission to enquire into the country's financial and economic situation and, on the basis of its findings, to frame constitutional recommendations. The Commission submitted that there were only two practical options: Responsible Government or, substantially at least, the existing system. If Whitehall wanted the people to vote on other constitutional possibilities, an enquiry would be necessary to define them, as a national convention, being a representative body, could not define the clear-cut choices a vote would require. Given all that was at stake, the Commission suggested that one or more of its members go to London for talks with Cranborne before he completed his plans.[26]

Two dissenting views complicated this report from St. John's. Dunn, the British commissioner of natural resources, argued that after the reconstruction plan was drafted and funded, a vote should be held in late 1944 on the restoration of Responsible Government. He detected "a strong though as yet unexpressed desire for a change in the form of Government." If the United Kingdom did not satisfy this, she would, given an economic downturn, face a political crisis and have to give way under pressure. The longer Newfoundlanders were kept in the "cotton wool" which had protected them since 1934, the more difficult it would be for them to resume self-government. An electoral verdict in favour of continuing the Commission system would also be beneficial. The Commission's weakness was that it lacked a popular mandate. Only with this would it be able to take the "drastic action against vested interests" that reconstruction might involve. Otherwise its work would be impaired and badly needed reforms delayed.[27]

Governor Walwyn thought that Dunn was "unsettled" and "rather fed up," but his own views were no less outspoken, though they changed nothing in Whitehall. According to Walwyn, the constitutional outcome would have to be "in the nature of a half way house." The commissioners, he reported, rejected this solution because of their belief that "having once enjoyed self responsibility you can't step down," but only a "noisy minority" in Newfoundland wanted old style Responsible Government. In any case the whole debate hinged on the meaning of self-supporting. "The country," Walwyn wrote, "could no doubt carry on in a Robinson Crusoe style and standard now, but with the present standard, which is far in advance of what it was several years ago, definitely *no*; with the reconstruction in sight, schools, sanitoria, cottage hospitals, settlements, roads etc., in fact nearly up to English standard, it is too obviously impossible to contemplate without heavy or continuous grants-in-aid." The United Kingdom should launch the general enquiry the Commission was advocating, but should not call it a royal commission lest it "be greeted with hoots of derision, because we have had so many missions." Though the Commission of Government could itself best guide the proposed national convention, it could not command public acceptance in this role.[28]

The Dominions Office readily agreed to receive a delegation from St. John's but, for the moment at least, dismissed the policy objections heard from there. Dunn's case for an immediate vote was rejected because the arguments against a wartime election of any kind were "decisive." Equally, the worries of the other commissioners about the national convention proposal were dismissed as insubstantial. To say that by accepting the Amulree recommendations, Newfoundlanders had limited themselves, when the moment for constitutional change arrived, to either the restoration of Responsible Government or the continuation of the Commission system, seemed to the Dominions Office to be absurd. It was "only reasonable" that before deciding their constitutional future the people "should be given the opportunity through their representatives of taking stock of the position in all its aspects." Whitehall was, however, willing to be "guided by the advice of the Commission" on the "means" by which the convention should be called together and agreed that that body would need expert and independent economic and financial advice.[29] A discussion followed over which commissioners should go to England. A party of three, including two Newfoundlanders, was readily decided upon; Dunn, Puddester, and Emerson were chosen for the mission, which was to arrive in London late in July.[30] When the British suggested that H.A. Winter (another Newfoundlander) replace Emerson, who was expected to resign shortly to become Chief Justice, the Commission insisted that the latter be included because of his greater knowledge of legal questions.[31] In early June, after the commissioner for finance, Ira Wild, had visited London, more detailed instructions were sent to St. John's about the preparation of the reconstruction program. Specifically, the Commission was told that the plan should emphasize "measures for expanding the economy of the country and adding to its earning power.[32]

The talks which followed in London in August 1944, between Lord Cranborne and Commissioners Dunn, Emerson, and Puddester produced significant advances both constitutionally and economically. Cranborne told the commissioners that, while he had not yet broached the matter with his government colleagues, he favoured the passing of a special act of Parliament to fund over ten years the capital cost of development schemes in Newfoundland which he and the chancellor of the exchequer might approve. The United Kingdom might also, he now indicated, take over Newfoundland's sterling debt if she in turn would put an amount equal to the annual charges on this towards the recurring cost of the development projects to be undertaken. This would be generous assistance indeed, and the commissioners were quick to point out that its announcement before Newfoundlanders voted in a referendum on their constitutional future would guarantee "an overwhelming vote in favour of a return to responsible Government." This being so, the United Kingdom would need to establish a "controlling Corporation" which would remain independent of any future Newfoundland Responsible Government.[33]

Cranborne agreed and proposed that a joint development board be established when Parliament approved the development grant for Newfoundland and while the Commission of Government was still in office. This board would be chaired by a judge of the Newfoundland Supreme Court, and the United Kingdom and Newfoundland would each nominate three members to it.[34] Future United Kingdom members might be the comptroller and auditor general of Newfoundland, who would remain a British appointee for the development period, the United Kingdom trade commissioner in Newfoundland, and "one prominent Newfoundlander outside political life."[35] The board, which would also have a secretary appointed from the United Kingdom, would consider and approve all schemes put forward for funding before they were submitted to London. Proposals to alter schemes approved before the board came into existence would have to be submitted through it to Whitehall for approval. The board would supervise the carrying out of funded projects and report to both the Newfoundland government and the secretary of state for dominion affairs. Newfoundland would be required to produce for publication both locally and in the United Kingdom an annual report, including audited statements, on all funded items. Likewise, it would not be allowed to borrow externally without British agreement while the assistance program was in effect. The advantages of these arrangements to the United Kingdom were manifest; the proposed timing of the establishment of the board was also in her interest. If the board was functioning and accepted when Newfoundlanders decided their constitutional future, the United Kingdom would avoid a direct and potentially embarrassing link between the reintroduction of Responsible Government and the imposition of new financial controls. Again, by the time a decision could be made in favour of Responsible Government the reliability of the board would be known. Finally, the membership of the board would enlarge Newfoundland representation under the Commission of Government and thereby answer local complaints on that subject.[36]

After Dunn, Emerson, and Puddester arrived back in St. John's, the reconstruction proposals made in London were accepted in principle by the whole Commission.[37] But the Newfoundland government, given its administrative resources, questioned both the practicability of emphasizing schemes of economic growth and the wisdom of appointing a development board while the existing constitution was in force. Schemes for economic growth, the Commission argued, would require time to develop and in some cases would necessitate a trial and error approach. It would be a mistake in a published program even to outline projects that had not been thought through. To do so would only "excite public hopes" and perhaps encourage waste. Further, it would be unwise to have two local bodies responsible to London, the more so since Newfoundlanders would not take the coincidence of the establishment of a development board and the reintroduction of elected government as a sign of British distrust. The opposite would be true: "The fact is," the Commission ventured, "that in all discussions of return to responsible government with or without financial aid from the United Kingdom, the hope is universally expressed that 'financial controls' will be established."[38] In reply the Dominions Office informed the Commission that only "a general outline" of the program for reconstruction would be needed for publication. On the other hand, detailed estimates, giving priority to development over social services, would be required for departmental use in London. Nor did the Commission win its point about the development board. The establishment of this body on the annnouncement of the reconstruction program, it was told, would encourage the idea that the economic plan stood "on its own merits" and would be carried out whatever happened constitutionally. In any case, while the Commission governed, the three Newfoundland members of the board would "doubtless" be drawn from its ranks, a procedure which in itself should obviate any problem vis à vis Westminster.[39]

With these explanations the various strands of the Commission of Government's planning effort could at last be woven together, and on 25 September 1944, Governor Walwyn forwarded to London the comprehensive program which had been requested.[40] It was one of the major documents of the Commission period and anticipated much that would happen in Newfoundland during the next two decades. It was above all a fund of ideas for the future and as such belies the notion that the origins of the "unlikely" revolution that would occur in Newfoundland in the 1950s and 1960s are to be found in those decades alone.[41] The Commission's proposals were organized under four headings: "Economic Development Scheme"; "Improvement of Communications"; "Social Improvement Schemes"; and "Government Buildings." The amounts to be spent in these categories were, respectively, $39,000,000, $30,000,000,

$26,300,000, and $4,100,000, for a grand total of $100,000,000. Under economic development, the part of the program the Commission had most haggled over, $10,500,000 was set aside for "Supplementary Schemes ... and Contingencies." Of the remainder, $9,500,000 was to be dedicated to fisheries research and development; $9,100,000 to land settlement and research and to geodetic surveying and aerial photography; $1,000,000 to forest research and operations; $6,000,000 to industrial research and government participation in new enterprises; $1,000,000 to mineral exploration in Newfoundland and Labrador; and $2,500,000 to tourism. Under improvement of communications, the largest appropriation was $16,000,000 for roads and bridges, but $6,000,000 was provided for railway improvement (including dock facilities and steamer services) and $5,000,000 for air service. The communications category also featured wharves and breakwaters ($2,000,000) and telegraphs and telephones ($1,000,000). In the area of social policy, the Commission's plan included major changes in education, health and welfare, housing, and local government services. For education the provision of $8,500,000 included $5,000,000 for school building and curriculum improvement and $1,500,000 for the construction of regional high schools. A vocational institute was to be built in St. John's and Memorial College expanded. The expenditure proposed for the building and equipping of hospitals together with other health care improvements was $7,400,000 while $5,000,000 was to be devoted to housing schemes outside St. John's. Local government was to be fostered with a like sum, while $2,000,000 was to be spent on central government buildings in St. John's.[42]

While the reconstruction plan was thus being completed, important developments were also occurring on constitutional matters. In July the Commission decided to assign Magistrate Nehemiah Short of Corner Brook to look into the mechanics of returning a national convention by primary or secondary elections, or otherwise as his findings indicated.[43] In taking this step, however, the commissioners again disputed in principle Cranborne's entire approach, arguing that in Newfoundland's circumstances a national convention would not be able to convert "wide and complicated issues" into clear electoral choices, but the talks that followed in London in August 1944 buried this criticism.[44] For his part, Magistrate Short quickly concluded that primary and secondary elections would be expensive, difficult to administer, and unpopular.[45] His alternative recommendation, communicated to London on 6 September, was that members be returned to the convention according to the traditions of the House of Assembly, that is, by secret ballot, using the electoral districts described in the redistribution act of 1925 with slight alterations as population change required. In this scheme of things a candidate for the national convention would have to be a voter in and a bona fide resident of a district in order to be nominated for it.[46] Other proposals about the national convention generally agreed on between London and St. John's by September 1944 were that it should be presided over by a judge of the Supreme Court of Newfoundland and that it should be assisted by a British constitutional lawyer. While the convention would not be preceded by the comprehensive enquiry into Newfoundland's situation and prospects which the Commission had long advocated, its members would be provided by the United Kingdom with a survey of the country's financial and economic position.[47] This would be prepared by two officials, one each from the Dominions Office and Treasury, who would go to Newfoundland, not immediately as the Commission requested, but once the calling of the national convention had been announced in Parliament.[48]

The completion of the reconstruction plan and the refinement by the Dominions Office of its national convention policy set the stage for a broader debate within the British government on the future of Newfoundland. On 22 September 1944, Cranborne sent a lengthy note to the chancellor of the exchequer explaining developments to date. While Newfoundlanders, this document argued, would "choose their own course for themselves after the war," the United Kingdom could not "just leave it at that and wait and see what happens." Left to themselves Newfoundlanders would probably opt for a constitutional "half-way house" but this, it was now stated, would be "most embarrassing" to the United Kingdom because experience had shown its impracticality. With the Commission system unlikely to be acceptable after the war and Confederation ruled out as "wholly adverse" to Newfoundland public opinion, the United Kingdom had to prepare for the restoration of self-government. But self-government by itself would not work; an independent Newfoundland would soon reach another financial impasse. Since London "could not contemplate a repetition of the 1933 chapter of events," the only answer was to underwrite Newfoundland for a transitional period. Hence the policy the Dominions Office had worked out, with its interlocking political and economic elements.[49]

Treasury responded to this appeal with a resounding no. Not surprisingly, its opposition was a result of the United Kingdom's dollar situation. Except for purchases in the United Kingdom, the expenditures proposed in the development plan would have to be paid for in dollars; since Newfoundland's banking system was an extension of Canada's, this meant Canadian dollars. It would be possible, of course, to issue Newfoundland currency, but this would inconvenience import trade, much of which was with Canada and the United States. Such a step might also be construed as totally ruling out Confederation. The United Kingdom could also attempt to borrow dollars from Canada to finance the planned reconstruction, but she might thereby prejudice larger financial negotiations of her own with the Dominion. When American Lend-Lease and Canadian Mutual Aid ended, the United Kingdom would have to increase her exports by 50 per cent over pre-war figures in order to feed her people and supply them with essential raw materials. This meant that she must avoid dollar expenditures for anything but her own pressing and immediate needs. Additional and inessential borrowing would increase the danger of "unacceptable conditions" from her creditors and threaten her position "as one of the three great Powers." The conclusion for Newfoundland was inescapable: "We have ... to face the fact that the expenditure now proposed and many other forms of expenditure may be in themselves politically and economically very desirable, but it is a melancholy fact that we cannot afford them."[50] It was a measure of the separation of ministries in Whitehall that so much effort in the Dominions Office could lead to so swift, simple, and stark a conclusion at the Treasury.

Lord Keynes's first impression of the Dominions Office's proposed reconstruction plan for Newfoundland was that "$100 million must be a misprint for $10 million." When the whole of the suggested British expenditure was taken into account, the result would be equivalent, on a per capita basis, to a grant from the United States to the United Kingdom of $30 billion. "Even if we were stuffed with money," Keynes wrote, "this would seem to be somewhat out of proportion." To meet her own needs, the United Kingdom was looking to borrow dollars from Canada up to her ability to pay interest charges and to suddenly find or attempt to borrow a big sum to assist Newfoundland would make her "look extremely silly." Nor did the proposed reconstruction plans make much sense in political terms: "the political argument by which this bounty is justified seems odd. It is agreed that the right long-term solution is for Newfoundland to be taken over by Canada. The argument seems to be that the Newfoundlanders will overcome their reluctance to leave us and put themselves in the hands of Canada if we give them these great sums. It would have been natural to conclude the exact opposite, namely that, after this signal mark of our favour, the Newfoundlanders would be still more reluctant to part company with us."[51]

While admitting the dollar problem, the Dominions Office countered the prevailing Treasury view with the claim that the choice was not whether Newfoundland would have to be helped, but when. By standing aloof until Newfoundland had exhausted her own surplus, the United Kingdom would merely postpone her involvement and risk intervention in more difficult circumstances.[52] Initially, Cranborne agreed both to consider the revision of his department's estimates so as to eliminate immediate British expenditure and "to make some informal and noncommital soundings of the Canadians" before discussions with Treasury continued, but he was soon fighting back as best he could. Eliminating the aid package, he argued, would unbalance and fundamentally alter a laboriously constructed policy and expose the government to "very strong" parliamentary attack. "It would," he wrote, "be an anomalous and hardly tenable position if Newfoundland, alone of the dependent Empire, were to be left to fend for herself from her own limited resources over the whole field of reconstruction and development." Nor was the moment ripe for talks with Canada. Ottawa was preoccupied with transatlantic financial plans for Stage II of the war – the period between the end of hostilities in Europe and the defeat of Japan – while the future of Newfoundland was a topic for Stage III – the period of post-war planning. This being so, "the best course" would be to postpone any further parliamentary statement on Newfoundland. This would cause disappointment both there and at home, but it would also afford a "breathing space" in which the Canadians might be consulted as opportunity arose.[53] On 19 January 1945, the Commission of Government was told of this development, and Parliament was informed eleven days later that detailed proposals on Newfoundland would not be forthcoming until later in the year.[54]

This standstill lasted for several months, although in June 1945 the Dominions Office accepted a Newfoundland proposal that Magistrate Short quietly get on with the work of preparing for an election to a national convention election on a district by district basis.[55] The same month Lord Cranborne, who was in San Francisco attending the conference that led to the founding of the United Nations, had the subject of the future of Newfoundland brought up to him by Associate Under-Secretary Hume Wrong of the Canadian Department of External Affairs. Cranborne's impression from this conversation was that Ottawa "would not be very happy" if the United Kingdom "put Newfoundland in so stable a financial position that all incentive for her to join Canada was removed." Wrong further revealed that the Canadian government had prepared figures on the annual cost of "bringing the Newfoundland social services etc. up to date," but for his part Cranborne said nothing of the reconstruction proposals worked out between London and St. John's.[56] Later in the summer, however, with their own financial negotiations with Ottawa settled for the moment, the British seized on this and other informal expressions of Canadian interest in the Newfoundland question. After the change of government in the United Kingdom in July, Lord Addison, the new secretary of state for dominion affairs, and Hugh Dalton, the new chancellor of the exchequer, confirmed the decision of their predecessors that the next step with regard to Newfoundland should be taken in Ottawa, and determined that Clutterbuck should go there to assist the High Commission in discussions.[57] Significantly, in accepting these arrangements, Dalton reiterated the previous view of his Department.

"I fully agree," he told Addison on 30 August, "that progress must be made with restoring Newfoundland's constitutional independence, but I see no prospect whatever of this country being able to provide the finance for the Reconstruction programme. After taking into account the proposed remission of the sterling debt, we should be committed to providing some $200 million. Quite apart from the effect on our own Exchequer, this presents us with an exchange problem which is quite insoluble. If the money is to be provided, it will have to come from Canada." Clutterbuck's mission, he concluded, would have to take account of this reality.[58]

How were the Canadians likely to react? Clutterbuck himself was reasonably optimistic, as shown in a joint Dominions Office-Treasury minute of November 1944, which he had helped to draft and which surveyed the history of Canadian-Newfoundland relations. According to this document, the accuracy of parts of which the high commissioner in Ottawa questioned, Newfoundlanders and Canadians got on well together individually, but collectively their dealings had "been marred by a long background of mutual suspicion and distrust" which was traceable to Newfoundland's rejection of Confederation in 1869. Canadians had traditionally viewed Newfoundland with "detachment, condescension and even contempt," believing that their neighbour was too small to manage alone in the modern world and would one day "fall into ... the Canadian lap." On the other hand, there was no need to hurry the process of union, as the island would be a liability rather than an asset. Not surprisingly, the result of these views had been to strengthen the determination of Newfoundlanders to remain independent and to promote among them the view that "nothing could be so disastrous ... as entry into the cold and comfortless Canadian fold." The effect of the war had been to change Canadian but not Newfoundland attitudes. Canada had finally come to see that Newfoundland's "full partnership" was necessary not only for her own security but to round off Confederation. The American presence in Newfoundland had driven this lesson home, and the Canadians had come to realize that their previous parochialism had not served them well. Canada's self-interest now dictated a policy towards Newfoundland which would "gradually ... build up an atmosphere of comradeship and practical co-operation in which the union of the two countries could be seen to be in the common interest." But it would take time to overcome the "golden opinions" American forces had won in Newfoundland as compared to the impression left by their Canadian counterparts. This in turn gave the United Kingdom an opening. Knowing that an offer to Newfoundland would certainly be rejected, the Canadians were confining themselves to "friendly expressions of interest" and to "assurances that if Newfoundlanders themselves should wish to turn to Canada they would be given a warm and sympathetic welcome." Confederation was desirable but might not yet be palatable in Newfoundland. What therefore should Canada do? In Clutterbuck's view the answer was "something which was calculated to ensure reasonable stability in the Island until there had been opportunity for a policy of breaking down the barriers to take effect." The plans London had devised met this requirement admirably and might thus command Canadian support. If a self-governing Newfoundland had to stand alone, the inevitable crisis would "arrive *before* there had been any change in outlook towards Canada and while Newfoundlanders were still under the glamorous spell of the lavish American war-time expenditure in the Island." What the United Kingdom intended would eliminate this danger while lessening the expenditure Canada would face in Newfoundland should the union of the two countries be later realized.[59]

This was the background of opinion when Clutterbuck arrived in Ottawa on 15 September 1945. Three days later he and two High Commission officials met with four representatives of the Department of External Affairs: Robertson, Wrong, MacKay, and Macdonald, who was back in Ottawa from St. John's. Clutterbuck opened the meeting by explaining the agenda that had been worked out for Newfoundland and the financial impasse that had now been reached. The United Kingdom, he said, would have to reconsider her plans for Newfoundland and would be helped greatly in this task by knowing Canada's attitude. To Clutterbuck's surprise, the initial response of the Canadian negotiators was "almost entirely negative." There was in Canada, he was told, little public or political interest in Newfoundland affairs. Accordingly, it would not be possible for Canada to provide the United Kingdom with the money needed to back reconstruction in Newfoundland. Nor could the government of Canada fund reconstruction directly, for fear of provoking her own provinces. When Clutterbuck countered with the American threat, he got a more "helpful" response. Specifically, he was asked how the United Kingdom would react if Canada said she would welcome a recommendation from the national convention in favour of Confederation. Such an initiative, Clutterbuck quickly replied, would be "warmly received" in London, union with Canada being Newfoundland's "natural destiny."[60]

Having thus cleared the preliminary hurdle, Clutterbuck moved on to talks with MacKay and Macdonald on the financial implications of Confederation. The focus here was on whether Newfoundland could function as a normal province or whether she would need special treatment, a potentially difficult point. Leaving debt charges aside and assuming the carry over of the existing surplus, it was agreed that a provincial government in St.John's would be able to meet its current expenditures out of normal provincial revenue sources. When this was reported to the larger group of officials, Clutterbuck detected an improved attitude on the

Canadian side. While it was true, they now conceded, that, taking social security payments into account, Newfoundland would not initially pay her own way, there was more at stake than a balance sheet; the potential benefits to Canada were "both tangible and intangible ... through the rounding off of the Confederation." Clutterbuck's triumph was made complete when Prime Minister King told Malcolm MacDonald, now the high commissioner in Canada, that he regarded the union of Newfoundland with Canada "as natural, desirable and inevitable." If the national convention led Newfoundlanders to seek Confederation, the government of Canada "would do the handsome thing by them." But the initiative had to come from Newfoundlanders themselves, and the United Kingdom and Canada had to avoid any suspicion that they were conspiring to achieve Confederation. Newfoundland public opinion changed slowly and King doubted whether "a move towards union" could really be expected. Still he hoped he was wrong, for the convention would offer "a grand chance, which might not recur for a long time, of getting the Confederation question settled without it being made an issue in party politics in Newfoundland." Delay, he agreed, might bring an embarrassing drift towards the United States. In a different vein, Clutterbuck told the Canadians that while in his forthcoming statement to Parliament the secretary of state could not make "any overt reference to union with Canada," he would no doubt want "to deal ... with Newfoundland's reconstruction needs in such a way as not to impede the swing of opinion towards Canada." The Canadian negotiators were less delicate. London, Clutterbuck was told in no uncertain terms, would have to make it clear to Newfoundlanders that they "should not count on receiving further financial assistance from the United Kingdom." This would "accord with the realities of the position" and "assist" Newfoundlanders in turning "their thoughts to Canada." How to influence Newfoundland opinion "behind the scenes" should be the subject of Anglo-Canadian discussions after the British parliamentary statement was out of the way.[61]

Once this understanding had been reached in Ottawa, events moved swiftly to a conclusion in London. On 25 October Addison submitted a memorandum with three appendices, including a draft parliamentary statement, to Cabinet. He told his colleagues that union with Canada should now be the United Kingdom's objective in Newfoundland but that no hint of this should be given either at home or abroad. Newfoundlanders must take the initiative themselves, and the United Kingdom must not appear to influence them; equally, she must avoid words or deeds which clashed with her overall objective. The moment was propitious for Confederation, Addison argued, because the war had "greatly strengthened" Newfoundland's "numerous ties with Canada." Another factor, "perhaps of overwhelming significance," was the attractiveness to

Newfoundlanders of Canada's new social security program, another war-time development. For "most Newfoundlanders," the Canadian family allowance program, approved by Parliament in 1944 and now in effect, "would make all the difference between poverty and comfort." "Once the full implications" of such measures, Addison concluded, had "penetrated the consciousness of Newfoundlanders in their remote settlements," there might occur "a rapid swing of opinion towards Canada."[62]

On 1 November 1945, Addison's recommendations were discussed by Cabinet and given general approval.[63] He was, however, asked to consider further the proposed method of election to the national convention and to address himself to the question of whether an imperial conference should be called to consider a change in Newfoundland's status. The first of these points was raised by Prime Minister Attlee, whose knowledge of Newfoundland was, of course, detailed and extensive. After leaving the Dominions Office, he had kept in touch with policy making toward Newfoundland and had welcomed the plan which Cranborne had devised in 1944.[64] Churchill, he noted in a September 1945 minute, had always favoured generosity towards Newfoundlanders, "the amount required for them being a drop in the ocean of our own liabilities." Attlee also commented in this minute, written after Clutterbuck's mission, about the recent "forthcomingness of the Canadians." Ottawa, he observed, would "have to make a very good offer to overcome the particularity and local prejudice of the Newfoundlanders, to say nothing of the vested interests of the Water Street Merchants."[65]

It was to the latter group that the prime minister addressed himself in Cabinet on 1 November. His worry was that even if, as Addison intended, a candidate for the national convention would have to be resident in a particular constituency to be nominated for it, the "business and financial interests" might still secure undue representation. Reopening a debate the Dominions Office and the Commission thought they had concluded, Attlee wondered whether in Newfoundland's special circumstances it would not be better to have interest groups rather than districts return members. Alternatively, the two approaches might be combined to produce a convention which truly expressed "the interests of the Islanders."[66] Having consulted St. John's, Addison put the Commission of Government's case against this and in favour of a geographically based election. Vocationally based representation, the Commission believed, would be open to "grave objection" because many Newfoundlanders, the majority of fisherman included, were not organized. The groupings that did exist, moreover, were "very divided" in constitutional and political outlook. Again, it would be impossible to decide how many members each organization should have. Nor in the organizations to be represented could the method of election be effectively controlled. This defect was conducive to "intrigues and manœuvres" which might well pervert the popular will. Finally, a vocational approach would be unfamiliar to Newfoundlanders, who would expect the national convention to resemble in form the House of Assembly which had agreed to give up Responsible Government. Admitting the importance of ensuring that workers and fishermen received "full representation," the Commission asserted that this could be achieved by requiring that a candidate have two years residence (war service included) in a constituency in order to be nominated for it. This in itself would prevent business or other special interests from dominating the convention. Addison accepted the Commission's position: "the geographical basis of election," he wrote, "has the great advantage of being unassailable in democratic theory, and I feel that, with the safeguards mentioned, it should give us the results we desire."[67] When Cabinet considered the matter again on 27 November, it was this view that carried.[68] The wishes of the Dominions Office on the question of calling an imperial conference to consider the future of Newfoundland also prevailed. Such an approach would negate the arrangements made in 1933 and be considered "derogatory" by Newfoundlanders.[69] It might also be "highly embarrassing" to the other Dominions, especially Canada.

On 11 December the government's plans for Newfoundland were at last announced in the House of Commons and the House of Lords.[70] Attlee himself made the statement in the Commons, which was a shortened version of the announcement read by Addison in the Lords. The national convention was to be elected on the basis of adult franchise and would be an advisory body only. The job of its members was spelled out as follows:

> To consider and discuss amongst themselves, as elected representatives of the Newfoundland people, the changes that have taken place in the financial and economic situation of the Island since 1934, and bearing in mind the extent to which the high revenues of recent years have been due to wartime conditions, to examine the position of the country and to make recommendations to His Majesty's Government as to possible forms of future government to be put before the people at a national referendum.[71]

In keeping with the 27 November Cabinet decision, a candidate for election to the convention would have to be a bona fide resident of the district he sought to represent. Once the national convention's recommendations had been considered in London, the constitutional issue could be put to the people in a referendum.[72] In the meantime, the short-term reconstruction schemes which the Commission of Government had devised could be pressed forward without delay. On the other hand, the carrying out of the Commission's long-term economic plans would hinge on the constitutional decision, thereby leaving any new administration with a free hand in the field of development. A new, post-referendum government in Newfoundland would have to be given "the fairest possible start," but the United Kingdom must not promise what she could not deliver.[73] "The special difficulties of our own financial position over the next few years," both Houses of Parliament heard in a wonderful piece of British understatement, "may well preclude us from undertaking fresh commitments."[74] Subsequently, in keeping with other provisions of the parliamentary announcements and earlier understandings with the Commission of Government, Chadwick of the Dominions Office and Edgar Jones of the Treasury were sent to St. John's to prepare a "factual and objective survey of the Island's financial and economic situation" to be given the convention and Parliament; K.C. Wheare, Fellow of All Souls College, Oxford, was named constitutional advisor to the convention.[75] The result of the work of Chadwick and Jones was the publication in June 1946 of the useful and informative *Report on the Financial and Economic Position of Newfoundland*.[76] For its part the Commission of Government passed a National Convention Act, dated 21 May 1946.[77] The stage was now set for a tumultuous political drama.

SYNOPSIS: 1942-45

The economic revival that began in Newfoundland in the early years of the war gave the Commission of Government a new lease on life that was sustained after the defence construction boom passed. The war highlighted the Commission's strengths and enhanced its legitimacy. Armed conflict and bureaucracy go hand in hand in the modern world, and the Commission was at its best in planning and day to day administration, skills that were in great demand in wartime. With the clear goal before it of assisting the Allied victory, the government was able to act decisively and get what it wanted. Its intervention on behalf of Newfoundlanders going abroad to work on contract typified its style and approach. Firm government is often popular government and despite the occasional flareups that occurred against it, the Commission's wartime rule appears to have been no exception. Furthermore, increased financial resources permitted Newfoundland's administration to carry out some of the reforms that had been part of its reconstruction agenda for the 1930s. It was also able to build up a financial reserve against the more difficult days which it believed and feared might follow the end of the war. In general the years 1942-45 marked a period of continuing prosperity and progress for the country; individual Newfoundlanders enjoyed the fruits of steady employment and their government took advantage of the fortunate turn economic events had taken to build and plan for the future. Because of their geographical location, Newfoundlanders had "reserved seats" for the war, but in spite of rationing and other wartime impositions the war years turned out on the whole to be very comfortable.[78] In his plan for Newfoundland, Gorvin had imagined an Icelandic- or Scandinavian-like future for the country, brought about by rural revival and the building of co-operative institutions. The war experience probably doomed any such experiment, if indeed it had ever been viable, by pulling Newfoundlanders more than ever before away from the sea and towards North American tastes, habits, and values. Once outport Newfoundlanders saw what was available in an American forces post exchange, they were poor candidates for a rural arcadia, if indeed they ever had been. For all that, however, social planners and theorists, often disillusioned with urban life elsewhere and ignorant of local history, would long imagine otherwise.

The Commission's dealing with the United States and Canada after the arrival of the forces of those countries were cautious and correct. Its purpose was to accede as far as possible to legitimate defence requests from the visiting forces, while keeping the Americans and Canadians within the limits of the agreements they had made and reserving for itself the greatest possible freedom of manœuvre for the post-war period. In general, the Commission seems to have done a better job of keeping track of what the visiting forces were up to in the country than Ottawa did in relation to American forces operating in parts of the Canadian north. Though there were some tense moments in the Commission of Government's dealings with the visiting forces in the country, its own assessment that in the long run things worked out smoothly seems to be essentially correct. Nothing occurred during the war and post-war years in Newfoundland comparable to what occurred in Halifax, Nova Scotia, on VE Day. There servicemen, feeling frustrated and believing themselves to have been unjustly treated by the civilian population, rioted and took revenge on the city.

Politically, thanks largely to the continuing prosperity, the Commission's position was probably stronger in the latter stages of the war than it had been earlier on. The argument that there should be no constitutional change while the war was in progress was, if anything, stronger in 1945 that it had been in 1940, the more so after the British announcement in December 1943 of the action that would be taken after the victory was won. Earlier in the year, speaking at Grand Falls, Walwyn had said: "Let us win the war first, the lads over seas do not want representation handed down to them on a platter while they are away."[79] This was hard to counter. Favouring the Commission too was the continuing division among those Newfoundlanders who were interested in such matters; this division was not only about the substance of constitutional change but about procedures for achieving such change. In June 1943, commenting on sarcastic newspaper references to the announcement of the parliamentary mission, Charles S. Reed II of the United States Consulate General in St. John's gave the State Department this astute assessment of the situation in the country:

In all fairness it must be pointed out that it would be difficult to please everybody in the Island as there are numerous factions, each with its own idea of the politically desirable future: responsible government immediately, responsible government when the time is ripe, responsible government if a better class of officials could be assured, responsible government if it did not debar the country from financial and economic aid from Great Britain, modified constitutional government for the time being, union with the Canadian federation, and, in a very small minority, continuance of the commission form of government. With such a diversity of opinions, one comment is well worth noting - if the Newfoundlanders themselves do not know what to do with their political problems how can an agency abroad know what to do about them. The old jibe, yet still very true, appears to state the case wisely; "Newfoundlanders want responsible government, but without responsibility."[80]

Though patronizing, this assessment was also discerning, but it missed one other crucial consideration - that constitutional questions can perhaps only attract popular attention when they are associated with leaders and policies; in Newfoundland, because of the Commission system and what lay behind it, such political discourse was difficult if not impossible. In the spring of 1943 the announcement of the British decision to grant representative government, with an elected assembly and appointed legislative council, to Jamaica fanned the discontent that erupted over the government's taxation policies. If this, it was claimed, could "be done for a colony of 'niggers,' it should be granted to Newfoundlanders, whose racial purity ... [was] close to 100 percent."[81] But the truth was that Newfoundland had no mass movement for change and no public figures of the stature that Norman Manley and Alexander Bustamante had achieved in Jamaica. And given the history of business-worker relations in the country, the Newfoundland Board of Trade was simply not credible as the saviour of the people. At the same time the labour movement, though growing in strength, was divided about what to do and was as yet only working its way into a formal political role. Prudently, the government made sure that when the going got rough its critics were answered by Newfoundland commissioners, who were drawn from the same class as the members of the Newfoundland Board of Trade. In the case of the Goose Bay deal, H.A. Winter played the role that Emerson and Puddester had played so effectively before him. The Commission showed considerable political acumen also in keeping potential critics busy at war-related work and in advisory capacities, especially in regard to the investigations of the committee on demobilization, civil re-establishment, and post-war planning.

A lingering defeatism in the population and traditional attitudes towards authority among Newfoundlanders may also have worked to the Commission's political advantage during the war. As it was, most of the political debate in the country went on in St. John's and in particular in the newspapers of the self-centred capital. This fact was noted by Hopper in September 1944, after he had spent a vacation travelling on the west and south coasts and on the Avalon Peninsula:

> In talking with various persons of different walks of life I was impressed with the apparent indifference manifested towards their government, and their lack of interest in the discussion (mainly in St. John's) as to what kind of government is best for Newfoundland. Most of my informants seemed to be content with the present state of affairs, as they were busy with their work, their crops, and other matters. Prosperity seemed to have dulled their minds as to politics, and as long as employment and good wages are forthcoming they do not respond very promptly to the appeals of the politicians of the metropolis. Most of them said that they read the newspapers and listen to the radio, but they stated that the criticisms of the Government appearing in the press are written by "paid writers who do not represent much of public opinion." Without so stating I fully agreed with the latter statement of these honest farmers and fishermen.[82]

This was probably realistic. Certainly, Newfoundlanders did not in large numbers seize upon wartime prosperity to demand more representative institutions or a voice in planning their own future. Rather, prosperity seems to have become an end in itself. After visiting Springdale in July 1943, Walwyn noted that only six men in the settlement had enlisted, "as compared with about 30 or 40" during the Great War. "The reason, of course," he observed, "is that all the able-bodied men are drawing big money in the woods."[83]

Yet the war period left an important domestic political legacy, especially in the St. John's business community: this was the sense that the Commission of Government had made some bad deals on Newfoundland's behalf, turning over valuable resources for too little in return. Before 1934 the business and professional elite of the country, based within the narrow confines of St. John's, had been to the fore in advocacy of the Commission system. After 1934 many members of it had come to oppose the Commission on some important issues, most notably the Bowaters deal and Gorvin's plans. During the war, seeing that Newfoundland had substantial assets, they wanted control of the country back. Failure to obtain this left them resentful and retributive: when Newfoundlanders got control of their country again, some of the work of the Commission would have to be undone, old scores would have to be settled, and – this notion runs through Newfoundland's whole history – bad agreements changed. In particular a bright economic future was seen for Newfoundland in civil aviation, provided the Commission did not in the meantime fritter the country's advantages away.[84] The changed mood of Newfoundland's upper class was well evident at the time of the Goose Bay Agreement. Whereas the Anglo-American Leased Bases Agreement, with all its sweeping concessions, had been accepted in 1941 with limited public protest, the deal made with Canada in 1944 touched off loud opposition. If the disaffected members of the Newfoundland elite did not get their way during the war, they emerged from that conflict with a burning sense of grievance and an agenda that was at once new and old: to undo the recent past of the country, to revise international agreements that operated to its detriment, and to drive a harder bargain than the allegedly weak-kneed Commission had done for Newfoundland's resources. In a sense, a phase of Newfoundland's history had come full circle.

In his pivotal November 1942 telegram to St. John's, Attlee conjectured that "if Newfoundland could be regarded as self-supporting and there were a general demand in Newfoundland for the restoration of self-government, it would not be practicable to refuse it."[85] The British could always have fought a rearguard action over the meaning of "self-supporting," but in fact this was not necessary. The attitudes of Newfoundlanders and the deep divisions among them and between the Newfoundland commissioners and their politically active compatriots left the initiative in the crucial constitutional field to Whitehall. By asserting without challenge her right to establish the timetable for political change in Newfoundland, the United Kingdom positioned herself to influence strongly what that change would be. The British began defining constitutional means for Newfoundland while still debating constitutional ends. When, however, they had to invoke the procedure for constitutional review promised in 1943, they had come to favour strongly and were promoting actively a decision by Newfoundlanders in favour of Confederation. What brought them to this position was the difficulty ultimately posed by the reconstruction they had also promised. Financing this, they eventually came to see, was beyond them. Political change was unavoidable in St. John's, but an independent Newfoundland would need a backer. If the United Kingdom could not play this role, Canada would have to shoulder the responsibility. Yet the British had to work towards the goal of Confederation within the framework of the promises made to Newfoundlanders in the parliamentary statement of December 1943. But if that statement had imposed limitations on their subsequent policy-making, its general wording had also left considerable room for manoeuvre – in relation to both Canada and Newfoundland.

Because of the United Kingdom's growing financial dependence on Canada, the balance of power in Anglo-Canadian relations shifted in Ottawa's favour as the war progressed. This was evident in the tactical retreat the British made in the Goose Bay negotiations but as far as Canada's post-war rights in Newfoundland more generally were concerned, the British, because they were sovereign there, remained in a position to bargain hard. Essentially, whatever direction Newfoundland might take after the war would have to be acceptable to London. As the war drew to a close, the reality facing Ottawa was that despite all Canada had done in Newfoundland, she had simply not carved out for herself rights there equivalent to what the United States had obtained in the Anglo-American Leased Bases Agreement of 1941. This made the future of Canada-Newfoundland relations problematic and set the stage for a mutually advantageous deal which the British orchestrated. In September 1945 with Clutterbuck's mission to Ottawa, the very different interests of the United Kingdom and Canada converged in the understanding that the two countries would henceforth work towards the goal of Confederation, Newfoundland's "natural destiny." Because of the public promises she had already made, of course, the United Kingdom could not dictate a choice to Newfoundlanders, but in the arrangements she announced in 1945 for the national convention she retained the last word on what they would decide and how they would decide it. As matters developed, this, along with so much else the British had done in Newfoundland since 1934, showed great foresight. Of all the players in a complex game, they remained the best informed and most clever. Their country had been battered by war, but the United Kingdom's diplomats were still unbowed even if their mission in many parts of the world, including Newfoundland, was now to arrange an orderly retreat. The post-colonial era had dawned and in terms of direct political responsibilities overseas the British were in the business of going out of business. Newfoundland was but a case in point.

The 1933 Royal Commission that recommended the introduction to Newfoundland of Commission of Government. Seated (left to right) are Charles A. Magrath, Lord Amulree, and Sir William Stavert. Standing is P.A. Clutterbuck of the Dominions Office, the Secretary of the Royal Commission. (National Archives, Washington, D.C., RG 59, 843.51/98, encl. in Dow to Secretary of State, 3 May 1933.)

Left to right: Thomas Lodge, Frederick C. Alderdice, Lord Mayor George A. Strong of Liverpool, and Sir John Hope Simpson, aboard the SS *Montclare*, 2 February 1934. Lodge, Alderdice, and Hope Simpson were en route to St. John's for the inauguration of the Commission of Government. (J.B. Hope Simpson and CP Rail Corporate Archives.)

The original members of the Commission of Government at work. Left to right: William R. Howley, Thomas Lodge, Frederick C. Alderdice, Governor Sir David Murray Anderson, John Hope Simpson, John C. Puddester, E.N.R. Trentham. Standing is William J. Carew, the Secretary of the Commission. (Courtesy J.B. Hope Simpson.)

On 10 November 1940 seven Hudson bombers left Gander, Newfoundland, for the United Kingdom, beginning thereby a ferry operation vital to the Allied war effort. Shown above are personnel of the first ferry mission standing in front of one of the cars supplied by the Newfoundland railway to house them at Gander. D.C.T. Bennett, who led the first mission, is standing at the far right. The photograph was taken by Griffith Powell. The historic departure from Newfoundland of 10 November 1940 highlighted the island's strategic importance in an age of air and submarine warfare. (Department of National Defence, Canada, DND/CF Photo, PMR 85/475.)

HRH the Duke of Kent (centre) with Governor Sir Humphrey Walwyn and Lady Walwyn, Newfoundland, 12 September 1941. The Duke arrived for a visit to St. John's by aircraft that landed at Bay Bulls Big Pond. (National Archives of Canada, NA-159578/Smith/DND.)

With many local helping hands, United States soldiers on a reconnaissance trip set up camp for the night, Newfoundland, June 1942. (National Archives, Washington, D.C., RG 111-SC-138732.)

Left to Right: HRH Princess Alice, Countess of Athlone (wife of the Governor General of Canada); The Honourable Ariel Baird (lady-in-waiting to the Countess of Athlone); and Lady Walwyn (wife of the Governor of Newfoundland), 27 August 1942. The party was on a tour of the enlisted men's barracks, Fort Pepperrell, St. John's, Newfoundland. (National Archives, Washington, D.C., RG 111-SC-147862.)

Deputy Prime Minister and Secretary of State for Dominion Affairs Clement Attlee (wearing hat and holding pipe) with members of the Newfoundland Forestry Unit, Glenmuick Camp, Aberdeenshire. Attlee met the Newfoundlanders shortly before his crucial visit to their country in September 1942. (Public Record Office, DO 35/745/N264/209.)

Commissioner for Justice and Defence L.E. Emerson (left) and Fiorello H. La Guardia, Mayor of New York and Chairman, United States section, Permanent Joint Board on Defence, standing on a fire truck at Torbay air base, September 1942. (National Archives, Washington, D.C., RG 111-SC-144649.)

Funeral of thirty-five victims of the Knights of Columbus Hostel fire, Mount Pleasant Cemetery, St. John's, Newfoundland, 15 December 1942. (National Archives of Canada, NA-114424/ Mahoney/DND.)

Restaurant scene, Fort Pepperrell, St. John's, Newfoundland, 3 February 1943. (National Archives, Washington, D.C., RG 111-SC-401565.)

George D. Hopper, United States Consul General, St. John's, Newfoundland, addressing soldiers and civilians, USO Club, St. John's, 3 August 1943. (National Archives, Washington, D.C., RG 111-SC-173722.)

Civilian and army ordnance workers, men and women, at Fort Pepperrell, St. John's, Newfoundland, 1943. (National Archives, Washington, D.C., RG 111-SC-234592.)

Cpl. George Chakedis of Philadelphia (left) with a member of the Newfoundland Constabulary who is directing traffic at the corner of Duckworth and Prescott Streets, St. John's, Newfoundland, 11 October 1943. (National Archives, Washington, D.C., RG 111-SC-350165.)

The Commission of Government circa 1947-49. Seated, left to right: Herman W. Quinton (1947-49), R.L.M. James (1946-49), Albert J. Walsh (1944-49), Governor Sir Gordon Macdonald (1946-49), William H. Flinn (1945-49), James S. Neill (1945-49), and Herbert L. Pottle (1947-49). Standing: William J. Carew, Secretary of the Commission (1934-49). (Courtesy Patricia James.)

Joseph Roberts Smallwood (left of Union Jack and wearing hat and bow-tie) campaigning in 1948. Having led the Confederate forces to victory in the referendum of 22 July 1948, Smallwood, a Liberal, held the office of Premier of the Province of Newfoundland from 1 April 1949 to 18 January 1972. (Centre for Newfoundland Studies Archives, Joseph R. Smallwood Collection/Coll-75.)

CHAPTER NINE

Post-War Adjustment, 1945-49

We accept the general principle that new schemes should not be undertaken, or existing schemes continued at the proposed rate (in cases where the rate of progress can in fact be modified) if it means making serious inroads on our accumulated surplus ... We have, as you know, had to make out a case that money was required for post-war reconstruction as well as for the establishment of *a reserve against a rainy day*.

Commissioner for Finance Ira Wild to H.N. Tait, Dominions Office, July 1946

Thirteen June 1946, the King's official birthday and a public holiday, was designated Victory Day in Newfoudland. In St. John's the day was sunny, and starting at 11 AM, there was a big parade.[1] That evening there was a fireworks display in the capital and bonfires were lit on Gibbet Hill and on the South Side hills. Altogether, it was a glorious and happy occasion, a time to pause, remember, and be thankful for the country's contribution to a good job well done - the defeat of Hitler and all his hideous works. Newfoundlanders were proud of their war record, and indeed there was much of which to be proud. By the end of September 1945, 7,075 men and 524 women, a total of 7,599, had come forward for active service abroad.[2] Taking into account service in the Newfoundland Regiment, the Forestry Unit and the merchant marine more than 12,000 Newfoundlanders were at one time or another directly or indirectly involved in the war effort. This was a sizeable contribution from a small country which did not have conscription and whose population according to the census taken in 1945 was 321,819, including 5,525 in Labrador.[3]

By the time the 1946 victory celebration was held in St. John's, the program of civil re-establishment the Commission had devised during the war was in full swing. The terms of this had previously been explained to the public in March 1945, in a radio address given by Walsh who was now commissioner for home affairs and education.[4] The government also issued a pamphlet entitled *When You Come Home* for the benefit of those to whom the scheme would mainly apply.[5] The model for what the Commission set out to do for returning veterans was similar to the Canadian scheme, but adapted to take account of the particular nature of the local economy and, as always with the Commission, the "financial ability" of the country.[6] As presented by Walsh, the government's plans were made to seem both generous and comprehensive, but in fact they were designed to minimize eligibility for benefits and to keep costs within strict bounds. To this end the thousands of Newfoundlanders who had served in the Forestry Unit and the merchant marine were excluded from the scheme. When the Dominions Office questioned the exclusion of merchant seamen – their United Kingdom counterparts would be eligible for benefits – the Commission refused to budge. While it was true that merchant seamen "had incurred great risks," they had also received "high wages." In any case most of them had been seamen before the war and should be encouraged to continue working in this capacity. As for members of the Forestry Unit, they had "been in civilian employment in comparative safety" and many of them had accumulated "considerable savings." Their circumstances did not justify putting them on the same footing as veterans.[7] Like all post-war Allied governments, the Commission had the delicate task of translating into dollar terms the debt of gratitude the country owed to those who had served it. In the Newfoundland government's case, though there unquestionably was a desire to do the honourable thing, there was also a clear determination that this would not result in a spending spree. In the years after 1945 the parsimonious mentality of the government on occasion made for strained relations with veterans, who had their own sense of what was fair. In their dealings with the Commission, the country's World War II veterans had the assistance of a citizen's re-establishment committee and the Great War Veterans' Association.

The body of Commissioners that actually oversaw the carrying out of the civil re-establishment plan was considerably changed from the one that had presided over Newfoundland's affairs in the glory days of the base building boom. Emerson had left the government in the autumn of 1944 to become chief justice of the Supreme Court, the biggest prize available to a Newfoundland lawyer. He was joined on the bench in November 1946, by H.A. Winter, whereupon Walsh replaced the latter as commissioner for justice and defence from 1 January 1947. In May 1947, after Puddester's death, Walsh became vice-chairman of the Commission. On the British side of the Commission, there were a series of changes between 1944 and 1947 which saw the departure of Woods, Dunn, and Wild and the arrival in turn of Sir George London (Public Utilities and Supply, 1944-45), James S. Neill (Public Utilities and Supply, 1945-49), Major William H. Flinn (Natural Resources, 1945-49), and R.L.M. James (Finance, 1946-49).[8]

The most symbolic change of all, however, was the departure of Walwyn. He left St. John's for Stephenville on 17 January 1946, aboard the "Terra Nova," the private car which the Newfoundland railway made available to the governor. He and Lady Walwyn, who had gained a glowing reputation for her charitable and wartime work, were seen off by a large crowd and, while the police band played "Auld Lang Syne," waved back to their well wishers from the rear of the train under a banner that read "God Guard Thee Newfoundland."[9] Walwyn's entry and exit said much about Newfoundland's progress and orientation. His arrival in 1936 was on a passenger liner on her regular run from Liverpool; his departure ten years later from Stephenville was by air on an American military plane. The picture of him and his wife in the *Evening Telegram* the day he departed St. John's was credited to an American government photographer. Walwyn's successor in St. John's was the recently knighted Welsh native Sir Gordon Macdonald, a teetotaller, former Labour member of Parliament, and good friend of Attlee. He came to Newfoundland to carry out the policy of promoting Confederation on which the United Kingdom had now embarked and about which an understanding with Canada had been reached. Considering the delicacy of his mission, it is no surprise to find that he chose to play his cards close to the chest in gossipy old St. John's, so close in fact that he made his son Kenneth his private secretary.[10]

The budgetary approach of the Commission in the post-war years was shaped by a series of exchanges with London that began with a letter Clutterbuck addressed to Walwyn in January shortly before the latter's departure from St. John's. This called on the Commission "to take stock" of its reconstruction plans in view of what had now to be assumed from the December announcement in Parliament, namely, that the United Kingdom would not assist financially in carrying them out. In these altered circumstances, Clutterbuck wrote, the "general view" in London favoured a policy of steering "a balanced course in regard to reconstruction expenditure generally, in order to avoid at this stage the piling up of too many commitments for the future." Reconstruction expenditure as such, however, should not be slowed down "on account of present uncertainties." Rather its purpose should be "to meet the more pressing needs of the Island." In sum, "fresh schemes with long-term implications" were to be avoided if possible, but this should not prevent the government "from pressing forward energetically" with reconstruction schemes already in hand. Accordingly, Clutterbuck asked the Commission to submit a full list of reconstruction projects on which work would be in progress in 1946 and to suggest additional projects on which work could be carried out in the shortrun, i.e., while the constitutional issue was being resolved. The Commission was now also requested to review its original draft reconstruction program of 1944 with a view to preparing a revised version for submission to the National Convention, a version that would take into account the inability of the United Kingdom to help Newfoundland. The preparation of this document was in accordance with a promise Addison had made in his December 1945 announcement in the Lords, to the effect that the Commission would make available to the National Convention its view of the reconstruction requirements of the country during the following decade.[11]

Clutterbuck's letter triggered a sharp reply from St. John's which went out over the signature of Emerson who, between the departure of Walwyn and the arrival of Macdonald, was administrator of the country. The proposal, Emerson wrote, that the Commission "should evolve a plan covering short-term and long-term policy depending entirely upon revenue" was "somewhat staggering." It would be impossible to carry out such a plan, or perhaps even its short-term component, without dipping into the country's accumulated surplus. But this would be dangerous; for while the government's revenues were holding up, "the ugly heads of unemployment and relief" had reappeared and the prospect for the immediate future was one of "falling revenues" and "substantial payments on account of relief." It was thought necessary, Emerson concluded, thus to warn Clutterbuck so that when he received the proposals called for from St. John's, he would "not be taken by surprise."[12]

Clutterbuck countered that his original instruction had been misunderstood. London's intention was that the Commission should "press forward as rapidly as possible" with reconstruction projects already started or authorized and "any fresh schemes of a priority character" it might wish to provide for in the 1946-47 estimates. In the case of the latter, the intention was that the Commission should focus on "short-term projects," which could be financed entirely from current revenue or "without any substantial call on surplus funds." Some surplus funds might be needed even for the short-term projects contemplated, but in general the use of these should be kept within the "narrowest possible limits." In sum, in a period of transition the Commission should concentrate on schemes that would "meet the most pressing needs of the Island in the immediate future" while leaving longer-term schemes "for further consideration in the light of constitutional developments," so as not to "tie the hands of a future Government." This would form the basis of a satisfactory interim policy for the Government. As for the memorandum on reconstruction to be prepared for the National Convention, Clutterbuck now advised that in making use of the 1944 reconstruction plan the Commission should delete items which would not have been included "but for [the] assumption of United Kingdom assistance." In short, the list of projects to be submitted to the convention should "be made as realistic as possible having regard to probable financial conditions." Items of "high priority" should not, however, be excluded because it was thought "Newfoundland could never afford them." Rather the list to be given the convention should be pared down to what the Commission believed to be "essential" in the following decade for "development ... to proceed and reasonable standards ... to be maintained."[13]

The revised reconstruction proposals the Commission produced based on these exchanges were forwarded to London by Emerson on 15 April. These were divided into three groups: projects already provided for in the draft estimates for 1946-47; short-term projects mainly involving construction not included in the 1946-47 estimates but which the government believed "should be undertaken without deferment"; and long-term schemes "important and essential for the proper development and welfare of the Island." The total cost of the items listed was estimated at $60,916,800 and the average annual cost of a full program in 1947-48 and 1948-49 was $10,534,000. An unspecified part of this latter amount, the Commission argued, would have to come from the surplus because it had to be assumed that revenue would soon fall from its present "abnormal level" and that ordinary spending could be expected to increase. Looking beyond 1948-49, the Commission was decidedly pessimistic: there were "grave reasons to doubt" whether, over the decade under review, Newfoundland would, without loans, be able to sustain even the long-term schemes already started and covered by the 1946-47 estimates. Concern for the future also governed the Commission's request for permission to carry out the additional short-term projects proposed, to begin in 1947-48. New means of employment might be "greatly needed" by then, for although the country's basic industries were still doing well, the number of veterans looking for work was "steadily increasing."[14]

The Commission's plan of action was poorly received at the Treasury. As Lt. Col. W. Russell Edmunds explained, it was questionable whether the term "reconstruction" really applied to what the Commission had in mind. The line between "ordinary" and "reconstruction" expenditure had become blurred in Newfoundland over the years, and the program the Commission now proposed was really nothing more than "an extenuation of the annual budgetary estimates for ten years." The Commission's program was "not an economic plan but [a] means of bringing about certain public and social improvements" and as such was overly ambitious.

It covered too many years and projected costs that were unrealistic in terms of likely revenue. It was indeed "simply a catalogue of how departments would like to spend money if it were available." Given Newfoundland's "unstable economy," which would remain dependent on the vagaries of the export market place, the accumulated surplus should be treated as a reserve "not to be touched, except in times of great need." To want "to use savings (albeit fortuitous) for improving social conditions" was understandable, but Newfoundland had "had too many 'rainy days' to disregard them." Accordingly, all that the Treasury could approve was the $15,373,500 of spending proposed for the continuation of work during 1947-48 and 1948-49 on the reconstruction projects already underway. This approval would be conditional, moreover, on something else: as previously indicated in relation to the Commission's 1946-47 estimates, if surplus funds were to be used in any year for reconstruction projects, a minimum of 75 per cent of the funding for these projects would have to come from ordinary revenue. Reconstruction expenditure, in other words, should take second place in the Commission's plans to maintaining "the surplus balances."[15]

This position was accepted in the Dominions Office, and Newfoundland was told about it in July 1946. In keeping with what Treasury wanted "and on general grounds," the Commission was now informed, the document on reconstruction to be submitted to the National Convention must be framed so as to avoid any "question of the programme being presented as one which His Majesty's Government ... have approved, even in principle." This being the case, the Commission should couch its submission in general terms, avoid detailed estimates, emphasize the need to conserve the existing surplus, and argue the case for funding at least 75 per cent of the cost of reconstruction schemes out of ordinary revenue. As a further precaution, because of the "constitutional position," the Commission was advised to avoid committing itself in the document to spending even what the Treasury was willing to approve for reconstruction over the period 1947-49 provided the 75 per cent rule was observed.[16]

The Commission's reaction to the latest directive was mixed. It accepted the "general principle" that spending on reconstruction schemes should not be allowed to erode the accumulated surplus but questioned whether the 75 per cent rule could be strictly observed. This was because, in spite of a decline in ordinary revenue, the government was inescapably committed to certain major items of expenditure - the civil re-establishment and public works programs already in progress, the chief of which was the building of a West Coast sanitorium and of three coastal steamers. It would also be difficult to deny further funds for school building and communications. If the government came up against the 75 per cent rule, the only "alternative to ... stern measures" would in fact lie in increased taxation and that was "not practical politics." In fact the government would "almost certainly" have to reduce the tax burden in its 1947-48 budget by, for example, adjusting the excess profits tax. The existing level of taxation had been justified in the face of budgets that provided for surpluses, on the grounds that the country had to provide for reconstruction after the war and put aside "a reserve against a rainy day." With the passage of time and the growth of the accumulated surplus, this was a line of argument that had already worn thin. Everything considered, the Commission now asserted, the best course for the immediate future would be to disregard the two-year conditional reconstruction budget approved by Treasury for 1947-48 and 1948-49 and to maintain the existing procedures in the reconstruction field, that is to say "individual submission of any new schemes coupled with annual approval of Estimates provision." This would permit the "somewhat wider discretion" that might be needed.[17]

The Commission encountered no great difficulty in meeting London's requirements about the memorandum on reconstruction to be submitted to the National Convention. Following a series of exchanges with the Dominions Office, this was soon ready to be presented.[18] Pared down from an original draft that was itself designed to minimize information and discourage debate about previous reconstruction discussions between London and St. John's, it was as notable for what it did not say as for what it did. Nonetheless, in the course of its preparation, two crucial points for the future were addressed. The first was whether the Commission was authorized, if asked, to tell the National Convention point blank that no assistance could be expected from the United Kingdom to carry out proposals described in the government's reconstruction memorandum. The second was whether or not "any financial assistance could be expected from the United Kingdom to meet ordinary expenditure, after exhaustion of present reserves, in case the Island chose continuation of Government by Commission or some form of Representative Government." Put another way, the question was, "would there be any expectation of help if there were continuation of control?" It was to be expected, the Commission contended, that this delicate matter would be raised almost as soon as the National Convention assembled.[19]

London's reply was delivered in a letter from C.G.L. Syers of the Dominions Office to Wild. Concerning aid for reconstruction, the Commission was advised to refer the convention, if need be, to the statement Addison had made in the House of Lords: "Our relations with Newfoundland have been so special and Newfoundlanders have played such a gallant part in the war, that it would, I know, be the wish of us all to assure to any new Government which may take over in the Island the fairest possible start. But we must all be careful not to promise what we may not be able to perform and the special difficulties of our financial position over the next few years, may well preclude us from undertaking fresh commitments." This should be sufficiently discouraging but if the convention persisted the Commission should simply refer the matter to London.[20]

With respect to an enquiry from the National Convention about the possibility of British assistance to keep Newfoundland going in the event of another financial crisis, the Commission was given a twofold instruction. If a representative government were in power when such a crisis occurred, the answer would be no, and the convention could be so informed in no uncertain terms. "Political responsibility" meant "financial independence," and that was that. If, however, "a continuing form of Commission Government" were in effect when the projected crisis occurred, the British government would have to intervene. On this point Syers wrote as follows:

> As regards grants-in-aid to a continuing form of Commission Government, I think I may say for your *confidential* information that, given such circumstance as complete exhaustion of all reserves on approved expenditure, and failure of revenue despite all remedial measures possible, then the deficit on ordinary expenditure at approved levels of the strictest economy would doubtless be met by a grant-in-aid of administration by His Majesty's Government....

However, it would be "highly inadvisable" for the Commission to tell the National Convention this. Instead, it should refer directly to London any enquiry the convention might make about what would happen if worse came to worse under future Commission rule.[21] All of this was indicative, of course, of just how much the project of Confederation was being advanced by the British within a framework, albeit self-imposed, of considerable policy constraint. In the last analysis, the British could only get their way if Newfoundlanders would go along with them. This made it necessary for London to have contingency plans ready in case it should fail to achieve its decided objective.

For all the foreboding that ran through the financial correspondence between London and St. John's in 1946, the Commission in fact sailed through the immediate post-war period with relative ease. For 1945–46 the government's budget had called for a surplus of $683,000, but a surplus of more than four times that amount was achieved.[22] For 1946–47 Wild brought in a budget that forecast a deficit but, happily, the out-turn was another surplus, albeit a small one.[23] Only in 1947–48 did the government record a deficit, and even then it was only slightly in the red.[24] Moreover, even though the 1948–49 budget provided for a cutback in total expenditure, spending on reconstruction during the years 1947–49 ran far ahead of the figure the Treasury had been willing to authorize in 1946 for this period. Nor was the increased spending on reconstruction a result of deficit financing. Thanks to high current revenues, the Commission was able, except in 1947-48, to pay its way on an annual basis. To the delight of Whitehall, the accumulated surplus Newfoundland carried into the post-war period was not only preserved but actually increased.

This was a measure of just how good, despite a few problems, times generally continued to be in Newfoundland. Employment remained high after the war, and the basic industries of the country continued to thrive, something that was reflected in the government's revenue figures. At Corner Brook, Bowaters announced an expansion in 1947 that would help carry the economy of this region to new heights. In mining, the discovery of iron ore in western Labrador along the Canadian-Newfoundland border held great promise for the future. In connection with this, the Commission passed legislation which became law in February 1948, whereby the Quebec North Shore and Labrador Railway Company was permitted to build a line through Newfoundland territory in Labrador toward the St. Lawrence.[25] After the war both Canada and the United States sold large quantities of their equipment in Newfoundland, but employment on American bases nevertheless remained important and was given a new lease on life as the Cold War developed. Nor, despite nagging worry within the government, did relief become much of a problem. In the winter of 1947-48, following a failure in the Labrador fishery, poor inshore catches in some areas, and a shorter than usual logging season, the able-bodied relief total rose sharply, but not so as to compare with the relief situation the Commission had faced in 1939.[26] Simply put, Newfoundland had risen out of the economic mire during the war and did not fall back into it thereafter. In a self-congratulatory passage in his 1948-49 budget speech, James surveyed what would be accomplished by the end of that financial year through the three-year limited reconstruction program the government had begun in 1946-47. Total reconstruction expenditure in the period under review, he said, would amount to more than $30,000,000.[27]

In natural resource development, the Commission concentrated after the war, both in its modified reconstruction program and in its overall administration, on the modernization and restructuring of the fishing industry and on a revitalized program of land settlement. The direction of policy favoured for the fisheries had been worked out during the war, beginning with the submission to London by Walwyn in January 1943 of the report of the fisheries rehabilitation subcommittee of the civil re-establishment and post-war reconstruction committee. This abandoned the wholesale co-operative approach, called for by Gorvin, which had so vexed Water Street, and proposed instead the adoption of a plan which offered businessmen the prospect of government assistance and a leading place in a new order, albeit within a tighter framework of government regulation than ever before. Significantly, the existing saltfish industry, to which so many venerable and vested interests were tied, would be left substantially untouched under the new scheme of things. While acknowledging that the "consuming countries" would always have "the last word" on the fate of the fishing industry, the subcommittee recommended the adoption by the government of a co-ordinated plan for fisheries development, the objective being to raise fishermen's incomes. To achieve this goal, the marketing of frozen fish would have to be emphasized, additional species taken, and new methods introduced both to increase catches and to extend and improve the existing product range. In order to make these changes, production would have to be concentrated in a few primary "fishing centres," which would be connected to outlying areas by improved road transportation. Each fishing centre would have integrated production facilities which would comprehend shipping, filleting, freezing, drying, canning, smoking, storage, salting, and fish meal and oil making operations. On the south and southwest coasts, deep sea draggers would operate from the designated fishing centres. These would ensure adequate fish supplies and keep the freezing plants going at full capacity. To give fishermen a steady market for their product, fish that could not be handled by the freezing, canning, and smoking operations at a particular production centre would be salted, thereby avoiding waste. Inshore fishermen who sold directly to the operator at one of the new fishing centres would be paid in cash, while dragger men would be paid a weekly wage, augmented by a bonus that would depend on the size of the week's catch. One company would operate at each fishing centre under regulations to be promulgated by the Newfoundland Fisheries Board. Workers and fishermen would be able to buy shares in these companies, if government assisted, "by instalment." When appropriate, the local operating company would be organized co-operatively and profits distributed to its shareholding "local employees and fishermen."[28]

The subcommittee identified eleven areas where primary fishing centres should be located and recommended the development of fifteen such centres in them. The capital needed to start each centre was estimated at anywhere from $150,000 to $400,000, depending on the range of services offered. The estimated cost of the whole scheme was $4,000,000. If needed, the government should provide "a portion of the capital of each company in the form of ordinary shares and debentures," putting its shares up for sale "at par in small lots" to the fishermen and workers connected with the enterprise. Companies starting without government help would not be required to encourage shareholding by their fishermen and workers, but self-interest would make this advisable. To assist operations at the fishing centres, the government would have to enlarge its technical staff and make the expertise of that staff readily available to those involved in the industry. Likewise "adult and vocational educational facilities" would have to be directed towards "increasing knowledge and efficiency" in the industry. The sale of Newfoundland fish products abroad, the subcommittee recommended, "should be effected through the agency of the principal distributors in each country." Their "goodwill and co-operation" was essential since they were in "a position to destroy all possibility of successful marketing." A successful sales effort also required that no Newfoundland producer "should be able for the sake of a temporary selfish advantage to take action which would ultimately prejudice the welfare of the whole industry." The subcommittee concluded that to get this scheme underway the government should issue whatever additional regulations were needed to control "the construction of plants, the production of processed fish and the marketing of fishery products."[29]

In a covering letter, Walwyn explained the philosophy behind the subcommittee's recommendations, recommendations the government had endorsed. It had been noted in the deliberations leading to the report, he wrote, "that the f.o.b. value of salt fish in 1938–39 had risen only fractionally above the value in 1870." Accordingly, it had been concluded "that the fishery of Newfoundland had been maintained at the expense of the standard of living of the people." The scheme of centralization and development now proposed would end the baneful credit system in the fisheries, while leaving the businessmen who ran the saltfish trade free to go about their business as usual. Nor was there anything to be feared in giving each operating company "a limited monopoly" in the area defined by its licence. This was because the record of the local frozen fish industry, though brief, showed that plants followed the price lead of the highest bidder among them. Government assistance to carry out development was considered essential because private enterprise on its own would "not be able or willing to carry out reorganization on the lines proposed." No doubt opposition might be encountered "to the Government taking a share in industry" and investing in companies that would compete for at least some business with existing enterprises, but this could be countered by allowing traders established at each fishing centre to acquire shares in the new company to be launched locally. The "most effective answer" to such criticism was that the future of a key industry was too important to be "left to the vagaries of individual traders with the very real risk of repeating the chaos prevalent in the salt codfish industry prior to 1936."[30]

In an accompanying memorandum, which specified fifteen communities that were candidates for development as fishery centres, Dunn hammered the same point home as follows:

> As regards finance, it is clear that the bulk of the finance required will have to be provided by the Government. Some of the firms already engaged in the fish trade are, unfortunately, not progressive, and they do not wish to change their methods so long as a profit can be made. They are not prepared to invest their capital in new schemes. Their attitude appears to be that someone else should take the initial risks and not until it is proved that profits can be made will they consider coming into the business. It is also unfortunate that at present the profits to be made on salt fish is of the order of four cents a pound and, that being so, it is difficult to interest persons earning such profits in ventures where the profit will have to be restricted to one cent per pound or even less.

Yet for all the failings of Newfoundland businessmen, "the alternative to development by private enterprise," namely, the adoption of an outright "co-operative system" was not feasible. This might "ultimately prove to be the form of enterprise most likely to survive in Newfoundland," but there could be "no doubt" that as things stood "a reorganization wholly on a co-operative basis, would be bitterly opposed by many and could not be successfully carried out." Only in a few locations would a co-operative approach be likely to work, and in these areas alone should it be attempted. Dunn's sense of the "most profitable arrangement" overall for a reorganized fishing industry was that this "would lie in the formation of companies which would have production and processing centres on the south coast or south-west coast as well as on the east or north-east coast." This linkage would permit integrated year-round work with southern deep sea dragger operations offsetting the disadvantage of a relatively short fishing season on the east and northeast coast and the fact that only limited improvement could be made on the catch in this region.[31]

On the marketing side of the plan, Dunn justified the proposed "central control" of the frozen fish production on the grounds that production capacity in Newfoundland had to take account of "distributive facilities" abroad if failure were not to ensue. This was a job for government, and the co-ordinating agency should be the Department of Natural Resources, acting through the Newfoundland Fisheries Board. Accordingly, the board should be empowered, through licensing arrangements, to regulate output, price, and product quality. While there was reason to believe that "American interests" were willing to put money into the Newfoundland frozen fish industry, Dunn thought it would be undesirable for them to obtain control of it. Using large scale production methods a big American company like General Seafoods could, given a base of operations on say the south coast, turn out a large volume of frozen fish. But this would only help the immediate area at the price of development elsewhere in the country. By contrast, the scheme the Commission contemplated would create work around the island and was specifically designed to create "as large a number of prosperous settlements as possible."[32]

The major criticism voiced by London about the scheme sent to it from St. John's concerned the proposal that development should proceed through a multiplicity of private enterprises but be assisted and tightly regulated by government. Despite the supervising role of the Newfoundland Fisheries Board, it was feared that these companies might end up "competing with each another for capital assistance, staff, equipment, etc., as well as for catch." This situation "might be all the more anomalous if the Government held shares in each company and had a director on each Board." A better arrangement would be for the Commission to work through some "central organization" which would in turn control local companies and deal with the particular circumstances each required. Since the reorganization of the fisheries after the war would hinge on government investment, the Commission had to be "in [a] position to exercise effective control." If it paid the piper, in other words, it must also call the tune. This would be done by setting up a central development agency that was "organized on public utility lines." Under this arrangement a "board or company" would be "established under statute with its profits limited and its membership appointed wholly by [the] Commission." The British also questioned the wisdom of setting up so many fully integrated production centres and while acknowledging the limiting factors of "regional interests and difficulties of transport," asked whether greater centralization and specialization by product might not be desirable.[33]

The answer given by the Commission to these points revealed much about the conservative drift of its thinking since the heady days of the Special Areas Bill and its aftermath. Beginning in 1941, it was pointed out, the government had indeed attempted to promote "the idea of one overall company for production of frozen fish and other fishery developments." It had, however, been impossible "to reconcile the conflicting interests involved in setting up such a company." Reluctantly, therefore, the Commission had had to drop the project in favour of what it now advocated, which was in any case an improvement on what had been sought before. Given the extent of Newfoundland's coastline, it made sense to have "independent companies ... managed by firms with experience of the locality concerned." Fishery operations varied considerably from area to area, and in the past "large firms operating the fish business from a distance" had failed because "centralized management" could not "appreciate the peculiarities and deal with [the] unanticipated difficulties of local operations." There was also the further problem that "a large company might ultimately tend to centralize its operations at a few of the most remunerative ports." By contrast, what the Commission sought to achieve was to maximize the number of areas benefiting from "increased earnings," even though some would be more profitable than others. Yet another consideration in favour of acting through independent companies was that American firms had the right under the Anglo-American Convention of 1818 to establish themselves on the treaty shore that this agreement had defined. At the same time, Newfoundland had the right under the Hague Tribunal Arbitration of 1910 to subject American plants to the same regulations that applied to Newfoundland companies. This would obviously be more tenable if there were a number of Newfoundland companies in the field. Beyond all this was perhaps a large consideration. There would be "much opposition" to the creation of a single company, "and it would be in the interests of many merchants to see that its operations were unsuccessful." Moreover, "even among fishermen" the government could "not count on wholehearted co-operation."[34] In the Commission's view these considerations were decisive. Having stirred up the wrath of the business community in 1940–41, the government was obviously not anxious to do it again.

For the moment, the British remained sceptical about the financial and ownership arrangements being pushed by St. John's. In June 1943, Clutterbuck told Dunn that the Treasury did not agree with all the Commission's objections to the creation of a "central public utility company" though it realized that any such venture "would probably founder in the face of attacks from vested interests coupled with the indifference of fishermen themselves." Treasury also held that when the government invested in the industry, it would be better, pending the disposal of its holdings to workers or operating companies, for it to own physical assets rather than ordinary shares. By taking shares, the government would "run the risk of ownership without control." Alternatively, Treasury suggested, the Newfoundland government could give the industry the financial help it required by buying both "first" and "income" debentures. These would be secured alike, but in the case of the income debentures interest would have to be paid only after a company had declared "necessary profits."[35]

In response to this suggestion and various other points about its overall scheme of development, the Commission returned, over the signature of Dunn, the most detailed account to date of what it intended. This concluded with a spirited defence of the financial structure proposed for the frozen fish industry. Co-operation, the British were told again, did not provide a basis on which to proceed. Indeed, some existing co-operative societies were having to be closed down. Except in a few areas, Newfoundland fishermen did "not know the most elementary facts of business" and were "unable to understand the necessity for the simplest form of bookkeeping." They saw their role exclusively as catching fish and did not want to be bothered "with the details of management." This was a harsh reality Gorvin had overlooked. Moreover, in the existing climate of political uncertainty it would be difficult even for the government itself to recruit suitable managers for a co-operative experiment that might be "swept away" immediately upon the return of Responsible Government. The "only alternative" therefore was "to make the best arrangement possible with private enterprise," and in the government's view this "ought to include a provision for ultimate share-interests for fishermen." For the government to build plants itself, even with the intention of selling them off "to workers or traders" as circumstances allowed, would deter private investment in the industry: "We have been told repeatedly by merchants that they would not consider a financial arrangement which would put them in any way at the mercy of Government and this objection would be even stronger with Responsible Government than now. We feel sure that they will not consider any proposal that the Government should hold a majority of the shares or should own the premises from which they might be ejected for political reasons." The Commission's answer to a complex problem was to assist the industry both by making loans and buying shares. This would satisfy businessmen while keeping the way open for eventual worker shareholding, an outcome the debenture purchase strategy recommended by Treasury would preclude. It was true that by owning shares the government risked "ownership without control," but all investors would be in the same boat and it was doubtful whether a debenture arrangement would produce a very different result. If the government bought debentures, it would be able to foreclose on the company issuing them, but only in case of default would it be able to control the company's affairs. Furthermore, the reality of government lending was that "the whole tendency" in the case of default would be "to lend more money in order to save the undertaking." All in all,what the Commission was proposing represented the best way forward, and the government should now be authorized to act.[36]

In October 1943 after Dunn had visited London and discussed matters further, the Dominions Office pressed the Treasury to approve in principle what the Commission advocated so that it could begin detailed costing of the proposed development. "As a long-term objective," Clutterbuck told C.M. Wilcox of the Treasury, it was "clear that the goal must be to revitalize the Newfoundland industry by concentrating more and more on the production of frozen fish for the rich, largely untapped, and virtually unlimited market in the United States, and retaining the production of salt fish which is sold to relatively poor markets largely as a means of disposing of surplus fish or fish which could not otherwise be marketed." On the question of "fifteen separate companies as against one central body," Clutterbuck now explained that Dunn's purpose would in practice be to encourage the expansion of the big firms already operating in the frozen fish business, such as the Harvey and Monroe interests. Ultimately, it was intended, these firms "might well control as many as three plants" each, something the fishing enterprise of the Monroe family had already achieved. Building on existing strength in this fashion would prevent foreign ownership and keep profits in Newfoundland for reinvestment.[37]

On the other hand, to turn over development to one big company would run counter to the "intensely local outlook of the merchants and fishermen who would be affected by the scheme." Expanding on this key point, Clutterbuck wrote as follows:

> As you will appreciate the outport merchant is in many ways guide, philosopher and friend to the fishermen. He provides their gear, tackle, clothing and food, and buys their fish in return. In many instances, although driving a hard bargain for goods provided on credit, he sees his men through a hard winter, and if the fishery is bad, he banks to lose heavily himself. If, therefore, a central organization were to endeavour to impose an alien manager on a long established outport business, or to attempt to set up a rival concern in the same locality, it is more than likely, however great the financial inducements offered, that the merchant and the local fishermen would make common cause against the new venture, and in nine cases out of ten make its working impossible.

In short, Dunn was on solid ground in his contention that the best chance to succeed was in working though "local companies, controlled to a considerable extent by existing business organizations." The Commissioner had a good case, too, Clutterbuck maintained, with respect to the question of the government owning shares in the companies that would be assisted to develop the industry. In sum, the Treasury should drop its advocacy of a debenture approach to financing development and support a scheme which, though speculative, was well thought out and sought to ensure the future of Newfoundland's biggest employer and therefore its most basic industry.[38]

This appeal succeeded, and in November 1943, the Treasury gave its "general approval in principle" to the Newfoundland scheme on the understanding that development would proceed gradually and that each stage would be explained in detail by the Commission in its annual estimates. In thus conceding ground to the "prejudices and sentiments existing in Newfoundland," Treasury took comfort in the fact that in the Newfoundland Fisheries Board the Commission had a ready made instrument for controlling the industry which was "not regarded by the fishing interests with the same suspicion as the Government itself."[39] The Commission itself heard the good news from London in December, and thereafter was guided in its fisheries policy by what had been agreed upon.[40] At a crucial moment in its history the rapidly expanding frozen fish business, where in fact the whole future of the fishing industry lay, had been cast in a mould which in its essentials – private ownership combined with government backing and regulation – would not be broken until the world wide recession of the early 1980s when the frozen fish business suffered a setback akin to that which the saltfish industry had suffered in the 1930s. The Commission had scored a big planning success but it can be argued that it had also followed the path of least resistance. The negative consequence of this was a privately owned frozen fish sector whose chronic dependence on the state would haunt Newfoundland for decades to come. The Commission achieved a long sought after goal in 1947 when saltfish export was handed over to a single company, the Newfoundland Associated Fish Exporters Limited (NAFEL).[41] This body was licensed by the Newfoundland Fisheries Board but was run by the trade in keeping with the ameliorative approach of that agency. In short, the role of businessmen was not usurped. Hence David Alexander's perceptive remark that during the Commission era Newfoundland's fish traders were not "beaten or overthrown" but "more-or-less house-trained."[42] In its fishing industry for all that had been achieved, the Commission left Newfoundland with all the myths of free enterprise but without much of the reality.

Though much less ambitious than the development scheme for the fishing industry, the revised land policy worked out by the Commission during the war and followed by it afterwards also attempted to improve on past performance. Following the submission of Gorvin's 1938 reports on land settlement and long range reconstruction and Hanley's report on agriculture and land settlements, the Commission had carried out a modified resettlement program.[43] This had run through three financial years beginning in July 1939 and had been designed to achieve self-sufficiency both for the older land settlements and for four new communities started in 1939, Winterland and Creston (near Marystown), Sandringham (near Eastport, Bonavista Bay) and Point au Mal (on the Port au Port Peninsula).

A new land settlement proposal, based on the findings of the agricultural subcommittee of the committee on post-war rehabilitation, was brought forward in March 1944. This divided prospective settlers, who would not number more than 1,000, into six categories. Preference under this scheme would be given to ex-servicemen first, members of the Forestry Unit second, and civilian settlers third. The estimated maximum cost of the program was $5,274,000.[44] In May 1944 a Land Development Act, which provided an administrative framework for carrying out this plan and applied as well to existing land settlements, became law.[45] Later the same year, the Commission was authorized to distribute a questionnaire to Newfoundland servicemen and Forestry Unit personnel overseas to see how many would be interested in participating in the proposed scheme.[46] In practice, however, the number of veterans who chose this route back into civilian life was comparatively small. Thus, in his 1948–49 budget speech James noted that by the end of 1948–49, ninety-six ex-servicemen would have been settled in a development area on the Upper Humber and 180 given agricultural assistance elsewhere.[47]

Another long-standing commitment the Commission pursued with renewed vigour after the war, was civil service reform. The civil service act which became law in December 1947 provided for a civil service selection board to assess the qualifications of candidates for government positions and recommend suitable appointees. Like its counterparts elsewhere, this board was intended to operate without fear or favour and to select on the basis of merit. Rules were laid down governing the working conditions of civil servants and the payment of pensions to them and of death benefits to their dependents. The Commission believed that these arrangements, which drew their inspiration from the United Kingdom, would be among its most important legacies to succeeding governments.[48]

The attitude of the Commission towards labour matters after the war was cautious. In March 1946 the government decided to set up a Department of Labour, for which the commissioner for public utilities and supply would be responsible.[49] Walsh was named secretary of this department, a move that guaranteed him a job after his days on the Commission had run their course, but no temporary appointment was made in his stead. Thereafter, in November, the government decided to phase out the wartime regulations governing strikes, lockouts and dispute settlement in two stages ending 1 March 1947.[50] Instead these changes did not come into effect until the original decision was confirmed at the end of March.[51] The following October, the Commission approved in principle An Act to Regulate Trade Unions and Trade Disputes, something for which the Newfoundland Federation of Labour had long lobbied hard; this was not proceeded with, however, and in September 1948 was dropped from the government's agenda.[52] Meanwhile, in December 1947, a minimum wage act had become law.[53]

In October 1948 the Commission was faced with its trickiest post-war labour problem when the nine unions representing employees of the Newfoundland Railway, having threatened a walkout as early as January of the previous year, actually went on strike.[54] This work stoppage, the biggest event of its kind in a year of strikes, lasted for a month and only ended when the government conceded a ten cent an hour increase in hourly wages and a twenty dollars per month increase to employees paid on a monthly basis.[55] Throughout this whole dispute the government consistently resisted pressure to refer its difference with the railway employees for settlement by arbitration. This course, it was decided early on (though not unanimously), could not be followed without setting a precedent that would apply to civil servants, teachers, and other public employees, a development that would in turn mean an "abdication by the Government of its responsibilities for the national finances."[56]

Intertwined with labour relations issues was the question of a still rapidly rising cost of living. This was an ever present source of concern to the government after the war, but, thanks to continuing good times and the maintenance of many wartime controls, this issue, like its labour relations counterpart, never become politically unmanageable. In November 1946 the government announced a number of changes in the Newfoundland tariff schedule so as to moderate the prices of some essential commodities.[57] At the same time the public was told that a commission of enquiry would be appointed to look into wholesale and retail profit margins. This commission was chaired by Henry Smith, Vice-Principal of Ruskin College, Oxford, and had as its other four members, well-known business and professional figures as well as a prominent labour leader.[58] If the commission did nothing else, it bought the government time, allowing it to present itself once more as the guardian of the public interest, beholden neither to business nor labour, but willing to listen to both.

An entirely different post-war venture of the Commission was changing the rule of the road as of 1 January 1947, from left hand to right hand driving. Puddester's despatch informing London that the Commission was considering this change and inviting comment on it noted that the left hand rule had been adopted in Newfoundland because the first cars in the country had been imported from the United Kingdom. Now, however, ninety-nine per cent of the motor vehicles in Newfoundland were built for right hand driving. Nonetheless, opposition could be expected either because of "pure aversion to change" or else because of the benefit perceived in allowing drivers "to keep the near side ditch on a narrow road continuously in view." The commissioner noted that "some argument will also, no doubt, centre on the ingrained 'left-handedness' of the local draught-horse, but as horse-drawn traffic is supposed to be under the control of a driver, it is difficult to avoid the conclusion that this school of thought has mainly in mind the interests of the inebriated individual whose fortunes are, temporarily, in the care of the instincts of his homeward plodding steed." What was bringing the whole issue to a head, Puddester further explained, was that the City of St. John's was discussing with the capital's public transport companies the possibility of replacing the existing tram car and motor bus system with an electric trolley bus network. Since the transport companies involved in St. John's were

Canadian, they wanted the rule of the road changed to accommodate the Canadian equipment they would bring in to introduce the new service. The proposed change-over would likewise facilitate the greater tourist traffic the government was hoping for and which would originate "almost entirely" in Canada and the United States.[59] No objection was raised to this reasoning in London, and following a public relations campaign the Commission made the change. In a visible and highly personal fashion this development made plain just how North American Newfoundland had recently become.

Diplomatically, the Commission was kept busy after the war dealing with the interrelated issues of defence and civil aviation. The possibilities for air passenger travel had been revolutionized by the war; the future held the promise of great commercial advantage for the world's airlines, both domestically and internationally. In anticipation of this boom, a basis was established during the war, through a tangled series of events, for a new framework of international relations in civil aviation. When this was developed, it favoured the point of view of the United States, the world's foremost aviation power, that "nationally designated airlines should compete in a loosely regulated universal framework." A competing British vision of the future, carried over from the 1930s and eventually abandoned in the face of United States power and Commonwealth disunity, had favoured "an imperial network whose control of bases and routes could balance the American lead in producing large aircraft."[60]

Though a minor player, Newfoundland was present at the creation of the new world civil aviation order, and the policy pursued by the Commission was to maximize the country's return from its strategic position in the air lanes of the North Atlantic. What this meant in practice was to funnel traffic through a repossessed Gander airport and to keep American and Canadian civil aviation rights at their Newfoundland military bases at a minimum. In pursuing these goals, the Commission had to take account of a growing public opinion in the country as the war progressed, well evident at the time of the Goose Bay Agreement, that Newfoundland's geographic position would be an asset of great economic importance in the age of mass air travel. Mixed with this, not surprisingly, was the fear, especially on the part of the business community, that an unrepresentative government would make for Newfoundland unjust, inadequate, and compromising deals with other countries. In their view the Goose Bay Agreement was such a deal and must not be repeated.

The situation facing the government by 1945 was thus decidedly complex, both domestically and internationally, and the product of a long series of wartime changes. In October 1942 there was a major development for the future of Commonwealth air relations when Canada served notice that she wished to withdraw from the Transatlantic Air Agreement of December 1935 between herself, the United Kingdom, Eire, and Newfoundland. The joint operating company proposed in that agreement had never been established and Ottawa now held that because of intervening changes, the existing understanding would not form "a useful basis for dealing with the post-war situation."[61] In October 1943 an attempt was made to work out a new joint Commonwealth position at a meeting held in London which Woods and Pattison attended as observers.[62] This gathering in effect buried the 1935 agreement while pronouncing itself in favour of the creation of an International Air Transport Authority to regulate many aspects of international civil aviation. Subsequently, the St. John's businessman, V.S. Bennett and two associates launched a company, Air Transport (later North Atlantic Airways) which sought to capitalize on Newfoundland's international bargaining position in civil aviation by obtaining landing rights abroad.[63] This ambition, however, ran counter to the Dominions Office view that no private Newfoundland international airline could operate successfully without government support.[64] Accordingly, Bennett did not get very far with the Commission and his death in June 1945 extinguished one of the grander dreams of a Newfoundland business elite anxious to be back in charge of the country's assets again.[65] In the end, there was no Newfoundland version, public or private, of Loftleidir ("Skyway"), the airline launched in Iceland in 1944 that eventually became an international carrier.

For civil aviation policy more generally, the biggest event of the latter stages of the war was the International Civil Aviation Conference, held at Chicago in late 1944. This was preceded by Commonwealth talks at Montreal and was attended by delegations from fifty-two countries. The conference dealt with two large matters: "technical regulations governing all forms of international flying" and "international relationships in air transport development." In practice much of the work of the conference focused on what were defined as the five freedoms (the British preferred to call them privileges) of the air. These were: (1) "the right of transit without landing" across another country (i.e., the right of innocent passage); (2) the right to land in another country "for non-traffic purposes"; (3) "the right to disembark passengers, mails and freight from the country of origin of the aircraft"; (4) "the right to embark passengers, mails and freight destined for the country of origin of the aircraft"; and (5) "the right to pick up and set down traffic to and from destinations *neither* of which is the country of origin of the aircraft." The Chicago conference failed to produce a general international understanding, but it did produce a number of agreements important to the future of civil aviation. An interim arrangement was made to establish a provisional international civil aviation organization (PICAO), and by September 1945, this had been formally accepted by thirty-five countries including the United Kingdom and the United States. The headquarters of the new body was established in Montreal. The 1944 convention also drew up the International Air Services Transit Agreement and the International Air Transport Agreement. The first, generally known as the two freedoms agreement (because of its grant of freedoms 1 and 2), was adhered to by both the United Kingdom and the United States. The second, which provided for the reciprocal grant of all five freedoms by its signatories, was opposed by the British but accepted and promoted enthusiastically by the Americans.[66]

Newfoundland was represented at the Montreal Commonwealth talks and the subsequent Chicago conference by London, Walsh, and Pattison, and they acted in an advisory capacity to the United Kingdom delegation in the American city.[67] The Newfoundland party was empowered to agree to the grant of the rights of innocent passage and landing for non-traffic purposes (freedoms 1 and 2) provided these were generally accepted.[68] But when on 7 December, the two freedoms agreement was actually signed by Lord Winster, the head of the British delegation, Newfoundland was exempted from its provisions by him in the following words: "I declare that, failing later notification of inclusion, my signature to this agreement does not cover Newfoundland."[69] This exception was made at the insistence of the Newfoundland representatives, when it became known that Canada would withhold signature from the document pending the working out of acceptable bilateral arrangements with the United States for air service between the two countries. If their country was covered by the agreement and Canada was not, the Newfoundland representatives maintained, the Commission might face the politically explosive charge of another giveaway.[70] Hence the necessity for the exception Winster made. This, however, prompted an angry response from the chief American negotiator, Adolph Berle, who, apparently unaware of Winster's action on signing, had praised the United Kingdom at the final session of the conference for giving up "a possible stranglehold on the Atlantic crossing," arising out of her geographical advantage in Newfoundland, where, pending the development of longer range aircraft, transatlantic flights must stop.[71] Berle's subsequent reaction alarmed Winster, who told London in a message repeated to St. John's that the Americans could now be expected to say that what the United Kingdom had "given with one hand" she had "taken away with another"; in short, that there had been a doublecross. Newfoundland's interest, according to Winster, lay in encouraging the maximum use of her airfields, and she had nothing to gain by holding back on the two freedoms agreement. This being so, he expressed the hope that the Newfoundland government could "be brought to see reason."[72] Churchill was more blunt. In a personal note to Attlee commenting on the latter's efforts to extricate the United Kingdom from what he termed "an untenable position," the prime minister, obviously referring to contemporary reconstruction plans for Newfoundland, challenged his deputy thus:

> If, as you contend, Newfoundland's position will be more favourable to that of Great Britain after the war, ought you not to reconcile this view with the many demands for expenditure on betterment which you make and to which we have bent our energies? I am all for Newfoundland and helping her, but I will not admit for a moment that she can claim to exercise a stranglehold upon Freedoms I and II and thus bring us into a most undesirable clash with the United States on a large question vital to the British nation upon the weakest of all grounds. Obstruction of this kind will be perfectly futile and the attempt to exercise it deeply injurious to our life and safety. You must not expect me to defend such a position in public.[73]

In a letter to Beaverbrook, Churchill maintained that Newfoundland would "never be considered as an entity for itself against the general view of the British Empire and against the needs of world society ... Everybody knows," he continued, "that Newfoundland is bankrupt and a pauper and has no power apart from us. Therefore nothing we can say will make the Americans believe that we are not pulling the strings of a puppet."[74] These were harsh strictures, disputed in subsequent high level discussion in London;[75] but as in the case of the Leased Bases Agreement of 1941, it is hard to see how, given the country's limited resources and likely post-war employment needs, any Newfoundland government could have defied the Anglo-American understanding now in the making.

How matters would have developed on the issue that had arisen at Chicago if Newfoundland had stood her ground, can only be speculated upon. But in fact after a flurry of telegrams had passed between St. John's, Ottawa, and London, the Commission decided to adhere to the two freedoms agreement.[76] A potentially explosive episode had passed without a public split, but in the process the Dominions Office had been explicitly told by the Commission that public opinion locally was "very definitely opposed to leaving the disposal of Newfoundland territory and rights to the United Kingdom. We must advise," the British were informed, "that any attempt on the part of the United Kingdom to disregard Newfoundland opinion on this subject may lead to serious and unfortunate consequences."[77]

The Newfoundland public was told of their government's decision to adhere to the two freedoms agreement in a statement published in St. John's on 15 January 1945. Since the maintenance of international airports in the country would be an expensive proposition, the Commission suggested that Newfoundland's interest lay in encouraging their maximum use. The adoption of the two freedoms agreement was a step in this direction. Over time the benefit to be derived from this approach would "far outweigh any temporary immediate benefit which might conceivably accrue from bargaining with other countries for civil aviation rights."[78] In other words, as Sir George London once put it elsewhere, "Newfoundland was in a special position of geographical advantage and financial disadvantage."[79]

The next major development affecting the country's civil aviation future came at a conference initiated by Ottawa.[80] This was held in Bermuda, 17-19 December 1945, and brought together British, Canadian, and Newfoundland officials. Canada's principal representatives on this occasion were C.D. Howe and H.J. Symington, the president of Trans-Canada Air Lines, both of whom had been present at the Chicago conference, while the main British negotiator was Lord Winster, now his country's minister of civil aviation. Newfoundland's spokesmen at Bermuda were Neill, Walsh and Pattison.[81] Walsh was sent, Walwyn explained to the Dominions Office in advance, because it was "politically important" that a Newfoundland commissioner be present.[82] Winster's confidential report on the proceedings noted that Walsh reflected "the feelings of the Newfoundlanders" and "was inclined to show distinct opposition to any permanent Canadian infiltration" of his country. In private Howe expressed doubt to the British whether Newfoundland could run Gander satisfactorily, but at the negotiating table Canada did not dispute Newfoundland's intention to take back control of the airport.[83] With an eye to British plans for the political future of Newfoundland, however, Winster successfully put forward proposals whereby Canada would continue to provide certain services at Gander until Newfoundland was ready or wanted to take them over. With respect to future financing of Gander, the conference accepted Winster's proposal that a memorandum should be addressed to the Provisional International Civil Aviation Organization calling for governments that benefited from the existence of "uneconomic airports" to contribute to their maintenance. Once this was done, Gander's claim could be advanced as an example.[84]

The deal worked out at Bermuda in relation to Goose Bay was a compromise between Canada's desire to have it "thrown open as an international airport" and Newfoundland's desire to funnel business through Gander. Canada herself, it was agreed, would be allowed to use Goose Bay for civil aviation purposes but planes of other countries would only be allowed to go there if the weather at Gander was unsuitable for landing. It was also agreed that Canadian title to the land on which Torbay airport was built should be confirmed by legislation in Newfoundland.

Newfoundland's right to use this facility for her own civil aviation purposes would be equal to that of Canada, but any additional civil use would be subject to bilateral agreement. The question of the military use of Torbay was left for subsequent discussion, but it was agreed that the base should be run by Canada with Newfoundland having customs and immigration facilities there. Newfoundland would also reserve the right to designate Torbay for use in service to and from the North American continent and to schedule it as a bad weather alternative to Gander in transatlantic operations through the country. Landing fees charged at Torbay would accrue to Canada as at Goose Bay. At the close of the Bermuda conference, the "conclusions and recommendations" agreed upon were embodied in a summary which Winster and Howe initialled on 21 December.[85] In July 1945, Sir George London had told W.P. Hildred, the director general of civil aviation in the United Kingdom, that Newfoundland's problem in the civil aviation field was whether to be a "Western outpost of the U. K. or an Eastern outpost of the American Continent."[86] The Bermuda settlement contained elements of both these positions but like so much else that happened internationally in relation to Newfoundland immediately after the war, this outcome was merely temporary.

Following the Bermuda talks, an Anglo-Canadian-Newfoundland conference on post-war defence and civil aviation arrangements met in St. John's from January to February 1946. Canada was represented at this gathering by a seven-man party that included Minister of Fisheries Frank Bridges, MacKay, and Macdonald. The Newfoundland delegation was led by Neill, who chaired the sessions, and Winter, the commissioner for justice and defence.[87] The United Kingdom was represented by M.W. Low of the Air Ministry, Group Captain S.H.V. Harris, and Chadwick of the Dominions Office. British preparations for the conference reflected the reality of the war just ended, namely that Newfoundland "was primarily in the [Canadian] defence orbit" and that Canada's geographical position made her "the only power which could go immediately to the Island's assistance in the event of an emergency."[88] The British aimed, therefore, at maintaining their own existing access to all the bases in the country (except for those leased to the United States) and at encouraging Canadian participation in the defence of Newfoundland, up to the stationing of Canadian troops there in peacetime. In the case of Goose Bay, what the British wanted was the continuation of their right to wartime use of the base "particularly for G.R. [general reconnaissance] purposes, in the unlikely event of our being at war and Canada neutral."[89] While not requiring permanent facilities at the base, the British wanted to be able to use it in peacetime for transit and training purposes. Otherwise they approached the negotiations with the following "political considerations" in view:

a) We should encourage both the Canadian and Newfoundland Governments to regard their defence interests as extending beyond their own borders and as bound up with the defence interests of the rest of the Commonwealth.
b) Although we should restrain the Commission government ... from taking an attitude inconsistent with (a), we should not force on them solutions that will leave the people of Newfoundland resentful against ourselves or the Canadians or both.
c) Although we attach considerable importance to obtaining rights at Goose Bay, since Gander by itself would not cover our requirements, securing rights at Goose Bay is not important enough to justify antagonizing the Canadians.
d) In general we should avoid suggesting that we regard this matter as a subject for hard bargaining; we should show that we do not seriously visualize the possibility of one part of the Commonwealth being at war and another not.
e) We should avoid accepting the principle that if one country, in the pursuance of the common war effort, builds facilities on the territory of another, the former can expect to enjoy rights of user after the war. (This is relevant in particular to Torbay.)[90]

The Canadian negotiating position was set forth in a telegram to London on 21 January 1946. Canada's existing defence plans, it was explained did not require "the stationing of Canadian forces in Newfoundland in normal times." At the same time, however, it was "thought desirable that essential facilities be maintained" there and "that an understanding be reached with Newfoundland in order that Canadian forces might be able to operate promptly in the area in the event of another emergency." Accepting that the Commission of Government would be "naturally reluctant to make extensive commitments" while the constitutional question was pending, the Canadians nonetheless held that an "effective management" arrangement could be devised which "would be unobjectionable to the Newfoundland and Canadian people." This would be all the more likely to be accepted by Newfoundlanders if the United Kingdom were party to it.[91] This telegram suggested a willingness on the part of Canada to conclude an interim arrangement, something the British were prepared to accept also, even though it might mean that they would have to negotiate later on with an independent Newfoundland government about their own base rights in the country. A British official noted that a general argreement would be possible if Gander could be opened up for civil operations and "Canadian influence" were removed from there, as well as from Botwood and Bay Bulls, where with the approval of the Commission and on the promise of a ninety-nine year lease Canada had built a marine railway. If these changes were made, Newfoundlanders would be more easily convinced "of the need for Canadian defence facilities at Torbay and Goose Bay and of the right of Canada to use Gander and the

St. John's Naval base in the event of emergency."[92]

As matters developed, it was on the term of the proposed agreement rather than on its actual provisions that the St. John's conference ultimately hinged. The key player on the Newfoundland side, although he was not a member of his country's delegation to the conference, was Walsh. He was not adverse to Confederation but "was resolutely opposed to the granting of any rights to Canada in Newfoundland." Acting on prior instructions, the British delegation initially pushed for a ten-year agreement, something that was acceptable to both the Canadian and Newfoundland delegations. But Walsh threatened to resign rather than be party to such an agreement. This was unprecendented in the history of the Commission and indicative of the changing political times in Newfoundland.[93]

On 1 February a special meeting of the Commission, attended by Bridges, Macdonald, MacKay, Low, and Chadwick, considered the situation which had arisen in the talks. They discussed a draft agreement which had been prepared by the British and Canadian delegations; but Walsh, supported by Emerson, the administrator of the country at the time, Puddester and Wild, "remained intransigent." Convinced by this encounter that a ten-year agreement was now impossible, the British and Canadians next met and produced a draft that would have a minimum term of three years. This document included clauses providing for defence consultations among the three governments as circumstances required and for the right of military aircraft to use Gander, Torbay, and Goose Bay. Chadwick later noted that the inclusion of Goose Bay had been agreed to by the Canadians "after only slight hesitation." The latest draft agreement was considered by the whole conference on 2 February with the result that Neill agreed to recommend it, with amendments, to his government colleagues for adoption. Subsequently, Chadwick lobbied Emerson and Wild and eventually heard favourable responses from both of them. The climax came on the morning of 5 February when a stormy session of the Commission ended with the Newfoundland government approving the draft, despite Walsh's "continuing suspicions" about it. The document, having been further amended, was then adopted by the conference at its final session the same afternoon.[94] At a crucial moment, the British had not only been able to hold the Commission together but to advance their ultimate design for Newfoundland. This had meant on the one hand dampening down the fires of a rising nationalism in Newfoundland, and on the other keeping Ottawa committed to a common objective with London.

The agreement thus negotiated was signed by Macdonald and Neill in St. John's on 8 April and by Addison in London on 3 May.[95] It had an initial three-year term, beginning on 31 March 1946, and, as events unfolded, would expire on a fateful date in Newfoundland's political and constitutional history. The agreement embodied a preamble and six articles, the first of which specified that the term "Newfoundland" meant "Newfoundland and its Dependencies and the territorial waters thereof." This wording was crucial from the British point of view because it ensured that the agreement covered Goose Bay, even though this base was not specifically mentioned in the document.[96] Article two dealt with the Newfoundland Airport at Gander and the seaplane bases at Botwood and Gleneagles. These were transferred back to Newfoundland control and operation, and Canada gave up her right under the 1941 Air Bases Agreement to the fifty-year lease of land at Gander on which she had built facilities during the war. For her part Newfoundland agreed to pay Ottawa $1,000,000 – truly a bargain price – for the transfer to her of various Canadian buildings, works, equipment, and supplies at Gander. Newfoundland also agreed, subject to provisos that followed the 1941 bases accord, to transfer the Newfoundland Airport to Canadian control again should the two countries once more have to fight a common enemy. By article three, Canada gave up her rights under the 1941 agreement to leases at Botwood and Gleneagles. Article four dealt with Torbay. It provided for Canadian title in fee simple to the base and formalized understandings arrived at in Bermuda on the civil aviation use of the facility. Militarily, Canada was authorized to construct and maintain whatever installations she deemed necessary at the base and to station aircraft and personnel there. To the extent practicable, Canada agreed to employ Newfoundland labour at the airport. Article five of the agreement covered the matter of tripartite defence consultations and the right of Canadian and United Kingdom military aircraft to fly over the country and use all airports under Canadian or Newfoundland control. The sixth and final article of the agreement specified its duration. After the initial three-year term, the agreement would remain in force, unless revised "by mutual agreement" or terminated by one of the contracting parties on twelve months' notice. On 29 July 1946 Macdonald and Neill signed a complementary agreement on air transport in St. John's.[97] This specified the terms on which Trans-Canada Air Lines would henceforth provide air service between Newfoundland and the North American continent; this too was subject to cancellation by either party on twelve months' notice. It also formalized those civil aviation understandings reached at Bermuda in relation to Torbay, Goose Bay, and a landing field Canada had built at Buchans not covered by the defence agreement.

The fate of the Admiralty naval base at St. John's was the subject of separate negotiations. In April 1945, Clutterbuck told Walwyn that the Admiralty was anxious "that Canada's interest in Imperial defence should be maintained and developed" and so felt "it very important that the Canadian Government should be encouraged to play a preponderant part in the defence of Newfoundland." Accordingly, the Admiralty would be pleased to see Canada take over responsibility for the maintenance of the Newfoundland base. The "political implications of anything which might be represented as encroachment by Canada on Newfoundland Sovereignty," especially in relation to St. John's harbour, was, however, recognized in London, and the reaction of the Newfoundland public to the Goose Bay agreement had been explained to the Admiralty. "We have made it clear," Clutterbuck wrote, "that the position of the Commission and ourselves as trustees for Newfoundland - particularly when the constitutional question is so much in our minds - is by no means an easy one." He wondered how the government and people of Newfoundland were likely to take a proposal for the Canadian financing of what had to be kept at a base that would not be needed in peacetime.[98]

Having made soundings, Walwyn gave a positive report. If Canada agreed to pay the bills, while acting on the Admiralty's behalf and giving preference to Newfoundland labour, all would be well politically: "What Newfoundland does not want is that this base should become a Canadian base, but that Newfoundland should remain part of the United Kingdom, and so long as Canada merely acts as caretaker for Admiralty property, honour would be satisfied and their sentiments would not be offended. They would, I feel sure, prefer to have a British administration in charge, but the Admiralty point of view is pretty obvious."[99] Following this exchange, a four-man Admiralty mission led by J.A.C. Champion visited St. John's in November 1945. The eventual outcome of its work was a compromise proposal to the Commission that Newfoundland should itself become responsible to the Admiralty for the care and maintenance of the core of properties that would have to be kept up in order to make the base quickly operational again in an emergency. The Admiralty would in turn invite the Royal Canadian Navy to carry out periodic technical inspections of the facilities retained in St. John's and to set appropriate naval maintenance standards. Within limits, Newfoundland would be able to make use of the properties to be kept up, while looking after them. Financially, it was proposed that Newfoundland keep a record of costs and benefits (actual or imputed rent) for a year, whereupon the accounts would be assessed "to see if settlement on any broader or more formal basis was practicable." The properties that made up the wartime base which did not need to be maintained would, except as otherwise agreed upon, be disposed of by the Newfoundland government acting on the Admiralty's behalf.[100] After Champion had visited St. John's again, the Commission of Government agreed, subject to certain amendments, to the terms proposed.[101] In May 1947 an act became law in Newfoundland, vesting indefeasibly in the Admiralty various pieces of land it had acquired in St. John's and its environs in connection with the development of the naval base.[102] All told, yet another potentially divisive question in the long post-war Newfoundland agenda had been quietly resolved.

Newfoundland's resumption of control of Gander produced a mixed result. Walwyn told Addison in January 1946 that he foresaw a half million dollar annual deficit in the operation of the airport, a loss Newfoundland could not avoid. "I want to get the public wise to this," he explained, "before they are confronted with the bill, but they all think an airport is a fine source of revenue."[103] In July 1946, a secret report from Neill to the Dominions Office confirmed Walwyn's pessimistic analysis. The running of the airport was turning out to be "no easy job." The government was making good progress with the provision of a terminal building and with the job of converting barracks into living quarters, but had encountered supply problems. Life was also being made more difficult for the government by the activities of J.R. Smallwood, who had moved to Gander in 1943 to run a pig farm there. He was "urging all employees, radio staff and maintenance workers, to demand higher wages with the threat of strike action." Politically and financially, the situation facing the government with respect to the airport was summed up by Neill as follows:

> The point locally made is – "Why should the Newfoundland taxpayer be saddled with the upkeep of an airport which is used only by trans-Atlantic operators and which confers no benefit on Newfoundland?" There is a certain cogency in the question from the point of view of a Newfoundlander. T.C.A. uses Gander on the regional service to Canada. We get direct labour benefits. We also get publicity benefit. These points are forgotten, or overlooked, in the general question. The old idea that Newfoundland should "cash in" on her strategic position remains in the minds of a certain section. If we attempted to turn strategic position into profits by charging a landing fee to cover all costs we would probably drive operators away.[104]

While the financial future of the airport could not yet be accurately predicted, Neill anticipated a normal annual expenditure of $2,000,000 and an income, from landing fees (to be set, it was decided in London in May, at twice the single landing rate at La Guardia, New York),[105] rents, and other charges, of $1,500,000. The resulting deficit, he cautioned, was a charge which Newfoundland could not "be expected to meet," and there was restiveness abroad about it.[106]

Faced with this situation, the British at first contemplated an approach to the Provisional International Civil Aviation Organization for financial assistance to Newfoundland, but this was ultimately deemed impracticable, at least for the moment.[107] Instead, after Neill had visited London, a proposal was put to St. John's whereby the United Kingdom would undertake "to meet such portion of the deficit of the running costs of the airport as could not be attributed to the Newfoundland Government on account of the benefits accruing to Newfoundland from the operation of Gander."[108] The term of this undertaking would be from the date of the transfer of the airport back to Newfoundland and for as long as the existing constitution remained in force. As a first step towards introducing the new system, an expert party from the Ministry of Civil Aviation would shortly visit Newfoundland to examine costs and make recommendations for deficit reduction.

This party, three in number, led by L.S. Mills, arrived in Newfoundland towards the end of February 1946, and met with the Commission itself in mid-March. In the course of these discussions, it was pointed out by Mills that 1,150 people were now employed at Gander by the Newfoundland government at a cost of $1,250,000 annually, while 500 others worked for the airlines and their subsidiaries operating through the airport. The British official's estimate of the likely 1946-47 deficit on the airport was $750,000, for Newfoundland, a substantial sum.[109] As a result of the work of the expert party, the United Kingdom agreed to assume two-thirds of the net operating deficit of the airport. Newfoundland would bear the remainder but would have to contribute a minimum of $250,000 annually. Coincidentally, the United Kingdom sold to Newfoundland, for $200,000, the wartime buildings and assets of the Royal Air Force and Ministry of Aircraft Production at Gander which were valued at $2,500,000.[110]

While the Commission was wrestling with Gander's financial troubles and the myriad other problems connected with the running of an international airport, it was involved in some hard bargaining with the United States over the status, so far as civil aviation was concerned, of that country's leased bases in Newfoundland. In August 1945 Hopper urged the Newfoundland government to allow Trans-Canada Air Lines to begin operating a commercial service through Harmon Field at Stephenville.[111] This action was prompted by an appeal to the consulate in St. John's from the Bay of Islands Businessmen's Association at Corner Brook, which wanted to improve transportation facilities on the west coast of the island.[112] This appeal enjoyed Canadian support. The United States, Hopper explained, hoped for a general understanding about the use of its leased bases in Newfoundland by commercial aircraft and would welcome the use of Harmon Field by Trans-Canada Air Lines on its Newfoundland-Canada service as an interim measure.[113]

The conjunction of west coast, Canadian, and American interests on this issue highlighted the difficulty of working out truly "national" economic policies in Newfoundland and illustrated again a long history of rivalry between St. John's and the Bay of Islands area.[114] But in this particular instance the Commission was well placed to take on all comers in its defence of Gander's pre-eminence as Newfoundland's international gateway. The strength of the Newfoundland government's position lay in Article XI (5) of the 27 March 1941, Anglo-American Leased Bases Agreement:

Commercial aircraft will not be authorised to operate from any of the Bases (save in case of emergency or for strictly military purposes under supervision of the War and Navy Departments) except by agreement between the United States and the Government of the United Kingdom; provided that in the case of Newfoundland such agreement shall be between the United States and the Government of Newfoundland.[115]

Thus secured, Newfoundland refused to allow Trans-Canada Air Lines into Harmon Field lest this action prejudice the future of Gander by setting an unfortunate precedent in the use of the leased bases. The American submission, Walwyn explained to Addison, expressed "solicitude for the convenience of the Newfoundland travelling public," but it was doubtful whether this was "the sole basis of the present representations." Even the interim arrangement contemplated had its dangers, no matter how "hedged about with limitations and conditions." In short, "the temporary convenience of a comparatively small group of potential air passengers" was outweighed by "the risk of a false step."[116]

Subsequently, Newfoundland authorized three United States airlines, Pan American, American Export, and Trans-Continental and Western, to operate through Gander on a two freedoms basis.[117] The first actual American use of the airport under this arrangement occurred on 23 October 1945, when an American Export Airlines plane, en route overseas from the United States, landed. To the dismay of Pattison, who was on the scene, the aircraft in question disembarked one passenger and 1,600 pounds of mail in clear violation of the two freedoms understanding. Pattison immediately telephoned Puddester in St. John's – it was around midnight – and was told that both passenger and mail would have to be taken back on board and carried on to England. The commissioner changed his mind about the passenger, however, when Pattison explained that it was none other than His Excellency James F. O'Neill, the Roman Catholic bishop of Harbour Grace. He could hardly be sent winging out over the Atlantic in order to maintain the letter of the law, and his unorthodox arrival was excused by the government because of his "high position in the Church." When the Americans refused to take the mail back on board, it was agreed that it would be held by Newfoundland customs pending the return journey of the plane, when it would be picked up and carried back to the United States. Newfoundland did not make a written protest about this incident, but an indignant Puddester saw Robert J. Cavanaugh, the United States vice consul in St. John's, and through him called on the State Department to remonstrate with the offending airline.[118]

During 1946, the situation facing the Commission over the future of United States leased bases in the country was further complicated by the preparation of a general Anglo-American leased base fields agreement.[119] This dealt with civil aviation rights in the other jurisdictions covered by the 1941 agreement, and was designed to open up Bermuda and the Caribbean for air travel by making use of local United States base facilities. Because of Article XI (5), Newfoundland was a separate case; but the Americans made their ultimate acceptance of the larger deal, in which they had conceded much, conditional on a satisfactory arrangement being made between themselves and Newfoundland and Canada about civil aviation rights at Gander, Harmon Field, Torbay, Argentia, and Goose Bay. The Commission agreed in principle to negotiate the issue, and in July 1946 its representatives in Washington were given a draft agreement. This document was examined in London and, having been discussed there by Neill at the beginning of 1947, amended considerably. In April 1947 the negotiations entered a new phase when the British pressed the United States informally to drop Gander from the list of airfields to be covered by the proposed agreement with Newfoundland.[120] This facility, it was explained, was not a leased base, and Newfoundland could not be reasonably expected to agree to its inclusion. The Americans now went along with this but the State Department remained committed to the American operators using Gander "to secure some safeguard concerning landing fees there."[121] This was a matter about which there had been many complaints but which Newfoundland claimed was in her sovereign domain. In May the United States proposed to Newfoundland that there be an exchange of notes on the signing of the base fields agreement whereby any dispute about the charges imposed on American carriers by Newfoundland would be referred to an ad hoc tribunal.[122] Newfoundland and the United States would each name one member to such a panel and the two national members would then select a third colleague. Newfoundland rejected this and a similar British offer on the grounds that landing fees affected many countries and could not therefore be dealt with bilaterally, that the issue was one of domestic concern, and that in any case aggrieved parties had an appeal procedure under article 15 of the International Civil Aviation Organization Convention.[123] Earlier, in calling for a resumption of negotiations with the United States, London had told St. John's that it would be made clear to the State Department by the embassy in Washington that there could be "no question of linking landing fees at Gander with commercial use of leased bases."[124]

This was the situation, then, when Neill held further talks in Washington in June. An understanding was reached on this occasion whereby the United States and the United Kingdom would together enjoin the Council of ICAO (the provisional body had now been made permanent) to spell out a precise procedure for dealing with "disputes and disagreements" referred to it, with particular reference to Article 15. The purpose of this joint effort would be to guarantee that such business would be handled by the international body with despatch and "to allay ... anxiety" about article 15 arising from the concern that if disputes had to be dealt with by the Council of ICAO acting as a whole, they would not be handled "adequately promptly and fairly."[125] With the landing fees issue thus shunted aside, Neill was able to reach agreement with his United States counterparts, but his own government colleagues in St. John's balked at the document he had negotiated. From Newfoundland's point of view, the problem with the draft lay in a provision which ran as follows: "In the event of Gander airfield being closed temporarily or permanently or otherwise unavailable as a regular civil international airport, the Government of Newfoundland *will* designate (subject in the case of Argentia and Stephenville to the concurrence of the United States Military Authorities) another suitable airport in Newfoundland either temporarily or permanently, as the case may be, as a regular civil international airport."[126] The Commission, with Neill dissenting, wanted the word "will" in this clause changed to "may" on the grounds that to make the designation of an alternate airport compulsory would be to commit "their eventual successors to a state of affairs where in the event, for instance, of Gander being closed for financial reasons, they would have no recourse but to accept the dictates of ICAO and/or the powerful American operators." The Commission also feared that Newfoundland "would be debarred from stepping up the landing fees at Gander on the grounds that American bases were readily available at economic rates." In sum, what Newfoundland wanted was "to make alternate designation *permissive* instead of *compulsory*." The British believed Newfoundland was "splitting hairs" in all this, but the Commission stood firm on the issue and in the end the Americans climbed down.[127]

Washington suspended negotiations with Newfoundland in October 1947, but then proceeded to complete the long delayed Anglo-American Base Fields Agreement, an action that took the heat from London over the delay of that agreement off St. John's.[128] The Commission had won a round, and Stephenville and Argentia, so far as civil aviation was concerned, retained their existing status as bad weather alternatives, a service they had been providing for over a year based on an informal understanding. Meanwhile, Gander, whose primacy the Commission had so vigorously defended, was a going concern, and an advance guard of what would in time be a large host of often surprised transatlantic travellers had already experienced its delights. In 1948 the flavour of what had by then become one of the world's exotic way stations was nicely captured by Nevil Shute in his novel *No Highway*.[129] Typically, apart from wanting directions to food, drink, and other creature comforts, the transatlantic passenger in transit through Gander, who often woke up to find himself there or almost there, had three questions in mind. In order, these were: where am I? what am I doing here? and when do I leave? For all that, and vulnerable as it might be to technological change, Newfoundland had found a new industry - at least of sorts.

SYNOPSIS: 1945-49 (DIPLOMATIC AND ADMINISTRATIVE DEVELOPMENTS)

After the war the Commission of Government was faced domestically and internationally with extensive and potentially troublesome agendas in its administration of Newfoundland's day to day affairs. It was then that Walsh emerged as the dominant Newfoundland member of the Commission. In 1946, with its nationalist critics keeping vigilant watch, the Commission carried through a tricky defence and civil aviation settlement with Canada. This satisfied the immediate needs of the parties involved, while leaving open the possibility for a future Newfoundland government to bargain afresh if it saw fit. The initial three-year term of the Newfoundland-Canada defence agreement also gave Ottawa an additional incentive to pursue the goal of Confederation and a timetable for achieving it, in order to be able to make defence arrangements in Newfoundland after 31 March 1949 a matter of domestic policy. This in turn well suited the United Kingdom's present purpose in Newfoundland. The British also had reason to be satisfied with the agreement in that it guaranteed during its term access for their military aircraft to all Canadian bases in the country including, implicitly, the much debated Goose Bay. In 1946-47 the Commission and the British and Canadian authorities were also able, without stirring up trouble in Newfoundland, to make a mutually satisfactory arrangement on the future of the Admiralty's St. John's naval base. Yet another potentially tricky negotiation for the Commission was successfully concluded in 1948 by the completion of the second supplementary lease between Newfoundland and the United States on American bases in the country. For their part, the Americans were pleased to tidy up this delicate matter before the Commission of Government went "out of ... business."[130]

A major preoccupation of the Commission after the war was the resumption of control of the Newfoundland Airport at Gander and the commercial development of the airport as a vital stopover facility for transatlantic passenger flights. The Commission succeeded in its purpose at Gander, and if it had not always bargained as aggressively about international civil aviation rights as some Newfoundland businessmen might have wished, it showed itself, perhaps through fear of public opinion, a determined defender of Newfoundland interests when it came to the American ambition to use their leased bases in the country for civil aviation purposes. Though its critics bemoaned the cost to the country of running Gander and trumpeted another sellout, the Commission was able both to generate considerable employment there and to prevent business from being siphoned off to landing fields outside its jurisdiction. Through all this, moreover, the Commission had to contend with the influence of the American transatlantic carriers, a powerful lobby in Washington, who were unhappy with landing fees at Gander and bent on constraining Newfoundland's freedom of action to set such charges.

The economic policy of the Commission after 1945, closely supervised from London, was one of cautious pump priming and investment. A scaled down version of the 1944 reconstruction plan which still included a long-term scheme for the development of the frozen fish industry was carried out alongside the not always well-received civil re-establishment plan. The country enjoyed a relatively smooth peacetime adjustment; the whole period was in Newfoundland, as in so many other places, a notable contrast to the turbulent immediate post World War I years. The level of employment remained high, the number of relief recipients correspondingly low, and markets good.

Furthermore, when major problems did arise, for example, the marketing of fish in the sterling area or the railway strike of 1948, they did not get out of hand. Nor did concern about the rising cost of living become an unmanageable political issue. Whitehall might regret various increases in public service salaries, but the good news was that the Commission had the revenue to meet the demands of its own employees. Contrary to earlier expectations, not only did public spending in Newfoundland reach new heights in the second half of the 1940s but the government's accumulated surplus also continued to grow. In these happy circumstances the Commission was able to improve further the country's social and educational services. At the same time it refined and consolidated its earlier civil service reforms, an achievement it considered one of its finest accomplishments.

Nonetheless, for all the welcome and encouraging reports out of St. John's, the underlying assumption of British policy towards Newfoundland remained what it had been through the war, namely, that a rainy day would soon dawn in the country. If this, fortunately, had not yet arrived, the prevailing view was that it had merely been delayed. Accordingly, the touchstone of the Commission's administration had to be the preservation of the surplus to meet a future emergency. If the downturn did not come during the time of the Commission, that would be all to the good, but it could not be assumed that things would work out this way. Moreover, for the Commission to pass on a big surplus to the next government would have a benefit of another kind. The surplus would bear witness to the United Kingdom's good stewardship while Newfoundland's trustee since 1934. The British had lived through the past in Newfoundland and believed that the country could not go it alone in the modern world. They knew, as well, that one possible constitutional future there – turning the clock back to 1934 – would not work. As the Newfoundlanders themselves debated their constitutional future, it turned out that a good many of them also subscribed to this view.

CHAPTER TEN

The National Convention, 1946-48

Some of the old politicians are already *creeping out of the jungle* and appealing for the support of their old constituencies.

Governor Sir Humphrey Walwyn to Lord Addison, January 1946

Politically, events immediately after the war were dominated by the run-up to the National Convention. In June 1945, former minister of finance, Peter Cashin, fired the opening salvo in what would be for him a long and bruising campaign when he gave the first of a series of radio addresses in which he styled himself the "Voice of Liberty."[1] Walwyn characterized his performance as "typical of the old time politician, hurling abuse at everybody. A very good advertisement of what people may expect if they get responsible government."[2] Clutterbuck was no less harsh, but he saw potential advantage in Cashin's initiative just the same:

> Knowing Mr. Cashin's record the odds are that he has nothing more in mind than to steer opinion towards the resumption of the old form of self-gov[ernmen]t so that he and his like can once more get the pickings. It obviously suits him in these circ[umstance]s not only to belittle the Comm[ission]'s doings but also the help given by the UK since 1934. However he is so discredited that he will probably upset more people than he is likely to convert. By and large it is not a bad thing that somebody - even a man of his stamp - sh[oul]d be taking the field, since his campaign if continued ought to do something to stir N[ewfound]landers out of their present apathy and draw some of the better type into the arena.[3]

The stirring of new political life in Newfoundland was also evident during 1945 in various calls to London for the restoration of self-government. In July 1945, a resolution to this effect was passed by the Bell Island

Miners' Union.[4] The next month, by a vote of 17 to 16, the annual convention of the Newfoundland Federation of Labour, after considering three resolutions dealing with constitutional change and political action, came out in favour of "the responsible form of government." At the same time, it was decided that a committee should "be appointed to investigate the economic position of the country in relation to this form of government."[5] Then, after the formation of the Labour government in the United Kingdom, the Newfoundland Lumbermen's Association called on Prime Minister Attlee, in a telegram signed by President J.J. Thompson, to give Newfoundland "a government by the people for the people and of the people," something that was at present "sadly lacking."[6] In November Walwyn forwarded to London a resolution in favour of the restoration of self-government which had been passed at a meeting in Cape Broyle where Cashin had been born in 1890 and where his family influence remained strong.[7] These developments in Newfoundland caused no particular concern in London. In the case of the Bell Island protest, one British official wrote that D.I. Jackman, the president of the local union, was a "nee'r-do well and a misguided agitator." Other industrial unions, it was believed at the Dominions Office, would be unlikely to respond to "Cashin's blandishments" because they felt "they never had a fair deal in the old days."[8] In short, when the announcement about the calling of the National Convention was made in December 1945,[9] London believed that it had the situation in Newfoundland well under control. If anything, the job would be to bring Newfoundlanders in general back to life again politically. In these circumstances, subsequent protests to the Dominions Office by the Newfoundland Labourers' Union of Corner Brook, the Botwood Longshoremen's Protective Union, and the Newfoundland Lumbermen's Association against the turn events had taken, got nowhere.[10] London also routinely brushed aside a petition to the King requesting the restoration of Responsible Government that Cashin circulated in the spring of 1946.[11]

Walwyn told Addison in January 1946 that the news of the National Convention had "produced little reaction locally." "It was really," the soon-to-depart Governor wrote in a vintage passage, "what most people expected although there is a certain element that appears disappointed in the absence of financial assistance. Generally speaking there is a feeling of alarm that the baby is now being handed to them and they don't know how to handle it. Some of the old politicians are already creeping out of the jungle and appealing for the support of their old constituencies." Walwyn's fear was that the "right people" wouldn't run for election, through fear "of being labelled for carrying responsibility" for what ultimately might happen.[12]

For whatever reason, the actual turnout of candidates varied considerably throughout the country. Under the terms of the National Convention Act, polling day was set by the government for 21 June in thirty-five of the thirty-eight electoral districts the country was divided into for the purpose at hand.[13] In three remote districts, including Labrador, which would be returning a member to an elected Newfoundland body for the first time, the election was scheduled to be held at later dates.[14] In the districts to vote on 21 June, a total of 123 candidates stood for election, but seven of them were unopposed.[15]

Ultimately, eight members or delegates – there were forty-five altogether – were returned to the convention by acclamation, all in rural districts. The districts with the largest numbers of candidates were St. John's City (West) (12) and St. John's City (East) (9), each of which was to elect three candidates. Only two women were nominated in the whole country but neither succeeded.[16] Although there were some lively contests, especially in the St. John's area, overall the turnout in the election, for which Magistrate Short, assisted by Wallace Halfyard, served as chief electoral officer, was lacklustre.[17] The United States consul in St. John's attributed the "light vote" to, among other things, "the absence of party rivalry, the failure by many to appreciate the importance of the Convention and the fact that many voters were absent from their districts in pursuit of their avocations, such as the fishermen and woodsmen." It was also noted that candidates for the election had been "placed in the position of having to toot their own horn without being able to campaign on any particular issue." In the outports, moreover, there had been candidates apparently with "no notion" of what the election was all about, who had run campaigns "consisting of making promises of what they would do for their constituents if elected." Whatever the validity of these observations about the campaign, this assessment of the electorate's response to it was correct. On an issue of "transcending importance" and in the first countrywide vote held in more than fourteen years, participation had been "disappointingly low."[18]

Nonetheless, the first objective of British policy had been achieved: the National Convention members were chosen; the convention's legitimacy was accepted. Furthermore the members elected to it represented a variety of interests and outlooks, though fully 60 per cent of them, according to one high level 1946 British document, "belonged to the merchant class."[19] Denominationally, the successful candidates consisted of seventeen members of the Church of England, thirteen Roman Catholics, twelve adherents of the United Church of Canada, two members of the Salvation Army, and one Presbyterian.[20] Occupationally, the largest single group returned consisted of thirteen merchants but a number of prominent unionists were also elected. A district labour party which had sprung up in St. John's supported eight candidates in the capital area but only five of these were actually labour leaders and only two were successful in the election.[21] They were Gordon Higgins (St. John's City East), a prominent lawyer one of whose clients was the Newfoundland Seamen's Association, and Frank Fogwill (St. John's East). Five of the members returned had previously sat in the House of Assembly, a group that included Gordon Bradley (Bonavista East) and Roland Starkes (Green Bay), the only two members of the old Liberal Party to have survived its electoral debacle in 1932.[22] No member of the convention - this spoke volumes about power relationships in local society - was identified either as a fisherman or a logger, though a number of fishermen had run for election. In Bonavista Centre, which included Gander, the voters made a fateful choice for the future of the country when they returned J.R. Smallwood. Having published a series of eleven newspaper letters in the *Daily News* during March 1946 on the advantages to Newfoundland of Confederation with Canada, he went on to win election to the convention by the widest margin of any candidate.[23]

Smallwood, whose name had occasionally surfaced earlier in the official correspondence of the Commission, was to say the least a most unconventional and unorthodox Newfoundlander.[24] He was the son of Charles William Smallwood and Mary (Minnie) Ellen Devanna and was born at Gambo, Bonavista Bay, on 24 December 1900. He was the grandson of David Smallwood, who had migrated from Prince Edward Island and established a sawmill at Gambo. In Newfoundland the term "bayman" is used, affectionately or pejoratively, depending on the context, to describe the male outporter. Later on Smallwood claimed to have a special affinity with the "bay" people, because of his place of birth, although he grew up in St. John's. There he lived in several different houses and attended several schools. He finished his education at Bishop Feild College, the leading boys' school of the Church of England, leaving it at age fifteen after a quarrel with a housemaster. He worked variously as an apprentice printer, journalist, author, and union organizer. In connection with the latter work, he undertook to walk across Newfoundland in 1925 in order to organize sectionmen threatened with a pay cut. This journey took him from Port aux Basques to a point near Avondale, not far from St. John's; it was one of many enterprises that helped give him an intimate and detailed knowledge of his country and its inhabitants. In 1925 Smallwood launched a short-lived Newfoundland Federation of Labour.[25] His newspaper career included a stint with the leftist New York *Call*. He also lived abroad for a brief period in London, England, where he moved in left wing circles and produced his first book, *Coaker of Newfoundland: The Man Who Led the Deep Sea Fishermen to Political Power*. From 1927 to 1930

Smallwood put out the *Humber Herald* at Curling, near Corner Brook, and in 1931 he published *The New Newfoundland*, which eulogized the policy of resource development favoured by Richard Squires.[26]

In the 1932 general election Smallwood ran as a Liberal in Bonavista South but lost to Herman Quinton by a wide margin. Thereafter he promoted a Fishermen's Co-operative Union with himself as "national chairman" and served as President of the Bonavista Co-operative Society, which he also organized.[27] While thus engaged, he came unfavourably to the attention of the authorities in St. John's through letters written by his erstwhile fellow Liberal candidate and future close political associate Gordon Bradley. Although Bradley's report of his public enquiry into logging had been poorly received by the Commission, the government nevertheless had appointed him magistrate at Bonavista. Bradley accused Smallwood of financial mismanagement of the affairs of the co-operative. Smallwood, he wrote, was unreliable "in money matters" and though having "quite a considerable theoretical acquaintance with the history of the co-operative movement" was "entirely lacking" in "practical experience." Looking to the future of co-operative development locally, Bradley recommended: "If the Government has any intention of giving financial assistance to a co-operative movement in Bonavista, (and I heartily support the idea) both its policy and funds should be wholly free from the control or even the influence of Mr. Smallwood. I think he might be quite useful as a propagandist to travel about the country teaching the idea of co-operation, but as a business executive he is hopeless. No reliance is to be placed upon him where steady work or sound judgment is required. He is not stable."[28]

When Bradley had suggested to Smallwood, who was at this time apparently himself living hand to mouth, that he "get a position which would give him sufficient income to keep his family in comfort," the latter had always replied that "he could not work at a job in which he was not interested." To Bradley this was evidently wrong-headed, but in fact it showed a high degree of self-knowledge. The pattern of Smallwood's life had been and would remain the pursuit of a series of enthusiasms. These led to many ups and downs, which mixed brilliant successes with notable misadventures but which above all ensured that Smallwood could never be considered ordinary. In May 1936 Bradley reported that Smallwood, who had now moved on, had been lucky to get away from Bonavista without having had a "rough time" at the hands of some members of his co-operative.[29] At this stage of his life Smallwood seems to have been between the millstones of the Commission and the masses he sought to lead. Legally, however, nothing came of the accusations, and in fairness that fact must be weighed against Bradley's charges, whatever their motive; in history as in law, the dictum "innocent until proven guilty" is fundamental. Still the incident is important in assessing Smallwood's career, if only because it likely confirmed for the authorities his reputation as a rabble-rouser and potential troublemaker. This was an impression that had already resulted in at least one undercover police report on his political speechmaking to an ever vigilant and suspicious Department of Justice.[30]

For his own part, Smallwood, ever the optimist in a land of tenacious survivors whose focus understandably was on the next catch or crop, quickly moved on from the Bonavista fiasco to new ventures. In 1937 he brought out the substantial two volume *The Book of Newfoundland*, which he then peddled door to door.[31] Considering the economic condition of the country at the time, this was a monumentally quixotic, if from a literary point of view prodigious and praiseworthy, undertaking. It was the action of a dreamer and a creative spender far removed from the world of cost accounting, for whom money seems to have been a means rather than an end. In 1937 also, Smallwood struck it lucky when he began broadcasting as "The Barrelman" over VONF.[32] He had previously used this pseudonym, a name given the crew member of a whaling or sealing ship who went to the masthead to direct his comrades below, in a column entitled "From the Masthead" that he had contributed to the *Daily News*. The purpose of "The Barrelman" was to make "Newfoundland better known to Newfoundlanders," and the program proved a big hit. More to the point politically, it gave Smallwood one of the best known radio voices in Newfoundland. It was while he was basking in this success that he criticized the government for the Bowaters deal.

In 1941 while editor of *The Express*, he aroused the Commission's suspicions in connection with a possible public protest against the Anglo-American Leased Bases Agreement. The backers of the Express Publishing Company were F.M. O'Leary, a prominent Water Street merchant and the sponsor of "The Barrelman" radio program, Gordon Higgins, and Eric Cook,[33] all of whom were also active in the Newfoundland National Association of St. John's which was decidedly oriented to business and the professions. If Smallwood and his 1941 business and legal associates were strange ideological bedfellows, brought together by a common desire for political and constitutional change, the connection had advantages for all concerned. For the politically ambitious Smallwood, after his organizational disappointments in the 1930s at a different level of Newfoundland society, it might have seemed that learning to live with rather than fighting the elite of the country represented a possible way forward. He had mixed with the masses and knew their limitations as well as their yearnings. Conversely, as a highly skilled newspaperman and broadcaster with a substantial following who knew how to whip up support for a cause, he was a useful propagandist for Water Street – provided he could be kept under control. Thus began a complex relationship between a populist and an elite oligarchy that would be central to the future of Newfoundland politics.

From *The Express* itself, which had as its motto "National Patriotism, National Unity, National Progress," came one of the strongest attacks ever directed against the Commission of Government.[34] Beginning in the first issue, Smallwood wrote a series of scathing articles for the paper on "The Story of Commission Government," while Eric Cook contributed an incisive critique, in several parts, of the report of the Amulree Royal Commission, a document described as "The Commission Government's 'Bible.'" The 15 March issue of *The Express* featured a wickedly funny satire of a Commission of Government press communiqué in which the administration was referred to as "The Ommission of Government" and individual commissioners were described as the "Ommissioner for Natural Reverses," etc.[35] But for all its journalistic bravura, the paper and the larger movement behind it faced an insuperable obstacle in the view, cleverly disseminated by the Commission in the critical spring of 1941, that wartime was no time to rock the boat. Following the demise of *The Express*, which lasted for only nine weekly issues, Smallwood stayed in St. John's for two years but, restless spirit that he was, soon moved again, this time to Gander. His pig farming days there dated from 1943, time enough to allow him to meet the residence requirement for candidacy in a particular district as specified in the National Convention Act.

The Commission of Government's preliminary estimate of the constitutional preferences of the winning candidates in the election was that a "quarter or slightly more" of them wanted Responsible Government. Another quarter was thought to be "sympathetic" to this option but wanted "to examine all facts and evidence available before making a final decision." A third group, again a quarter, leaned to the view that the time was not ripe for the return of Responsible Government. The remaining election winners were "sympathetic to confederation with Canada."[36] Raymond Gushue's sense of how things would work out, which he explained to Hickerson in Washington before the election, was that a decision would ultimately be made to continue with Commission of Government. The "more serious Newfoundland voters," he told the American official, "had been frightened ... by the performance of some of the old line politicians." Their "antics" had "scared" the voters against a return to Responsible Government, about which Gushue said he had "felt confident" shortly before. Confederation, Hickerson noted, was a course viewed darkly by this particular Newfoundland official.[37]

Whatever else the National Convention might or might not accomplish, one thing was clear about it from the beginning: it would not be allowed to put the Commission of Government in the witness box. Unlike a legislature, the convention could not call the executive branch of government to account. Rather, it was constrained in all its activities by the terms of the National Convention Act and the decisions of the Commission under that act. The convention was empowered by the legislation to establish rules for its own governance and for "the attendance of members and the conduct of business," but it was left to the Governor in Commission to provide the convention with "advisers, officers and servants" as might be seen fit. The allowances and expenses paid to members were likewise to be determined. In sum, the convention had no budget of its own and could only run up whatever expenses the Commission would allow. Nor did the convention even have the right to name its own chairman: by the terms of the act, this position was reserved for a judge of the Newfoundland Supreme Court appointed by the Governor in Commission.[38] In practice the first appointee to the post was Judge Cyril J. Fox, a Roman Catholic who had been named to the bench in 1944.[39] Last, but not least, the convention was hemmed in by the fact that the act specified precisely what it was created to do.

> It shall be the duty and function of the Convention to consider and discuss among themselves as elected representatives of the people of Newfoundland the changes that have taken place in the financial and economic situation of the Island since 1934, and, bearing in mind the extent to which the high revenues of recent years have been due to wartime conditions, to examine the position of the country and to make recommendations to His Majesty's Government in the United Kingdom as to possible forms of future government to be put before the people at a national referendum.[40]

To add to all this, it was agreed in advance between Fox and the government that "no member of the Commission of Government should appear before the Convention in session convened, but that at the discretion of Commissioners information would be placed before Committees of the Convention by the Commissioners concerned upon request of the Chairmen on behalf of the Convention."[41] Under the act the calling together of the convention in the first instance was to be by proclamation of the governor, but thereafter the convention could decide where and when it would meet.[42]

The formal opening took place on 11 September in the House of Assembly Chamber in the Colonial Building. Wheare was present, and the proceedings were in two parts, the second of which was broadcast live by the Broadcasting Corporation of Newfoundland. By prior agreement between Fox and the Commission the occasion was marked with the "formalities customary in connection with the opening of the House of Assembly," adapted as circumstances required.[43] The members of the convention were not, however, required to take the oath of allegiance, as the elected members of a legislature had to. This was a subtle but intentional distinction. The secretary named to the convention by the Commission and chosen in part because of his war service, was Captain W. Gordon Warren, who had run in St. John's City (East) in the election and been defeated.[44] No sooner had the convention got underway than the question of the attendance of commissioners at its sessions was raised in debate. This delicate point was discussed again by Fox and the government on 13 September and understandings were reached which confirmed and made more explicit the relationship agreed upon earlier. These Fox undertook to pass on to the convention. Under "no circumstances" would commissioners be "willing to appear before the Convention in public session." To assist the work of the convention, however, individual commissioners would be willing to attend meetings of its committees in private and to bring along with them members of their staff for the purpose of discussing matters relevant to the activities of their own departments. If instead committees chose, for the sake of convenience, to go to the office of individual commissioners for the same purpose, this too would be acceptable, whereupon "the appropriate officers and the Departmental records would be available for consultation." Any request or supplementary request to a commissioner for information would have to be submitted "in writing in duplicate." Should "oral explanations" be required of them, commissioners would have to give these privately. If a committee required information "immediately," its chairman could communicate directly "with the Commissioner or the Head of the Division concerned."[45]

After a plethora of questions had been tabled in the first days of the convention, these procedures were further refined at a meeting of the government which Fox attended on 20 September. At this time he indicated that measures were under consideration which would "ensure that only information necessary to the work of the Convention would be sought." Henceforth, it was intended, all questions would be vetted by an information committee. It would be the job of this committee to avoid duplication in questions, to apply the test of relevance to all information sought, and to see "that a certain restraint was exercised" on the enquiries made so as not to put an "undue burden" on government departments. Only questions thus approved would be passed on to the various investigative committees through which the convention proposed to work with the government. Accordingly, there was no need for the Commission to address any of the questions already put until these had been sifted by the Information Committee.[46] Subsequently, the government directed officials who were required to attend committee meetings of the convention to ask for notice, preferably in writing, "of difficult or complicated questions."[47]

The National Convention created thirteen committees in its preliminary phase, leaving all appointments to them to Fox. This number included the Information Committee (also referred to in the minutes as a subcommittee)[48] agreed to between the chairman and the Commission. The first three committees to be launched were the rules and procedure, steering, and library committees.[49] Thereafter the convention created nine investigative committees, each of which would enquire, with the help of subcommittees if necessary, into a particular aspect of the country's economy and society. Specifically, committees were created to study fisheries, finance, forestry, mining, agriculture, local industries, education, public health and welfare, and transportation and communications.[50] The plan of the convention was to receive the reports of these committees and then, using the information thus obtained, move on to the constitutional issue. By its own rules the convention was scheduled to meet in full session Monday to Friday, 3 to 6 PM, unless adjourned for committee meetings, which frequently occurred.[51] Once the nine investigative committees on the economy began their work and debate on the constitutional issue progressed, night sessions were called. Sometime in October (probably around the twentieth) the Broadcasting Corporation of Newfoundland recorded a session of the convention and subsequently broadcast it. This presentation proved such a hit that the corporation then began recording and broadcasting the sessions on a regular basis.[52] These broadcasts more than anything else drew the attention of the Newfoundland public to what was now happening. They also helped create a new generation of Newfoundland political stars, the chief of whom would be Smallwood, a polished performer on the airwaves. In his quarterly report of 20 November 1946, W.F. Galgay, the General Manager of the Broadcasting Corporation, noted that its National Convention broadcasts had been the organization's most important work in the period under review.[53] If anything, this understated the importance of what the corporation had done.

Not surprisingly, the reports produced by the convention's committees mixed frustration with hopes and dreams.[54] But in the long run they may also have had the effect of awakening Newfoundlanders generally to some harsh realities, of giving local politics a badly needed focus, and of providing the prospective leaders of the country with a working agenda. From the British point of view the reports turned out to be harmless, if somewhat windy, and at times, ungrateful and wrong-headed exercises, that allowed some steam to be vented politically without threatening either normal commission rule or their own grand design. The first of the documents in question to be ready for consideration by the convention as a whole was the interim report of the fisheries committee, which was presented by R.B. Job (St. John's City East), one of the fishing industry's most prominent businessmen, on 10 October.[55] Of this report and the debate on it, George K. Donald, the United States Consul General in St. John's, and an official with a good eye for Newfoundland politics, made this harsh but revealing comment to the State Department: "The idea that developed was that the world owes Newfoundland a living and [that] an appeal to the humanitarian instincts of the great white fathers in Washington, Ottawa and London might bring that about – emphasis being placed on Washington which had more to offer in the way of markets and which is so deeply indebted to this country for the protection afforded the United States by Newfoundland's strategic position." According to Donald, Raymond Gushue had to talk the fisheries committee out of sending a delegation to Washington to look for "customs concessions."[56]

With this episode behind it, the convention busied itself again with committee work until 28 October, when it received what Donald termed the "relatively unprovocative" education and forestry committee reports. The first dealt mainly with financial matters, but the second was made "slightly less boring," for Donald at least, by the fact that in reviewing it Peter Cashin (St. John's City West) "rehashed" the 1938 Bowaters deal, claiming that this was costing the country three quarters of a million dollars annually in lost revenue.[57] Following the committee presentations on the twenty-eighth, Smallwood electrified the convention with a motion calling for the "appropriate authorities" (i.e. the Commission) to be advised that the convention desired to find out from the government of Canada its attitude towards the federal union of the two countries and wished to send a delegation to Ottawa to determine the "terms and conditions" upon which the Canadian authorities might be willing to take this step. The proposed delegation would have "no authority whatsoever to negotiate or conclude any agreement or in any manner to bind the Convention or the people of Newfoundland." Its justification rather lay in the fact that the convention itself and the people at large "should be fully informed so far as possible of all facts having any bearing upon forms of government that might be submitted to the people in a National Referendum."[58]

In August, Smallwood had visited Ottawa on a fact finding mission of his own, though his plans to go there had alarmed High Commissioner Macdonald, who feared that his journey would stir up resentment in Newfoundland against Canada.[59] In fact his visit passed off without incident.[60] Smallwood himself later gave this description of how he was received in the Canadian capital: "I expected to have a warm welcome in Ottawa. If the plague had descended on them, I didn't think they would have been any more scared. They were scared. They were really scared; I was almost an untouchable."[61] Nevertheless, as MacKay would recall,

Smallwood made a vivid and favourable impression on many of those he met in what turned out to be a busy round of high level engagements.[62] More importantly, the articulate, cheeky, resourceful, and immensely energetic Newfoundlander who had with mixed results embraced many causes, returned convinced of success for his latest enthusiasm. He had avidly taken up the cause of Confederation.

Smallwood's motion of 28 October, however, was given a rough reception by many of his convention colleagues. Michael F. Harrington (St. John's City West), a journalist and Smallwood's successor as the Barrelman, spoke for many when he got up and said that the motion was premature. Union with Canada, he implied, might be unconstitutional. Moreover, behind the scenes Smallwood was involved in "the lowest kind of political chicanery."[63] For his part, Cashin claimed that the Commission and the Dominions Office were behind Smallwood's motion. There were, he said, only two constitutional options the convention could legitimately consider. These were Commission of Government and Responsible Government. Confederation was not covered by the National Convention Act, and a resolution "to seek terms from Moscow" would make as much sense as the motion Smallwood had introduced.[64] Early on in the debate, Albert E. Penney (Carbonear) introduced an amendment to the resolution whereby consideration of the question of sending a delegation to Ottawa would be deferred until the reports of all the investigative committees had been presented.[65] By an amendment to the amendment, Gordon Bradley moved that in any event the proposed delegation would not go to Ottawa before 1 January 1947.[66] On 30 October, as the debate ignited by Smallwood was in its third day, Brown, (Bonavista South), the President of the Fishermen's Protective Union, who had earlier said that 75 per cent of Newfoundland fishermen wanted Commission of Government continued, was stricken with a cerebral hemorrhage and collapsed while speaking.[67] The convention adjourned the following day until 4 November. Debate was finally concluded on Smallwood's resolution the day after the convention resumed; Bradley's sub-amendment was defeated 25 to 17 and Penney's amendment carried 25 to 18. The weakened main motion as amended was then also carried.[68]

Despite this outcome, Wheare's assessment of this first skirmish on the constitutional front was by no means pessimistic. Smallwood's opening speech in which he had "boldly and provocatively" declared that Confederation was "the only hope of Newfoundland" had been met with "dismay and confusion" by his seconder, Gordon Higgins, and the other members who had agreed to support him. Their understanding was that the motion was not for or against Confederation as such but merely about obtaining information on the subject. By leaving the impression that "the Convention was being 'railroaded,'" Smallwood's rhetorical fireworks had "roused the suspicions of many cautious neutral delegates, and the positive fury of those delegates already committed to Responsible Government." On the other hand, if "the first round ... [had] gone to Responsible Government," Confederation had not been "knocked out." The decision had hinged on "timing" rather than substance and except for two or three "complete enthusiasts for Responsible Government," almost all delegates had "asserted their desire to know the terms of Confederation." The issue of sending a delegation to Ottawa, therefore, had not been definitively decided but simply postponed.[69]

J.S. Macdonald's view, given while the debate was still in progress, was that Smallwood had been "indiscreet" and had "dealt a heavy blow to the cause of Confederation." His motion had been "deplorably ill-timed ... and tactlessly presented." Moreover, instead of "setting forth [the] desirability of securing information," he had made "an impassioned plea for Confederation, in the course of which he had painted a dark picture of Newfoundlanders and their position."[70] However, Macdonald afterwards admitted that Smallwood's action had shown the public that Bradley and the members who looked to him for leadership were identified with the idea of Confederation.[71] From the United States Consulate, Donald reported that, rightly or wrongly, Smallwood was a "much hated man" whom he had heard referred to as "'that dirty swine,' 'that dirty politician, etc.'"[72] Such epithets notwithstanding, at one stroke Smallwood had succeeded in pushing himself to where he liked to be and would long remain - in the limelight at centre stage. In short order he had become the convention's lightning rod, a figure upon whom the Newfoundland conservative social and economic elite would heap their scorn but whom they would not soon silence. The country at last had a leader in the making but one decidedly not to the taste of the comfortable upper class. Having brought in the Commission and then largely turned against it, this group now considered itself the natural inheritor of power in the country. Ironically, as the convention unfolded, it was Smallwood, widely regarded in polite local society as a dangerous upstart, who had lined up with what the United Kingdom and Canada wanted for Newfoundland. Having tried his fortune in many ventures which mixed fancy with unorthodoxy, Smallwood had at last chanced on a winner. If he was intelligent, he was also phenomenally lucky. Furthermore, as would become clear, he was blessed with one of the finest assets of the successful politician - incompetent and myopic opponents who lacked both realistic expectations and political savvy. Following the uproar of 28 October 1948 the convention would not proceed as originally intended, from committee reports to constitutional choices.

Once the smell had cleared from Smallwood's "stink bomb" (so called by Donald),[73] the convention returned to its normal routine of debating committee reports and adjourning for committee meetings. But proceedings were disrupted again by the sudden death on 16 November of Judge Fox.[74] Quickly and boldly, the convention seized the initiative with regard to the choice of his successor and on 23 November an informal meeting of its members passed a resolution detailing what was wanted. This called on the Commission to empower the convention to select its own chairman henceforth, to appoint Bradley in the present instance, and to leave him as chairman with his right to vote as an elected member.[75] The Commission immediately consulted the Dominions Office about these requests and the matter was discussed in London with Wheare, who was just back from St. John's.[76] The decision taken was to go along with the choice of Bradley,[77] and the National Convention Act was duly amended to allow this. The amendment left the power of appointment of the chairman in the hands of the Commission and eliminated the requirement that the appointee be a judge of the Supreme Court. It provided further that the chairman would only be entitled to vote if he were an elected member of the convention.[78]

With Bradley as chairman, the convention convened on 11 December in open session to receive and debate the report of the Committee on Transportation and Communications.[79] In the course of this debate, three sections of the report were covered, namely, those dealing with Gander Airport, broadcasting, and tourism. The Commission was fiercely attacked for its alleged neglect of the tourist industry and its treatment of the Newfoundland Tourist Board, a voluntary but government-supported body formed in 1925, whose members had resigned on 15 November over what they considered government inaction.[80] Governor Macdonald was so disturbed by the tendency shown by some participants in this debate "to discredit the Commission of government and if possible to undermine its authority" that he contemplated having Bradley in to discuss the matter, but in the end decided not to do so.[81] On 12 December the convention unanimously passed a motion introduced by businessman Ches Crosbie (St. John's City West) to the effect that, pending the decision of the people on the constitutional question, "there should be no further negotiations in connection with nor any disposal of the natural resources or liquid assets of Newfoundland, other than current liquid assets, at present in the control of the Commission of Government other than those already contracted for, either in Newfoundland or Labrador."[82] This quintessentially St. John's motion had, of course, no legal standing, but it highlighted the critical and cranky mood of the convention as it ended its first round. The Commission may have erected strong defences for itself against the incursions of the convention, but there was nonetheless a determination in that body to show that Newfoundland's administration was, as one still remembered popular characterization would have it, the "Ommission of Government."[83] Donald's summation of what the convention had done in its first phase was that it "seemed to have adopted the role of an opposition party" and was spending its time "in useless condemnation" of the government's every deed.[84] Still, for all the mud being thrown at it, the Commission was not without resources of its own in the game of thrust and counter thrust now in progress. It decided that while members of the convention would qualify to have their return passages paid to their homes for the period of the adjournment, the payment of per diem allowances to them would cease from 15 December until 8 January when the convention would reconvene.[85]

An important political development that occurred outside the convention in December was the quiet formation in St. John's of a league for responsible government.[86] The principal organizer of this new movement was F.M. O'Leary, Smallwood's erstwhile radio sponsor, now widely known and respected for his wartime fund raising on behalf of servicemen and his participation in the annual Christmas Seal sale in support of a campaign in the country to eradicate tuberculosis. To begin with, O'Leary and a number of associates, mainly fellow Water Street merchants but including also Leo Earle, the president of the Longshoremen's Protective Union, drew up a circular letter and a draft declaration of principles.[87] The intention was to keep these private until "a sufficient number of satisfactory signers with varied interests and from all strata of society" had been obtained. When this had been achieved, the league proposed to go public with a big print and radio campaign. No member of the National Convention was included in the original list of sponsors used by the league to recruit a wider membership, but O'Leary told Donald that Crosbie and Edgar Hickman (St. John's City East), another important businessman, were supporters of the movement. Because they were members of the convention, however, they did not for the moment want to be publicly identified with the organization.

A notable omission from the list of sponsors, public or private, was Peter Cashin, whose blustering style did not endear him to Water Street, where he was identified, as he was at the Dominions Office, with the bad old politics of the past. If many Newfoundland businessmen wanted Responsible Government again they did not want the country handed back to a demagogic rabble-rouser like the former minister of finance. As in 1933–34, what businessmen hankered after was a government above politics, only this time within a parliamentary structure. In this respect, fourteen years of Commission rule had taught them nothing. When O'Leary told Donald that Cashin was not included because the league had "not got around to approaching him," his explanation was rightly dismissed by the American official as "hardly ... plausible." If Smallwood was persona non grata to polite society on one side, Cashin was on another. The interest of Newfoundland, the Responsible Government League explained in its circular letter, could "best be served by first returning to a self-government pledged to investigate all possibilities from the development of our own resources," and to negotiation "with other countries with a view to securing the full benefits from such assets as we may possess in our strategic position in a shrinking world."[88]

The accompanying draft declaration of "principles and policies" held out the prospect of "sound and progressive development of the national resources"; the maintenance of existing social services and their extension as the "country's capacity" allowed; careful examination of all "feasible" constitutional options to determine whether there was "any course other than dominion status" that would "better further the interests of the people"; the safeguarding of "the integrity of the Civil Service"; the adoption of such measures as might be required "to prevent the emergence of graft and corruption in any form in the public life of Newfoundland"; the examination of "the strategic position of Newfoundland in the light of conditions now existing" combined with international negotiations, to obtain from other countries benefits commensurate with any advantage wanted by them in Newfoundland; and the use of the power of government within reason to raise living standards and make "able-bodied relief ... an unpleasant memory." Item five in the league's ten-point list stated that it would be the "primary duty" of a new government "to study closely all commitments of a long-term nature entered into during the war." The object of this exercise would be to open negotiations that would "lead to appropriate reciprocity from those other countries which have obtained valuable strategic and other concessions in Newfoundland without the consent of the people."[89]

On 2 January 1947 a few days before the National Convention resumed sitting, Albert Walsh, speaking to the St. John's Rotary Club, issued what amounted to a stern warning about expecting any such redress. Newfoundland, he said, hoped to sell more fish in the United States, but there were vested interests there that had to be contended with and the bases agreement simply could not be used to lever tariff concessions. There were indeed several compelling reasons why a quid pro quo for the bases was beyond Newfoundland's reach:

> Whatever the position relating to the grant of bases might have been, it cannot be overlooked that these formed part of a plan of defence of the whole Western Hemisphere and were a large contribution to our own security at a time when the outcome of the war was most uncertain and we were not in a position to undertake our own defence. A proposal that by unilateral action this agreement be reviewed

> is unusual. It entirely overlooks the wider international questions of inviolability of agreements and assumes willingness on the part of the other party. Moreover, it overlooks the implications of results upon most favoured nation clauses of trade and tariff agreements, conventions and treaties and would introduce a new factor in international arrangements, arising from a change from reciprocal agreements in trade matters.

Those Newfoundlanders who imagined that "air rights" could be used to extract trade concessions were equally mistaken. Such "extraneous considerations" were ruled out of international civil aviation discussions, and other countries would "scarcely countenance being held to ransom for use of the air or of services existing on the ground below by ships of the air carrying on the commercial business of the world." As for the charge that Gander constituted a burden on the country, the cost of running the airport had to be weighed against all the benefits it had brought since work had started on it and the employment and transportation benefits it currently provided. In any event, the commercial phase of the airport's history had just started, and it was too soon to say what the balance sheet of the operation would ultimately look like.[90] Forgotten in Walsh's speech, and apparently also ignored by the convention, was the informal promise from the Americans that J.H. Penson had made public on returning from the vital mission he and Emerson had undertaken in the spring of 1941.[91] Much, of course, had happened since Penson had spoken on the radio in defence of the Leased Bases Agreement.

When proceedings resumed on 8 January the convention met in public session for five days while it continued its debate on the six-part Transportation and Communications Committee report.[92] On the ninth Smallwood moved that Neill be asked to come to a session of the convention, either public or private, to give further details of the financing of Gander.[93] Job used the occasion of the debate on this motion to pronounce further on what Donald described as his "favourite subject," namely, how Newfoundland might capitalize on her strategic position. What Job wanted was a round table conference which would bring together representatives of Newfoundland, the United Kingdom, the United States, and Canada. The purpose of this gathering would be to discuss Gander and Newfoundland's economic situation generally and to give Newfoundland the opportunity to make its case for compensation in lieu of the defence advantages other countries had been given on its soil. Newfoundland's claim in this regard, he believed, would be "irresistible."[94] In keeping with these sentiments Smallwood's motion was subsequently broadened so as to raise in the proposed discussion with Neill "any other public matter" he was prepared to talk about.[95] It was then carried as amended, but Neill refused the invitation, agreeing only to receive a delegation in his office. The convention went along with this, but the encounter that ensued – Smallwood was a member of the relevant committee and therefore of the visiting delegation – produced sour feelings all round. On 3 February a special report on Gander, consisting of a transcript of the meeting with Neill, was the main item of business when the convention met in session again.[96] Smallwood was in full oratorical flight on this occasion and the Commission, which had cautioned the Dominions Office the previous month to act quickly on Gander financing to contain what was "fast becoming a real live issue in the country,"[97] was once again excoriated.

Having thus vented its spleen on a highly emotional issue but one which the British would soon defuse with further financial assistance, the convention moved back to the constitutional issue. The renewed debate on this began on 4 February and focused on a complex motion put that day by Job and carried, with one important procedural amendment, by thirty to eight. The Job resolution declared it "essential" that the convention take immediate action to ascertain the following:

1. What steps, if any, can be taken for establishing improved economic or fiscal relationships between the United States of America and Newfoundland particularly bearing in mind the present occupation of certain Newfoundland territory by the said United States of America and the fact that free entry is accorded to the United States for its importations into Newfoundland;
2. What financial and fiscal relationships could be expected between the Government of the United Kingdom and Newfoundland.
(1) Under a continuation of Commission Government in its present form,
(2) Under a revised form of Commission Government with elected representatives thereon,
(3) Under Responsible Government in approximately its previous form,
(4) Under any other suitable form of Government.
3. What would be a fair and equitable basis for Federal Union of the Dominion of Canada and Newfoundland, or what other fiscal, political or economic arrangements may be possible.[98]

As a first step the resolution provided that the government be informed that the convention wished to appoint a committee to confer with it about "ways and means" of gathering the information desired. If the government agreed to this, the convention would then elect a delegation which, along with Bradley, would constitute the committee called for to carry out the work envisaged. It would be the responsibility of this committee to report to the convention the results of its meetings with the government "before being in any way committed to the despatch of any delegation outside of Newfoundland."[99] Subsequent to the passing of his motion Job released copies of a pamphlet he had written expanding on his own pet scheme of an Anglo-American-Canadian condominium for the country.[100] Prominent among the eight members who voted against the Job motion were Cashin and ex-magistrate Malcolm Hollett (Grand Falls), the latter of whom said in the course of the debate that the territory occupied by United States bases in the country had been "stolen from us and given away ... by Great Britain."[101] Cashin's perspective was that Job's motion was "silly"; if Newfoundland had responsible government back, "it would have the power to go anywhere it liked."[102]

The choice of members to the crucial committee now to be formed was made at an informal and private session of the convention on 5 February and those elected included Job, Crosbie, Higgins, and Smallwood.[103] Accompanied by Bradley, the committee met with Macdonald and all of the commissioners except Neill, who was in England patching up the Gander financial settlement, on 8 February. This was Smallwood's first acquaintance with the seat of power in the country that he would soon capture and hold for a generation. In retrospect, therefore, it was a bigger moment in Newfoundland history than was realized at the time, though it was clear enough then that a turning point had been reached. With respect to measures "for establishing improved economic or fiscal relationships" with the United States, the committee was told by the Commission that this was a matter "for negotiation between Governments through the regular diplomatic channels." In any event it was "doubtful" whether the substance of clause 1 of the Job motion came within the convention's terms of reference. Moreover, with international talks looking towards a general agreement on tariffs and trade and the establishment of an international trade organization (the future GATT) pending at Geneva in April, the government was simply not in a position to broach with the Americans the issue raised by the convention. The United States and the United Kingdom as well as Newfoundland would be represented at Geneva, and it was unlikely that any country intending to participate in the conference would open separate tariff negotiations in the meantime.[104]

Clause 2 of the Job motion, dealing with the possible future "financial and fiscal relationship" between Newfoundland and the United Kingdom under the three forms of government specified, evoked an altogether different response. The government, the committee was told, would forward to the United Kingdom any relevant inquiries the convention wished to make. It would also forward a request to the British government that it receive a delegation from the convention to discuss what it wanted to know. But if the convention should decide to submit enquiries to London or to seek to send a delegation there, it would have to accompany its requests with detailed memoranda stating its questions precisely in the first case, and the proposed matters to be discussed in the second. This procedure, of course, which the committee recommended to the convention, would effectively prevent the British from being put in the witness box, just as the Commission itself was safeguarded. When asked by Job whether a delegation to London could discuss the Newfoundland-United States side of his motion, he was told that this would be up to the government of the United Kingdom, should the projected delegation raise the matter. As for clause 3 of the Job motion concerning "a fair and equitable basis for Federal Union of the Dominion of Canada and Newfoundland," the government offered to make the same approaches to Ottawa on behalf of the convention, either for information or the despatch of a delegation, that it agreed to make to London. The Commission insisted, however, that the reference in clause 3 to "what other fiscal, political or economic arrangements may be possible" would have to be dropped from any further action of the convention vis-à-vis Canada, as these matters were "entirely for discussion between Governments." If the convention was going to deal with Ottawa, it would be about Confederation and Confederation alone.[105]

The report of the committee that had met with the Commission, as agreed upon by Bradley and Walsh, was presented to the convention on 26 February. Two motions in regard to the report were passed on the twenty-eighth. The first, introduced by Hollett and carried unanimously, requested the government to arrange for the despatch of a delegation to London composed of Bradley and six other members the convention would elect by secret ballot once it had heard that the British government was receptive to its request. This motion further specified five matters to be discussed by the proposed delegation, while calling on the Steering Committee to prepare "a detailed statement of the questions to be submitted" in London. This statement would in turn have to be confirmed by the convention before being transmitted to London through the Newfoundland government. The five matters itemized by Hollett for discussion were: "1. National debt; 2. Military, Naval and Air Bases in this country; 3. Gander Airport; 4. Interest-free Loans; 5. Any matters relating to the future economic position of Newfoundland."[106]

The second resolution, introduced by Smallwood and carried by twenty-four votes to sixteen, called on the government to arrange if possible for the sending of a delegation to Ottawa for the purpose specified in the Job motion. The words the Commission objected to in this motion would be dropped. The Ottawa delegation would have the same number of members and be elected in the same fashion as the delegation it was hoped would go to the United Kingdom, but it would not leave the country until that delegation had returned home when it would "proceed ... as soon as possible." While it awaited word through the Commission from London and Ottawa, the convention met on 10 March to consider the report of the Steering Committee on the questions to be put by the delegation which it was hoped would go to Britain. The committee called for detailed discussion on seven matters: "1. The Public debt; 2. The Interest-free Loans; 3. Development Loans; 4. The position arising out of the various Base Deals; 5. The financing and control of Newfoundland Airports; 6. Trade and Tariffs; 7. Any other matters relative to Newfoundland affairs which the delegation may raise and His Majesty's Government in the United Kingdom be willing to discuss."[107] After ten days of meetings the Steering Committee had produced so skimpy a list and one so little changed from that included in Hollett's motion, that considerable criticism was provoked. But Hollett, who moved adoption of the report, insisted that it was not in the public interest to go further, and with Bradley's help the report was finally approved.

On 19 March having received a favourable response from the British government, the convention in private session chose the delegates who, along with Bradley, would go to London. Those elected were Cashin, Crosbie, Hollett, A.B. Butt (St. John's West), an insurance agent, W.J. Keough (St. George's), who worked in the co-operative movement, and Pierce Fudge (Humber), the President of the Newfoundland Labourers' Union.[108] The big loser was obviously Job, whose initiative had led to this development but who was elected only as an alternate and did not in fact go overseas. If nothing else, the selection of Cashin heralded more pyrotechnics. Though widely thought of as a problem case with a tendency to be a party of one, he nonetheless had rightly discerned that the Dominions Office was not above the fray but actually a supporter of one particular outcome - Confederation. Cashin was, moreover, now embroiled in a libel suit, the writ for which had been taken out on 14 March by none other than Chief Justice Emerson, Justice H.A. Winter, and J.A. Winter, the Registrar of the Supreme Court.[109] The basis of their action was a statement Cashin had made in the convention, whose members did not enjoy parliamentary immunity, to the effect that Commission of Government had been indirectly instituted by "bribery and corruption." By this Cashin meant that those who had supported the introduction of the Commission had been assured they would be taken care of under it. Cashin offered to apologize to the three litigants who had all sat in the House of Assembly elected in 1932, but not, as they insisted, in the National Convention. Hence the suit, in which Wheare pronounced the judges to "have acted foolishly," having given Cashin "a very good opportunity to pose as the friend of the people."[110] The case, described by G.K. Donald as "a one-day sensation," came to trial before Justice Dunfield on 17 April. The nine member jury was unable to reach a unanimous verdict and when Dunfield asked the parties whether they would accept a majority verdict, the plaintiffs accepted but Cashin refused. The jury was then dismissed and Cashin left the courthouse to a tumultuous welcome outside.[111] Thereafter the plaintiffs dropped the suit.

On 1 April when the convention had met to continue consideration of the report of the Committee on Public Health and Welfare, it had been read a message that the Canadian government was willing to receive the delegation it wished to send to Ottawa. Over the objection of some members who argued that they were being stampeded and of others who wanted to carry on with the business in progress, the convention proceeded to choose the members of the Ottawa delegation. Those selected in addition to Smallwood, Job, and Higgins, were T.W.G. Ashbourne (Twillingate), an outport merchant; Charles Ballam (Humber), a former President of the Newfoundland Federation of Labour who now worked as an insurance agent; and the Rev. Lester Burry (Labrador), a United Church of Canada clergyman who had worked for many years in the region that elected him.[112] Having reached the inner circle of authority in Newfoundland, Smallwood would soon be mixing officially with the highest levels of the Canadian government.

On 11 April, D.I. Jackman (Bell Island), described by Donald as "decidely a rough diamond and a graduate of the school of hard knocks," moved in the convention, seconded by Percy Figary (Burgeo), another trade unionist, that arrangements be made through the appropriate authorities for the sending of a fact-finding delegation to Washington as well. The task of this delegation would be to determine the attitude of the American government towards "the question of Federal Union of Newfoundland with the United States of America," and "to ascertain the terms and conditions" on which the United States would be willing to consider this. In a confused and rambling defence of his motion, Jackman, according to Donald's report, said that while he personally didn't "want any dealings with the U.S.," the people should be given the opportunity to decide the matter for themselves. That there was a considerable body of support in the country for linking up with the United States, he said, was shown in a straw vote on the public's own constitutional preferences being taken by the *Sunday Herald*.[113] Recently launched in St. John's, this paper was an American style, strongly pro-American tabloid run by Geoff Stirling, an aggressive young entrepreneur. Neither its advocacy, however, nor Jackman's intervention had much influence in the convention, which well understood the blunt message the Commission had delivered about what was and what was not possible in relation to Washington. When the vote was taken Jackman could muster only three votes with thirty-four against. The majority included Bradley, who not only voted first but cast his first vote as chairman.[114]

The delegation to London left Gander on 25 April and arrived the following day in the British capital to a mix-up over hotel rooms, an awkward beginning that presaged how proceedings generally would go. Before the delegates left Newfoundland, Wheare, writing from St. John's, gave Syers of the Dominions Office thumbnail sketches of them as follows:

> Butt has had some education, and so has Keough. Fudge is a union leader, a labour man (as they go here) and claims a friendship with Mr. Attlee. He does not speak English very well, but what he says is sensible. Crosbie, though a wealthy merchant, does not speak English very well either. Hollett is the oldest of them, a former Rhodes Scholar, of University College Oxford (Mr. Attlee's old college and mine), and a former magistrate at Grand Falls ... Cashin I find an attractive rascal, though not everybody agrees. I cannot believe that the ressources of the Dominions Office will fail to cope easily and happily with these men.[115]

As predicted, Whitehall did not fail: British officialdom's special gift for saying no was on this occasion employed to full advantage. Four meetings were held between the two sides, on 29 and 30 April, and on 1 and 7 May.[116] Governor Macdonald and Commissioner Walsh had been called to London to assist with the talks, and the Commission had earlier forwarded to London the precise questions the delegation wished to ask under the list of seven subjects approved by the convention.[117]

The Dominions Office and the Treasury prepared a carefully crafted set of answers, and these were used by the British at the first two meetings.[118] At the third meeting the British actually gave the Newfoundlanders written replies in order "to give firm and clear answers to the questions raised and to remove any ambiguity or wrong impression resulting from the first two talks."[119] On 6 May the delegation submitted a memorandum of its own for consideration, in answer to the document it had been handed by the British on the first. This reply was signed by only five of its members, the names missing at the end of the documents being those of Bradley and Keough. They, it was explained in the last paragraph, did not concur with "a few matters" covered by the submission.[120] At the meeting on the seventh, Addison read a statement, a copy of which was then given to each delegate. This was done "to put the whole talks in the right perspective (not omitting a rebuke)."[121]

An acerbic summary of the talks prepared afterwards by W. Russell Edmunds of the Treasury noted that it had been clear from the beginning that "some members of the delegation were prepared to take every opportunity of raising extraneous matters, criticising the Commission of Government and the U.K. Government and generally seeking to extract for their own ends expressions of opinion on a variety of hypothetical questions." By contrast Bradley and Keough had shown "much more restraint and kept their remarks within the questions raised." The "main grouse" of the Newfoundlanders had been the American bases agreement, about which "they all appeared to be hot under the collar."

> They took the petulant attitude of a spoiled child all along and seemed to lack balanced judgment in this matter. The main purpose of their remarks was that we had sold Newfoundland for our own ends - they seemed entirely thick headed that it was for their needs as well - and we should now make restitution by either getting trade concessions from the U.S.A. for fish, particularly, or wipe out, if not all, at least some part of the Public Debt.
>
> This matter is undoubtedly the big drum in Newfoundland politics and no opportunity was lost to beat it at meetings and I have no doubt it will sound loud and often in Newfoundland. I could not help thinking that on this it is so true that none are so blind as those who will not see.
>
> It is fantastic to try and saddle H.M.G. with this, to the extent that we must pay for what is a completely erroneous view.

By the same token, the delegation had been "unrealistic" about the financing of Gander airport and had "completely closed their eyes to any question of benefit to Newfoundland."[122]

On the trade and tariff side of things this official expressed "some sympathy on the fish problem," about which Crosbie had been "the chief protaganist" for Newfoundland. But it was really up to the Newfoundland industry to solve its own problems: "They must drop their conservative ways and employ modern methods not only in the general handling of fish but in their marketing and general sales effort." The United Kingdom could not "spare dollars" for the fisheries, and Newfoundlanders could "not expect the charity of the U.K. Government to carry the industry." Overall Russell Edmunds's impression of the talks was scathing, though he saw one possible benefit coming from them:

> It was obvious that the Delegation was out to test the form as to what the U.K. Government might be prepared to do for Newfoundland. They really wanted to know the price of further assistance. The Dominions Office quite properly took the line of giving firm answers to the questions raised and to this extent this suited our book. No prizes were dangled in their eyes ... The visit ran true to expected form: the peddling of wares; the attempt to belittle the work of the Commission of Government; to claim as a right U.K. financial responsibility for Newfoundland; to air personal grievances and political opinions. Nothing constructive emerged: neither was any indication forthcoming as to the trend of future events. The visit to Canada will round off their prospecting. It is to be hoped that they will speed up the work of [the] National Convention which has already frittered away so much time chasing the shadow of pipe dreams.[123]

As part of the very pointed statement he made and circulated on 7 May, Addison answered a further enquiry from the delegation, embodied in another memorandum. This concerned the meaning of section three of the National Convention Act, which defined "the duty and function of the Convention," in the context of the constitutional resolution the Newfoundland legislature had passed in 1933 and the subsequent Newfoundland Act passed by Parliament.[124] "Are we to assume," the delegation had asked, "that Section 3 ... is to be interpreted to mean that through the medium of the National Convention the forms of Government to be recommended to the people of Newfoundland would be: – 1. Retention of Commission Government; or 2. Restoration of Responsible Government?" Addison's terse reply was that the act clearly authorized the convention to recommend additional "possible future forms of Government." It was up to the convention to make to him whatever recommendations on the subject it wished. Addision then went on to address the question raised in the resolution which had led to the despatch of the delegation, that is to say the future "fiscal and financial relations" of the Newfoundland and United Kingdom governments in the event of any one of four constitutional outcomes being decided upon. If Newfoundlanders were to opt for "Commission of Government in its present form," relations would "continue ... as close as at present" and the United Kingdom would continue to assume responsibility for Newfoundland's "financial stability." If the choice were "A revised form of Commission Government," the relations in question would depend "upon the precise form of revision suggested." Under "Responsible Government," however, Newfoundland would be fully responsible for her own finances and the commitments made by the United Kingdom when the Commission was established would no longer apply. As for the category of "Any other suitable form of Government," relations would depend on exactly what was proposed constitutionally.[125] At no stage in the London talks did Addison put in writing that Confederation would be on the referendum ballot no matter what the convention decided to recommend. But he left this impression with the majority of the delegates, and his statement took care to leave the way open for this to be done if necessary.[126]

A largely resentful and dissatisfied Newfoundland party, with Bradley and Keough the exceptions, left London on 9 May, and on the nineteenth the convention received its report. This consisted of the various documents that had changed hands in connection with the talks. In the course of a spirited debate on the report, Cashin now charged that an Anglo-Canadian conspiracy was afoot to determine the future of Newfoundland. He and other aggrieved colleagues also made known their dissatisfaction over the role Macdonald and Walsh had played in London, charging that they had been brought there to sabotage the whole mission.[127]

Macdonald's own worry arising out of the London talks concerned the transcription of the proceedings of the last two meetings produced from the notes of the stenographer who had accompanied the Newfoundland delegation. This, he cautioned London in forwarding a copy, differed substantially from what had been taken down by the British reporters.[128]

On 19 May also the convention returned yet again to the much picked over question of sending a delegation to Washington. This time it actually passed unanimously a motion to this effect. Introduced by Penney and seconded by Fudge, the motion called for the despatch by the convention of a delegation of "some six members" to the American capital "if and when" this could be arranged. The purpose of the mission would be to hold discussions on trade and "and other relevant matters affecting the future economy of Newfoundland" with the United States government.[129] In reality the convention adopted the motion merely to get the Commissions's ruling on it. As expected, the Commission declared the resolution outside the convention's terms of reference, a judgment that buried the whole matter once and for all.[130]

The stage was now set for the departure of the delegation to Ottawa on 19 June. The Newfoundland party arrived there on 24 June and a dinner was given for them by the government of Canada that evening presided over by Prime Minister Mackenzie King. Bradley spoke in reply to King's toast to Newfoundland and gave what Clutterbuck, who had been knighted in January 1946 and moved over to Ottawa as high commissioner the following May (no doubt to complete the Newfoundland deal), described as an "excellent speech." The following day business began with a public session with King again present and presiding. Following this a private session was held at which Secretary of State for External Affairs, Louis St. Laurent, elected to chair the meetings, gave the Newfoundland delegates a 100 page brief explaining the workings of Canada's federal system and how Newfoundland would be accommodated by it. On the suggestion of the Newfoundlanders, sessions were then adjourned until 2 July. Clutterbuck's impression was that a "very good start" had been made.[131] Certainly, events in Ottawa were a decided contrast to what had occurred in London a few weeks before. Cashin had beforehand predicted in the National Convention that the delegation to Ottawa, unlike the one that had gone to England, would be welcomed "with a heart and a half" and that "joy bells" would sound on its arrival.[132]

There was an element of truth in this, but it was also the case that there were varying degrees of enthusiasm in Ottawa for the entry of Newfoundland into Confederation. The basic distinction was between senior civil servants and some ministers. The former group, with the Department of

External Affairs in the lead, were strongly behind the project and mainly constituted what Julian Harrington, counselor at the United States Embassy in Ottawa, called "the 'manifest destiny' school". But even within this group, it seems, there was cynicism. Thus Harrington also noted in the same report that Clifford Clark, the pro-Confederation deputy minister of finance and one of the most powerful mandarins in Ottawa, had told him that if Newfoundland did become the tenth province, Canada would "have a 'little Ireland' on its hand - a disgruntled people no matter what is done for them." On the other hand, Clark was clearly impressed by the Commission of Government's financial record and reckoned that Newfoundland's per capita debt was now less than Canada's. More importanly, he believed that Quebec could be reconciled to Newfoundland's entry into Confederation without any change being made in the existing Labrador boundary. For his part, Harrington noted that "Newfoundland as a tenth province without Labrador and its iron ore would have little political or economic sex appeal to Canadians."[133]

Within the Canadian ministry there was undoubtedly a strong desire for union, but King in particular, though fancying himself a latter day father of confederation, understood throughout that there were domestic political imperatives in the matter that would have to be respected. One of these, the attitude of the existing provinces, was evident in the spring of 1947 as the Canadians manoeuvered to have the arrival of the Newfoundland delegation timed so as not to jeopardize delicate Dominion-Provincial financial negotiations then in progress.[134] Nevertheless, much had already been accomplished in Ottawa by way of preparation for the possible opening of talks with Newfoundland. In 1946 the Department of External Affairs had taken the lead in establishing a temporary interdepartmental committee on Canadian-Newfoundland relations, which had held its first meeting on 13 May with MacKay in the chair.[135] Under his direction, this group had then proceeded to compile a wealth of background and policy memoranda, by far the biggest dossier on Newfoundland ever assembled by a Canadian administration.[136] On 30 October 1946 matters had been brought a stage further in Ottawa when the Cabinet decided to appoint a committee on Newfoundland.[137] King had named Secretary of State for External Affairs Louis St. Laurent to be chairman of this committee and Minister of National Health and Welfare Brooke Claxton, a strong supporter of union who was expected to do most of the work, deputy chaiman. At the same time A.P. Baldwin of the Privy Council Office had been named secretary of the commitee and given the task of organizing its work and co-ordinating its activites with those of a now formally constituted interdepartmental committee, which MacKay also chaired.[138] On 16 June 1947 just before the delegation from St. John's arrived, Baldwin submitted for Cabinet information memoranda on the benefits to be expected from taking Newfoundland into Confederation, on the "financial aspects" of union, and – this was the document handed to the Newfoundland delegation on 25 June – on the myriad workings of Canada's federal system.[139]

The "benefits" memorandum was divided into eight sections which dealt in turn with "*Area and Population*," "*Trade*," "*Balance of payments*," "*Fisheries*," "*Natural Resources*," "*Strategic Considerations*," "*The Possibility of Closer Affiliation of Newfoundland with the United States*," and "*Completion of Confederation*." The trade section pointed out that Newfoundland was now Canada's eighth largest customer and that annual sales there had risen in value from a pre-war figure of approximately $10,000,000 to a current total of about $40,000,000. This figure was inflated by the abnormal trade conditions caused by the war, but Canada should be left with a market worth about $25,000,000 annually in Newfoundland. Confederation would increase this figure roughly in the order of $16,000,000 to $20,000,000 annually. Factors that would lead to increased trade would be the elimination of tariff barriers and the higher purchasing power in Newfoundland made possible by federal government expenditures there and Dominion-wide transfer payments to individuals, in particular the family allowance scheme Canada had introduced in 1944. Should Newfoundland not join Canada but instead manage to strike a deal with the United States involving "economic concessions in return for defence concessions," the projected normal level of Canadian sales to the country would fall drastically, a development that "would bear with special severity on the Maritime Provinces."[140]

The entry of Newfoundland into Confederation would also help Canada's balance of payments situation with the United States, in that goods at present imported by Newfoundland from that country and paid for with Canadian dollars could be supplied domestically. In resource terms, union would give Canada a greatly enlarged economic base for her fisheries, permit broader conservation measures in relation to the use of fish stocks, and overcome the "disadvantages" caused by the existing "severe competition" between the fishing industries of the two countries. By contrast, should Newfoundland obtain special consideration in fish sales from the United States, as had been broached at the Geneva trade talks, Canada would be adversely affected. This could in fact cost the Canadian industry in the Maritime Provinces and Quebec as much as $20,000,000 annually. Otherwise, Newfoundland would bring her lucrative forest and iron ore mining industries and the possibility of an exciting new economic development in the future from the discovery of large deposits of iron ore in Labrador. The latter region also possessed extensive undeveloped timber stands and at the Grand Falls (now Churchill Falls), a site whose potential for hydro electric development rivalled that of Niagara.[141]

Strategically, Canada was manifestly caught up in a race with the United States for influence in Newfoundland. If Newfoundland regained self-government, Canada would face a situation whereby, except at Goose Bay, she would "almost certainly" lose her existing defence rights in the country and only get them back "on condition of substantial payments or other considerations." While it was true that under the terms of the Protocol to the 1941 Anglo-American Leased Bases Agreement, the United States had to consult Canada before acquiring additional defence rights in Newfoundland territory, this didn't mean very much. Canada was "in a very secondary defence position in the area" and poorly placed to resist "determined" American pressure, already being felt, to expand its regional defence establishment. Therefore, unless Canada acted the prospect before her was stark: "Should Newfoundland remain outside of Canada, the present United States ascendancy in the Newfoundland-Labrador region will almost certainly increase and might very well lead to a virtual withdrawal from the area by Canada in favour of the United States." It might be held that this wouldn't make any difference, but so far as defence was concerned it "would inevitably point to absorption of Canada within the United States orbit." It might also "hamper Canadian air communication with the United Kingdom and Europe" and would ipso facto make her "freedom of action on her north-eastern borders almost entirely dependent on the goodwill of the United States." The plain, unvarnished truth was that circumstances were ripe for a comprehensive future deal between the United States and Newfoundland: "The possibility, in due course, of closer affiliation of Newfoundland with the United States should not be discounted. Such affiliation might take a form of either commercial or political union and might be brought about as a result of the growing prestige of the United States in Newfoundland, the attractiveness of the United States as a free market for Newfoundland products and by a desire on the part of the United States to further strengthen its position in the Newfoundland region." If Canada did not seize the present opportunity to effect union, the likelihood was that this possibility would not "become a live issue again for many years, if ever." The annual dollar cost to the federal treasury of carrying Newfoundland as a province, the "financial aspects" memorandum prepared for Cabinet predicted, would be in the order of $10,000,000 - $20,000,000 with $12,000,000 - $15,000,000 a reasonable expectation during the first decade.[142]

Compelling as the case was, and despite the extensive spadework that had been done in the Canadian capital, the talks with the Newfoundland delegation in the summer of 1947 dragged on intermittently for many weeks. On 3 July King told Clutterbuck that it would be "a great mistake to hurry the delegation," and that it was unlikely that discussions would be over before the end of July. This might forestall an autumn referendum in Newfoundland, but the delegation sensibly did not want to be "hurried at this stage." Moreover, putting off the referendum for some time after the delegation reported would allow the Confederates in Newfoundland more time to gather their forces and give public opinion a better opportunity to appreciate the benefits of union. (Clutterbuck believed that this idea originated with Smallwood and Bradley).[143] The British were not disturbed by this timetable, but the slow pace of events in Ottawa soon stirred up trouble in St. John's. On 16 July five members of the convention, Cashin, Hollett, Butt, Harrington, and Reuben Vardy (Trinity North), wired Bradley to the effect that they had met Governor Macdonald that morning as a delegation from a gathering of twenty-five convention delegates who had called on the governor the previous week. This message claimed that Macdonald had told Bradley that the Commission wanted an autumn referendum and that the National Convention must have its recommendations in to the Dominions Office by 15 August in order to meet this deadline. The governor had also said that if the project for an autumn referendum failed, "he personally would place responsibility for such failure on the proper shoulders, and this responsibility would not be on the shoulders of the Commission of Government." Since things were evidently not working out in Ottawa as planned, it was apparent that a scheme was afoot to prevent the people from voting when it was intended they should vote. Thus Bradley should authorize the secretary of the convention to reconvene it immediately.[144] This rebuff from his colleagues was brushed aside by Bradley, who was informed by Macdonald that the construction put on his remarks by Cashin and his associates was incorrect.[145]

A more serious threat to the negotiations, however, soon manifested itself. This was the death, on 10 August, of New Brunswick's sole reprensentative in the Cabinet, Frank Bridges. New Brunswick was soon given another Cabinet spokesman in the person of Milton F. Gregg, who became minister of fisheries on 2 September, but in a decision that Clutterbuck called "remarkable" the government decided to put off a final decision about the Newfoundland negotiations until Gregg had faced the voters in a by-election to be held in Bridges's riding of York-Sunbury.[146] Earlier on, the ever cautious King had taken the position that the question of Newfoundland's entry into Confederation should be regarded as being above party consideration and that the leaders of the opposition parties represented in Parliament should be taken into the government's confidence on the issue.[147]. Subsequently, however, he and his Cabinet colleagues had concluded that the opposition could not be trusted to this extent and that, if necessary, the government would have to go it alone on the matter.[148] King's attitude was also influenced by evidence of provincial feelings on the issue. Like many citizens of his province, the combative Union Nationale premier of Quebec, Maurice Duplessis, had never been able to swallow the 1927 Privy Council award on Labrador and saw the negotiations with Newfoundland now in progress as an opportunity to rectify matters. He also feared a "plot to bring three hundred thousand more 'Britishers'" into Canada.[149] Both Duplessis and Angus L. Macdonald, the premier of Nova Scotia, apparently claimed the right for their provinces to be consulted before Newfoundland was admitted.[150] King did not admit this claim, but to avoid a damaging by-election fight over the admission of Newfoundland he took the position that the government could not release proposed terms of union until New Brunswick had secure representation in the cabinet. King's principle, in other words, was that while the existing provinces need not be consulted, the final decision would have to be taken by a cabinet in which each province had a well-established representative.

The state of public opinion in Canada justified the prime minister's caution. Thus, according to a Gallup Poll released in July 1947, when a representative sample of Canadians had been asked whether "Canada should invite Newfoundland to become the tenth province, or not," 49 per cent had said yes compared to 57 per cent a year earlier.[151] Regionally the highest no percentage, some 23 per cent, was in the Maritime Provinces. There, and in Quebec, those answering yes constituted 40 per cent and 38 per cent respectively. Moreover, though only 18 per cent of the Quebecers polled had answered no, 44 per cent had described themselves as undecided. By contrast, support for union came in at 54 per cent in Ontario and 55 per cent on the Prairies and in British Columbia. In sum, once past Quebec, the further Canadians got from Newfoundland, the better it looked. Among voters who identified themselves as Liberals – no doubt this reflected the strenght of the party in Quebec – 48 per cent answered in the affirmative, one percent below the national average. On the other hand, among Progressive Conservative and CCF supporters polled, the yes totals were 56 per cent and 57 per cent respectively. As usual, King was a good barometer of his party and his country.

The delay caused by Frank Bridges's death and King's political calculations based on it, put the Newfoundland delegation in a dilemma, whether to stay or go. Smallwood later recounted that one of his contributions to keeping the mission alive through the long hot summer of 1947 was his willingness to humour Bradley, who was "fed up with the heat of Ottawa," by going on long walks with him.[152] But in the end the fate of the delegation hinged on more momentous considerations. To return home empty-handed would create one set of problems: to stay on in Ottawa in defiance of the wishes of a substantial group of the members of the National Convention would create another.

On 8 September the latter possibility took on a new aspect when twenty-one convention members sent Bradley a telegram calling on the delegation to break off negotiations and return home at once. Accusing the chairman of having "dictatorially refused" the earlier request sent him to call the convention together again, the signatories to this latest message declared that the delegation had exceeded its terms of reference. The disgruntled convention members also dissociated themselves from anything done by the delegation beyond its legal powers and drew the attention of Bradley and his colleagues to a newspaper report of Quebec's continuing claim on Labrador as evidence of that province's antagonism towards Newfoundland.[153] Bradley shot back a sharp rebuttal but soon received a further salvo from St. John's, this one signed by twenty-seven members and again emphasizing the Labrador issue. To this Bradley promptly gave another stiff reply, but he indicated also that the delegation expected to finish its work on 29 September, and that the Convention could therefore resume sitting about 8 October.

On 13 September the day after this message was sent, the first plenary session since July was held between the Newfoundland delegation and their Canadian counterparts. On this occasion it was agreed that, contrary to what had been previously contemplated, the Canadian side would alone report to Cabinet. This would avoid the charge that the Newfoundland delegation had been negotiating Confederation as such and therefore exceeding its mandate. Once the representation of New Brunswick was resolved, the cabinet would then decide "the terms they were prepared to recommend to Parliament as the basis for union," whereupon these would be made known to the National Convention.[154] In order, however, that the Newfoundlanders would have some document to take home with them, the final session on the twenty-ninth approved a joint public summary of proceedings.[155] This was to be made available first to the National Convention by the Newfoundland delegation and would remain confidential until then. Thus fortified, Bradley and his colleagues left the Canadian capital on 30 September. For all the risks they had run and the abuse they had taken, the Commission later denied their request for $15 rather than $10 per diem for the time they were in transit to and from Ottawa.[156]

The National Convention finally resumed sitting on 10 October, when the preliminary section of the document brought back from Ottawa was introduced, and then the whole report tabled. These each had black covers and were commonly referred to thereafter as "the Black Books." The sensation of the day, however, was Bradley's announcement of his resignation as chairman. The events of the summer had obviously made it difficult for him to carry on, and when the first words of criticism were levelled against him, he seized the opportunity to leave in a huff, scolding the members as he did for their conduct.[157] He was succeeded in the chair on 13 October by the lawyer J.B. McEvoy, a former student of MacKay at Dalhousie University.[158] McEvoy presided over his first meeting on 15 October and on the sixteenth the convention moved on to consider the report of the Finance Committee.[159] This key committee had been chaired by Cashin and essentially had concluded that Newfoundland was indeed now self-supporting. While the convention was thus preoccupied, Paul Bridle of the Canadian Department of External Affairs, who had previously been posted to St. John's and was now secretary of the Interdepartmental Committee on Canada-Newfoundland Relations, arrived in the Newfoundland capital with Canada's proposed terms of union for delivery to Governor Macdonald.[160] The way had been cleared for this action by Gregg's big victory in York-Sunbury on 20 October, when he had been able to widen substantially the margin by which the Liberals had won the seat in the general election of 1945.[161] In a letter to Macdonald accompanying the Canadian proposal, King explained that the financial side of the proposed arrangement was definitive but that in relation to matters referred to in the offer that were "primarily of provincial concern" (e.g., education), the government of Canada would be prepared to consider reasonable adjustments.[162]

From Ottawa, a pleased and enthusiastic Clutterbuck reported to London that the Canadian offer was "exceptionally generous" and went far beyond "any expectations previously entertained." Financially, Newfoundland would not only enjoy benefits comparable to those of the other provinces but would receive a special transitional grant of $3,500,000 for the first three years of union and have her whole financial position as a province reviewed within eight years. Ottawa would also assume responsibility for Newfoundland's sterling debt and for the country's expensive railway and steamship services, while leaving St. John's with the surplus funds the Commission had accumulated. All this, Clutterbuck believed, would have a "marked effect" on public opinion in Newfoundland. Moreover, the beneficial effect the elimination of tariff barriers between the two countries would have on the cost of living in Newfoundland, and the advantages individual Newfoundlanders would gain from Canadian family allowances, unemployment insurance, and more substantial old age pensions and veterans benefits would in themselves give Confederation "a wide appeal" with the voters. The net annual cost to Canada of incorporating Newfoundland on the basis proposed would be in the order of $15,000,000, but it had long been recognized in Ottawa that, to begin with at least, Newfoundland would "be a serious financial liability." Weighing against this from the Canadian point of view were the "cogent political, strategic and economic advantages" of union. "In drawing up their terms," Clutterbuck concluded, "the Canadian Government made it their guiding principle, notwithstanding possible criticism from some of the Provinces, to err always on the side of generosity, and the offer now made should ensure that, whatever the ultimate decision in Newfoundland, the people of Canada will at least have no cause to reproach themselves for any failure on their part to extend to their sensitive friends and neighbours the most open-handed and open-hearted of welcomes."[163]

The National Convention was handed the Canadian offer on 6 November and a raucus debate on it commenced on the twentieth.[164] With Bradley ill, Smallwood took the lead from the pro-Confederation side. Then, on 12 December the convention came to what Wainwright Abbott, Donald's recently arrived successor as United States consul general, called "a sudden and undignified adjournment," when anti-Confederate members denied a quorum to Smallwood, who had just bested Cashin in a contest to get the floor.[165] When the convention reassembled on 5 January 1948, it more or less picked up where it had left off, with Smallwood at one electrifying moment on the first day back challenging Pierce Fudge "to go outside." When, however, Fudge rose to accept the invitation, the wily Smallwood chose to ignore him and continued his speech.[166]. The next day, Cashin began a speech - Abbott called it a "long drawn out harangue" - that dominated proceedings until 9 January, when he gave way to Higgins. Higgins, of course, had been a member of the delegation to Ottawa; but now, to the surprise of nobody in the know, he came down firmly on the side of a return to Responsible Government.[167] The debate on the terms finally ended on 15 January, when the speakers included the venerable R.B. Job, who rose from his sick bed to claim that without further information being available, the choice of Confederation would be folly. If Newfoundland returned to Responsible Government or if the Commission system were continued for a time, Confederation would still be possible but could be better negotiated. Before the issue of Conderation was ever put before the people, Newfoundland should have the opportunity to investigate for herself all the international possibilities open to her.[168]

The curtain now rose on the last tumultuous act of the convention drama. On 19 January, Higgins moved to recommend to the United Kingdom government that the wishes of the people as between "Responsible Government as it existed in Newfoundland prior to its suspension in 1934" and the existing form of government be determined "at the earliest moment."[169] Higgins's motion passed unanimously on 22 January.[170] The next day Smallwood, in one of his greatest speeches, introduced a resolution by which the convention would recommend that the referendum ballot also include the choice of "Confederation with Canada upon the basis submitted to the National Convention on November 6th, 1947, by the Prime Minister of Canada."[171]

Hours of highly charged discussion followed. Finally, after an all-night sitting, ending at 5:30 AM on the morning of 28 January, Smallwood's resolution was defeated, twenty-nine to sixteen.[172] In a division that foreshadowed later electoral developments, all those voting in the affirmative represented constituencies off the Avalon Peninsula. On the afternoon of the twenty-ninth, the convention approved in private session a final report to the secretary of state for commonwealth relations on its work.[173] Drafted by a six-man committee composed equally of known supporters of Responsible Government and Confederation,[174] this was presented in ceremonial public session to Emerson (Macdonald was in England at the time) on 30 January.[175] Following a polite speech by the administrator, the convention then disbanded. Soon afterwards Abbott gave it this mixed review:

> By no stretch of imagination can it be credited with having achieved with distinction and success its appointed task of considering possible forms of future government and objectively weighing their advantages and disadvantages. With the introduction of the Confederation issue, the Convention was split from the beginning with this issue dominating the debates to the extent of their revolving principally about it and nothing else; their usefulness suffered proportionately. If the Convention has served no other purpose, it has aroused political interest in this country which for 14 years has lived in a political vacuum. It is generally expected that a bitterly partisan campaign will now commence and be waged in preparation for the coming referendum.[176]

In retrospect his summation seems fair enough.

CHAPTER ELEVEN

The Political Settlement, 1948-49

A successful outcome to the negotiations had been generally expected but was none the less gratifying to Canadians. There is a feeling in Ottawa that the errant and high-spirited son who is now at last *joining the rest of the family after running wild for so long* a period may prove to be both unruly and prodigal, but that any sacrifice and inconveniences entailed will be well repaid in the long run. Even the French-Canadian newspapers have for the most part forborne to criticize.

P.A. Clutterbuck to Secretary of State for Commonwealth Relations, December 1948

After so much talk, the final report of the National Convention was mercifully brief. Following a description of the work of the committees and of the delegations sent abroad, it gave the text of the Higgins and Smallwood motions on constitutional choices to be recommended and detailed lists of the members who had voted for and against them. The report concluded with a name by name summary of the constitutional preferences of the members of the convention themselves, as required by standing order 39 of the Rules of Procedure of the convention. The choices posed and preferences expressed were as follows: for Responsible Government, 28 in favour; for Commission of Government, nil; for Confederation as against Responsible Government, 12 in favour; for Confederation as against Commission of Government, 12 in favour; for Responsible Government as against either Confederation or Commission of Government, 28 in favour.

Annexed to the report were copies of the minutes of the decisive meetings of 22, 27, and 29 January, and the finance committee's economic report, which had been adopted unanimously on 14 January.[1] But only one item really mattered: the recommendation that the referendum ballot incorporate the two choices embodied in the Higgins resolution. In the opinion of thirty-two of the thirty-four practicing lawyers in St. John's, these were the only choices that could legitimately be offered to the people. They gave their opinion on 9 February in a telegram to Philip Noel-Baker, who had succeeded Addison as secretary of state for commonwealth relations in October 1947.[2] Constitutionally, the question of Confederation could only be decided in a general election.

Smallwood, to whom Bradley was now clearly playing second fiddle on the pro-Confederation side, characterized the members of the convention who had voted against his final resolution as "twenty-nine dictators," men who would deny the Newfoundland people a choice that was rightfully theirs.[3] From the convention floor Smallwood took the fight to get Confederation on the ballot to Noel-Baker and to the Newfoundland people. He organized, with many helping hands, a petition in favour of what he wanted. All this was no doubt politically very useful for Smallwood himself, and convenient for the British who, however, hardly needed persuading. Though he did not know it, Smallwood was pushing against an open door. Much has been made of his success in this period, but he was really facilitating the inevitable. The masterful British response to the convention's recommendations was issued on 11 March, following close consultation with officials in St. John's and Ottawa. The referendum would offer three choices: revised versions of the two recommended by the National Convention, and Confederation.[4] The actual wording on the ballot as eventually printed was as follows: "1. COMMISSION OF GOVERNMENT for a period of five years"; "2. CONFEDERATION WITH CANADA"; "3. RESPONSIBLE GOVERNMENT as it existed in 1933."[5]

Interestingly, the formal justification given to the Governor of Newfoundland by Noel-Baker for including Confederation did not mention the petition Smallwood and his associates had organized. The United Kingdom's initiative was justified because the issues involved in union with Canada had been "sufficiently clarified" to enable the people of Newfoundland to pronounce on Confederation and because of the support this additional choice had received in the National Convention.[6] The five-year time limit (Canada initially wanted ten) placed on the continuation of Commission of Government was designed to make this choice as unappetizing as possible, though it ran the the danger of having the opposite effect by encouraging some voters to put off a final choice until it could be better seen how Newfoundland would fare economically in the post-war world.[7] The simple phrase "Confederation with Canada" was designed to obtain approval in principle for this particular option, but it was clearly understood between St. John's, Ottawa, and London in advance of the British announcement that this did not mean the negotiation of terms de novo. Rather, what was intended, the British assured a nervous Canadian government, fearful of misunderstanding later on, was that the offer submitted by Canada to the National Convention in November 1947, would "serve to the voters as a guide to the kind of terms which would be obtained."[8] To guarantee that matters would proceed as intended, the British specified in their statement that if Newfoundlanders chose either Responsible Government or Confederation, the Commission of Government would nonetheless remain in office "for the period required to arrange for the establishment of the new form of Government." Should Confederation be the people's choice, "means would be provided to enable the full terms and arrangements for the constitution of Newfoundland as a Province of Canada to be discussed and settled between authorized representatives of Newfoundland and Canada."[9]

To secure further his country's own position, King made an announcement to Parliament the same day the British intentions were made known in Newfoundland. In this speech he quoted, from the covering letter he had sent to Governor Macdonald with the Canadian offer, the section, which distinguished between the possibility of further modification of the proposed financial terms and those relating to "matters ... primarily of Provincial concern."[10] Afterwards the question of exactly what the country would be voting for if it chose "Confederation with Canada" became a hot political issue in Newfoundland, but no further clarification of the phrase was issued by any of the governments concerned beyond what was made known from London and Ottawa on 11 March. Three choices rather than two meant, of course, that a referendum might not produce an absolute majority for any one. Recognizing this and believing that majority support was crucial on so basic a decision, the British ruled that a second referendum would have to be held if the first failed to meet this requirement.[11]

A proclamation, issued on 7 May under the terms of a referendum act that had become law on 27 April, set the date of the referendum for 3 June; it remained to be seen whether there would have to be a second one.[12] Magistrate Short was again named chief electoral officer, and the balloting was to be organized through twenty-five electoral districts, twenty-four as described, with slight variations, in the 1932 redistribution act, and the district of Labrador as defined in the first schedule to the National Convention Act.[13] The voters lists to be used were those compiled under the Lists of Electors Act 1947,[14] but a qualified person not thus enumerated could vote on taking a prescribed oath. Smallwood later pressed the Commision – unsuccessfully – to set up polling booths "on bankers, draggers and trawlers."[15] The Commission did, however, provide for advance voting at specified times and places in eight electoral districts for electors who met certain requirements.[16]

By the time the date of the first referendum was announced, the campaign leading up to it, which had really begun during the convention period, was in full swing. Support for Confederation was mobilized by the Newfoundland Confederate Association, which was launched on 21 February at a meeting in the ballroom of the Newfoundland Hotel. Bradley was chosen to be president and Smallwood, general secretary.[17] Prominent also in the pro-Confederation inner circle were Philip Forsey, Harold Horwood, and Gregory Power, men of diverse backgrounds but all politically adept. According to Horwood, funding for the campaign was provided variously: through a one dollar initiation fee (a limited source), through the opening up of a market in senatorial futures, and, most importantly, through contacts made in Canada by courtesy of Senator Gordon Fogo, a prominent fund-raiser for the Liberal Party.[18] On 7 April the Confederate Association brought out the first issue of *The Confederate*, an enormously successful propaganda tool that showed to full advantage the well-honed literary skills of Smallwood and many of his closest colleagues.[19] The paper countered the arguments of the opponents of Confederation, spread the good news of the benefits that union with Canada would bring to families, workers, and veterans, and promoted the populist notion that a return to Responsbile Government would mean government of Water Street, by Water Street, and for Water Street.

Those in favour of Responsible Government were divided about their ultimate goals, a circumstance that highlighted the variety of opinions on what a return to self-government would bring. The initially high tory Responsible Government League, having completed its preliminary organizational work, made a public declaration of purpose and issued on 21 July 1947, a pamphlet entitled *The Case for Responsible Government*. It then began a radio campaign on 20 September with the lawyer Charles Hunt leading off.[20] Cashin, who had eventually come under the League's umbrella and was by now one of its leading spokesmen, gave the organization a conservative populist appeal. Funding came largely from Newfoudland businessmen and professionals anxious to seize the opportunities they believed independence would bring but fearful too of the increased competition they would face from better situated rivals within Canada.[21] On 22 March the League began distributing its own newspaper, *The Independent*.[22] The cause of Responsible Government had received another boost of sorts in February when *The Monitor*, the newspaper of the Roman Catholic Archdiocese of St. John's, reaffirmed its earlier stand that self-government was prerequisite to any other constitutional step.[23] High Commissioner Macdonald's observation on this position, probably correct, was that once self-government with a two-party system was restored, both political parties would be dominated by Water Street and the issue of Confederation would be smothered.[24]

On 25 November 1947, a shadowy "Union with America Party" had publicly announced its existence.[25] Following the dissolution of the National Convention, D.I. Jackman, much abused in the diplomatic correspondence emanating from St. John's, sent a petition to London, intended to be a counterpart to Smallwood's, calling for economic union with the United States to be put on the referendum ballot.[26] Not surprisingly, he was turned down; but on 20 March the whole issue took on a different complexion when Ches Crosbie announced the launching of the Party for Economic Union with the United States, with himself as president.[27] Since its objective was not specifically included on the ballot, Crosbie's party campaigned for Responsible Government as a first step in the direction it favoured. The unofficial mouthpiece of the Economic Union party was Geoff Stirling's now well-established and popular *Sunday Herald*.[28] Abbott's preliminary analysis for the State Department of Crosbie's move was that the Economic Union party was likely to attract votes that would otherwise go to Confederation.[29]

If ever there was a suitor whose attentions were unwanted, it was Crosbie's party. The last thing the United States wanted to see in Newfoundland was a government, however nominally well disposed, that might be tempted to reopen for discussion – here is a leitmotif of Newfoundland political history – a one-sided agreement considered to have been forced on the country and negotiated by a sellout government. The 1941 bases deal gave the Americans what they wanted in Newfoundland, and not unnaturally they wanted to keep it. As an American official once succinctly and memorably wrote, Newfoundland was "a mortgaged property."[30] In these circumstances the United States had no reason to go counter to the wishes of the United Kingdom and Canada so far as the constitutional future of Newfoundland was concerned. On the contrary they had every reason to go along, as a guarantee of their own position, with what was the decided policy of those countries in relation to Newfoundland. From Washington's perspective, if through force of circumstance the United Kingdom had to give up its role in Newfoundland, Canada promised to be a reliable alternative partner. Large countries often prefer to deal with other large countries so that interests within a broad spectrum can be traded off. Better to deal with a government in Ottawa whose interests in relation to the United States were multifarious and continental in scope than with an independent government in St. John's driven by an idée fixe.

In November 1946 while the National Convention was in its first phase, Raymond Gushue had visited Washington and been given an earful by the Americans. J. Graham Parsons of the Division of British Commonwealth Affairs wrote to Hickerson that both within and without the convention Newfoundlanders were busy persuading themselves that they were "owed a *quid pro quo* for the bases, preferably in the form of a substantial concession to their fishing interests." It was, they held, "the *moral* obligation of the U.S. to give them some return!" Gushue should be encouraged to "use his influence to quell this sort of argument." Thus, there was "no reason, moral or otherwise," why the United States should give a quid pro quo, and there was "no chance in the world" of the Newfoundlanders "getting anything" in return for the bases. Accordingly it would perhaps be well to nip the current agitation in the bud. Newfoundland's war effort, Parsons acidly concluded, had "contained a larger element of *get* than *give*."[31] Gushue listened sympathetically, telling Hickerson on 8 November that not only did Washington not owe St. John's anything but that Newfoundland owed "her wartime prosperity and her tidy Government surplus almost wholly to the United States for its expenditures on the bases and in Newfoundland during the war." Gushue, to the approval of the American official, also reported that he had told the National Convention when consulted that the sending of a mission to Washington to enquire into the possibility of getting fish put "on the free list in return for reductions in the Newfoundland tariff ... would do positive harm and no good whatever."[32]

For his part Hickerson told his Newfoundland visitor that he did not consider a "political union between the United States and Newfoundland ... desirable." Nor would Congress be likely to approve a "unanimous application in that sense" from the National Convention. In keeping with all this, the Division of British Commonwealth Affairs in March 1948 gave all officers in Canada and Newfoundland the following summary of where the United States stood on the Newfoundland constitutional question: "There appears to be increasing agitation in Newfoundland for union with the United States. There is, however, no expectation that the people will be given a chance to vote on this alternative. The position of the Department on this question is that there has been no official approach whatever from the United Kingdom or the Government of Newfoundland, that the matter is entirely one of internal concern in Newfoundland, and that this Government has no views and no comment."[33] This hands-off approach was also evident when the commissioner for home affairs approached Abbott to allow polling booths for the 3 June referendum to be set up on United States bases in the country.[34] When Abbott expressed a preference that this not be done, the Newfoundland official dropped the issue.[35]

Abbott himself argued after Crosbie had thrown his hat in the ring that even by standing aloof the State Department might influence the outcome of events in Newfoundland. This particular stance might be interpreted "by the majority of the unlettered voters as tacit approval of the Crosbie proposal." From their point of view it was inconceivable that the United States was not interested in what Newfoundland, especially in Labrador, had to offer strategically and developmentally. The big drawing card of Confederation was Canadian social security, especially the baby bonus, and to match this Crosbie might eventually have to come out for a "closer union" than he now advocated. Indeed, some of his supporters, were already interpreting economic union to mean unrestricted immigration to the United States and the extension to Newfoundland of that country's social security program. Abbott's own estimate of how events would likely proceed, should Newfoundland get back self-government, was as follows:

> There is no doubt that one of the first acts of any Responsible Government party returned to power would be an endeavour to obtain a review of the Bases Agreement. The value of the Bases to the country's economy is fully realized but a strong feeling persists that the United States has obtained something for nothing and that in justice to the country the Agreement should be reviewed. The requested revision may take the form of a demand for customs privileges, which would improve the island's economy, for a substantial rent for the base areas, which could be used for a social security program in Newfoundland, or for both. There would, however, be no attempt to cancel the agreement with a view to the removal of the United States armed forces.[36]

Crosbie eventually told a consulate official in St. John's "confidentially and categorically" that should his party come to power it would not attempt to renegotiate the bases agreement.[37] But this, of course, was merely the word of an individual and in any case his was only one of two organizations campaigning in favour of Responsible Government. Significantly, the Responsible Government League went into the election still committed to the policy of using Article XXVIII of the bases agreement to lever economic concessions from the United States for the "free gift" that country had been given in Newfoundland. Under this article the signatories to the agreement had undertaken "to give sympathetic consideration" to representations from each other, looking towards the modification of the document "in the light of experience" and on a mutually acceptable basis.[38]

In his own attempts to counteract the undoubted appeal of economic union with the United States, Smallwood made much of Manley O. Hudson's opinion about its feasibility. In a memorandum which he addressed to McEvoy, who had visited him in the United States on a fact finding mission, Hudson, a prominent international jurist at Harvard Law School, did not rule economic union out theoretically but severely questioned its practicality. Hudson's memorandum was published in the *Evening Telegram* on 8 May together with letters McEvoy had also received from A.H. Monroe (son of Walter Monroe and a major figure in the export trade in frozen fish to the United States) and from the Gloucester (Mass.)

Fisheries Association. From the former McEvoy heard that a campaign to pressure the United States to grant special privileges to Newfoundland producers would not only be futile but might well backfire. From the Gloucester organization McEvoy heard that if local fishing interests were threatened by concessions to any foreign producer, they would ask Congress for protection.[39] When the Broadcasting Corporation of Newfoundland refused McEvoy air time to discuss his findings on the grounds that he wanted to make a political speech as an individual and not on behalf of any recognized party or group, Smallwood came to his rescue, extending to him the sponsorship of the Newfoundland Confederate Association.[40]

Meanwhile the *Sunday Herald* had individually contacted all the members of the United States Senate to find out how many would be willing to meet with a Newfoundland delegation to discuss economic union, should this cause succeed with the electorate. Abbott analyzed the seventy replies in hand by 14 May as follows: twenty-nine were "unreservedly favorable," ten were "favorable" but wanting the approach to be made through the State Department, nine were "conditionally favourable," nine were unwilling "for various reasons," thirteen had "no opinion owing to illness or absence." On 11 May the *Herald* wrote to those Senators who had responded favourably to its initial appeal, asking them to get in touch with the paper before accepting at face value any request for a retraction they might receive from the Confederation side, which was now portrayed as an "anti-Amerian minority party spreading class hatred."[41] Later on in May, Stirling popped up in the United States and on the twenty-fourth "called without prior appointment" at the State Department, where he was poorly received. He fished for "something in repudiation" of the Hudson memorandum but heard only that Hudson was not a government official and that the State Department understandably had no comment to make on his private views.[42] When Stirling returned to St. John's, he attempted to obtain air time for broadcasting a recording of a statement made by Senator C. Wayland Brooks, an Illinois Republican, which was favourable to his cause.[43] On receipt of a public complaint, however, the Commission banned such a broadcast over the facilities of the Broadcasting Corporation of Newfoundland, on the grounds that the stations of the publicly owned system should not be available for persons not resident of Newfoundland to comment on the constitutional issues now before the country. On the other hand, quotation from outside commentators was declared permissible.[44]

The 3 June 1948 referendum produced the indecisive result the British had anticipated it might. Responsible Government led the poll with 69,400 votes. Confederation with Canada was a reasonably close second at 64,066 and Commission of Government a distant third at 22,311.

In percentage terms these figures worked out to 44.55 per cent, 41.13 per cent, and 14.32 per cent respectively of the votes cast. Turnout in the election was 88.36 per cent of the registered electors, a marked improvement on what had happened in the National Convention election.[45]. Geographically, Responsible Government had done best on the Avalon Peninsula, and Confederation best elsewhere in the country. Proportionately, the highest votes for Commission of Government were in Twillingate (42.44 per cent), Fogo (25.65 per cent), Grand Falls (24.05 per cent), Bonavista South (22.93 per cent) and St. Barbe (21.09 per cent), where the result may have been influenced by the idea that Commission rule had marked a refreshing change from the St. John's-centred governments of the past.[46] Though the Commission vote overall was small, it was nonetheless substantial given that no organized public campaign had been conducted in favour of it. Towards the end of the campaign Job had prepared a speech repeating his well-worn themes in favour of the Commission option, but like McEvoy he had been denied the use of the Broadcasting Corporation's facilities because he planned to speak as an individual and not on behalf of an organized group.[47] He had, however, released the speech to the press.

Altogether the supporters of Responsible Government constituted a majority in eight districts, all of them on the Avalon Peninsula, where only Trinity South resisted the prevailing trend and gave a plurality to Confederation. The supporters of Confederation formed a majority in another nine districts. In the eight districts that did not produce a majority for any option (Grand Falls, Twillingate, Fogo, Bonavista South, Trinity North, Trinity South, Placentia West, and St. George's-Port au Port) Confederation had a plurality in all but Bonavista South, the only district off the Avalon where Responsible Government had come in first. Because the Roman Catholic population was concentrated on the Avalon Peninsula, there was obviously a high correlation between being Roman Catholic and voting for Responsible Government. But at root the vote seems to have been regional rather than denominational. Thus, there were two districts on the Avalon (Port de Grave and Carbonear-Bay de Verde) with large Protestant majorities that gave a majority to Responsible Government, while there were two districts with Roman Catholic majorities off the Avalon (Placentia West and St. George's-Port au Port) which gave pluralities to Confederation. This choice was also known to enjoy the support of prominent Roman Catholics both on and off the Avalon. Clearly, Roman Catholic voters, like the electorate generally away from the Avalon, were subject to different influences than were their co-religionists there.

On 14 June it was announced that the second referendum, in which the Commission of Government option would be dropped from the ballot, would be held on Thursday, 22 July.[48] The campaign leading up to this repeated much that had been heard before but at a higher level of intensity. Not surprisingly, in a do or die situation both sides were able to attract prominent new recruits to battle on their behalf. In addition to the well-established casts of the Responsible Government League and the Economic Union Party, speakers on the Responsible Government side now included Andrew Carnell, the mayor of St. John's; John S. Currie, whose *Daily News* was virulently anti-Confederation; P.F. Halley, a well know St. John's wholesaler and retailer and a member of the House of Assembly elected in 1932; J.G. Higgins, a prominent Roman Catholic lawyer; Roy Cheeseman, whose family was prominent in the fish export business; Charles Hunt; Donald Jamieson; R.B. Job, whose own cherished solution had now gone by the board; P.E. Outerbridge, the brother of Leonard Outerbridge; A.M. Fraser of Memorial Univerity College; Calvert C. Pratt, a businessman with diverse interests and president of the Newfoundland Industrial Development Board; the pugnacious Fanny Ryan Fiander of Harbour Grace, who ended her direct campaigning with a letter to the *Daily News* which she entitled "Over the top with Fanny"; and Raymond Gushue, who, to use Abbott's words, had "at last been 'flushed.'"[49]

Among the new faces supporting Confederation were the lawyers J.B. McEvoy and Leslie R. Curtis, Will Roberts, a politically active physician, and a number of prominent businessmen including Leonard Outerbridge, whose presence in any group always suggested legitimacy.[50]. The participation of the businessmen who stepped forward was important, of course, because it indicated that, as in previous showdowns during the Commission period, the economic elite of the country was divided. Confederation also now attracted the public support of Commissioners Herman Quinton and H.L. Pottle, who in 1947 had been the last two Newfoundlanders to be named to the Commission of Government.[51] They spoke out in their private capacities as Newfoundland residents and voters. Abbott's impression was that some of the "best people" who had now lined up on the Confederation side hoped to dump Smallwood once Confederation was carried, but that this would prove illusory. "Other people had the same idea about Hitler if you remember," he told Andrew Foster of the State Department's Division of British Commonwealth Affairs.[52]

For his part Smallwood was now in overdrive, presenting himself as the champion of the little man against big interests determined to get back control of the country seemingly at almost any cost. In a radio address on the evening of the nineteenth, he recounted that he had been variously threatened, twice physically attacked, and now had to have a bodyguard during his public appearances and nighttime police protection for his house. Cashin was identified as one assailant, with the occasion of his attack having been a meeting of the Steering Committee of the National Convention. Such, Smallwood theatrically proclaimed, was the measure of the desperation of his opponents.[53] Another notable incident of the second referendum campaign was the accusation by *The Confederate* that American personnel within base limits had actively supported Responsible Government before the 3 June vote.[54] Abbott refused comment to the editor of the *Evening Telegram* on what he termed "an absurd assertion."[55]

A figure never liked, respected, or trusted by many advocates of Responsible Government, but who came to be detested by them in the period between the referanda, was Governor Macdonald. Their reason was his alleged intervention in favour of Confederation. One incident, according to Abbott, that had sparked protest and bitter feeling was a remark Macdonald had made to a Methodist (United Church of Canada) convention in St. John's to the effect "that one sect (the Catholics) had influenced the first referendum and that it was time that the Protestants pulled together."[56] Macdonald was also accused of having inspired a circular letter sent out to his fellow members by Chelsey Fillier, the Grand Master of the Provincial Grand Orange Lodge of Newfoundland. This incorporated a resolution of the Provincial Grand Lodge denouncing the interference of the Roman Catholic Church in the electoral process and calling on Orangemen to act to ensure that "efforts at sectional domination" would not prevail.[57] In a similar vein Smallwood had played up Confederation as "British Union," while some of his opponents, appealing to another local prejudice and fears about the future of Labrador, described it as "French-Canadian Union."[58] Abbott's perhaps justifiable impression of the effect of Macdonald's performance on the pro-Responsible Government side was that he had "proved conclusively their charge that the British Government at the instigation of Canada had connived to 'railroad' Newfoundland into union with Canada."[59]

At the end of the contest, the voters endorsed Confederation by 78,323 votes (52.34 per cent) to 71,344 (47.66 per cent) in an election that repeated the basic pattern of the 3 June contest.[60] The turnout in the referendum was 84.89 per cent of the number of registered electors, and in two districts, Ferryland and Labrador, more people voted than were registered. This outcome was made possible, not, as has sometimes been hinted at by uninformed commentators looking for an easy laugh, because of peculiar Newfoundland electoral mores, but by the normal workings of the swearing in system which allowed people to vote who had not been previously enumerated. Responsible Government carried in seven of the eight districts, all on the Avalon, in which it had obtained a majority in June (the one exception in this regard, by a narrow margin, was

Carbonear-Bay de Verde) and Confederation won everywhere else. In percentage terms Responsible Government obtained its best results in Ferryland (84.56 per cent) and Harbour Main-Bell Island (82.58 per cent) with Placentia and St. Mary's (81.60 per cent) a close third. In St. John's East and West, Responsible Government was supported by 68.78 per cent and 66.89 per cent respectively, a modest increase in both cases from the June figures. By contrast, the Confederation vote even in these ridings grew by 7.71 per cent and 8.17 per cent respectively. On the Confederation side the districts producing the best percentage results were Burgeo and La Poile, Burin, and Fortune Bay and Hermitage, all on the south coast of the island, a region hit hard during the Depression and which had long enjoyed close economic links of its own with the Maritime provinces. Overall the Confederation total grew by 11.21 per cent between the June and July votes and the Responsible Government total by only 3.11 per cent. This left little doubt about who had won the battle for support among those who had initially opted for the continuation of Commission of Government. The same Catholic-Protestant split was evident in July as in June, but so too was the same regional variation in this. Catholic votes off the Avalon may indeed have been crucial in putting Confederation over the top. The Commission's assessment of the occupational basis of support was that Responsible Government had done best among the professional and commercial classes and among the miners on Bell Island. Confederation had done best among lumbermen and fishermen. On the other hand, the campaign had shown that "members of business, professional and workmen's interests" could be found on both sides of the issue.[61]

When the balloting was over, Abbott gave the State Department this prophetic forecast of how things would be likely to develop politically in Newfoundland:

> Barring an objection from the Canadian Parliament, which is hardly to be expected, it is clear that Newfoundland will become a part of Canada within the next ten months or less. Had it not been for the success of the Governor in obtaining the aid of the United Church, the Orangemen, two of the Commissioners and a few other prominent citizens at the last moment the result would probably have been different. Mr. Joseph Smallwood attracted a large following with his promises of family allowances; but he repelled a great many of the more substantial class by his extreme claims and by his injection of class hatred and regional differences into the campaign. The new men who came out at the last moment reassured the more conservative voters and cast an aura of respectability about the Confederate party which had been lacking before. Having made use of Smallwood's undoubted organizing and demagogic talents, these new accessions to Confederation are now faced with the problem of how to get rid of him, which they privately state they wish and intend to do. He is reported to have an almost hypnotic influence over

the audiences which he addresses, and the more conservative elements may well find that it is easier to release a genie from the bottle than to persuade him to return.[62]

The Newfoundland electorate had spoken, but would Canada listen? In his 1975 book *My Years with Louis St. Laurent*, J.W. Pickersgill, who was working in Mackenzie King's office in 1948 and was an ardent supporter of Confederation, recounts a memorable telephone conversation with the Canadian prime minister the morning following the second referendum. Fearful of how the cautious King would react to so close a vote for union, Pickersgill, whose budding friendship with Smallwood would eventually lead him into Parliament via a safe Newfoundland seat, had taken the precaution of having had some calculations done in advance. With these in hand he was able, when King sought his opinion, to place the result in Newfoundland in a most favourable context indeed. Confederation, he told the prime minister, had carried by a higher percentage of the popular vote than the Liberal Party of Canada had been able to muster in any general election from 1921, that is to say during King's leadership of it.[63] Whatever the effect this appeal to an old man's vanity might have been, there were of course compelling reasons of high policy why Canada should have accepted the margin of victory in Newfoundland as sufficient to proceed and on 27 July the Cabinet in fact made the decision.[64]

Having plucked up his courage, King afterwards portrayed himself in his diary as a man of vision and foresight who had finished the design of the Fathers of Confederation.[65] Posturing such as this was typical of him. Whether it mattered or not, the British had done a little judicious elbowing in Ottawa immediately after the second vote. "There must be no hesitation on the part of the Canadian authorities," Governor Macdonald wrote Machtig in a warning London immediately brought to Clutterbuck's attention.[66] Having earlier forecast that a decision to go ahead with Confederation on the basis of a small majority in its favour might produce "civil disorders" in the country,[67] the governor now nonetheless pronounced that "any sign whatever of hesitation" would be "fatal."[68] This sentiment accorded with established British policy, long since made plain to Ottawa, that so far as the United Kingdom was concerned "any majority for Confederation, however small," would be binding.[69] If Confederation momentarily hung in the balance after 22 July 1948, the indecision was in Ottawa.

Needless to say, Whitehall was immensely pleased with the eventual decision taken in Canada, its satisfaction marred only by an embarrassing and unusual mixup in London over the appropriate timing of the announcements to be made there, in Ottawa, and St. John's. What

Macdonald told the Newfoundland people in his statement, dated 30 July like its Canadian and British counterparts, was that since Canada was now ready to receive a delegation from Newfoundland to negotiate terms of union, such a group would be appointed shortly. The delegation to Ottawa would be led by Walsh, but he would be the only member of the Commission of Government on it. Macdonald's statement further revealed that the Newfoundland, Canadian, and United Kingdom governments were consulting as to "the precise procedure, parliamentary and otherwise, to be followed for effecting Confederation."[70] The names of those chosen to serve along with Walsh on the delegation were then announced on 5 August. They were Bradley, Crosbie, Philip Gruchy (General Manager of the Anglo-Newfoundland Development Company's operations at Grand Falls), McEvoy, Smallwood, and Gordon Winter (second vice president of the T. & M. Winter Company and 1947 President of the Board of Trade).[71] Crosbie's appointment was an obvious gesture of reconciliation but was no doubt influenced by the apparent willingness of the Economic Union Party, unlike the Responsible Government League, to lay down arms.[72] The Newfoundland Federation of Labour later complained to the Commission and the Commonwealth Relations Office that no labour representative had been named to the delegation, but this protest, like so many others in Newfoundland since 1934, failed to move the authorities and then was forgotten.[73] Meanwhile on 7 August the British had heard from their High Commission in Ottawa that the union of the two countries would probably not be practical until 31 March 1949.[74] Reference previously made to 1 April as the possible day of the big event was being quietly discouraged in the Canadian capital because of the jokes it might unleash.

The Newfoundland delegation (except for Crosbie, who was absent for some time because he had been involved in a motor accident) held its first meeting with the seven-member Canadian cabinet committtee on 6 October.[75] The chairman of the Canadian negotiating group, and co-chairman with Walsh of the meetings of the two parties, was St. Laurent, who had been chosen leader of the Liberal Party at a convention in August which Bradley and Smallwood had attended as observers. In fact, however, he was frequently absent from the sessions on other business; in October he attended the Commonwealth prime ministers conference in London in place of King and on 15 November succeeded him as prime minister of Canada. When St. Laurent was unavailable, the chair was taken by Brooke Claxton, who was now Minister of National Defence. Another frequent absentee from the talks was Lester B. Pearson, who had moved over from the civil service to become secretary of state for external affairs on 10 September, and was busy in the autumn of 1948 fighting a by-election in Algoma East (Ontario). For the United Kingdom,

Clutterbuck kept a watching brief on the negotiations with a view to defending his country's interests.

On 15 October Clutterbuck told London that negotiations had "got off to a slow and sticky start" over the question of financial arrangements. The Newfoundland delegation was advancing the view that under the scheme of payments from Ottawa embodied in Canada's 1947 offer the new province of Newfoundland would soon be threatened with bankruptcy. The reason this had not been recognized before was that the delegation sent by the National Convention had been "working with rough estimates calculated by Smallwood." Now, however, expert opinion obtained both from the Newfoundland government and the delegation's own financial adviser, the accountant J.S. Thompson of Montreal, made it evident that this would be the case. The Newfoundland delegation conceded, Clutterbuck reported, that it would be difficult for Ottawa to discriminate any more in favour of Newfoundland than was contemplated already, but was insistent nonetheless that somehow, "without giving rise to claims from other provinces," extra funds would have to be found for Newfoundland.[76]

The Newfoundlanders' own suggestions as to how this might be done was for Canada to ask the United Kingdom to take over Newfoundland's sterling debt, but Clutterbuck immediately sought to prevent this as unfair "to the already highly-taxed people of the United Kingdom," a position in which the Canadians eventually acquiesced. Smallwood, according to Clutterbuck, had advanced to him the "idea that [the] Federal Government should lease Labrador from Newfoundland for say 50 years at a rental of dollars 6 or 7 millions," an amount which would cover the estimated budgetary deficit of the province of Newfoundland. But this scheme was rejected by the delegation as a whole lest it encourage the idea in Newfoundland "that Canadian willingness for Confederation sprang solely from [a] desire to get their hands on Labrador resources." Both Smallwood and Walsh, the high commissioner further reported, had told him the present mood of the delegation was such that unless the Canadians became "more responsive and sympathetic," Confederation was "doomed." As things stood, "at least three members would refuse to sign the 1947 terms without substantial financial improvement," and the delegation was unanimous in the view that if Newfoundland was destined for bankruptcy, "they would sooner go down as an independent country than as an impecunious Canadian province."[77]

These were harsh sentiments, but Clutterbuck was not alarmed, believing that both parties were in too far to pull back now. His optimism was well placed, for a deal was shortly struck whereby the Canadians agreed to increase the amount of their twelve-year sliding scale transitional grant from the $26,250,000 originally proposed to $42,750,000.[78] Another important matter on which the Canadians conceded ground in this round of negotiations was the future of the Newfoundland Fisheries Board. This organization, they agreed, could continue in existence for five years from the date of union to administer the existing saltfish export marketing regulatory system, provided the powers under Newfoundland law in this respect vested in the commissioner for natural resources and the Governor in Commission were transferred to the minister of fisheries and the Governor General in Council respectively.[79] The negotiations faltered over the Newfoundland demand for a watertight guarantee that financial arrangements similar to those the United Kingdom had made in 1948 concerning sales in sterling of Newfoundland saltfish be made by Canada for 1949. But this difficulty was overcome when London agreed at Ottawa's request to extend conditionally the existing practice for a transitional year.[80]

Yet another tricky matter on which agreement was now reached was how in general Newfoundland would be governed in the period between union and the election of a provincial legislature. From the outset, it was decided, the administration of the province would be "by a Lieutenant-Governor with an Executive Council."[81] This, of course, left one crucial question hanging, namely, who would be in this first government. The initial instinct of the Canadians was to have the members of the Commission remain in office under a Lieutenant Governor but this was adamantly refused by the Newfoundlanders, who instead pushed for an interim government formed from people who had worked for the cause of Confederation. Fearful of making Confederation an issue in party politics in the new province, the Canadians instead turned to the idea of "a caretaker administration under the Lieutenant Governor composed only of Newfoundland members of the Commission," but this also was dropped.[82] On 18 November Clutterbuck told London that the question of who should be in the first government had been "transferred to [the] political level" and that Smallwood and Bradley were vigorously arguing the case that those who had "fought the battle of Confederation should be entitled as [reward] for their labours to take over administration of [the] country as from date of union, and form interim government to conduct affairs pending provincial elections." Whoever was in power when the first general election was held, Clutterbuck noted, would have an obvious political advantage. Nonetheless, he correctly predicted, that despite "Canadian qualms," Bradley and Smallwood were likely to get what they wanted.[83]

The terms of union as finally laid out were signed on 11 December at a ceremony held in the Senate chamber and broadcast in both countries. St. Laurent and Claxton signed for Canada, and all the members of the Newfoundland delegation, except for Crosbie, signed for their country. Crosbie refused to sign mainly on the grounds that the financial terms were not satisfactory.[84] The gathering heard speeches by St. Laurent and Walsh, and the ceremony concluded with the playing of "God save the King" and "O Canada." The "Ode to Newfoundland" was omitted because the band recruited for the occasion could not locate the music for it. In its stead and as a final gesture, St. Laurent led a rousing three cheers for Newfoundland. In his report of this event a justifiably proud and self-satisfied Clutterbuck noted "a feeling in Ottawa that the errant and high-spirited son ... now at last joining the rest of the family after running wild for so long a period" might "prove to be both unruly and prodigal." But it was also thought that any "sacrifice and inconveniences entailed" would "be well repaid in the long run." Even Crosbie's dissent, the high commissioner wryly observed in this same despatch, had its positive side, for "if the entire delegation had accepted the Terms without any reservation, the existing Provinces would certainly have complained that they were too generous!"[85] If Clutterbuck and his colleagues knew how to play on the strengths and limitations of Newfoundlanders, they also understood the multiple parochialisms and parish pump federalism of Canada.

The fifty terms of union were embodied in a memorandum of agreement which, following a preamble, was subdivided into eight parts, some of which were themselves subdivided by topic. The terms were to "come into force immediately before the expiration of the thirty-first day of March, 1949," and the province was to "comprise the same territory as at the date of union, that is to say, the island of Newfoundland and the islands adjacent thereto, the Coast of Labrador as delimited in the report delivered by the Judicial Committee of His Majesty's Privy Council on the first day of March, 1927, and approved by his Majesty in His Privy Council on the twenty-second day of March, 1927, and the islands adjacent to the said Coast of Labrador." The general provisions of the British North America Acts, 1867–1946, were to apply to Newfoundland as to the existing provinces except as varied by the terms of union themselves. Newfoundland was initially to have six senators and seven members in the House of Commons, both numbers to be revisable according to procedures spelled out in the British North America Acts. The constitution of Newfoundland as it existed before Commission of Government was to come back into force at the union except as specified and subject to the provisions of the British North America Acts, 1867–1946.[86]

As in the other provinces, the executive was to consist of a lieutenant governor, appointed by the Governor General in Council and advised by an Executive Council, that is to say, a cabinet headed by a premier. The legislature was now to consist of the elected House of Assembly only, unless it decided to re-establish the old Legislative Council or create a new one. By contrast with what the British had favoured for Newfoundland, existing denominational school rights were guaranteed by term 17, which was to apply to the province in lieu of the much-fought-over section 93 of the British North America Act of 1867. This enshrined the victory the churches had won during the Commission years. The existing laws of Newfoundland were to continue in force after the union, subject to the will of the Parliament of Canada and the Newfoundland legislature within their respective spheres of constitutional jurisdiction. Canadian statute law in effect at the union was, with certain provisos, to come into force in Newfoundland as specified by act of the Parliament of Canada or proclamation of the Governor General in Council. While the Newfoundland Fisheries Board was to continue in existence, the "Fisheries Laws" establishing it and the regulatory system it administered in the exporting of saltfish were to be subject to repeal or alteration by the Parliament of Canada during the five-year transitional period agreed upon. Such action would, however, during this period require the consent of the Lieutenant Governor in Council of the province. Financially, in addition to what has already been noted, Canada was to assume responsibility for the interest payments and the redemption of the whole of the 3 per cent sterling debt owed by Newfoundland under its 1933 Loan Act for which the United Kingdom was guarantor.[87]

At the same time Newfoundland was to retain control of its financial surplus, subject to various conditions as to its use. The review of Newfoundland's financial position within Confederation to be undertaken within eight years of union was provided for in term 29, a term which would be the subject of a fierce federal-provincial fight later on. Newfoundland was to have the same ownership rights in relation to "all lands, mines, minerals and royalties" that the other provinces enjoyed, but the term specifying this, number 37, omitted any specific reference to ownership of offshore resources, another matter that would greatly disturb future federal-provincial relations. It is noteworthy, however, that the international standing Newfoundland had established with respect to the use of her air space and civil aviation generally became subject to normal Canadian jurisdictional arrangements once union was complete; that is to say, came under federal rather than provincial control. Included among various works, properties, and services that Canada was to "take over" was the Newfoundland Railway together with its "steamship and other marine services." What the phrase "take over" meant in practice in relation to the railway would also be a matter of contention later, but there was no doubt about another Canadian transportation commitment. This was to "maintain in accordance with the traffic offering a freight and passenger steamship service between North Sydney and Port aux Basques." Newfoundland veterans were to be eligible for specified Canadian veterans benefits as though they had served in the Canadian armed forces. By the same token, Newfoundland merchant seamen who had done wartime duty on British or Allied ships were to be eligible for a variety of benefits on an equivalent basis.[88]

By term 46 Newfoundland residents were to have the constitutional right within Confederation to produce and sell margarine within the province and to ship it wherever else in the country its distribution was legal. The reason for the inclusion of this term lay in the fact that for many years, thanks to the influence of politically well placed farm and dairy interests, the sale of the product in question had been illegal in Canada. Since there was only a small dairy industry in Newfoundland, and margarine was relatively cheap there while butter was a luxury item, this arrangement made good economic and political sense when it was drafted. Union with Canada would have been off to a shaky start indeed if it had immediately disrupted the eating habits of Newfoundlanders.[89] The Newfoundland people also brought with them into Confederation the benefit of the arrangements for local labour preference which their government had negotiated for any "concession or privilege granted." A schedule to the terms of union spelled out the boundaries of the constituencies through which Newfoundlanders would initially return members to the House of Commons.[90] In a separate memorandum, which St. Laurent enclosed in a letter he addressed to Walsh on 11 December, the Canadian government put on record its policy and intentions with respect to various administrative and other matters not of a constitutional nature arising out of the talks with the Newfoundland delegation.[91] For its part, the Commission of Government approved the terms of union on 26 January 1949.[92] Generally speaking, the Commission was kept in the background constitutionally after the first referendum, in which its continuance had been rejected.[93]

On 7 February, with Smallwood, Cashin, and Clutterbuck present in the Gallery and Mackenzie King in his seat,[94] a bill to approve the terms of union with Newfoundland was introduced into the Canadian House of Commons by St. Laurent, following debate on a preliminary resolution also proposed by him.[95] The bill passed second reading the next day.[96] Then, on 14 February after the bill had passed all stages and gone to the Senate, the prime minister moved in the House a resolution embodying an address to the King asking that an act as specified be passed by the Parliament of the United Kingdom to give effect to the terms of union.[97] His resolution was challenged by the Leader of the Opposition, George Drew, who had succeeded John Bracken at the head of the Progressive Conservative Party in October 1948. Drew moved an amendment that would have required the government "to consult at once the governments of the several provinces" and to present the address to His Majesty only "upon a satisfactory conclusion of such consultations.[98] This was opposed by the leader of the CCF, M.J. Coldwell, but supported by Solon Low, the Social Credit leader. Next, Wilfrid LaCroix and Jean François

Pouliot, the members for the Quebec constituencies of Quebec-Montmorency and Témiscouata respectively, moved to amend Drew's amendment "so as to provide that the Government should secure consent of all Provincial Governments and not merely consult them before [the] Address was forwarded to His Majesty."[99] This was unacceptable to the Tories because it would have given each province a veto which Quebec might well use; the amendment to Drew's proposal lost 191 to 12.[100]

The minority was made up of eight Alberta and four Quebec members, a provincial combination that foreshadowed the turbulent debate of a later time about Canadian federalism. Drew's own amendment was then defeated 137 to 66.[101] Finally, on 16 February St. Laurent's motion was carried 140 to 74, with Tories, Social Crediters, and Quebec Nationalists joined in opposition. At the conclusion of the vote the members rose and sang "O Canada" and "God Save the King."[102] This was stirring, but in truth the whole occasion had shown something of the shabby underside of the political system Newfoundlanders were about to enter.

As part of a general tidying up of Anglo-Canadian affairs consequent on Newfoundland's impending union with Canada, a temporary civil aviation agreement was reached between Ottawa and London in March 1949.[103] Under this the operating rights currently enjoyed by the United Kingdom at Gander would be continued until 30 June 1949, pending the revision of the existing bilateral air agreement between the two countries. Later this deadline was extended, but in the meantime a revised general bilateral agreement between the two countries was signed on 19 August.[104] This permitted service, by British-designated carriers, from London and Prestwick to Gander and through Gander to New York, Bermuda, and beyond. In January 1950 London accepted a Canadian offer for the purchase of the Admiralty properties in St. John's for $7,000,000.[105] Earlier Canada had given an assurance that if this offer were accepted, the St. John's base would be kept up so as to be quickly convertible to wartime use again, and that in the event of hostilities it would be available to the United Kingdom.[106]

A much stickier item of business concerned the status within Confederation of the rights Bowaters enjoyed in Newfoundland as contained in twelve separate pieces of legislation.[107] The advantages conferred by this body of law, especially the tax advantages were substantial to say the least, and the Bowater-Lloyd Group had a considerable stake in the constitutional position of Newfoundland, especially in the continuity of the country's laws. Accordingly, in November 1948, as negotiations of the final terms of union proceeded in Ottawa, Sir Eric Bowater acted in defence of his company's interests. In cables to Governor

Macdonald and Commissioner of Finance R.L.M. James, who was one of the Newfoundland government-appointed directors of Bowaters Newfoundland Pulp and Paper Mills, he promised "the strongest representations, in London, Ottawa and St. John's," if his company's position was not respected.[108] What this position amounted to in tax terms was the difference between an annual upper limit of $150,000 the company was required to pay under Newfoundland law and the $1,000,000 it would have paid on its previous year's operations had it been subject to Canadian law.[109] In one telegram Bowater told St. Laurent that for Canada to disavow the arrangements his company had with Newfoundland threatened "all confidence in the moral sanctions binding upon Sovereign Government."[110]

When its transatlantic lobbying failed, Bowaters stepped up the pressure on London for help. With an important British overseas business venture claiming to be at risk and an important principle at issue, there was a case for Whitehall's intervention. Ottawa, however, was firm in its conviction that Bowaters must operate in Canada on the same basis as all other paper companies. The most Canada would agree to was to give the Newfoundland subsidiary of the British enterprise "full opportunity" to present its case but only after Newfoundland had entered Confederation.[111] There could be no deal in advance of union. British diplomacy had scored a point on procedure, and the Commonwealth Relations Office had a plausible answer for Bowaters; but Canada had conceded nothing in principle and the matter would be settled as a matter of domestic rather than international concern. Though the idea of mobilizing further support for Bowaters lingered on in London, the matter was ultimately decided as Ottawa wanted, that is to say, by reference to the Supreme Court of Canada. In a June 1950 ruling, the first involving the terms of union with Newfoundland, the court decreed in effect that Bowaters had to operate in Canada so far as the jurisdiction of the Parliament of Canada was concerned comme les autres.[112] Accordingly, Canadian law took precedence over any conflicting pre-Confederation arrangement between the company and the government of Newfoundland.

The events leading to Newfoundland's entry into Confederation also opened up a new chapter in Canadian-American relations with respect to the Leased Bases Agreement of 1941. In effect, unless the terms of that agreement were modified, union would now require Canada to swallow eight years later the same strong medicine Newfoundland had taken in 1941. Not surprisingly, this was resisted in Ottawa, where much was made of the reference in a joint statement, issued by the two countries on 12 February 1947, to the "underlying principle" of Canadian-American defence understandings. This was that "*all cooperative arrangements*" between the two countries would be "*without impairment of the control of either country over all activities in the territory*" concerned. Ottawa took comfort too in a 20 November 1946 recommendation of the Permanent Joint Board on Defence, which both governments had accepted, "that defence cooperation projects in either country should be agreed to by both governments, should confer no permanent rights or status upon either country, and should be without prejudice to the sovereignty of either country."[113] Nonetheless, the Americans were obviously in a strong bargaining position. They had a treaty in hand, knew its value, and while no doubt anxious to accommodate a trusted and valued ally, had sizeable investment to protect and connected rights elsewhere to think about. In sum, from the point of view of the State Department the bases question was seen as both "delicate" and of "prime significance."[114]

In September 1947 after Brooke Claxton had spoken out about the need to modify the 1941 agreement should Confederation go forward, Julian Harrington alerted the State Department from Ottawa of the need to give the issue consideration. Harrington's impression was that the Canadians might look to reopen the agreement "for face-saving purposes" and that the United States "as a gesture might agree to a modification of some sort." There was no doubt, however, in his mind as to who would be in the stronger negotiating position; if the United States agreed to revisions, it would do so voluntarily since the agreement made no provision for adjustment in the event of a change in Newfoundland's sovereignty. In these circumstances, the United States might be "in a position to do a lot of bargaining."[115] The eventual drift of Ottawa's thinking about the Newfoundland bases was that, both because of the expense and military commitments involved, it would not be practical to seek to take them over and run them. This policy option indeed would only make sense if Canada were willing to assume responsibility for northern defence operations as well and this was manifestly impractical. Still, there was no doubt "that a continuation of the extraterritorial rights of the United States in Newfoundland would be exceedingly embarrassing." The "best solution" for Canada, therefore, lay in steering a middle course, "to recognize the leases but try to secure their modification both as to term and as to extraterritorial rights."[116]

A formal statement of the Canadian position was forthcoming in a letter which Hume Wrong, Canada's ambassador in Washington, addressed to Robert A. Lovett, the American acting secretary of state, on 19 November 1948. This noted that the agreement on bases had been made when "the war had reached its most anxious stage," when the United Kingdom and the Allied countries generally had been "in desperate need of assistance from the United States," and when Newfoundland's "self-governing powers ... were suspended." It was assumed, Wrong also wrote, that "in the interest of continental security" the United States would continue to station forces at its Newfoundland bases after Confederation. But to avoid embarrassing complications, this would have to be on a different basis than was at present provided for by an agreement that was greatly at variance with existing Canadian-American defence understandings. These understandings were based on "complete equality" and had never been thought of by Canadians as "imposed ... by the overwhelming strength of their great neighbour." What Canada took exception to in the present arrangements was "the extent of the extraterritorial jurisdiction exercised by the United States authorities over non-military activites in the leased areas." Canada would not seek to restrict "the effective use by the United States of the leased areas for military purposes," but at the same time believed that the 1941 agreement needed to be revised to bring it "more closely into accord with the spirit that governs the existing joint defence arrangements between the two countries.[117] Soon afterwards in a reassuring exchange Pearson explained to Harrington what this would mean. According to a State Department note on the conversation, Pearson spoke as follows: "It would not have to be much, merely a matter of shading down the jurisdictional clauses in the lease and possibly the display of two flags instead of one. The Canadians had no intention whatever of interfering with our maintenance and operation of the bases; they merely wished to gain some revision which would square the Government with the public."[118]

In the meantime Wrong had reported from Washington that Lovett foresaw difficulty in persuading Congress that what Canada wanted would be in the American "national interest." Trouble could also be expected from the United States Air Force (now a separate service), which in fact was looking to expand operations in Newfoundland. Equally, if Canada were to push for the shortening of the term of the leases, she would only stir up opposition to any change at all.[119]

The sense conveyed to Ottawa by the ambassador that the way forward would not necessarily be smooth was borne out by later events. In February 1949 when he met St. Laurent, President Harry S. Truman promised prompt and sympathetic consideration by his administration of whatever detailed proposals Canada put forward on the whole issue.[120] But when these were forthcoming on 19 March 1949,[121] a long delay ensued as the United States Air Force apparently remained a big stumbling block. In October when the United States embassy in Ottawa came into possession of the second draft of a forthcoming *Maclean's* article on the Newfoundland bases question, a disturbing new factor was introduced into the equation. Harrington described this article as a "stinker":

> It harps continually on the question of legal jurisdiction and makes no pretense of being objective. It highlights all of the unpleasant incidents and makes no

> attempt to mention the countless favourable actions of the Air Force or the benefits to Canada of having the United States maintain these Bases.
>
> When discussing the article some time ago with Blair Fraser he expressed the hope that his story "would not upset any applecart." It definitely will. It intentionally is slanted to emphasize the sore spots. Fraser's first draft apparently was more objective and cited both favourable and unfavourable aspects. It was returned by the editor with instructions to emphasize the factors that demonstrate the need for modifying the agreement ... It implies that no action has been taken since the Canadian request for modification was received.

The effect of the piece might be to "induce the Air Force to stand pat and say 'nuts' to the Canadians," a position for which Harrington confessed he himself "would have a certain amount of sympathy."[122]

Harrington took the matter of the forthcoming article up with Arnold Heeney, the under-secretary of state for external affairs, and was relieved when, for whatever reason, the version of the story that appeared in the magazine on 9 November was "greatly watered down" from the draft he had seen. "I feel," he told Sidney Belovsky, the present consul general in St. John's, "that the Embassy has achieved a major victory in obtaining a more objective slant."[123] Meanwhile, Wrong had been instructed from Ottawa to point out to Secretary of State Dean Acheson the "keen disappointment" felt by the Canadian side about the lack of progress, "high level assurances" notwithstanding, on the bases issue. This development led the American embassy in Ottawa to warn Washington that the question was a "dangerous threat" to Canadian-American relations generally; the adjustment of the bases agreement was "in the best interests of the US" and "prompt action"was required.[124] This episode apparently did the trick, for on 3 November after he had discussed the matter with Truman and been told the issue must not jeopardize good relations with Canada, Acheson proposed to Pearson that the whole matter be referred to the Permanent Joint Board on Defence.[125] This recourse eventually led to an agreement between the two countries, which was completed by an exchange of notes in February and March 1952. The agreement altered in Canada's favour income tax, customs and excise, and post office arrangements under the 1941 deal. Furthermore, and most importantly, the United States waived in 1952 "its rights of jurisdiction under the Leased Bases Agreement over Canadian citizens, other British subjects, and alien civilians other than those subject to U.S. military law by reason of their accompanying or serving with the U.S. Forces." At the same time the operation of the jurisdictional article (no.IV) of the 1941 Agreement was otherwise suspended on the understanding that an amended Visiting Forces (USA) Act would be extended to Newfoundland by Ottawa; that the suspension could be lifted by either side on due notice; and that in practice "jurisdictional conditions would remain substantially as now exercised" in Newfoundland.[126] By a June 1949 agreement Canada and the United States had already reached an accord on the use of United States leased bases in Newfoundland for domestic and international civil aviation.[127]

Undoubtedly, Canada won important concessions in the 1952 agreement, but that document nonetheless left the United States in a position on Canadian soil in Newfoundland that was unique. For Ottawa this was part of the price of Confederation. But it was a price perhaps more easily paid in the early 1950s than it would have been earlier on because of the cold war with the Soviet Union that now dominated world politics. In this, as in World War II, Newfoundland and Labrador were strategically important. At bottom, the 1952 bases settlement was indicative of something else; namely, that in their very different ways, Canada and Newfoundland had been caught up through the 1940s in the same seachange. The locus of leadership in the larger affairs of the world had shifted for both of them from London to Washington.

In Newfoundland itself, a drama of a very different sort was acted after the second referendum as the Responsible Government League, unlike the Economic Union Party, battled on against Confederation and at every turn opposed the procedure being followed to determine the country's constitutional future. After floundering about for a time after the vote, the league decided to present a petition to the House of Commons in favour of the restoration of Responsible Government in accordance with the Letters Patent of 1934 and against negotiations with Canada "other than by representatives of a duly elected Government of the people of Newfoundland." Launched at a meeting in St. John's on 2 September, the petition was widely circulated thereafter.[128] A broadcast the league had scheduled for 9 October over radio station VONF of the Broadcasting Corporation of Newfoundland in support of the petition campaign was cancelled by the Commission as part of a general prohibition against the resumption of political broadcasts over the facilities of the government-owned corporation.[129]

Whether this decision helped or hindered the efforts of the league is debatable, but in any event three of its representatives, Cashin, John G. Higgins, and Major F.W. Marshall, left for London on 12 November with the petition, which bore some 50,000 names.[130] At the request of A.P. Herbert, who supported the league's position, Noel-Baker received the three Newfoundlanders, led by Marshall, on 30 November. They were accompanied and introduced by Herbert and, as might be expected, were given a very frosty reception indeed. When they complained about

Governor Macdonald's alleged political intervention on behalf of Confederation, Noel-Baker lashed back, telling them that they would have to produce "detailed written evidence" in support of their charges before these could be given any attention.[131] On 23 November Herbert had presented the league's petition to the House of Commons and on 26 November had tabled a motion to do what it asked.[132] This motion, which was supported by ten other members (seven Tories, two Labourites and one Liberal) called on the government to bring in a bill "to restore self-government to Newfoundland, so that an election may be held in May 1949, after which the people of the island, through their own elected Legislature and Government, may determine their future, whether by way of Confederation with Canada or otherwise." The motion, however, failed to come up for debate, a fate that also befell a "Newfoundland Liberation Bill" circulated by Herbert in January 1949. A complementary attempt by Lord Sempill in the House of Lords also sputtered out.[133] Indirectly, the efforts of Herbert and his fellow protagonists in Parliament in support of a self-governing Newfoundland may have helped the British government's position by making plain that the Newfoundland opponents of Confederation were not without recourse and were being given a fair hearing.

Meanwhile, on the evening of 10 December, the league delegation that had gone to London had reported back at a crowded public meeting in St. John's. A resolution was adopted at this meeting, demanding that the Commission instruct the delegation in Ottawa not to sign the terms of union.[134] This resolution was then taken directly by the league executive, accompanied by a large body of supporters (estimated by Abbott at 2,000), to Government House, where they insisted that Macdonald, who was in bed, get up to receive the protest.[135] The governor obliged, but next day, when the terms of union were actually signed in Ottawa, the government, which had long feared an outbreak of disorder, especially in St. John's, finally slammed the door on its critics.[136]

A separate attempt made through the courts to block Confederation also came a cropper. A writ was issued in November on behalf of six members of the last Newfoundland parliament against the governor and the commissioners.[137] If successful, this would have prevented the government from carrying through with Confederation. The case was heard before Justice Dunfield, who found against the applicants on 13 December.[138] An appeal was heard by Justices Emerson and Winter, both former members of the Commission, who upheld Dunfield's decision.[139] Subsequently leave was granted to carry the case to the Judicial Committee of the Privy Council, but this effort was overtaken by events.[140]

On 22 February the bill to amend the British North America Act which Canada had requested in order to confirm the terms of union with

Newfoundland was given first reading by the British House of Commons.[141] The legislation was challenged by A.P. Herbert and his determined little band of supporters, but it was moved forward easily and received royal assent on 23 March.[142] With everything apparently under full control, Macdonald had departed St. John's on 6 March, leaving Emerson once more as administrator of the country.[143] Two days after the last British governor had left, the *Evening Telegram* allowed a poem, signed by "E.A.," in praise of him to slip into its letters to the editor section, not noticing that the first letter of each line, read from top to bottom, formed the words "THE BASTARD."[144] This summed up a widespread feeling about Macdonald in the capital, but, relieved as he must have been to get away, he had succeeded in his governorship all the same. During the previous summer a rumour had gone around St. John's that he would be "ducked" in Quidi Vidi Lake while attending the city's annual regatta. A police guard had been mounted for his protection on this occasion, but nothing happened.[145] Such bluster and anticlimax was typical of Newfoundland's inward-looking little capital in the days after the electoral decision to join Canada, although a steely Macdonald seems not to have been intimidated by it. On the contrary, he seems to have had the full measure of his quixotic opponents, whose efforts in retrospect might perhaps have been better directed, as were Crosbie's, at the terms of union rather than the issue of Confederation itself.

The one thousand ninety-eighth, and last, meeting of the Commission, presided over by Emerson and held at his office in the judges' chambers, took place at 12:30 PM on Thursday, 31 March 1949.[146] Then, as scheduled, Newfoundland became a province of Canada "immediately before the expiration" of the same day. Thus, the United Kingdom achieved a longstanding objective, Canada was made geographically more secure, and Newfoundland traded a precarious nationhood for the benefit, if not always the dignity, of provincial status. In sum, there were gains all round. On the morning of 1 April, Bradley was sworn into the federal cabinet as secretary of state and at noon a nationally broadcast ceremony began on Parliament Hill to celebrate the entry of the new province. This opened with the assembled gathering listening to a loudspeaker relay of the broadcast of a simultaneous ceremony held at Government House in St. John's, which began with the playing of the "Ode to Newfoundland."[147] Next, at the St. John's end, Emerson swore in Walsh as the Province's first lieutenant governor. Thereafter, Colin Gibson, who vacated the portfolio taken over by Bradley to become minister of mines and resources, presented Walsh with a general certificate of Canadian citizenship. This covered all Newfoundland British subjects "coming within the relevant provisions of the Canadian citizenship Act," who would henceforth enjoy the status of "natural-born" Canadian citizens.[148]

At the close of the Newfoundland ceremony, the carillon of the Peace Tower rang out in Ottawa, whereupon a party of dignitaries led by the governor general and including Clutterbuck arrived at a dais beneath the Peace Tower. St. Laurent and Bradley then spoke in turn, and the prime minister afterwards made the first symbolic marks on a blank escutcheon on the Arch of the Peace Tower, where the arms of the existing provinces were already displayed. The blank would henceforth bear the arms of Newfoundland, though in his report on the proceedings, Clutterbuck noted that the suggestion had been made that the blank might have been intended for the Yukon. Nonetheless, he wryly observed, it had "come in very handy for Newfoundland." When St. Laurent had finished his task, the governor general spoke and, following his remarks, the ceremony concluded with the singing of "God Save the King," "The Ode to Newfoundland" (this time the music was at hand in Ottawa), and "O Canada." One of the tunes played on the carillon of the Peace Tower, was the "Squid Jiggin' Ground," an enduring Newfoundland favourite composed in 1928 by Arthur Scammell. A few diehard anti-confederates in St. John's hung out black drapery on 1 April, but this now mattered not a whit. For better or for worse, the deed had been done.[149]

Walsh's choice as lieutenant governor was a tribute both to his talents and the need for continuity in administration, but his appointment was also intended as a sop to his Roman Catholic co-religionists, especially in the hierarchy.[150] It was, however, understood that he would not stay long in the job, and five months later he was sworn in as chief justice of the Supreme Court in succession to Emerson, who died on 19 May. By prior arrangement, Walsh's successor at Government House would be Leonard Outerbridge, who had been knighted in 1946. Shortly after his own swearing in as lieutenant governor, Walsh had sworn in the first government of the Province of Newfoundland. For all the denigration of him that had gone on, not least in the correspondence of McEvoy with his old mentor MacKay,[151] Smallwood was chosen as premier.[152] Nine other members of the Executive Council were sworn in with him. They were Pottle and Quinton, the two commissioners who had spoken out in favour of Confederation; Gordon Winter, who had been a member of the delegation that had negotiated the final terms of union and whose presence gave the new administration a useful link to St. John's business; W.J. Keough and Charles Ballam, who had supported the cause of Confederation in the National Convention and campaigned for it thereafter; and Leslie R. Curtis, Samuel J. Hefferton, Philip Forsey, and Michael J. Sinnott. Denominationally – as always in Newfoundland, this was significant – the first cabinet included four adherents of the Church of England (Winter,

Quinton, Hefferton and Ballam), four non-conformists (Smallwood, Curtis, Pottle and Forsey) and two Roman Catholics (Keough and Sinnott).[153] Winter was initially made minister of finance and Curtis minister of justice, a position he would hold continuously until 1966.[154] Another key position, that of minister of natural resources, went to Keough.

On 30 April the founding convention of the Newfoundland Liberal Party, held in St. John's, chose Smallwood and Bradley to be the leaders of its provincial and federal wings respectively. Philosophically, they were both of the left, but there was undoubtedly an element of opportunism, appropriate in the circumstances, about their choice of a Canadian party label. No matter what party had been in power in Ottawa when Confederation was negotiated, they would, understandably, have probably ended up in it. Smallwood described the Newfoundland Liberal Party as belonging to the "toiling masses" and on 27 May led it to a decisive victory in the first provincial election, winning twenty-two of twenty-eight seats.[155] In the course of the campaign he was stopped by the United States commander at Argentia, supported by the consulate general in St. John's, from speaking on the base.[156] The opposition members returned to the first post-Confederation House of Assembly consisted of five Progressive Conservatives and Cashin, who was returned as an independent. All the opposition members were known anti-Confederates, five of them were Roman Catholics, and all were returned from areas that had supported Responsible Government in the 1948 referenda. When a federal general election was held on 27 June, the St. Laurent Liberals carried five of Newfoundland's seven seats and the Progressive Conservatives two, St. John's East and West. Following the bitter electoral contests of 1948, politics in the new province had been cast in a mould that would not soon or easily be broken.

In January 1950, while in Ottawa for a Dominion-Provincial conference, Smallwood also addressed himself to the matter of Newfoundland's interest free loans to the United Kingdom. Overall, these had amounted to $12,300,000 and had, along with other such borrowings from dependent governments, been repayable "three months after the conclusion of a Treaty of Peace."[157] In 1946 the Treasury had announced itself willing to repay any lender who wished to be reimbursed. Prior to Confederation, Newfoundland had called in $3,232,000 preparatory to the repayment of sterling loans redeemable in 1950 and 1952. This left a total loan balance of $9,068,000 at the time of union. The position regarding this amount was further complicated by the fact that term 24(3) of the terms of union gave Newfoundland the right, within a year of the date of Confederation, "to deposit with the Government of Canada all or any part of its financial surplus held in dollars" and to receive thereon interest at the annual rate of 2 5/8 per cent.[158] This term amounted to an incentive to Newfoundland to call in its loan to the United Kingdom, a circumstance that posed difficulty for a British government itself now chronically in need of Canadian dollar credit. The British looked to Ottawa to help them out but to their surprise found that, union notwithstanding, the matter remained one between London and St. John's.[159] Having made this point, the Canadian government did its best to be accommodating, and in September 1949 Smallwood indicated to Finance Department officials in Ottawa that he would be willing to forego the recall of the loan for a three- to five-year period if the British would themselves begin making annual interest payments at 2 5/8 per cent.[160] The Treasury view was that this rate was "excessive" as far as the United Kingdom was concerned. At the same time, it was feared that the repayment of the loan, however awkward, by a government that was itself living in part on Canadian credit might cause "surprise and displeasure" in Ottawa, the more so since the United Kingdom was reducing its Canadian imports.[161]

This was roughly the situation when Smallwood landed in Ottawa in January 1950, in what Clutterbuck described as an "excitable frame of mind." The source of the premier's concern was a series of economic reversals in the province which had left him "worried over immediate prospects." One of the setbacks that had occurred involved the export sale of saltfish; between them, Smallwood pronounced, "by holding back ... on sterling fish sales," London and Ottawa had together cost Newfoundland dearly in the Italian market. According to Clutterbuck, Deputy Minister of Finance Clifford Clark succeeded in calming Smallwood, but the most the Newfoundland leader would now consider in relation to the United Kingdom loan was a two-year extension with interest from 1 April 1950.[162]

After Smallwood left Ottawa, Clutterbuck and Clark met with Herman Quinton, who had became Newfoundland's minister of finance in August 1949.[163] He suggested that for the Newfoundland government to go further than Smallwood had contemplated, some "fresh factor" would have to be introduced into the equation. Fearing that this meant "1950 fish sales," and believing that even a marginally better deal would be difficult to make and carry a high cost, Clutterbuck advised caution: "I am not impressed by Smallwood's reliability and if Newfoundland is now getting into a difficult position economically there seems much to be said for making [a] clean break by repayment. Even if we can secure [a] *modus vivendi* for [a] short period, Newfoundland Government will no doubt regard this as [a] concession to us and there is risk that they will expect something in return later, e.g. in connection with 1950 fish sales."[164] If through force of circumstances, the British had been well served in Newfoundland by Smallwood, they had also kept their distance from him. Clutterbuck's advice was heeded in London and the balance owing St. John's was repaid on 30 March.[165] Having got their way constitutionally with Newfoundland, the British, to their great relief, had now also squared their accounts with her.

SYNOPSIS: 1945–49 (POLITICAL AND CONSTITUTIONAL DEVELOPMENTS)

Once the United Kingdom and Canada reached a working understanding in 1945 about the future of Newfoundland, the issue before them was what they could do to forward their common cause. They believed that the one thing they must not do was to intervene directly in the constitutional debate in Newfoundland. Any hint of Anglo-Canadian co-operation to promote Confederation would be disastrous; the initiative for union had to come from Newfoundlanders themselves. It would, however, be possible for both parties to influence the development of Newfoundland opinion. Canada could do this best by welcoming any expression of interest in Confederation arising out of the National Convention. If a signal came across the Gulf of St. Lawrence, Canada had to be prepared to do "the handsome thing" by Newfoundlanders. The United Kingdom could "assist" the latter "to turn their thoughts to Canada" by making clear to them that they could not rely on London for further financial help.[166] The British, of course, had another important lever in their ability to define the purposes for which the National Convention would meet and the electoral procedure by which Newfoundlanders would subsequently make their constitutional choice.

The British had good cards and they played them skilfully. Newfoundland's would-be political leaders were turned loose in the National Convention, but that body was also kept on a short leash. Thus in calling the convention together, the Attlee government left itself great freedom for manoeuvre, while emphasizing to Newfoundlanders its inability to offer them much future help. The convention was an advisory body only, and its job was to recommend to the United Kingdom constitutional choices that might be put before the Newfoundland people in a referendum. Its views would clearly carry weight and be difficult to ignore; but it was not given the say on what would be on the referendum. This prerogative the British kept carefully to themselves; when the National Convention failed to recommend what they wanted to hear, they used their power to place the option they favoured on the ballot.

All elections hinge upon particular historical circumstances, and there can be no doubt that the decisions made by the United Kingdom and Canada from 1945 onwards were important in establishing the framework of politics in which Newfoundlanders voted in 1948. But to influence is not to engineer. Once the form of the ballot and the procedure for voting were decided upon, the choice belonged to the Newfoundlanders. Rumours persist of electoral irregularities in Newfoundland in 1948, but not a shred of evidence has been produced to substantiate them. The United Kingdom and Canada had certainly worked together to put the choice of Confederation before Newfoundlanders, but it was Newfoundlanders, not they, who made the choice. The British were uncertain of the outcome in Newfoundland and had well-developed contingency plans to reintroduce Responsible Government should the vote go that way. If Smallwood's role in the National Convention and in getting Confederation on the referendum ballot was perhaps less important than has heretofore been thought, there is no denying his achievement on the hustings. He did not win a rigged bout but a winner-take-all, bare-knuckle fight-to-the-finish. Ultimately, Smallwood triumphed, and the United Kingdom and Canada succeeded but only just.

In 1985 one Newfoundland commentator on the period concluded from his researches that "a plot to manœuvre Newfoundland into Confederation by fair means or foul, was not only true" but "much worse" than he had previously thought.[167] Is it surprising to find it confirmed in the historical record that the United Kingdom and Canada favoured a particular outcome in Newfoundland after the war? The answer is no. Given the substantial interests both countries had in Newfoundland, the real surprise would have been to find that they did not have clearly defined goals. Nor is it surprising to find that the United Kingdom and Canada had reached an understanding about the future of Newfoundland. Historians may not have known until recently the details of Anglo-Canadian negotiations in the 1940s, but they have never doubted that the United Kingdom and Canada were players rather than spectators. Newfoundland's union with Canada was a complex diplomatic, constitutional, and political event. It could not have been anything else and cannot otherwise be understood. The United Kingdom and Canada undoubtedly pursued their self-interest vis-à-vis Newfoundlanders but that too is neither surprising nor shocking. And it does not follow that because they did so they had necessarily to disregard the best interest of Newfoundland. Again, there were limits to what the British and Canadians could do to achieve their objectives. It is one thing to have the last word on what appears on a referendum ballot, as the British did in Newfoundland in 1948; it can be quite another thing to win the referendum, as René Levesque discovered in Quebec in 1980. Ultimately, in a fair and democratic electoral contest, Newfoundlanders had to decide their constitutional future themselves. If they had not wanted Confederation, they had other substantial choices before them. This was well understood at the time and should not now be obscured.

Perhaps the one real surprise in the British records is not that the United Kingdom wanted Newfoundland to join Canada but that the Dominions Office for so long clung to the notion that Newfoundland could resume self-government with British financial support. Critics of Confederation and the means by which it was brought about in Newfoundland would do well to ponder the plan the Dominions Office had worked out for Newfoundland in 1944. If this had been implemented, Newfoundland might well have regained self-government, but her freedom of action as an independent country would have been severely limited by the financial controls the British intended as the price for their continued support. As premiers of a Canadian province, Joey Smallwood and his Progressive Conservative successors have had no such constraints. Arguably, Newfoundland found greater independence within the loose structure of Canadian federalism than it could ever have achieved on its own. When Clutterbuck made a nostalgic visit to Newfoundland in 1950, he was amazed at how much Smallwood's government was attempting and how far it intended to go.[168] If the administration he had helped plan in 1944 had come into existence, things would have been very different. In effect, the relationship St. John's achieved with Ottawa through Confederation was the very one that London was above all determined to avoid for itself. Newfoundland had found a backer, but her guarantor could not necessarily control her financial course. There was no Dominions Office or Treasury in Ottawa to rein in Joey Smallwood or his Progressive Conservative successors, Frank Moores and Brian Peckford.

All this, of course, means nothing if one believes as an article of faith that Newfoundland was the victim of an Anglo-Canadian plot. The fact that some British files relating to Newfoundland affairs in the 1930s and 1940s remain either closed or, in one case at least, are "wanting" (in British archival parlance), will encourage such thinking. What has been held back, however, may well have more to do with personality than policy, though here there can be no certainty. On the other hand, the voluminous and comprehensive body of information that has been released lends cold comfort to those Newfoundlanders who now seem to hold a grudge against their own past and dream of a glory that might have been but never was – before or after the upheaval of 1934. Conspiracy theories of history have a life of their own; no amount of contrary evidence can ever conclusively refute them. After all, it is always possible to believe that the "real" evidence has been destroyed or hidden or the official record cunningly falsified, and that the "true story" will only be told when the secret archives are opened or the long-lost diary found. Such notions are long-lived especially in regard to historic events where the margin between success and failure, victory and defeat, was razor-thin. Manifestly, this was the case in Newfoundland in 1948.

CHAPTER TWELVE

Conclusion

In the collective memory of Newfoundlanders, the Commission era, to the extent that it is remembered at all, tends to get harsh or at most mixed reviews. Like much else in history, the Commission of Government is perhaps best known by what its enemies and heirs, often one and the same, have had to say about it. Those who first governed Newfoundland after Confederation had a vested interest in spreading the notion that 1949 was the year one, and that all good things began with their accession to power. Doubtless the Commission was all the more easily condemned because of the embarrassment felt by many Newfoundlanders that their country, alone of the Dominions of the British Empire, had failed in its self-government. Understandably, despite the idealistic conservatism of those who had launched the Commission, the experiment was not always later on a source of pride. It is not pleasant to be reminded that, as the British Conservative P.V. Emrys-Evans wrote in June 1942, Newfoundland represented the "only failure in the history of the British Empire of our own people to govern themselves."[1] Unsettling, too, in a democracy is the thought that unrepresentive government could be better government.

In retrospect then, the Commission came to be associated in the minds of Newfoundlanders with a few simple ideas: the Commission had made Newfoundlanders on relief live on a pittance in the 1930s; the Commission had made Newfoundlanders work for Americans and Canadians during the war on slave wages; it was not the Commission that had rescued Newfoundlands from the Depression but rather the establishment of American bases in the country; and – here is a familiar Newfoundland complaint – the Commission had given the country away.[2] And so on. In 1947 a Grand Bank merchant wrote to a correspondent in St. John's: "I do not want any more commission of government – you will probably know many of my reasons. A government getting two and one half times the revenue of the peak years of the past ought certainly to have been able to do a lot for the country or save a lot more than it has done ... I do not like absentee government nor do I like the secrecy we have had which resulted in Nflders getting up in the morning to find the interests of the country have been given away overnight. Apparently 'Empire' comes first and 'Nfld' afterwards – I think it should be the other way round."[3]

As time passed, this was the sort of recollection heard of the Commission of Government. The best generally said of it was that it had left behind a big surplus that Joey Smallwood promptly wasted. Beyond that, the line of defence, such as it was, usually fell back to the distribution of cod liver oil to children, their introduction of the Junior Red Cross program into schools, the good work of the cottage hospitals, and a few other oddments. The Commission did not leave many defenders behind it; but as always, the inheritors of power had good reason to provide their own version of history, a version in which, typically, past and present were contrasted with great advantage to the latter.

Yet one does not have to look very far into the documentary record to see that the stereotypes about the Commission belie a complex historical reality. To begin with, it is clear that the period of Commission rule cannot be treated as a single entity. Manifestly, this was a government that passed through several distinct phases. The first of these, which ran to 1936, was a period of improvement and cautious optimism. The Depression generally had risen from its nadir, and there were small signs, or so it seemed, of economic revival in Newfoundland. Thanks to grants-in-aid, more money was available for social spending. Miserable as the Commission's dole was, it was nonetheless an improvement on what Newfoundland's able-bodied poor had been receiving in the earlier period of reduction in goverment spending. It was at this time, too, that the Commission took up the policy of land settlement, an abiding interest in one form or another thereafter. A second chapter in the career of the Commission began in 1936 with the start of comprehensive long-term planning. This followed more serious setbacks in the economy, especially in the fishing industry, and a consequent deeper appreciation than before, both in London and in St. John's, of just how intractable Newfoundland's problems really were and of just how long it would take to get the country back on its feet. Fortified by the 1936 plan of reconstruction, the Commission hoped for a future of slow but steady progress; instead it encountered a menacing crisis when the country was struck by the Roosevelt Recession.

In short order, to meet urgent political, economic, and social necessities, carefully crafted and settled plans had to be radically revised. The ultimate expression of this shift was J.H. Gorvin's 1940 Special Areas bill, which set the stage for the introduction of entirely new economic and social institutions into rural Newfoundland. Though the Commission was divided on it, the bill marked the government's high point in experimentation, and its withdrawal with the outbreak of the war in 1939 meant that another corner had been turned. The immediate response of the Commission to the war was to cut back on planned ordinary and reconstruction expenditure in order to meet the cost of the country's participation. In fact, Newfoundland enjoyed an economic boom beginning in the early 1940s because of the military spending there by the United States and Canada, and the ensuing general prosperity was sustained for the rest of the war years and into the post-war period. With this sudden change of economic fortune and with the consequent favourable balance sheets, the Commission got a new lease on life. Accordingly, while dealing with the exigencies of war and the consequences of having thousands of American and Canadian military personnel in the country, the Commission was able both to carry out some important social and economic reforms and build up a healthy surplus to meet the needs of an uncertain future. Nothing as daring as what Gorvin had contemplated was attempted, and while some of the changes may only have breathed new life into old ways, as in education for example, they were nonetheless substantial and important. As it administered the new prosperity and got on with the business of the war, the Commission was producing fresh plans for the future, a process which tied in with London's preparations for constitutional change. The high point of the Commission's planning effort was the submission to London of the 1944 reconstruction plan. This was in the tradition of the step-by-step, conciliatory, and restorative approach of the 1936 plan rather than the radical approach of the Gorvin period. From the British perspective, the 1944 plan was part and parcel of a larger scheme whereby self-government might be restored to Newfoundland with, of course, important financial safeguards. When this particular constitutional option was abandoned, much of the 1944 plan went with it.

Nevertheless, after London and Ottawa had agreed to act in concert to encourage Confederation, the Commission, in its final post-war phase, did more than fence its way out of the room and slam the door behind it. In these years it carried out, with varying degrees of success, some of the plans drawn up during the war, including the scheme for civil re-establishment and parts of a master plan for the development of the frozen fish industry, where, it believed, much of the future of Newfoundland lay. At the same time, the Commission adroitly handled the constitutional issue and fulfilled London's hopes by bequeathing to the country a fat surplus, proof of sound and far-seeing administration.

The supreme irony of the 1934–49 period was that the St. John's business and professional class (including Archbishop Roche) which had been instrumental in bringing the Commission system in, also produced the most sustained and systematic opposition to it. Businessmen in particular, especially those in the Newfoundland Board of Trade, believed that a government above politics would naturally listen to them because they too were above politics and dealt in objective realities. When, however, they came up against commissioners like Lodge, Hope Simpson, and, later on, Gorvin, who believed that much of Newfoundland's trouble lay with its conservative elite, they were soon disillusioned. After a number of preliminary skirmishes about such matters as denominational education and after the Wes Kean affair, elite opposition to the Commission erupted over the 1938 Bowaters agreement. In this case the Commission adopted a populist stance common in Newfoundland politics and appealed to the unemployed and the under-employed over the heads of the elite which, as usual, had proclaimed its interest as the national interest. At the time of the Leased Bases Agreement in 1941, the Commission feared another outburst along economic nationalist lines, but this did not materialize. Subsequently, however, the return of prosperity to the country whetted the appetite of the gentry to regain control of Newfoundland assets. The two most serious episodes in the wartime opposition to the rule of the Commission occurred in 1943, over taxes, and in 1944, over the Goose Bay agreement. The Commission in both cases easily overcame its critics. After 1945, when a new constitution was in the making, the opponents of the Commission again had their plans thwarted: first, by the British over the recommendations of the National Convention, and then by the general populace in the referenda. Not surprisingly, with its days more than likely numbered, the Commission was criticized on all sides in the National Convention, but here too the elite, best represented perhaps by R.B. Job and Ches Crosbie, failed. Confederation, which both the United Kingdom and Canada favoured, became the cause of Joey Smallwood, an outsider. After two referenda, which together constituted what is described in American politics as a realigning election, that is to say, one that sets the pattern for many subsequent elections, Smallwood went on to hold power for a generation. He understood well the appeal of nationalist rhetoric, as his performance during the Bowaters matter and his subsequent editorship of *The Express* had shown. Yet later as premier, he was frequently accused of giving the province away. On the other hand, nationalism did not become the dominant ideology of the Newfoundland government until the Progressive Conservatives came to power in 1972. It is this party, therefore, that became the true heir of the disaffected elite of the 1940s, and it is striking that John Crosbie, Ches Crosbie's son, was instrumental in its success.

What explains the political failure of the Newfoundland elite from 1934 to 1949? Clearly, in countering their critics, the Commission and the British had many advantages. One was that when the push came, Newfoundland businessmen and professionals were invariably divided and compromised. In 1938 the government had prominent business supporters for the Bowaters deal, most notably Leonard Outerbridge, a key figure in the local establishment. When the Leased Bases Agreement went through, the war made criticism appear disloyal. Patriotism likewise helped keep the tax revolt of 1943 and the Goose Bay outburst of 1944 within limits. Given a choice between burning the Union Jack and running it up the staff, Newfoundland's elite, Catholic and Protestant alike, had long chosen the latter course in spite of a succession of disappointments with the mother country. Sentiment favoured the British position in Newfoundland, and they well knew how to play on it. In the last act of the Confederation drama, important members of the elite again served the British well by speaking out in favour of Confederation although too late to derail Smallwood's express and run their own.

Another factor working against the elite critics of the Commission was the attitude of organized labour. As long as the labour movement did not challenge the state and worked within the law, the Commission welcomed its growth and development as part of a general policy of nurturing collective activity among ordinary Newfoundlanders. Thanks to this benign attitude and the big wartime and post-war demand for labour in the country, unions made considerable headway in Newfoundland after 1934. Labour, however, was neither united nor very vocal on the constitutional issue. Indeed, there were elements of the labour movement that saw considerable merit in Commission rule, at least in the short run; not surprisingly, Gorvin was especially popular in labour circles. In one respect, however, labour tended to react strongly and instinctively: it believed that Water Street and the Newfoundland Board of Trade should not decide the post-Commission future, and that anything they favoured in this regard was probably a bad idea. In short, business in Newfoundland had but to say yea for labour, or important elements of it, to say nay. The opportunities for Whitehall in this sort of division were not missed.

The British were likewise able to exploit regional tensions within Newfoundland. Attlee's 1942 observation that the west was "more awake"[4] had its counterpart in government policy; the substantial support given the Commission option in 1948 in Corner Brook, Grand Falls, and some relatively satisfied rural areas, in spite of what amounted to official discouragement, was probably indicative of hinterland satisfaction that the government had looked beyond the Avalon peninsula and not allowed itself to be dominated by St. John's.

Yet another advantage the British had in dealing politically with Newfoundlanders was the fact that the events of 1929–34 had not only produced a fundamental constitutionnal change, but had also smashed the party apparatus of the country and largely discredited politicians as a type. This sentiment lingered on after Newfoundland became a province of Canada.

Obviously the British enjoyed great latitude in the loose arrangement for the restoration of self-government that a trusting Alderdice administration had agreed to in 1933, but the transformation of the party man into a pariah was important to them also. Not until the British were themselves ready to bring back party politics did the country produce the charismatic leader it had so visibly lacked. The British were helped in all this, of course, by the special circumstances of the war which gave them a moral advantage, enhanced by good times, over potential troublemakers in Newfoundland while in no way inhibiting their own freedom to plan and act. By the time the war was over Newfoundlanders were in a procedural box on the constitutional question that was not of their own making but from which they could only escape by a fundamental challenge to the legitimacy of the existing government. The political basis for such a challenge did not exist in the country and it was not attempted, even by Peter Cashin, who in a sense delivered himself over to Whitehall the moment he entered the National Convention and accepted the terms of its existence. At every turn after 1934, the Newfoundland critics of the Commission and the Dominions Office were intellectually outclassed. Generally speaking, the Newfoundland critics of the Commission reacted to particular events on an ad hoc basis and lacked vision, common purpose, and systematic organization. By contrast the British thought far ahead and in detail, always had contingency plans ready, and were superbly informed. Though he would have been like a fish out of water in the Whitehall of Clutterbuck and Machtig, Smallwood possessed similar strengths and was able, after 1945, to use them to like advantage. "Frankly," he wrote in his 1973 memoirs *I Chose Canada*, "I do not know of one single step taken in the National Convention by the opponents of Confederation that was sound, or shrewd, or such as to win the support of our Newfoundland people."[5] Though exaggerated, like much else in this idiosyncratic work, even perhaps including the title, Smallwood's assessment of his opponents was not far off the mark. Much the same judgment might be made of the business and professional opposition to the Commission of Government. When all was said and done, the struggle of minds and wills between Whitehall and Water Street was no contest.

Added to everything else was the unswerving loyalty to London of the Newfoundland commissioners. No member of the government ever resigned in protest, and the Commission did not divide in practice along United Kingdom-Newfoundland lines, even though the British on occasion feared it might do so. Moreover, at every critical moment there was a Newfoundland commissioner ready and able to defend the government in public. At the time of the Bowaters deal Puddester filled this role. In 1941 Emerson took the lead in defending the Leased Bases Agreement, and in 1944 Harry Winter argued the government's case over the Goose Bay deal. After 1945 Albert Walsh, who was hated in anti-Confederate St. John's, took on this role.

Why were the Newfoundland commissioners so reliable? No definitive answer can be given to a question that involves personal motives but a number of factors were obviously at play. No doubt, there was an element of idealism, a sincere belief both in the system and in the actions of the government. Furthermore, within the administration there was ample scope for debate and dissent; protest from within could and did get results. The cardinal sin in the Commission, as in the higher British public service on which it was modelled, was not disagreement, but making such disagreement public. Implicit in this was the understanding that if one did not break ranks, honourable service would be followed by honourable appointment or honourable retirement. This is not to imply that the Newfoundland commissioners were bought off either with power or the promise that they would always be looked after, but that they were incorporated willingly and easily into a mandarin tradition with a well-established and comfortable career path. Two of the Newfoundland commissioners, the unfortunate Frederick Alderdice and the old war-horse John Puddester, died in office. Two others, William Howley and J.A. Winter, moved on to the position of registrar of the Supreme Court. Three commissioners, Harry Winter, Edward Emerson, and Albert Walsh, became judges, with the latter two becoming chief justice. Emerson went straight to this position in 1944, and Walsh succeeded him in 1949 after a brief stint as lieutenant governor and as part of an understanding about his future worked out before Confederation. Herman Quinton and H.L. Pottle were exceptional in the history of the Commission in that they chose subsequent political careers, but they had just joined the administration when, for all intents and purposes, it was coming to an end.

If the Newfoundland members of the Commission of Government could almost as a matter of course look forward to continued service to the state, the price of breaking ranks was also clear enough. For his efforts, Thomas Lodge, himself a disagreeable man, came up against that special nastiness official London reserved for one of its own who had become a bounder. At the Dominions Office the lexicon of supercilious scorn and contempt was scarcely adequate to convey what was felt about him, especially after he went back to Newfoundland as a private citizen, spoke out there, and then published *Dictatorship in Newfoundland*. In the end Lodge received the bureaucratic equivalent of being dishonourably discharged. Gorvin was also treated roughly at the end of his Newfoundland days, but he ultimately swallowed his pride and settled dutifully into another job. Open rebellion by a Newfoundlander would probably have been a sure road to public and political oblivion. In all likelihood any Newfoundland commissioner who left could easily have been replaced and, though all this is speculative, it is doubtful whether on any issue of the period a rebellious commissioner could have sparked an uprising in the country. Still, this was theoretically possible and was part of the complex equation governing the intricate relationships of dependency and accommodation that existed among the Newfoundland commissioners, their United Kingdom colleagues, the different governors, and the Dominions Office. The British, of course, had long experience of working through the local elite in many parts of the world, and in this respect the experience of the Commission of Government was but a variation on a familiar imperial theme. Silencing opposition through judicious recruitment and reward was for Whitehall a fine art.

In March 1935, Joey Smallwood told a protest meeting of sealers in St. John's, as reported by a police detective, that every government of Newfoundland in the previous century had "been merely a false face for the real Government," that is to say "the Government on Water Street." "The Commission Government," he continued, "is different from all other governments we have had in this country in one way and that is that they have more power and more authority than ever any government ever had before. They have strong power and strong authority. They have the British Government behind them; they have the British Treasury behind them and they have absolutely no opposition. Everything they want they got. Never had a government such a marvelous opportunity." But would the new administration live up to its promise? In Smallwood's view the evidence was already there that it might not:

> They have got the power and the authority to run this country as it should be run but they lack the courage and the determination to look after the producers and to give the working man a square deal ... I saw Sir John Hope Simpson three or four times and when I met him I said to myself, if ever a man was sent from God to help the poor people of the country, it was Sir John Hope Simpson. That was my opinion of Sir John Hope Simpson and I kept on believing that, but I say tonight and I say it in all charity, I don't want to hurt his feelings, I say in all charity that in my opinion Sir John Hope Simpson would like to come to the rescue and assistance of the poor people. But the trouble with him and Mr. Lodge, they are the only two that count, is that they lack the courage and determination and backbone. Every time they look down through the windows of their offices they get frightened. Sir John Hope Simpson said to me in my last interview: "Mr. Smallwood, the merchants think we have the whip hand over them, I think it is the other way about, they have the whip hand over us." When the biggest man in the land has that feeling we cannot hope to expect anything from them. The only way we can force anything out of them is by fighting the merchants of Newfoundland, and you will then help the Commission as nothing else can do.[6]

His analysis was perceptive, for it was certainly true that Lodge and Hope Simpson had a poor opinion of upper crust Newfoundland.

In other respects, however, Smallwood's case was overstated. The British had been forced to undertake the Commission experiment under the threat of a potentially very damaging bankruptcy and because their efforts to work in concert with Canada to keep Newfoundland financially afloat had failed. Their preferred solution for Newfoundland in the crisis of the 1930s, as it had been in the 1860s, was Confederation, but this was not possible. Of necessity they had to put a good face on their intervention and they certainly improved matters, but they were not in Newfoundland to promote and pay for a social revolution. Their overall approach was ameliorative and gradual; when they came up against strong opposition they were willing to compromise and, if need be, retreat. Lodge and Hope Simpson were bent on a bare-knuckle fight with important local vested interests, but London did not have the stomach for this potentially very costly and divisive battle. After the Commission's difficult and confrontational opening phase, the Dominions Office replaced most of the new administration's personnel. The United Kingdom's reliance was henceforth placed on civil servants either nearing the end of sedate and steady careers or, more especially, on others for whom Newfoundland would be but a way station, who could advance themselves by not getting into unnecessary trouble and by keeping expenses under control. Emerson's appointment as a Newfoundland commissioner in 1937 was especially revealing. Highly regarded in the increasingly restive Newfoundland elite, he had shown through his performance in the Kean affair that he had both the intelligence and stamina to become troublesome. His elevation to the government demonstrated the willingness and ability of the British to head off establishment opposition by bringing key members of it on board. The benefit of this approach was shown in 1941 when the formerly dangerous commissioner of justice and defence resourcefully defended the government at one of its most trying moments. For all their privately stated detestation of it, the British also showed themselves adept at playing the denominational game in Newfoundland. From beginning to end the Newfoundland commissioners were chosen with an eye to denominational balance. The severe economic crisis of the late 1930s once again brought the British close to a battle with vested interests in Newfoundland; only a real war precluded this fight. Developments during World War II, moreover, especially the arrival in the country of American forces, gave Whitehall fresh ammunition to use in Ottawa to promote Confederation, the master plan for which was a British rather than a Canadian product. When it came to Confederation, the United Kingdom led, Canada followed, and Newfoundland consented. Throughout the period of this study, Canada was more influenced than influencing.

Confederation relieved the British of a burden they had not wanted in the first place, and which in post-war circumstances they believed they could no longer sustain. The British had plumbed the social and economic depths in Newfoundland in the second half of the 1930s, knew well how big and expensive a reconstruction job was needed there, and did not want to be on the scene when the next economic and financial storm struck. But more than self-interest was involved in their preference for Confederation. Manifestly, this constitutional option would bring great benefits to Newfoundlanders themselves. The obvious case in point was the extension to them of the increasingly comprehensive and sophisticated Canadian welfare state. Newfoundland families with young children could look forward to receiving Canada's family allowances; the elderly would receive Canada's old age pensions; many workers (but not including fishermen) would qualify for inclusion in Canada's unemployment insurance scheme; and Newfoundland veterans (but not including foresters), a big group of voters in the late 1940s, would qualify for Canadian veterans benefits. The Commission of Government had created a rudimentary welfare state in Newfoundland, but this could not be compared to the benefits Newfoundlanders would enjoy as Canadians. Additionally Newfoundlanders would, in law at least, be able to move freely in the Dominion in search of work. Collectively, Confederation would ensure that in a financial emergency Newfoundlanders would ipso facto have somewhere to turn. The Dominion of Newfoundland had relied on "that thin red cord of sentiment and of blood." By contrast, the Province of Newfoundland would be able to look to a senior government. This promised Newfoundland a financial latitude she might never have achieved as a separate country. In a sense, therefore, the greatest boon of Confederation was provincial status itself, a status that would put Newfoundland into a relationship with Canada that the United Kingdom would never have accepted for herself and Newfoundland. For fairly obvious reasons the British did not involve themselves in the substantive negotiation of terms of union between Newfoundland and Canada. Such a role would have been politically risky in Newfoundland but it would also have been offensive to Canada. Furthermore British expertise and bargaining power at the negotiating table might well have weakened Canadian resolve in the matter, a resolve in any case not always strong. Both the delegation that went to Ottawa from the National Convention and the one that negotiated the final terms of union were authorized by the Commission, but the approval given the final terms by Newfoundland's British appointed administration was merely pro forma. Nor was the British government challenged in Parliament on the substance of the terms of union. Rather, debate there centred on the legitimacy of the general procedure being followed for constitutional change in Newfoundland.

For Canada the costs were high, although taking Newfoundland into Confederation would bring several important benefits. For one thing this would increase her wealth of natural and human resources. Newfoundland brought with her sizeable inland forests, mineral and waterpower resources, and rich fishing grounds offshore. Canada also stood to gain from Confederation by acquiring control of the busy airport at Gander, a move that would enhance her standing and bargaining power in international civil aviation. Most important of all, perhaps, Confederation would secure Canada's eastern frontier, simplify her defence administration, and head off the looming threat of a Newfoundland ever more closely tied to the United States. The transformation of Newfoundland into "a garrison country" during the Second World War and the entry of the United States into the region had fundamentally altered Anglo-Canadian-Newfoundland relations.

At war's end, the secure niche the Americans had carved out for themselves in Newfoundland made problematic the future of Canada-Newfoundland relations. Despite the hard bargaining their country had done in 1940–41, American forces had won high praise in Newfoundland both from the Commission of Government and from the people at large. Canada was caught up during the war in a competition with the United States for advantage in Newfoundland; here as elsewhere the Allies were engaged in what the British historian David Reynolds has called, with reference to the building of the Anglo-American alliance, 1937–41, "competitive co-operation."[7] In Newfoundland this process worked to the advantage of the British; nothing perhaps whets the Canadian appetite as much as American involvement, and after 1940 Newfoundland was no exception. From Ottawa's perspective "defensive expansionism,"[8] a phenomenon notable in other phases of Canadian history, gradually became the order of the day towards Newfoundland as well. The terms on which United States forces had arrived in Newfoundland did not in themselves dictate the outcome to be Confederation, but as matters developed they were a powerful force pointing to it.

The United States' own post-war interest in Newfoundland was relatively straightforward. The Americans wanted to keep whatever they had there that was of continuing military importance to them. If the British could no longer act as guarantor of their rights, it was better that this be done by Ottawa than by a petty national government in St. John's, even one which claimed to favour economic union with the United States. Essentially, Washington could sit back and enjoy the show and that is what it did. After Confederation, however, without really giving up anything vital, the United States moved to satisfy Canadian opinion by putting a better face on the 1941 Leased Bases Agreement in what was now a Canadian province.

Confederation, then, was one of those exceptional international deals that conferred benefits on all, even in the end on its Newfoundland opponents. But it was not an unmixed blessing; perhaps no change of such magnitude ever is or can be. At a time of rapid social and economic expansion in the world generally, Confederation required Newfoundlanders to adjust for the second time in fifteen years to a new form of government. How well that adjustment was made remains to be studied, though there can be no doubt about the complexity of the federal system Newfoundlanders had joined. Confederation also ended the integrated reconstruction plans of the Commission of Government; nonetheless for all their professed contempt of this regime, Newfoundland's post-Confederation leaders were not averse to looking back to it for ideas. Undeniably, Confederation marked a new beginning for Newfoundland, but it was not quite the sharp break with the past that its protagonists, for perfectly understandable political reasons, made it out to be. Nor was everything necessarily for the better after 1949. Arguably, in one crucial area of development, namely the expansion of the frozen fish industry, events after 1949 represented a retreat from the restructuring proposed in the 1940s. Thus the Canadian and Newfoundland governments between them continued to ladle out money to private enterprise to expand the industry but without advancing the cause of worker shareholding that the Commission had in view. When the great recession of the early 1980s hit Newfoundland the privately owned but heavily state-subsidized frozen fish business reached a crisis comparable in its proportions and severity to the one that had overtaken the saltfish industry in the 1930s. The result was a drastic reorganization of the industry and the emergence of a super company, Fishery Products International, owned jointly, until privatized, by the federal and provincial governments and the Bank of Nova Scotia. In relation to these events and the economic and social history of the province of Newfoundland more generally, the plans and actions of the Commission provide a standard against which government activities after 1949 can be usefully measured. By the same token, the thinking of the mandarins in London who dealt with Newfoundland affairs between 1934 and 1949 begs comparison with that of their counterparts in Ottawa who have dealt with the province since 1949.

If Confederation buried a particular set of social and economic plans for Newfoundland, it may also, more importantly, have altogether limited Newfoundland's ability to plan. One of the most successful administrative units of the Commission of Government was the Department of Natural Resources, which attempted to co-ordinate policy across the basic fishery, forestry, mining, and agricultural sectors of the economy. With the coming of Confederation, the jurisdiction that this department had enjoyed was divided between Ottawa and St. John's with planning thereby made administratively more complex. Moreover, though Newfoundland was placed on the same footing as the existing provinces with respect to the ownership of inland resources, her principal resource, at least in employment, was to be found in her offshore fish stocks. Within Confederation, the fishing industry has been managed mainly by Ottawa, and in respect of her major resource Newfoundland therefore has a diminished stature among the provinces. Provincial control of all fishing policy would not, of course, necessarily mean better management and direction, but in this case it would perforce mean a higher priority in consideration. In Ottawa questions relating to fisheries are invariably secondary; in St. John's their prime importance is in the long run hard to avoid. The 1948 terms of union did not deal directly with resources under the seabed of the continental shelf, but in 1984, after the discovery of oil offshore, the Supreme Court of Canada ruled that this resource too was the nation's, rather than the province's, to explore, exploit, and govern.[9] This ruling made good legal and historical sense, but it confirmed anew that in some respects geography made a coastal province a less than perfect fit into a continental dominion.

Compounding all this was something else about the events of 1945–49. On one side the union of Newfoundland and Canada was the decision of a people made at the polls; on the other it was the choice of a government, prompted, some would say pushed, by an ambitious bureaucracy. When all was said and done, it was the Canadian government that chose and the Canadian people who followed. Even granting that an issue that was central in Newfoundland could not be expected to have the same prominence in Canada, the different perspectives of the two parties to the union remain important. The Confederates in Newfoundland held out to their countrymen the prospect of full partnership in a welcoming, caring, committed, and dynamic nation. In Ottawa, on the other hand, the idea seems to have been ingrained that what Canada was getting was the equivalent of another Maritime Province. Deputy Minister of Finance Clifford Clark's devastating remark to the American diplomat Julian Harrington in June 1947 that Newfoundland would in all likelihood be "a little Ireland" full of "disgruntled people" went to the heart of this point of view.[10] That Clark should have chosen the same point of comparison that his former minister E.N. Rhodes had employed against Amulree in 1933, suggests that for all that had changed in Canada's attitude towards Newfoundland as a result of the war, some things had remained the same. After 1934, the United Kingdom had searched for a social and economic model applicable to Newfoundland. For Canada, however, the Maritime Provinces provided a readily available one. By the late 1940s, these provinces were firmly dependent on the federal government, and in spite of all the brave and high-minded talk that accompanied Newfoundland's entry into the union, Ottawa could scarcely have imagined that Newfoundland would be different. In the differing outlooks and expectations of Canada and Newfoundland at the start lay the seeds of much future acrimony. In *Colony to Nation*, Arthur R.M. Lower wrote that "some peoples are born nations, others achieve nationhood, and others have nationhood thrust upon them. Canadians seem to be among these last."[11] Newfoundland's entry into Confederation may have been yet another example of "nationhood thrust upon" Canadians.

But these are the observations of hindsight made when difficult economic times have returned to Newfoundland and after a period of intense conflict between St. John's and Ottawa reminiscent of the 1930s and 1940s quarrels with Water Street economic nationalists on one side and the Commission of Government and the Dominions Office on the other. In the short run, the great success of Confederation was undeniable. The 1950s constituted a decade of optimism and expansion in Newfoundland as it did in Canada as a whole. Ten years after the fierce electoral battles of 1948, it would have been difficult to find much sentiment in the province in favour of turning the constitutional clock back to 1934. Just how rapidly things were settling down was already evident when Clutterbuck undertook a tour of the Maritime Provinces and Newfoundland - the Atlantic provinces - in 1950. His report to London on the findings of his journey was characteristically comprehensive and detailed, capturing at once the big picture and the fine point. In St. John's he met with Joe Smallwood. The premier, he wrote, "obviously enjoys his position as the head of a 'one-man Government' and commented to me on the benefits of 'democratic dictatorship' which he said was only possible in a small place like Newfoundland." Smallwood's self-proclaimed economic policy was "'make or break', in other words to indulge in a series of gambles in the hope that some at least will come off." The wisdom of this course of action remained to be seen but Smallwood's high-risk financial course clearly had the potential for "lively embarrassment to the Federal Government."[12] These were memorable observations, made at another turning point in Newfoundland's history. But memorable too is the sense of detachment conveyed by Clutterbuck's account. For one who had been immersed in Newfoundland affairs for so long, the high commissioner wrote with a distance that was truly remarkable. He might have been Jeeves on the eastern marches of an old but now abandoned domain. Still his stance was not inappropriate. Thanks in no small measure to his own efforts, the United Kingdom had arranged her departure from Newfoundland with a hard logic and clinical precision she would not always manage in other parts of her far-flung but now crumbling empire. Because she had taken on so much responsibility in Newfoundland, the United Kingdom had to walk away from it altogether. Paradoxically, France, her old rival in the region, though coming close to losing the islands of St. Pierre and Miquelon during the war, managed to recoup her position and today negotiates with Canada to carve up the resources off Newfoundland. Clutterbuck and his associates, sly old foxes that they were, would not be amused.

Appendices

APPENDIX ONE

Government of Newfoundland, 1934-49

Governors	*Date of Appointment*
David Murray Anderson	20 October 1932
Humphrey Thomas Walwyn	3 December 1935
Gordon Macdonald	5 March 1946

Commissioners	*Date of Appointment*
Frederick Charles Alderdice	31 January 1934
Sir John Hope Simpson	31 January 1934
William Richard Howley	31 January 1934
Thomas Lodge	31 January 1934
John Charles Puddester	31 January 1934
Everard Noel Rye Trentham	31 January 1934
James Alexander Winter (in the place of Alderdice, deceased)	20 April 1936
Robert Benson Ewbank (in succession to Sir John Hope Simpson)	28 July 1936
Sir Wilfrid Wentworth Woods (in succession to Thomas Lodge)	15 January 1937
John Hubert Penson (in succession to Everard Noel Rye Trentham)	10 May 1937
Lewis Edward Emerson (in succession to William Richard Howley)	15 September 1937
John Henry Gorvin (in succession to Robert Benson Ewbank)	31 May 1939

Ira Wild (in succession to John Hubert Penson)	14 February 1941
Harry Anderson Winter (in succession to James Alexander Winter)	20 May 1941
Peter Douglas Hay Dunn (in succession to John Henry Gorvin)	30 June 1941
Sir George Ernest London (in succession to Sir Wilfrid Wentworth Woods)	5 September 1944
Albert Joseph Walsh (in succession to Sir Lewis Edward Emerson)	5 September 1944
James Scott Neill (in succession to Sir George Ernest London)	28 September 1945
William Henry Flinn (in succession to Peter Douglas Hay Dunn)	28 September 1945
Richard Lewis Malcolm James (in succession to Ira Wild)	12 September 1946
Herman William Quinton (in succession to Harry Anderson Winter)	1 January 1947
Herbert Lench Pottle (in the place of Puddester, deceased)	19 September 1947

Source: *The London Gazette*

APPENDIX TWO

Revenue and Expenditure of Newfoundland Government, 1934-35 to 1948-49 in $ million

Year Ending	*Revenue**	*Expenditure +*	*Deficit (–) or Surplus (+)*
30 June 1935	9.6	11.6	– 2.0
30 June 1936	9.8	13.0	– 3.2
30 June 1937	11.0	13.0	– 2.0
30 June 1938	12.3	14.1	– 1.8
30 June 1939	11.2	15.3	– 4.1
30 June 1940	12.6	17.4	– 4.8
30 June 1941	16.2	15.8	+ 0.4
30 June 1942	23.3	16.1	+ 7.2
31 March 1943	19.5	15.8	+ 3.7
31 March 1944	28.6	25.2	+ 3.4
31 March 1945	33.3	26.3	+ 7.0
31 March 1946	33.4	30.3	+ 3.1
31 March 1947	37.2	37.1	+ .1
31 March 1948	40.7	41.0	– .3
31 March 1949	41.1	40.0	+ 1.1

Source: Report on the Financial & Economic Position of Newfoundland, Cmd. 6849, p. 5; *Reports of the Comptroller and Auditor General, Newfoundland*, 1946-49

* Excluding Grants and Loans

\+ Including debt servicing but excluding loans and gifts to the United Kingdom

Abbreviations

AIR	Air Ministry, United Kingdom (Air Ministry documents cited are located in the Public Record Office, Kew)
AP	William Warrender Mackenzie, first Baron Amulree Papers (Bodleian Library, Oxford)
AVIA	Air Ministry, Civil Aviation Files, United Kingdom (Documents cited are located in the Public Record Office, Kew)
BEW	British Embassy, Washington, D.C.
CAB	Cabinet Papers, United Kingdom (Public Record Office, Kew)
CAM	Charles A. Magrath Papers (National Archives of Canada)
CG	Commission of Government
Cmd.	Parliamentary Papers, United Kingdom
CNS(A)	Centre for Newfoundland Studies (Archives), Queen Elizabeth II Library, Memorial University, St. John's, Newfoundland
DN	*Daily News*, St. John's, Newfoundland
DO	Dominions Office, United Kingdom (Dominions Office documents cited are located in the Public Record Office, Kew)
ET	*Evening Telegram*, St. John's, Newfoundland
FO	Foreign Office, United Kingdom (Foreign Office documents cited are located in the Public Record Office, Kew)
GC	Government of Canada
GN	Government of Newfoundland (Newfoundland government documents cited are located in the Provincial Archives of Newfoundland and Labrador, St. John's, Newfoundland)
Govr.	Governor of Newfoundland
HCC	High Commissioner of the United Kingdom in Canada
HCUK	High Commissioner of Canada in the United Kingdom
HCN	High Commissioner of Canada in Newfoundland

HS	J. B. Hope Simpson manuscript, "Newfoundland. The Commission of Government"
JRM	J. Ramsay MacDonald Papers, United Kingdom (Public Record Office, Kew)
JWGP	John W. Greenslade Papers (Manuscript Division, Library of Congress, Washington, D.C.)
NA	National Archives, Washington, D.C.
NAC	National Archives of Canada, Ottawa
NG	*Newfoundland Gazette*
NRC	Washington National Records Center, Suitland, Maryland
PANL	Provincial Archives of Newfoundland and Labrador, St. John's, Newfoundland
PREM	Papers of the Prime Minister's Office, United Kingdom (Public Record Office, Kew)
PRO	Public Record Office, Kew
RBB	R. B. Bennett Papers (Microfilm) (Harriet Irving Library, University of New Brunswick, Fredericton)
SSCR	Secretary of State for Commonwealth Relations, United Kingdom
SSD	Secretary of State for Dominion Affairs, United Kingdom
SSEA	Secretary of State for External Affairs, Canada
SSW	Secretary of State, Washington, D.C.
T	Treasury, United Kingdom (Treasury documents cited are located in the Public Record Office, Kew)
USSEA	Under-Secretary of State for External Affairs, Canada

Notes

CHAPTER ONE

1 For details of topography, climate, etc., see my "Newfoundland."

2 Paul West, "A Lullaby too Rough."

3 From 1713 to 1763 the French Shore extended from Cape Bonavista around the north coast of the island to Pointe Riche, an arrangement confirmed by the Treaty of Paris of 1763. By the Treaty of Versailles of 1783 the French Shore was redefined so as to run from Cape St. John around the north coast to Cape Ray. The advantages given United States fishermen in 1783 were scaled down by an Anglo-American convention of 20 October 1818. By this they could fish within coastal waters on the south, west, and north coasts of Newfoundland from the Ramea to the Quirpon islands, on the coast of Labrador (provided the exclusive rights of the Hudson Bay Company were respected), and at the Magdalen Islands in the Gulf of St. Lawrence. They were also authorized to land and dry fish in unsettled places on the south coast of Newfoundland from the Ramea Islands to Cape Ray and on the coast of Labrador. For a full discussion of the history of French and American rights, see my "The French and American Shore Questions."

4 Head, *Eighteenth Century Newfoundland*, p. 82; Mannion, *The Peopling of Newfoundland*, p. 20.

5 *Journal of the House of Assembly of Newfoundland*, 1858, Appendix, p. 124.

6 Ibid, p. 125; *Census of Newfoundland and Labrador, 1874*, p. 190.

7 Robert G. Reid, the founder of the Reid Newfoundland Company, was born in Scotland in 1847. A stonemason by trade, he emigrated to Canada where he enjoyed great success as a contractor for the Canadian Pacific Railway. His controversial and complex Newfoundland career began in 1890, when he and G. H. Middleton of Toronto contracted to complete the trans-island railway to Halls Bay, its original western

terminus. On his own Reid eventually undertook to continue the line to Port aux Basques and to operate it and a previously constructed Placentia branch line for ten years. A contract negotiated in 1898 between Reid and the Tory government of James S. Winter was given a frosty reception by the imperial authorities and touched off an uproar in Newfoundland itself. In 1900 the opposition Liberals came to power, led by Robert Bond who had accused Winter of a sellout. In 1901 Bond successfully renegotiated the 1898 contract, but the revised deal was sufficiently sweeping to leave the Reids in charge of the country's railway until 1951. For further details, see Hiller, "The Railway and Local Politics in Newfoundland."

8 For Newfoundland's relations with the United States around the turn of the century, see Neary and Noel, "Newfoundland's Quest for Reciprocity."

9 See Rowe, Haxby, and Graham, *The Currency and Medals of Newfoundland*, pp. 30-7; Mitchell, "Canada's Negotiations with Newfoundland."

10 For details, see Thompson, *The French Shore Problem in Newfoundland*, pp. 183-7, and Appendix 6, p. 199.

11 See Noel, *Politics in Newfoundland*, pp. 77-115; McDonald, "W.F. Coaker and the Balance of Power Strategy."

12 To 30 June 1932, Newfoundland's borrowing for "War Purposes" together with interest payments on this amount, other wartime expenditures, and war pensions amounted to $37,064,289. CAM, vol. 12, Newfoundland Royal Commission file, financial memoranda enclosed in Trentham to Secretary, Royal Commission, 7 March 1933.

13 For the impact of the Great War on Newfoundland, see Noel, *Politics in Newfoundland*, pp. 116-33.

14 Alexander, *Atlantic Canada and Confederation*, p. 74.

15 Ibid., p. 17. Newfoundland's total population, however, apparently continued to grow, while Nova Scotia's population actually dropped from 523,837 to 512,846 over the decade 1921-31. See Dominion Bureau of Statistics, *Seventh Census of Canada, 1931*, vol. 1, p. 348.

16 See my "The Supreme Court of Canada and 'the Bowater's law,' 1950," pp. 202-3.

17 RBB, reel 139, p. 168867, Vanier to Bennett, 27 June 1935.

18 Supreme Court of Canada, "IN THE MATTER OF Section 55," "Factum of the Attorney General of Canada," pp. 53-4. The arguments and document collections prepared by the governments of Canada and Newfoundland in connection with this reference form a rich source of information for the study of Newfoundland's modern history. Section 2 of the Statue of Westminster empowered a dominion to repeal or amend imperial statutes. Section 3 empowered a dominion to legislate extraterritorially. Section 4 provided that no Act of the United Kingdom

Parliament would apply to a dominion unless "it is expressly declared in that Act that the dominion has requested and consented to the enactment thereof." Sections 5 and 6 dealt with dominion powers "in relation to merchant shipping" and "Courts of Admiralty" respectively. According to Section 10, Sections 2-6 would be inapplicable to Australia, New Zealand, or Newfoundland unless adopted by the dominion in question. See *The Public General Acts*, 1931-32, pp. 13-17. Australia did not assume the powers provided for in Sections 2-6 until 1942 nor did New Zealand until 1947.

19 See William C. Gilmore, "Newfoundland and the League of Nations."

20 Noel, *Politics in Newfoundland*, pp. 181-2; *Acts of the General Assembly of Newfoundland passed in the eighth and ninth years of the reign of His Majesty King George V*, pp. 80-96; *Acts of the General Assembly of Newfoundland passed in the twelfth and thirteenth years of the reign of His Majesty King George V*, pp. 92-116; *Acts of the General Assembly of Newfoundland passed in the fifteenth year of the reign of His Majesty King George V*, pp. 159-62.

21 *Acts of the General Assembly of Newfoundland passed in the twentieth year of the reign of His Majesty King George V*, pp. 128-74.

22 *Acts of the General Assembly of Newfoundland passed in the twenty-second year of the reign of His Majesty King George V*, pp. 454-5.

23 See *Newfoundland Illustrated Tribune*, p. 8.

24 NA, RG 59, 843.50/2-2845, Hopper to SSW, 28 February 1945. Socially, the haunts of this commercial elite and a connected group of lawyers and accountants were the Bally Haly Golf and Country Club in the eastern suburbs of the City; the City Club, a men's retreat in the centre of the business district; and a fishing and country club at Murray's Pond on Portugal Cove Road.

25 In addition to the cutting of pulpwood, trees were harvested for pitprops, saw-logs, firewood, and fencing material, and for use in the fishing industry. See my "The Bradley Report on Logging Operations."

26 Best, *War and Society in Revolutionary Europe,"* p. 10.

27 McCann, "The Educational Policy of the Commission of Government," p. 206.

28 *Acts of the General Assembly of Newfoundland passed in the eighteenth year of the reign of His Majesty King George V*, pp. 134-5; Andrews, *Integration and other Developments in Newfoundland Education*, p. 123.

29 Alexander, *Atlantic Canada and Confederation*, p. 74.

30 DO 117/58, Allardyce to Amery, 24 February 1927.

CHAPTER TWO

1 Cmd. 4480, pp. 70-1

2 The account that follows of Squires's career and of Newfoundland

politics, 1918-29, is based generally on Noel, *Politics in Newfoundland*, pp. 134-85.

3 Calculated from Cmd. 4480, pp. 57, 63.
4 For the history of the Canadian dollar in this period, see Mackintosh, *The Economic Background*, pp. 173-8.
5 RBB, reel 139, pp. 168946-7, encl. in Dodds to Bennett, 20 June 1931; DO 414/58, "Newfoundland Affairs: Correspondence and Papers 1931-1933," pp. 7-8, desp. to GN, 21 September 1931.
6 RBB, reel 139, pp. 168307-10, Barnes, Cashin, Coaker, and Mosdell to Bennett, 7 October 1931.
7 Ibid., p. 168893, Dodds to Bennett, 2 January 1932.
8 *ET*, 1 February 1932, p. 4; 5 February 1932, p. 5.
9 Ibid., 6 April 1932, p. 4.
10 *Acts of the General Assembly of Newfoundland 1932*, pp. 168-80.
11 *ET*, 25 May 1932, p. 9.
12 Smallwood, *Encyclopedia, 1*, pp. 717-19.
13 DO 414/58, p. 33, tel. to GN, 17 November 1932; pp. 36-7, tel. to GN, 25 November 1932.
14 Ibid., pp. 35-6, tel. to GN, 24 November 1932. In July 1933, interest payments amounted to approximately $5,200,000 per annum. See ibid., p. 78.
15 Ibid., pp. 41-2, tel. to GN, 20 December 1932.
16 Noel, *Politics in Newfoundland*, p. 310.
17 DO 414/58, p. 43, tel. from GN, 22 December 1932.
18 For his career, see *Who's Who 1934*, p. 55.
19 Roberts and Tunnell, *The Canadian Who's Who*, pp. 1026-7.
20 For details of his career, see ibid., pp. 701-2; den Otter, *Civilizing the West*.
21 Cmd. 4480, p. ii.
22 AP, Dep. c. 391, p. 102, Thomas to Amulree, 20 November 1933.
23 Cmd. 4480, p. ii.
24 *Who Was Who 1971-1980*, p. 156.
25 For details of these meetings, see DO 414/58, pp. 50-6.
26 *The Public General Acts*, 1931-32, p. 14.
27 DO 414/58, pp. 54-5.
28 CAM, vol. 8, file 39, Magrath to Bennett, 18 March 1933.
29 DO 414/58, p. 57, Amulree to Harding, 3 April 1933; Cmd. 4480, p. 69.
30 CAM, vol. 8, file 39, Magrath to Bennett, 13 April 1933. Magrath, who came to chafe under this approach, later regretted the way the commission had gone about its work. For this, see his memo "Re The Newfoundland Royal Commission," August 1942.
31 DO 414/58, p. 57, Amulree to Harding, 3 April 1933.
32 Ibid., pp. 58-9, Amulree to Thomas, 3 April 1933.

33 Ibid., p. 59; *DN*, 15 April 1933, p. 4.
34 DO 414/58, pp. 60-1, tel. to HCC, 1 May 1933.
35 Ibid., pp. 61-2, tel. to HCC, 3 May 1933.
36 CAM, vol. 8, file 39, Magrath to Bennett, 13 April 1933.
37 Ibid., "Memorandum re Newfoundland," 13 April 1933, p. 4.
38 Ibid., Magrath to Bennett, 13 April 1933.
39 Ibid., "Memorandum re Newfoundland," 13 April 1933, p. 11.
40 Ibid., Magrath to Bennett, 13 April 1933.
41 Ibid., "Memorandum re Newfoundland," 13 April 1933, p. 11.
42 AP, Dep. c. 390, pp. 140-2, Amulree to Harding, 21 May 1933.
43 DO 414/58, p. 62, tel. from HCC, 13 May 1933.
44 AP, Dep. c. 390, p. 140, Amulree to Harding, 21 May 1933.
45 DO 414/58, p. 63, tel. from HCC, 13 May 1933.
46 Ibid., pp. 62-3, tel. to HCC, 11 May 1933; pp. 66-7, tel. to HCC, 22 May 1933.
47 Ibid., pp. 63-4, tel. from HCC, 13 May 1933, and tels. to HCC, 16 May 1933.
48 Ibid., pp. 65-6, tel. from HCC, 21 May 1933.
49 Ibid., pp. 69-73, memo encl. in Amulree to Thomas, 22 May 1933.
50 Ibid., p. 68, tel. to HCC, 30 May 1933.
51 Ibid., pp. 68-9, tel. from GN, 31 May 1933.
52 Ibid., p. 67, tel. from HCC, 22 May 1933.
53 Ibid., pp. 73-4, tel. from GN, 2 June 1933.
54 Ibid., pp. 74-5, tel. from GN, 3 June 1933.
55 RBB, reel 140, pp. 169429-31, Magrath to Bennett, 26 May 1933.
56 Ibid., pp. 169542-3, Magrath to Bennett, 2 June 1933.
57 Ibid., p. 169484, draft reply. See also pp. 169483, 169487, Bennett to Perley, 16, 19 June 1933.
58 DO 414/58, pp. 75-6, tel. to GN, 22 June 1933.
59 Ibid., p. 78; Cmd. 4480, pp. 2-3.
60 AP, Dep. c. 390-1, p. 166, Alderdice to Amulree, 13 August 1933; pp. 168-9, Stavert to Amulree, 14 August 1933; Dep. c. 390, p. 105, Sutphen to Amulree, 13 April 1933. For the completion, in November 1933, of the Labrador sub-plot and E.W. Sutphen's role in it, see DO 414/58, pp. 106-7, tel. to GN, 21 November 1933.
61 DO 414/58, pp. 78-81.
62 Ibid., pp. 81-3, "Note of Meeting held at Treasury on 18 July 1933."
63 Ibid., p. 83.
64 Ibid., p. 83, Harding to Hopkins, 25 July 1933.
65 Ibid., p. 85, DO Note, 5 August 1933.
66 Ibid., p. 86-8, Chamberlain to Amulree, 31 August 1933.
67 Ibid.
68 Ibid., pp. 88-90, "Note of meeting held in the Dominions Office,

1st September, 1933."
69 Ibid., pp. 90-3, "Note of meeting held in Sir E. Harding's room on 2nd September, 1933."
70 Ibid.
71 Ibid., pp. 88-90, "Note of meeting held in the Dominions Office, 1st September, 1933."
72 Ibid.
73 Ibid., pp. 93-5, "Note of meeting held in Sir Edward Harding's room on 7th September, 1933."
74 AP, Dep. c. 391, p. 37, Amulree to Alderdice, 16 September 1933.
75 DO 414/58, pp. 95-6, tel. from GN, 20 September, 1933.
76 JRM, 679/124-26, Amulree to MacDonald, 28 September 1933.
77 AP, Dep. c. 391, p. 37, Amulree to Alderdice, 16 September 1933.
78 DO 414/58, pp. 95-6, tel. from GN, 20 September 1933.
79 JRM, 679/124-26, Amulree to MacDonald, 28 September, 1933.
80 Ibid., 6/3-79, MacDonald to Alderdice, 9 October 1933; 6/3-80-81, Alderdice to MacDonald, 31 October 1933.
81 DO 414/58, pp.96-7, tel. to Secretary, Royal Commission, 29 September 1933.
82 Ibid., pp. 97-8, tel. from GN, 13 October 1933.
83 AP, Dep. c. 391, pp. 62-3, Magrath to Amulree, 3 October 1933. Afterwards, looking back over his correspondence with Magrath, Amulree decided that it would be wise to get his signature on a copy of the report "so that no question can arise hereafter." See ibid., p. 105, Amulree to Clutterbuck, 22 November 1933.
84 Ibid., Dep. c. 391, pp. 98-9, Harding to Amulree, 15 November 1933.
85 Ibid., Alderdice to Amulree, 26 February 1934.
86 AP, Dep. c. 391, pp. 98-9, Harding to Amulree, 15 November 1933.
87 DO 35/499/N1024/1, Clutterbuck minute, 12 March 1934.
88 Ibid., marginal note by Clutterbuck in Alderdice to Amulree, 26 February 1934.
89 Ibid., Clutterbuck minute, 12 March 1934.
90 Ibid., Alderdice to Amulree, 26 February 1934.
91 DO 414/58, p. 98, Amulree to Thomas, 10 November 1933.
92 Cmd. 4480, p. 224.
93 DO 414/58, p. 100, tel. to HCC, 18 November 1933.
94 Cmd. 4479.
95 Ibid., pp. 4-8
96 DO 414/58, pp. 107-9, tel. to GN, 22 November 1933.
97 See, for example, *ET*, 22 November 1933, p. 6; *DN*, 22 November 1933, p. 4.
98 AP, Dep. c. 391, p. 111, Stavert to Amulree, 25 November 1933.
99 Ibid., pp. 194-6, Alderdice to Amulree, 28 April 1934.

100 Ibid., pp. 134-5, Alderdice to Amulree, 2 December 1933.
101 *Journal of the House of Assembly*, 1933, pp. 7-14.
102 *Journal of the Legislative Council*, 1933, pp. 33-5.
103 *Journal of the House of Assembly*, 1933, pp. 15-17.
104 For Bradley's views, see my *The Political Economy of Newfoundland*, pp. 48-51.
105 *Journal of the House of Assembly*, 1933, pp. 15-19.
106 DO 414/58, p. 110, tel. to GN, 22 November 1933.
107 Ibid., p. 115, Coaker to SSD, 25 November 1933; Noel, *Politics in Newfoundland*, p. 203.
108 DO 414/58, p. 118, tel. from Sir Richard Squires, 30 November 1933.
109 Ibid., p. 132, desp. from GN, 1 December 1933.
110 *Parliamentary Debates* (Commons), 5th ser., 283 (1933-34), cols. 1845-1914; Cmd. 4481, 1933.
111 *Parliamentary Debates* (Commons), 5th ser., 283 (1933-34), cols. 2065-8.
112 Ibid., 284 (1933-34), cols. 215-310.
113 For Attlee's speech, see ibid., cols. 223-31.
114 Ibid., cols. 307-10.
115 Ibid., cols. 565-811.
116 For the debate on third reading, see ibid., cols. 931-88. For Bevan's speech, see ibid., cols. 964-96.
117 *Parliamentary Debates* (Lords), 5th ser., 90 (1933-34), col. 594.
118 Ibid., cols. 655-75, 681-4.
119 *Parliamentary Debates* (Commons), 5th ser., 284 (1933-34), cols. 1447-9, 1508.
120 For the act, see, *The Public General Acts*, 1933-34, pp. 5-14.
121 DO 414/59, "Newfoundland Affairs: Correspondence, 1934-1936," pp. 48-9, tel. to GN, 27 January 1934.
122 In his *The Ottawa Men*.
123 McKenty, *Mitch Hepburn*, p. 120. For King's attitude, see Struthers, *No Fault of Their Own*, pp. 140-1.
124 Cmd. 4480, p. 195.
125 CAM, vol. 18, "Newfoundland Royal Commission - Evidence, Nos. 96-107, 1933," Evidence of The Merchants' Committee, No. 101, 9 June 1933, p. 10.
126 DO 35/490/N1004A/2, note by Harding, 10 May 1934.
127 AP, Dep. c. 391, p. 135, Alderdice to Amulree, 2 December 1933.
128 Ibid., p. 225, Alderdice to Amulree, 7 September 1935.
129 RBB, reel 139, p. 168685, tel. Squires to Bennett, received 2 January 1932.

CHAPTER THREE

1 For a chronology of appointments to the Commission, see Appendix One.

2 JRM, 679/907, MacDonald to Walker, 25 December 1933.

3 DO 35/489/N1004/7, Harding to Anderson, 10 January 1934.

4 For his career, see *Who Was Who 1951-1960*, p. 671; *Times* (London), 12 February 1958, p. 10, col. d. The sketches of the commissioners that follow also draw on *ET*, 22 January 1934, p. 4.

5 For his career, see *Who Was Who 1961-1970*, pp. 1035-6; *Times* (London), 12 April 1961, p. 15, col. a, and 22 April 1961, p. 13, col. c.

6 DO 35/489/N1004/7, Anderson to Thomas, 26 December 1933 and Anderson to Harding, 26 December 1933.

7 Ibid., Anderson to Harding, 26 December 1933.

8 Ibid., Harding to Anderson, 10 January 1934.

9 DO 414/59, tel. to NG, 27 January 1934.

10 For the Letters Patent, see DO 35/492/N1005/4. The first commissioners "were appointed for three years from February, 1934 ... in each case subject (a) to the possibility of extension after the three year period (b) to the right of the Secretary of State to give three months' notice of termination at the end of the first or second years." See DO 35/490/N1004/66, Harding to Walwyn, 11 February 1936.

11 For these, see DO 35/492/N1005/4.

12 GN 38/S1-1, pp. 1-3, 17 February 1934.

13 For the act creating the office of secretary to the Commission of Government, see *Acts of the Commission of Government*, 1934, p. 10.

14 GN 38/S1-1, pp. 4-7, 21 February 1934.

15 Ibid., p. 8, 23 February 1934.

16 Supreme Court of Canada, "IN THE MATTER OF Section 55," "Case on Appeal," 10, p. 1338.

17 *Acts of the General Assembly of Newfoundland*, 1921, p. 8; GN 38/S1-1, p. 41, 1 May 1934.

18 HS, p. 12

19 Ibid., pp. 7-13.

20 AP, Dep. c. 391, p. 189, Carew to Amulree, 14 March 1934.

21 For the background, see DO 35/499/N1024/1, Clutterbuck memo, 12 March 1935.

22 Ibid., Alderdice to Amulree, 26 February 1934.

23 Ibid., Clutterbuck minute, 12 March 1934.

24 Ibid., Clutterbuck note on conversation with Amulree, 12 March 1934.

25 Ibid., SSD to Govr., 12 March 1934.

26 DO 35/499/N1024/2, Govr. to SSD, 12 March 1934.

27 DO 35/499/N1024/3, Govr. to SSD, 13 March 1934.

28 DO 35/499/N1024/4, Govr. to SSD, 14 March 1934.

29 Ibid., SSD to Govr., 21 March 1934.

30 DO 35/499/N1024/5, Govr. to SSD, 22 March 1934.

31 DO 35/499/N1024/4, Machtig to Craig, 23 March 1934.

32 DO 35/499/N1024/5, SSD to Govr., 28 March 1934.

33 HS, p. 4

34 AP, Dep. c. 391, p. 211, Walsh to Amulree, 3 September 1934.

35 Cmd. 5117, p. 5.

36 The first of these, issued in January 1935, dealt with the economic situation in Newfoundland (Cmd. 4788). The second, which appeared the following May (Cmd. 4910), reported on unemployment, while the other four papers (Cmds. 5117, 5425, 5741 and 6010) incorporated, seriatim, annual reports for the years 1935-38 inclusive. Thereafter the practice of publishing annual reports was discontinued, and no other parliamentary paper relating to Newfoundland was issued until 1946.

37 See DO 35/506/N1083/5, note for SSD. The British commissioners would cheerfully have dismantled the St. John's Council, but the Council proved adept at defending itself. Its enemies were in any case loath to risk inflaming public opinion by moving against the last vestige of self-government in the country.

38 For the history of the force, see Alice M. Tuck, "The Newfoundland Ranger Force." See also Horwood, *A History of the Newfoundland Ranger Force* (St. John's, 1986).

39 Tuck, "The Newfoundland Ranger Force," pp. 47, 56.

40 Cmd. 5425, p. 26.

41 This account is based on ibid., pp. 47-9 and Cmd. 5117, pp. 12-14. Quinton was one of the new generation of magistrates. All the district magistrates and their assistants were Newfoundlanders.

42 This account is based on Cmd. 4788, pp. 9-10; Cmd. 5117, pp. 23-30; and Cmd. 5425, pp. 6-12.

43 Cmd. 5425, p. 10.

44 See Struthers, *No Fault of Their Own*, pp. 6-7.

45 Cmd. 5425, p. 12.

46 The monthly "Scale for Relief Allowances" was as follows:

Persons in family	*Total amount monthly order*	*Amount of old order*
1.	$2.00	$2.00
2.	4.00	3.75
3.	5.85	5.35
4.	7.70	6.53
5.	9.50	7.88
6.	11.20	9.25
7.	13.00	10.60
8.	14.75	11.94
9.	16.00	13.29
10.	17.00	14.64

In a minute dated 7 December 1934 on the despatch from the Commission of Government that included this information, Clutterbuck described the relief system in effect in rural Newfoundland as follows: "Relieving Officers stationed throughout the country ... report to and are supervised by the Dept of Public Health; these officers enquire into the cir[cumstance]s. of each applicant for relief and if satisfied that the application is genuine they then give the applicant a dole order on the nearest store in accordance with the approval scale; relief is thus given in accordance with local necessities and no cash is handled locally, the storekeepers sending their dole orders up to St. John's for payment - a system which enables the Dept of Public Health to maintain a thorough check & prevents collusion between the storekeeper and the Relieving Officer." For both the scale of allowances and Clutterbuck's minute, see DO 35/494/N1028/4.

47 DO 35/494/N1028/4, Clutterbuck minute.
48 Ibid., letter from CG, 17 November 1934.
49 Cmd. 4910 (1935), p. 5.
50 DO 35/499/N1028/4, CG memo.
51 Cmd. 4910, pp. 6-7.
52 DO 35/499/N1012/161, Walwyn to Harding, 1 September 1936.
53 DO 35/723/N2/40, note on discussion of Newfoundland affairs at DO, 4 April 1939.
54 HS, p. 19.
55 DO 35/504/N1051/7, Lodge memo on general policy.
56 Ibid.
57 AP, Dep. c. 391, p. 220, Alderdice to Amulree, 24 September 1934.
58 For a detailed account of educational reform in this period, see McCann, "The Educational Policy of the Commission of Government," pp. 201-6.
59 HS, p. 27.
60 *Acts of the Commission of Government*, 1935, pp. 40-2.
61 McCann, "The Educational Policy of the Commission of Government," p. 206.
62 HS, p. 27.
63 DO 35/493/N1007/16, Machtig memo, 21 May 1935.
64 Ibid., Clutterbuck memo.
65 Ibid., Roche to Howley, 29 April 1935.
66 Ibid., Clutterbuck memo.
67 Ibid., Machtig memo, 21 May 1935.
68 DO 35/490/N1004/45, Anderson to Harding, 22 June 1935.
69 AP, Dep. c. 391, p. 255, Alderdice to Amulree, 7 September 1935.
70 Cmd. 4788, p. 5. For a summary of public finance under the Commission of Government, see Appendix Two.

71 Cmd. 5117, p. 7; Cmd. 5425, p. 57.
72 Cmd. 4788, p. 7.
73 Cmd. 5117, pp. 14-15.
74 Cmd. 5425, pp. 16-17.
75 HS, p. 12.
76 Cmd. 4788, p. 1.
77 DO 35/497/NF1017/38, pt. 1, Hope Simpson to Harding, 11 November 1935.
78 *Acts of the General Assembly of Newfoundland 1933* (St. John's, 1933), pp. 293-302; *Acts of the Commission of Government*, 1935, pp. 137-45.
79 DO 35/497/NF1017/38, pt. 1, Hope Simpson to Harding, 11 November 1935.
80 HS, p. 14.
81 Ibid., p. 22.
82 Ibid., p. 35.
83 Ibid., p. 11.
84 The economic historian David Alexander concluded that the Newfoundland Fisheries Board was "relative to its size and resources, the best fisheries service in North America." See his *The Decay of Trade*, p. 29.
85 *Acts of the Commission of Government*, 1936, pp. 31-6. The Department of Natural Resources had been established by an act dated 29 November 1934. See *Acts of the Commission of Government*, 1934, pp. 181-8. On 5 May "the Commissioner for Natural Resources (Powers) Act, 1934" had become law. See ibid, pp. 46-7.
86 For business reaction to the creation of the Newfoundland Fisheries Board, see HS, p. 42; *Observer's Weekly* (St. John's), 14 April 1936.
87 DO 35/498/NF1020/16, draft desp. for SSD.
88 For his terms of reference, see GN 1/3/A, file 627. See also my "The Bradley Report," p. 194.
89 HS, pp. 8-9.
90 For the full report, see GN 1/3/A, file 627.
91 See my "The Bradley Report," pp. 211-12.
92 DO 35/498/N1020/16, draft despatch by Hope Simpson to SSD.
93 DO 35/498/NF1020/16, Hope Simpson to Harding, 1 November 1934.
94 Ibid., Anderson to Thomas, 2 November 1934.
95 Ibid., Hope Simpson to Harding, 1 November 1934.
96 Cmd. 5117, p. 16; DO 35/490/N1004A/5, Anderson to Thomas, 20 September 1934.
97 See, for example, Cmd. 5117, pp. 16-17.
98 Ibid., pp. 17-18; Cmd. 5425, p. 18.
99 Cmd. 5117, p. 17.
100 *Acts of the Commission of Government*, 1935, pp. 233-9.

101 Cmd. 4788, p. 8. Cmd. 4479 includes a map of the road system in 1933. The legend on this map gives the following information: first class roads completed, 490 miles; first class roads projected, 27 miles; second class roads completed, 385 miles; second class roads projected, 5 miles; second class roads proposed, 80 miles; third class roads completed, 2,700 miles. The third class road mileage covered "roads in all settlements" under the jurisdiction of the Department of Public Works. In 1939 the Commission reported that the highway system of the country consisted of "600 miles in the Avalon Peninsula and 500 outside." In addition there were "2,000 miles of secondary roads" for the maintenance of which the government accepted "a measure of responsibility." See DO 114/80, N. 11/43, No. 37, p. 8, desp. from GN, 13 February 1939.

102 Cmd. 5117, p. 19.

103 Cmd. 4788, pp. 8-9

104 Cmd. 5425, p. 41. The railway had been operated by the government since 1923.

105 DO 35/504/N1051/7, Lodge memo on general policy.

106 DO 35/490/N1004A/5, encl. in Anderson to Thomas, 20 September 1934.

107 Cmd. 5117, pp. 22-3.

108 Cmd. 4910, p. 5.

109 Cmd. 5117, pp. 22-3.

110 Cmd. 6010, p. 30.

111 These figures are taken from DO 35/740/157/53, note by Clutterbuck. The highest and lowest monthly relief totals, 1933–36, were as follows:

	Highest	*Lowest*
1933	91,817 (April)	34,597 (August)
1934	85,050 (March)	21,475 (September)
1935	73,669 (April)	26,315 (August)
1936	76,629 (March)	41,609 (August)

112 For the chronology of the Kean affair, see DO 35/497/NF1017/38, pt. 1, Anderson to Harding, 12 November 1935.

113 The presiding judge was William J. Browne.

114 For his career, see Hibbs, *Who's Who in and from Newfoundland*, p. 100. For a British assessment of him, see DO 35/490/N1004/82, "Notes on Possible Candidates for the Post of Newfoundland Commissioner."

115 See DO 35/497/NF1017/38, pt. 1, note, "The case of Captain Kean."

116 Ibid.

117 Ibid.

118 Ibid., Anderson to Harding, 12 November 1935.

119 DO 35/490/N1004/45, Anderson to Harding, 22 June 1935.

120 DO 35/497/NF1017/38, pt. 1, Lodge to Machtig, 25 October 1935.

121 For his departure for Liverpool, see *ET*, 15 October, 1934, p. 4.

122 DO 35/497/NF1017/38, pt. 1, Lodge to Machtig, 15 October 1934, p. 4.
123 Ibid.
124 For the Commission's case, see DO 35/497/NF1017/38, pt. 1, note, "The case of Captain Kean."
125 For the argument against the Commission, see ibid., note, "The Constitutional Position in Newfoundland."
126 Ibid., document beginning "The three Commissioners now in England."
127 Ibid., "Note of meeting on 18th December, 1935."
128 Ibid., pt. 3, Walwyn to Harding, 19 June 1936.
129 DO 35/497/NF1017/38, pt. 2, Howley to Private Secretary, Government House, and encl., 23 February 1937. This file also contains copies of Kean's complaint against Gaze and the warrant, signed by Magistrate Hugh O'Neill, for Gaze's arrest.
130 DO 35/497/NF1017/38, pt. 3, DO to Govr., 31 December 1936; GN 38/S1-1, p. 366, 17 December 1937.
131 GN 38/S1-1, p. 377, 21 January 1937.
132 *Times* (London), 8 December 1936, p. 15.
133 For his career, see *Who Was Who 1951-60*, p. 1132; *Times* (London), 30 December 1957, p. 8, col. e.
134 DO 35/490/N1004/77, Walwyn to Harding, 22 February 1936.
135 HS, pp. 41-2.
136 For his career, see *Who Was Who 1971-1980*, p. 873.
137 Ibid., p. 359; *Times* (London), 5 September 1967, p. 10, col. h.
138 See *Who Was Who 1941-1950*, p. 1261; *Times* (London), 9 January 1947, p. 4, col. g; and 10 January, p. 7, col. e.
139 DO 35/490/N1004/77, Walwyn to Harding, 22 February 1936.
140 DO 35/496/N1012/131, Walwyn to MacDonald, 14 March 1936.
141 DO 35/496/N1012/161, Walwyn to Harding, 1 September 1936.
142 See ibid., Hale to Tait, 7 October 1936.
143 Ibid., Walwyn to Harding, 1 September 1936.
144 Ibid.

CHAPTER FOUR

1 DO 414/59, desp. to GN, 22 October 1936.
2 DO 35/506/N1083/5, minute by Malcolm MacDonald, 8 March 1936
3 See DO 35/497/NF1017/38, pt. 3, tel. to Govr., 31 December 1936; DO 35/725/N11/2, Walwyn to Batterbee, 28 December 1936.
4 For the Commission's plan, see DO 114/80, "Newfoundland Affairs: Correspondence 1937-1939," N.11/1, No. 32, desp. from GN, 24 December 1936. For quotations in this paragraph, see pp. 2, 5, 25.
5 Ibid., pp. 5, 13, 15.
6 Ibid., p. 10.

7 Ibid., pp. 15-16.
8 Ibid., pp. 6-8.
9 Ibid., p. 16.
10 Ibid., p. 21.
11 Ibid., pp. 24-5.
12 GN 38/S1-1, p. 363, 11 December 1936.
13 DO 35/725/N11/2, Walwyn to Batterbee, 28 December 1936.
14 NA, RG 59, 843.00/74, Quarton to SSW, 31 December 1934.
15 Ibid., 843.00/77, Quarton to SSW, tel., 11 May 1935; 843.00/78, Quarton to SSW, 11 May 1935; 843.00/80, Quarton to SSW, 3 July 1935.
16 Ibid., 843.00/82, Quarton to SSW, 1 October 1935.
17 I am grateful to James Overton, who has research in progress on the social history of the period, for this information.
18 DO 35/723/N2/1, Walwyn to MacDonald, 15 March 1937.
19 DO 114/80, N.11.3., No. 33, desp. to GN, 31 March 1937.
20 DO 35/725/N11/3, MacDonald to Walwyn, 31 March 1937.
21 *Times* (London), 7 April 1937, p. 15, col. b.
22 DO 35/725/N11/5, Penson to Machtig, 14 April 1937.
23 See ibid., Hale to Machtig, 15 April 1937.
24 Ibid., Clutterbuck note, 29 April 1937.
25 See *ET*, 14 July 1937, pp. 5, 7.
26 DO 35/723/N2/30, Lodge to MacDonald and encl., 27 September 1937.
27 NA, RG 59, 843.00/96, Sundell to SSW, 3 October 1938. Lodge's book was published in London in 1939. Walwyn once described it as "a clever, but caddish book that would be better unwritten." See DO 35/725/N8/17, Walwyn to Machtig, 12 June 1939.
28 See DO 35/723/N2/30, Machtig minute, 1 October 1937.
29 Cmd. 6010, p. 7.
30 Ibid., pp. 7-8.
31 Ibid., pp. 3, 5, 16.
32 Ibid., p. 6.
33 DO 114/80, N.11/43., No. 37, p. 4, desp. from GN, 13 February 1939.
34 For the impact of the recession on this industry, see Cmd. 6010, pp. 6-7, 21-2.
35 DO 35/740/157/53, Clutterbuck note.
36 Cmd. 6010, p. 10.
37 This account of the negotiations is based generally on DO 35/746/N271/1, Clutterbuck note, 25 February 1939. For other useful summaries of the negotiations, see DO 35/747/N271/81, Machtig to Rae Smith, 2 February, 19 July 1938.
38 DO 35/746/N271/1, note by Clutterbuck, 25 February 1939.
39 For a summary of the terms of the agreement, see Ewbank, *Public Affairs in Newfoundland*, pp. 10-11.
40 GN 38/S1-1, p. 430, 9 July 1937. This account of the strike is based on

GN 1/8/2, 1937 (N.R. 64-37), "Report on LOGGERS STRIKE AT ROBERTS ARM, N.D. Bay," by the chief ranger, 3 November 1937.

41 GN 1/8/2, 1937 (N.R. 64-37), "Report on LOGGERS STRIKE," pp. 1, 6, 10-11.

42 GN 1/8/2, 1937 (N.R. 64-37), "Memorandum submitted by Commissioner for Natural Resources for Consideration of Commission of Government."

43 MacDonald's account of his conversation with Bowater is in DO 35/746/N271/76.

44 DO 35/747/N241/81, Machtig to Rae Smith, 2 February 1938.

45 See *ET*, 18 February 1938, pp. 4, 6.

46 DO 35/747/N271/93A, tel. to GN, 12 May 1938.

47 See Ewbank, *Public Affairs in Newfoundland*, p. 23.

48 For the terms of the agreement, see ibid., pp. 14-18.

49 Ibid., pp. 9-23. The quotation from Ewbank's radio address is on pp. 21-2.

50 For his minute, see GN 38/S2-3-1, file 5.

51 DO 35/747/N271/113, GN to DO, 9 December 1938.

52 DO 35/747/N271/110, Nfld. Board of Trade to DO, 7 December 1938.

53 DO 35/747/N271/112, Carnell to MacDonald, 9 December 1938; GN 38/S2-3-1, file 4, newspaper item entitled "Petitions Received from 38 Settlements."

54 See DO 35/747/N271/112.

55 GN 38/S2-3-1, file 5, letter by J.R. Smallwood to Editor, *DN*, "Bowater-Lloyd's Anxiety."

56 DO 35/747/N271/113, GN to DO, 9 December 1938.

57 See NA, RG 59, 843.00/83, Quarton to SSW, 3 March 1938; *Acts of the Commission of Government*, 1939, pp. 252-92.

58 Brown was another of the ministers Alderdice had wanted kept on "in an advisory capacity." See AP, Dep. c. 391, pp. 98-9, Harding to Amulree, 15 Nov. 1933 and DO 35/499/1024/1, Clutterbuck minute, 12 March 1934.

59 DO 34/747/N271/113, GN to DO, 9 December 1938.

60 For Puddester's speech, see *ET*, 20 December 1938, pp. 7, 13-16.

61 See GN 38/S2-3-1, file 3, Walwyn to MacDonald, 6 January 1939, and file 5, newspaper item, "Government Passes Bowater Act."

62 For the attitude of the Fishermen's Protective Union, see DO 34/747/N271/117, DO to GN, 22 December 1938. On 19 December the Company had sent the Government a reassuring letter in this regard. See Lewin to Ewbank, 19 December 1938, *ET*, 20 December 1938; and GN 38/S2-3-1, file 5, draft tel. to SSD, 24 December 1938.

63 GN 38/S2-3-1, file 3, Walwyn to MacDonald, 6 January 1939.

64 Ibid., file 4, newspaper item, "Bd of Trade Protests Arbitrary Method of

Ratifying Gander Deal."
65 Ibid., file 3, Walwyn to MacDonald, 6 January 1939.
66 DO 35/729/N31/25, Clutterbuck note, 8 December 1938.
67 DO 35/729/N45/11, Clutterbuck note, 10 December 1937.
68 For Gorvin's career, see *Who Was Who 1951-1960*, p. 437; *Times* (London), 22 January 1960, p. 15, col. b.
69 DO 35/724/N3/54A, Hankinson to Hardinge, 2 May 1939.
70 For the background to his appointment, see DO 35/729/N45/11, Clutterbuck note, 10 December 1937.
71 *Interim Report of J.H. Gorvin*, p. 5. See also his *Report on Land Settlements in Newfoundland*.
72 GN 38/S1-1, p. 529, 6 June 1938.
73 DO 35/725/N8/12, Walwyn to Harding, 4 July 1938.
74 *Interim Report of J.H. Gorvin*.
75 Ibid., pp. 3, 5, 14.
76 DO 35/726/N11/51, Clutterbuck note.
77 Ibid.
78 *Interim Report of J.H. Gorvin*, pp. 16, 19–20.
79 Ibid., pp. 20, 24.
80 Ibid., pp. 20–7.
81 Ibid., p. 28–9.
82 The items published with Gorvin's *Interim Report* make up vol. 2 of Newfoundland, *Papers Relating to a Long Range Reconstruction Policy in Newfoundland*.
83 See DO 35/726/N11/34, Clutterbuck minutes, 26, 27 October 1938 and tel. to GN, 28 October 1938.
84 Ibid., tel. from GN, 25 October 1938.
85 Ibid., GN 38/S1-1, p. 627, 14 January 1939.
86 DO 114/80, N.11/43., No. 37, p. 4, desp. from GN, 13 February 1939.
87 Ibid., pp. 2-3.
88 Ibid., pp. 3-4.
89 Ibid., pp. 11-13.
90 Ibid., N.11/44., No. 38, p. 1, encl. in desp. from GN, 13 February 1939.
91 Ibid., N.11/46., No. 39, p. 1, tel. to GN, 20 March 1939.
92 GN 38/S1-1, p. 650, 23 March 1939.
93 The record of this meeting is in DO 35/726/N11/51.
94 Ibid.
95 See DO 35/724/N3/54A, Machtig memo, 27 April 1939.
96 Ibid., memo, 3 May 1939.
97 GN 38/S1-1, p. 693, 5 July 1939.
98 For a summary of this, see DO 114/80, N.11/43., p. 14, appendix to desp. from GN, 13 February 1939.
99 GN 38/S1-1, p. 639, 20 February 1939.

100 Ibid., p. 705, 25 August 1939; Lillian Bouzane, "Mary Arnold and her work in Newfoundland."

101 GN 38/S1-1, p. 694, 10 July 1939; p. 699, 26 July 1939.

102 In December 1938, Clutterbuck described Emerson and Dunfield as becoming "a somewhat dangerous combination." See DO 35/729/N31/25, note by Clutterbuck, 12 December 1938.

103 See, for example, DO 35/723/N2/26, memo, 16 December 1938.

104 See *Daily Express* (London), 3 March 1939, p. 9; 25 March 1939, p. 1; 27 March 1939, pp. 1, 10; 28 March 1939, p. 8; 29 March 1939, p. 8; 30 March 1939, pp. 1-2, 4; 31 March 1939, p. 8; 1 April 1939, p. 4.

105 DO 35/740/157/53, Clutterbuck memo.

CHAPTER FIVE

1 Supreme Court of Canada, "IN THE MATTER OF Section 55," "Factum of the Attorney General of Canada," p. 57.

2 GN 38/S4-1-5, memo by Emerson, 31 May 1939.

3 GN 38/S4-1-2, memo by Emerson, 8 June 1939; *Acts of the Commission of Government*, 1939, p. 76.

4 DO 35/725/N8/14, Clutterbuck note, 5 November 1938.

5 GN 38/S4-2-1, file 1, Administrator to Inskip, March 1939.

6 DO 114/57, "1934-1936, Aviation: Correspondence and Papers," pp. 91, 93, "Transatlantic Air Service."

7 See AVIA 2/2285, 40B, DO draft memo, "Newfoundland Obligations under the Transatlantic Air Service Agreement and the Ottawa Negotiations, 1935," May, 1943.

8 AVIA 2/1946, 10A, "Report on the selection of bases in Newfoundland for the Ireland-Newfoundland air route," 23 August 1935.

9 Ibid., 8. For a further reference to Vatcher, see GN 38/S1-1, 3 April 1934, p. 24.

10 AVIA 2/1943, 123A, "Bases In Newfoundland For The N. Transatlantic Air Service."

11 Ibid., Batterbee to Lodge, 23 July 1936.

12 Ibid., 125B, tel. to GN, 30 July 1936.

13 Ibid., 141B, Lodge to Batterbee, 23 July 1936.

14 AVIA 2/1946, 23B, Lodge to Batterbee, 20 August 1936.

15 AVIA 2/1943, 132B, tel. to GN, 6 August 1936.

16 AVIA 2/2285, 40B, DO draft memo, "Newfoundland Obligations under the Transatlantic Air Service Agreement and the Ottawa Negotiations, 1935," May 1943.

17 See AVIA 2/2303, 20B, "United States of American Civil Aeronautics Authority: In the matter of the application of Imperial Airways Limited for a Foreign Air Carrier Permit."

18 AVIA 2/1063, 164B, "Extract from confidential despatch from the Governor of Newfoundland to the Secretary of State for Dominion Affairs, dated 4th October, 1937."
19 AVIA 2/1943, 8A, Golpin to Pattison, 11 December 1936; NAC, RG 24, Fraser, "History," p. 103.
20 GN 38/S4-2-1, file 1, Administrator to Inskip, March 1939.
21 GN 38/S4-2-2, file 14, "Newfoundland Defence Scheme 1936."
22 Ibid., file 13, Committee of Imperial Defence, Overseas Defence Committee, "Newfoundland Defence Scheme 1936: Remarks by the Oversea Defence Sub-Committee of the Committee of Imperial Defence," June 1937.
23 GN 38/S1-1, p. 483, 7 January 1938.
24 Ibid., p. 643, 2 March 1939.
25 GN 38/S4-2-1, file 1, Administrator to Inskip, March 1939.
26 GN 38/S4-1-2, file 1, joint memo by the Acting Commissioner for Justice and the Commissioner for Finance.
27 *Acts of the Commission of Government*, 1939, pp. 197-204.
28 NG (extraordinary), 1 September 1939.
29 *Acts of the Commission of Government*, 1939, pp. 205-14 and 215-18.
30 NG, 12 September 1939, p. 6.
31 NAC, RG 24, Fraser, "History," pp. 48-58; NG, 19 September 1939, p. 1. Eventually, on the authority of the Supreme Court of Newfoundland - Admiralty in Prize, the *Christopher V Doornum* was handed over to the British Ministry of Shipping. Renamed the *Empire Commerce*, she was then chartered to Bowater's Newfoundland Pulp and Paper Mills Ltd., in whose service she was destroyed by enemy action.
32 NG (extraordinary), 16 September 1939, pp. 1-2.
33 V. Calver, who had come over from the United Kingdom to work in the Department of Finance, was named secretary to the board, a position he held through the war. See *ET*, 18 September 1939, p. 7.
34 GN 38/S4-1-4, memo by Emerson, 4 September 1939.
35 GN 38/S4-1-2, J. 59-1939, memo by Emerson, 3 October 1939.
36 *Acts of the Commission of Government*, 1939, pp. 245-7.
37 NAC, RG 24, Fraser, "History," p. 39; *ET*, 1 November 1939, p. 5.
38 NG, 21 November 1939, p. 1.
39 GN 38/S1-1, p. 750, 17 November 1939.
40 GN 38/S4-1-2, file 1, memo by Emerson, 23 November 1939.
41 NAC, RG 24, Fraser, "History," pp. 62-5.
42 Bridle, *Documents*, 1, pp. 43, 45.
43 AVIA 2/2285, Herbertson to Dixon, 30 October 1939.
44 Bridle, *Documents*, 1, pp. 53-4.
45 NAC, RG 24, Fraser, "History," pp. 1, 7-8.
46 Ibid., p. 6.
47 *Acts of the Commission of Gouvernment*, 1939, pp. 11-26.

48 NG (extraordinary), 26 January 1940.
49 NAC, RG 24, Fraser, "History," pp. 9-10.
50 DO 35/725/N8/14, pp. 10-11, Clutterbuck note, 5 November 1938.
51 NAC, RG 24, Fraser, "History," p. 10.
52 NG, 6 February 1940, p. 1.
53 This account is based on NAC, RG 24, Fraser, "History," pp. 11-16, 25-6.
54 Ibid., pp. 26-30.
55 NG, 21 May 1940, p. 1.
56 NAC, RG 24, Fraser, "History," pp. 20-1.
57 NG, 25 June 1940, p. 1.
58 NAC, RG 24, Fraser, "History," pp. 22-5.
59 *Acts of the Commission of Government*, 1939, pp. 250-1.
60 For a detailed account of the early history of the Unit, see GN 38/S2-1-18, memo by Gorvin enclosing report by Claude Fraser (Secretary, Dept. of Natural Resources) on "the formation, organisation, enlistment and transportation of the Newfoundland Forestry Unit," 10 September 1940. Fraser's report is dated 17 August 1940.
61 NAC, RG 24, Fraser, "History," p. 32.
62 GN 38/S4-1-2, file 2, Martin to Carew, 9 November 1939.
63 Ibid., Secretary for Home Affairs to Martin, 22 November 1939.
64 Ibid., Martin to Carew, 18 December 1939.
65 For the sequence of events, see GN 38/S4-2-9, file 12, Renouf to Carew, 13 February 1940.
66 For the memo, dated 15 January 1940, see GN 38/S4-1-2, file 2.
67 GN 38/S4-1-2, file 2, memo by Emerson, 7 February 1940.
68 Ibid., Emerson to Outerbridge, 6 February 1940.
69 GN 38/S4-2-9, Renouf to Carew, 13 February 1940.
70 For Dunfield's appointment, see NG, 7 November 1939, p. 1. His place at the Justice Department had been taken by G. Bernard Summers, a barrister who had been secretary of the enquiry Gordon Bradley had undertaken into logging, shortly after the Commission was formed. See NG, 5 December 1939, p. 1.
71 For the letter, dated February 3, sent to Dunfield and the others invited, see GN 38/S4-1-2, file 2.
72 Ibid., Emerson to Outerbridge, 6 February 1940.
73 *ET*, 27 February 1940, p. 5.
74 GN 38/S4-1-4, memo by Emerson, 8 August 1940.
75 See GN 38/S4-2-9, file 9, Howitt and Macgillivray to Puddester, 5 October 1940; NAC, RG 24, Fraser, "History," p. 7.
76 GN 38/S4-1-4, Macgillivray to Puddester, 13 July 1945; Margaret Duley, *The Caribou Hut* (Toronto, [1949]).
77 *ET*, 4 July 1939, pp. 5, 7, 11 (original 1939-40 budget) and

21 November 1939, p. 5; NAC, RG 24, Fraser, "History," pp. 209-11.
78 GN 38/S1-1, p. 788, 14 March 1940.
79 See ibid., pp. 791-5, 19-21, 23-4 March 1940.
80 DO 35/723/N2/57, tel. from the GN, 28 March 1940.
81 NG (extraordinary), 29 April 1940; 30 April 1940, p. 1.
82 *Observer's Weekly*, 7 May 1940, p. 2.
83 Ibid., 21 May 1940, pp. 1-2.
84 GN 38/S2-1-19, memo from the Newfoundland Board of Trade on the Special Areas Development Bill, 1940, encl. in Renouf to Carew, 21 September 1940.
85 GN 38/S1-1, p. 814, 17 May 1940 and p. 816, 25 May 1940.
86 For the budget, see *ET*, 4 July 1940, pp. 5, 12, 14. See also NAC, RG 24, Fraser, "History," pp. 213-17.
87 *Acts of the Commission of Government*, 1940, pp. 24-5; NAC, RG 24, Fraser, "History," pp. 211-12.
88 *Acts of the Commission of Government*, 1940, pp. 31-3; Fraser, "History," pp. 217-19.
89 *Acts of the Commission of Government*, 1940, pp. 50-4; NAC, RG 24, Fraser, "History," pp. 219-20.
90 GN 38/S2-1-17, memo by Gorvin, 4 September 1940.
91 GN 38/S1-1, p. 882, 30 September 1940.
92 *ET*, 5 October 1940, p. 7.
93 See DO 34/724/N3/82, p. 102, Govr. to DO, 25 April 1941.
94 Ibid., Govr. to DO, 30 May 1941.
95 Ibid., pp. 7-8, minute by Tait, 12 May 1941.
96 Ibid.
97 Ibid., Gorvin to Tait, 26 June 1941.
98 *ET*, 5 July 1941, pp. 5, 14, 16.
99 GN 38/S1-1, p. 989, 15 July 1941; *ET*, 10 July 1941, p. 6.
100 GN 38/S1-1, p. 963, 22 May 1941; p. 1014, 30 September 1941.
101 DO 35/725/N8/26, Walwyn to Machtig, 17 July 1941.
102 GN 38/S1-1, p. 803, 19 April 1940.
103 NG, 28 May 1940, p. 1.
104 GN 38/S1-1, p. 820, 31 May 1940.
105 NG, 5 November 1940, pp. 3-4.
106 *Acts of the Commission of Government*, 1940, p. 27.
107 Ibid., p. 26.
108 GN 38/S1-1, p. 830, 21 June 1940.
109 G.B. Summers to author, 13 December 1986.
110 *Acts of the Commission of Government*, 1940, p. 29; *ET*, 6 October 1945, p. 6.
111 GN 38/S1-1, p. 830, 21 June 1940.
112 NG, 23 July 1940, pp. 2-4.

113 Ibid., 30 July, pp. 1-2; 6 August 1940, p. 4. Defence alarm areas were established for the Exploits Valley (Grand Falls, Windsor, Bishop's Falls, and Botwood) on 18 March 1941 and for Corner Brook on 24 March 1942. See NAC, RG 24, Fraser, "History," pp. 86-7.
114 GN 38/S1-1, p. 827, 13 June 1940; NAC, RG 24, Fraser, "History," pp. 65-6, 79, 98-100.
115 See information in GN 38/S4-2-1, file 11. This camp was never used.
116 GN 38/S1-1, p. 847, 16 July 1940.
117 *Acts of the Commission of Government*, 1940, pp. 73-8.
118 GN 38/S4-1-4, memo by Emerson, 11 September 1940.
119 *Acts of the Commission of Government*, 1940, p. 73.
120 GN 38/S1-1, p. 2183, 30 March 1949.
121 NG, 3 September 1940, p. 6.
122 Bridle, *Documents*, 1, pp. 66, 68.
123 Ibid., pp. 70-1.
124 Ibid., p. 73.
125 Ibid., p. 74.
126 Ibid., p. 75–80, 116.
127 Ibid., pp. 116-17.
128 NAC, RG 24, Fraser, "History," pp. 118–19.
129 DO 114/79, "1937-1942, Civil Aviation: Further Correspondence and Papers," p. 188, HCC to GN, 5 August 1940.
130 Ibid., GN to HCC, 6 August 1940.
131 For the minutes of this meeting, see Bridle, *Documents*, 1, pp. 159-62.
132 *Acts of the Commission of Government*, 1940, pp. 106-17.
133 See GN 38/S4-1-4, memo by Emerson, 9 October 1940.
134 NG, 3 December 1940, p. 1.
135 Bridle, *Documents*, 1, pp. 404-6.
136 Ibid., p. 53; NAC, RG 24, Fraser, "History," p. 141.
137 See AIR 38/20, "Summary of information covering the organization of the Atlantic ferry bomber service by the Canadian Pacific," pp. 1-4.
138 NAC, RG 24, Fraser, "History," pp. 141-2.
139 For his memoirs, see Griffith Powell, *Ferryman* (Shrewsbury 1982).
140 NAC, RG 24, Fraser, "History," pp. 143-4. The PBY flying boat was an amphibious-type aircraft, also know as the Canso (Canadian) or Catalina (American).
141 Powell, *Ferryman*, p. 27.
142 NAC, RG 24, Fraser, "History," p. 446.
143 AIR 38/20, "Summary of information covering the organization of the Atlantic ferry bomber service by the Canadian Pacific," pp. 4-5.
144 Powell, *Ferryman*, pp. 27-8.
145 NAC, RG 24, Fraser, "History," pp. 145-6.

146 AIR 38/20, "Summary of information covering the organization of the Atlantic ferry bomber service by the Canadian Pacific," p. 8.
147 Powell, *Ferryman*, p. 117; AIR 29/467, Operations Record Book and Appendices, Staging Post 83, orders of the day, no. 1, 21 July 1944.
148 NAC, RG 24, Fraser, "History," pp. 146-7.
149 For this and the other personnel information, see ibid., pp. 147-8. I am grateful to Carl Christie, Directorate of History, Department of National Defence, Ottawa, for information about individual Newfoundland servicemen.
150 GN 38/S4-2-4, file 3, tel. to SSD, 19 June 1940.
151 Ibid., SSD to Govr., 22 June 1940.
152 GN 38/S1-1, p. 833, 23 June 1940.
153 For his report, addressed to Gorvin and dated 5 July 1940, see GN 38/S4-2-4, file 3.
154 Douglas, G. Anglin, *The St. Pierre and Miquelon* Affaire, pp. 49-50, 65.
155 Ibid., p. 65.
156 Ibid., pp. 82-4.
157 Ibid., pp. 85, 100-7.
158 Cmd. 6624, 1940.
159 See Granatstein, *Canada's War*, p. 128.
160 GN 38/S4-2-1, file 13, SSD to Govr., 15 August 1940.
161 Ibid., Govr. to SSD, 16 August 1940.
162 Ibid., Govr. to SSD, 23 August 1940.
163 Ibid., SSD to Govr., 4 September 1940.
164 Ibid., SSD to Govr., 6 September 1940.
165 Ibid., SSD to Govr., 6 September 1940; Govr. to SSD, 7 September 1940.
166 Ibid., Govr. to SSD, 12 September 1940.
167 For the record of these events, see JWGP, box 3, file 22.
168 GN 38/S4-2-1, file 13, Govr. to SSD, 17 September 1940.
169 Ibid., Govr. to SSEA, 17 September 1940.
170 Ibid., SSD to Govr., 21 September 1940.
171 Ibid., SSD to Govr., 22 September 1940.
172 For the report of the "Board of Experts" of which Greenslade was President, see JWGP, box 3, file 22.
173 DO 114/111, "Newfoundland: United States Leased Bases, Correspondence 1940-1947," p. 12, tel. from GN, 21 September 1940.
174 JWGP, box 3, file 22, Walwyn to Greenslade, 21 September 1940.
175 GN 38/S4-2-1, file 8, Govr. to SSD, n.d. This refers to tel. no. 2744 from BEW to FO, 19 November 1940.
176 Bridle, *Documents*, 1, p. 225.
177 The report, dated 7 October, submitted by Emerson and Penson on this meeting, is in GN 38/S4-1-2, file 10.
178 GN 38/S4-2-1, file 13, Govr. to SSD, 8 October 1940.

179 Ibid., BEW to Govr., 11 October 1940.

180 Ibid., BEW to GN, 21 October 1940; GN to BEW, 26 October 1940; GN 38/S4-2-1, file 12, BEW to GN, 4 November 1940, and Govr. to SSD, 30 December 1940; GN 38/S4-2-1, file 8, memo by Emerson, 6 November 1940, with draft lease attached; GN 38/S5-1-2, file 10, memo by Emerson, 28 November 1940.

181 GN 38/S4-2-1, file 12, Butler to Knox, 11 November 1940.

182 Ibid., Govr. to SSD, 23 November 1940.

183 Ibid., Govr. to SSD, 30 December 1940.

184 Ibid., BEW to GN, 22 December 1940.

185 Ibid., Govr. to SSD, 23 December 1940; Govr. to BEW, 30 December 1940; GN 38/S4-2-3, file 16, Govr. to BEW, 9, 23 January 1941.

186 CAB 21/991, BEW to GN, 8 January 1941; GN 38/S4-2-3, file 16, BEW to Govr., 22 January 1941.

187 NG (extraordinary), 6 March 1941. The other members named to the Board were Francis W. Bradshaw, a businessman, and John Boyd Baird, an appraiser.

188 GN 38/S4-2-3, file 16, Govr. to BEW, Washington, 18 February 1941.

189 GN 38/S4-2-1, file 12, Govr. to SSD, 20 December 1940.

190 GN 38/S5-1-2, file 10, memo by Emerson, 28 November 1940.

191 GN 38/S4-2-3, file 16, encl. in Renouf to Walwyn, 2 January 1941.

192 Ibid., SSD to Govr., 13 January 1941; Govr. to SSD, 14 January 1941; GN 38/S4-2-1, file 13, SSD to Govr., 22 September 1940.

CHAPTER SIX

1 GN 38/S4-2-3, file 16, BEW to Govr., 17 January 1941.

2 CAB 98/17, note by Cranborne, 12 February 1941.

3 Ibid.

4 CAB 21/1913, memo by Cranborne and Moyne, 3 March 1941.

5 Ibid.

6 CAB 21/1913, Halifax to FO, 5 March 1941.

7 GN 38/S4-2-3, file 16, SSD to Govr., 19 March 1941.

8 Joe Garner, *The Commonwealth Office 1925-68* (London 1978), p. 250.

9 DO 114/111, p. 16, Churchill to Emerson, 22 March 1941.

10 Ibid., p. 17, Emerson to Churchill, 24 March 1941, p. 17.

11 GN 38/S4-2-3, file 16, SSD to Govr.

12 Cmd. 6259.

13 This summary is from a 1949 British commentary on the agreement. See DO 114/111, p. 3.

14 Ibid.

15 CAB 122/1051, "United States Bases in Newfoundland, Bermuda and the West Indies," p. 2.

16 GN 38/S4-2-3, file 16, SSD to Govr., 24 March 1941.
17 Ibid.
18 R.A. MacKay, in "Introduction," pp. xxxii-xxxv.
19 Cmd 6259, p.43.
20 GN 38/S4-2-3, file 16, SSD to Govr., 24 March 1941.
21 GN 38/S4-2-4, file 14a, Puddester to Emerson, 6 April 1941.
22 Copies of letters, dated 28 March 1941, to C.E.A., Jeffery and J.S. Currie are in ibid. See also "Sacrifice for Freedom," *ET*, 27 March 1941, p. 6; "The American Bases," *DN*, 28 March 1941, p. 4.
23 GN 38/S4-2-4, file 14a, Puddester to Emerson, 6 April 1941.
24 For information on the Newfoundland National Association, see *DN*, 28 February 1941, p. 3; 12 March 1941, p. 3; 19 March 1941, p. 3; 26 March 1941, p. 3. There is a copy of the prospectus of the Association, whose motto was "*Let our object be our country, our whole country and nothing but our country*," in CNS(A), John G. Higgins Collection. The date of the formation of the Association is given in CNS(A), Walter Sparkes Collection, Howell to Secretary, Brotherhood of Railway Clerks, Freight Handlers, n.d.
25 GN 38/S4-2-4, file 14a, Puddester to Emerson, 6 April 1941.
26 This account is based on GN 38/S4-2-5, file 2, "Discussions in Washington April 7th to 12th, 1941," memo by Penson, 25 April 1941.
27 Ibid. For the magazine articles, see Davenport, "Defense on Ice," and Clark, "Outpost No. 1: Newfoundland."
28 *ET*, 26 April 1941, pp. 6, 16.
29 Ibid., 28 April 1941, p. 5.
30 GN 38/S4-2-3, file 15, Dunn to Butler, 9 June 1941.
31 Ibid. Butler to Dunn, 20 May 1941.
32 Ibid. Dunn to Butler, 9 June 1941.
33 Cmd. 6259, pp. 39-40.
34 *Acts of the Commission of Government*, 1941, pp. 107-42.
35 *ET*, 16 June 1941, p. 10.
36 By section 7 of the act.
37 U.S., Dept. of the Navy, "Commander Task Force Twenty-Four," pp. 3-4.
38 See GN 38/S4-2-4, file 4d, memo by Emerson, 6 January 1941. Population figures are taken from the 1935 census.
39 See GN 38/S4-1-6, memo by Emerson and attachments, 6 January 1941.
40 *ET*, 11 February 1941, p. 4.
41 Ibid., 21 February 1941, p. 3.
42 *DN*, 22 February 1941, p. 9.
43 GN 38/S4-2-4, file 13, Silliman to Woods, 14 March 1941, annexed to memo by Woods, 15 March 1941.
44 Ibid., memo by Woods, 15 March 1941.
45 GN 38/S4-2-3, Vice Chairman of Commission to Halifax, 16 March 1941.

46 GN 38/S4-2-4, file 14a, memo by Woods, 1 April 1941.
47 Ibid., draft letter from Woods to Secretary, Argentia Committee, April 1941.
48 GN 38/S4-2-5, file 2, memo by Woods, 8 May 1941; GN 38/S5-1-2, file 10, memo by Gorvin, 6 June 1941.
49 GN 38/S4-2-4, file 15, tel. to Walwyn, 17 July 1941.
50 GN 38/S4-2-7, file 7, "Report of the Chief Health Inspector on the Exhumation and removal of the dead bodies from the Cemeteries at Argentia," 12 August 1942.
51 GN 38/S4-2-4, file 4b, copy of letter to Woods, 13 February 1941.
52 Noel, *Politics in Newfoundland*, p. 243.
53 GN 38/S4-2-7, file 8, Woods to Puddester, 21 April 1941.
54 Ibid., encl. in Berry to Mosdell, 20 February 1941.
55 GN 38/S4-2-3, file 16, Govr. to BEW, 18 February 1941.
56 GN 38/S4-2-5, file 2, memo by Woods, 17 January 1941.
57 GN 38/S4-2-4, file 4c, attachments to memo by Woods, 25 February 1941.
58 *DN*, 8 March 1941, p. 3.
59 Ibid., 10 March 1941, p. 3.
60 GN 38/S5-1-2, file 10, memo by Woods, 28 April 1941.
61 For a visitor's reaction to driving arrangements inside and outside the American base at Argentia, see Morton, *Atlantic Meeting*, pp. 111-12.
62 Bridle, *Documents*, 1, pp. 167-72.
63 Ibid., pp. 432-5.
64 Ibid., pp. 1409-13.
65 Ibid., pp. 1409, 1411, 1413.
66 Ibid., pp. 436-7.
67 Ibid., p. 433.
68 Ibid., pp. 443.
69 Ibid., p. 462.
70 GN 38/S4-2-3, file 16, SSEA to Govr., 16 September 1941.
71 Bridle, *Documents*, 1, pp. 484-5, 488; GN 38/S4-2-3, file 15, SSD to Govr., 23 October 1941.
72 DO 35/1376/N665/35, "Goose Bay," memo by Clutterbuck, 27 January 1944.
73 Bridle, *Documents*, 1, p. xlv.
74 GN 38/S4-2-3, file 15, SSEA to Govr., 16 September 1941.
75 Ibid., SSEA to Govr., 30 August 1941.
76 Bridle, *Documents*, 1, p. 199.
77 For Burchell's career, see Kathryn Ellen Hayman, "The Origins and Function of the Canadian High Commission," pp. 26-7.
78 Bridle, *Documents*, 1, pp. 194-8.
79 For the negotiations leading to the agreement, see ibid., pp. 1117-31.

80 This account is based on DO 35/1369/N517/13, 117-20, note, n.d.
81 NAC, RG 24, Fraser, "History," p. 445.
82 See Leonard Outerbridge, "Churchill and Roosevelt in Newfoundland."
83 Dilks, *The Diaries of Sir Alexander Cadogan*, p. 398.
84 See "Newfoundland Seamen" in *Collected Poems of E.J. Pratt*, p. 115.
85 *ET*, 16 November 1940, p. 7.
86 Ibid., 21 November 1940, p. 3.
87 E.J. Pratt's "Newfoundland Seamen" in *Collected Poems*, p. 115.
88 Ibid. For the history of this disaster, see Cassie Brown, *Standing Into Danger*.
89 The ships sunk were the SS *Lord Strathcona* and the SS *Saganaga* (5 September) and the SS *Rose Castle* and the *PLM 27* (5 November). (The last mentioned ship was named for the Paris-Lyon-Marseilles railway.) No one was lost on the *Lord Strathcona*, but thirty-three went down with the *Saganaga*. There were thirty-eight survivors from the *PLM 27* and nineteen from the *Rose Castle*. I am grateful to Carl Christie of the Directorate of History, Dept. of National Defence, Ottawa, for assistance with this note. See also Hadley, *U-Boats against Canada*, pp. 116, 142, 152.
90 See *ET*, 15-17, 19-24 October, and 14 November 1942, p. 3, for the official report on the sinking.
91 Ibid., 14-19 December 1942.
92 *Report of the Hon. Mr. Justice Dunfield*, p. 11.
93 Alec Douglas, "The Nazi weather station in Labrador."
94 DO 35/1143/N409/1, "Report for 1941 Commission of Government St. John's Newfoundland," p. 57.
95 DO 35/1143/N409/2, "Abbreviated Annual Report for the year 1942," p. 6.
96 Ibid., p. 47.
97 Cmd. 6849, p. 42.
98 *Acts of the Commission of Government*, 1939, pp. 229-44.
99 Cmd. 6849, p. 44.
100 GN 38/S1-1, p. 748, 3 November 1939.
101 Cmd. 6849, p. 24.
102 GN 38/S1-1, p. 1066, 14 February 1942.
103 Cmd. 6849, pp. 26, 27.
104 Ibid., p. 26; Neary, *Bell Island*. The ship that sailed from Bell Island on 26 August was the *SS Pajola*. She was bound for Emden and carried 9,700 tons of iron ore. See *ET*, 28 August 1939, p. 4.
105 Cmd. 6849, p. 27.
106 Ibid., p. 30.
107 DO 35/1143/N409/2, "Abbreviated Annual Report for the Year 1942," p. 6.

108 GN 38/S1-1, p. 1145, 8 August 1942.

109 GN 38/S1-1, p. 838, 3 July 1940; *ET*, 18 November 1940, p. 5.

110 The information on 1940-41 out-turn and the Government's financial plans for the following year is taken from Penson's 1941-42 budget speech, *ET*, 4 July 1941, pp. 8-9, and "Revenue Estimates 1940-41 and 1941-42," *ET*, 5 July 1941, p. 12.

111 For the 1939-40 figures, see *ET*, 3 July 1940, p. 4.

112 Ibid., 15 July 1942, pp. 2, 11.

113 *Acts of the Commissions of Government*, 1941, pp. 213-21; Cmd. 6849, p. 16.

114 *Acts of the Commission of Government*, 1942, pp. 135-42.

115 See DO 35/746/N265/99, note, "Education in Newfoundland," n.d.

116 See *Acts of the Commission of Government*, 1939, pp. 33-6. For details of events between 1935 and the 1939 act, see McCann, "The Educational Policy of the Commission of Government," pp. 206-7.

117 GN 38/S1-1, p. 1094, 1 May 1942.

118 DO 35/746/N265/99, note, "Education in Newfoundland."

119 GN 38/S1-1, p. 1187, 30 October 1942.

120 Ibid., p. 1093, 30 April 1942.

121 *Acts of the Commission of Government*, 1937, pp. 11-31.

122 GN 38/S1-1, p. 959, 10 May 1941.

123 *Acts of the Commission of Government*, 1941, pp. 104-5.

124 *NG*, 3 June 1941, p. 1.

125 Ibid., 17 June 1941, p. 7.

126 Ibid., 25 June, 1941, p. 1; 16 September 1941, p. 1.

127 *Acts of the Commission of Government*, 1942, pp. 161-84.

128 Ibid., pp. 185-214.

129 GN 38/S1-1, p. 702, 4 August 1939.

130 See ibid., p. 885, 4 October 1940.

131 GN 38/S1-1, pp. 877-8, 23 September 1940.

132 *Acts of the Commission of Government*, 1942, pp. 1-5.

133 Cmd. 6849, pp. 15-16.

134 Newfoundland, Liddell, *Industrial Survey of Newfoundland*, pp. 138-41.

135 The membership of this Union was described in one British document as comprising "a considerable proportion of undesirables" whose attitude had "nearly always been one of suspicion and non-co-operation." See DO 35/746/N265/99, note, "Trade Unionism and Conciliation Machinery." For the background of the January 1940 labour trouble, see *ET*, 15 January 1940, p. 4.

136 GN 38/S1-1, p. 769, 13 January 1940.

137 Ibid., p. 777, 2 February 1940.

138 Ibid., p. 805, 30 April 1940.

139 Liddell, *Industrial Survey of Newfounland*, pp. 16-19, 41-4.

140 For biographical information on Walsh, see DO 35/1142/N403/14.

141 NG, 2 July 1941, p. 1.

142 For a detailed account of the Buchans strike, see NAC, RG 24, Fraser, "History," pp. 286-97.

143 GN 38/S1-1, p. 1013, 13 October 1941.

144 Ibid., p. 1020, 15 October 1941.

145 NG (extraordinary), 23 October 1941, pp. 1-2.

146 NAC, RG 24, Fraser, "History," p. 321. The report of the Board was printed in the *ET* beginning 16 March 1942, p. 7.

147 NAC, RG 24, Fraser, "History," pp. 307-8.

148 Liddell, *Industrial Survey of Newfoundland*, p. 138.

149 DO 35/1144/N449/7, *Report of the Labour Relations Officer for the period June 1st, 1942, to February 8th, 1944*, p. 1.

150 GN 38/S1-1, p. 1085, 11 April 1942.

151 DO 35/746/N265, note, "Trade Unionism and Conciliation Machinery."

152 *Acts of the Commission of Government*, 1944, pp. 1-8.

153 DO 35/746/N265, note, "Trade Unionism and Conciliation Machinery"; DO 35/1156/N693/4, Clutterbuck to Woods, 8 July 1944 and Woods to Clutterbuck, 12 September 1944.

154 *Statutes of Newfoundland*, 1950, pp. 50-89.

155 DO 35/1144/N449/7, *Report of the Labour Relations Officer for the period from June 1st, 1942, to February 8th, 1944*, p. 11.

156 See my "Canada and the Newfoundland Labour Market, 1939-49," pp. 475-6.

157 DO 35/749/N321/1, Walwyn to Attlee, 5 December 1942.

158 DO 35/1143/N409/2, "Abbreviated Annual Report for the year 1942," p. 48.

159 GN 38/S1-1, p. 1032, 22 November 1941.

160 GN, 30 December 1941, pp. 1-4.

161 NAC, RG 24, Fraser, "History," p. 252–4.

162 *NG*, 30 December 1941, pp. 3-4.

163 *ET*, 31 December 1941, p. 11.

164 This account is based on NAC, RG 24, Fraser, "History," pp. 256-84.

165 NA, RG 59, 843.00/128, section of report by Hopper, "Political Developments During the Month of April, 1942," 20 May 1942, p. 4.

166 Encl. in ibid.

167 NA, RG 59, 843.00/128, section of report by Hopper, "Political Developments During the Month of April, 1942," 20 May 1942, p. 5.

168 DO 35/1141/N402/11, Walwyn to Machtig, 31 August 1943.

169 DO 35/1154/N653/15, encl. in Parsons to Chadwick, 25 March 1946.

170 DO 35/724/N3/82, Lush to Secretary of State, 12 May 1941.

171 DO 35/1342/N402/29, note encl. in Cranborne to Anderson, 22 September 1944.

172 DO 35/1141/N402/11, Walwyn to Machtig, 31 August 1943.

173 DO 35/723/N2/73, note by Emrys-Evans, 10 June 1942.

174 For McKenzie's submission, see DO 121/92. For a detailed account of Attlee's visit, see my "Clement Attlee's Visit to Newfoundland."

175 DO 35/744/N230/8, Machtig to Walwyn, 14 July 1942.

176 Ibid., Machtig to Walwyn, 14 August 1942; GN 38/S1-1, p. 1155, 29 August 1942.

177 *ET*, 15 September 1942.

178 Ibid., 18 September 1942.

179 For this see my "Clement Attlee's Visit to Newfoundland," p. 109. The original note is filed in DO 35/723/N2/73, pp. 58-67.

180 Bridle, *Documents*, 1, pp. 839-51.

181 Ibid., p. 475, "Memorandum concerning Torbay Aerodrome."

182 When a hangman was needed in May 1942, to carry out the execution of "the only white man to be convicted of murder in Newfoundland since 1899," (Emerson's words), one was supplied by Canada. See GN 38/S4-1-7, file 10; *ET*, 22 May 1942, p. 3.

183 Bridle, *Documents*, 2, pt. 1, pp. 295-300, extracts from memo by HCN, 12 October 1946.

184 Brebner, *North Atlantic Triangle*.

185 See Cuff and Granatstein, "Canada and the Perils of 'Exemptionalism.'"

186 DO 114/103, "Newfoundland Correspondence and Papers 1940-1949," pt.1, "Confederation with Canada," p. 1, tel. to GN, 25 November 1942.

187 As often happens in wartime, bureaucracy grew apace in Newfoundland after 1939. The civil service increased from 2,900 in 1937-38 to 4,126 in 1945-46 - but overshadowing this was the remarkable transformation whereby the country had traded in its begging bowl. For the civil service figures, see Cmd. 6849, p. 17.

188 Bridle, *Documents*, 2, pt. 1, pp. 32-3, Burchell to Robertson, 22 August 1942.

CHAPTER SEVEN

1 PANL, HC 117N4, 1943, "Abbreviated Annual Report for the Year 1943," p. 1; HC 117N4, 1944, "Abbreviated Annual Report for the Year 1944," p. 28.

2 PANL, HC 117N4, "Abbreviated Annual Report for the Year 1943," pp. 1-2.

3 Ibid., p. 13; Roll, *The Combined Food Board*, p. 55

4 Alexander, *The Decay of Trade*, p. 33.

5 PANL, HC 117N4, "Abbreviated Annual Report for the Year 1943," pp. 1-2.

6 Courage, *Newfoundland Who's Who 1961*, pp. 99-100. Gushue was Chairman of the International Emergency Food Council (Fisheries

Branch), 1945-46. For his intended 1940 resignation see GN 38/S1-1, p. 811, 11 May 1940; p. 814, 17 May 1940; p. 816, 25 May 1940; p. 871, 12 September 1940; and p. 882, 30 September 1940.

7 PANL, HC 117N4, "Abbreviated Annual Report for the Year 1943," p. 2.

8 PANL, HC 117N4, "Abbreviated Annual Report for the Year 1944," p. 1.

9 Ibid., p. 28; PANL, HC 117N4, "Abbreviated Annual Report for the Year 1943," p. 2.

10 For a full account of the labour aspect of Newfoundland's relations with Canada in this period, see my "Canada and the Newfoundland Labour Market."

11 NAC, RG 25, vol. 2405, file 4995-40, pt. 1, MacNamara to Robertson, 3 May 1943.

12 Ibid. Canadian ambassador to the United States to SSEA, 17 March 1944.

13 NRC, RG 84, vol. 13, 1943, Hopper to SSW, 5 April 1943.

14 In his 1945 annual report Selby Parsons, the Labour Relations Officer, summarized Canadian and United States recruitment in Newfoundland since 1943 as follows:

	Number recruited		*Number still on the job*	
	Men	Women	Men	Women
Canada	1,505	159	298	20
United States	1,947	-	895	-
Total by sex	3,452	159	1,193	20
Total of men and women	3,611		1,213	

15 See my "Canada and the Newfoundland Labour Market."

16 NAC, RG 25, file 4995-40, pt. 4, encl. in Bridle to SSEA, 3 July 1946.

17 For the 1944 appointments of Walsh and Parsons, see GN 38/S1-1, p. 1428, 16 June 1944; p. 1433, 3 July 1944; p. 1474, 23 September 1944; p. 1478, 3 October 1944.

18 "Report of the Labour Relations Office for the Year 1945," 8 December 1945.

19 *ET*, 28 April 1943, p. 3.

20 Ibid, 22 April 1945, p. 2. This figure included "a small cash balance" on hand in June 1940, and "certain gains on exchange transactions." Excluding these amounts the accumulated surplus as of the 1946 budget speech was $28,332,900. For a further account of revenue and expenditure, see *ET*, 6 April 1945, p. 12 and 28 April 1945, p. 17.

21 Cmd. 6849, p. 5.

22 *ET*, 3 March 1943, p. 3; DO 35/1333/N402/1/2, Clark to Hardinge, 2 June 1943.

23 *ET*, 9 March 1943, pp. 2, 3, 6, 11. For the tea party reference see

NA, RG 59, 843.00/137, Hopper to SSW, 13 March 1943. The resolution was moved by F.M. O'Leary and seconded by Harold Mitchell.

24 *ET*, 9 March 1943, pp. 6,11. The resolution to form the committee was moved by former Primer Minister Walter S. Monroe and seconded by J.B. McEvoy, a prominent St. John's lawyer.

25 *ET*, 30 March 1943, pp. 2, 5, 11.

26 GN 38/S1-1, p. 1237, 6 March 1943; p. 1247, 25 March, 1943.

27 *ET*, 30 March 1943, p. 2.

28 For an astute assessment of this, see DO 35/1333/N402/1/2, note by Clutterbuck, n.d.

29 Ibid. Cramm to Maxton, 24 April 1943.

30 For their resolution, see ibid., 72-3 and *DN*, 13 April 1943, p. 5. The signatories were William Thompson, President of the Longshoremen's Protective Union, Botwood; H.M. Barrett, Secretary of the Longshoremen's Protective Union, Botwood; J.J. Thompson, President, Newfoundland Lumbermen's Association; A. Hayes, President, Newfoundland Coasters' Association; Pierce Fudge, President, Newfoundland Labourers' Union; D.I. Jackman, President, Wabana Mine Workers' Union; and G.C. Tulk, President, Workers' Central Protective Union.

31 DO 35/1333/N402/1/2, Cramm to Maxton, 24 April 1943.

32 Ibid. Cramm's letter to Winterton is also in this file.

33 Ibid., note by Clutterbuck, n.d.

34 Newfoundland Federation of Labour, *Report of Proceedings of the Seventh Annual Convention*, p. 28.

35 Ibid., pp. 19-20, 29-30

36 DO 35/1356, Walwyn to Cranborne, 11 October, 1943.

37 *Acts of the Commission of Government*, 1944, pp. 52-61.

38 See Lewis and Shrimpton, "Policymaking in Newfoundland during the 1940s," pp. 209-39.

39 *Acts of the Commission of Government*, 1944, pp. 132-41, 142-53.

40 Ibid., pp. 122-4, 274-89, 290-375; *Acts of the Commission of Government*, 1943, pp. 22-52.

41 NRC, RG 84, vol. 11, 1943, Puddester to Brooks, 28 July 1943.

42 The account that follows is based on Nicholson, "Our Fighting Forces in World War II," and his *More Fighting Newfoundlanders*.

43 *ET*, 6 August, 1985, p.3.

44 Outerbridge, "Churchill and Roosevelt in Newfoundland," p. 436

45 Nicholson, "Our Fighting Forces in World War II," pp. 499-502

46 *ET*, 9 December 1942, pp. 3-4.

47 See ibid., 16 July 1941, p. 7.

48 For a summary of Davies's career, see ibid., 6 April 1946, p.7.

49 Nicholson, *More Fighting Newfoundlanders*, p. 82.

50 See GN 38/S1-1, p. 857, 9 August, 1940

51 Nicholson, "Our Fighting Forces in World War II," p. 487.
52 See ibid., pp. 498-9.
53 NG, 16 March 1943, p. 1.
54 GN 38/S1-1, p. 1041, 16 December, 1941.
55 NG, 6 January 1942, p. 6.
56 GN 38/S1-1, p. 1053, 12 January, 1942.
57 NAC, RG 24, Fraser, "History," pp. 88-9.
58 *ET*, 10 January 1942, p. 11.
59 Ibid., 31 January 1942, p. 6.
60 For an account of his career, see NRC, RG 84, vol. 8, 1941, 844.
61 NG, 28 July 1941, pp. 1-2.
62 Ibid., 16 December 1941, p. 1.
63 GN 38/S1-1, p. 1044, 19 December 1941.
64 Ibid., p. 1539, 9 March 1945; GN 38/S4-1-2-, file 7, memo by Haig-Smith, 27 January 1945, attached to memo by Commissioner for Justice and Defence, 31 January 1945.
65 GN 38/S4-1-2, file 7, memo by Haig-Smith, 27 January 1945.
66 NG, 31 December 1942, pp. 1-2; *ET*, 2 January 1943, p. 5. For Hopper's views see, for example, NRC, RG 84, vol. 11, 1942, Hopper to SSW, 13 April 1942; NA, RG 59, 843.00/136, Hopper to SSW, 9 February 1943; 843.00/137, Hopper to SSW, 13 March 1943. Coupon rationing was an already well-established feature of life in Canada and the United States. See Wartime Information Board, *Canada at War*, p. 147, and Polenberg, *War and Society*, p. 32.
67 See various orders in the NG, 1943-44.
68 Ibid., 11 May 1943, pp. 6-7; 29 June 1943, pp. 1-2.
69 Ibid., 31 August 1943, p. 3.
70 PANL, HC 117N4, "Abbreviated Annual Report for the year 1943," pp. 1-2.
71 GN 38/S1-1, p. 1392, 31 March 1944.
72 PANL, HC 117N4, "Abbreviated Annual Report for the year 1944," p. 34.
73 Galbraith, *A Life in Our Times*, p. 172.
74 NRC, RG 84, vol. 9, 1942, Doyle to Hopper, 30 November 1943.
75 Ibid. Hopper to Doyle, 3 December 1943.
76 Cmd. 6849, p. 21.
77 GN 38/S1-1, p. 1085, 11 April 1942.
78 Ibid., p. 1188, 6 November 1942.
79 NG, 11 August 1942, p. 3.
80 GN 38/S1-1, p. 865, 30 August 1940.
81 Ibid., p. 909, 13 December 1940.
82 Ibid., p. 1011, 26 September 1941.
83 Ibid., p. 1028, 12 November 1941.
84 Ibid., pp. 1036-7, 29 November 1941.

85 Ibid. Those the government initially decided to ask to serve were John Boyd Baird, K.M. Brown, A.F. Buffett, W.R. Dawe, Gerald S. Doyle, Professor R. Duder, Harold Earle, Cyril F. Horword, Hon. Harold Macpherson, James McIntyre, F.M. O'Leary, Leonard Outerbridge, Calvert C. Pratt and James Stowe. The representatives of Corner Brook and Grand Falls decided upon later were H.M.S. Lewin and J.C. Fitzgerald of the former place and L.R. Cooper and A.G. Duggan of the latter (ibid., pp. 1044-5, 19 December 1941). Duggan was a founding father of the Newfoundland Federation of Labour.
86 Ibid., pp. 1036-7, 29 November 1941.
87 Ibid., p. 1211, 6 January 1943; DO 35/1156/N718/1, "Review of the Dominions Press," Series E, No. 180, 16 April 1943, "Newfoundland's Post-War Planning."
88 GN 38/S1-1, p. 1090, 18 April 1942.
89 Orwell and Angus, *Collected Essays, Journalism and Letters of George Orwell*, p. 113.
90 Bridle, *Documents*, 1, p. 496, HCN to SSEA, 12 October 1942. For a detailed account of the negotiation of the Goose Bay agreement, see my "The Diplomatic Background."
91 GN 38/S1-1 p. 117, 10 October 1941. For the Canadian draft, see Bridle, *Documents*, 1, pp. 493-6.
92 For the minutes of the meeting which was held on 26 January 1942, see Bridle, *Documents*, 1 pp. 498-504.
93 Ibid., p. 509, Govr. to SSD, 6 February 1943.
94 Ibid.
95 For the Newfoundland draft, see Bridle, *Documents*, 1, pp. 505-8, encl. in Woods to Burchell, 2 February 1943.
96 Ibid.
97 Ibid., p. 508-10, Govr. to SSD, 6 February 1943.
98 DO 35/1375/665/5, Woods to Clutterbuck, 17 June 1943.
99 DO 35/1356, Walwyn to Cranborne, 11 October 1943.
100 Bridle, *Documents*, 1 p. 514, No. 226, SSD to Govr., 14 May 1943.
101 Ibid., pp. 523-4, HCUK to SSEA, 15 September 1943.
102 Ibid., pp. 522-3, HCUK to SSD, 25 August 1943.
103 Ibid., pp. 523-4, HCUK to SSEA, 15 September 1943.
104 DO 35/1375/665/5, minute by Clutterbuck, 23 October 1943.
105 Bridle, *Documents*, 1, pp. 534-6, HCN to Commissioner for Public Utilites, 30 December 1943.
106 Bridle, *Documents*, 1, p. 542, memo from HCUK to USSEA [10 March 1944].
107 Ibid., pp. 543-5, memo from USSEA to HCC, 27 June 1944.
108 DO 35/1376/N665/35, tel. to DO from HCC, 17 August 1944.
109 Bridle, *Documents*, 1 pp. 545-7, SSD to Govr., 23 August 1944.

110 Ibid., p. 549, HCN to SSEA, 10 October 1944.
111 Ibid., pp. 549-51, HCN to SSEA, 23 October 1944.
112 *ET*, 4 November 1944, p. 3.
113 Ibid., 17 November 1944, pp. 2, 12
114 Bridle, *Documents*, 1, pp. 554-5, HCN to SSEA, 2 December 1944.
115 Ibid., p. 557, HCN to SSEA, 15 January 1944.
116 Ibid., pp. 555-6, memo from Legal Adviser to Special Counsellor to USSEA, 18 December 1944.
117 DO 35/1363/N516/8, Woods to Clutterbuck 23 February 1944.
118 See Bridle *Documents*, 1 pp. 478-80, Burchell to Reid, 30 October 1943; pp. 787-90, Winter to Read, 2 May 1945.
119 Ibid., pp. 774-5, memo from Department of External Affairs to Cabinet War Committee.
120 Canada had, however, been promised in 1941 that if the Admiralty ever considered "relinquishing title and control of the Naval Base and shore facilities," the Royal Canadian Navy would be consulted first. See Bridle, *Documents*, 1 p. 591, MacDonald to Pearson, 6 September 1941.
121 Ibid., pp. 623-4, SSD to Govr., 27 October 1943; DO 35/1369/N517/13, Dixon to Garner, 29 October 1943 and minute by Clutterbuck, 3 June 1943.
122 NRC, RG 84, vol. 13, 1943, Hopper to SSW, 3 June 1943.
123 DO 114/111, p. 48, desp. from GN, 15 October 1945.
124 Ibid.
125 Ibid.
126 DO 35/1736, Walwyn to Machtig, 4 March 1944.
127 This account is based on ibid, note encl. in Machtig to Walwyn, 27 January 1944 and CAB 122/85, 55A, Govr. to Viscount Halifax, 9 May 1942.
128 DO 114/111, p. 26, tel. to GN, 14 May 1943.
129 Ibid., tel. from GN, 11 May 1943.
130 Ibid., p. 27, tel. from GN, 1 June 1943.
131 GN 38/S4-1-2, file 5, Emerson memo, 17 May 1943.
132 DO 114/111, pp. 29-30, DO to FO, 14 August 1944.
133 Ibid., p. 33 United States Embassy, London, to FO, 6 February 1945.
134 Ibid., tel. from GN, 27 August 1942
135 Ibid., tel. from GN, 2 November 1943
136 Ibid., p. 35, tel. from GN, 25 November 1942
137 NRC, RG 84, vol. 13, memo of conversation 15 January 1943. Clara L. Borjes, a State Department divisional assistant, was also present at this meeting.
138 DO 114/111, pp. 38-9, desp. from GN, 27 February 1943.
139 Ibid., p. 39, tel. to GN, 30 April 1943.
140 Ibid., p. 40, tel. to GN, 5 June 1943.

141 NRC, RG 84, vol. 1, 1941, Moffat to Hopper, 23 August 1941.
142 Ibid., Hopper to Emerson, 19 December 1941.
143 Ibid., vol. 6, 1941, Hopper to SSW, 15 January 1942.
144 Ibid.
145 GN 38/S1-1, p. 1228, 12 February 1943.
146 Ibid., and NA, RG 59, 843.00/136, Hopper to SSW, 9 February 1943.
147 NA, RG 59, 843.00/1-645, Hopper to SSW, 6 January 1945; 843.00/142, Hopper to SSW, 15 December 1943; 843.00/134, Hopper to SSW, 19 December 1942. The examples given here are selective.
148 NRC, RG 84, vol. 11, 1942, Hopper to SSW, 26 February, 1942.
149 NA, RG 59, 843.00/149, Hopper to SSW, 8 April 1944.
150 Ibid., 843.00/142 Hopper to SSW, 15 December 1943; NRC, RG 84, vol. 14, 1943, Brooks to Hopper, 7 October 1943.
151 NRC, RG 84, vol. 10, 1942, Hand to Secretary for Home Affairs, 25 February 1942.
152 Ibid., vol. 11, 1942, Hopper to SSW, 27 May 1942.
153 Ibid., vol. 10, 1942, Hopper to Meaden, 7 February 1942; vol. 11, 1942, Caldwell to Hopper, 9 September 1942 and Hopper to Hutchings, 25 September 1942.
154 For the order issued in Newfoundland, see NA, RG 59, 811.22/381, encl. in Hickerson to Henry, 27 March 1944. The order was issued under the authority of War Department Circular No. 305 of 8 September 1942.
155 NA, RG 59, 843.00/126, Hopper to SSW, 15 January 1942; NRC, RG 84, vol. 11, 1942, Hopper to Hutchings, 25 September 1942.
156 NA, RG 59, 811.22/386, Hopper to SSW, 21 April 1944.
157 Ibid.
158 NA, RG 59, 811.22/374B, memo from the Canadian Legation, Washington, 3 January 1944; 811.22/381, memo of conversation, 24 March 1944.
159 Ibid., 811.22/386, Hopper to SSW, 21 April 1944.
160 See, for example, NRC, RG 84, vol. 2, 1941, Quarton to SSW, "Semi-annual report on the purpose, object and results of representation allotment," 8 July 1941.
161 DO 35/1376, Walwyn to Machtig, 4 March 1944.
162 DO 114/111, pp. 46-9, desp. from GN, 15 October 1945.
163 DO 35/1736, notes encl. in Machtig to Walwyn, 27 January 1941.

CHAPTER EIGHT

1 DO 114/103, 1, pp. 1-2, SSD to GN, 25 November 1942.
2 Ibid. pp. 2-5, GN to SSD, 15 January 1943.
3 Ibid.
4 See DO 35/1343/N402/32, Cranborne to Attlee, 13 November 1944 and encl. "Lectures to Newfoundlanders serving in the United Kingdom on

local and parliamentary government."

5 DO 114/103, 1, p. 5-6, tel. to GN, 17 March 1943.

6 Ibid.

7 Ibid., p. 15, tel. to GN, 5 May 1943; DO 35/1333/N402/1/2, SSD to GN, 11 June 1943.

8 DO 114/103, 1, p. 17, tel. from GN, 21 June 1943; DO 35/1336/N402/1/10, "Report on Newfoundland by the Chairman of the Parliamentary Mission."

9 DO 35/1334/N402/1/8, Gunston and Herbert to Chadwick, 10 September 1943.

10 Ibid. For the reports of Ammon and Gunston, see DO 35/1336/N402/1/10.

11 DO 114/103, 1, pp. 18-19, 22, 25, tels. to GN, 8, 13 November, 3 December 1943; tels. from GN, 31 October, 25 November 1943.

12 For reaction in the Dominions Office, see DO 35/1339/N402/1/13.

13 Their constitutional recommendations are summarized in DO 35/1335/N402/1/9.

14 DO 35/1142/1/12, note, 8 December 1943.

15 DO 35/1335/N402/1/9.

16 DO 35/1356, Walwyn to Cranborne, 11 October 1943.

17 There is a copy of Cranborne's memorandum in DO 35/1337/N402/1/11.

18 Ibid.

19 This is also in ibid.

20 Ibid., "War Cabinet 158 (43), Extract from Conclusions of a Meeting held on Friday, 19th November, 1943, at 12 Noon."

21 *Parliamentary Debates* (Commons), 5th ser., 345 (1943-44), cols. 599-600.

22 DO 114/103, 1, 32-4., tel. to GN, 6 January 1944.

23 Ibid., pp. 19-20, tel. to GN, 19 November 1943, 32.

24 Ibid., pp. 32-4, tel. to GN, 6 January 1944.

25 Ibid., p. 34.

26 Ibid., pp. 35-7, tel. from GN, 12 February 1944.

27 Ibid.

28 DO 35/1338/N402/1/11, Walwyn to Clutterbuck, 13 February 1944.

29 DO 114/103, 1, p. 38, SSD to GN, 14 March 1944.

30 Ibid., p. 41, DO to GN, 18 May 1944; p. 45, SSD to GN, 1 August 1944.

31 Ibid., p. 42, SSD to GN, 18 May 1944 and GN to SSD, 25 May 1944.

32 Ibid., p. 44, SSD to GN, 7 June 1944.

33 DO 35/1142/N402/31, "Second Meeting with the Newfoundland Commissioners held at the Dominions Office at 3 P.M. on Tuesday August 8th."

34 Ibid., "Third Meeting with the Newfoundland Commissioners held at the Dominions Office at 10:30 a.m. on Thursday August 10th."

35 DO 35/1342/N402/29, Appendix B to note, "Newfoundland."

36 See DO 35/1342/N402/31, "Third Meeting with the Newfoundland Commissioners."

37 DO 114/103, 1, p. 46, tel. from GN, 31 August 1944.

38 Ibid., pp. 46-7, tel. from GN, 6 September 1944.

39 Ibid., p. 48, tel. to GN, 13 September 1944.

40 Ibid., pp. 49-51, desp. from GN, 25 September 1944.

41 The word "unlikely" comes from Gwyn, *Smallwood: The Unlikely Revolutionary*.

42 DO 35/1342/N402/29, "Summary of Outline Reconstruction Programme Covering a Period of Ten Years." See also, "Summary of Proposals Contained in Reconstruction Scheme." Housing in the capital was provided for by the St. John's Housing Corporation.

43 DO 114/103, 1, p. 45, tel. from GN, 28 July 1944.

44 Ibid. p. 46, tel. from GN, 31 August 1944.

45 Ibid., p. 45, tel. from GN, 15 August 1944.

46 Ibid., p. 47, tel. from GN, 6 September 1944.

47 DO 35/1342/N402/29, p. 179, note, "Newfoundland."

48 DO 114/103, 1, p. 46, tel. from GN, 31 August 1944; p. 48, tel. to GN, 13 September 1944; DO 35/1342/N402/29, "Sequence of Events," August 1944.

49 DO 35/1342/N402/29, note, "Newfoundland."

50 For the Treasury view, see DO 35/1343/N402/32, "Newfoundland, Joint Note by Treasury and Dominions Office."

51 T 220/60, Keynes note, 18 December 1944.

52 DO 35/1343/N402/32, "Newfoundland, Joint Note by Treasury and Dominions Office."

53 DO 35/1343/N402/32, Cranborne to Anderson, 19 January 1945.

54 DO 114/103, 1, pp. 52-3, tel. to GN, 19 January 1945; p. 55, tel. to HCC, 29 January 1945.

55 Ibid., p. 56, tel. from GN, 15 May 1945 and tel. to GN, 7 June 1945.

56 T 220/60, tel. from Cranborne to Machtig, 14 June 1945.

57 DO 35/1334/N402/39, Addison to Dalton, 15 August 1945.

58 Ibid., Dalton to Addison, 30 August 1945.

59 DO 35/1343/N402/32, "Newfoundland, Joint Note by Treasury and Dominions Office," and tel. from HCC, 9 December 1944.

60 DO 35/1347/N402/54, "Report by Mr. Clutterbuck," Appendix D, "Newfoundland, Memorandum by the Secretary of State for Dominion Affairs."

61 Ibid.

62 Ibid. "Newfoundland, Memorandum by the Secretary of State for Dominion Affairs."

63 DO 35/1345/N402/43, "Extract From: *C.M. (45) 48th Conclusions*."

64 See DO 35/1342/N402/29, Cranborne to Attlee, 19 October 1944; DO 35/1343/N402/32, note by Clutterbuck, 6 November 1944.
65 DO 35/1344/N402/39, Attlee to SSD, 7 September 1945.
66 DO 35/1345/N402/43, "Extract From: *C.M. (45) 48th Conclusions.*"
67 Ibid., "Newfoundland, Memorandum by the Secretary of State for Dominion Affairs," 21 November 1945.
68 Ibid., "*C.M. (45) 56th Conclusions.*"
69 Ibid., "Newfoundland, Memorandum by the Secretary of State for Dominion Affairs," 21 November 1945.
70 *Parliamentary Debates* (Commons), 5th ser., 417 (1945-46), cols. 210-11; (Lords), 5th ser., 138 (1945-46), cols. 541-5.
71 *Parliamentary Debates* (Lords), 5th ser., 138 (1945-46), col. 542.
72 Ibid., col. 543.
73 Ibid., col. 544.
74 Ibid., and *Parliamentary Debates*, (Commons), 5th ser., 417 (1945-46) col. 211.
75 DO 114/103, 1, p. 68, tel. to GN, 26 February 1946; p. 71, tel. to GN, 31 May 1946. Wheare was the author of *Federal Government* (London 1946).
76 Cmd. 6849.
77 *Acts of the Commission of Government*, 1946, pp. 108-206.
78 NA, RG 59, 843.00/123, Hopper to SSW, 13 November 1941.
79 Ibid., 843.00/139, Hopper to SSW, 2 April 1943.
80 Ibid., 843.00/141, Reed to SSW, 5 June 1943.
81 Ibid., 843.00/137, Hopper to SSW, 13 March 1943.
82 Ibid., 843.00/9-1544, Hopper to SSW, 15 September 1944.
83 DO 35/1356, Walwyn to Cranborne, 11 October 1943.
84 See, for example, the interview with John S. Currie, of the *DN* in the *Montreal Gazette*, 3 October 1944, pp. 13-14.
85 DO 114/103, 1, p. 1, tel. to GN, 25 November 1942.

CHAPTER NINE

1 *NG*, 4 June 1946, p. 2; *ET*, 4 June 1946 p. 3.
2 NAC, RG 24, Fraser, "History," pp. 430-40; *ET*, 3 November 1945, p. 7. The figures of the Department of Defence were subdivided as follows: Males: Royal Navy, 3,419; Royal Artillery, 2,343; Royal Air Force, 713; Canadian Forces (estimate), 660; Females: Women's Royal Canadian Naval Service, 74; Canadian Women's Army Corps, 190; Royal Canadian Air Force (Women's Division), 260. In a letter dated 6 March 1987, J.R. Walsh, Sub Regional Director (Nfld.), Veterans Affairs Canada, provided "the following record of enlistments for all branches of the service as obtained from Nominal Rolls in this office":

Royal Artillery, 2,390; Royal Navy, 3,232; Royal Air Force, 734; Nfld. Regiment (Militia), 1,668; Nfld. Overseas Forestry Corps, 3,596.

3 *Eleventh Census of Newfoundland and Labrador 1945*, 1, p. 1.

4 *ET*, 15 March 1945, pp. 2, 5, 7.

5 This was published by the Division of Civil Re-establishment, 1945.

6 *ET*, 15 March 1945, p. 2.

7 DO 114/103, 2, p. 39, desp. from GN, 3 March 1945.

8 The changes noted here can be traced in the minutes of the Commission of Government, the appropriate volumes of the British *Who Was Who*, and DO 114/103, pt. 2, "Miscellaneous," pp. 49-60, "Commission of Government: Appointment of Commissioners." London came to Newfoundland from the Gold Coast. Neill had been administrator of Dominica since 1938. Flinn had been colonial secretary of Jamaica since 1942 and acting governor there in 1943. James was another Treasury official. See also Appendix One.

9 *ET*, 17 January 1946, p. 3.

10 *NG*, 7 May 1946, p. 1; 14 May 1946, p. 1.

11 DO 114/103, 1, pp. 64-5, Clutterbuck to Walwyn, 16 January 1946.

12 Ibid., p. 67, Emerson to Clutterbuck, 18 February 1946.

13 Ibid., p. 67-8, tel. to GN, 20 February 1946.

14 Ibid., pp. 69-70, desp. from GN, 15 April 1946.

15 Ibid., pp. 76-7.

16 Ibid., pp. 75-6, Tait to Wild, 6 July 1946.

17 Ibid., pp. 78-9, Wild to Tait, 26 July 1946.

18 Ibid., p. 82, "Memorandum by the Commission of Government: Reconstruction and Development Schemes."

19 Ibid., pp. 78-9, Wild to Tait, 26 July 1946.

20 Ibid., pp. 80-1, Syers to Wild, 23 August 1946.

21 Ibid.

22 *ET*, 22 April 1946, p. 7.

23 Ibid., 8 May 1947, p. 20.

24 Ibid., 30 April 1948, p. 15.

25 *Acts of the Commission of Government*, 1948, pp. 10-27.

26 *ET*, 30 April 1948, p. 14.

27 Ibid., p. 15.

28 DO 114/103, 2, pp. 78-9, "Rehabilitation and Post-War Planning Committee," 17 December 1942.

29 Ibid., p. 79.

30 Ibid., pp. 77-8, desp. from GN, 9 January 1943.

31 Ibid., pp. 80-1, "Memorandum for consideration of Commission of Government by Commissioner for Natural Resources: Reorganization of Fisheries."

32 Ibid.

33 Ibid., pp. 93-4, tel. to GN, 23 April 1943.
34 Ibid., pp. 94-5, tel. from GN, 30 April 1943.
35 Ibid., pp. 81-2, Clutterbuck to Dunn, 16 June 1943.
36 Ibid., pp. 83-6, Dunn to Clutterbuck, 9 July 1943.
37 Ibid., pp. 86-7, Clutterbuck to Wilcox, 18 October 1943.
38 Ibid., p. 87.
39 Ibid., p. 89, Wilcox to Clutterbuck, 4 November 1943.
40 Ibid., p. 90, Clutterbuck to Dunn, 2 December 1943.
41 Alexander, *The Decay of Trade*, p. 34.
42 Ibid., p. 33.
43 DO 114/103, 2, pp. 107-13, desp. from GN, 28 April 1941.
44 Ibid., pp. 116-17, desp. from GN, 29 March 1944.
45 *Acts of the Commission of Government*, 1944, pp. 72-89.
46 DO 114/103, 2, p. 119, tel. to GN, 2 September 1944.
47 *ET*, 30 April 1948, p. 15.
48 *Acts of the Commission of Government*, 1944, pp. 320-46.
49 GN 38/S1-1, p. 1689, 15 March 1946.
50 Ibid., p. 1800, 29 November 1946.
51 Ibid., p. 1857, 28 March 1947; *NG*, 1 April 1947, p. 4.
52 GN 38/S1-1, p. 1941, 17 October 1947; p. 2096, 30 September 1948.
53 *Acts of the Commission of Government*, 1947, pp. 313-19.
54 See GN 38/S1-1, p. 1829, 1 February 1947.
55 *ET*, 12 November 1948, p. 1.
56 GN 38/S1-1, p. 2101, 8 October 1948.
57 DO 114/103, 2, pp. 64-5, tel. from GN, 9 November 1946; *ET*, 12 November 1946, p. 3.
58 See *Report of Commission of Enquiry into the Cost of Living*, p. 1. Smith's commission colleagues were Herbert R. Brookes of Harvey and Company; Eric Cook and James A. Gibbs, both lawyers; and the trade unionist, C.W. Strong.
59 DO 114/103, 2, pp. 131-2, desp. from GN, 1 September 1945.
60 Christopher Brewin, "British Plans for International Operating Agencies for Civil Aviation, 1941-1945," p. 91.
61 DO 114/79, p. 47, Massey to Attlee, 24 October 1942. For a detailed account of Canadian civil aviation policy through the war, see Bothwell and Granatstein, "Canada and the Wartime Negotiations over Civil Aviation."
62 CAB 104/232, "Civil Air Transport. British Commonwealth Conversations. List of Delegates, Advisers, Observers and Secretariat," 9 October 1943, p. 3.
63 For a full account of this venture and of the ideas behind it, see NA, RG 59, 843.796/17, Hopper to SSW, 25 April 1944; 843.796/20, Hopper to SSW, 19 May 1944; 843.796/9-2144, Hopper to SSW, 21 September 1944.

64 Bridle, *Documents*, 1, pp. 1091-2, SSD to Govr., 19 May 1944.
65 GN 38/S1-1, pp. 1481-2, 13 October 1944; NRC, RG 84, 1945, 864-891, report by Hopper on "Civil Aviation in Newfoundland," 6 June 1945.
66 This account is based on CAB 104/233, memo by the Minister of Civil Aviation, 3 September 1945.
67 For London's report to the Commission on the Chicago conference, see GN 1/8/5, 1944, Public Utilities and Supply 147(h)–44. For the status of the Newfoundland party at the Chicago talks, see DO 114/102, "1943-1944 Civil Aviation: Correspondence and Papers," p. 165, tel. from GN, received 23 December 1944.
68 GN 38/S1-1, p. 1481, 13 October 1944.
69 GN 1/8/5, 1944, Public Utilities and Supply 147(h)–44.
70 Ibid., pp. 13-14.
71 DO 114/102, p. 162, tel. from HCC, 8 December 1944.
72 Ibid., pp. 163-4, tel. to GN, 9 December 1944.
73 CAB 104/233, minute by Churchill, 14 January 1945.
74 PREM 4/5/7, Churchill to Lord President of the Council, Lord Privy Seal, 24 December 1944.
75 See CAB 104/233, minutes of a meeting held in the Lord President's Room, 29 December 1944.
76 See DO 114/102, pp. 163-5.
77 Ibid., p. 165, tel. from GN, 22 December 1944.
78 Ibid., pp. 149-50, encl. in desp. from GN, 19 January 1945.
79 AVIA 2/2285, "Newfoundland," memo by W.P. Hildred, 17 July 1945.
80 DO 114/109, "1945-1951, Civil Aviation: Further Correspondence and Papers," p. 47, Hudd to Addison, 5 September 1945.
81 For a list of the Canadian and Newfoundland delegations, see DO 35/1110/A201/54, memo on the Bermuda civil aviation talks by the Minister of Civil Aviation, 8 January 1946.
82 Bridle, *Documents*, 1, p. 1110, Govr. to SSD, 7 December 1945.
83 DO 35/1110/A201/59, Winster to Addison, 27 December 1945.
84 See DO 114/109, pp. 48-50, "Bermuda Civil Aviation Conservations: Summary of Conclusions and Recommendations."
85 Ibid.
86 AVIA 2/2285, "Newfoundland," memo by W.P. Hildred, 17 July 1945.
87 For a list of the delegations to the conference, see DO 114/109, p. 155, "Newfoundland Air Conference: Notes of Proceedings by Mr. G.W. St. J. Chadwick, Dominions Office."
88 DO 35/1378/N665/55, pp. 3-4, minutes.
89 DO 114/109, pp. 153-4, "Military Use of Newfoundland Bases," encl. in AIR to DO, 28 January 1946.

90 Ibid.
91 Ibid., p. 152, tel. from GC, 21 January 1946.
92 DO 35/1378/N665/55, minute by Chadwick. For the arrangement between Canada and Newfoundland about Bay Bulls, see Bridle, *Documents*, 1, p. 606, Commissioner for Public Utilities to HCN, 24 August 1942, and pp. 574-5, acting USSEA to deputy minister of national defence for naval service, 21 June 1945.
93 This account is based on DO 114/109, pp. 155-6, "Newfoundland Air Conference: Notes on Proceedings by Mr. G.W. St. J. Chadwick, Dominions Office."
94 Ibid.
95 For the agreement, see Bridle, *Documents*, 1, pp. 1418-21.
96 See DO 114/109, p. 156, tel. to GN, 28 March 1946.
97 For this, see Bridle, *Documents*, 1, pp. 1422-5.
98 DO 114/103, p. 145, Clutterbuck to Walwyn, 25 August 1946.
99 Ibid., p. 146, Walwyn to Clutterbuck, 18 September 1945.
100 Ibid., pp. 149-50, desp. to GN, 16 May 1946.
101 Ibid., pp. 151-2, desp. from GN, 22 August 1946; desp. to GN, 19 November 1946.
102 *Acts of the Commission of Government*, 1947, pp. 16-29.
103 DO 35/1359, Walwyn to Addison, 4 January 1946.
104 DO 35/1359/N516/26, Neill to Syers, 30 July 1946.
105 Ibid., "Gander Airport, Newfoundland: Note of Meeting ... 22nd May 1946."
106 DO 35/1359/N516/26, Neill to Syers, 30 July 1946.
107 Ibid., Wilson to Syers, 17 August 1946.
108 DO 35/3482, DO to GN, 5 February 1947.
109 Ibid., for copies of the minutes of these meetings.
110 DO 35/3464/N2005/81, memo "Union of Newfoundland with Canada."
111 NRC, RG 84, 1945, 864-891, Hopper "Memorandum of oral representations concerning air traffic," 13 August 1945.
112 See ibid., House to Hopper, 1 June 1945 and Macdonald to London, 21 August 1945.
113 NRC, RG 84, 1945, 864-891, Hopper "Memorandum of oral representations concerning air traffic," 13 August 1945.
114 For intimations of this, see my "The French and American Shore Questions," pp. 95-122.
115 Cmd. 6259, p. 8.
116 DO 35/1365/516/22, Walwyn to Addison, 31 August 1945.
117 *DN*, 24 October 1945, p. 3.
118 This account is based on NRC, RG 84, 864-891, memo by Robert J. Cavanaugh, 24 October 1945.
119 DO 114/109, pp. 157-8, "Memorandum: Newfoundland/United States

Base Fields Agreement," encl. in Macdonald to Machtig, 27 August 1947.

120 DO 35/3483/N2570/8, "Informal note on the use for civil aviation purposes of the leased bases," encl. in Maclean to Merchant, 15 April 1947.

121 DO 35-3482, tel. from BEW to FO, 16 April 1947.

122 NA, RG 59, 843.7962/5-2847, tels. from State Dept. to Consul, St. John's, 28 May 1947 and from Donald to State Dept., 30 May 1947.

123 See DO 35/3483/N2570/8, tel. from HCC to SSD, 28 May 1947; tel. from BEW to FO, 4 June 1947.

124 Ibid. tel. from SSD to GN, 10 April 1947.

125 Ibid., tel. from BEW to FO, 4 June 1947.

126 DO 114/109, pp. 157-8, "Memorandum: Newfoundland/United States Base Fields Agreement," encl. in Macdonald to Machtig, 27 August 1947.

127 DO 35/3483/N2570/8, note by Chadwick, "Newfoundland/U.S. Basefields Agreement," 15 August 1947.

128 DO 114/109, p. 160, tel. from GN, 18 October 1947; NA, RG 59, 811.34544/11-747, State Dept. to Consul, St. John's, et al, 7 November 1947.

129 This novel was published in London in 1948.

130 NA, RG 59, 843.00/7-2048, Abbott to Foster, 20 July 1948.

CHAPTER TEN

1 DO 35/1359, Walwyn to Cranborne, 30 June 1945; DO 35/1144/N412/3, Dunn to Clutterbuck, 28 July 1945. For Cashin's own account of his 1945 broadcasts, see his "My Fight for Responsible Government," pp. 111-12.

2 DO 35/1359, Walwyn to Cranborne, 30 June 1945.

3 DO 35/1144/N412/3, minute by Clutterbuck, 6 August 1945.

4 DO 35/1142/N402/38, encl. in Emerson to Cranborne, 19 July 1945.

5 *Report of Proceedings of the Ninth Annual Convention of the Newfoundland Federation of Labour*, p. 61.

6 DO 35/1142/N402/40, Thompson to Attlee, 4 October 1945.

7 Ibid., encl. in Walwyn to Addison, 6 November 1945.

8 DO 35/1142/N402/38, minute by Chadwick, 26 July 1945, and minute by Clutterbuck following.

9 *ET*, 12 December 1945, p. 2.

10 DO 35/1142/N402/40, Addison to administrator, 23 January 1946, and encls.

11 DO 35/1144/N412/3, Cashin to Attlee, 11 March 1946, with copy of petition encl. and Macdonald to Addison, 4 June 1946.

12 DO 35/1359, Walwyn to Addison, 4 January 1946.

13 *Acts of the Commission of Government*, 1946, pp. 108-206; *NG*, 21 May 1946, p. 1.

14 *NG*, 11 June 1946, p. 1; 23 July 1946, p. 1; DO 114/103, 1, p. 72, tel. from GN, 7 June 1946. The other districts where the election was delayed were White Bay and St. Barbe. The latter eventually produced a member by acclamation.

15 The information that follows about the election is taken from Smallwood, *Encyclopedia*, 1, pp. 719-21, and *NG*, 30 July 1946, p. 2. Nomination day for the districts that voted on 21 June was 31 May. See *NG*, 21 May 1946, p. 1.

16 They were Martha Hann in Humber and Frances Blaikie Holmes in St. John's City West.

17 For the appointments of Short and Halfyard, see *NG*, 21 May 1946, p. 1.

18 NA, RG 59, 843.00/7-1746, Donald to SSW, 17 July 1946.

19 DO 35/1349/N402/68, "Newfoundland-Constitutional Developments," encl. in Addison to Prime Minister, 4 November 1946.

19 DO 35/1349/N402/68, "Newfoundland-Constitutional Developments," encl. in Addison to Prime Minister, 4 November 1946.

20 DO 114/103, 1, p. 78, tel. from GN, 16 July 1946. Two members, Burry (Labrador)) and Newell (White Bay), who had yet to be elected, were not accounted for in this tabulation. The first was a United Church Minister and the second an adherent of the Church of England. I am grateful to Barbara Kelland of the CNS for this information about Newell.

21 See NA, RG 59, 843.00/4-846, Donald to SSW, 8 April 1946; 843.00/6-1046, Donald to SSW, 10 June 1946; 843.00/7-1746, Donald to SSW, 17 July 1946; Bill Gillespie, *A Class Act*, pp. 96-7.

22 Smallwood, *Encyclopedia*, 1, p. 720.

23 *DN*, 1 March 1946, pp. 4-5; 2 March, pp. 4-5; 4 March, pp. 4, 7; 5 March, pp. 4, 7; 6 March, pp. 4-5; 8 March, pp. 4, 9; 9 March, pp. 4-5; 11 March, pp. 4-5; 12 March, p. 4; 13 March, pp. 4, 7; 14 March, p. 5.

24 The account of Smallwood's career that follows is based mainly on his *I Chose Canada*, and Gwyn, *Smallwood: The Unlikely Revolutionary*.

25 This federation should not be confused with the present-day Newfoundland Federation of Labour which developed from the Newfoundland Trades and Labour Council formed in 1937.

26 *Coaker of Newfoundland* was published in London in 1927 by the Labour Publishing Company. *The New Newfoundland* was published in New York by the Macmillan Company.

27 GN 13/1, box 233, file 95, Bradley to Dunfield, 8 November 1935 and 2 May 1936.

28 Ibid., Bradley to Dunfield, 8 November 1936.
29 Ibid., Bradley to Dunfield, 2 May 1936.
30 Ibid., box 155, file 14, Mahoney to O'Neill, 5 March 1935. See also Mahoney's report in ibid, box 135, file 74, "Re: meeting convened by Reuben T. Vardy in Board of Trade Rooms last night," 4 February 1937. Here Mahoney writes of Smallwood as follows: "J.R. Smallwood was editor of the Humber Herald which is published in Corner Brook. I have known this man for eight years. He was a strong supporter of the Squires Government and was defeated in one election during the regime of that Government. He was made a J.P. during the Squires regime and later his commission was cancelled. Smallwood is a mysterious man, getting along so to say solely on his wits. Actually, I cannot say anything about him by way of a criminal nature, but he is what we usually term a 'shady' character. From time to time he has been associated with all these men who are opposed to Commission of Government. Reports were current that he misappropriated certain monies in connection with the Fisherman's Organization which he organized the last couple of years."
31 Vols. 3 and 4 of this work appeared in 1967 and vols 5 and 6 in 1975.
32 See Peter Narváez, "Joseph R. Smallwood, 'The Barrelman,'" pp. 60-78.
33 Newfoundland, Registry of Deeds, Companies and Securities, "The Express Publishing Company, Limited. Memorandum of Association."
34 There is a complete run of the paper in the Newfoundland Division of the Provincial Reference and Resource Library, Arts & Culture Centre, St. John's, Newfoundland.
35 The other fictional members of the government were "The Ommissioner for Finance and Bust 'em," "The Ommissioner for Public Humilities," "The Ommissioner for Public Wealth," "The Ommissioner for Unknown Affairs and Speculation," and "The Ommissioner for Just What."
36 DO 114/103, 1, p. 73, tel. from GN, 22 June 1946.
37 NRC, RG 84, 350-811.11, Parsons to Donald, 21 May 1946.
38 *Acts of the Commission of Government*, 1946, p. 115-16.
39 *NG*, 21 May 1946, p. 1.
40 *Acts of the Commission of Government*, 1946, p. 115.
41 GN 38/S1-1, p. 1747, 9 August 1946.
42 *Acts of the Commission of Government*, 1946, p. 116.
43 GN 38/S1-1, p. 1747, 9 August 1946.
44 *NG*, 10 September 1946, p. 1.
45 GN 38/S1-1, p. 1765-6, 13 September 1946.
46 Ibid., p. 1768, 20 September 1946; *ET*, 18 September 1946, p. 3.
47 GN 38/S1-1, p. 1771, 27 September 1946.
48 GN 10/C, box 2, "Precis of Minutes," National Convention, 20 September 1946; *ET*, 21 September 1946, p. 6.

49 GN 10/C, box 2, "Precis of Minutes," 12, 17 September 1946.
50 Ibid., 20 September 1946.
51 The mechanics of the Convention are described in NA, RG 59, 843.00/10-446, Donald to SSW, 4 October 1946.
52 I am grateful to Philip Hiscock of the Folklore Archive, Memorial University, St. John's, for this information.
53 Ibid.
54 These reports are available in a 6 vol. set at the CNS(A). O'Dea, Alexander, *Bibliography of Newfoundland*, 1, p. 446, no. 2708.
55 *ET*, 11 October 1946, pp. 3, 6, 7, 9.
56 NA, RG 59, 843.00/11-846, Donald to SSW, 8 November 1946.
57 Ibid; see also *ET*, 29 October 1946, pp. 2-3, 6.
58 GN 10/C, box 2, "Precis of Minutes," 28 October 1946.
59 Bridle, *Documents*, 2, pt. 1, pp. 262-3, Macdonald to MacKay, 29 June 1946.
60 Hume Wrong agreed with Macdonald but cautioned that Smallwood might "be too valuable a friend to risk antagonizing." See ibid., p. 264, Wrong to Macdonald, 4 July 1946.
61 Smallwood, *I Chose Canada*, p. 565.
62 See MacKay, "Smallwood's visit to Ottawa," pp. 230-2.
63 CNS(A), Collection of National Convention Proceedings, 28 October 1946.
64 GN 10/A, box 1, National Convention Proceedings, September–December 1946, file 13.
65 GN 10/C, box 2, "Precis of Minutes," 28 October 1946.
66 Ibid., 5 November 1946.
67 DO 35/1349/N402/68, Addison to Prime Minister, 4 November 1946.
68 GN 10/C, box 2, "Precis of Minutes," 5 November 1946.
69 DO 35/1335/N402/71, "Memorandum for His Excellency the Governor," by K.C. Wheare, 6 November 1946, encl. in Macdonald to Addison, 7 November 1946.
70 Bridle, *Documents*, 2, pt. 1, pp. 316-17, Macdonald to Acting SSEA, 4 November 1946.
71 Ibid., pp. 322-3, Macdonald to SSEA, 7 November 1946.
72 NA, RG 59, 843.00/11-846, Donald to SSW, 8 November 1946.
73 Ibid.
74 DO 114/103, 1, p. 84, tel. from GN, 17 November 1946.
75 Ibid., p. 85, tel. from GN, 27 November 1946.
76 Ibid., p. 84, tel. from GN, 21 November 1946.
77 Ibid., p. 85, tel. to GN, 2 December 1946.
78 *Acts of the Commission of Government*, 1946, p. 481.
79 GN 38/S1-1, p. 1803, 6 December 1946; DO 114/103, 1, p. 86, tel. from GN, 14 December 1946; GN 10/C, box 2, "Precis of Minutes," 11 December 1946.

80 The history of the Tourist Board is nicely summarized in NA, RG 59, 843.00/12-2746, Donald to SSW, 27 December 1946.

81 DO 114/103, 1, p. 86, tel. from GN, 14 December 1946.

82 GN 10/C, box 2, "Precis of Minutes," 12 December 1946.

83 The author heard this phrase used by a resident of Freshwater, Placentia Bay, on 2 May 1986, during one of the sessions of the conference on "Newfoundland in the Era of the Commission of Government." This conference was held in St. John's, Markland, Argentia, and Freshwater, 30 April–2 May 1986.

84 NA, RG 59, 843.00/1-847, Donald to SSW, 8 January 1947.

85 GN 38/S1-1, p. 1804, 6 December 1946.

86 This account is based on NA, RG 59, 843.00/1-1447, Donald to SSW, 14 January 1947 and encls.

87 The other members of the original sponsoring group were James S. Ayre, president of Ayre & Sons Ltd.; Lewis Ayre, a director of the same firm; Harold Mitchell, president of J.B. Mitchell & Sons, Ltd.; Hon. Harold Macpherson, president of the Royal Stores; Eric White, managing director of the White Clothing Co.; W.R. Dawe, president, Dominion Command, Great War Veterans' Association; Hon. Judge Francis J. Morris; Robert J. Murphy, president, United Towns Electric Co. Ltd.; S. Richard Steele; Charles R. Bell, managing director, C.R. Bell, Ltd.; Walter Chafe, Mutual Life Insurance; R.C.B. Mercer; John S. Currie and Albert B. Perlin of the *Daily News*; and Charles Hunt.

88 See NA, RG 59, 843.00/1-1447, Donald to SSW, 14 January 1947 and encls.

89 Ibid.

90 For this see *ET*, 3 January 1947, p. 2.

91 Penson had spoken as follows: "There is one message to Newfoundland which I am definitely authorised to give. It is that: that when the present emergency is over the United States will be disposed to consider sympathetically the commercial relations between Newfoundland and herself with a view to the development of mutual trade. The Newfoundland Government of the day will be very willing, I feel assured, to co-operate in that study ... We are assured that the United States desires closer economic relations with Newfoundland and we hope the day may not be far distant when this prospect will be realized." See *ET*, 28 April 1941, p. 5.

92 GN 10/C, box 2, "Precis of Minutes," 8, 9, 10, 14, 15, January.

93 Ibid., 9 January 1947.

94 NA, RG 59, 843.00/2-147, Donald to SSW, 1 February 1947.

95 GN 10/C, box 2, "Precis of Minutes," 9 January 1947.

96 *ET*, 4 February 1947, p. 2; GN 10/C, box 2, "Precis of Minutes," 3 February, 1947.

97 DO 114/103, 2, p. 87, tel. from GN, 12 January 1947.
98 GN 10/C, box 2, "Precis of Minutes," 4 February 1947.
99 Ibid.
100 See NA, RG 59, 843.00/2-947, Donald to SSW, 9 February 1947.
101 GN 10/A, box 2, file 7, National Convention Proceedings, 4 February 1947.
102 *ET*, 5 February 1947, p. 3.
103 GN 10/C, box 2, "Precis of Minutes," 7 February 1947. The other members of the committee were T.W.G. Ashbourne (Twillingate), Issac Newell (White Bay) and Frank Fogwill (St. John's East).
104 GN 38/S1-1, p. 1834-5, 8 February 1947.
105 Ibid.
106 For a draft of the report, see DO 114/103, 1, p. 90, tel. from GN, 13 February 1947. For the motions, see GN 10/C, box 2, "Precis of Minutes," 28 February 1947.
107 GN 10/C, box 2, "Precis of Minutes," 10 March 1947. See also *ET*, 11 March 1947, p. 6.
108 GN 10/C, box 2, "Precis of Minutes," 19 March 1947.
109 *ET*, 14 March 1937, p. 3.
110 DO 35/3446/N2005/13, Wheare to Syers, 20 March 1947.
111 NA, RG 59, 843.00/5-547, Donald to SSW, 5 May 1947; *ET*, 18 April 1947, p. 2. For Cashin's own account of events see Wade, *Regionalism in the Canadian Community*, pp. 237-8.
112 GN 10/C, box 2, "Precis of Minutes," 1 April 1947; *ET*, 2 April 1947, p. 3. Because of an illness in his family, R.B. Job resigned from the delegation before it went to Ottawa. He was replaced by P. Wellington Crummey (Bay de Verde), an outport shopkeeper and one of the alternates elected in April. See Bridle, *Documents*, 2, pt. 1, p. 483.
113 NA, RG 59, 843.00/4-1247, Donald to SSW, 12 April 1947; GN 10/C, box 2, "Precis of Minutes," 11 April 1947.
114 NA, RG 59, 843.00/5-547, Donald to SSW, 5 May 1947; *ET*, 12 April 1947, p. 6. The others voting in favour of the motion were Figary (Burgeo) and Reddy (Burin East).
115 DO 35/3446/N2005/13, Wheare to Syers, 20 March 1947.
116 T 220/61, Lt. Col. W. Russell Edmunds, "Memorandum on visit of Newfoundland Delegation from the National Convention to discuss certain questions with the Dominions Secretary," 8 May 1947.
117 DO 114/103, 1, p. 97, tels. to GN, 15, 17 March; pp. 99-100, desp. from GN and encl., 27 March 1947.
118 For the British background material, see T 220/61 generally.
119 T 220/61, Russell Edmunds, "Memorandum on visit of Newfoundland Delegation from the National Convention," 8 May 1947. For the British

replies, see DO 114/103, 1, pp. 104-7, encl. (b) in desp. to GN, 15 May 1947.

120 T 220/61, "Memorandum submitted by the Newfoundland Delegation."

121 Ibid., Russell Edmunds, "Memorandum on visit of Newfoundland Delegation from the National Convention," 8 May 1947. For the statement, see DO 114/103, 1, 107-8, encl. (d) in desp. to GN, 15 May 1947.

122 T 220/61, Russell Edmunds "Memorandum on visit of Newfoundland Delegation from the National Convention," 8 May 1947.

123 Ibid.

124 T 220/61, "Memorandum with reference to section 3 of the Convention Act, 1946."

125 DO 114/103, 1, pp. 107-8, encl. (d) in desp. to GN, 15 May 1947.

126 See "In the News" by "Wayfarer" (A.B. Perlin), *DN*, 26 May 1947, p. 4; 28 May 1947, p. 4.

127 NRC, RG 84, file 800, 1947, Donald to SSW, 21 May 1947; *ET*, 20 May 1947, p. 3.

128 DO 114/103, 1, p. 108, desp. from GN, 22 May 1947.

129 Ibid., p. 109, encl. 1 in desp. from GN, 27 May 1947; *ET*, 23 May 1947, p. 2.

130 DO 114/103, 1, p. 109, Carew to Warren, 26 May 1947, encl. 2 in desp. from GN, 27 May 1947.

131 DO 114/103, 1, pp. 111-12, tel. from HCC, 26 June 1947.

132 NRC, RG 84, 1947, file 800, Donald to SSW, 21 May 1947; *DN*, 20 May 1947, p. 11.

133 NRC, RG 84, 1947, file 800, Harrington to Foster, 23 June 1947.

134 See, for example, DO 114/103, 1, pp. 96-7, tel. from HCC, 12 March 1947.

135 Bridle, *Documents*, 2, pt. 1, pp. 240-1, Wrong to Mackenzie, 7 May 1946; pp. 245-8, "Minutes of a Meeting of Interdepartmental Committee on Canadian-Newfoundland Relations.".

136 There is a set of the background memoranda, dated 16 October 1946, in NAC, R.A. MacKay Papers, MG 30 E159, vol. 2.

137 Bridle, *Documents*, 2, pt. 1, pp. 310-11, memo of Department of External Affairs, 30 October 1946.

138 Ibid., pp. 319-20, memo from secretary of the cabinet to USSEA.

139 Ibid., pp. 495-6, memo from secretary, Cabinet Committee on Newfoundland Relations, to cabinet.

140 Ibid., pp. 496-9.

141 Ibid.

142 Ibid., pp. 499-500, "Financial aspects of union with Newfoundland."

143 DO 114/103, 1, pp. 112-13, tel. from HCC, 4 July 1947.

144 Ibid., p. 115, tel. from HCC, 17 July; *ET*, 17 July 1947, p. 1.

145 DO 114/103, 1, p. 118, tel. from GN, 20 July 1947.
146 Ibid., pp. 120-1, tel. from HCC, 6 September 1947.
147 *The Mackenzie King Diaries 1932-1949*, 2 June 1947, microfiche 242, pp. 486-7.
148 Ibid., 18 July 1947, transcript/typescript 244, p. 644.
149 Dale C. Thomson, *Louis St. Laurent: Canadian* (Toronto 1967), p. 234.
150 DO 114/103, 1, pp. 120-1, tel. from HCC, 6 September 1947.
151 Bridle, *Documents*, 2, pt. 1, pp. 574-6, Press release of the Canadian Institute of Public Opinion.
152 Smallwood, *I Chose Canada*, p. 570.
153 For this message and the exchange that followed, see Bridle, *Documents*, 2, pt. 1, pp. 632-5, encls. in Britton to SSEA, 13 September 1947; *DN*, 11 September 1947, p. 3.
154 Bridle, *Documents*, 2, pt. 1, pp. 636-42, "Minutes of a meeting between the delegation to Ottawa from the National Convention of Newfoundland and Representatives of the Government of Canada."
155 Ibid., pp. 651-7, encl. to "Minutes of a meeting between the delegation to Ottawa from the National Convention of Newfoundland and Representatives of the Government of Canada."
156 GN 38/S1-1, p. 1989, 13 February 1948.
157 Bridle, *Documents*, 2, pt. 1, pp. 671-2, Macdonald to SSEA, 11 October 1947.
158 DO 114/103, 1, p. 125, tel. from GN, 12 October 1947.
159 *ET*, 16 October 1947, p. 1; 17 October 1947, p. 14.
160 Bridle, *Documents*, 2, pt. 1, p. 681, SSEA to HCN, 3 November 1947.
161 In 1945 Bridges had carried the riding by a plurality of 875. See Canada, *Twentieth General Election 1945: Report of the Chief Electoral Officer*, p. 489. In 1947 Gregg outpolled his two rivals combined by 604 votes. See Canada, *By-Elections held during the year 1947: Report of the Chief Electoral Officer*, p. 14.
162 Bridle, *Documents*, 2, pt. 1, pp. 682-3. Prime Minister to Govr. 29 October 1947.
163 DO 114/103, 1, pp. 128-30, desp. from HCC, 7 November 1947.
164 Bridle, *Documents*, 2, pt. 1, p. 723, HCN to SSEA, 6 November 1947; 736-7, extract from desp. from HCN to SSEA, 21 November 1947; *ET*, 21 November 1947, p. 2.
165 NA, RG 59, 843.00/1-548, Abbott to SSW, 5 January 1948.
166 GN 10/A, box 6, file for 5 January 1948.
167 NA, RG 59, 843.00/1-1248, Abbott to SSW, 12 January 1948.
168 *ET*, 16 January 1948, p. 2.
169 GN 10/C, box 2, "Precis of Minutes," 19 January 1948.
170 Ibid., 22 January 1948.
171 Ibid., 23 January 1948.

172 Ibid., 27 January 1948; *ET*, 28 January 1948, pp. 2, 11.

173 For this, see DO 114/103, 1, pp. 134-6.

174 The members of the drafting committee were Cashin (Convenor), Higgins, Butt, Smallwood, Ashbourne and Starkes. See Bridle, *Documents*, 2, pt. 1, p. 799.

175 See *ET*., 31 January 1948, p. 2.

176 NA, RG 59, 843.00/20548, Abbott to SSW, 5 February 1948.

CHAPTER ELEVEN

1 Bridle, *Documents*, 2, pt. 1, pp. 793-9.

2 Ibid., p. 819. See also NA, RG 59, 843.00/3-948, Abbott to SSW, 9 March 1948.

3 Smallwood, *I Chose Canada*, p. 283.

4 DO 114/103, 1, p. 143, desp. to GN, 2 March 1948.

5 *Acts of the Commission of Government*, 1948, p. 49.

6 DO 114/103, 1, p. 143, desp. to GN, 2 March 1948.

7 See ibid., pp. 137-8, tel. from HCC, 17 February 1948; DO 35/3456/N2005/51, Addison to the prime minister, 3 February 1948; NA, RG 59, 843.00/4-1248, Richardson to SSW, 12 April 1948.

8 DO 114/103, 1, p. 141, tel. to GN, 26 February 1948.

9 Ibid., p. 143, desp. to GN, 2 March 1948.

10 Ibid., p. 145, tel. from HCC, 11 March 1948.

11 Ibid., p. 143, desp. to GN, 2 March 1948.

12 *NG*, 11 May 1948, p. 2.

13 *Acts of the Commission of Government*, 1948, pp. 49-50.

14 *Acts of the Commission of Government*, 1947, pp. 305-8.

15 GN 38/S1-1, p. 2025, 21 April 1948.

16 *Acts of the Commission of Government*, 1948, pp. 62-7. For the second referendum, the number of districts with advance polls was increased to 17. See ibid., pp. 125-7.

17 Smallwood, *I Chose Canada*, p. 286.

18 Wade, *Regionalism in the Canadian Community*, pp. 249-51.

19 Stacey, "1000 days that changed our destiny," p. 136.

20 NA, RG 59., 843.00/10-2347, Millet to SSW, 23 October 1947; NA, RG 84, 1947, file 800, Snow to SSW, 24 July 1947; *ET*, 21 July 1947, p. 7; 20 September 1947, p. 27.

21 There is a large body of information on the League's financial affairs in the CNS(A), John G. Higgins Collection.

22 NA, RG 59, 843.00/4-548, Abbott to SSW, 5 April 1948.

23 Bridle, *Documents*, 2, pt. 1, p. 826 (Bridle minute); *The Monitor*, 15, no. 2 (February 1948), p. 4.

24 Bridle, *Documents*, 2, pt. 1, p. 851, Macdonald to SSEA, 24 March 1948.

25 NA, RG 59, 843.00/12-247, Abbott to SSW, 2 December 1947; *DN*, 25 November 1947, p. 5.

26 NA, RG 59, 843.00/3-948, Abbott to SSW, 9 March 1948. Jackman was refused access to the facilities of the government-owned Broadcasting Corporation of Newfoundland to promote his scheme but spoke over the privately owned VOCM, St. John's, on 7 and 11 February.

27 *ET*, 20 March 1948, pp. 3, 19.

28 Closely associated with Stirling was the golden-tongued Donald Jamieson, a future minister in the government of Canada.

29 NRC, RG 84, 1948, file 800, Abbott to SSW, 23 March 1948.

30 NA, RG 59, 843.7962/11-1048, Snow memo to Hickerson and Wailes, 10 November 1948.

31 NA, RG 59, FW843.628/10-2146, memo by J. Graham Parsons to Hickerson, 8 November 1946.

32 Ibid., memo by Hickerson to Parsons, 14 November 1946.

33 NRC, RG 84, 1948, file 800, circular newsletter no. 2 from Division of British Commonwealth Affairs, Department of State, 15 March 1948.

34 NRC, RG 59, 843.00/6-248, Abbott to SSW, 2 June 1948.

35 For a further expression of the United States' position in this period, see NRC, RG 84, 1948, file 800, memo by Abbott, 14 January 1948, encl. in Abbott to SSW, 16 January 1948.

36 NA, RG 59, 843.00/3-3048, Abbott to SSW, 30 March 1948.

37 NRC, RG 84, 1948, file 800, Abbott to SSW, 27 May 1948.

38 Ibid., Abbott to SSW, 28 May 1948. For Article 28, see Cmd. 6259, p. 13.

39 NA, RG 59, 843.00/5-1448, Abbott to SSW, 14 May 1948.

40 Bridle, *Documents*, 2, pt. 1, pp. 863-5, Macdonald to SSEA, 8 May 1948.

41 NA, RG 59, 843.00/5-1448, Abbott to SSW, 14 May 1948.

42 Ibid., 843.00/5-1948, memo by Andrew Foster on visit from Geoffrey Stirling, 24 May 1948.

43 Ibid., 843.00/6-248, Abbott to SSW, 2 June 1948. Someone other than Brooks read the statement on the recording.

44 GN 38/S1-1, pp. 2044-5, 29 May 1948.

45 *NG*, 31 August 1948, p. 5.

46 In order, moving from highest to lowest, per cent support for the various options, constituency by constituency, was as follows: For Responsible Government - 1. Ferryland (90.48), 2. Harbour Main-Bell Island (82.56), 3. Placentia and St. Mary's (78.63), 4. St. John's East (65.87), 5. St. John's West (65.63), 6. Harbour Grace (64.16), 7. Port de Grave (52.40), 8. Carbonear-Bay de Verde (50.39), 9. Bonavista South (43.16), 10. Trinity South (41.40), 11. Placentia West (39.70), 12. St. George's-Port au Port (36.84), 13. Grand Falls (35.59), 14. Trinity North (32.39), 15. Fogo (27.54), 16. Humber (25.85), 17. Bonavista North (24.80),

18. Green Bay (20.78), 19. White Bay (20.17), 20. Fortune Bay and Hermitage (18.99), 21. St. Barbe (14.59), 22. Twillingate (14.43), 23. Burin (13.51), 24. Labrador (11.52), 25. Burgeo and La Poile (11.38); For Confederation with Canada - 1. Labrador (81.38), 2. Burin (78.56), 3. Burgeo and La Poile (72.74), 4. St. Barbe (64.32), 5. White Bay (63.71), 6. Bonavista North (63.57), 7. Fortune Bay and Hermitage (63.54), 8. Green Bay (60.52), 9. Humber (53.72), 10. Placentia West (48.78), 11. Trinity North (47.93), 12. Trinity South (47.86), 13. St. George's-Port au Port (47.22), 14. Fogo (46.81), 15. Carbonear-Bay de Verde (43.36), 16. Twillingate (43.13), 17. Port de Grave (40.62), 18. Grand Falls (40.37), 19. Bonavista North (33.90), 20. Harbour Grace (30.55), 21. St. John's West (24.94), 22. St. John's East (23.51), 23. Placentia and St. Mary's (15.21), 24. Harbour Main-Bell Island (12.12), 25. Ferryland (5.77); For Commission of Government - 1. Twillingate (42.44), 2. Fogo (25.65), 3. Grand Falls (24.05), 4. Bonavista South (22.93), 5. St. Barbe (21.09), 6. Humber (20.43), 7. Trinity North (19.67), 8. Green Bay (18.70), 9. Fortune Bay and Hermitage (17.47), 10. White Bay (16.12), 11. St. George's-Port au Port (15.93), 12. Burgeo and La Poile (15.88), 13. Bonavista North (11.63), 14. Placentia West (11.51), 15. Trinity South (10.74), 16. St. John's East (10.61), 17. St. John's West (9.43), 18. Burin (7.93), 19. Labrador (7.10), 20. Port de Grave (6.98), 21. Carbonear-Bay de Verde (6.25), 22. Placentia and St. Mary's (6.10), 23. Harbour Main-Bell Island (5.32), 24. Harbour Grace (5.29), 25. Ferryland (3.75).

47 NRC, RG 84, 1948, file 800, Abbott to SSW, 28 May 1948.

48 *NG*, 22 June 1948, p. 9. Macdonald's proclamation announcing the date of the second referendum was itself dated 18 June 1948.

49 Bridle, *Documents*, 2, pt. 1, p. 941 (footnote 72); pp. 938-9, Briddle to SSEA, 20 July 1948; NA, RG 59, 843.00/7-2048, Abbott to Foster, 20 July 1948.

50 Bridle, *Documents*, 2, pt. 1, pp. 940-1, memo from Pearson to SSEA, 21 July 1948. Other businessmen who now spoke up for Confederation were A.H. Monroe, Eric Bowring and H.B. Clyde Lake.

51 Quinton had left the magistracy in 1944 to become local government officer in the Department of Public Health and Welfare. A native of Flatrock, Carbonear, and a graduate of the University of Toronto in educational psychology, Pottle had been appointed in 1943 to the newly created posts of director of child welfare and judge of the St. John's Juvenile Court.

52 NA, RG 59, 843.00/7-2048, Abbott to Foster, 20 July 1948.

53 Bridle, *Documents*, 2, pt. 1, pp. 936-9, Bridle to SSEA, 20 July 1948.

54 *The Confederate*, 1, no. 10 (16 June 1948), p. 1.

55 NRC, RG 84, 1948, file 800, Abbott to SSW, 23 June 1948.
56 Ibid.
57 NA, RG 59, 843.00/7-3048, Abbott to SSW, 30 July 1948.
58 Smallwood, *I Chose Canada*, p. 293, 310-11.
59 NA, RG 59, 843.00/7-3048, Abbott to SSW, 30 July 1948.
60 *NG*, 31 August 1948, p. 5. In order, moving from highest to lowest, per cent support for the two options, constituency by constituency, was as follows: Confederation with Canada - 1. Burgeo and La Poile (88.91), 2. Burin (84.96), 3. Fortune Bay and Hermitage (81.40), 4. St. Barbe (78.80), 5. Labrador (77.78), 6. White Bay (75.81), 7. Twillingate (75.25), 8. Bonavista North (74.49), 9. Green Bay (71.36), 10. Humber (68.73), 11. Trinity North (65.09), 12. Fogo (61.93), 13. Trinity South (60.27), 14. St. George's-Port au Port (56.73), 15. Grand Falls (56.46), 16. Placentia West (54.81), 17. Carbonear-Bay de Verde (52.71), 18. Bonavista South (51.90), 19. Port de Grave (49.04), 20. Harbour Grace (37.68), 21. St. John's West (33.11), 22. St. John's East (31.22), 23. Placentia and St. Mary's (18.40), 24. Harbour Main-Bell Island (17.42), 25. Ferryland (15.44); For Responsible Government - 1. Ferryland (84.56), 2. Harbour Main-Bell Island (82.58), 3. Placentia and St. Mary's (81.60), 4. St. John's East (68.78), 5. St. John's West (66.89), 6. Harbour Grace (62.32), 7. Port de Grave (50.96), 8. Bonavista South (48.10), 9. Carbonear-Bay de Verde (47.29), 10. Placentia West (45.19), 11. Grand Falls (43.54), 12. St. George's-Port au Port (43.27), 13. Trinity South (39.73), 14. Fogo (38.07), 15. Trinity North (34.91), 16. Humber (31.27), 17. Green Bay (28.64), 18. Bonavista North (25.51), 19. Twillingate (24.75), 20. White Bay (24.19), 21. Labrador (22.22), 22. St. Barbe (21.20), 23. Fortune Bay and Hermitage (18.60), 24. Burin (15.04), 25. Burgeo and La Poile (11.09).
61 DO 114/103, 1, pp. 169-70, tel. from GN, 26 July 1948.
62 NA, RG 59, 843.00/8-248, Abbott to SSW, 2 August 1948.
63 Pickersgill, *My Years with Louis St. Laurent*, pp. 79-80.
64 Bridle, *Documents*, 2, pt. 1, pp. 964-5, memo by Dept. of External Affairs, 27 July 1948.
65 Ibid., p. 965.
66 Ibid., pp.. 961-2, SSCR to HCC, 26 July 1948; DO 35/3460/N2005, Macdonald to Machtig, 23 July 1948.
67 DO 114/103, 1, pp. 153-4, tel. from HCN to CG, 1 July 1948.
68 Bridle, *Documents*, 2, pt. 1, pp. 961-2, SSCR to HCC, 26 July 1948.
69 DO 114/103, 1, pp. 153-4, HCC to CG, 1 July 1948.
70 Ibid., p. 183, statement by Govr., 30 July 1948.
71 NG, 10 August 1948, p. 1.
72 Bridle, *Documents*, 2, pt. 1, p. 963, Acting HCN to SSEA, 26 July 1948.

73 DO 114/103, 1, p. 189, Strong to SSCR, received 25 August 1948; p. 190, tel. from GN, 27 August 1948.

74 Ibid., p. 185, tel. from HCC, 7 August 1948.

75 Ibid., pp. 219-21, desp. from HCC, 23 December 1948; Bridle, *Documents*, 2, pt. 2: 1116-17, minutes of a meeting between Cabinet Committee and Delegation from Newfoundland.

76 DO 114/103, 1, pp. 200-1, tel. from HCN, 15 October 1948.

77 Ibid., p. 200.

78 Ibid., pp. 219-21, desp. from HCC, 23 December 1948.

79 Ibid., pp. 205-6, tel. from HCC, 13 November 1948.

80 Ibid., pp. 206-7, tel. from HCC, 18 November 1948; p. 212, tel. to HCC, 27 November 1948.

81 Ibid., pp. 208-9, tel. from HCC, 18 November 1948.

82 Ibid., pp. 205-6, tel. from HCC, 13 November 1948.

83 Ibid., pp. 208-9, tel. from HCC, 18 November 1948.

84 For his position, see ibid., pp. 246-8, encls. in desp. from GN, 19 February 1949.

85 Ibid., pp. 219-21, desp. from HCC, 23 December 1948.

86 Bridle, *Documents*, 2, pt. 2, pp. 1244-5, 1259.

87 Ibid., pp. 1245-50

88 Ibid., pp. 1250-1, 1253-7.

89 In fact, because of a decision of the Supreme Court of Canada in 1948, the manufacture and sale of margarine, except in Quebec, were increasing in Canada by the time Newfoundland actually became a province.

90 Bridle, *Documents*, 2, pt. 2, pp. 1258-61.

91 Ibid., pp. 1279-88.

92 GN 38/S1-1, p. 2154, 26 January 1948; p. 2183, 30 March 1948.

93 See DO 35/3465, Macdonald to Machtig, 31 August 1948.

94 DO 35/3474/N2005/114, Clutterbuck to Noel Baker, 11 February 1949.

95 Canada, House of Commons, *Journals*, 1949, 90, p. 46; Canada, House of Commons, *Debates*, 1949, 1, pp. 283-310.

96 Canada, House of Commons, *Journals*, 1949, 90, p. 51.

97 Canada, House of Commons, *Debates*, 1949, 1, pp. 493-4.

98 Ibid., p. 501.

99 Ibid., p. 562; DO 114/103, 1, p. 241, tel. from HCC, 16 February 1949. The sub-amendment read as follows: "That the words 'after they will have given their consent' be substituted for the words 'upon a satisfactory conclusion of such consultation' in the last paragraph of the amendment."

100 Canada, House of Commons, *Debates*, 1949, 1, p. 579.

101 Ibid., p. 580.

102 Ibid., p. 606.

103 DO 114/109, p. 171, HCC to SSCR, 31 March 1949 and encls.

104 Canada, *Treaty Series*, 1949, No. 21 (Ottawa, 1950), "Agreement between the Government of Canada and the Government of the United Kingdom for air services between and beyond their respective territories."
105 DO 114/103, 1, p. 263, tel. from HCC, 26 January 1950.
106 Ibid., p. 262, desp. from HCC, 23 December 1949 and encl.
107 For a full account of this, see my "The Supreme Court of Canada and 'the Bowater's law,' 1950," pp. 201-15.
108 DO 35/3470, James to Tait, 30 November 1948.
109 Ibid., minute in Shannon to Tait, 16 December 1948.
110 Ibid., Bowater to St. Laurent, 22 December 1948.
111 Ibid., Noel-Baker to Bowater, 14 February 1949.
112 Richard and des Rivières, eds., *Canada Law Reports*, pp. 608-64.
113 The announcement followed discussions by the Permanent Joint Board on Defence. See Dept. of State, *Foreign Relations 1947*, 3 (Washington, 1972), pp. 104-5; Bridle *Documents*, 2, pt. 2, pp. 1922-3, oral message from SSEA and Minister of National Defence to Ambassador of United States.
114 NA, RG 59, 811.24543/8-3048, Snow to Harrington, 30 August 1948.
115 Ibid., 811.24542/9-2647, Harrington to Foster, 26 September 1947.
116 Bridle, *Documents*, 2, pt. 2, pp. 1899-1900, memo from Minister of National Defence to SSEA.
117 Ibid., pp. 1900-1, Ambassador in United States to Acting SSW, 19 November 1948.
118 NA, RG 59, 843.7962/12-2848, Snow to Hickerson, 28 December 1948.
119 Bridle, *Documents*, 2, pt. 2, pp. 1902-3, Ambassador in United States to SSEA, 19 November 1948.
120 Ibid., p. 1918, memo from Secretary of the Cabinet to Secretary, Cabinet Defence Committee, 15 February 1949.
121 Ibid., pp. 1922-3, oral message from SSEA and Minister of National Defence to Ambassador of United States, 19 March 1949.
122 NA, RG 59, Permanent Joint Board on Defence, box 22, file "Newfoundland Bases (Oct-Dec 1949)," Harrington to Snow, 14 October 1949.
123 Ibid., Harrington to Belovsky, 9 November 1949.
124 Ibid., file "Newfoundland Bases (general) (Sept. 1949)," unsigned tel. to SSW from Ottawa embassy, 26 October 1949.
125 Ibid., file "Newfoundland Bases (Oct-Dec 1949)," memo by SSW of conversation with the President, 27 October 1949; Acheson to Pearson, 3 November 1949.
126 Canada, *Treaty Series*, 1952, No. 14 (Ottawa, 1954), "Agreement Concerning Leased Bases in Newfoundland: 1941-1952."
127 Canada, *Treaty Series*, 1949, No. 15 (Ottawa, 1950), "Exchange of Notes (June 4, 1949) between Canada and the United States of America constituting an understanding relating to civil aviation at the leased bases in Newfoundland."

128 *ET*, 4 September 1949, p. 18.

129 GN 38/S1-1, p. 2103, 9 October 1948.

130 *ET*, 13 November 1948, p. 1.

131 DO 114/103, 1, pp. 213-4, tel. to GN, 3 December 1948.

132 Bridle, *Documents*, 2, pt. 2, p. 1342, tels. from HCUK to SSEA, 24, 27 November 1948; *Parliamentary Debates*, 5th ser., 458 (1948-49), cols. 1049-51.

133 Bridle, *Documents*, 2, pt. 2, pp. 1365-6, HCUK to SSEA, 29 January 1949; pp. 1493-4, Acting HCUK to SSEA, 10 February 1949; p. 1524, HCUK to SSEA, 18 February 1949.

134 DO 114/103, 1, pp. 218-19, encl. in desp. from GN, 13 December 1948.

135 See NRC, RG 84, file 800, Abbott to SSW, 11 December 1948.

136 DO 114/103, 1, pp. 218-19, encl. 2 in desp. from GN, 13 December 1948.

137 Ibid., p. 206, tel. from GN, 14 November 1948. The plaintiffs were Hon. J.S. Currie, Hon. F. McNamara and Hon. J.V. O'Dea, who had been members of the Legislative Council, and W.C. Winsor, Harold Mitchell and W. J. Browne, who had been members of the House of Assembly. Solicitors for the plaintiffs were John G. Higgins and Richard A. Parsons. See *ET*, 15 November 1948, p. 1.

138 *ET*, 13 December 1948, p. 3.

139 DO 114/103, 1, pp. 234-5, Noel-Baker to Shawcross, 3 February 1949.

140 Ibid., pp.. 251-2, Commonwealth Relations Office to Messrs. Burns and Berridge, 5 March 1949; Browne, "Case for the restoration of Responsible Government," 3, p. 130.

141 *Parliamentary Debates*, 5th ser., 461 (1949), col. 1700.

142 *The Public General Acts*, 1949, 1, pp. 52-71. The short title of the act embodying the terms of union was "The British North America Act, 1949."

143 *ET*, 7 March 1949, p. 3.

144 Ibid., 8 March 1949, p. 6.

145 NRC, RG 84, file 800, Abbott to SSW, 20 August 1948.

146 GN 38/S1-1, p. 2188, 31 March 1949.

147 DO 114/103, 1, pp. 252-3, desp. from HCC, 5 April 1949.

148 For this, see Neary and O'Flaherty, *Part of the Main*, p. 170.

149 DO 114/103, 1, p. 253, desp. from HCC, 5 April 1949.

150 DO 35/3477/N2005/130, tel. from HCC, 27 March 1949; Bridle, *Documents*, 2, pt. 2, pp. 1583-4, St. Laurent to Walsh, 8 March 1949; pp. 1591-3, Walsh to St. Laurent, 16 March 1949; p. 1595, extract from tel. from SSEA to HCN, 25 March 1949.

151 See, for example, ibid., pp. 1988-9, McEvoy to MacKay, 11 March 1949.

152 *NG*, 1 April 1949, p. 2.

153 See Bridle (ed.), *Documents*, 2, pt. 1, pp. 1590-1, memo by Parliamentary Assistant to Prime Minister.

154 *NG*, 1 April, 1949, p. 2.

155 For post-Confederation political developments, see my "Party Politics in Newfoundland," pp. 205-45.

156 NA, RG 59, Permanent Joint Board on Defence, box 22, file "Newfoundland Bases (Oct-Dec 1949)," Belovsky to SSW, 25 October 1949.

157 DO 35/3511, "Newfoundland Interest-free Loan," 7 December 1949.

158 Bridle, *Documents*, 2, pt. 2, p. 1251.

159 DO 35/3475/N2005/110, "Note on the Discussion between Mr. John Deutsch of the Canadian Department of Finance and Sir Henry Wilson-Smith, on 26th January, 1949, about the Treatment of the Newfoundland Debt after Confederation with Canada, and certain other related matters," 27 January 1949; tel. to HCC, 7 February 1949.

160 DO 35/3480/N2455/7, tel. from HCC, 27 September 1949.

161 DO 35/3511, "Newfoundland Interest-free Loan," 7 December 1949.

162 Ibid., tel. from HCC, 19 January 1950.

163 *NG*, 2 August 1949, p. 1. Quinton was appointed Minister of Public Health on 5 April 1949 (ibid., 5 April 1949, p. 10) and Acting Minister of Finance on 22 June 1949 (ibid., 28 June 1949, p. 1).

164 DO 35/3511, tel. from HCC, 19 January 1950.

165 DO 35/3511, tel. to HCC, 29 March 1950.

166 DO 35/1347/N402/54, Appendix D, "Report by Mr. Clutterbuck."

167 Walsh, *More Than a Poor Majority*, p. 5.

168 DO 35/3121, "Note of impressions on visit to Newfoundland between 20th and 30th August, 1950," 11 October 1950, encl. in Clutterbuck to Gordon-Walker, 11 October 1950.

CHAPTER TWELVE

1 Garner, *The Commonwealth Office 1925-68*, p. 251.

2 For a recent statement of this position in relation to the establishment of United States Bases in Newfoundland, see Peckford, *The Past in the Present*, pp. 47-9.

3 CNS(A), John G. Higgins Collection, 3.01.019, Correspondence O'Leary/Collins, Jan.-Sept. 1947, Buffett to O'Leary, 16 June 1947.

4 See my "Clement Attlee's Visit," p. 108.

5 Smallwood, *I Chose Canada*, p. 273.

6 GN 13/2/1, box 155, file 14, Mahoney to O'Neill, 5 March 1935.

7 Reynolds, *The Creation of the Anglo-American Alliance*.

8 See Aitken, "Defensive Expansionism," pp. 183-221.

9 This decision was followed by the negotiation of the Atlantic Accord, which provides for joint management of the resource by the governments of Canada and of the Province of Newfoundland.

10 NRC, RG 84, file 800, Harrington to Foster, 23 June 1947.

11 Lower, *Colony to Nation*, p. 330.

12 DO 35/3121, "Note of impressions on visit to Newfoundland between 20th and 30th August, 1950," 11 October 1950, encl. in Clutterbuck to Gordon-Walker, 11 October 1950.

Bibliography

The basic bibliography of Newfoundland and Labrador to 1975 is the two-volume *Bibliography of Newfoundland* (Toronto, 1986), compiled by Agnes O'Dea and edited by Anne Alexander. For work published since 1975 the most comprehensive source of information is the catalogue of the Centre for Newfoundland Studies, Queen Elizabeth II Library, Memorial University, St. John's, Newfoundland. The Centre also has a bibliography of articles relating to Newfoundland and Labrador. For the records of the Newfoundland government in the Provincial Archives of Newfoundland and Labrador, *A Guide to the Government Records of Newfoundland* (St. John's, 1983), compiled by Margaret Chang, is indispensable. The arguments and document collections prepared by the governments of Canada and Newfoundland in connection with the dispute between them concerning "legislative jurisdiction over the seabed and subsoil of the continental shelf offshore Newfoundland," referred to the Supreme Court of Canada in 1982, form another important source for the study of Newfoundland's modern history. For an account of the historiography of Newfoundland, see my "The Writing of Newfoundland History: An Introductory Survey," in *Newfoundland in the Nineteenth and Twentieth Centuries: Essays in Interpretation*, edited by J.K. Hiller and Peter Neary (Toronto, 1980).

MANUSCRIPT SOURCES

Canada

National Archives of Canada

Department of External Affairs. Record Group 25.

Department of Labour. Record Group 27.

Fraser, A.M. "History of the Participation by Newfoundland in World War II." Record Group 24. Records of the Department of National Defence. Vol. 10995, file 290-NFD-013-(DI). I am grateful to Barbara Wilson of the National

Archives of Canada for directing me to the Fraser manuscript.

MacKay, R.A. Papers. Manuscript Group 30 E159.

Magrath, Charles A. Papers. Manuscript Group 30 E82.

New Brunswick

Harriet Irving Library, University of New Brunswick, Fredericton, New Brunswick

Bennett, R.B. Papers. Microfilm.

Newfoundland

Centre for Newfoundland Studies (Archives). Queen Elizabeth II Library, Memorial University, St. John's, Newfoundland

John G. Higgins Collection.

Walter Sparkes Collection.

Provincial Archives of Newfoundland and Labrador, St. John's, Newfoundland

Commission of Government

"Abbreviated Annual Report for the Year 1943." HC 117N4, 1943.

"Abbreviated Annual Report for the Year 1944." HC 117N4, 1944.

Commission Papers, Governor's Set, 1934–48. Originals. GN 1/8.

Department of Justice. Departmental Files. GN 13/2/1.

Department of Justice and Defence. Defence. GN 38/S4–2.

Department of Justice and Defence. General Administration. GN 38/S4–1.

Department of Natural Resources. Forestry Division. GN 38/S2–3.

Department of Natural Resources. General Administration. GN 38/S2–1.

Department of Public Utilities. General Administration. GN 38/S5–1.

Governor's Office. Miscellaneous Despatches and Local Correspondence Received 1850–1952. GN 1/3/A-B.

Secretary of the Commission. Minutes of Meetings. GN 38/S1–1.

National Convention

Proceedings Sessions 1-5, 1946–48, including Orders of the Day. GN 10/A.

Reports of National Convention Committees, 1946–48. GN 10/C.

Registry of Deeds, Companies and Securities. Confederation Building, St. John's, Newfoundland

"The Express Publishing Company, Limited. Memorandum of Association." No. 1682. 23 January 1941.

United Kingdom

Bodleian Library, Oxford

Amulree, first Baron (William Warrender Mackenzie). Papers.

Public Record Office, Kew

Air Ministry. Civil Aviation Files, 1909–58. AVIA 2.

Air Ministry. Ferry and Transport Commands. 1940–65. AIR 38.

Air Ministry. Operation Record Books: Miscellaneous Units, 1912–67. AIR 29.

Cabinet Papers. British Joint Staff Mission: Washington Office Files, 1940–49. CAB 122.

Cabinet Papers. Registered Files, 1916–59. CAB 21.

Cabinet Papers. Supplementary Registered Files, 1923–51. CAB 104.

Cabinet Papers. War Cabinet Miscellaneous Committees, 1939–47. CAB 98.

Dominions Office. Confidential Print Dominions, 1924–51. DO 114.

Dominions Office. "Newfoundland Affairs: Correspondence and Papers 1931–1933." DO 414.

Dominions Office. Private Office papers, 1911–55. DO 121.

Dominions Office. Supplementary Original Correspondence, 1926–29. DO 117.

Dominions Office and Commonwealth Relations Office. Original Correspondence, 1926–61. DO 35.

MacDonald, J. Ramsay. Papers.

Prime Minister's Office. Confidential Papers, 1939–46. PREM 4.

Treasury. Imperial and Foreign Division: Files, 1920–59. T 220.

United States

Library of Congress, Manuscript Division

John W. Greenslade Papers.

National Archives, Washington, D.C.

Department of State

General Records. Record Group 59.

Washington National Records Center, Suitland, Maryland

Department of State

Records of the Foreign Service Posts. Record Group 84.

Privately Held

Hope Simpson, J. B. Manuscript: "Newfoundland. The Commission of Government."

Walwyn, Vice-Admiral Sir Humphrey and Lady Walwyn. Papers.

GOVERNMENT DOCUMENTS

Canada

Bridle, Paul, ed. *Documents on Relations between Canada and Newfoundland.* Vol. 1, 1935–49. Vol. 2 in 2 pts., 1940–49. Vol. 1, Introduction by R.A. MacKay. Vol. 2, pt. 1, Introduction by Paul Bridle. Ottawa, 1974–84.

[Chief Electoral Officer]. *By-Elections held during the year 1947: Report of the Chief Electoral Officer.* Ottawa, 1947.

- *Twentieth General Election 1945: Report of the Chief Electoral Officer.* Ottawa, 1946.

A Consolidation of the Constitution Acts 1867 to 1882. Ottawa, 1983.

Dominion Bureau of Statistics. *Eleventh Census of Newfoundland and Labrador 1945.* 2 vols. Ottawa, 1949.

- *Seventh Census of Canada, 1931.* 13 vols. Ottawa, 1936.

Gazetteer of Canada: Newfoundland Terre-Neuve. 2d ed. Ottawa, 1983.

House of Commons. *Debates*, vol. 1, 1949.

- *Journals*, vol. 90, 1949.

Richard, Adrien E. and Francois des Rivières, eds. *1950 Canada Law Reports: Supreme Court of Canada.* Ottawa, 1951.

Supreme Court of Canada. "IN THE MATTER OF Section 55 of the Supreme Court Act, R.S.C. 1970, Chapter S-19, as amended; AND IN THE MATTER OF a reference by the Governor in Council concerning property in and legislative jurisdiction over the seabed and subsoil of the continental shelf offshore Newfoundland and set out in Order-in-Council P.C. 1982-1509 dated the 19th day of May, 1982," "Factum of the Attorney General of Canada."

- "Case on Appeal." Government of Canada. 18 vols.

Treaty Series. 1949. Nos. 15 and 21. Ottawa, 1950.

- 1952, No. 14. Ottawa, 1954.

Wartime Information Board. *Canada at War.* No. 45. Ottawa, 1945.

Newfoundland

Acts of the General Assembly of Newfoundland.

Acts of the Honourable Commission of Government of Newfoundland.

Budget Speeches. 1934-48.

Census and Return of the Population, &c., of Newfoundland and Labrador, 1874. St. John's, 1876.

Commission of Enquiry. *Report of the Commission of Enquiry into the Cost of Living.* St. John's, 1947.

Comptroller and Auditor General. *Reports.* 1946-49.

Division of Civil Re-establishment. *When You Come Home.* St. John's, 1945.

Dunfield, Brian E.S. *Report of the Hon. Mr. Justice Dunfield, Special Commissioner under Public Enquiries Act 1934.* St. John's, 1943.

Gorvin, J.H. *Report on Land Settlements in Newfoundland.* Department of Agriculture and Rural Reconstruction. Economic Series no. 1. St. John's, 1938.

- *Papers Relating to a Long Range Reconstruction Policy in Newfoundland.* 2 vols. Vol. 1, *Interim Report of J.H. Gorvin C.B.E.* Vol. 2 [Supporting Documents]. St. John's, 1938.

Journal of the House of Assembly of Newfoundland. 1858. Appendix, "Abstract Census and Return of the Population, &c. of Newfoundland, 1857."

Journal of the House of Assembly and Legislative Council of Newfoundland in the Second Session of the Twenty-Ninth [sic Eighth] General Assembly. 1933.

Journal of the Legislative Council of the Dominion of Newfoundland, Second Session of the Twenty-Eighth General Assembly. 1933.

Labour Relations Officer. "Report of the Labour Relations Officer for the Year 1945." (Typescript available in the Library, Department of Labour, Ottawa).

Liddell, T.K. *Industrial Survey of Newfoundland*. St. John's, 1940.

National Convention. *Reports of Committees*. 6 vols. Ottawa, [1948].

Newfoundland Gazette.

Statutes of Newfoundland. 1950. St. John's, [1950].

United Kingdom

The London Gazette.

Parliament. Command Papers (in numerical order).

Cmd. 4479. *Newfoundland: Papers relating to the Report of the Royal Commission, 1933*. 1933.

Cmd. 4480. *Newfoundland Royal Commission 1933 Report*. 1933.

Cmd. 4481. *Newfoundland: Memorandum on Proposed Financial Resolution*. 1933.

Cmd. 4788. *Newfoundland: Report of the Commission of Government on the Economic Situation December, 1934*. 1935.

Cmd. 4910. *Newfoundland: Report by the Commission of Government on the Unemployment Situation May, 1935*. 1935.

Cmd. 5117. *Newfoundland: Report by the Commission of Government on the Work of the Commission January, 1936*. 1936.

Cmd. 5425. *Newfoundland: Annual Report of the Commission of Government for the year 1936*. 1937.

Cmd. 5741. *Newfoundland: Annual Report of the Commission of Government for the Year 1937*. 1938.

Cmd. 6010. *Newfoundland: Annual Report by the Commission of Government on the Work of the Commission during 1938*. 1939.

Cmd. 6224. *Exchange of Notes regarding United States Destroyers and Naval and Air Facilities for the United States in British Transatlantic Territories*. 1940.

Cmd. 6259. *Agreement between the Governments of the United Kingdom and the United States of America relating to the Bases Leased to the United States of America (and exchange of notes) together with Protocol between the Governments of the United Kingdom, Canada and the United States of America concerning the Defence of Newfoundland: London, March 27, 1941*. 1941.

Cmd. 6849. *Report on the Financial and Economic Position of Newfoundland*. 1946.

1932 Supplementary Estimate. No. 65. London, 1933.

Parliamentary Debates. House of Commons. 5th Series.

Parliamentary Debates. House of Lords. 5th Series.

Privy Council. Judicial Committee. *In the matter of the boundary between the Dominion of Canada and the Colony of Newfoundland in the Labrador Peninsula*. 12 vols. London, 1927.

The Public General Acts.

United States

Department of the Navy, Navy Historical Center, Washington Navy Yard, Washington, D.C. "Commander Task Force Twenty-Four." Commander in Chief United States Atlantic Fleet, 1946.

Department of State. *Foreign Relations of the United States 1947*. 8 vols. Washington, 1972.

NEWSPAPERS AND REVIEWS

Call. New York.

The Confederate. St. John's.

Daily Express. London.

Evening Telegram. St. John's.

The Express. St. John's.

Fishermen's Advocate. Port Union, Newfoundland.

Fishermen-Workers Tribune. St. John's.

Humber Herald. Curling, Newfoundland.

The Independent. St. John's.

The Monitor. St. John's.

The Newfoundlander. (J.T. Meaney). St. John's.

Observer's Weekly. St. John's.

Sunday Herald. St. John's.

The Times. London.

Trade Review. St. John's.

PERSONAL CORRESPONDENTS AND INFORMANTS

Christie, Carl

Hiller, J.K.

Hiscock, Philip

Kelland, Barbara

Overton, James

Summers, G.B.

Walsh, J.R.

OTHER SOURCES

Aitken, H.G.J. "Defensive Expansionism: The State and Economic Growth in Canada." In *Approaches to Canadian Economic History*, edited by W.T. Easterbrook and M.H. Watkins, pp. 183-221. Toronto, 1967.

Alexander, David. *Atlantic Canada and Confederation.* Compiled by Eric W. Sager, Lewis R. Fischer, and Stuart O. Pierson. Toronto, 1983.

– *The Decay of Trade: An Economic History of the Newfoundland Saltfish Trade, 1935–1965.* Newfoundland Social and Economic Studies, no. 19. Memorial University of Newfoundland: Institute of Social and Economic Research, 1977.

Ammon, Charles G. *Newfoundland: The Forgotten Island.* London, 1944.

Andrews, Ralph L. *Integration and other Developments in Newfoundland Education 1915–1949.* St. John's, 1985.

Anglin, Douglas G. *The St. Pierre and Miquelon* Affaire *of 1941.* Toronto, 1966.

Best, Geoffrey. *War and Society in Revolutionary Europe, 1770–1870.* Leicester, 1982.

Bothwell, Robert and J.L. Granatstein. "Canada and the Wartime Negotiations over Civil Aviation: The Functional Principle in Operation." *The International History Review* 2, no. 4 (October 1980), pp. 585-601.

Bouzane, Lillian. "Mary Arnold and her work in Newfoundland during the proposed reconstruction programme, 1939–1940." Address to the Newfoundland Historical Society, St. John's, Newfoundland, 7 December 1966. (Available through the Society at the Colonial Building, St. John's).

Brebner, John Bartlett. *North Atlantic Triangle: The Interplay of Canada, the United States and Great Britain.* New York, 1945.

Brewin, Christopher. "British Plans for International Operating Agencies for Civil Aviation, 1941–1945." *The International History Review* 4, no. 1 (February 1982), pp. 91-110.

Bridle, Paul. "Introduction," In *Documents on Relations between Canada and Newfoundland*, vol. 2, pt. 1. See above under Government Documents, Canada.

Bridle, Paul, ed. *Documents on Relations between Canada and Newfoundland.* See above under Government Documents, Canada.

Brown, Cassie. *Standing Into Danger.* Toronto, 1979.

Browne, W.J. "The Case for the Restoration of Responsible Government." In *The Book of Newfoundland*, edited by J.R. Smallwood, vol. 3, pp. 119-30. St. John's, 1967.

Cashin, Peter. "My Fight for Responsible Government." In *The Book of Newfoundland*, edited by J.R. Smallwood, vol. 3, pp. 105-118, St. John's, 1967.

Clark, Malcolm H. "Outpost No. 1: Newfoundland." *Harper's Magazine*, February 1941, pp. 248-54.

Courage, J.R, ed. *Newfoundland Who's Who 1961.* St. John's, 1961.

Cuff, R.D. and J.L. Granatstein. "Canada and the Perils of 'Exemptionalism.'" In their book, *Canadian American Relations in Wartime: From the Great War to the Cold War*, pp. 151-63. Toronto, 1975.

Davenport, Walter, "Defense on Ice." *Collier's*, 12 April 1941, pp. 16, 26, 28, 31–32, 34.

den Otter, A. A. *Civilizing the West: The Galts and the Development of Western Canada.*

Edmonton, 1982.

Dilks, David, ed. *The Diaries of Sir Alexander Cadogan O.M. 1938–1945*. London, 1971.

Douglas, Alec. "The Nazi Weather Station in Labrador." *Canadian Geographic* 101, no. 6 (December 1981/January 1982), pp. 42-7.

Duley, Margaret. *The Caribou Hut*. Toronto, [1949].

Ewbank, R.W. *Public Affairs in Newfoundland*. Cardiff, 1939.

Fraser, A.M. "History of the Participation by Newfoundland in World War II." See above under Manuscript Sources, Canada.

Galbraith, John Kenneth. *A Life in Our Times: Memoir*. Boston 1981.

Garner, Joe. *The Commonwealth Office 1925–68*. London, 1978.

Gillespie, Bill. *A Class Act: An Illustrated History of the Labour Movement in Newfoundland and Labrador*. St. John's. 1986.

Gilmore, William C. "Newfoundland and the League of Nations." In *The Canadian Yearbook of International Law*. 1980. Vol. 18, pp. 201-17. Vancouver, 1981.

Gorvin, J.H. *Papers Relating to a Long Range Reconstruction Policy in Newfoundland*. See above under "Government Documents, Newfoundland."

– *Report on Land Settlements in Newfoundland*. See above under "Government Documents, Newfoundland."

Granatstein, J.L. *Canada's War: The Politics of the Mackenzie King Government, 1939–1945*. Toronto, 1975.

– *The Ottawa Men: The Civil Service Mandarins, 1935–1957*. Toronto, 1982.

Gwyn, Richard. *Smallwood: The Unlikely Revolutionary*. Rev. ed. Toronto, 1972.

Hadley, Michael. *U-Boats against Canada: German Submarines in Canadian Waters*. Montreal, 1985.

Hayman, Kathryn Ellen. "The Origins and Function of the Canadian High Commission in Newfoundland, 1941–1949." Master's thesis, University of Western Ontario, 1979.

Head, C. Grant. *Eighteenth-Century Newfoundland*. Toronto, 1970.

Hibbs, R., ed. *Who's Who in and from Newfoundland*. 3d ed. St. John's, 1937.

Hiller, J.K. *The Newfoundland Railway 1881–1949*. Newfoundland Historical Society Pamphlet No. 6. St. John's, 1981.

– "The Railway and Local Politics in Newfoundland, 1870–1901." In *Newfoundland in the Nineteenth and Twentieth Centuries: Essays in Interpretation*, edited by J.K. Hiller and Peter Neary, pp. 123-47. Toronto, 1980.

Hiller, J.K., and Neary, Peter, eds. *Newfoundland in the Nineteenth and Twentieth Centuries: Essays in Interpretation*. Toronto, 1980.

Horwood, Harold. *A History of the Newfoundland Ranger Force*. St. John's, 1986.

Lewis, Jane, and Mark Shrimpton. "Policymaking in Newfoundland during the 1940s: The Case of the St. John's Housing Corporation." *Canadian Historical Review* 64, no. 2 (June, 1984), pp. 209-39.

Liddell, T.K. *Industrial Survey of Newfoundland*. See above under Government

Documents, Newfoundland.

Lodge, Thomas. *Dictatorship in Newfoundland*. London, 1939.

Lower, A.R.M. *Colony to Nation*. 4th ed. Toronto, 1964.

McCann, Philip. "The Educational Policy of the Commission of Government." *Newfoundland Studies* 3, no. 2 (Fall, 1987), p. 201-15.

McDonald, Ian. "W.F. Coaker and the Balance of Power Strategy: The Fishermen's Protective Union in Newfoundland Politics." In *Newfoundland in the Nineteenth and Twentieth Centuries: Essays in Interpretation*, edited by J.K. Hiller and Peter Neary, pp. 148-80. Toronto, 1980.

MacKay, R.A. "Introduction," In *Documents on Relations between Canada and Newfoundland*, vol. 1. See above under Government Documents, Canada.

- "Smallwood's visit to Ottawa, 1946." *Dalhousie Review* 50, no. 2 (Summer, 1970), pp. 230-2.

- ed. *Newfoundland: Economic, Diplomatic and Strategic Studies*. Toronto, 1946.

McKenty, Neil, *Mitch Hepburn*. Toronto, 1967.

Mackintosh, W.A. *The Economic Background of Dominion-Provincial Relations*. Toronto, 1964.

Mannion, John J., ed. *The Peopling of Newfoundland*. St. John's, 1977.

Mitchell, Harvey. "Canada's Negotiations with Newfoundland, 1887–1895." *Canadian Historical Review* 40, no. 4 (December 1959), pp. 277-93.

Morton, H.V. *Atlantic Meeting*. London, 1943.

Narváez, Peter, "Joseph R. Smallwood, 'The Barrelman': The Broadcaster as Folklorist." *Canadian Folklore Canadien* (Journal of the Folklore Studies Association of Canada) 5, nos. 1-2, pp. 60-78.

Neary, Peter. *Bell Island: A Newfoundland Mining Community 1895–1966*. Ottawa, 1974.

- "Canada and the Newfoundland Labour Market, 1939–49." *Canadian Historical Review* 62, no. 4 (December 1981), pp. 470-95. I want to thank the editors of the *Canadian Historical Review* for permission to draw upon work published in this journal.

- "Clement Attlee's Visit to Newfoundland, September 1942." *Acadiensis* 13, no. 2 (Spring, 1984), pp. 101-9. I want to thank the editor of *Acadiensis* for permission to draw upon work published in this journal.

- "The Diplomatic Background to the Canada-Newfoundland Goose Bay Agreement of October 10, 1944." *Newfoundland Studies* 2, no. 1 (1986), pp. 39-61. I want to thank the editors of *Newfoundland Studies* for permission to draw upon work published in this journal.

- "The French and American Shore Questions as Factors in Newfoundland History." In *Newfoundland in the Nineteenth and Twentieth Centuries: Essays in Interpretation*, edited by J.K. Hiller and Peter Neary, pp. 95-122. Toronto, 1980.

- "Newfoundland." In *Encyclopedia Americana*, vol. 20, pp. 258-70. Danbury, Conn., 1986.

- Newfoundland and the Anglo-American Leased Bases Agreement of 27 March

1941." *Canadian Historical Review* 67, no. 4 (December 1986), pp. 491-519.

- "Great Britain and the Future of Newfoundland, 1939–45," *Newfoundland Studies* 1, no. 1 (Spring, 1985), pp. 29-56.
- Newfoundland's Union with Canada, 1949: Conspiracy or Choice?" *Acadiensis* 12, no. 2 (Spring, 1983), pp. 110-19.
- "Party Politics in Newfoundland, 1949–71: A Survey and Analysis." In *Newfoundland in the Nineteenth and Twentieth Centuries: Essays in Interpretation*, edited by J.K. Hiller and Peter Neary, pp. 205-45. Toronto, 1980.
- *The Political Economy of Newfoundland, 1929–1972*. Toronto, 1973.
- "The Supreme Court of Canada and 'the Bowater's law,' 1950." *Dalhousie Law Journal* 8, no. 1 (January 1984). I want to thank the editor of the *Dalhousie Law Journal* for permission to draw upon work published in this journal.
- ed. "The Bradley Report on Logging Operations in Newfoundland, 1934: A Suppressed Document." *Labour/Le Travail*, no. 16 (Fall, 1985), pp. 193-232.

Neary, Peter, and S.J.R. Noel. "Newfoundland's Quest for Reciprocity, 1890–1910." In *Regionalism in the Canadian Community, 1867–1967*, edited by Mason Wade, pp. 210-26. Toronto, 1969.

Neary, Peter, and Patrick O'Flaherty, eds. *By Great Waters: A Newfoundland and Labrador Anthology*. Toronto, 1974.

- *Part of the Main: An Illustrated History of Newfoundland and Labrador*. St. John's, 1983.

Newfoundland Federation of Labour. *Report of Proceedings of the Ninth Annual Convention of the Newfoundland Federation of Labour held at Grand Falls, Newfoundland, August 20th to August 25th, 1945*. St. John's, [1945].

- *Report of Proceedings of the Seventh Annual Convention of the Newfoundland Federation of Labour held at the Newfoundland Hotel, St. John's, August 30th, to September 5th (inclusive) 1943*. St. John's, [1943].

The Newfoundland Illustrated Tribune, 1909. (Available through the Newfoundland Historical Society, Colonial Building, St. John's).

Nicholson, G.W.L. *More Fighting Newfoundlanders*. St. John's, 1969.

- "Our Fighting Forces in World War II." In *The Book of Newfoundland*, edited by J.R. Smallwood, vol. 4, pp. 468-502. St. John's, 1967.

Noel, S.J.R. *Politics in Newfoundland*. Toronto, 1971.

Orwell, Sonia, and Ian Angus, eds. *The Collected Essays, Journalism and Letters of George Orwell*. 4 vols. Harmandsworth, 1970.

Outerbridge, Leonard. "Churchill and Roosevelt in Newfoundland." In *The Book of Newfoundland*, edited by J.R. Smallwood, vol. 4, pp. 430-6. St. John's, 1967.

Peckford, A. Brian. *The Past in the Present: A Personal Perspective on Newfoundland's Future*. St. John's, 1983.

Pickersgill, J.W. *My Years with Louis St. Laurent*. Toronto, 1975.

Polenberg, Richard. *War and Society: The United States 1941–1945*. Philadelphia, 1972.

Powell, Griffith. *Ferryman*. Shrewsbury, 1982.

Pratt, E.J. *The Collected Poems of E.J. Pratt*. 2d ed. with an intro. by Northrop Frye. Toronto, 1958.

Responsible Government League of Newfoundland. *The Case for Responsible Government*. St. John's, 1947.

Reynolds, David. *The Creation of the Anglo-American Alliance 1937-41: A Study in Competitive Co-operation*. London, 1981.

Richard, Adrien E. and Francois des Rivières, eds. *1950 Canada Law Reports: Supreme Court of Canada*. See above under Government Documents, Canada.

Roberts, Charles G.D. and Arthur L. Tunnell, eds. *The Canadian Who's Who*. Toronto, 1936.

Roll, Eric. *The Combined Food Board: A Study in Wartime International Planning*. Stanford, 1956.

Rowe, C. Francis, James A. Haxby, and Robert J. Graham. *The Currency and Medals of Newfoundland*. Willowdale, 1963.

Shute, Nevil. *No Highway*. London, 1948.

Smallwood, J.R., ed. *The Book of Newfoundland*. 6 vols. St. John's, 1937–75.

– *Coaker of Newfoundland: The Man Who Led the Deep Sea Fishermen to Political Power*. London, 1927.

– *Encyclopedia of Newfoundland and Labrador*. 2 vols. St. John's, 1981–84.

– *I Chose Canada: The Memoirs of the Honourable Joseph R. "Joey" Smallwood*. Toronto, 1973.

– *The New Newfoundland*. New York, 1931.

Stacey, Alec G. "1000 Days that Changed Our Destiny." In *The Book of Newfoundland*, edited by J.R. Smallwood, vol. 3, pp. 132-39. St. John's, 1967.

Stacey, C.P. *Arms, Men and Governments: The War Policies of Canada, 1939–1945*. Ottawa, 1970.

– *Six Years of War: The Army in Canada, Britain and the Pacific*. Ottawa, 1966.

Struthers, James. *No Fault of Their Own: Unemployment and the Canadian Welfare State, 1914–1941*. Toronto, 1983.

Thompson, Frederic F. *The French Shore Problem in Newfoundland: An Imperial Study*. Toronto, 1961.

Thomson, Dale C. *Louis St. Laurent: Canadian*. Toronto, 1967.

Tuck, Alice M. "The Newfoundland Ranger Force, 1935–1950." Master's thesis, Memorial University, 1983.

Wade, Mason, ed. *Regionalism in the Canadian Community, 1867–1967*. Toronto, 1969.

Walsh, Bren. *More Than a Poor Majority: The Story of Newfoundland's Confederation with Canada*. St. John's, 1985.

West, Paul. "A Lullaby too Rough." In *By Great Waters: A Newfoundland and Labrador Anthology*, edited by Peter Neary and Patrick O'Flaherty, pp. 225-9. Toronto, 1974.

Wheare, K.C. *Federal Government*. London, 1946.

Who's Who 1934. London, 1934.

Who Was Who 1941–1950. London, 1952.
Who Was Who 1951–1960. London, 1961.
Who Was Who 1961–1970. London, 1972.
Who Was Who 1971–1980. New York, 1981.

Index